## Get the eBook FREE!
(PDF, ePub, Kindle, and liveBook all included)

We believe that once you buy a book from us, you should be able to read it in any format we have available. To get electronic versions of this book at no additional cost to you, purchase and then register this book at the Manning website.

Go to https://www.manning.com/freebook and follow the instructions to complete your pBook registration.

## That's it!
## Thanks from Manning!

MW01196824

*Causal AI*

# Causal AI

ROBERT OSAZUWA NESS

FOREWORD BY LINDSAY EDWARDS

MANNING
SHELTER ISLAND

For online information and ordering of this and other Manning books, please visit
www.manning.com. The publisher offers discounts on this book when ordered in quantity.
For more information, please contact

Special Sales Department
Manning Publications Co.
20 Baldwin Road
PO Box 761
Shelter Island, NY 11964
Email: orders@manning.com

| | |
|---|---|
| Manning Publications Co. 20 Baldwin Road PO Box 761 Shelter Island, NY 11964 | Development editor: Frances Lefkowitz<br>Technical editor: Emily McMilin<br>Review editor: Dunja Nikitović<br>Production editor: Kathy Rossland<br>Copy editor: Andy Carroll<br>Proofreader: Jason Everett<br>Technical proofreader: Jeffrey Finkelstein<br>Typesetter and cover designer: Marija Tudor |

ISBN 9781633439917
Printed in the United States of America

*To Dad, Professor Ness*

# brief contents

# *contents*

# *foreword*

*Twenty-seven lawyers in the room, anybody know 'post hoc, ergo propter hoc?'*
—*President Josiah Bartlett (The West Wing)*

"Post hoc ergo propter hoc" is a logical fallacy regarding causation: "After it, therefore because of it." The idea dates back at least to Aristotle (the fallacy appears in *On Sophistical Refutations*). More than two thousand years after Aristotle, Welsh economic theorist Sir Clive Granger inverted "post hoc ergo propter hoc" to provide one of the two principles underlying what is now known as Granger Causality, namely that something cannot *cause* something if it happened *before* it.

Humans have been fascinated by the notion of causality—what causes what—since their early recorded writing. Indeed, causal reasoning is a major distinguishing feature of human cognition. On a practical level, the importance is obvious: one cannot control something if one does not understand cause and effect. *Causal AI* is the first book I know of that draws together the necessary theory, the technical foundations (i.e., the packages and libraries), and a host of real examples, to allow anyone with a decent grounding in basic probability theory and software engineering to get started using causal AI to tackle any problem they choose.

In my own field—the application of machine learning to problems in biology and drug discovery—understanding causality is essential. New drugs currently cost $2–3B to develop, with most of this cost coming from the 95% failure rate of new drugs in clinical trials. A significant proportion of these costs can be explained by failures to understand (particularly biological) causality. Approximately 60% of all drug failures can be traced back to a poor selection of drug target, and many of these poor drug targets are errors of causal attribution.

While machine learning and artificial intelligence are rapidly transforming our world, they are dogged by a number of technical problems, including poor explainability, robustness, and generalizability. Causal reasoning addresses all of these directly. Often, one will hear AI algorithms being described as "black boxes" (in other words, impossible to "peer into" and explain). Yet, intuitively (and increasingly backed up by research), machine learning models that are robustly predictive *must* have learned causality.

Models that learn causality *explicitly* (such as the methods outlined in this book) will be both predictive *and* explainable. Models regularly fail to generalize when a correlate of the true cause is used to predict an effect (or output). Let us assume a chain of events: A causes B causes C. If a model, trained on this data, has learned to predict A from C, it is inherently fragile. It will fail completely if, in a new setting, the link between A and B is somehow broken. Again, explicit causal models tackle this issue directly, greatly increasing the chances that a performant model will generalize well.

In this excellent book, Robert Ness uses vignettes drawn from business, retail, and technology. While these are perfect teaching tools, readers should be under no illusion: The scope for these methods is vast and important, including medicine, biology, and policy-making. Understanding and modeling causality has extraordinary potential to improve human lives. Yet, as Robert points out, much of the knowledge required to understand and apply causal AI effectively is distributed across disciplines, including traditional statistics, Bayesian inference, computer science, and probabilistic machine learning. Hence, learning about and applying causal AI has (till now) been far more arduous than it should be.

Robert is also an inspired teacher—all the better, as this stuff can be hard! I hope you enjoy *Causal AI* as much as I did. It is essential reading for anyone interested in applying these powerful methods (cause) and, hopefully, having a positive impact in the world (effect).

—LINDSAY EDWARDS
CTO at Relation, London

# *preface*

I wrote this book because I wanted a code-first approach to causal inference that seamlessly fit with modern deep learning. It didn't make sense to me that deep learning was often presented as being at odds with causal reasoning and inference, so I wanted to write a book that proved they combine well to their mutual benefit.

Second, I wanted to close an obvious gap. Deep generative machine learning methods and graphical causal inference have a common ancestor in probabilistic graphical models. There have been tremendous advances in generative machine learning in recent years, including in the ability to synthetize realistic text, images, and video. Yet, in my view, the low-hanging fruit of connections to related concepts in graphical causality was left to rot on the vine. Chances are that if you're reading this, you sensed this gap as well. So here we are.

This book evolved from the Causal AI workshop I run through Altdeep.ai, an educational company that runs workshops and community events devoted to advanced topics in modeling. Participants in this causal AI workshop have included data scientists, machine learning engineers, and product managers from Google, Amazon, Meta, and other big tech companies. They've also included data scientists and ML experts from retailers such as Nike, consultancies like Deloitte, and pharmaceuticals like AstraZeneca. We've worked with quantitative marketing experts trying to take causal approaches to channel attribution. We've worked with economists and molecular biologists trying to get a more general perspective on the causal methods popular in their domains. We've worked with professors, post-docs, and PhD students across departments looking for a code-first approach to learning causal inference.

I wrote this book for all of these people, based on the real-world problems they care about and their feedback. If you belong to or relate to any of these groups, this book is for you, too.

How is this book different from other causal inference books? Causal inference relies mainly on three different skill sets: the ability to turn your domain knowledge into a causal model rendered in code, deep skills in probability theory, and deep skills in statistical theory and methods. This book focuses on the first skill by using libraries that enable bespoke causal modeling, and by leveraging the deep learning machinery in tools such as PyTorch to do the statistical heavy lifting.

I hope this sounds like what you are looking for.

# acknowledgments

I was very fortunate to have Emily McMilin, senior research scientist at Meta, and Kevin Murphy, principal research scientist at Google AI and author of the best book on probabilistic ML, both give a careful review of each chapter. Finally, Jeffrey Finkelstein, the most talented research engineer I've ever met, provided a thorough code review.

My colleagues at Microsoft Research, Emre Kiciman and Amit Sharma, provided helpful advice with the DoWhy code. Fritz Obermeyer and Eli Bingham got me unstuck on Pyro code. The book also builds on work with many collaborators, including Karen Sachs, Sara Taheri, Olga Vitek, and Jeremy Zucker.

My editors Frances Lefkowitz, Michael Stephens, and Andy Carroll at Manning Publications provided frequent and invaluable edits and feedback, as did many others on the Manning team.

To all the reviewers—Adi Shavit, Alain Couniot, Camilla Montonen, Carlos Aya-Moreno, Christian Sutton, Clemens Baader, German Vidal, Guillermo Alcántara González, Igor Vieira, Jeremy Loscheider, Jesús Juárez, Jose San Leandro, Keith Kim, Kyle Peterson, Maria Ana, Mikael Dautrey, Nick Decroos, Pierluigi Riti, Pietro Alberto Rossi, Sebastian Maier, Sergio Govoni, Simone Sguazza, and Thomas Joseph Heiman—your suggestions helped make this a better book.

# *about this book*

## Who should read this book

This book is for

- Machine learning engineers looking to incorporate causality into AI systems and build more robust predictive models
- Data scientists who are looking to expand both their causal inference and machine learning skillsets
- Researchers who want a wholistic view of causal inference and how it connects to their domain of expertise without going down stats theory rabbit holes
- AI product experts looking for case studies in business settings, especially tech and retail
- People who want to get in on the ground floor of causal AI

## What is the required mathematical and programming background?

Rest assured, this book doesn't require a deep background in probability and statistics theory. The relationship between causality and statistics is like the relationship between engineering and math. Engineering involves a lot of math, but you need only a bit of math to learn core engineering concepts. After learning those concepts and digging into an applied problem, you can focus on learning the extra math you need to go deep on that problem.

This book assumes a level of familiarity with probability and statistics typical of a data scientist. Specifically, it assumes you have basic knowledge of

- Probability distributions
- Joint probability and conditional probability and how they relate to each other (chain rule, Bayes rule)

- What it means to draw samples from a distribution
- Expectation, independence, and conditional independence
- Statistical ideas such as random samples, identically and independently sampled data, and statistical bias

Chapter 2 provides a primer on these and other topics key to the ideas presented in this book for those who need refreshing.

## What programming tools will we use?

This book assumes you are familiar with data science scripting in Python. The three open source Python libraries we rely on in this book are DoWhy, pgmpy, and Pyro. DoWhy is a library for the open source PyWhy suite of Python libraries for causal inference. pgmpy is a probabilistic graphical modeling library built on SciPy and NetworkX. Pyro is a probabilistic machine learning library that extends PyTorch.

Our code-first goal is unique because, rather than going deep into the statistical theory needed to do causal inference, we rely on these supporting libraries to do the statistics for us. DoWhy tries to be as end-to-end as possible in terms of mapping domain knowledge inputs to causal inference outputs. When we want to do more bespoke modeling, we'll use pgmpy or Pyro. These libraries provide probabilistic inference algorithms that take care of the estimation theory. pgmpy has graph-based inference algorithms that are extremely reliable. Pyro, as an extension of PyTorch, extends causal modeling to deep generative models on high dimensional data and *variational inference*—a cutting-edge deep learning–based inference technique.

If your background is in R or Julia, you should still find this book useful. There are numerous R and Julia packages that overlap in functionality with DoWhy. Graphical modeling software in these languages, such as bnlearn, can substitute for pgmpy. Similarly, the ideas we develop with Pyro will work with similar probabilistic programming languages, such as PyMC. See www.altdeep.ai/causalAIbook for links to code notebooks related to the book.

## Navigating this book

This book is divided into four parts. In part 1, we'll establish the conceptual foundations for the models we'll build in this book.

Chapter 1 illustrates our probabilistic machine learning approach to causality with some practical examples. We'll then dive right into a causal inference workflow using the MNIST data—the "hello world" of machine learning. Throughout the rest of the book, we'll do code-first explorations of various parts of this workflow.

Chapter 2 provides a primer on the core concepts from probabilistic modeling, generative machine learning, and Bayesian modeling that we'll build upon in this book. We'll also explore key ideas from statistical inference, such as conditional independence and Monte Carlo, which we'll leverage to build, validate, and do inference with causal models.

In part 2, you'll learn to build and validate causal graphs, including deep causal generative models.

Chapter 3 starts by giving you a solid foundation for the causal directed acyclic graph (DAG) as a model of the causal structure of a data generating process. We'll begin with a practical example of building a causal graph based on domain knowledge and train a causal graphical model on the structure of that causal graph. I'll also introduce parameter modularity and independence of mechanism—ideas that make a causal graphical model special, relative to other types of probabilistic graphical models.

Chapter 4 dives into performing empirical validation of a causal DAG. The true causal DAG constrains the statistical structure of the data. I'll show how to articulate those constraints, and how to use them to design statistical tests that evaluate how well our proposed DAG stands up against empirical evidence in the data. We'll also look at how causal discovery algorithms automate this process, and you'll learn how to avoid the pitfalls of these algorithms.

Chapter 5 explores the connection between deep learning and causal inference. First, we'll use deep learning to build a more powerful causal graphical model using a causal DAG as a scaffold. Then we'll explore ways in which causality can improve the traditional deep learning workflow. We'll use semi-supervised learning as a case study.

In part 3, we'll take a code-first dive into the conceptual heart of causal inference, namely structural causal models, interventions, counterfactual inference, and causal identification.

Chapter 6 introduces the structural causal model. Though often regarded as a difficult approach to causal inference, I'll show that it is a simple kind of generative model and thus easy to implement with generative modeling tools like Pyro. We'll see how to implement these models with deep learning frameworks.

Chapter 7 introduces the concept of interventions, meaning actions that change the data generating process. Using our code-first approach and Pyro's do function, we'll ground the idea of interventions in generative modeling to show how causal models can emulate real-world interventions. Generative modeling of interventions will become the keystone of our causal inference methods going forward.

Chapter 8 introduces parallel-world counterfactual reasoning. Once we observe a causal event and its effect, counterfactual reasoning asks how the effect might have been different if the cause had been different. We'll see how to model this idea by building a causal DAG that crosses *parallel worlds*. We'll look at practical examples of counterfactual reasoning, such as in marketing and in deal-making at Netflix.

Chapter 9 introduces the algorithm for general counterfactual inference. The algorithm combines a structural causal model with the parallel-world approach we saw in chapter 8. We'll look at several examples of how to implement this approach, including using a deep learning image model in PyTorch.

Chapter 10 provides a guide to causal identification, which concerns how we make causal inferences from data. While this is typically a theory-dense topic, we'll take a code-first approach. For example, we'll introduce the concept of the do-calculus with a Python library whose algorithms apply the do-calculus automatically.

In part 4, we'll take a deeper look at applications.

Chapter 11 dives into building a causal effect estimation workflow. We'll work with the DoWhy library and explore different statistical algorithms for identifying, estimating, and then stress-testing a causal effect estimate. We'll cover traditional techniques, such as propensity scores and instrumental variables, as well as newer methods, such as double machine learning. We'll then use Pyro to implement a Bayesian approach to estimating a causal effect using a Monte Carlo simulation of interventions on a deep causal graphical model trained with latent variables.

Chapter 12 explores the connection of causality with automated decision-making and reinforcement learning. We'll start with a famous causal decision problem called Newcomb's paradox and then extend to bandits, Markov decision processes, partial Markov decision processes, and reinforcement learning. We'll connect interventions to reward functions, show how agents make decisions under confounding, and see how policies are intervention generators.

Finally, chapter 13 introduces causality in the context of large language models and other multimodal foundation models. First, we'll explore how to use a large language model to solve causal problems. We'll then explore how to chain large language models over a causal DAG, and use causal interventions to generate text from these models, as well as the benefits of doing so.

## About the code

In each chapter, I provide a list of the Python libraries and versions you'll need to get the code working as well as guidance in setting up your environment. Note that different versions of the same library are sometimes used in different chapters. All the code in the book is implemented in Jupyter notebooks that are available online at www.altdeep.ai/causalAIbook. The notebooks were all tested in Google Colab, and they include links that automatically load the notebooks in Google Colab, where you can run them directly. This can save time and aggravation if you hit issues in setting up your environment. You'll find links to the notebooks and other book resources at www.altdeep.ai/causalAIbook.

This book contains many examples of source code, both in numbered listings and in-line with normal text. In both cases, source code is formatted in a `fixed-width font like this` to separate it from ordinary text.

In many cases, the original source code has been reformatted; I've added line breaks and reworked indentation to accommodate the available page space in the book. In rare cases, even this was not enough, and listings include line-continuation markers (➥). Additionally, comments in the source code have often been removed from the listings when the code is described in the text. Code annotations accompany many of the listings, highlighting important concepts.

You can get executable snippets of code from the liveBook (online) version of this book at https://livebook.manning.com/book/causal-ai. The complete code for the examples in the book is available for download from the Manning website at https://www.manning.com/books/causal-ai and from https://www.altdeep.ai/causalAIbook.

## liveBook discussion forum

Purchase of *Causal AI* includes free access to liveBook, Manning's online reading platform. Using liveBook's exclusive discussion features, you can attach comments to the book globally or to specific sections or paragraphs. It's a snap to make notes for yourself, ask and answer technical questions, and receive help from the author and other users. To access the forum, go to https://livebook.manning.com/book/causal-ai/discussion. You can also learn more about Manning's forums and the rules of conduct at https://livebook.manning.com/discussion.

Manning's commitment to our readers is to provide a venue where a meaningful dialogue between individual readers and between readers and the author can take place. It is not a commitment to any specific amount of participation on the part of the author, whose contribution to the forum remains voluntary (and unpaid). We suggest you try asking the author some challenging questions lest his interest stray! The forum and the archives of previous discussions will be accessible from the publisher's website as long as the book is in print.

# *about the author*

**ROBERT OSAZUWA NESS** researches generative AI at Microsoft Research. He is an adjunct professor in the Khoury School of Information Sciences at Northeastern University. He studied at Johns Hopkins University and Purdue University. He has a PhD in statistics.

# *about the cover illustration*

The figure on the cover of *Causal AI*, titled "La Religieuse," or "The Nun," is taken from a book by Louis Curmer published in 1841. Each illustration is finely drawn and colored by hand.

In those days, it was easy to identify where people lived and what their trade or station in life was just by their dress. Manning celebrates the inventiveness and initiative of the computer business with book covers based on the rich diversity of regional culture centuries ago, brought back to life by pictures from collections such as this one.

# Part 1

# Conceptual foundations

Part 1 lays the essential groundwork for understanding and building causal models. Here, I'll introduce key concepts from statistics, probabilistic modeling, generative machine learning, and Bayesian methods that will serve as our building blocks for this book's approach to causal modeling. This part is all about arming you with the core concepts you need to start solving causal problems with machine learning tools.

# Why causal AI

**This chapter covers**
- Defining causal AI and its benefits
- Incorporating causality into machine learning models
- A simple example of applying causality to a machine learning model

Subscription streaming platforms like Netflix are always looking for ways to optimize various indicators of performance. One of these is their *churn rate*, meaning the rate at which they lose subscribers. Imagine that you are a machine learning engineer or data scientist at Netflix tasked with finding ways of reducing churn. What are the types of *causal questions* (questions that require causal thinking) you might ask with respect to this task?

- *Causal discovery*—Given detailed data on who churned and who did not, can you analyze that data to find causes of the churn? *Causal discovery* investigates what causes what.
- *Estimating average treatment effects* (ATEs)—Suppose the algorithm that recommends content to the user is a cause of the churn; a better choice of

3

algorithm might reduce churn, but by how much? The task of quantifying how much, on average, a cause drives an effect is the *ATE estimation*. For example, some users could be exposed to a new version of the algorithm, and you could measure how much this affects churn, relative to the baseline algorithm.

Let's go a bit deeper. The mockumentary *The Office* (the American version) was one of the most popular shows on Netflix. Later, Netflix learned that NBCUniversal was planning to stop licensing the show to Netflix to stream in the US, so that US streaming of The Office would be exclusive to NBCUniversal's rival streaming platform, Peacock. Given the popularity of the show, churn was certainly affected, but by how much?

- *Estimating conditional average treatment effects* (CATEs)—The effect of losing *The Office* would be more pronounced for some subscriber segments than others, but what attributes define these segments? One attribute is certainly having watched the show, but there are others (demographics, other content watched, etc.). *CATE estimation* is the task of quantifying how much a cause drives an effect for a particular segment of the population. Indeed, there are likely multiple segments we could define, each with a different within-segment ATE. Part of the task of CATE estimation is finding distinct segments of interest.

Suppose you had reliable data on subscribers who quit Netflix and signed up for Peacock to continue watching *The Office*. For some of these users, the recommendation algorithm failed to show them possible substitutes for *The Office*, like the mockumentary *Parks and Recreation*. That may lead to a different type of question.

- *Counterfactual reasoning and attribution*—If the algorithm had placed *Parks and Recreation* more prominently in those users' dashboards, would they have stayed on with Netflix? These *counterfactual questions* ("counter" to the "fact" that the show wasn't prominent in their dashboard) are essential for *attribution* (assigning a root cause and credit/blame for an outcome).

Netflix worked with Steve Carrel (star of *The Office*) and Greg Daniels (writer, director, and producer of *The Office*) to create the show *Space Force* as Netflix original content. The show was released just months before *The Office* moved to Peacock. Suppose that this show was Netflix's attempt to create content to retain subscribers who were fans of *The Office*. Consider the decisions that would go into the creation of such a show:

- *Causal decision theory*—What actors/directors/writers would tempt *The Office* fans to stay subscribed? What themes and content?
- *Causal machine learning*—How could we use generative AI, such as large language models to create scripts and pilots for the show in such a way that optimizes for the objective of reducing churn amongst fans of *The Office*?

*Causal inference* is about breaking down a problem into these types of specific *causal queries*, and then using data to answer these queries. *Causal AI* is about building algorithms that automate this analysis. We'll tackle both of these problem areas in this book.

# 1.1    *What is causal AI?*

To understand what causal AI is, we'll start with the basic ideas of causality and causal inference, and work our way up. Then we'll review the kinds of problems we can solve with causal AI.

*Causal reasoning* is a crucial element of how humans understand, explain, and make decisions about the world. Anytime we think about cause ("Why did that happen?") or effect ("What will happen if I do this?"), we are practicing causal reasoning.

In statistics and machine learning, we use data to lend statistical rigor to our causal reasoning. But while cause-and-effect relationships drive the data, statistical correlation alone is insufficient to draw causal conclusions from data. For this, we must turn to *causal inference*.

Statistical (non-causal) inference relies on statistical assumptions. This is true even in deep learning, where assumptions are often called "inductive bias." Similarly, causal inference relies on causal assumptions; causal inference refers to a body of theory and practical methods that constrain statistical analysis with causal assumptions.

*Causal AI* refers to the automation of causal inference. We can leverage machine learning algorithms, which have developed robust approaches to automating statistical analyses and scale up to large amounts of data of different modalities.

The goal of AI is automating reasoning tasks that until now have required human intelligence to solve. Humans rely heavily on causal reasoning to navigate the world, and while we are better at causal reasoning than statistical reasoning, our cognitive biases still make our causal reasoning highly error prone. Improving our ability to answer causal questions has been the work of millennia of philosophers, centuries of scientists, and decades of statisticians. But now, a convergence of statistical and computational advances has shifted the focus from discourse to algorithms that we can train on data and deploy to software. It is a fascinating time to learn how to build causal AI.

---

**Key definitions underpinning causal AI**
- *Inference*—Drawing conclusions from observations and data
- *Assumptions*—Constraints that guide inferences
- *Inductive biases*—Another word for *assumptions*, often used to refer to assumptions implicit in the choice of machine learning algorithm
- *Statistical model*—A framework using statistical assumptions to analyze data
- *Data science*—An interdisciplinary field that uses statistical models along with other algorithms and techniques to extract insights and knowledge from structured and unstructured data
- *Causal inference*—Techniques that use causal assumptions to guide conclusions
- *Causal model*—A statistical model built on causal assumptions about data generation

*(continued)*
- *Causal data science*—Data science that employs causal models to extract causal insights
- *Causal AI*—Algorithms that automate causal inference tasks using causal models

## 1.2 How this book approaches causal inference

The goal of this book is the fusion of two powerful domains: causality and AI. By the end of this journey, you'll be equipped with the skills to

- *Design AI systems with causal capabilities*—Harness the power of AI, but with an added layer of causal reasoning.
- *Use machine learning frameworks for causal inference*—Utilize tools like PyTorch and other Python libraries to seamlessly integrate causal modeling into your projects.
- *Build tools for automated causal decision-making*—Implement causal decision-making algorithms, including causal reinforcement learning algorithms.

Historically, causality and AI evolved from different bodies of research, they have been applied to different problems, and they have led to experts with different skill sets, books that use different languages, and libraries with different abstractions. This book is for anyone who wants to connect these domains into one comprehensive skill set.

There are many books on causal inference, including books that focus on causal inference in Python. The following subsections discuss some features that make this book unique.

### 1.2.1 Emphasis on AI

This book focuses on causal AI. We'll cover not just the relevance of causal inference to AI, or how machine learning can scale up causal inference, but also focus on implementation. Specifically, we'll integrate causal models with conventional models and training procedures from probabilistic machine learning.

### 1.2.2 Focus on tech, retail, and business

Practical causal inference methods have developed from econometrics, public health, social sciences, and other domains where it is difficult to run randomized experiments. As a result, examples in most books tend to come from those domains. In contrast, this book leans heavily into examples from tech, retail, and business.

### 1.2.3 Parallel world counterfactuals and other queries beyond causal effects

When many think of "causal inference," they think of estimating causal effects, namely average treatment effects (ATEs) and conditional average treatment effects (CATEs). These are certainly important queries, but there are other kinds of causal queries as well. This book gives due attention to these other types.

For example, this book provides in-depth coverage of the *parallel worlds* account of counterfactuals. In this approach, when some cause and some effect occur, we imagine a parallel universe where the causal event was different. For example, suppose you asked, "I married for money and now I'm sad. Would I have been happier had I married for love?" With our parallel worlds approach, you'd use your experience of marrying for money and being sad as inputs to a causal model-based probabilistic simulation of your happiness in a parallel universe where you married for love. This type of reasoning is useful in decision-making. For example, it might help you choose a better spouse next time.

Hopefully this example of love and regret illustrates how fundamental this kind of "what could have been" thinking is to human cognition (we'll see more applied examples in chapters 8 and 9). It therefore makes sense to learn how to build AI with the same capabilities. But although they're useful, some counterfactual inferences are hard or impossible to verify (you *can't* prove you would have been happier if you had married for love). Most causal inference books only focus on the narrow set of counterfactuals we can verify with data and experiments, which misses many interesting, cognitive science-aligned, and practical use cases of counterfactual reasoning. This book leans into those use cases.

### 1.2.4 An assumption of commodification of inference

Many causal inference books go deep into the statistical inference nuts and bolts of various causal effect estimators. But a major trend in the last decade of developing deep learning frameworks is the *commodification of inference*. This refers to how libraries like PyTorch abstract away the difficult aspects of estimation and inference—if you can define your estimation/inference problem in terms minimizing a differentiable loss function, PyTorch will handle the rest. The commodification of inference frees up the user to focus on creating ever more nuanced and powerful models, such as models that represent the causal structure of the data-generating process.

In this book, we'll focus on leveraging frameworks for inference so that you can learn a universal view of modeling techniques. Once you find the right modeling approach for your domain, you can use other resources to go deep into any statistical algorithm of interest.

### 1.2.5 Breaking down theory with code

One of the standout features of this book is its approach to advanced topics in causal inference theory. Many introductory texts shy away from subjects like identification, the do-calculus, and the causal hierarchy theorem because they are difficult. The problem is that if you want to create causal-capable AI algorithms, you need an intuition for these concepts.

In this book, we'll make these topics accessible by relying on Python libraries that implement their basic abstractions and algorithms. We'll build intuition for these advanced topics by working with these primitives in code.

## 1.3  *Causality's role in modern AI workflows*

There is great value in positioning ourselves to build future versions of AI with causal capabilities, but the topics covered in this book will also have an impact on applications common today. In this section, we'll review how causality can enhance some of these applications.

### 1.3.1  *Better data science*

Big tech and tech-powered retail organizations have recognized the significance of causal inference, offering premium salaries to those proficient in it. This is because the essence of data science—deriving actionable insights from data—is inherently causal.

When a data scientist examines the correlation between a feature on an e-commerce site and sales, they do so because they want to know whether the feature causally drives sales. Causal inference can help answer this question in several ways. First, it can help them design an experiment that will quantify the causal effect of the feature on sales, especially in the case where a perfect randomized experiment is not possible. Second, if a proposed experiment is not feasible, the data scientist can use past observational data and data from related but different past experiments to infer the value of the causal effect that would result from the proposed experiment without actually running it. Finally, even if the data scientist has complete freedom in running experiments, causal inference can help select which experiment to run and what variables to measure, minimizing the opportunity cost of running wasteful or uninformative experiments.

### 1.3.2  *Better attribution, credit assignment, and root cause analysis*

Causal inference also supports attribution. The "attribution problem" in marketing is perhaps best articulated by a quote credited to advertising pioneer John Wanamaker:

> *Half the money I spend on advertising is wasted; the trouble is*
> *I don't know which half.*

In other words, it is difficult to know what advertisement, promotion, or other action *caused* a specific customer behavior, sales number, or other key business outcome. Even in online marketing, where the data has gotten much richer and more granular than in Wanamaker's time, attribution remains a challenge. For example, a user may have clicked after seeing an ad, but was it that single ad view that led to the click? Or were they going to click anyway? Perhaps there was a cumulative effect of all the nudges to click that they received over multiple channels. Causal modeling addresses the attribution problem by using formal causal logic to answer "why" questions, such as "why did this user click?"

Attribution goes by other names in other domains, such as "credit assignment" and "root cause analysis." The core meaning is the same; we want to understand why a particular event outcome happened. We know what the causes are in general, but we want to know how much a particular cause is to blame in a given instance.

### 1.3.3 More robust, decomposable, and explainable models

For organizations that use machine learning to build software, incorporating causal modelling can improve both the process and the product. In particular, causality adds value by making machine learning more robust, decomposable, and explainable.

#### MORE ROBUST MACHINE LEARNING

Machine learning models lack robustness when differences between the environment where the model was trained and the environment where the model is deployed cause the model to break down. Causality can address the lack of robustness in the following ways:

- *Overfitting*—Overfitting occurs when learning algorithms place too much weight on spurious statistical patterns in the training data. Causal approaches can orient machine learning models toward learning statistical patterns that are rooted in causal relationships.
- *Underspecification*—Underspecification occurs when there are many equivalent configurations of a model that perform equivalently on test data but perform differently in the deployment environment. One sign of underspecification is sensitivity to arbitrary elements of the model's configuration, such as a random seed. Causal inference can tell you when a causal prediction is "identified" (i.e., not "underspecified"), meaning a unique answer exists given the assumptions and the data.
- *Data drift*—As time passes, the characteristics of the data in the environment where you deploy the model differ or "drift" from the characteristics of the training data. Causal modeling addresses this by capturing causal invariance underlying the data. For example, suppose you train a model that uses elevation to predict average temperature. If you train with data only from high-elevation cities, it should still work well in low-elevation cities if the model successfully fit the underlying physics-based causal relationship between altitude and temperature.

This is why leading tech companies deploy causal machine learning techniques—they can make their machine learning services more robust. It is also why notable deep learning researchers are pursuing research that combines deep learning with causal reasoning.

#### MORE DECOMPOSABLE MACHINE LEARNING

Causal models decompose into components, specifically tuples of effects and their direct causes, which I'll define formally in chapter 3. To illustrate, let's consider a simple machine learning problem of predicting whether an individual who sees a digital ad will go on to make a purchase.

We could use various characteristics of the ad impression (e.g., the number of times the ad was seen, the duration of the view, the ad category, the time of day, etc.) as the feature vector, and predict the purchase using a neural network, as depicted in figure 1.1. The weights in the hidden layers of the model are mutually dependent, so the model cannot be reduced to smaller independent components.

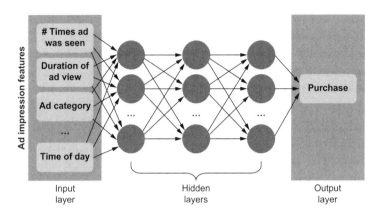

Figure 1.1   A simple multilayer perceptron neural network that uses features associated with ad impressions to predict whether a purchase will result

On the other hand, if we take a causal view of the problem, we might reason that an ad impression drives engagement, and that the engagement drives whether an individual makes a purchase. Using engagement metrics as another feature vector, we could instead train the model shown in figure 1.2. This model aligns with the causal structure of the domain (i.e., ad impressions causing engagement, and engagement causing purchases). As such, it decomposes into two components: {ad impression, engagement} and {engagement, purchase}.

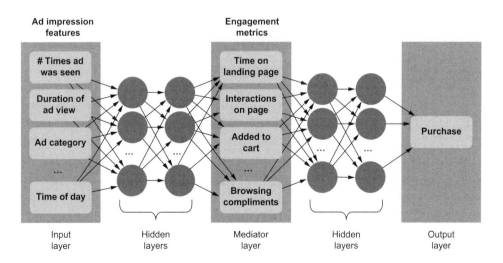

Figure 1.2   A model that captures how ad impressions drive engagement, which in turn drives purchases. This model decomposes into {ad impression, engagement} and {engagement, purchase}.

There are several benefits of this decomposability:

- Components of the model can be tested and validated independently.
- Components of the model can be executed separately, enabling more efficient use of modern cloud computing infrastructure and enabling edge computing.
- When additional training data is available, only the components relevant to the data need retraining.
- Components of old models can be reused in new models targeting new problems.
- There is less sensitivity to suboptimal model configuration and hyperparameter settings, because components can be optimized separately.

The components of the causal model correspond to concepts in the domain that you are modeling. This leads to the next benefit, explainability.

#### MORE EXPLAINABLE MACHINE LEARNING

Many machine learning algorithms, particularly deep learning algorithms, can be quite "black box," meaning the internal workings are not easily interpretable, and the process by which the model produces an output for a given input is not easily explainable.

In contrast, causal models are eminently explainable because they directly encode easy-to-understand causal relationships in the modeling domain. Indeed, causality is the core of explanation; explaining an event means describing the event's causes and how they led to the event occurring. Causal models provide explanations in the language of the domain you are modeling (semantic explanations) rather than in terms of the model's architecture (such as syntactic explanations of "nodes" and "activations").

Consider the examples in figures 1.1 and 1.2. In figure 1.1, only the input features and output are interpretable in terms of the domain; the internal workings of the hidden layers are not. Thus, given a particular ad impression, it is difficult to explain how the model arrives at a particular purchase outcome. In contrast, the example in figure 1.2 explicitly provides engagement to explain how we get from an ad impression to a purchase outcome.

The connections between engagement and ad impression, and between purchase and engagement, are still black boxes, but if we need to, we can make additional variables in those black boxes explicit. We just need to make sure we do so in a way that is aligned with our assumptions about the causal structure of the problem.

### 1.3.4   *Fairer AI*

Suppose Bob applies for a business loan. A machine learning algorithm predicts that Bob would be a bad loan candidate, so Bob is rejected. Bob is a man, and he got ahold of the bank's loan data, which shows that men are less likely to have their loan applications approved. Was this an "unfair" outcome?

We might say the outcome is "unfair" if, for example, the algorithm made that prediction *because* Bob is a man. To be a "fair" prediction, it would need to be formulated from factors relevant to Bob's ability to pay back the loan, such as his credit history, his line of business, or his available collateral. Bob's dilemma is another example of why we'd like machine learning to be explainable: so that we can analyze what factors in Bob's application led to the algorithm's decision.

Suppose the training data came from a history of decisions from loan officers, some of whom harbored a gender prejudice that hurt men. For example, they might have read studies that show men are more likely to default in times of financial difficulty. Based on those studies, they decided to deduct points from their rating if the applicant was a man.

Furthermore, suppose that when the data was collected, the bank advertised the loan program on social media. When we look at the campaign results, we notice that the men who responded to the ad were, on average, less qualified than the women who clicked on the ad. This discrepancy might have been because the campaign was better targeted toward women, or because the average bid price in online ad auctions was lower when the ad audience was composed of less-qualified men. Figure 1.3 plots various factors that might influence the loan approval process, and it distinguishes fair from unfair causes. The factors are plotted in a directed acyclic graph (DAG), a popular and effective way to represent causal relationships. We'll use DAGs as our workhorse for causal reasoning throughout the book.

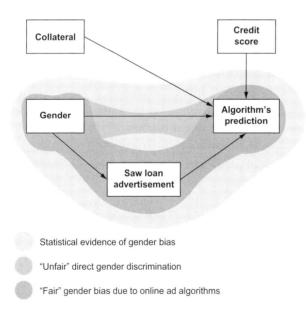

Figure 1.3   A causal directed acyclic graph (DAG) showing how statistical bias against a particular gender could come from an algorithm directly penalizing that gender (unfair) and indirectly through gender discrepancies in applicants targeted by digital advertising algorithms (fair). Causal inference can parse the bias into fair and unfair sources.

Thus, we have two possible sources of statistical bias against men in the data. One source of bias is from the online ad that attracted men who were, on average, less qualified, leading to a higher rejection rate for men. The other source of statistical bias comes from the prejudice of loan officers. One of these sources of bias is arguably "fair" (it's hard to blame the bank for the targeting behavior of digital advertising algorithms), and one of the sources is "unfair" (we *can* blame the bank for sexist loan policies). But when we only look at the training data without this causal context, all we see is statistical bias against men. The learning algorithm reproduced this bias when it made its decision about Bob.

One naive solution to this problem is simply to remove gender labels from the training data. But even if those sexist loan officers didn't see an explicit indication of the person's gender, they could infer it from elements of the application, such as the person's name. Those loan officers encode their prejudicial views in the form of a statistical correlation between those proxy variables for gender and loan outcome. The machine learning algorithm would discover this statistical pattern and use it to make predictions. As a result, you could have a situation where the algorithm produces two different predictions for two individuals who had the same repayment risk but differed in gender, even if gender wasn't a direct input to the prediction. Deploying this algorithm would effectively scale up the harm caused by those loan officers' prejudicial views.

For these reasons, we can see how many fears about the widespread deployment of machine learning algorithms are justified. Without corrections, these algorithms could adversely impact our society by magnifying the unfair outcomes captured in the data that our society produces.

Causal analysis is instrumental in parsing these kinds of algorithmic fairness issues. In this example, we could use causal analysis to parse the statistical bias into "unfair" bias due to sexism and bias due to external factors like how the digital advertising service targets ads. Ultimately, we could use causal modeling to build a model that only considers variables *causally relevant* to whether an individual can repay a loan.

It is important to note that causal inference alone is insufficient to solve algorithmic fairness. Causal inference can help parse statistical bias into what is fair and what's not. And yet, even that depends on all parties involved agreeing on definitions of concepts and outcomes, which is often a tall order. To illustrate, suppose that the social media ad campaign served the loan ad to more men because the cost of serving an ad to men is cheaper. Thus, an ad campaign can win the online ad spot auctions with lower bids when the impression is coming from a man, and, as a result, more men see the ad, though many of these men are not good matches for the loan program. Was this process unfair? Is the result unfair? What is the fairness tradeoff between balanced outcomes across genders and pricing fairness to advertisers? Should some advertisers have to pay more due to pricing mechanisms designed to encourage balanced outcomes? Causal analysis can't solve these questions, but it can help understand them in technical detail.

## 1.4 How causality is driving the next AI wave

Incorporating causal logic into machine learning is leading to new advances in AI. Three trending areas of AI highlighted in this book are representation learning, reinforcement learning, and large language models. These trends in causal AI are reminiscent of the early days of deep learning. People already working with neural networks when the deep learning wave was gaining momentum enjoyed first dibs on new opportunities in this space, and access to opportunities begets access to more opportunities. The next wave of AI is still taking shape, but it is clear it will fundamentally incorporate some representation of causality. The goal of this book is to help you ride that wave.

### 1.4.1   *Causal representation learning*

Many state-of-the-art deep learning methods attempt to learn geometric representations of the objects being modeled. However, these methods struggle with learning causally meaningful representations. For example, consider a video of a child holding a helium-filled balloon on a string. Suppose we had a corresponding vector representation of that image. If the vector representation were causally meaningful, then manipulating the vector to remove the child and converting the manipulated vector to a new video would result in a depiction of the balloon rising upwards. Causal representation learning is a promising area of deep representation learning that's still in its early stages. This book provides several examples in different chapters of causal models built upon deep learning architectures, providing an introduction to the fundamental ideas used in this exciting new growth area of causal AI.

### 1.4.2   *Causal reinforcement learning*

In canonical reinforcement learning, learning agents ingest large amounts of data and learn like Pavlov's dog; they learn actions that correlate positively with good outcomes and negatively with bad outcomes. However, as we all know, correlation does not imply causation. Causal reinforcement learning can highlight cases where the action that causes a higher reward differs from the action that correlates most strongly with high rewards. Further, it addresses the problem of credit assignment (correctly attributing rewards to actions) with counterfactual reasoning (i.e., asking questions like "how much reward would the agent have received had they been using a different policy?"). Chapter 12 is devoted to causal reinforcement learning and other areas of causal decision-making.

### 1.4.3   *Large language models and foundation models*

Large language models (LLMs) such as OpenAI's GPT, Google's Gemini, and Meta's Llama are deep neural language models with many billions of parameters trained on vast amounts of text and other data. These models can generate highly coherent natural language, code, and content of other modalities. They are foundation models, meaning they provide a foundation for building more domain-specific machine learning models and products. These products, such as Microsoft 365 Copilot, are already having a tremendous business impact.

A new area of investigation and product development investigates LLMs' ability to answer causal questions and perform causal analysis. Another line of investigation is using causal methods to design and train new LLMs with optimized causal capabilities. In chapter 13, we'll explore the intersection of LLMs and causality.

## 1.5    A machine learning-themed primer on causality

Now that you've seen the many ways that causal inference can improve machine learning, let's look at the process of incorporating causality into AI models. To do this, we will use a popular benchmark dataset often used in machine learning: the MNIST dataset of images of handwritten digits, each labeled with the actual digit represented in the image. Figure 1.4 illustrates multiple examples of the digits in MNIST.

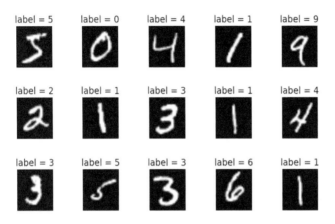

**Figure 1.4   Each image in the MNIST dataset is an image of a written digit, and each image is labeled with the digit it represents.**

MNIST is essentially the "Hello World" of machine learning. It is primarily used to experiment with different machine learning algorithms and to compare their relative strengths. The basic prediction task is to take the matrix of pixels representing each image as input and return the correct image label as output. Let's start the process of incorporating causal thinking into a probabilistic machine learning model applied to MNIST images.

### 1.5.1    Queries, probabilities, and statistics

First, we'll look at the basic process without including causal inference. Machine learning can use probability in analyses about quantities of interest. To do so, a probabilistic machine learning model learns a probabilistic representation of all the variables in that system. We can make predictions and decisions with probabilistic machine learning models using a three-step process.

   1   *Pose the question*—What is the question you want to answer?
   2   *Write down the math*—What probability (or probability-related quantity) will answer the question, given the evidence or data?
   3   *Do the statistical inference*—What statistical analysis will give you (or will *estimate*) that quantity?

There is more formal terminology for these steps (*query, estimand,* and *estimator*) but we'll avoid the jargon for now. Instead, we'll start with a simple statistical example problem. Your step 1 might be "How tall are Bostonians?" For step 2, you might decide that knowing the *mean* height (in probability terms, the "expected value") of everyone who lives in Boston will answer your question. Step 3 might involve randomly selecting 100 Bostonians and taking their average height; statistical theorems guarantee that this sample average is a close estimate of the true population mean.

Let's extend that workflow to modeling MNIST images.

### STEP 1: POSE THE QUESTION

Suppose we are looking at the MNIST image in figure 1.5, which could be a "4" or could be a "9". In step 1, we articulate a question, such as "given this image, what is the digit represented in this image?"

### STEP 2: WRITE DOWN THE MATH

In step 2, we want to find some probabilistic quantity that answers the question, given the evidence or data. In other words, we want to find something we can write down in probability math notation that can answer the question from step 1.

**Figure 1.5   Is this an image of the digit 4 or 9? The canonical task of the MNIST dataset is to classify the digit label given the image.**

For our example with figure 1.5, the "evidence" or "data" is the image. Is the image a 4 or a 9? Let the variable $I$ represent the image and $D$ represent the digit. In probability notation, we can write the probability that the digit is a 4, given the image, as $P(D=4|I=\textbf{9})$, where $I=\textbf{9}$ is shorthand for $I$ being equal to some vector representation of the image. We can compare this probability to $P(D=9|I=\textbf{9})$, and choose the value of $D$ that has the higher probability. Generalizing to all ten digits, the mathematical quantity we want in step 2 is shown in figure 1.6.

$$argmax_d \, P(D = d|I = \textbf{9})$$

**Figure 1.6   Choose the digit with the highest probability, given the image.**

In plain English, this is "the value $d$ that maximizes the probability that $D$ equals $d$, given the image," where $d$ is one of the ten digits (0–9).

### STEP 3: DO THE STATISTICAL INFERENCE

Step 3 uses statistical analysis to assign a number to the quantity we identified in step 2. There are any number of ways we can do this. For example, we could train a deep neural network that takes in the image as an input and predicts the digit as an output; we could design the neural net to assign a probability to $D=d$ for every value $d$.

## 1.5.2   *Causality and MNIST*

So how could causality feature in the previous section's three-step analysis? Yann LeCun is a Turing Award winner (computer science's equivalent of the Nobel prize) for his work on deep learning, and he's director of AI research at Meta. He is also one of the three researchers behind the creation of MNIST. He discusses the *causal* backstory of the MNIST data on his personal website, https://yann.lecun.com/exdb/mnist/index.html:

> *The MNIST database was constructed from NIST's Special Database 3 and Special Database 1 which contain binary images of handwritten digits. NIST originally designated SD-3 as their training set and SD-1 as their test set. However, SD-3 is much cleaner and easier to recognize than SD-1. The reason for this can be found on the fact that SD-3 was collected among Census Bureau employees, while SD-1 was collected among high-school students. Drawing sensible conclusions from learning experiments requires that the result be independent of the choice of training set and test among the complete set of samples. Therefore, it was necessary to build a new database by mixing NIST's datasets.*

In other words, the authors mixed the two datasets because they argue that if they trained a machine learning model solely on digits drawn by high schoolers, it would underperform when applied to digits drawn by bureaucrats. However, in real-world settings, we want robust models that can learn in one scenario and predict in another, even when those scenarios differ. For example, we want a spam filter to keep working when the spammers switch from Nigerian princes to Bhutanese princesses. We want our self-driving cars to stop even when there is graffiti on the stop sign. Shuffling the data like a deck of cards is a luxury not easily afforded in real-world settings.

Causal modeling leverages knowledge about the causal mechanisms underlying how the digits are drawn that will help models generalize beyond high school students and bureaucrats in the training data to high schoolers in the test data. Figure 1.7 illustrates a causal DAG representing this system.

This particular DAG imagines that the writer determines the thickness and curviness of the drawn digits, and that high schoolers tend to have a different handwriting style than bureaucrats. The graph also assumes that the writer's classification is a cause of what digits they draw. Perhaps bureaucrats write more 1s, 0s, and 5s, as these

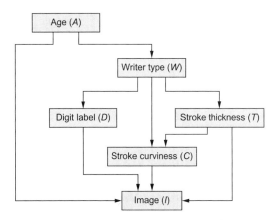

**Figure 1.7   An example causal DAG representing the generation of MNIST images. The nodes represent objects in the data generating process, and edges correspond to causal relationships between those objects.**

numbers occur more frequently in census work, while high schoolers draw other digits more often because they do more long division in math classes (this is a similar idea to how, in topic models, "topics" *cause* the frequency of words in a document). Finally, the DAG assumes that age is a common cause of writer type and image; you have to be below a certain age to be in high school and above a certain age to be a census official.

A causal modeling approach would use this causal knowledge to train a predictive model that could extrapolate from the high school training data to the bureaucrat test data. Such a model would generalize better to new situations where the distributions of writer type and other variables are different than in the training data.

### 1.5.3  *Causal queries, probabilities, and statistics*

At the beginning of this chapter, I discussed various types of causal questions we can pose, such as causal discovery, quantifying causal effects, and causal decision-making. We can answer these and various other questions with a causal variation on our previous three-step analysis (pose the question, write down the math, do the statistical inference):

1. *Pose the causal question*—What is the question you want to answer?
2. *Write down the causal math*—What probability (or expectation) will answer the causal question, given the evidence or data?
3. *Do the statistical inference*—What statistical analysis will give you (or "estimate") that causal quantity?

Note that the third step is the same as in the original three steps. The causal nuance occurs in the first and second steps.

#### STEP 1: POSE THE CAUSAL QUESTION

These are examples of some causal questions we could ask about our causal MNIST model:

- "How much does the writer's type (high schooler vs. bureaucrat) affect the look of an image of the digit 4 with level 3 thickness?" (*Conditional average treatment effect estimation* is discussed in chapter 11).
- Assuming that stroke thickness is a cause of the image, we might ask, "What would a 2 look like if it were as curvy as possible?" (This is *intervention prediction*, discussed in chapter 7).
- "Given an image, how would it have turned out differently if the stroke curviness were heavier?" (See *counterfactual reasoning*, discussed in chapters 8 and 9).
- "What should the stroke curviness be to get an aesthetically ideal image?" (*Causal decision-making* is discussed in chapter 12).

Let's consider the CATE in the first item. CATE estimation is a common causal inference question applied to ordinary tabular data, but rarely do we see it in the applied in the context of an AI computer vision problem.

#### STEP 2: WRITE DOWN THE CAUSAL MATH

Causal inference theory tells us how to mathematically formalize our causal question. Using special causal notation, we can mathematically formalize our CATE query as follows:

$$E(I_{W=\text{"high school"}}|D = 4, T = 3) - E(I_{W=\text{"bureaucrat"}}|D = 4, T = 3)$$

where $E(.)$ is an expectation operator. We'll review expectation in the next chapter, but for now we can think of it as an averaging of pixels across images.

The preceding use of subscripts is a special notation called "counterfactual notation" that represents an *intervention*. A random assignment in an experiment is a real-world intervention, but there are many experiments we can't run in the real world. For example, it wouldn't be feasible to run a trial where you randomly assign participants to either be a high school student or be a census bureau official. Nonetheless, we want to know how the writer type causally impacts the images, and thus we rely on a causal model and its ability to represent interventions.

To illustrate, figure 1.8 visualizes what CATE might look like. The challenge is deriving the differential image at the right of figure 1.8. Causal inference theory helps us address potential age-related "confounding" bias in quantifying how much writer type drives the image. For example, the *do-calculus* (chapter 10) is a set of graph-based rules that allows us to take this DAG and algorithmically derive the following equation:

$$E(I_{W=w}|D = 4, T = 3) = \sum_a E(I|W = w, A = a, D = 4, T = 3)P(A = a, D = 4, T = 3)$$

The left side of this equation defines the expectations used in the CATE definition in the second step—it is a theoretical construct that captures the hypothetical condition "if writer type were set to 'w'". But the right side is actionable; it is composed entirely of terms we could estimate using machine learning methods on a hypothetical version of NIST image data labeled with the writers' ages.

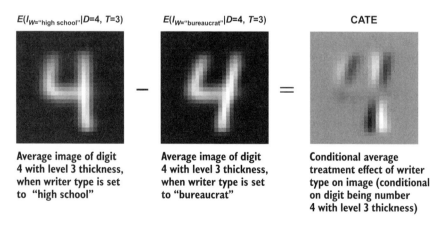

$E(I_{W=\text{"high school"}}|D{=}4, T{=}3)$    $E(I_{W=\text{"bureaucrat"}}|D{=}4, T{=}3)$    **CATE**

**Average image of digit 4 with level 3 thickness, when writer type is set to "high school"**

**Average image of digit 4 with level 3 thickness, when writer type is set to "bureaucrat"**

**Conditional average treatment effect of writer type on image (conditional on digit being number 4 with level 3 thickness)**

**Figure 1.8  Visualization of an example CATE of writer type on an image. It is the pixel-by-pixel difference of the expected image under one intervention ($W{=}_{\text{"high school"}}$) minus the expected image under another intervention ($W{=}_{\text{"bureaucrat"}}$), with both expectations conditional on being images of the digit 4 with a certain level of thickness.**

### STEP 3: DO THE STATISTICAL INFERENCE

Step 3 does the statistical estimation, and there are several ways we could estimate the quantities on the right side of that equation. For example, we could use a convolutional neural network to model $E(I|W=w, A=a, D=d, T=t)$, and build a probability model of the joint distribution $P(A, D, T)$. The choice of statistical modeling approach involves the usual statistical trade-offs, such as ease-of-use, bias and variance, scalability to large data, and parallelizability.

Other books go into great detail on preferred statistical methods for step 3. I take the strongly opinionated view that we should rely on the "commodification of inference" trend in statistical modeling and machine learning frameworks to handle step 3, and instead focus on honing our skills on steps 1 and 2: figuring out the right questions to ask, and representing the possible causes mathematically.

As you've seen in this section, our journey into causal AI is scaffolded by a three-step process, and the essence of causal thinking emerges prominently in the first two steps. Step 1 invites us to frame the right causal questions, while step 2 illuminates the mathematics behind these questions. Step 3 leverages patterns we're well-accustomed to in traditional statistical prediction and inference.

Using this structured approach, we'll transition in the coming chapters from purely predictive machine learning models—like the deep latent variable models you might be familiar with from MNIST—to causal machine learning models that offer deeper insights into and answers to our causal questions. First, we will review the underlying mathematics and machine learning foundations. Then, in part 2 of the book, we'll delve into crafting the right questions and articulating them mathematically for steps 1 and 2. For step 3, we'll harness the power of contemporary tools like PyTorch and other advanced libraries to bridge the causal concepts with cutting-edge statistical learning algorithms.

## *Summary*

- Causal AI seeks to augment statistical learning and probabilistic reasoning with causal logic.
- Causal inference helps data scientists extract more causal insights from observational data (the vast majority of data in the world) and experimental data.
- When data scientists can't run experiments, causal models can simulate experiments from observational data.
- They can use these simulations to make causal inferences, such as estimating causal effects, and even to prioritize interesting experiments to run in real life.
- Causal inference also helps data scientists improve decision-making in their organizations through algorithmic counterfactual reasoning and attribution.
- Causal inference also makes machine learning more *robust*, *decomposable*, and *explainable*.
- Causal analysis is useful for formally analyzing *fairness* in predictive algorithms and for building fairer algorithms by parsing ordinary statistical bias into its causal sources.

- The *commodification of inference* is a trend in machine learning that refers to how universal modeling frameworks like PyTorch continuously automate the nuts and bolts of statistical learning and probabilistic inference. The trend reduces the need for the modeler to be an expert at the formal and statistical details of causal inference and allows them to focus on turning domain expertise into better causal models of their problem domain.
- Types of causal inference tasks include *causal discovery, intervention prediction, causal effect estimation, counterfactual reasoning, explanation,* and *attribution.*
- The way we build and work with probabilistic machine learning models can be extended to causal generative models implemented in probabilistic machine learning tools such as PyTorch.

# A primer on probabilistic generative modeling

**This chapter covers**

- A primer on probability models
- Computational probability with the pgmpy and Pyro libraries
- Statistics for causality: data, populations, and models
- Distinguishing between probability models and subjective Bayesianism

Chapter 1 made the case for learning how to code causal AI. This chapter will introduce some fundamentals we need to tackle causal modeling with probabilistic machine learning, which roughly refers to machine learning techniques that use probability to model uncertainty and simulate data. There is a flexible suite of cutting-edge tools for building probabilistic machine learning models. This chapter will introduce the concepts from probability, statistics, modeling, inference, and even philosophy that we will need in order to implement key ideas from causal inference with the probabilistic machine learning approach.

This chapter will not provide a mathematically exhaustive introduction to these ideas. I'll focus on what is needed for the rest of this book and omit the rest. Any data scientist seeking causal inference expertise should not neglect the practical nuances of probability, statistics, machine learning, and computer science. See the chapter notes at www.altdeep.ai/causalAIbook for recommended resources where you can get deeper introductions or review materials.

In this chapter, I'll introduce two Python programming libraries for probabilistic machine learning:

- *pgmpy* is a library for building probabilistic graphical models. As a traditional graphical modeling tool, it is far less flexible and cutting-edge than Pyro but also easier to use and debug. What it does, it does well.
- *Pyro* is a general probabilistic machine learning library. It is quite flexible, and it leverages PyTorch's cutting-edge gradient-based learning techniques.

Pyro and pgmpy are the general modeling libraries we'll use in this book. Other libraries we'll use are designed specifically for causal inference.

## 2.1   Primer on probability

Let's review the probability theory you'll need to work with this book. We'll start with a few basic mathematical axioms and their logical extensions without yet adding any real-world interpretation. Let's begin with the concrete idea of a simple three-sided die (these exist).

### 2.1.1   Random variables and probability

A *random variable* is a variable whose possible values are the numerical outcomes of a random phenomenon. These values can be discrete or continuous. In this section, we'll focus on the discrete case. For example, the values of a discrete random variable representing a three-sided die roll could be {1, 2, 3}. Alternatively, in a 0-indexed programming language like Python, it might be better to use {0, 1, 2}. Similarly, a discrete random variable representing a coin flip could have outcomes {0, 1} or {True, False}. Figure 2.1 illustrates three-sided dice.

The typical approach to notation is to write random variables with capitals like $X$, $Y$, and $Z$. For example, suppose $X$ represents a die roll with outcomes {1, 2, 3}, and the outcome represents the number on the side of the die. $X=1$ and $X=2$ represent the events of rolling a 1 and 2 respectively. If we want to abstract

**Figure 2.1   Three-sided dice each represent a random variable with three discrete outcomes.**

away the specific outcome with a variable, we typically use lowercase. For example, I would use "*X*=*x*" (e.g., *X*=1) to represent the event "I rolled an '*x*'!" where *x* can be any value in {1, 2, 3}. See figure 2.2.

X=2

**Figure 2.2    *X* represents the outcome of a three-sided die roll. If the die roles a 2, the observed outcome is *X*=2.**

Each outcome of a random variable has a *probability value.* The probability value is often called a *probability mass* for discrete variables and a *probability density* for continuous variables. For discrete variables, probability values are between zero and one, and summing up the probability values for each possible outcome yields 1. For continuous variables, probability densities are greater than zero, and integrating the probability densities over each possible outcome yields 1.

Given a random variable with outcomes {0, 1} representing a coin flip, what is the probability value assigned to 0? What about 1? At this point, we just know the two values are between zero and one, and that they sum to one. To go beyond that, we have to talk about how to *interpret* probability. First, though, let's hash out a few more concepts.

### 2.1.2    *Probability distributions and distribution functions*

A *probability distribution function* is a function that maps the random variable outcomes to a probability value. For example, if the outcome of a coin flip is 1 (heads) and the probability value is 0.51, the distribution function maps 1 to 0.51. I stick to the standard notation $P(X=x)$, as in $P(X=1) = 0.51$. For longer expressions, when the random variable is obvious, I drop the capital letter and keep the outcome, so $P(X=x)$ becomes $P(x)$, and $P(X=1)$ becomes $P(1)$.

If the random variable has a finite set of discrete outcomes, we can represent the probability distribution with a table. For example, a random variable representing outcomes {1, 2, 3} might look like figure 2.3.

| X | 1 | 2 | 3 |
|-----|------|------|------|
| P(X) | 0.45 | 0.30 | 0.25 |

**Figure 2.3    A simple tabular representation of a discrete distribution**

In this book, I adopt the common notation $P(X)$ to represent the probability distribution over all possible outcomes of *X*, while $P(X=x)$ represents the probability value of a specific outcome. To implement a probability distribution as an object in pgmpy, we'll use the `DiscreteFactor` class.

**Listing 2.1  Implementing a discrete distribution table in pgmpy**

The values
each variable
in the factor
can take

```
from pgmpy.factors.discrete import DiscreteFactor
dist = DiscreteFactor(
    variables=["X"],
    cardinality=[3],
    values=[.45, .30, .25],
    state_names= {'X': ['1', '2', '3']}
)
print(dist)
```

A list of the names of the variables in the factor

The cardinality (number of possible outcomes) of each variable in the factor

A dictionary, where the key is the variable name and the value is a list of the names of that variable's outcomes

This code prints out the following:

```
+------+----------+
| X    | phi(X)   |
+======+==========+
| X(1) |   0.4500 |
+------+----------+
| X(2) |   0.3000 |
+------+----------+
| X(3) |   0.2500 |
+------+----------+
```

**Setting up your environment**

This code was written with pgmpy version 0.1.24 and Pyro version 1.8.6. The version of pandas used was 1.5.3.

See www.altdeep.ai/causalAIbook for links to the Jupyter notebooks for each chapter, with the code and notes on setting up a working environment.

### 2.1.3  Joint probability and conditional probability

Often, we are interested in reasoning about more than one random variable. Suppose, in addition to the random variable $X$ in figure 2.1, there was an additional random variable $Y$ with two outcomes $\{0, 1\}$. Then there is a *joint probability* distribution function that maps each combination of $X$ and $Y$ to a probability value.

| Y \ X | 1 | 2 | 3 |
|---|---|---|---|
| 0 | 0.25 | 0.20 | 0.15 |
| 1 | 0.20 | 0.10 | 0.10 |

**Figure 2.4  A simple representation of a tabular joint probability distribution**

As a table, it could look like figure 2.4.

The DiscreteFactor object can represent joint distributions as well.

**Listing 2.2  Modeling a joint distribution in pgmpy**

```
joint = DiscreteFactor(
    variables=['X', 'Y'],
    cardinality=[3, 2],
```

X has 3 outcomes, Y has 2.

Now we have two variables instead of one.

```
values=[.25, .20, .20, .10, .15, .10],
    state_names= {
        'X': ['1', '2', '3'],
        'Y': ['0', '1']
    }
)
print(joint)
```

◁— **Now there are two variables, so we name the outcomes for both variables.**

◁— **You can look at the printed output to see how the values are ordered of values.**

The preceding code prints this output:

```
+------+------+------------+
| X    | Y    |  phi(X,Y)  |
+======+======+============+
| X(1) | Y(0) |    0.2500  |
+------+------+------------+
| X(1) | Y(1) |    0.2000  |
+------+------+------------+
| X(2) | Y(0) |    0.2000  |
+------+------+------------+
| X(2) | Y(1) |    0.1000  |
+------+------+------------+
| X(3) | Y(0) |    0.1500  |
+------+------+------------+
| X(3) | Y(1) |    0.1000  |
+------+------+------------+
```

Note that the probability values sum to 1. Further, when we marginalize (i.e., "sum over" or "integrate over") $Y$ across the rows, we recover the original distribution $P(X)$, (aka the marginal distribution of $X$). Summing up over the rows in figure 2.5 produces the marginal distribution of $X$ on the bottom.

| Y \ X | 1 | 2 | 3 |
|---|---|---|---|
| 0 | 0.25 | 0.20 | 0.15 |
| 1 | 0.20 | 0.10 | 0.10 |
| **P(X)** | 0.45 | 0.30 | 0.25 |

**Figure 2.5   Marginalizing over $Y$ yields the marginal distribution of $X$.**

The marginalize method will sum over the specified variables for us.

```
print(joint.marginalize(variables=['Y'], inplace=False))
```

This prints the following output:

```
+------+----------+
| X    |  phi(X)  |
+======+==========+
| X(1) |  0.4500  |
+------+----------+
| X(2) |  0.3000  |
+------+----------+
| X(3) |  0.2500  |
+------+----------+
```

Setting the `inplace` argument to `False` gives us a new marginalized table rather than modifying the original joint distribution table.

| Y \ X | 1 | 2 | 3 | P(Y) |
|---|---|---|---|---|
| 0 | 0.25 | 0.20 | 0.15 | 0.60 |
| 1 | 0.20 | 0.10 | 0.10 | 0.40 |

**Figure 2.6** Marginalizing over *X* yields the marginal distribution of *Y.*

Similarly, when we marginalize $X$ over the columns, we get $P(Y)$. In figure 2.6, summing over the values of $X$ in the columns gives us the marginal distribution of $Y$ on the right.

```
print(joint.marginalize(variables=['X'], inplace=False))
```

This prints the following output:

```
+------+----------+
|  Y   |  phi(Y)  |
+======+==========+
| Y(0) |  0.6000  |
+------+----------+
| Y(1) |  0.4000  |
+------+----------+
```

I'll use the notation $P(X, Y)$ to represent joint distributions. I'll use $P(X=x, Y=y)$ to represent an outcome probability, and for shorthand, I'll write $P(x, y)$. For example, in figure 2.6, $P(X=1, Y=0) = P(1, 0) = 0.25$. We can define a joint distribution on any number of variables; if there were three variables $\{X, Y, Z\}$, I'd write the joint distribution as $P(X, Y, Z)$.

In this tabular representation of the joint probability distribution, the number of cells increases exponentially with each additional variable. There are some (but not many) "canonical" joint probability distributions (such as the multivariate normal distribution—I'll show more examples in section 2.1.7). For that reason, in multivariate settings, we tend to work with *conditional probability* distributions.

The conditional probability of $Y$, given $X$, is

$$P(Y = y | X = x) = \frac{P(X = x, Y = y)}{P(X = x)}$$

Intuitively, $P(Y|X=1)$ refers to the probability distribution for Y conditional on $X$ being 1. In the case of tabular representations of distributions, we can derive the conditional distribution table by dividing the cells in the joint probability distribution table with the marginal probability values, as in figure 2.7. Note that the columns on the conditional probability table in figure 2.7 now sum to 1.

| Y \ X | 1 | 2 | 3 |
|---|---|---|---|
| 0 | 0.25 | 0.20 | 0.15 |
| 1 | 0.20 | 0.10 | 0.10 |
| P(X) | 0.45 | 0.30 | 0.25 |

| Y \ X | 1 | 2 | 3 |
|---|---|---|---|
| 0 | 0.25/0.45 | 0.20/0.30 | 0.15/0.25 |
| 1 | 0.20/0.45 | 0.10/0.30 | 0.10/0.25 |

$$P(Y = y | X = x) = \frac{P(X = x, Y = y)}{P(X = x)}$$

**Figure 2.7** Derive the values of the conditional probability distribution by dividing the values of the joint distribution by those of the marginal distribution.

The pgmpy library allows us to do this division using the "/" operator:

```
print(joint / dist)
```

That line produces the following output:

```
+------+------+------------+
| X    | Y    |  phi(X,Y)  |
+======+======+============+
| X(1) | Y(0) |     0.5556 |
+------+------+------------+
| X(1) | Y(1) |     0.4444 |
+------+------+------------+
| X(2) | Y(0) |     0.6667 |
+------+------+------------+
| X(2) | Y(1) |     0.3333 |
+------+------+------------+
| X(3) | Y(0) |     0.6000 |
+------+------+------------+
| X(3) | Y(1) |     0.4000 |
+------+------+------------+
```

Also, you can directly specify a conditional probability distribution table with the TabularCPD class:

```
from pgmpy.factors.discrete.CPD import TabularCPD
PYgivenX = TabularCPD(
    variable='Y',
    variable_card=2,
    values=[
        [.25/.45, .20/.30, .15/.25],
        [.20/.45, .10/.30, .10/.25],
    ],
    evidence=['X'],
    evidence_card=[3],
    state_names = {
        'X': ['1', '2', '3'],
        'Y': ['0', '1']
    })
```

A conditional distribution has one variable instead of DiscreteFactor's list of variables.

variable_card is the cardinality of Y.

Elements of the list correspond to outcomes for Y. Elements of each list correspond to elements of X.

```
print(PYgivenX)
```

That produces the following output:

```
+------+--------------------+--------------------+------+
| X    | X(1)               | X(2)               | X(3) |
+------+--------------------+--------------------+------+
| Y(0) | 0.5555555555555556 | 0.6666666666666667 | 0.6  |
+------+--------------------+--------------------+------+
| Y(1) | 0.4444444444444445 | 0.33333333333333337| 0.4  |
+------+--------------------+--------------------+------+
```

The variable_card argument  is the cardinality of $Y$ (meaning the number of outcomes $Y$ can take), and evidence_card is the cardinality of $X$.

### Conditioning as an operation

In the phrase "conditional probability," "conditional" is an adjective. It is useful to think of "condition" as a verb (an action). You condition a random variable like *Y* on another random variable *X*. For example, in figure 2.5, I can condition *Y* on *X*=1, and essentially get a new random variable with the same outcome values as *Y* but with a probability distribution equivalent to *P*(*Y*|*X*=1).

For those with more programming experience, think of conditioning on *X* = 1 as filtering on the event *X* == 1; for example, "what is the probability distribution of *Y* when *X* == 1?" Filtering in this sense is like the WHERE clause in a SQL query. *P*(*Y*) is the distribution of the rows in the *Y* table when your query is SELECT * FROM Y, and *P*(*Y*|*X*=1) is the distribution of the rows when your query is SELECT * FROM Y WHERE X=1.

Thinking of "conditioning" as an action helps us better understand probabilistic machine learning libraries. In these libraries, you have objects representing random variables, and conditioning is an operation applied to these objects. As you'll see, the idea of conditioning as an action also contrasts nicely with the core causal modeling concept of "intervention," where we "intervene" on a random variable.

Pyro implements conditioning as an operation with the `pyro.condition` function. We'll explore this in chapter 3.

### 2.1.4 *The chain rule, the law of total probability, and Bayes Rule*

From the basic axioms of probability, we can derive the chain rule of probability, the law of total probability, and Bayes rule. These laws of probability are especially important in the context of probabilistic modeling and causal modeling, so we'll highlight them briefly.

The *chain rule of probability* states that we can factorize a joint probability into the product of conditional probabilities. For example *P*(*X*, *Y*, *Z*) can be factorized as follows:

$$P(x, \ y, \ z) \ = \ P(x)P \ (y|x)P(z|x, \ y)$$

We can factorize in any order we like. Above, the ordering was *X*, then *Y*, then *Z*. However, *Y*, then *Z*, then *X*, or *Z*, then *X*, then *Y*, and other orderings are just as valid.

$$P \ (x, \ y, \ z) = P \ (y) \ P \ (z| \ y) \ P \ (x| \ y, z)$$
$$= P \ (y) \ P \ (z| \ y) \ P \ (x| \ z, y)$$
$$= P \ (z) \ P \ (x| \ z) \ P(y|z, \ x)$$

The chain rule is important from a modeling and a computational perspective. The challenge of implementing a single object that represents *P*(*X*, *Y*, *Z*) is that it needs to map each combination of possible outcomes for *X*, *Y*, and *Z* to a probability value. The chain rule lets us break this into three separate tasks for each factor in a factorization of *P*(*X*, *Y*, *Z*).

The *law of total probability* allows you to relate marginal probability distributions (distributions of individual variables) to joint distributions. For example, if we want to derive the marginal distribution of $X$, denoted $P(X)$, from the distribution of $X$ and $Y$, denoted $P(X, Y)$, we can sum over $Y$.

$$P(x) = \sum_y P(x, y)$$

In figure 2.5, we did this by summing over $Y$ in the rows to get $P(X)$. In the case where $X$ is a continuous random variable, we integrate over $Y$ rather than summing over $Y$.

Finally, we have *Bayes rule*:

$$P(x \mid y) = \frac{P(y|x)P(x)}{P(y)}$$

We derive this by taking the original definition of conditional probability and applying the chain rule to the numerator:

$$P(x \mid y) = \frac{P(x, y)}{P(y)} = \frac{P(y|x)P(x)}{P(y)}$$

By itself, the Bayes rule is not particularly interesting—it's a derivation. The more interesting idea is *Bayesianism*, a philosophy that uses Bayes rule to help the modeler reason about their subjective uncertainty regarding the problems they are modeling. I'll touch on this in section 2.4.

### 2.1.5   *Markovian assumptions and Markov kernels*

A common approach to modeling when you have chains of factors is to use *Markovian assumptions*. This modeling approach takes an ordering of variables and makes a simplifying assumption that every element in the ordering depends only on the element that came directly before it. For example, consider again the following factorization of $P(x, y, z)$:

$$P(x, y, z) = P(x)P(y|x)P(z|x, y)$$

If we applied a Markovian assumption, this would simplify to:

$$P(x, y, z) = P(x)P(y|x)P(z|y)$$

This would let us replace $P(z|x, y)$ with $P(z|y)$, which is easier to model. In this book, when we have a factor from a factorization that has been simplified using the Markov assumption, like $P(z|y)$, we'll call it a *Markov kernel*.

The Markov assumption is a common simplifying assumption in statistics and machine learning; $Z$ may *actually* still depend on $X$ after accounting for $Y$, but we're *assuming* that the dependence is weak and we can safely ignore it in our model. We'll see that the Markovian assumption is key to graphical causality, where we'll assume effects are independent of their indirect causes, given their direct causes.

### 2.1.6 *Parameters*

Suppose I wanted to implement in code an abstract representation of a probability distribution, like the tabular distribution in figure 2.1, that I could use for different finite discrete outcomes. To start, if I were to model another three-sided die, it might have different probability values. What I want to keep is the basic structure as in figure 2.8.

| *X* | 1 | 2 | 3 |
|-----|---|---|---|
| *P(X)* | | | |

**Figure 2.8** The scaffolding for a tabular probability distribution data structure

In code, I could represent this as some object type with a constructor that takes two arguments, $\rho_1$ and $\rho_2$, as in figure 2.9 ("$\rho$" is the Greek letter "rho").

The reason the third probability value is a function of the other two (instead of a third argument, $\rho_3$) is because the probability values must sum to one. The set of two values $\{\rho_1, \rho_2\}$ are the parameters of the distribution. In programming terms, I could create a data type that represents

| *X* | 1 | 2 | 3 |
|-----|---|---|---|
| *P(X)* | $\rho_1$ | $\rho_2$ | $1-\rho_1-\rho_2$ |

**Figure 2.9** Adding parameters to the data structure

a table with three values. Then, when I want a new distribution, I could construct a new instance of this type with these two parameters as arguments.

Finally, in my three-sided die example, there were three outcomes, $\{1, 2, 3\}$. Perhaps I want my data structure to handle a different prespecified number of outcomes. In that case, I'd need a parameter for the number of outcomes. Let's denote that with the Greek letter kappa, $\kappa$. My parameterization is $\{\kappa, \rho_1, \rho_2, \dots \rho_{\kappa-1}\}$, where $\rho_\kappa$ is 1 minus the sum of the other $\rho$ parameters.

In the pgmpy classes `DiscreteFactor` and `TabularCPD`, the $\rho$'s (rhos) are the list of values passed to the `values` argument, and the $\kappa$ corresponds to the values passed to the `cardinality`, `variable_card`, and `evidence_card` arguments. Once we have a representation of a probability distribution like `TabularCPD`, we can specify an instance of that distribution with a set of parameters.

### Greeks vs. Romans

In this book, I use Roman letters (*A*, *B*, and *C*) to refer to random variables representing objects in the modeling domain, such as a "dice roll" or "gross domestic product," and I use Greek letters for so-called *parameters*. *Parameters* in this context are values that characterize the probability distributions of the Roman-lettered variables. This distinction between Greeks and Romans is not as important in statistics; for example, a Bayesian statistician treats both Roman and Greek letters as random variables. However, in causal modeling the difference matters, because Roman letters can be causes and effects, while Greek letters serve to characterize the statistical relationship between causes and effects.

### 2.1.7    *Canonical classes of probability distribution*

There are several common classes of distribution functions. For example, the tabular examples we just studied are examples from the class of *categorical distributions*. Categorical distributions are distributions on discrete outcomes we can view as categories, such as {"ice cream", "frozen yogurt", "sherbet"}. A Bernoulli distribution class is a special case of the categorical class where there are only two possible outcomes. A discrete uniform distribution is a categorical distribution where all outcomes have the same probability. In implementation, categorical distributions are defined either on the categories directly (like "tails" and "heads") or on indices to the category (like 0 and 1).

> **Discrete vs. continuous random variables**
>
> For discrete random variables, we have been using have probability distribution functions with the notation $P(X=x)$. Probability distribution functions return the probability that a variable takes a specific value. With continuous random variables, we also have *probability density functions*, which describe the relative likelihood of observing any outcome within a continuous range and that integrate over an interval to give a probability.
>
> When we have specific cases where discrete or continuous parameterizations matter, we'll call them out and use $p(X=x)$ to denote a probability density function. However, in this book, we'll focus on framing our causal questions independently of whether we're in a discrete or continuous setting. We'll stick mostly to the probability distribution function notation $P(X=x)$, but keep in mind that the causal ideas work in the continuous case as well.

There are other canonical distribution classes appropriate for continuous, bounded, or unbounded sets of variables. For example, the normal (Gaussian) distribution class illustrates the famous "bell curve." I use the term "class" (or, perhaps more ideally, "type") in the computer science sense because the distribution isn't realized until we assign our Greek-lettered parameters. For a normal (Gaussian) distribution class, the probability density function is

$$p(X = x) = \frac{1}{\sqrt{2\pi\sigma^2}} e^{-\frac{1}{2\sigma^2}(x-\mu)^2}$$

Here, $\mu$ and $\sigma$ are the parameters.

Figure 2.10 is a popular figure that illustrates several commonly used canonical distributions. The arrows between the distributions highlight relationships between the distributions (e.g., Bernoulli is a special case of the binomial distribution) that we won't dive into here.

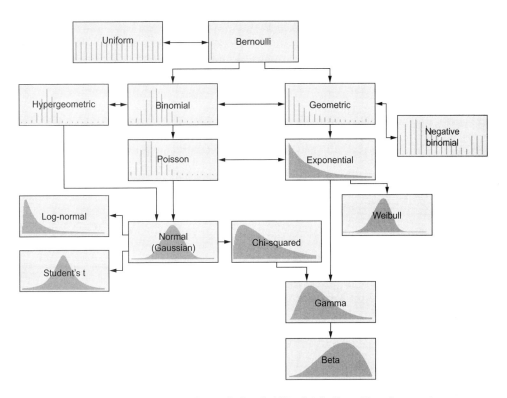

**Figure 2.10** **A popular common set of canonical probability distributions. The edges capture mathematical relationships between the distributions (that we won't get into here). Light-colored distributions are discrete and dark-colored distributions are continuous. An arrow represents the existence of a transformation that converts one distribution to another.**

### TYPES OF PARAMETERS

In probabilistic modeling settings, it is useful to have an intuition for how to interpret canonical parameters. To that end, think of the probability in a distribution as a scarce resource that must be shared across all the possible outcomes. Some outcomes may get more than others, but at the end of the day, it all must sum or integrate to 1. Parameters characterize how the finite probability is distributed to the outcomes.

As an analogy, we'll use a city with a fixed population. The parameters of the city determine where that population is situated. Location parameters, such as the normal distribution's "$\mu$" ($\mu$ is the mean of the normal, but not all *location parameters* are means), are like the pin that drops down when you search the city's name in Google Maps. The pin characterizes a precise point we might call the "city center." In some cities, most of the people live near the city center, and it gets less populated the further away from the center you go. But in other cities, other non-central parts of the city are densely populated. *Scale parameters*, like the normal's "$\sigma$" ($\sigma$ is the standard deviation of a normal distribution, but not all scale parameters are standard deviation parameters), determine the spread of the population; Los Angeles has a high scale parameter. A *shape parameter* (and its inverse, the *rate parameter*) affects the shape of a distribution in a manner that does not simply shift it (as a location parameter does) or stretch or shrink it (as a scale parameter does). As an example, think of the skewed shape of Hong Kong, which has a densely packed collection of skyscrapers in the downtown area, while the more residential Kowloon has shorter buildings spread over a wider space.

The Pyro library provides canonical distributions as modeling primitives. The Pyro analog to a discrete categorical distribution table is a `Categorical` object.

---

**Listing 2.3   Canonical parameters in Pyro**

```
import torch
from pyro.distributions import Bernoulli, Categorical, Gamma, Normal

print(Categorical(probs=torch.tensor([.45, .30, .25])))
print(Normal(loc=0.0, scale=1.0))
print(Bernoulli(probs=0.4))
print(Gamma(concentration=1.0, rate=2.0))
```

> **Pyro includes the commonly used canonical distributions.**

> **The Categorical distribution takes a list of probability values, each value corresponding to an outcome.**

---

This prints the following representations of the distribution objects:

```
Categorical(probs: torch.Size([3]))
Normal(loc: 0.0, scale: 1.0)
Bernoulli(probs: 0.4000)
Gamma(concentration: 1.0, rate: 2.0)
```

Rather than providing a probability value, the `log_prob` method will provide the natural log of the probability value, because log probabilities have computational advantages over regular probabilities. Exponentiating (taking $e^l$ where $l$ is the log probability) converts back to the probability scale. For example, we can create a Bernoulli distribution object with a parameter value of 0.4.

```
bern = Bernoulli(0.4)
```

That distribution assigns a 0.4 probability to the value 1.0. For numerical reasons, we typically work with the natural log of probability values.

We can use the `exp` function in the math library to convert from log probability back to the probability scale:

```
lprob = bern.log_prob(torch.tensor(1.0))

import math
print(math.exp(lprob))
```

Exponentiating the log probability returns the following probability value:

```
0.3999999887335489
```

It is close, but not the same as 0.4 due to rounding error associated with floating-point precision in computer calculations.

**CONDITIONAL PROBABILITY WITH CANONICAL DISTRIBUTIONS**

There are few canonical distributions commonly used to characterize sets of individual random variables, such as random vectors or matrices. However, we can use the chain rule to factor a joint probability distribution into conditional distributions that we can represent with canonical distributions. For example, we could represent $Y$ conditioned on $X$ and $Z$ with the following normal distribution,

$$p(y|x, z) = \frac{1}{\sqrt{2\pi\sigma^2}} e^{-\frac{1}{2\sigma^2}(y-\mu(x,z))^2}$$

where the location parameter $\mu(x,z)$ is a function of $x$ and $z$. An example is the following linear function:

$$\mu(x,\ z) = \beta_0 + \beta_x x + \beta_z z$$

Other functions, such as neural networks, are possible as well. These $\beta$ parameters are typically called *weight parameters* in machine learning.

### 2.1.8 *Visualizing distributions*

In probabilistic modeling and Bayesian inference settings, we commonly conceptualize distributions in terms of visuals. In the discrete case, a common visualization is the bar plot. For example, we can visualize the probabilities in figure 2.3 as the bar plot in figure 2.11. Note that this is not a histogram; I'll highlight the distinction in section 2.3.

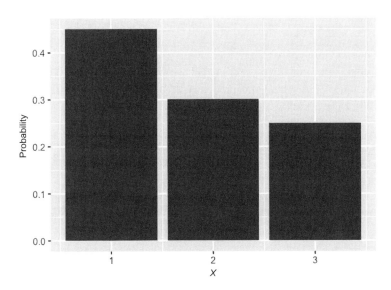

**Figure 2.11**
**Visualization of a discrete probability distribution. The outcomes in the distribution are on the horizontal axis, and probability is on the vertical axis.**

We still use visualizations when the distribution has a non-finite set of outcomes. For example, figure 2.12 overlays two distributions functions: a discrete Poisson distribution and a continuous normal (Gaussian) distribution (I specified the two distributions in such a way that they overlapped). The discrete Poisson has no upper bound on outcomes (its lower bound is 0), but the probability tapers off for higher numbers, resulting in smaller and smaller bars until the bar becomes too infinitesimally small to draw. We visualize the normal distribution by simply drawing the probability distribution function as a curve in the figure. The normal has no lower or upper bound, but the further away you get from the center, the smaller the probability values get.

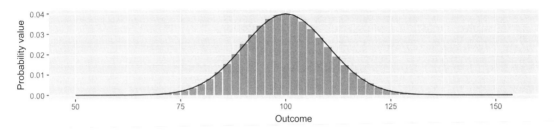

**Figure 2.12    A continuous normal distribution (solid line) approximates a discrete Poisson distribution (gray bars). Again, the outcomes are on the horizontal axis, and the probability values are on the vertical axis.**

Visualizing conditional probability distributions involves mapping each conditioning variable to some element in the image. For example, in figure 2.13, $X$ is discrete, and $Y$ conditioned on $X$ has a normal distribution where the location parameter is a function of $X$.

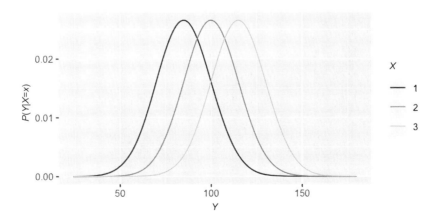

**Figure 2.13    A visualization of the conditional probability distribution of continuous $Y$, given discrete $X$. For different values of $X$, we get a different distribution of $Y$.**

Since $X$ is discrete, it is simplest to map $X$ to color and overlay the curves for $P(Y|X=1)$, $P(Y|X=2)$, and $P(Y|X=3)$. However, if we wanted to visualize $P(Y|X, Z)$, we'd need to map $Z$ to an aesthetic element other than color, such as a third axis in a pseudo-3D image or rows in a grid of images. But there is only so much information we can add to a 2D visualization. Fortunately, conditional independence helps us reduce the number of conditioning variables.

### 2.1.9 *Independence and conditional independence*

Two random variables are *independent* if, informally speaking, observing an outcome of one random variable does not affect the probability of outcomes for the other variable, i.e., $P(y|x) = P(y)$. We denote this as $X \perp Y$. If two variables are not independent, they are *dependent.*

Two dependent variables can become *conditionally independent* given other variables. For example, $X \perp Y | Z$ means that $X$ and $Y$ may be dependent, but they are conditionally independent given $Z$. In other words, if $X$ and $Y$ are dependent, and $X \perp Y | Z$, then it is not true that $P(y|x) \neq P(y)$ but it is true that $P(y|x, z) = P(y|z)$.

#### INDEPENDENCE IS A POWERFUL TOOL FOR SIMPLIFICATION

Independence is a powerful tool for simplifying representations of probability distributions. Consider a joint probability distribution $P(W, X, Y, Z)$ represented as a table. The number of cells in the table would be the product of the number of possible outcomes each for $W$, $X$, $Y$, and $Z$. We could use the chain rule to break the problem up into factors $\{P(W), P(X|W), P(Y|X, W), P(Z|Y, X, W)\}$, but the total number of parameters across these factors wouldn't change, so the aggregate complexity would be the same.

However, what if $X \perp W$? Then $P(X|W)$ reduces to $P(X)$. What if $Z \perp Y|X$? Then $P(Z|Y, X, W)$ reduces to $P(Z|X, W)$. Every time we can impose a pairwise conditional independence condition as a constraint on the joint probability distribution, we can reduce the complexity of the distribution by a large amount. Indeed, much of model building and evaluation in statistical modeling, regularization in machine learning, and deep learning techniques such as "drop-out" are either direct or implicit attempts to impose conditional independence on the joint probability distribution underlying the data.

#### CONDITIONAL INDEPENDENCE AND CAUSALITY

Conditional independence is fundamental to causal modeling. Causal relationships lead to conditional independence between correlated variables. For example, a child's parents' and grandparents' blood types are all causes of that child's blood type; these blood types are all correlated. But all you need is the parents' blood type, the direct causes, to fully determine the child's blood type, as illustrated in figure 2.14. In probabilistic terms, the child's and grandparents' blood types are conditionally independent, given the parents.

The fact that causality induces conditional independence allows us to learn and validate causal models against evidence of conditional independence. In chapter 4, we'll explore the relationship between conditional independence and causality in formal terms.

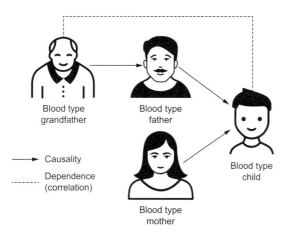

**Figure 2.14   How causality can induce conditional independence.** The blood types of the parents cause the blood type of the child. The grandfather's blood type is correlated with that of the child's (dashed line). But the parents' blood types are direct causes that fully determine that of the child. These direct causes render the child's and grandfather's blood types conditionally independent.

### 2.1.10  *Expected value*

The *expected value* of a function of a random variable is the weighted average of the function's possible output values, where the weight is the probability of that outcome.

$$E\left(f\left(X\right)\right) = \sum_{X=x} f\left(x\right) P\left(x\right)$$

$$E\left(f(X)\mid Y=y\right) = \sum_{X=x} f(x) P\left(x\mid y\right)$$

In the case of a continuum of possible outcomes, the expectation is defined by integration.

$$E\left(f(X)\right) = \int_{X=u} f\left(u\right) p\left(u\right) du$$

$$E\left(f(X)\mid Y=y\right) = \int_{X=u} f(u) p\left(u\mid y\right) du$$

Some of the causal quantities we'll be interested in calculating will be defined in terms of expectation. Those quantities only reason about the expectation, not about how the expectation is calculated. It is easier to get an intuition for a problem when working with the basic arithmetic of discrete expectation rather than integral calculus in the continuous case. So, in this book, when there is a choice, I use examples with discrete random variables and discrete expectation. The causal logic in those examples all generalize to the continuous case.

There are many interesting mathematical properties of expectation. In this book, we care about the fact that conditional expectations simplify under conditional independence: If $X \perp Y$, then $E(X|Y) = E(X)$. If $X \perp Y|Z$, then $E(X|Y,Z) = E(X|Z)$. In simpler terms, if two variables ($X$ and $Y$) are independent, our expectation for one does not change with information about the other. If their independence holds conditional on a third variable $(Z)$, our expectation for one, given that we know the third variable, is unaffected by information about the other variable.

Other than this, the most important property is the linearity of the expectation, meaning that the expectation passes through linear functions. Here are some useful reference examples of the linearity of expectation:

- For random variables $X$ and $Y$: $E(X + Y) = E(X) + E(Y)$ and

$$E(\sum_i X_i) = \sum_i E(X_i)$$

- For constants $a$ and $b$: $E(aX + b) = aE(X) + b$
- If $X$ only has outcomes 0 and 1, and $E(Y|X) = aX + b$, then $E(Y|X=1) - E(Y|X=0)$ $= a$. (This is true because $a*1 + b - (a*0 + b) = a$. Spoiler alert: this one is important for linear regression-based causal effect inference techniques.)

The mean of the random variable's distribution is the expected value of the variable itself, as in $E(X)$ (i.e., the function is the *identity function*, $f(X) = X$). In several canonical distributions, the mean is a simple function of the parameters. In some cases, such as in the normal distribution, the location parameter is equivalent to the expectation. But the location parameter and the expectation are not always the same. For example, the Cauchy distribution has a location parameter, but its mean is undefined.

In the next section, you'll learn how to represent distributions and calculate expectations using computational methods.

## 2.2  Computational probability

We need to *code* probability distributions and expectations from probability to use them in our models. In the previous section, you saw how to code up a probability distribution for a three-sided die. But how do we code up *rolling* a three-sided die? How do we write code representing two dice rolls that are conditionally independent? While we're at it, how do we get a computer to do the math that calculates an expectation? How do we get a computer, where everything is deterministic, to roll dice so that the outcome is unknown beforehand?

### 2.2.1  The physical interpretation of probability

Suppose I have a three-sided die. I have some probability values assigned to each outcome on the die. What do those probability values mean? How do I interpret them?

Suppose I repeatedly rolled the die and kept a running tally of how many times I saw each outcome. First, the roll is random, meaning that although I roll it the same way each time, I get varying results. The physical shape of the die affects those tallies; if one face of the die is larger than the other two, that size difference will affect the count. As I repeat the roll many times, the proportion of total times I see a given outcome converges to a number. Suppose I use that number for my probability value. Further, suppose I interpret that number as the "chance" of seeing that outcome each time I roll.

This idea is called *physical* (or *frequentist*) *probability*. Physical probability means imagining some repeatable physical random process that results in one outcome among a set of possible outcomes. We assign a probability value using the convergent proportion of times the outcome appears when we repeat the random process ad infinitum. We then interpret that probability as the propensity for that physical process to produce that outcome.

### 2.2.2   *Random generation*

Given the preceding definition for physical probability, we can define random generation. In *random generation*, an algorithm randomly chooses an outcome from a given distribution. The algorithm's choice is inspired by physical probability; the way it selects an outcome is such that if we ran the algorithm ad infinitum, the proportion of times it would choose that outcome would equal the distribution's probability value for that outcome.

Computers are deterministic machines. If we repeatedly run a computer procedure on the same input, it will always return the same output; it cannot produce anything genuinely random (unless it has a random input). Computers have to use deterministic algorithms to emulate random generation. These algorithms are called pseudo-random number generators—they take a starting number, called a *random seed*, and return a deterministic series of numbers. Those algorithms mathematically guarantee that a series of numbers is statistically indistinguishable from the ideal of random generation.

In notation, I write random generation as follows:

$$x \sim P(X)$$

This reads as "x is generated from the probability distribution of *X*."

In random generation, synonyms for "generate" include "simulate" and "sample." For example, in pgmpy the `sample` method in `DiscreteFactor` does random generation. It returns a pandas DataFrame. Note that since this is random generation, you will likely get different outputs when you run this code:

$$x, y \sim P(X, Y)$$

Listing 2.4   Simulating random variates from `DiscreteFactor` in pgmpy

```
from pgmpy.factors.discrete import DiscreteFactor
dist = DiscreteFactor(
    variables=["X"],
    cardinality=[3],
    values=[.45, .30, .25],
    state_names= {'X': ['1', '2', '3']}
)
dist.sample(n=1)          n is the number of instances
                          you wish to generate.
```

This produces the table pictured in figure 2.15.

**X**

**0** 1

**Figure 2.15** Generating one instance from *P(X)* creates a pandas `DataFrame` object with one row.

We can also generate from joint probability distributions.

```
joint = DiscreteFactor(
    variables=['X', 'Y'],
    cardinality=[3, 2],
    values=[.25, .20, .20, .10, .15, .10],
    state_names= {
        'X': ['1', '2', '3'],
        'Y': ['0', '1']
    }
)

joint.sample(n=1)
```

This produces the table pictured in figure 2.16.

**X Y**

**0** 2 0

**Figure 2.16** Generating one instance from *P(X, Y)* creates a pandas `DataFrame` object with one row.

Pyro also has a `sample` method for canonical distributions:

```
import torch
from pyro.distributions import Categorical
Categorical(probs=torch.tensor([.45, .30, .25])).sample()
```

This generates a sample from that categorical distribution, i.e., either 0, 1, or 2.

```
tensor(1.)
```

### 2.2.3  *Coding random processes*

We can write our own random processes as code when we want to generate values in a particular way. A random process written as code is sometimes called a *stochastic function, probabilistic subroutine,* or *probabilistic program.* For example, consider the joint probability distribution $P(X, Y, Z)$. How can we randomly generate from this joint distribution? Unfortunately, software libraries don't usually provide pseudo-random generation for arbitrary joint distributions.

We can get around this by applying the chain rule and, if it exists, conditional independence. For example, we could factorize as follows:

$$P(x, y, z) = P(z)P(x|z)P(y|x, z)$$

Suppose that $Y$ is conditionally independent of $Z$ given $X$, then:

$$P(x, y, z) = P(z)P(x|z)P(y|x)$$

Finally, suppose we can sample from $P(Z)$, $P(X|Z)$, and $P(Y|X)$ given the basic random generation functions in our software library. Then we can use this factorization to compose an algorithm for sampling:

$$z \sim P(Z)$$
$$x \sim P(X|Z = z)$$
$$y \sim P(Y|X = x)$$

This is a random process that we can execute in code. First, we generate a $Z$-outcome $z$ from $P(Z)$. We then condition $X$ on that $z$, and generate an $X$-outcome $x$. We do the same to generate a $Y$-outcome $y$. Finally, this procedure generates a tuple $\{x, y, z\}$ from the joint distribution $P(X, Y, Z)$.

In pgmpy, we can create a random process using the class called `BayesianNetwork`.

---

**Listing 2.5   Creating a random process in pgmpy and Pyro**

```
from pgmpy.factors.discrete.CPD import TabularCPD
from pgmpy.models import BayesianNetwork
from pgmpy.sampling import BayesianModelSampling

PZ = TabularCPD(
    variable='Z',
    variable_card=2,
    values=[[.65], [.35]],          P(Z)
    state_names = {
        'Z': ['0', '1']
    })

PXgivenZ = TabularCPD(
    variable='X',
    variable_card=2,
    values=[                         P(X|Z=z)
        [.8, .6],
        [.2, .4],
```

```
    ],
    evidence=['Z'],
    evidence_card=[2],
    state_names = {
        'X': ['0', '1'],
        'Z': ['0', '1']
    })
```

P(X|Z=z)

```
PYgivenX = TabularCPD(
    variable='Y',
    variable_card=3,
    values=[
        [.1, .8],
        [.2, .1],
        [.7, .1],
    ],
    evidence=['X'],
    evidence_card=[2],
    state_names = {
        'Y': ['1', '2', '3'],
        'X': ['0', '1']
    })
```

P(Y|X=x)

**Create a BayesianNetwork object. The arguments are edges of a directed graph, which we'll cover in chapter 3.**

```
model = BayesianNetwork([('Z', 'X'), ('X', 'Y')])
model.add_cpds(PZ, PXgivenZ, PYgivenX)
```

**Add the conditional probability distributions to the model.**

```
generator = BayesianModelSampling(model)
generator.forward_sample(size=1)
```

**Create a BayesianModelSampling object from the BayesianNetwork object.**

**Sample from the resulting object**

This produces one row in a pandas DataFrame, shown in figure 2.17.

| | Z | X | Y |
|---|---|---|---|
| 0 | 0 | 1 | 1 |

**Figure 2.17** The `forward_sample` method simulates one instance of *X*, *Y*, and *Z* as a row in a pandas DataFrame.

Implementing random processes for random generation is powerful because it allows generating from joint distributions that we can't represent in clear mathematical terms or as a single canonical distribution. For example, while pgmpy works well with categorical distributions, Pyro gives us the flexibility of working with combinations of canonical distributions.

The following listing shows a Pyro version of the previous random process. It has the same dependence between *Z*, *X*, and *Y*, but different canonical distributions.

**Listing 2.6   Working with combinations of canonical distributions in Pyro**

```
import torch
from pyro.distributions import Bernoulli, Poisson, Gamma

z = Gamma(7.5, 1.0).sample()
x = Poisson(z).sample()
y = Bernoulli(x / (5+x)).sample()
print(z, x, y)
```

Represent P(Z) with a gamma distribution, and sample z.

Represent P(X|Z=z) with a Poisson distribution with location parameter z, and sample x.

Represent P(Y|X=x) with a Bernoulli distribution. The probability parameter is a function of x.

This prints out a sample set, such as the following:

```
tensor(7.1545) tensor(5.) tensor(1.)
```

*Z* comes from a gamma distribution, *X* from a Poisson distribution with mean parameter set to *z*, and *Y* from a Bernoulli distribution with its parameter set to a function of *x*.

Implementing a random function with a programming language lets us use nuanced conditional control flow. Consider the following pseudocode:

```
z ~ P(Z)
x ~ P(X|Z=z)
y = 0
for i in range(0, x){
    y_i ~ P(Y|X=x)
    y += y_i
}
```

We can use control flow, like this for loop, to generate values.

y is the sum of the values generated in the for loop. y still depends on x, but through nuanced control flow.

Here, *y* is still dependent on *x*. However, it is defined as the sum of *x* individual random components. In Pyro, we might implement this as follows.

**Listing 2.7   Random processes with nuanced control flow in Pyro**

```
import torch
from pyro.distributions import Bernoulli, Poisson, Gamma
z = Gamma(7.5, 1.0).sample()
x = Poisson(z).sample()
y = torch.tensor(0.0)
for i in range(int(x)):
    y += Bernoulli(.5).sample()
print(z, x, y)
```

y is defined as a sum of random coin flips, so y is generated from P(Y|X=x) because the number of flips depends on x.

In Pyro, best practice is to implement random processes as functions. Further, use the function `pyro.sample` to generate, rather than using the `sample` method on distribution objects. We could rewrite the preceding `random_process` code (listing 2.7) as follows.

Listing 2.8   Using functions for random processes and `pyro.sample`

```
import torch
import pyro
def random_process():
    z = pyro.sample("z", Gamma(7.5, 1.0))
    x = pyro.sample("x", Poisson(z))
    y = torch.tensor(0.0)
    for i in range(int(x)):                              ┐ f"y{i}" creates the
        y += pyro.sample(f"y{i}", Bernoulli(.5))    ◁─── │ names "y1", "y2", etc.
    return y
```

The first argument in `pyro.sample` is a string that assigns a name to the variable you are sampling. The reason for that will become apparent when we start running inference algorithms in Pyro in chapter 3.

### 2.2.4   *Monte Carlo simulation and expectation*

*Monte Carlo algorithms* use random generation to estimate expectations from a distribution of interest. The idea is simple. You have some way of generating from $P(X)$. If you want $E(X)$, generate multiple $x$'s, and take the average of those $x$'s. If you want $E(f(X))$, generate multiple $x$'s and apply the function $f(.)$ to each of those $x$'s, and take the average. Monte Carlo works even in cases when $X$ is continuous.

In pgmpy, you use the `sample` or `forward_sample` methods to generate a pandas DataFrame. You can then calculate the panda's `mean` method.

```
generated_samples = generator.forward_sample(size=100)
generated_samples['Y'].apply(int).mean()
```

In Pyro, we call the `random_process` function repeatedly. We can do this for the preceding Pyro generator with a `for` loop that generates 100 samples:

```
generated_samples = torch.stack([random_process() for _ in range(100)])
```

This code repeatedly calls `random_process` in a Python list comprehension. Recall that Pyro extends PyTorch, and the value of y it returns is a tensor. I use `torch.stack` to turn this list of tensors into a single tensor. Finally, I call the `mean` method on the tensor to obtain the Monte Carlo estimate of $E(Y)$.

```
generated_samples.mean()
```

When I ran this code, I got a value of about 3.78, but you'll likely get something slightly different.

Most things you'd want to know about a distribution can be framed in terms of some function $f(X)$. For example, if you wanted to know the probability of $X$ being greater than 10, you could simply generate a bunch of $x$'s and convert each $x$ to 1 if it is greater than 10 and 0 otherwise. Then you'd take the average of the 1's and 0's, and the resulting value would estimate the desired probability.

To illustrate, the following code extends the previous block to calculate $E(Y^2)$.

```
torch.square(generated_samples).mean()
```

When calculating $E(f(X))$ for a random variable $X$, remember to get the Monte Carlo estimate by applying the function to the samples first, and then take the average. If you apply the function to the sample average, you'll instead get an estimate of $f(E(X))$, which is almost always different.

### 2.2.5   *Programming probabilistic inference*

Suppose we implement in code a random process that generates an outcome $\{x, y, z\}$ from $P(X, Y, Z)$ as follows:

$$z \sim P(Z)$$
$$x \sim P(X|Z = z)$$
$$y \sim P(Y|X = x)$$

Further, suppose we are interested in generating from $P(Z|Y=3)$. How might we do this? Our process can sample from $P(Z)$, $P(X|Z)$, and $P(Y|Z)$, but it is not clear how we go from these to $P(Z|Y)$.

*Probabilistic inference algorithms* generally take an outcome-generating random process and some target distribution as inputs. Then, they return a means of generating from that target distribution. This class of algorithms is often called Bayesian inference algorithms because the algorithms often use Bayes rule to go from $P(Y|Z)$ to $P(Z|Y)$. However, the connection to Bayes rule is not always explicit, so I prefer "probabilistic inference" over "Bayesian inference algorithms."

For example, a simple class of probabilistic inference algorithms is called accept/reject algorithms. Applying a simple accept/reject technique to generating from $P(Z|Y=3)$ works as follows:

1  Repeatedly generate $\{x, y, z\}$ using our generator for $P(X, Y, Z)$.
2  Throw away any generated outcome where $y$ is not equal to 3.
3  The resulting set of outcomes for $Z$ will have the distribution $P(Z|Y=3)$.

Illustrating with Pyro, let's rewrite the previous `random_process` function to return $z$ and $y$. After that, we'll obtain a Monte Carlo estimate of $E(Z|Y=3)$.

Listing 2.9   Monte Carlo estimation in Pyro

```
import torch
import pyro
from pyro.distributions import Bernoulli, Gamma, Poisson
def random_process():
    z = pyro.sample("z", Gamma(7.5, 1.0))
    x = pyro.sample("x", Poisson(z))
    y = torch.tensor(0.0)
    for i in range(int(x)):
```

```
        y += pyro.sample(f"{i}", Bernoulli(.5))
    return z, y
```

**This new version of random_process returns both z and y.**

```
generated_samples = [random_process() for _ in range(1000)]
z_mean = torch.stack([z for z, _ in generated_samples]).mean()
print(z_mean)
```

**Generate 1000 instances of z and y using a list comprehension.**

**Turn the individual z tensors into a single tensor, and then calculate the Monte Carlo estimate via the mean method.**

This code estimates $E(Z)$. Since $Z$ is simulated from a gamma distribution, the true mean $E(Z)$ is the shape parameter 7.5 divided by the rate parameter 1.0, which is 7.5.

Now, to estimate $E(Z|Y=3)$, we'll filter the samples and keep only the samples where $Y$ is 3.

```
z_given_y = torch.stack([z for z, y in generated_samples if y == 3])
print(z_given_y.mean())
```

One run of this code produced `tensor(6.9088)`, but your result might be slightly different. That probabilistic inference algorithm works well if the outcome $Y=3$ occurs frequently. If that outcome were rare, the algorithm would be inefficient: we'd have to generate many samples to get samples that meet the condition, and we'd be throwing away many samples.

There are various other algorithms for probabilistic inference, but the topic is too rich and tangential to causal modeling for us to explore in depth. Nevertheless, the following algorithms are worth mentioning for what we cover in this book. Visit www.altdeep.ai/causalAIbook for links to some complementary materials on inference with pgmpy and Pyro.

### PROBABILITY WEIGHTING METHODS

These methods generate outcomes from a joint probability distribution and then weight them according to their probability in the target distribution. We can then use the weights to do weighted averaging via Monte Carlo estimation. Popular variants of this kind of inference include importance sampling and inverse probability reweighting, the latter of which is popular in causal inference and is covered in chapter 11.

### INFERENCE WITH PROBABILISTIC GRAPHICAL MODELS

Probabilistic graphical models use graphs to represent conditional independence in a joint probability distribution. The presence of a graph enables graph-based algorithms to power inference. Two well-known approaches include variable elimination and belief propagation. In figures 2.5 and 2.6, I showed that you could "eliminate" a variable by summing over its columns or rows in the probability table. Variable elimination uses the graph structure to optimally sum over the variables you wish to eliminate until the resulting table represents the target distribution. In contrast, belief propagation is a message-passing system; the graph is used to form different "cliques" of neighboring variables. For example, if $P(Z|Y=1)$ is the target distribution, $Y=1$ is a message iteratively passed back and forth between cliques. Each time a message is received, parameters in the clique are updated, and the message is passed on. Eventually, the algorithm converges, and we can derive a new distribution for Z from those updated parameters.

One of the attractive features of graph-based probabilistic inference is that users typically don't implement them themselves; software like pgmpy does it for you. There are theoretical caveats, but they usually don't matter in practice. This feature is an example of the "commodification of inference" trend I highlighted in chapter 1. In this book, we'll work with causal graphical models, a special type of probabilistic graphical model that works as a causal model. That gives us the option of applying graph-based inference for causal problems.

### VARIATIONAL INFERENCE

In *variational inference*, we write code for a new stochastic process that generates samples from an "approximating distribution" that resembles the target distribution. That stochastic process has parameters that we optimize using gradient-based techniques now common in deep learning software. The objective function of the optimization tries to minimize the difference between the approximating distribution and the target distribution.

Pyro is a probabilistic modeling language that treats variational inference as a principal inference technique. It calls the stochastic process that generates from the approximating distribution a "guide function," and a savvy Pyro programmer gets good at writing guide functions. However, it also provides a suite of tools for "automatic guide generation," another example of the commodification of inference.

### MARKOV CHAIN MONTE CARLO

*Markov chain Monte Carlo* (MCMC) is an inference algorithm popular amongst computational Bayesians. These are accept/reject algorithms where each newly generated outcome depends on the previous (non-rejected) generated outcome. This produces a chain of outcomes, and the distribution of outcomes in the chain eventually converges to the target distribution. *Hamiltonian Monte Carlo* (HMC) is a popular version that doesn't require users to implement the generator. Pyro, and similar libraries, such as PyMC, implement HMC and other MCMC algorithms.

### ADVANCED INFERENCE METHODS

Research in generative models continues to develop new inference techniques. Examples include techniques such adversarial inference, inference with normalizing flows, and diffusion-based inference. The goal of such techniques are to efficiently sample from the complex distributions common in machine learning problems. Again, see www.altdeep.ai/causalAIbook for references. We'll see an example of a structural causal model that leverages normalizing flows in chapter 6. The approach taken in this book is to leverage the "commodification of inference" trend discussed in chapter 1, such that we can build causal models that leverage these algorithms, as well as new algorithms as they are released.

## 2.3    Data, populations, statistics, and models

So far, we have talked about random variables and distributions. Now we'll move on to data and statistics. Let's start with defining some terms. You doubtless have an idea of what data is, but let's define it in terms we've already defined in this chapter. *Data* is a set of recorded outcomes of a random variable or set of random variables. A *statistic* is anything you calculate from data. For example, when you train a neural network on training data, the learned weight parameter values are statistics, and so are the model's predictions (since they depend on the training data via the weights).

The real-world causal process that generates a particular stream of data is called the *data generating process* (DGP). A *model* is a simplified mathematical description of that process. A *statistical model* is a model with parameters tuned such that the model aligns with statistical patterns in the data.

This section presents some of the core concepts related to data and statistics needed to make sense of this book.

### 2.3.1    Probability distributions as models for populations

In applied statistics, we take statistical insights from data and generalize them to a population. Consider, for example, the MNIST digit classification problem described in chapter 1. Suppose the goal of training a classification model on MNIST data was to deploy the model in software that digitizes written text documents. In this case, the population is all the digits on all the texts the software will see in the future.

Populations are heterogeneous, meaning members of the population vary. While a feature on a website might drive engagement among the population of users, on average, the feature might make some subpopulation of users less engaged, so you would want to target the feature to the right subpopulations. Marketers call this "segmentation."

In another example, a medicine might not be much help on average for a broad population of patients, but there some subpopulation might experience benefits. Targeting those subpopulations is the goal of the field of precision medicine.

In probabilistic models, we use probability distributions to model populations. It is particularly useful to target subpopulations with conditional probability. For example, suppose $P(E|F=\text{True})$ represents the distribution of engagement numbers among all users exposed to a website feature. Then $P(E|F=\text{True}, G=\text{"millennial"})$ represents the subpopulation of users exposed to the feature who are also millennials.

#### CANONICAL DISTRIBUTIONS AND STOCHASTIC PROCESSES AS MODELS OF POPULATIONS

If we use probability distributions to model populations, what canonical distributions should we use for a given population? Figure 2.18 includes common distributions and the phenomena they typically model.

These choices don't come from nowhere. The canonical distributions are themselves derived from stochastic functions. For example, the binomial distribution is the result of a process where you do a series of coin flips. When something is the result of adding together a bunch of independent (or weakly dependent) small changes, you

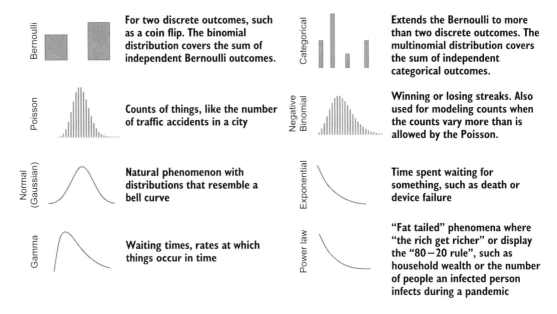

**Figure 2.18**   Examples of common canonical distributions and the types of phenomena and data they typically model

get a normal distribution. Waiting time distributions capture the distribution of the amount of time one must wait for an event (e.g., a device failure or a car accident). The exponential distribution is appropriate for waiting times when the amount of time you've already been waiting has no bearing on how much time you still must wait (e.g., for the amount of time it takes a radioactive atom to decay). If the time to event has an exponential distribution, the number of times that event has occurred within a fixed time period has a Poisson distribution.

A useful trick in probabilistic modeling is to think of the stochastic process that created your target population. Then either choose the appropriate canonical distribution or implement the stochastic process in code using various canonical distributions as primitives in the code logic. In this book, we'll see that this line of reasoning aligns well with causal modeling.

### SAMPLING, IID, AND GENERATION

Usually, our data is not the whole population but a small subset from the population. The act of randomly choosing an individual is called *sampling*. When the data is created by repeatedly sampling from the population, the resulting dataset is called a *random sample*. If we can view data as a *random sample*, we call that data *independent and identically distributed (IID)*. That means that the selection of each individual data point is *identical* in how it was sampled, and each sampling occurred *independently* of the others, and they all were sampled from the same population distribution. Figure 2.19 illustrates how an IID random sample is selected from a population.

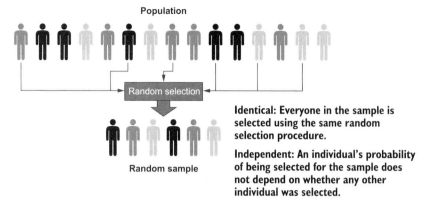

**Figure 2.19**   Creating a random sample by random selection from a population. Individuals
are randomly selected from the population such that the sample distribution resembles the
population distribution. The sample is identically and independently distributed (IID),
meaning that sample members are selected the same way, and whether an individual is
selected doesn't depend on whether another individual was selected.

The idea of sampling and IID data illustrates the second benefit of using probability
distributions to model populations. We can use generation from that distribution to
model sampling from a population. We can implement a stochastic process that represents the DGP by first writing a stochastic process that represents the population
and then composing it with a process that generates data from the population process, emulating IID sampling.

In pgmpy, this is as simple as generating more than one sample.

```
generator.forward_sample(size=10)
```

This produces the table showing in figure 2.20

|   | Z | X | Y |
|---|---|---|---|
| 0 | 0 | 1 | 3 |
| 1 | 0 | 0 | 3 |
| 2 | 0 | 0 | 2 |
| 3 | 0 | 0 | 3 |
| 4 | 0 | 0 | 3 |
| 5 | 0 | 0 | 3 |
| 6 | 1 | 0 | 3 |
| 7 | 1 | 0 | 3 |
| 8 | 1 | 0 | 2 |
| 9 | 0 | 0 | 3 |

**Figure 2.20**   A pandas DataFrame created by
generating ten data points from a model in pgmpy

The Pyro approach for IID sampling is `pyro.plate`.

**Listing 2.10   Generating IID samples in Pyro**

```
import pyro
from pyro.distributions import Bernoulli, Poisson, Gamma

def model():
    z = pyro.sample("z", Gamma(7.5, 1.0))
    x = pyro.sample("x", Poisson(z))
    with pyro.plate("IID", 10):
        y = pyro.sample("y", Bernoulli(x / (5+x)))
    return y

model()
```

pyro.plate is a context manager for generating conditionally independent samples. This instance of pyro.plate will generate 10 IID samples.

Calling pyro.sample generates a single outcome y, where y is a tensor of 10 IID samples.

Using generation to model sampling is particularly useful in machine learning, because often the data is not IID. In the MNIST example in chapter 1, the original NIST data was not IID—one block of data came from high school students and the other from government officers. You could capture the identity of the digit writer as a variable in your stochastic process. Then the data would be IID *conditional* on that variable.

### DON'T MISTAKE THE MAP FOR THE TERRAIN

Consider again the MNIST data. The population for that data is quite nebulous and abstract. If that digit classification software were licensed to multiple clients, the population would be a practically unending stream of digits. Generalizing to abstract populations is the common scenario in machine learning, as it is for statistics. When R.A. Fisher, the founding father of modern statistics, was designing experiments for testing soil types on crop growth at Rothamsted Research, he was trying to figure out how to generalize to the population of future crops (with as small a number of samples as possible).

The problem with working with nebulously large populations is that it can lead to the mistake of mentally conflating populations with the probability distributions. Do not do this. Do not mistake the map (the distribution used to model the population) for the terrain (the population itself).

To illustrate, consider the following example: While writing part of this chapter, I was vacationing in Silves, a town in the Portuguese Algarve with a big castle, deep history, and great hiking. Suppose I were interested in modeling the heights of Silves residents.

Officially, the population of Silves is 11,000, so let's take that number as ground truth. That means there are 11,000 different height values in Silves. Suppose I physically went down to the national health center in Silves and got a spreadsheet of every resident's height. Then the data I'd have is not a randomly sampled subset of the population—it is the full population itself.

I could then compute a *histogram* on that population, as shown in figure 2.21. A histogram is a visualization of the counts of values (in this case, heights) in a population or sample. For continuous values like heights, we count how many values fall into a range or "bin."

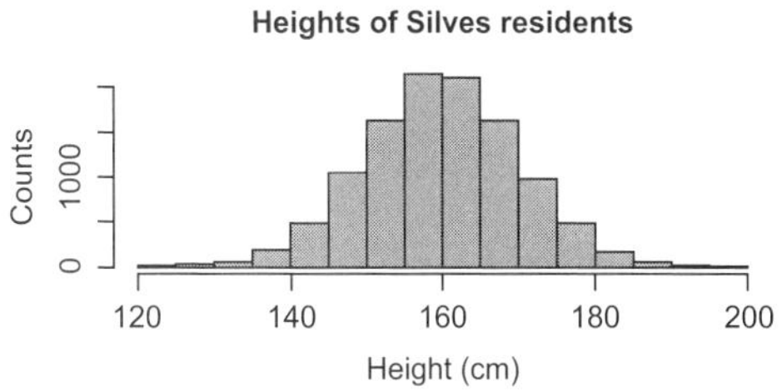


**Figure 2.21 A histogram illustrating the height distribution of all Silves residents**

This histogram represents the full population distribution. I can make it look more like a probability distribution by dividing the counts by the number of people, as in figure 2.22

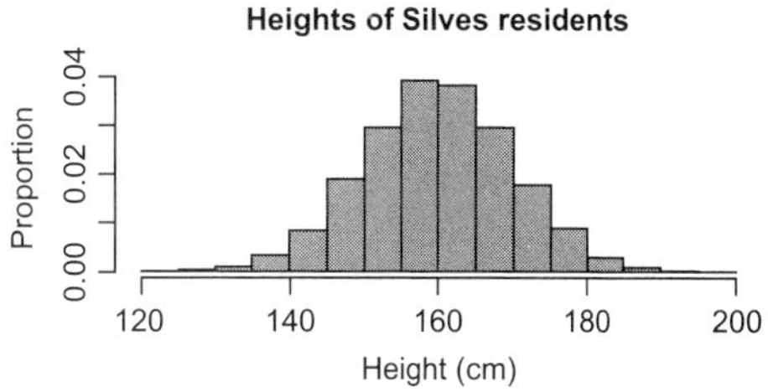


**Figure 2.22 Histogram of proportions of Silves residents with given height**

One might say this distribution follows the normal (Gaussian) probability distribution, because we see a bell curve, and indeed, the normal is appropriate for evolutionary bell-shaped phenomena such as height. But that statement is not precisely true. To see this, consider that all normal distributions are defined for negative numbers (though those numbers might have an infinitesimal amount of probability density), whereas heights can't be negative. What we are really doing is using the normal distribution as a *model*—as an *approximation* of this population distribution.

In another example, figure 2.23 shows the true distribution of the parts of speech in Jane Austen's novels. Note that this is not based on a sample of pages from her novels; I created this visualization from the parts-of-speech distribution of the 725 thousand words in *all* her six completed novels.

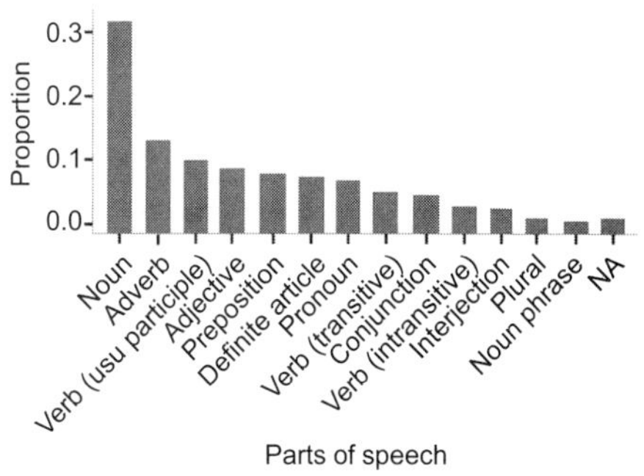


**Figure 2.23 Actual distribution of word types in all of Jane Austen's novels**

As modelers, we use canonical distributions to model the population distribution, but the model is not equivalent to the population distribution. This point may seem like trivial semantics, but in the era of big data, we often can reason about an entire population instead of just a random sample. For example, popular online social networks have hundreds of millions and sometimes billions of users. That's a huge size, yet the entire population is just one database query away.

In causal modeling, being precise in how we think about modeling data and populations is extremely useful. Causal inferences are about the real-world attributes of the population, rather than just statistical trends in the data. And different causal questions we want to answer will require us to bake different causal assumptions into our models, some of which are stronger or harder to validate than others.

### 2.3.2   *From the observed data to the data generating process*

In causal modeling, it is important to understand how the observed data maps back to the joint probability distribution of the variables in the data, and how that joint probability distribution maps back to the DGP. Most modelers have some level of intuition about the relationships between these entities, but in causal modeling we must be explicit. This explicit understanding is important because, while in ordinary statistical modeling you model the joint distribution (or elements of it), in causal modeling you need to model the DGP.

#### FROM THE OBSERVED DATA TO THE EMPIRICAL JOINT DISTRIBUTION
Suppose we had the dataset of five data points shown in table 2.1.

Table 2.1   A simple data set with five examples

|   | jenny_throws_rock | brian_throws_rock | window_breaks |
|---|---|---|---|
| 1 | False | True | False |
| 2 | True | False | True |
| 3 | False | False | False |
| 4 | False | False | False |
| 5 | True | True | True |

We can take counts of all the observed observable outcomes, as in table 2.2.

Table 2.2   Empirical counts of each possible outcome combination

|   | jenny_throws_rock | brian_throws_rock | window_breaks | counts |
|---|---|---|---|---|
| 1 | False | False | False | 2 |
| 2 | True | False | False | 0 |
| 3 | False | True | False | 1 |
| 4 | True | True | False | 0 |
| 5 | False | False | True | 0 |
| 6 | True | False | True | 1 |

**Table 2.2   Empirical counts of each possible outcome combination** *(continued)*

|   | jenny_throws_rock | brian_throws_rock | window_breaks | counts |
|---|---|---|---|---|
| 7 | False | True | True | 0 |
| 8 | True | True | True | 1 |

Dividing by the number of outcomes (5) gives us the *empirical joint distribution*, shown in table 2.3.

**Table 2.3   The empirical distribution of the data**

|   | jenny_throws_rock | brian_throws_rock | window_breaks | proportion |
|---|---|---|---|---|
| 1 | False | False | False | 0.40 |
| 2 | True | False | False | 0.00 |
| 3 | False | True | False | 0.20 |
| 4 | True | True | False | 0.00 |
| 5 | False | False | True | 0.00 |
| 6 | True | False | True | 0.20 |
| 7 | False | True | True | 0.00 |
| 8 | True | True | True | 0.20 |

So, in the case of discrete outcomes, we go from the data to the empirical distribution using counts.

In the continuous case, we could calculate a histogram or a density curve or some other statistical representation of the empirical distribution. There are different statistical choices you can make about how you create those summaries, but these are representations of the same underlying empirical distribution.

Importantly, the empirical joint distribution is not the actual joint distribution of the variables in the data. For example, we see that several outcomes in the empirical distribution never appeared in those five data points. Is the probability of their occurrence zero? More likely, the probabilities were greater than zero but we didn't see those outcomes, since only five points were sampled.

As an analogy, a fair die has a $1/6$ probability of rolling a 1. If you roll the die five times, you have a near $(1-1/6)^5=40\%$ probability of not seeing 1 in any of those rolls. If that happened to you, you wouldn't want to conclude that the probability of seeing a 1 is zero. If, however, you kept rolling, the proportion of times you saw the 1 would converge to $1/6$.

**NOTE**   More precisely, our frequentist interpretation of probability tells us to interpret probability as the proportion of times we get a 1 when we roll ad infinitum. Despite the "ad infinitum," we don't have to roll many times before the proportion starts converging to a number $(1/6)$.

The *observational joint probability* distribution is the true joint distribution of the variables observed in the data. Let's suppose table 2.4 shows the true observational joint probability distribution of these observed variables.

Table 2.4    Assume this is the true observational joint distribution.

|   | jenny_throws_rock | brian_throws_rock | window_breaks | probability |
|---|---|---|---|---|
| 1 | False | False | False | 0.25 |
| 2 | True | False | False | 0.15 |
| 3 | False | True | False | 0.15 |
| 4 | True | True | False | 0.05 |
| 5 | False | False | True | 0.00 |
| 6 | True | False | True | 0.10 |
| 7 | False | True | True | 0.10 |
| 8 | True | True | True | 0.20 |

Sampling from the joint observational distribution produces the empirical joint distribution, as illustrated in figure 2.24.

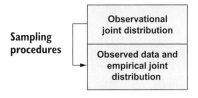

Figure 2.24    Sampling from the observational joint distribution produces the observed data and empirical distribution.

LATENT VARIABLES: FROM THE OBSERVED JOINT DISTRIBUTION TO THE FULL JOINT DISTRIBUTION

In statistical modeling, *latent variables* are variables that are not directly observed in the data but are included in the statistical model. Going back to our data example, imagine there were a fourth latent variable, "strength_of_impact", shown in table 2.5.

Table 2.5    The values in the strength_of_impact column are unseen "latent" variables.

|   | jenny_throws_rock | brian_throws_rock | strength_of_impact | window_breaks |
|---|---|---|---|---|
| 1 | False | True | 0.6 | False |
| 2 | True | False | 0.6 | True |
| 3 | False | False | 0.0 | False |
| 4 | False | False | 0.0 | False |
| 5 | True | True | 0.8 | True |

Latent variable models are common in disciplines ranging from machine learning to econometrics to bioinformatics. For example, in natural language processing, an example of a popular probabilistic latent variable model is *topic models*, where the observed variables represent the presence of words and phrases in a document, and the latent variable represents the topic of the document (e.g., sports, politics, finance, etc.)

The latent variables are omitted from the observational joint probability distribution because, as the name implies, they are not observed. The joint probability distribution of both the observed and the latent variables is the full joint distribution. To go from the full joint distribution to the observational joint distribution, we marginalize over the latent variables, as shown in figure 2.25.

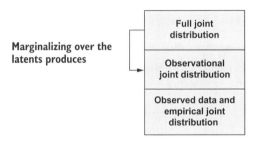

Figure 2.25  Marginalizing the full joint distribution over the latent variables produces the observational joint distribution.

#### FROM THE FULL JOINT DISTRIBUTION TO THE DATA GENERATING PROCESS

I wrote the actual DGP for the five data points using the following Python code.

Listing 2.11  An example of a DGP in code form

Jenny and Brian throw the rock if so inclined.

Input variables reflect Jenny and Brian's inclination to throw and the window's strength.

```python
def true_dgp(jenny_inclination, brian_inclination, window_strength):
    jenny_throws_rock = jenny_inclination > 0.5
    brian_throws_rock = brian_inclination > 0.5
    if jenny_throws_rock and brian_throws_rock:
        strength_of_impact = 0.8
    elif jenny_throws_rock or brian_throws_rock:
        strength_of_impact = 0.6
    else:
        strength_of_impact = 0.0
    window_breaks = window_strength < strength_of_impact
    return jenny_throws_rock, brian_throws_rock, window_breaks
```

If both Jenny and Brian throw the rock, the total strength of the impact is .8.

If either Jenny or Brian throws the rock, the total strength of the impact is .6.

Otherwise, no one throws and the strength of impact is 0.

If the strength of impact is greater than the strength of the window, the window breaks.

**NOTE**  In general, the DGP is unknown, and our models are making guesses about its structure.

In this example, `jenny_inclination`, `brian_inclination`, and `window_strength` are latent variables between 0 and 1. `jenny_inclination` represents Jenny's initial desire to throw, `brian_inclination` represents Brian's initial desire to throw, and `window_strength` represents the strength of the window pane. These are the initial conditions that lead to one instantiation of the observed variables in the data: (`jenny_throws_ball`, `brian_throws_ball`, `window_breaks`).

I then called the `true_dgp` function on the following five sets of latent variables:

```
initials = [
    (0.6, 0.31, 0.83),
    (0.48, 0.53, 0.33),
    (0.66, 0.63, 0.75),
    (0.65, 0.66, 0.8),
    (0.48, 0.16, 0.27)
]
```

In other words, the following `for` loop in Python is the literal sampling process producing the five data points:

```
data_points = []
for jenny_inclination, brian_inclination, window_strength in initials:
    data_points.append(
        true_dgp(
            jenny_inclination, brian_inclination, window_strength
        )
    )
```

The DGP is the causal process that generated the data. Note the narrative element that is utterly missing from the full joint probability distribution; Jenny and Brian throw a rock at a window if they are so inclined, and if they hit the window, the window may break, depending on whether one or both of them threw rocks and the strength of the window. The DGP entails the full joint probability distribution, as shown in figure 2.26. In other words, the joint probability distribution is a consequence of the DGP based on *how* it generates data.

In summary, the DGP entails the full joint distribution, and marginalizing over the full joint distribution produces the observational joint distribution. Sampling from that distribution produces the observed data and the corresponding empirical joint distribution. There is a many-to-one relationship as we move down this hierarchy that has implications for causal modeling and inference.

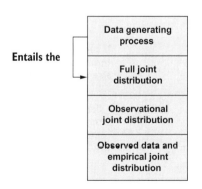

**Figure 2.26   The DGP entails the full joint distribution.**

**MANY-TO-ONE RELATIONSHIPS DOWN THE HIERARCHY**

As we move down from the DGP to full joint to observational joint to empirical joint distribution and observed data, there is a many-to-one relationship from the preceding level to the subsequent level, as illustrated in figure 2.27.

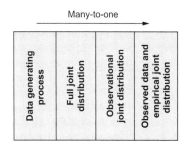

Similarly, an object at one of the levels is consistent with multiple objects at the next level up:

- *There could be multiple observational joint distributions consistent with the empirical joint distribution.* If we sample five points, then sample five more, we'll get different datasets and thus different empirical distributions.

**Figure 2.27   There is a many-to-one relationship as we move down the hierarchy. In summary, there are multiple DGPs consistent with the observed data.**

- *There could be multiple full joint distributions consistent with one observational joint distribution.* The difference between the two distributions is the latent variables. But what if we have different choices for the sets of latent variables? For example, if our observation distribution is $P(X, Y)$, the full joint would be $P(X, Y, Z, W)$ if our set of latent variables is $\{Z, W\}$, or $P(X, Y, Z, V)$ if our set of latent variables is $\{Z, V\}$.

- *There could be multiple DGP's consistent with one full joint probability distribution.* Suppose in our window-breaking example, Jenny had a friend Isabelle who sometimes egged Jenny on to throw the rock and sometimes did not, affecting Jenny's inclination to throw. This DGP is different from the original, but the relationship between the latent variable of Isabell's peer pressure and Jenny's inclination to throw could be such that this new DGP entailed exactly the same joint probability distribution. As a more trivial example, suppose we looked at the distribution of a single variable corresponding to the sum of the roll of three dice. The DGP is rolling three dice and then summing them together. Two DGPs could differ in terms of the order of summing the dice; e.g., (first + second) + third or (first + third) + second or (second + third) + first. These would all yield the same distribution.

Those last two many-to-one relationships are fundamental to the concept of *causal identifiability,* the core reason why causal inference is hard. This concept is the reason "correlation does not imply causation," as the saying goes.

### 2.3.3   *Statistical tests for independence*

Causality imposes independence and conditional independence on variables, so we rely on statistical tests for conditional independence to build and validate causal models.

Suppose $X$ and $Y$ are independent, or $X$ and $Y$ are conditionally independent given $Z$. If we have data observing $X$, $Y$, and $Z$, we can run a statistical test for independence. The canonical statistical independence procedure returns a test statistic that quantifies the statistical association between $X$ and $Y$, and a p-value that quantifies the probability of getting that degree of association, or one more extreme, by pure chance when $X$

and $Y$ are actually conditionally independent given $Z$. Put simply, the test quantifies the statistical evidence of dependence or independence.

Evidence suggesting that someone committed a murder is not the same as the definitive truth that they did. Similarly, statistical evidence indicating independence between two variables does not equate to the actual fact of their independence. In both cases, evidence can point toward a conclusion without definitively proving it. For example, given that independence is true, the strength of the statistical evidence can vary on several factors, such as how much data there is. And it is always possible to make false conclusions from these tests.

Remember that if $X$ and $Y$ are independent, then $P(Y|X)$ is equivalent to $P(Y)$. In predictive terms, that means $X$ has no predictive power on $Y$. If you can't use classical statistical tests (e.g., if $X$ and $Y$ are vectors) then you can try training a predictive model and subjectively evaluating how well the model predicts.

### 2.3.4   *Statistical estimation of model parameters*

When we "train" or "fit" a model, we are attempting to estimate the values of parameters of the model, such as the weights in a regression model or neural network. Generally, in statistical modeling and machine learning, the goal of parameter estimation is modeling the observational or joint probability distribution. In causal modeling, the objective is modeling the DGP. The distinction is important for making good causal inferences.

#### ESTIMATING BY MAXIMIZING LIKELIHOOD

In informal terms and in the context of parameter estimation, likelihood is the probability of having observed the data given a candidate value of the parameter vector. *Maximizing likelihood* means choosing the value of the parameter vector that has the highest likelihood. Usually, we work with maximizing the log of the likelihood instead of the likelihood directly because it is mathematically and computationally easier to do so; the value that maximizes likelihood is the same as the value that maximizes log-likelihood. In special cases, such as linear regression, the maximum likelihood estimate has a solution we can derive mathematically, but in general, we must find the solution using numerical optimization techniques. In some models, such as neural networks, it is infeasible to find the value that maximizes likelihood, so we settle for a candidate that has a relatively high likelihood.

#### ESTIMATING BY MINIMIZING OTHER LOSS FUNCTIONS AND REGULARIZATION

In machine learning, there are a variety of loss functions for estimating parameters. Maximizing likelihood is a special case of minimizing a loss function, namely the negative log-likelihood loss function.

*Regularization* is the practice of adding additional elements to the loss function that steer the optimization toward better parameter values. For example, L2 regularization adds a value proportional to the sum of the square of the parameter values to the loss. Since a small increase in value leads to a larger increase in the square of the value, L2 regularization helps avoid exceedingly large parameter estimates.

## BAYESIAN ESTIMATION

*Bayesian estimation* treats parameters as random variables and tries to model the conditional distribution of the parameters (typically called the *posterior* distribution) given the observed variables in the data. It does so by putting a "prior probability distribution" on the parameters. The prior distribution has its own parameters called "hyperparameters" that the modeler must specify. When there are latent variables in the model, Bayesian inference targets the joint distribution of the parameters and the latent variables conditional on the observed variables.

As mentioned before, in this book I use Greek letters for parameters and Roman letters for variables in the DGP, including latent variables. But for a Bayesian statistician, the distinction is irrelevant; both parameters and latent variables are unknown and thus targets of inference.

One of the main advantages of Bayesian estimation is that rather than getting a point value for the parameters, you get an entire conditional probability distribution of the parameters (more specifically, you get samples from or parameter values representing that distribution). That probability distribution represents uncertainty about the parameter values, and you can incorporate that uncertainty into predictions or other inferences you make from the model.

According to Bayesian philosophy, the prior distribution should capture the modeler's subjective beliefs about the true value of the parameters. We'll do something similar in causal modeling when we turn our beliefs about the causal structure and mechanisms of the DGP into causal assumptions in the model.

## STATISTICAL AND COMPUTATIONAL ATTRIBUTES OF AN ESTIMATOR

Given that there are many ways of estimating a parameter, let's look for ways to compare the quality of estimation methods. Suppose the parameter we want to estimate had a ground truth value. Statisticians think about how well an estimation method can recover that true value. Specifically, they care about the bias and consistency of an estimation method. An estimator is a random variable because it comes from data (and data has a distribution), which means an estimator has a distribution. An estimator is unbiased if the mean of that distribution is equal to the true value of the parameter it is estimating. Consistency means that the more data you have, the closer the estimate is to the true value of the parameter. In practice, the consistency of the estimator is more important than whether it is unbiased.

Computer scientists know that while consistency is nice in theory, getting an estimation method to work with "more data" is easier said than done. They care about the computational qualities of an estimator in relation to the amount of data. Does the estimator scale with the data? Is it parallelizable? An estimator may be consistent, but when its running on an iPhone app, will it converge to the true value in milliseconds and not eat up the battery's charge in the process?

This book decouples understanding causal logic from the statistical and computational properties of estimators of causal parameters. We will focus on the causal logic and rely on libraries like DoWhy that make the statistical and computational calculations easy to do.

When we estimate parameters, we can calculate various statistics to tell us how well we've done. One class of statistics is called *goodness-of-fit statistics*. Statisticians define goodness-of-fit as statistics that quantify how well the model fits the data used to train the model. Here's another definition: goodness-of-fit statistics tell you how well your model pretends to be the DGP for the data you used to train your model. However, as we saw, there are multiple possible DGPs for a given data set. Goodness-of-fit won't provide causal information that can distinguish the true DGP.

Cross-validation statistics generally indicate how well your model predicts data it was not trained on. It is possible to have a model with a decent goodness-of-fit relative to other models, but that still predicts poorly. Machine learning is usually concerned with the task of prediction and so favors cross-validation. However, a model can be a good predictor and provide completely bogus causal inferences.

## 2.4    *Determinism and subjective probability*

This section will venture into the philosophical underpinnings we'll need for probabilistic causal modeling. In this book, we'll use probabilistic models to model causal models. When training the model, we might want to use Bayesian parameter estimation procedures. When doing causal inference, we might want to use a probabilistic inference algorithm. When we do causal decision-making, we might want to use Bayesian decision theory. Further, *structural causal models* (chapter 6) have a rigid requirement on where randomness can occur in the model. That means being clear about the differences between Bayesianism, uncertainty, randomness, probabilistic modeling, and probabilistic inference is important.

The first key point is to view the DGP as deterministic. The second key point is to view the probability in our models of the DGP as subjective.

### 2.4.1    *Determinism*

The earlier code for the rock-throwing DGP is entirely *deterministic*; given the initial conditions, the output is certain. Consider our definition of physical probability again: if I throw a die, why is the outcome random?

If I had a superhuman level of dexterity, perception, and mental processing power, I could mentally calculate the die roll's physics and know the outcome with certainty. This philosophical idea of determinism essentially says that the DGP is deterministic. Eighteenth-century French scholar Pierre-Simon Laplace explained determinism with a thought experiment called *Laplace's demon*. Laplace imagined some entity (the demon) that knew every atom's precise location and momentum in the universe. With that knowledge, that entity would know the future state of the universe with complete deterministic certainty because it could calculate them from the laws of (Newtonian) mechanics. In other words, given all the causes, the effect is 100% entirely determined and not at all random.

To be clear, some systems, when we look closely enough, have inherently stochastic elements (e.g., quantum mechanics, biochemistry, etc.). However, this philosophical view of modeling will apply to most things we'll care to model.

### 2.4.2 *Subjective probability*

In our physical interpretation of probability, when I roll a die, probability represents my lack of the demon's superhuman knowledge of the location and momentum of all the die's particles as it is rolling. In other words, when I build probability models of the DGP, the probability reflects my lack of knowledge. This philosophical idea is called *subjective probability* or *Bayesian probability*. The argument goes beyond Bayes rule and Bayesian statistical estimation to say that probability in the model represents the modeler's lack of complete knowledge about the DGP and does not represent inherent randomness in the DGP.

Subjective probability expands our "random physical process" interpretation of probability. The physical interpretation of probability works well for simple physical processes like rolling a die, flipping a coin, or shuffling a deck of cards. But, of course, we will want to model many phenomena that are difficult to think of as repeatable physical processes. For example, how the mind turns thoughts into speech, or how an increased flow of fresh water into the ocean due to climate change is threatening to tip the global system of ocean currents. In these cases, we will still model these phenomena using random generation. The probabilities used in the random generation reflect that while we, as modelers, may know some details about the data-generating process, we'll never have the superhuman deterministic level of detail.

### Summary

- A random variable is a variable whose possible values are numerical outcomes of a random phenomenon.
- A probability distribution function is a function that maps the random variable outcomes to a probability value. A joint probability distribution function maps each combination of $X$ and $Y$ outcomes to a probability value.
- We derive the chain rule, the law of total probability, and Bayes rule from the fundamental axioms of probability. These are useful rules in modeling.
- A Markovian assumption means each variable in an ordering of variables only depends on those that come directly before in the order. This is a common simplifying assumption in statistical modeling, but it plays a large role in causal modeling.
- Canonical classes of distributions are mathematically well-described representations of distributions. They provide us with primitives that make probabilistic modeling flexible and relatively easy.
- Canonical distributions are instantiated with a set of parameters, such as location, scale, rate, and shape parameters.
- When we build models, knowing what variables are independent or conditionally independent dramatically simplifies the model. In causal modeling, independence and conditional independence will be vital in separating correlation from causation.
- The expected value of a random variable with a finite number of outcomes is the weighted average of all possible outcomes, where the weight is the probability of that outcome.

- Probability is just a value. We need to give that value an interpretation. The physical definition of probability maps probability to the proportion of times an outcome would occur if a physical process could be run repeatedly ad infinitum.
- In contrast to the physical interpretation of probability, the Bayesian view of subjective probability interprets probability in terms of belief, or conversely, uncertainty.
- When coding a random process, Pyro allows you to use canonical distributions as primitives in constructing nuanced random process models.
- Monte Carlo algorithms use random generation to estimate expectations from a distribution of interest.
- Popular inference algorithms include graphical model-based algorithms, probability weighting, MCMC, and variational inference.
- Canonical distributions and random processes can serve as proxies for populations we wish to model and for which we want to make inferences. Conditional probability is an excellent way to model heterogeneous subpopulations.
- Different canonical distributions are used to model different phenomena, such as counts, bell curves, and waiting times.
- Generating from random processes is a good model of real-life sampling of independent and identically distributed data.
- Given a dataset, multiple data generating processes (DGPs) could have potentially generated that dataset. This fact connects to the challenge of parsing causality from correlation.
- Statistical independence tests validate independence and conditional independence claims about the underlying distribution.
- There are several methods for learning model parameters, including maximum likelihood estimation and Bayesian estimation.
- Determinism suggests that if we knew everything about a system, we could predict its outcome with zero error. Subjective probability is the idea that probability represents the modeler's lack of that complete knowledge about the system. Adopting these philosophical perspectives will serve us in understanding causal AI.
- A great way to build models is to factorize a joint distribution, simplify the factors with conditional independence, and then implement factors as random processes.
- A powerful modeling technique is to use probability distributions to model populations, particularly when you care about heterogeneity in those populations.
- When we use probability distributions to model populations, we can map generating from random processes to sampling from the population.
- While traditional statistical modeling models the observational joint distribution or the full joint distribution, causal modeling models the DGP.

*Part 2*

# *Building and validating*
# *a causal graph*

In part 2, we'll focus on learning how to represent causal relationships through causal graphs. We'll also learn how to validate those causal graphs with data, as well as combine them with deep generative models. This part will equip you with the skills to systematically construct causal structures that represent real-world data generation processes and validate those structures empirically.

# Building a causal graphical model

In this chapter, we'll build our first models of the data generating process (DGP) using the *causal directed acyclic graph* (causal DAG)—a directed graph without cycles, where the edges represent causal relationships. We'll also look at how to train a statistical model using the causal DAG as a scaffold.

## 3.1 Introducing the causal DAG

Let's assume we can partition the DGP into a set of variables where a given combination of variable values represents a possible state of the DGP. Those variables may be discrete or continuous. They can be univariate, or they can be multivariate vectors or matrices.

A causal DAG is a directed graph where the nodes are this set of variables and the directed edges represent the causal relationships between them. When we use a causal DAG to represent the DGP, we assume the edges reflect true causality in the DGP.

To illustrate, recall the rock-throwing DGP from chapter 2. We started with Jenny and Brian having a certain amount of inclination to throw rocks at a window, which has a certain amount of strength. If either person's inclination to throw surpasses a threshold, they throw. The window breaks depending on whether either or both of them throw and the strength of the window.

> **Setting up your environment**
>
> The code in this chapter was written with pgmpy version 0.1.24, pyro-ppl version 1.8.6, and DoWhy version 0.11.1. Version 0.20.1 of Python's Graphviz library was used to draw an image of a DAG, and this depends on having the core Graphviz software installed. Comment out the Graphviz code if you would prefer not to set up Graphviz for now.
>
> See the book's notes at www.altdeep.ai/causalAIbook for links to the Jupyter notebooks with the code.

We'll now create a causal DAG that will visualize this process. As a Python function, the DGP is shown in the following listing.

**Listing 3.1   DAG rock-throwing example**

Jenny and Brian throw the rock if so inclined.

Input variables are numbers between 0 and 1.

```
def true_dgp(jenny_inclination, brian_inclination, window_strength):
    jenny_throws_rock = jenny_inclination > 0.5
    brian_throws_rock = brian_inclination > 0.5
    if jenny_throws_rock and brian_throws_rock:
        strength_of_impact = 0.8
    elif jenny_throws_rock or brian_throws_rock:
        strength_of_impact = 0.6
    else:
        strength_of_impact = 0.0
    window_breaks = window_strength < strength_of_impact
    return jenny_throws_rock, brian_throws_rock, window_breaks
```

If both throw the rock, the strength of impact is .8.

If neither throws, the strength of impact is 0.

If one of them throws, the strength of impact is .6.

The window breaks if the strength of impact is greater than the window strength.

Figure 3.1 illustrates the rock-throwing DGP as a causal DAG.

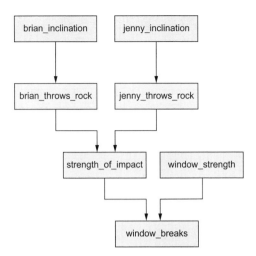

**Figure 3.1 A causal DAG representing the rock-throwing DGP. In this example, each node corresponds to a random variable in the DGP.**

In figure 3.1, each node corresponds to a random variable in the DGP. The directed edges correspond to cause-effect relationships (the source node is the cause and the target node is the effect).

### 3.1.1 Case study: A causal model for transportation

In this chapter, we'll look at a model of people's choice of transportation on their daily commutes. This example will make overly strong assumptions (to the point of being borderline offensive) that will help illustrate the core ideas of model building. You'll find links to the accompanying code and tutorials at www.altdeep.ai/causalAIbook.

Suppose you were an urban planning consultant trying to model the relationships between people's demographic background, the size of the city where they live, their job status, and their decision on how to commute to work each day.

You could break down the key variables in the system as follows:

- *Age (A)*—The age of an individual
- *Gender (S)*—An individual's reported gender (using "S" instead of "G," since "G" is usually reserved for DAGs)
- *Education (E)*—The highest level of education or training completed by an individual
- *Occupation (O)*—An individual's occupation
- *Residence (R)*—The size of the city the individual resides in
- *Travel (T)*—The means of transport favored by the individual

You could then think about the causal relationships between these variables, using knowledge about the domain. Here is a possible narrative:

- Educational standards are different across generations. For older people, a high school degree was sufficient to achieve a middle-class lifestyle, but younger people need at least a college degree to achieve the same lifestyle. Thus, age ($A$) is a cause of education ($E$).

- Similarly, a person's gender is often a factor in their decision to pursue higher levels of education. So, gender ($S$) is a cause of education ($E$).
- Many white-collar jobs require higher education. Many credentialed professions (e.g., doctor, lawyer, or accountant) certainly require higher education. So education ($E$) is a cause of occupation ($O$).
- White-collar jobs that depend on higher levels of education tend to cluster in urban areas. Thus, education ($E$) is a cause of where people reside ($R$).
- People who are self-employed might work from home and therefore don't need to commute, while people with employers do. Thus, occupation ($O$) is a cause of transportation ($T$).
- People in big cities might find it more convenient to commute by walking or using public transportation, while people in small cities and towns rely on cars to get around. Thus, residence ($R$) is a cause of transportation ($T$).

You could have created this narrative based on your knowledge about the domain, or based on your research into the domain. Alternatively, you could have consulted with a domain expert, such as a social scientist who specializes in this area. Finally, you could reduce this narrative to the causal DAG shown in figure 3.2.

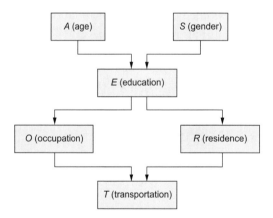

**Figure 3.2   A causal DAG representing a model of the causal factors behind how people commute to work**

You could build this causal DAG using the following code.

**Listing 3.2   Building the transportation DAG in pgmpy**

```
from pgmpy.models import BayesianNetwork
model = BayesianNetwork(
    [
        ('A', 'E'),
        ('S', 'E'),
        ('E', 'O'),
```

Input the DAG as a list of edges (tuples).

pgmpy provides a BayesianNetwork class where we add the edges to the model.

```
            ('E', 'R'),              △  Input the DAG as a list
            ('O', 'T'),             │  of edges (tuples).
            ('R', 'T')
        ]
    )
```

The `BayesianNetwork` object in pgmpy is built on the `DiGraph` class from NetworkX, the preeminent graph modeling library in Python.

---

### Causal abstraction and causal representation learning

In modeling, the *level of abstraction* refers to the level of detail and granularity of the variables in the model. In figure 3.2, there is a mapping between the variables in the data and the variables in the causal DAG, because the level of abstraction in the data generated by the DGP and the level of abstraction of the causal DAG are the same. But it is possible for variables in the data to be at a different levels of abstraction. This is particularly common in machine learning, where we often deal with low-level features, such as pixels.

When the level of abstraction in the data is lower than the level the modeler wants to work with, the modeler must use domain knowledge to derive the high-level abstractions that will appear as nodes in the DAG. For example, a doctor may be interested in a high-level binary variable node like "Tumor (present/absent)," while the data itself contains low-level variables such as a matrix of pixels from medical imaging technology.

That doctor must look at each image in the dataset and manually label the high-level tumor variable. Alternatively, a modeler can use analytical means (e.g., math or logic) to map low-level abstractions to high-level ones. Further, they must do so in a way that preserves causal assumptions about the DGP.

This task of creating high-level variables from lower-level ones in a causally rigorous way is called *causal abstraction*. In machine learning, the term "feature engineering" applies to the task of computing *useful* high-level features from lower-level features. Causal abstraction differs in that requirement for causal rigor. You'll find some sources for causal abstraction information in the book's notes at www.altdeep.ai/causalAIbook.

Another approach to learning high-level causal abstractions from lower ones in data is to use deep learning—this is called *causal representation learning*. We'll touch briefly on this topic in chapter 5.

---

### 3.1.2   Why use a causal DAG?

The causal DAG is the best-known representation of causality, but to understand its value, it's useful to think about other ways of modeling causality. One alternative is using a mathematical model, such as a set of ordinary differential equations or partial differential equations, as is common in physics and engineering. Another option is to use computational simulators, such as are used in meteorology and climate science.

In contrast to those alternatives, a causal DAG requires a much less mathematically detailed understanding of the DGP. A causal DAG only requires you to specify what causes what, in the form of a graph. Graphs are easy for humans to think about; they are the go-to method for making sense of complicated domains.

Indeed, there are several benefits of using a causal DAG as a representation of the DGP:

- DAGs are useful in communicating and visualizing causal assumptions.
- We have many tools for computing over DAGs.
- Causal DAGs represent time.
- DAGs link causality to conditional independence.
- DAGs can provide scaffolding for probabilistic ML models.
- The parameters in those probabilistic ML models are modular parameters, and they encode causal invariance.

Let's review these benefits one at a time.

### 3.1.3 DAGs are useful in communicating and visualizing causal assumptions

A causal DAG is a powerful communication device. Visual communication of information involves highlighting important information at the expense of other information. As an analogy, consider the two maps of the London Underground in figure 3.3. The map on the left is geographically accurate. The simpler map on the right ignores the geographic detail and focuses on the position of each station relative to other stations, which is, arguably, all one needs to find their way around London.

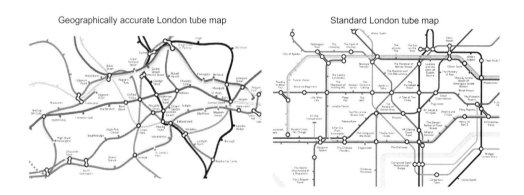

Geographically accurate London tube map          Standard London tube map

**Figure 3.3   Visual communication is a powerful use case for a graphical representation. For instance, the map of the London Underground on the left is geographically accurate, while the one on the right trades that accuracy for a clear representation of each station's position relative to the others. The latter is more useful for train riders than the one with geographic accuracy. Similarly, a causal DAG abstracts away much detail of the causal mechanism to create a simple representation that is easy to reason about visually.**

Similarly, a causal DAG highlights causal relationships while ignoring other things. For example, the rock-throwing DAG ignores the if-then conditional logic of how Jenny and Brian's throws combined to break the window. The transportation DAG says nothing about the types of variables we are dealing with. Should we consider age (*A*) in terms of continuous time, integer years, categories like young/middle-aged/elderly, or intervals like 18–29, 30–44, 45–64, and >65? What are the categories of the transportation variable (*T*)? Could the occupation variable (*O*) be a multidimensional tuple like {employed, engineer, works-from-home}? The DAG also fails to capture which of these variables are observed in the data, and the number of data points in that data.

### CAUSAL DAGS DON'T ILLUSTRATE MECHANISM

A causal DAG also doesn't visualize interactions between causes. For example, in older generations, women were less likely to go to college than men. In younger generations, the reverse is true. While both age (*A*) and gender (*S*) are causes of education (*E*), you can't look at the DAG and see anything about how age and gender interact to affect education.

More generally, DAGs can't convey any information about the causal mechanism or *how* the causes impact the effect. They only establish the *what* of causality, as in *what* causes *what*. Consider, for example, the various logic gates in figure 3.4. The input binary values for *A* and *B* determine the output differently depending on the type of logic gate. But if we represent a logic gate as a causal DAG, then all the logic gates have the same causal DAG. We can use the causal DAG as a scaffold for causal graphical models that capture this logic, but we can't *see* the logic in the DAG.

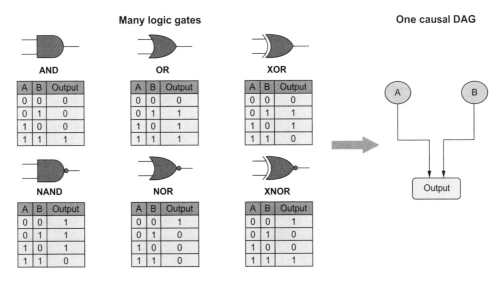

**Figure 3.4 The various kinds of logic gates all have the same causal DAG.**

This is a strength and a weakness. A causal DAG simplifies matters by communicating what causes what, but not *how*. However, in some cases (such as logic gates), visualizing the *how* would be desirable.

### CAUSAL DAGs REPRESENT CAUSAL ASSUMPTIONS

A causal DAG represents the modeler's assumptions and beliefs about the DGP, because we don't have access to that process most of the time. Thus, a causal DAG allows us to visualize our assumptions and communicate them to others.

Beyond this visualization and communication, the benefits of a causal DAG are mathematical and computational (I'll explain these in the following subsections). Causal inference researchers vary in their opinions on the degree to which these mathematical and computational properties of causal DAGs are practically beneficial. However, most agree on the fundamental benefit of visualization and communication of causal assumptions.

The assumptions encoded in a causal DAG are strong. Let's look again at the transportation DAG from figure 3.2, shown again in figure 3.5. Consider the alternatives to that DAG; how many possible DAGs could we draw on this simple six-node system? The answer is 3,781,503, so when we use a causal DAG to communicate our assumptions about this system, we're communicating our top choice over 3,781,502 alternatives.

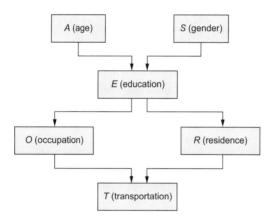

**Figure 3.5   A causal DAG model of transportation choices. This DAG encodes strong assumptions about how these variables do and do not relate to one another.**

And how about some of those competing DAGs? Some of them seem plausible. Perhaps baby boomers prefer small-town life while millennials prefer city life, implying that there should be an $A \rightarrow R$ edge. Perhaps gender norms determine preferences and opportunities in certain professions and industries, implying an $S \rightarrow O$ edge. The assumption that age and gender cause occupation and residence only indirectly through education is a powerful assumption that would provide useful inferences *if it is right*.

But what if our causal DAG is wrong? It seems it is likely to be wrong, given its 3,781,502 competitors. In chapter 4, we'll use data to show us when the causal assumptions in our chosen DAG fail to hold.

### 3.1.4 We have many tools for computing over DAGs

Directed graphs are well-studied objects in math and in computer science, where they are a fundamental data structure. Computer scientists have used graph algorithms to solve many practical problems with theoretical guarantees on how long they will take to arrive at solutions. The programming languages commonly used in data science and machine learning have libraries that implement these algorithms, such as NetworkX in Python. These popular libraries make it easier to write code that works with causal DAGs.

We can bring all that theory and tooling to bear on a causal modeling problem when we represent a causal model in the form of a causal DAG. For example, in pgmpy we can train a causal DAG on data to get a directed causal graphical model. Given that model, we can apply algorithms for graph-based probabilistic inference, such as *belief propagation*, to estimate conditional probabilities defined on variables in the graph. The directed graph structure enables these algorithms to work in typical settings without our needing to configure them to a specific problem or task.

In the next chapter, I'll introduce the concept of *d-separation*, which is a graphical abstraction for conditional independence and the fundamental idea behind the do-calculus theory for causal inference. D-separation is all about finding paths between nodes in the directed graph, which is something any worthwhile graph library makes easy by default. Indeed, conditional independence is the key idea behind the third benefit of the causal DAG.

### 3.1.5 Causal DAGs can represent time

The causal DAG has an implicit representation of time. In more technical terms, the causal DAG provides a *partial temporal ordering* because causes precede effects in time.

For example, consider the graph in figure 3.6. This graph describes a DGP where a change in cloud cover (Cloudy) causes both a change in the state of a weather-activated sprinkler (Sprinkler) and the state of rain (Rain), and these both cause a change in the state of the wetness of the grass (Wet Grass). We know that a change in the state of the weather causes rain and sprinkler activation, and that these both cause a change in the state of the wetness of the grass. However, it is only a *partial* temporal ordering, because the graph doesn't tell us which happens first: the sprinkler activation or the rain.

The partial ordering in figure 3.6 may seem trivial, but consider the DAG in figure 3.7. Visualization libraries can use the partial ordering in the hairball-like DAG on the left of figure 3.7 to create the much more readable form on the right.

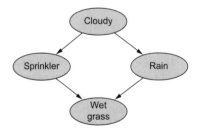

**Figure 3.6 A causal DAG representing the state of some grass (wet or dry). The DAG gives us a partial temporal ordering over its nodes because causes precede effects in time.**

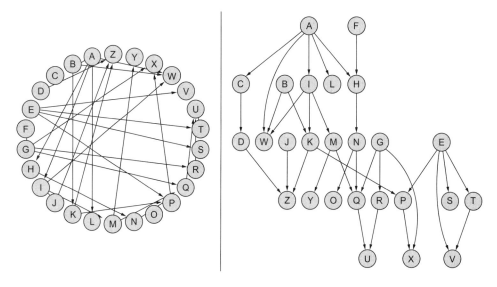

**Figure 3.7   A visualization library can use the DAG's partial ordering to unravel the hairball-like DAG on the left into the more readable form on the right.**

Sometimes we need a causal DAG to be more explicit about time. For example, we may be modeling causality in a dynamic setting, such as in the models used in reinforcement learning. In this case, we can make time explicit by defining and labeling the variables of the model, as in figure 3.8. We can represent continuous time with interval variables like "Δ." Chapter 12 will provide some concrete examples.

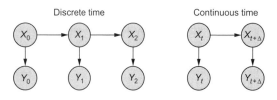

**Figure 3.8   If we need a causal DAG to be explicit about time, we can make time explicit in the definition of the variables and labeling of their nodes. We can represent continuous time with interval variables like "Δ."**

The causal DAG doesn't allow for any cycles. In some causal systems, relaxing the acyclicity constraint makes sense, such as with systems that have feedback loops, and some advanced causal models allow for cycles. But sticking to the simpler acyclic assumption allows us to leverage the benefits of the causal DAG.

If you have cycles, sometimes you can *unroll* the cycle over time and make the time explicit to get acyclicity. A graph $X \rightleftarrows Y$ can unroll as $X_0 \rightarrow Y_0 \rightarrow X_1 \rightarrow Y_1 \ldots$. For example, you may have a cycle between supply, price, and demand, but perhaps you could rewrite this as price at time 0 affects supply and demand at time 1, which then affects price at time 2, etc.

### 3.1.6 DAGs link causality to conditional independence

Another benefit of a causal DAG is that it allows us to use causality to reason about conditional independence. Humans have an innate ability to reason in terms of causality—that's how we get the first and second benefits of causal DAGs. But reasoning probabilistically doesn't come nearly as easily. As a result, the ability to use causality to reason about conditional independence (a concept from probability) is a considerable feature of DAGs.

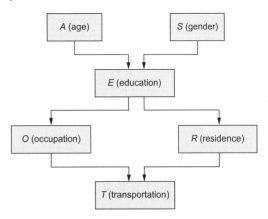

**Figure 3.9  The causal relationships in the transportation DAG encode key assumptions about conditional independence.**

Consider the transportation DAG, displayed again in figure 3.9.

The six variables in the DAG have a joint distribution $P(A,S,E,O,R,T)$. Recall the chain rule from chapter 2, which says that we can factorize any joint probability into a chain of conditional probability factors. For example,

$$P(a, s, e, o, r, t) = P(e) P(s|e) P(t|s, e) P(a|t, s, e) P(o|a, t, s, e) P(r|o, t, s, e)$$
$$= P(t) P(o|t) P(r|o, t) P(e|r, o, t) P(a|e, r, o, t) P(s|a, e, r, o, t)$$
$$= \ldots$$

The chaining works for any ordering of the variables. But instead of choosing any ordering, we'll choose the (partial) ordering of the causal DAG, since that ordering aligns with our assumptions of the causal flow of the variables in the DGP. Looking at figure 3.9, the ordering of variables is $\{(A, S), E, (O, R), T\}$. The pairs $(A, S)$ and $(O, R)$ are unordered. If we arbitrarily pick an ordering, letting $A$ come before $S$ and $O$ come before $R$, we get this:

$$P(a, s, e, o, r, t) = P(a) P(s|a) P(e|s, a) P(o|e, s, a) P(r|o, e, s, a) P(t|o, r, e, s, a)$$

Next, we'll use the causal DAG to further simplify this factorization. Each factor is a conditional probability, so we'll simplify those factors by *conditioning each node on only its parents* in the DAG. In other words, for each variable, we'll look at that variable's direct parents in the graph, then we'll drop everything on the right side of the conditioning bar (|) that isn't one of those direct parents. If we condition only on parents, we get the following simplification:

$$P(a, s, e, o, r, t) = P(a) P(s|a) P(e|s, a) P(o|e, s, a) P(r|o, e, s, a) P(t|o, r, e, s, a)$$
$$= P(a) P(s) P(e|s, a) P(o|e) P(r|e) P(t|o, r)$$

What is going on here? Why should the causal DAG magically mean we can say $P(s|a)$ is equal to $P(s)$ and $P(r|o,e,s,a)$ simplifies to $P(r|e)$? As discussed in chapter 2, stating that $P(s|a)=P(s)$ and $P(t|o,r,e,s,a)=P(t|o,r)$ is equivalent to saying that $S$ and $A$ are independent, and $T$ is conditionally independent of $E$, $S$, and $A$, given $O$ and $R$. In other words, the causal DAG gives us a way to impose conditional independence constraints over the joint probability distribution of the variables in the DGP.

Why should we care about things being conditionally independent? Conditional independence makes life as a modeler easier. For example, suppose you were to model the transportation variable $T$ with a predictive model. The predictive model implied by $P(t|o,r,e,s,a)$ requires having features $O$, $R$, $E$, $S$, and $A$, while the predictive model implied by $P(t|o,r)$ just requires features $O$ and $R$ to predict $T$. The latter model will have fewer parameters to learn, have more degrees of freedom, take less space in memory, train faster, etc.

But why does a causal DAG give us the right to impose conditional independence? Let's build some intuition about the connection between causality and conditional independence. Consider the example of using genetic data from family members to draw conclusions about an individual. For example, the Golden State Killer was a California-based serial killer captured using genetic genealogy. Investigators used DNA left by the killer at crime scenes to identify genetic relatives in public databases. They then triangulated from those relatives to find the killer.

Suppose you had a close relative and a distant relative on the same line of ancestry. Could the distant relative provide any additional genetic information about you once we had already accounted for that close relative? Let's simplify a bit by focusing just on blood type. Suppose the close relative was your father, and the distant relative was your paternal grandfather, as in figure 3.10. Indeed, your grandfather's blood type is a cause of yours. If we saw a large dataset of grandfather/grandchild blood type pairs, we'd see

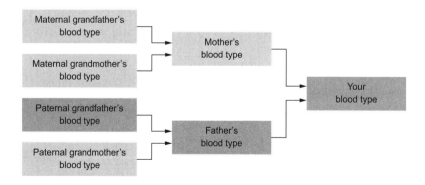

**Figure 3.10   Causality implies conditional independence. Your paternal grandfather's blood type is a cause of your father's, which is a cause of yours. You and your paternal grandfather's blood types are conditionally independent given your father's blood type because your father's blood type already contains all the information your grandfather's type could provide about yours.**

a correlation. However, your father's blood type is a more direct cause, and the connection between your grandfather's blood type and yours passes through your father. So, if our goal were to predict your blood type, and we already had your father's blood type as a predictor, your paternal grandfather's blood type could provide no additional predictive information. Thus, your blood type and your paternal grandfather's blood type are conditionally independent, given your father's blood type.

The way causality makes correlated variables conditionally independent is called the *causal Markov property*. In graphical terms, the causal Markov property means that variables are conditionally independent of their non-descendants (e.g., ancestors, uncles/aunts, cousins, etc.) given their parents in the graph.

This "non-descendants" definition of the causal Markov property is sometimes called the *local Markov property*. An equivalent articulation is called the *Markov factorization property*, which is the property that if your causal DAG is true, you can factorize a joint probability into conditional probabilities of variables, given their parents in the causal DAG:

$$P\,(a,s,e,o,r,t)\ =P\,(a)\,P(s)P\,(e|s,a)\,P\,(o|e)\,P\,(r|e)\,P\,(t|o,r)$$

If our transportation DAG is a true representation of the DGP, then the local Markov property should hold. In the next chapter, we'll see how to test this assumption with data.

### 3.1.7   *DAGs can provide scaffolding for probabilistic ML models*

Many modeling approaches in probabilistic machine learning use a DAG as the model structure. Examples include directed graphical models (aka Bayesian networks) and latent variable models (e.g., topic models). Deep generative models, such as variational autoencoders, often have an underlying directed graph.

The advantage of building a probabilistic machine learning model on top of a causal graph is, rather obviously, that you have a probabilistic *causal* machine learning model. You can train it on data, and you can use it for prediction and other inferences, like any probabilistic machine learning model. Moreover, because it is built on top of a causal DAG, it is a causal model, so you can use it to make causal inferences.

A benefit that follows from providing scaffolding is that *the parameters in those models are modular and encode causal invariance*. Before exploring this benefit, let's first build a graphical model on the transportation DAG.

`Building a probabilistic machine learning model on a causal DAG`

Recall our factorization of the joint probability distribution of the transportation variables over the ordering of the variables in the transportation DAG.

$$P\,(a,s,e,o,r,t)\ =P\,(a)\,P(s)P\,(e|s,a)\,P\,(o|e)\,P\,(r|e)\,P\,(t|o,r)$$

We have a set of factors, $\{P(a),\ P(s),\ P(e|s,a),\ P(o|e),\ P(r|e),\ P(t|o,r)\}$. From here on, we'll build on the term "Markov kernel" from chapter 2 and call these factors *causal Markov kernels*.

We'll build our probabilistic machine learning model by implementing these causal Markov kernels in code and then composing them into one model. Our implementations for each kernel will be able to return a probability value, given input arguments. For example, $P(a)$ will take an outcome value for $A$ and return a probability value for that outcome. Similarly, $P(t|o,r)$ will take in values for $T$, $O$, and $R$ and return a probability value for $T=t$, where $t$ is the queried value. Our implementations will also be able to generate from the causal Markov kernels. To do this, these implementations will require parameters that map the inputs to the outputs. We'll use standard statistical learning approaches to fit those parameters from the data.

### 3.1.8   *Training a model on the causal DAG*

Consider the DGP for the transportation DAG. What sort of data would this process generate?

Suppose we administered a survey covering 500 individuals, getting values for each of the variables in this DAG. The data encodes the variables in our DAG as follows:

- *Age (A)*—Recorded as young ("young") for individuals up to and including 29 years, adult ("adult") for individuals between 30 and 60 years old (inclusive), and old ("old") for people 61 and over
- *Gender (S)*—The self-reported gender of an individual, recorded as male ("M"), female ("F"), or other ("O")
- *Education (E)*—The highest level of education or training completed by the individual, recorded either high school ("high") or university degree ("uni")
- *Occupation (O)*—Employee ("emp") or a self-employed worker ("self")
- *Residence (R)*—The population size of the city the individual lives in, recorded as small ("small") or big ("big")
- *Travel (T)*—The means of transport favored by the individual, recorded as car ("car"), train ("train"), or other ("other")

**Labeling causal abstractions**

How we conceptualize the variables of a model matters greatly in machine learning. For example, ImageNet, a database of 14 million images, contains anachronistic and offensive labels for racial categories. Even if renamed to be less offensive, race categories themselves are fluid across time and culture. What are the "correct" labels to use in a predictive algorithm?

How we define our variables isn't just a question of politics and census forms. A simple thought experiment by philosopher Nelson Goodman shows how a simple change in label can change a prediction to a contradictory prediction. Suppose you regularly search for gems and record the color of every gem you find. It turns out 100% of the gems in your dataset are green. Now let's define a new label "grue" to mean "green if observed before now, blue otherwise." So 100% of your data is "green" or "grue," depending on your choice of label. Now suppose you predict the future based on extrapolating from the past. Then you can predict the next emerald will be green based on data where all past emeralds were green, or you can predict the next emerald will be "grue" (i.e., *blue*) based on the data that all past emeralds were "grue." Obviously, you would never invent such an absurd label, but this thought experiment is enough to show that the inference depends on the abstraction.

In data science and machine learning, we're often encouraged to blindly model data and not to think about the DGP. We're encouraged to take the variable names for granted as columns in a spreadsheet or attributes in a database table. When possible, it is better to choose abstractions that are appropriate to the inference problem and collect or encode data according to that abstraction. When it is not possible, keep in mind that the results of your analysis will depend on how other people have defined the variables.

In chapter 7, I'll introduce the idea of "no causation without manipulation"—an idea that provides a useful heuristic for how to define causal variables.

The variables in the transportation data are all *categorical* variables. In this simple categorical case, we can rely on a graphical modeling library like pgmpy.

##### Listing 3.3 Loading transportation data

```
import pandas as pd
url='https://raw.githubusercontent.com/altdeep/causalML/master/datasets
➥/transportation_survey.csv'
data = pd.read_csv(url)
data
```

> We'll load the data into a pandas DataFrame with the read_csv method.

This produces the DataFrame in figure 3.11.

|     | A | S | E | O | R | T |
|-----|------|---|------|-----|-------|-------|
| 0   | adult | F | high | emp | small | train |
| 1   | young | M | high | emp | big | car |
| 2   | adult | M | uni | emp | big | other |
| 3   | old | F | uni | emp | big | car |
| 4   | young | F | uni | emp | big | car |
| ... | ... | ... | ... | ... | ... | ... |
| 495 | young | M | high | emp | big | other |
| 496 | adult | M | high | emp | big | car |
| 497 | young | M | high | emp | small | train |
| 498 | young | M | high | emp | small | car |
| 499 | adult | M | high | emp | small | other |

500 rows × 6 columns

Figure 3.11 An example of data from the DGP underlying the transportation model. In this case, the data is 500 survey responses.

The `BayesianNetwork` class we initialized in listing 3.2 has a `fit` method that will learn the parameters of our causal Markov kernels. Since our variables are categorical, our causal Markov kernels will be in the form of conditional probability tables represented by pgmpy's `TabularCPD` class. The `fit` method will fit ("learn") estimates of the parameters of those conditional probability tables using the data.

**Listing 3.4   Learning parameters for the causal Markov kernels**

```
from pgmpy.models import BayesianNetwork
model = BayesianNetwork(
    [
        ('A', 'E'),
        ('S', 'E'),
        ('E', 'O'),
        ('E', 'R'),
        ('O', 'T'),
        ('R', 'T')
    ]
)
model.fit(data)
causal_markov_kernels = model.get_cpds()
print(causal_markov_kernels)
```

The fit method on the BayesianNetwork object will estimate parameters from data (a pandas DataFrame).

Retrieve and view the causal Markov kernels learned by fit.

This returns the following output:

```
[<TabularCPD representing P(A:3) at 0x7fb030dd1050>,
 <TabularCPD representing P(E:2 | A:3, S:2) at 0x7fb0318121d0>,
 <TabularCPD representing P(S:2) at 0x7fb03189fe90>,
 <TabularCPD representing P(O:2 | E:2) at 0x7fb030de85d0>,
 <TabularCPD representing P(R:2 | E:2) at 0x7fb030dfa890>,
 <TabularCPD representing P(T:3 | O:2, R:2) at 0x7fb0316c9110>]
```

Let's look at the structure of the causal Markov kernel for the transportation variable *T*. We can see from printing out the `causal_markov_kernels` list that *T* is the last item in the list.

```
cmk_T = causal_markov_kernels[-1]
print(cmk_T)
```

We get the following output:

| O        | O(emp)  | O(emp)   | O(self) | O(self)  |
|----------|---------|----------|---------|----------|
| R        | R(big)  | R(small) | R(big)  | R(small) |
| T(car)   | 0.70343 | 0.52439  | 0.44444 | 1.0      |
| T(other) | 0.13480 | 0.08536  | 0.33333 | 0.0      |
| T(train) | 0.16176 | 0.39024  | 0.22222 | 0.0      |

Note that in this printout, I truncated the numbers so the table fits on the page.

cmk_T is the implementation of the causal Markov kernel $P(T|O,R)$ as a conditional probability table, a type of lookup table where, given the values of $T$, $O$, and $R$, we get the corresponding probability mass value. For example, $P(T=$car$|O=$emp, $R=$big$) = 0.7034$. Note that these are conditional probabilities. For each combination of values for $O$ and $R$, there are conditional probabilities for the three outcomes of $T$ that sum to 1. For example, when $O=$emp and $R=$big, $P(T=$car$|O=$emp, $R=$big$) + (P(T=$other$|O=$emp, $R=$big$) + P(T=$train$|O=$emp, $R=$big$) = 1$.

The causal Markov kernel in the case of nodes with no parents is just a simple probability table. For example, `print(causal_markov_kernels[2])` prints the causal Markov kernel for gender ($S$), the third item in the `causal_markov_kernels` list.

```
+------+-------+
| S(F) | 0.517 |
+------+-------+
| S(M) | 0.473 |
+------+-------+
| S(O) | 0.010 |
+------+-------+
```

The `fit` method learns parameters by calculating the proportions of each class in the data. Alternatively, we could use other techniques for parameter learning.

### 3.1.9 *Different techniques for parameter learning*

There are several ways we could go about training these parameters. Let's look at a few common ways of training parameters in conditional probability tables.

#### MAXIMUM LIKELIHOOD ESTIMATION

The learning algorithm I used in the `fit` method on the `BayesianNetwork` model object was *maximum likelihood estimation* (discussed in chapter 2). It is the default parameter learning method, so I didn't specify "maximum likelihood" in the call to `fit`. Generally, maximum likelihood estimation seeks the parameter that maximizes the likelihood of seeing the data we use to train the model. In the context of categorical data, maximum likelihood estimation is equivalent to taking proportions of counts in the data. For example, the parameter for $P(O=$emp$|E=$high$)$ is calculated as:

$$\frac{\text{\# observations where } O = emp \text{ and } E = \text{high}}{\text{\# observations where } E = \text{high}}$$

#### BAYESIAN ESTIMATION

In chapter 2, I also introduced Bayesian estimation. It is generally mathematically intractable and relies on computationally expensive algorithms (e.g., sampling algorithms and variational inference). A key exception is the case of *conjugate priors*, where the prior distribution and the target (posterior) distribution have the same canonical form. That means the code implementation can just calculate the parameter values of the target distribution with simple math, without the need for complicated Bayesian inference algorithms.

For example, pgmpy implements a *Dirichlet conjugate prior* for categorical outcomes. For each value of *O* in *P(O|E=high)*, we have a probability value, and we want to infer these probability values from the data. A Bayesian approach assigns a prior distribution to these values. A good choice for a prior on a set of probability values is the *Dirichlet distribution*, because it is defined for a *simplex*, a set of numbers between zero and one that sum to one. Further it is *conjugate* to categorical distributions like *P(O|E=high)*, meaning the posterior distribution on the parameter values is also a Dirichlet distribution. That means we can calculate point estimates of the probability values using simple math, combining counts in the data and parameters in the prior. pgmpy does this math for us.

---

**Listing 3.5    Bayesian point estimation with a Dirichlet conjugate prior**

```
from pgmpy.estimators import BayesianEstimator
model.fit(
    data,
    estimator=BayesianEstimator,
    prior_type="dirichlet",
    pseudo_counts=1
)
causal_markov_kernels = model.get_cpds()
cmk_T = causal_markov_kernels[-1]
print(cmk_T)
```

Import BayesianEstimator and initialize it on the model and data.

Pass the estimator object to the fit method.

pseudo_counts refers to the parameters of the Dirichlet prior.

Extract the causal Markov kernels and view P(T|O,R).

---

The preceding code prints the following output:

```
+----------+--------------------+-----+--------------------+----------+
| O        | O(emp)             | ... | O(self)            | O(self)  |
+----------+--------------------+-----+--------------------+----------+
| R        | R(big)             | ... | R(big)             | R(small) |
+----------+--------------------+-----+--------------------+----------+
| T(car)   | 0.7007299270072993 | ... | 0.4166666666666667 | 0.5      |
+----------+--------------------+-----+--------------------+----------+
| T(other) | 0.1362530413625304 | ... | 0.3333333333333333 | 0.25     |
+----------+--------------------+-----+--------------------+----------+
| T(train) | 0.1630170316301703 | ... | 0.25               | 0.25     |
+----------+--------------------+-----+--------------------+----------+
```

In contrast to maximum likelihood estimation, Bayesian estimation of a categorical parameter with a Dirichlet prior acts like a smoothing mechanism. For example, the maximum likelihood parameter estimate says 100% of self-employed people in small towns take a car to work. This is probably extreme. Certainly, some self-employed people bike to work—we just didn't manage to survey any of them. Some small cities, such as Crystal City in the US state of Virginia (population 22,000), have subway stations. I'd wager at least a few of the entrepreneurs in those cities use the train.

## Causal modelers and Bayesians

The Bayesian philosophy goes beyond mere parameter estimation. Indeed, Bayesian philosophy has much in common with DAG-based causal modeling. Bayesians try to encode subjective beliefs, uncertainty, and prior knowledge into "prior" probability distributions on variables in the model. Causal modelers try to encode subjective beliefs and prior knowledge about the DGP into the form of a causal DAG. The two approaches are compatible. Given a causal DAG, you can be Bayesian about inferring the parameters of the probabilistic model you build on top of the causal DAG. You can even be Bayesian about the DAG itself and compute probability distributions over possible DAGs!

I focus on causality in this book and keep Bayesian discussions to a minimum. But we'll use the libraries Pyro (and its NumPy-JAX alternative NumPyro) to implement causal models; these libraries provide complete support for Bayesian inference on models as well as parameters. In chapter 11, we'll look at an example of Bayesian inference of a causal effect using a causal graphical model we build from scratch.

### OTHER TECHNIQUES FOR PARAMETER ESTIMATION

We need not use a conditional probability table to represent the causal Markov kernels. There are models within the generalized linear modeling framework for modeling categorical outcomes. For some of the variables in the transportation model, we might have used non-categorical outcomes. Age, for example, might have been recorded as an integer outcome in the survey. For variables with numeric outcomes, we might use other modeling approaches. You can also use neural network architectures to model individual causal Markov kernels.

*Parametric assumptions* refer to how we specify the outcomes of a node in the DAG (e.g., category or real number) and how we map parents to the outcome (e.g., table or neural network). Note that the causal assumptions encoded by the causal DAG are decoupled from the parametric assumptions for a causal Markov kernel. For example, when we assumed that age was a direct cause of education level and encoded that into our DAG as an edge, we didn't have to decide if we were going to treat age as an ordered set of classes, as an integer, or as seconds elapsed since birth, etc. Furthermore, we didn't have to know whether to use a conditional categorical distribution or a regression model. That step comes after we specify the causal DAG and want to implement $P(E|A, S)$.

Similarly, when we make predictions and probabilistic inferences on a trained causal model, the considerations of what inference or prediction algorithms to use, while important, are separate from our causal questions. This separation simplifies our work. Often we can build our knowledge and skill set in causal modeling and reasoning independently of our knowledge of statistics, computational Bayes, and applied machine learning.

### 3.1.10  *Learning parameters when there are latent variables*

Since we are modeling the DGP and not the data, it is likely that some nodes in the causal DAG will not be observed in the data. Fortunately, probabilistic machine learning provides us with tools for learning the parameters of causal Markov kernels of latent variables.

#### LEARNING LATENT VARIABLES WITH PGMPY

To illustrate, suppose the education variable in the transportation survey data was not recorded. pgmpy gives us a utility for learning the parameters of the causal Markov kernel for latent *E* using an algorithm called *structural expectation maximization*, which is a variant of parameter learning with maximum likelihood.

Listing 3.6  Training a causal graphical model with a latent variable

```
import pandas as pd
from pgmpy.models import BayesianNetwork
from pgmpy.estimators import ExpectationMaximization as EM
url='https://raw.githubusercontent.com/altdeep/causalML/master/datasets
/transportation_survey.csv'
data = pd.read_csv(url)
data_sans_E = data[['A', 'S', 'O', 'R', 'T']]
model_with_latent = BayesianNetwork(
    [
        ('A', 'E'),
        ('S', 'E'),
        ('E', 'O'),
        ('E', 'R'),
        ('O', 'T'),
        ('R', 'T')
    ],
    latents={"E"}
)
estimator = EM(model_with_latent, data_sans_E)
cmks_with_latent = estimator.get_parameters(latent_card={'E': 2})
print(cmks_with_latent[1].to_factor())
```

Download the data and convert to a pandas DataFrame.

Keep all the columns except education (E).

Indicate which variables are latent when training the model.

Run the structural expectation maximization algorithm to learn the causal Markov kernel for E. You have to indicate the cardinality of the latent variable.

Print out the learned causal Markov kernel for E. Print it as a factor object for legibility.

The print line prints a factor object.

```
+------+----------+------+--------------+
| E    | A        | S    | phi(E,A,S)   |
+======+==========+======+==============+
| E(0) | A(adult) | S(F) |      0.1059  |
+------+----------+------+--------------+
| E(0) | A(adult) | S(M) |      0.1124  |
+------+----------+------+--------------+
| E(0) | A(old)   | S(F) |      0.4033  |
+------+----------+------+--------------+
| E(0) | A(old)   | S(M) |      0.2386  |
+------+----------+------+--------------+
| E(0) | A(young) | S(F) |      0.4533  |
+------+----------+------+--------------+
```

```
| E(0) | A(young) | S(M) |        0.6080 |
+------+----------+------+---------------+
| E(1) | A(adult) | S(F) |        0.8941 |
+------+----------+------+---------------+
| E(1) | A(adult) | S(M) |        0.8876 |
+------+----------+------+---------------+
| E(1) | A(old)   | S(F) |        0.5967 |
+------+----------+------+---------------+
| E(1) | A(old)   | S(M) |        0.7614 |
+------+----------+------+---------------+
| E(1) | A(young) | S(F) |        0.5467 |
+------+----------+------+---------------+
| E(1) | A(young) | S(M) |        0.3920 |
+------+----------+------+---------------+
```

The outcomes for $E$ are 0 and 1 because the algorithm doesn't know the outcome names. Perhaps 0 is "high" (high school) and 1 is "uni" (university), but correctly mapping the default outcomes from a latent variable estimation method to the names of those outcomes would require further assumptions.

There are other algorithms for learning parameters when there are latent variables, including some that use special parametric assumptions (i.e., functional assumptions about how the latent variables relate to the observed variables).

### LATENT VARIABLES AND IDENTIFICATION

In statistical inference, we say a parameter is "identified" when it is theoretically possible to learn its true value given an infinite number of examples in the data. It is "unidentified" if more data doesn't get you closer to learning its true value. Unfortunately, your data may not be sufficient to learn the causal Markov kernels of the latent variables in your causal DAG. If we did not care about representing causality, we could restrict ourselves to a latent variable graphical model with latent variables that are identifiable from data. But we must build a causal DAG that represents the DGP, even if we can't identify the latent variables and parameters given the data.

That said, even if you have non-identifiable parameters in your causal model, you still may be able to identify the quantity that answers your causal question. Indeed, much of causal inference methodology is focused on robust estimation of causal effects (how much a cause affects an effect) despite having latent "confounders." We'll cover this in detail in chapter 11. On the other hand, even if your parameters are identified, the quantity that answers your causal question may not be identified. We'll cover causal identification in detail in chapter 10.

### 3.1.11 *Inference with a trained causal probabilistic machine learning model*

A probabilistic machine learning model of a set of variables can use computational inference algorithms to infer the conditional probability of an outcome for any subset of the variables, given outcomes for the other variables. We use the variable elimination algorithm for a directed graphical model with categorical outcomes (introduced in chapter 2).

For example, suppose we want to compare education levels amongst car drivers to that of train riders. We can calculate and compare $P(E|T)$ when $T$=car to when $T$=train by using variable elimination, an inference algorithm for tabular graphical models.

##### Listing 3.7  Inference on the trained causal graphical model

```
from pgmpy.inference import VariableElimination
inference = VariableElimination(model)
query1 = inference.query(['E'], evidence={"T": "train"})
query2 = inference.query(['E'], evidence={"T": "car"})
print("train")
print(query1)
print("car")
print(query2)
```

**VariableElimination is an inference algorithm specific to graphical models.**

This prints the probability tables for "train" and "car."

```
"train"
+---------+----------+
| E       |   phi(E) |
+=========+==========+
| E(high) |   0.6162 |
+---------+----------+
| E(uni)  |   0.3838 |
+---------+----------+
"car"
+---------+----------+
| E       |   phi(E) |
+=========+==========+
| E(high) |   0.5586 |
+---------+----------+
| E(uni)  |   0.4414 |
+---------+----------+
```

It seems car drivers are more likely to have a university education than train riders: $(P(E='uni'|T='car') > P(E='uni'|T='train')$. That inference is based on our DAG-based causal assumption that university education indirectly determines how people get to work.

In a tool like Pyro, you have to be a bit more hands-on with the inference algorithm. The following listing illustrates the inference of $P(E|T="train")$ using a probabilistic inference algorithm called importance sampling. First, we'll specify the model. Rather than fit the parameters, we'll explicitly specify the parameter values we fit with pgmpy.

##### Listing 3.8  Implementing the trained causal model in Pyro

```
import torch
import pyro
from pyro.distributions import Categorical
```

```
A_alias = ['young', 'adult', 'old']
S_alias = ['M', 'F']
E_alias = ['high', 'uni']
O_alias = ['emp', 'self']
R_alias = ['small', 'big']
T_alias = ['car', 'train', 'other']
```

**The categorical distribution only returns integers, so it's useful to write the integers' mapping to categorical outcome names.**

```
A_prob = torch.tensor([0.3,0.5,0.2])
S_prob = torch.tensor([0.6,0.4])
E_prob = torch.tensor([[[0.75,0.25], [0.72,0.28], [0.88,0.12]],
                        [[0.64,0.36], [0.7,0.3], [0.9,0.1]]])
O_prob = torch.tensor([[0.96,0.04], [0.92,0.08]])
R_prob = torch.tensor([[0.25,0.75], [0.2,0.8]])
T_prob = torch.tensor([[[0.48,0.42,0.1], [0.56,0.36,0.08]],
                        [[0.58,0.24,0.18], [0.7,0.21,0.09]]])
```

**For simplicity, we'll use rounded versions of parameters learned with the fit method in pgmpy (listing 3.4), though we could have learned the parameters in a training procedure.**

```
def model():
    A = pyro.sample('age', Categorical(probs=A_prob))
    S = pyro.sample('gender', Categorical(probs=S_prob))
    E = pyro.sample('education', Categorical(probs=E_prob[S][A]))
    O = pyro.sample('occupation', Categorical(probs=O_prob[E]))
    R = pyro.sample('residence', Categorical(probs=R_prob[E]))
    T = pyro.sample('transportation', Categorical(probs=T_prob[R][O]))
    Return {'A': A, 'S': S, 'E': E, 'O': O, 'R': R, 'T': T}

pyro.render_model(model)
```

**When we implement the model in Pyro, we specify the causal DAG implicitly using code logic.**

**We can then generate a figure of the implied DAG using pyro.render_model(). Note that we need to have Graphviz installed.**

The `pyro.render_model` function draws the implied causal DAG from the Pyro model in figure 3.12.

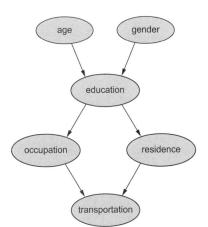

**Figure 3.12   You can visualize the causal DAG in Pyro by using the `pyro.render_model()` function. This assumes you have Graphviz installed.**

Pyro provides probabilistic inference algorithms, such as importance sampling, that we can apply to our causal model.

**Listing 3.9   Inference on the causal model in Pyro**

```
import numpy as np
import pyro
from pyro.distributions import Categorical
from pyro.infer import Importance, EmpiricalMarginal
import matplotlib.pyplot as plt

conditioned_model = pyro.condition(
    model,
    data={'transportation':torch.tensor(1.)}
)

m = 5000
posterior = pyro.infer.Importance(
    conditioned_model,
    num_samples=m
).run()
```

We'll use two inference-related classes, Importance and EmpiricalMarginal.

pyro.condition is a conditioning operation on the model.

It takes in the model and evidence for conditioning on. The evidence is a dictionary that maps variable names to values. The need to specify variable names during inference is why we have the name argument in the calls to pyro.sample. Here we condition on T="train".

We'll run an inference algorithm that will generate m samples.

Run the random process algorithm with the run method. The inference algorithm will generate from the joint probability of the variables we didn't condition on (everything but T) given the variables we conditioned on (T).

I use an inference algorithm called importance sampling. The Importance class constructs this inference algorithm. It takes the conditioned model and the number of samples.

Based on these samples, we produce a Monte Carlo estimation of the probabilities in P(E|T="train").

We are interested in the conditional probability distribution of education, so we extract education values from the posterior.

```
E_marginal = EmpiricalMarginal(posterior, "education")
E_samples = [E_marginal().item() for _ in range(m)]
E_unique, E_counts = np.unique(E_samples, return_counts=True)
E_probs = E_counts / m

plt.bar(E_unique, E_probs, align='center', alpha=0.5)
plt.xticks(E_unique, E_alias)
plt.ylabel('probability')
plt.xlabel('education')
plt.title('P(E | T = "train") - Importance Sampling')
```

Plot a visualization of the learned probabilities.

This produces the plot in figure 3.13. The probabilities shown are close to the results from the pgmpy model, though they're slightly different due to different algorithms and the rounding of the parameter estimates to two decimal places.

This probabilistic inference is not yet causal inference—we'll look at examples combining causal inference with probabilistic inference starting in chapter 7. In chapter 8, you'll see how to use probabilistic inference to implement causal inference. For now, we'll look at the benefit of parameter modularity, and at how parameters encode causal invariance.

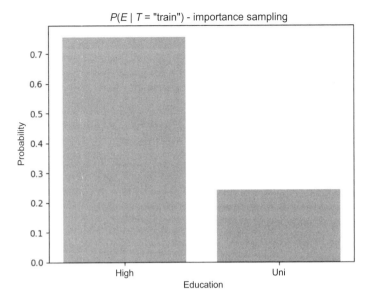

**Figure 3.13   Visualization of the P(E|T="train") distribution**

## 3.2   *Causal invariance and parameter modularity*

Suppose we were interested in modeling the relationship between altitude and temperature. The two are clearly correlated; the higher up you go, the colder it gets. However, you know temperature doesn't cause altitude, or heating the air within a city would cause the city to fly. Altitude is the cause, and temperature is the effect.

We can come up with a simple causal DAG that we think captures the relationship between temperature and altitude, along with other causes, as shown in figure 3.14. Let's have $A$ be altitude, $C$ be cloud cover, $L$ be latitude, $S$ be season, and $T$ be temperature. The DAG in figure 3.14 has five causal Markov kernels: $\{P(A), P(C), P(L), P(S), P(T|A, C, L, S)\}$.

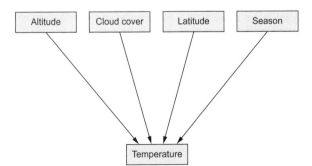

**Figure 3.14   A simple model of outdoor temperature**

To train a causal graphical model on top of this DAG, we need to learn parameters for each of these causal Markov kernels.

### 3.2.1    *Independence of mechanism and parameter modularity*

There are some underlying thermodynamic mechanisms in the DGP underlying the causal Markov kernels in our temperature DAG. For example, the causal Markov kernel $P(T|A, C, L, S)$ is the conditional probability induced by the physics-based mechanism, wherein altitude, cloud cover, latitude, and season drive the temperature. That mechanism is distinct from the mechanism that determines cloud cover (according to our DAG). *Independence of mechanism* refers to this distinction between mechanisms.

The independence of the mechanism leads to a property called *parameter modularity*. In our model, for each causal Markov kernel, we choose a parameterized representation of the causal Markov kernels. If $P(T|A, C, L, S)$ and $P(C)$ are distinct mechanisms, then our representations of $P(T|A, C, L, S)$ and $P(C)$ are representations of distinct mechanisms. That means we can change one representation without worrying about how that change affects the other representations. Such modularity is atypical in statistical models; you can't usually change one part of a model and expect the other part to be unaffected.

One way this comes in handy is during training. Typically, when you train a model, you optimize all the parameters at the same time. Parameter modularity means you could train the parameters for each causal Markov kernel separately, or train them simultaneously as decoupled sets, allowing you to enjoy some dimensionality reduction during training. In Bayesian terms, the parameter sets are a priori independent (though they are generally dependent in the posterior). This provides a nice causal justification for using an independent prior distribution for each causal Markov kernel's parameter set.

### 3.2.2    *Causal transfer learning, data fusion, and invariant prediction*

You may not be a climatologist or a meteorologist. Still, you know the relationship between temperature and altitude has something to do with air pressure, climate, sunlight, and such. You also know that whatever the physics of that relationship is, the physics is the same in Katmandu as it is in El Paso. So, when we train a causal Markov kernel on data solely collected from Katmandu, we learn a causal representation of a mechanism that is invariant between Katmandu and El Paso. This invariance helps with transfer learning; we should be able to use that trained causal Markov kernel to make inferences about the temperature in El Paso.

Of course, there are caveats to leveraging this notion of causal invariance. For example, this assumes your causal model is correct and that there is enough information about the underlying mechanism in the Katmandu data to effectively apply what you've learned about that mechanism in El Paso.

Several advanced methods lean heavily on causal invariance and independence of mechanism. For example, *causal data fusion* uses this idea to learn a causal model by combining multiple datasets. *Causal transfer learning* uses causal invariance to make causal inferences using data outside the domain of the training data. *Causal invariant prediction* leverages causal invariance in prediction tasks. See the chapter notes at www.altdeep.ai/causalAIbook for references.

### 3.2.3   *Fitting parameters with common sense*

In the temperature model, we have an intuition about the physics of the mechanism that induces $P(T|A, C, L, S)$. In non-natural science domains, such as econometrics and other social sciences, the "physics" of the system is more abstract and harder to write down. Fortunately, we can rely on similar invariance-based intuition in these non-natural science domains. In these domains, we can still assume the causal Markov kernels correspond to distinct causal mechanisms in the real world, assuming the model is true. For example, recall $P(T|O, R)$ in our transportation model. We still assume the underlying mechanism is distinct from the others; if there were changes to the mechanism underlying $P(T|O, R)$, only $P(T|O, R)$ should change—other kernels in the model should not. If something changes the mechanism underlying $P(R|E)$, the causal Markov kernel for $R$, this change should affect $P(R|E)$ but have no effect on the parameters of $P(T|O, R)$.

This invariance can help us estimate parameters *without* statistical learning by reasoning about the underlying causal mechanism. For example, let's look again at the causal Markov kernel $P(R|E)$ (recall $R$ is residence, $E$ is education). Let's try to reason our way to estimates of the parameters of this distribution without using statistical learning.

People who don't get more than a high school degree are more likely to stay in their hometowns. However, people from small towns who attain college degrees are likely to move to a big city where they can apply their credentials to get higher-paying jobs.

Now let's think about US demographics. Suppose a web search tells you that 80% of the US lives in an urban area ($P(R=\text{big}) = .8$), while 95% of college degree holders live in an urban area ($P(R=\text{big}|E=\text{uni}) = .95$). Further, 25% of the overall adult population in the US has a university degree ($P(E=\text{uni}) = .25$). Then, with some back-of-the-envelope math, you calculate your probability values as $P(R=\text{small}|E=\text{high})=.25$, $P(R=\text{big}|E=\text{high}) = .75$, $P(R=\text{small}|E=\text{uni}) = .05$, and $P(R=\text{big}|E=\text{uni}) = .95$. The ability to calculate parameters in this manner is particularly useful if data is unavailable for parameter learning.

## 3.3   *Your causal question scopes the DAG*

When a modeler meets a problem for the first time, there is often already a set of available data, and a common mistake is to define your DAG using only the variables in that data. Letting the data scope your DAG is attractive, because you don't have to decide what variables to include in your DAG. But causal modelers model the DGP, not the data. The true causal structure in the world doesn't care about what happens to be measured in your dataset. In your causal DAG, you should include causally relevant variables whether they are in your dataset or not.

But if the data doesn't define the DAG's scope, what does? While your data has a fixed set of variables, the variables that could comprise your DGP are only bounded by your imagination. Given a variable, you could include its causes, those causes' causes, those causes' causes' causes, continuing all the way back to Aristotle's "prime mover," the single cause of everything. Fortunately, there is no need to go back that far. Let's look at a procedure you can use to select variables for inclusion in your causal DAG.

### 3.3.1  *Selecting variables for inclusion in the DAG*

Recall that there are several kinds of causal inference questions. As I mentioned in chapter 1, causal effect inference is the most common type of causal question. I use causal effect inference as an example, but this workflow is meant for all types of causal questions.

1  *Include variables central to your causal question(s)*—The first step is to include all the variables central to your causal question. If you intend to ask multiple questions, include all the variables relevant to those questions. As an example, consider figure 3.15. Suppose that we intend to ask about the causal effect of $V$ on $U$ and $Y$. These become the first variables we include in the DAG.

2  *Include any common causes for the variables in step 1*—Add any common causes for the variables you included in the first step. In our example, you would start with variables $U$, $V$ and $Y$ in figure 3.15, and trace back their causal lineages and identify shared ancestors. These shared ancestors are common causes. In figure 3.16, $W_0$, $W_1$, and $W_2$ are common causes of $V$, $U$, and $Y$.

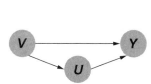

Figure 3.15   First include variables central to your causal question(s). Here, suppose you are interested in asking questions about $V$, $U$, and $Y$.

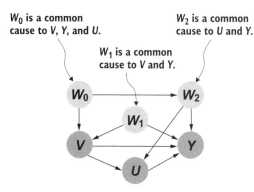

$W_0$ is a common cause to $V$, $Y$, and $U$.

$W_2$ is a common cause to $U$ and $Y$.

$W_1$ is a common cause to $V$ and $Y$.

Figure 3.16   Satisfy causal sufficiency; include common causes to the variables from step 1.

In formal terms, a variable is a common cause $Z$ of a pair of variables $X$ and $Y$ if there is a directed path from $Z$ to $X$ that does not include $Y$ and a directed path from $Z$ to $Y$ that does not include $X$. The formal principle of including common causes is called *causal sufficiency*. A set of variables is causally sufficient if it doesn't exclude any common causes between any pair of variables in the set.

Furthermore, once you include a common cause, you don't have to include earlier common causes on the same paths. For example, figure 3.17 illustrates how we might exclude variables' earlier common causes.

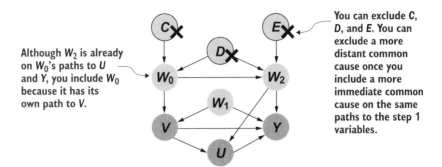

**Figure 3.17** **Once you include a common cause, you don't have to include any earlier common causes on the same paths to the step 1 variables.**

In figure 3.17, $W_2$ is on $W_0$'s path to $Y$ and $U$, but we include $W_0$ because it has its own path to $V$. In contrast, while $C$ is a common cause of $V$, $Y$, and $U$, $W_0$ is on all of $C$'s paths to $V$, $Y$ and $U$, so we can exclude it after including $W_0$. Similarly, $W_2$ lets us exclude $E$, and $W_0$ and $W_2$ together let us exclude $D$.

**3** *Include variables that may be useful in causal inference statistical analysis*—Now we include variables that may be useful in statistical methods for the causal inferences you want to make. For example, in figure 3.18, suppose you were interested in estimating the cause effect of $V$ on $Y$. You might want to include possible "instrumental variables." We'll define these formally in part 4 of this book, but for now in a causal effect question, an *instrument* is a parent of a variable of interest, and it can help in statistical estimation of the causal effect. In figure 3.18, $Z$ can function as an instrumental variable. You do not need to include $Z$ for causal sufficiency, but you might choose to include it to help with quantifying the causal effect.

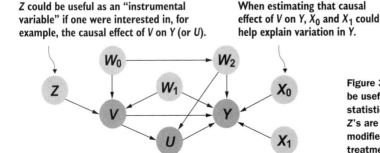

**Figure 3.18** **Include variables that may be useful in the causal inference statistical analysis. $W$'s are confounders, $Z$'s are instruments, $X$'s are effect modifiers, $Y$ is the outcome, $V$ is a treatment, and $U$ is a front door mediator.**

Similarly, $X_0$ and $X_1$ could also be of use in the analysis by accounting for other sources of variation in $Y$. We could potentially use them to reduce variance in the statistical estimation of a causal effect. Alternatively, we may be interested in the *heterogeneity* of the causal effect (how the causal effect varies) across subsets of the population defined by $X_0$ and $X_1$. We'll look at causal effect heterogeneity more closely in chapter 11.

4  *Include variables that help the DAG communicate a complete story*—Finally, include any variables that help the DAG better function as a communicative tool. Consider the common cause $D$ in figure 3.19.

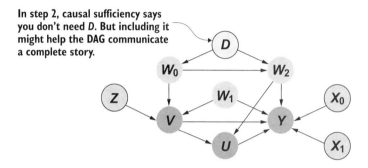

**Figure 3.19   Include variables that help the DAG tell a complete story. In this example, despite having excluded *D* in step 2 (figure 3.17) we still might want to include *D* if it has communicative value.**

In figure 3.17, we concluded that the common cause $D$ could be excluded after including common causes $W_0$ and $W_2$. But perhaps $D$ is an important variable in how domain experts conceptualize the domain. While it is not useful in quantifying the causal effect of $V$ on $U$ and $Y$, leaving it out might feel awkward. If so, including it may help the DAG tell a better story by showing how a key variable relates to the variables you included. When your causal DAG tells a convincing story, your causal analysis is more convincing.

### 3.3.2   *Including variables in causal DAGs by their role in inference*

Many experts in causal inference de-emphasize writing their assumptions in the form of a causal DAG in favor of specifying a set of relevant variables, according to their *role* in causal inference calculations. Focusing on variable-role-in-inference over a causal DAG is common in econometrics pedagogy. Examples of such roles include terms I've already introduced, such as "common cause," "instrumental variable," and "effect modifier." Again, we'll define these formally in chapter 11.

For now, I want to make clear that this is not a competing paradigm. An economist might say they are interested in the causal effect of $V$ on $U$, conditional on some "*effect modifiers*," and that they plan to "*adjust for* the influence of *common causes*" using an "*instrumental variable.*" These roles all correspond to structure in a causal DAG; common causes of $U$ and $V$ in figure 3.19 are $W_0$, $W_1$, and $W_2$. $Z$ is an instrumental variable, and $X_0$ and $X_1$ are effect modifiers. Assuming variables with these roles are important to your causal effect estimation analysis is implicitly assuming that your DGP follows the causal DAG with this structure.

In fact, given a set of variables and their roles, we can construct the implied causal DAG on that set. The DoWhy causal inference library shows us how.

**Listing 3.10 Creating a DAG based on roles in causal effect inference**

```
from dowhy import datasets

import networkx as nx
import matplotlib.pyplot as plt

sim_data = datasets.linear_dataset(
    beta=10.0,
    num_treatments=1,
    num_instruments=2,
    num_effect_modifiers=2,
    num_common_causes=5,
    num_frontdoor_variables=1,
    num_samples=100,

)
```

datasets.linear_dataset generates a DAG from the specified variables.

Add one treatment variable, like V in figure 3.19.

Front door variables are on the path between the treatment and the effect, like U in figure 3.19. Here we add one.

Z in figure 3.19 is an example of an instrumental variable; a variable that is a cause of the treatment, but its only causal path to the outcome is through the treatment. Here we create two instruments.

$X_0$ and $X_1$ in figure 3.19 are examples of "effect modifiers" that help model heterogeneity in the causal effect. DoWhy defines these as other causes of the outcome (though they needn't be). Here we create two effect modifiers.

We add 5 common causes, like the three $W_0$, $W_1$, and $W_2$ in figure 3.19. Unlike the nuanced structure between these variables in figure 3.19, the structure here will be simple.

```
dag = nx.parse_gml(sim_data['gml_graph'])
pos = {
 'X0': (600, 350),
 'X1': (600, 250),
 'FD0': (300, 300),
 'W0': (0, 400),
 'W1': (150, 400),
 'W2': (300, 400),
 'W3': (450, 400),
 'W4': (600, 400),
 'Z0': (10, 250),
 'Z1': (10, 350),
 'v0': (100, 300),
 'y': (500, 300)
}
options = {
    "font_size": 12,
    "node_size": 800,
    "node_color": "white",
    "edgecolors": "black",
    "linewidths": 1,
```

This code extracts the graph, creates a plotting layout, and plots the graph.

```
    "width": 1,
}
nx.draw_networkx(dag, pos, **options)
ax = plt.gca()
ax.margins(x=0.40)
plt.axis("off")
plt.show()
```

> This code extracts the graph, creates a plotting layout, and plots the graph.

This code produces the DAG pictured in figure 3.20.

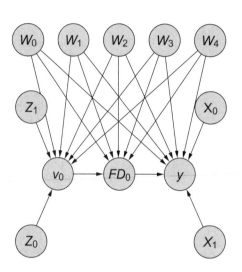

**Figure 3.20   A causal DAG built by specifying variables by their role in causal effect inference**

This role-based approach produces a simple template causal DAG. It won't give you the nuance that we have in figure 3.19, and it will exclude the good storytelling variables that we added in step 4, like $D$ in figure 3.19. But it will be enough for tackling the predefined causal effect query. It's a great tool to use when working with collaborators who are skeptical of DAGs but are comfortable talking about variable roles. But don't believe claims that this approach is DAG-free. The DAG is just implicit in the assumptions underlying the specification of the roles.

Such a template method could be used for other causal queries as well. You can also use this approach to get a basic causal DAG in a first step, which you could then build upon to produce a more nuanced graph.

## 3.4   *Looking ahead: Model testing and combining causal graphs with deep learning*

The big question when building a causal DAG is "what if my causal DAG is wrong?" How can we be confident in our selected DAG? In the next chapter, we'll look at how to use data to stress test our causal DAG. A key insight will be that while data can never prove that a causal DAG is right, it can help show when it is wrong. You'll also learn about causal discovery, a set of algorithms for learning causal DAGs from data.

In this chapter, we explored building a simple causal graphical model on the DAG structure using pgmpy. Throughout the book, you'll see how to build more sophisticated causal graphical models that leverage neural networks and automatic differentiation. Even in those more sophisticated models, the causal Markov property and the benefits of the DAG including causal invariance, and parameter modularity will still hold.

## *Summary*

- The causal directed acyclic graph (DAG) can represent our causal assumptions about the data generating process (DGP).

- The causal DAG is a useful tool for visualizing and communicating your causal assumptions.

- DAGs are fundamental data structures in computer science, and they admit many fast algorithms we can bring to bear on causal inference tasks.

- DAGs link causality to conditional independence via the causal Markov property.

- DAGs can provide scaffolding for probabilistic ML models.

- We can use various methods for statistical parameter learning to train a probabilistic model on top of a DAG. These include maximum likelihood estimation and Bayesian estimation.

- Given a causal DAG, the modeler can choose from a variety of parameterizations of the causal Markov kernels in the DAG, ranging from conditional probability tables to regression models to neural networks.

- A causally sufficient set of variables contains all common causes between pairs in that set.

- You can build a causal DAG by starting with a set of variables of interest, expanding that to a causally sufficient set, adding variables useful to causal inference analysis, and finally adding any variables that help the DAG communicate a complete story.

- Each causal Markov kernel represents a distinct causal mechanism that determines how the child node is determined by its parents (assuming the DAG is correct).

- "Independence of mechanism" refers to how mechanisms are distinct from the others—a change to one mechanism does not affect the others.

- When you build a generative model on the causal DAG, the parameters of each causal Markov kernel represents an encoding of the underlying causal mechanism. This leads to "parameter modularity," which enables you to learn each parameter set separately and even use common sense reasoning to estimate parameters instead of data.

- The fact that each causal Markov kernel represents a distinct causal mechanism provides a source of invariance that can be leveraged in advanced tasks, like transfer learning, data fusion, and invariant prediction.

- You can specify a DAG by the roles variables play in a specific causal inference task.

# Testing the DAG
# with causal constraints

4

## This chapter covers

- Using d-separation to reason about how causality constrains conditional independence
- Using NetworkX and pgmpy to do d-separation analysis
- Refuting a causal DAG using conditional independence tests
- Refuting a causal DAG when there are latent variables
- Using and applying causal discovery algorithm constraints

Our causal DAG, or any causal model, captures a set of assumptions about the real world. Often, those assumptions are testable with data. If we test an assumption, and it turns out not to hold, then our causal model is wrong. In other words, our test has "falsified" or "refuted" our model. When this happens, we go back to the drawing board, come up with a better model, and try to refute it again. We repeat this loop until we get a model that is robust to our attempts to refute it.

In this chapter, we'll focus on using statistical conditional independence-based testing to test our causal DAG. As you learn more about the assumptions we can pack into a causal model, and the inferences those assumptions allow you to make, you'll learn new ways to test and refute your model. The workflow you'll learn for running conditional independence tests in this chapter can be applied to new tests you may come up with.

## 4.1 How causality induces conditional independence

Causal relationships constrain the data in certain ways, one of which is by forcing variables to be conditionally independent. This forced conditional independence gives us a way to test our model with data using statistical tests for independence; if we find strong evidence that two variables are dependent when the DAG says they shouldn't be, our DAG is wrong.

In this chapter, we'll test our causal DAG using these statistical independence tests, including independence tests on *functions* of observed variables that we can run when other variables are latent in the data. At the end, we'll look at how these ideas enable *causal discovery algorithms* that try to learn the causal DAG directly from data.

But before that, let's see how causality induces conditional independence. Consider again our blood type example, shown in figure 4.1. Your father's blood type is a direct cause of yours, and your paternal grandfather's blood type is an indirect cause. Despite being a cause of your blood type, your paternal grandfather's blood type is conditionally independent of your blood type, given your father's.

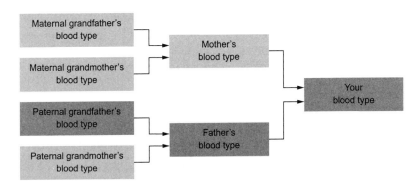

**Figure 4.1   Causality induces conditional independence. Your blood type is conditionally independent of your paternal grandfather's blood type (an indirect cause), given your father's blood type (a direct cause).**

We know this from causality; the parents' blood types completely determine the blood type of the child. Your paternal grandfather's and grandmother's blood types completely determined your father's blood type, but your father's and mother's blood types completely determined yours. Once we know your father's blood type, there is nothing more your paternal grandfather's blood type can tell us. In other words, your grandparent's blood type is independent of yours, given your parents.

### 4.1.1 Colliders

Now we'll consider the *collider,* an interesting way in which causality induces cases of dependence between variables that are typically independent. Consider the canonical example in figure 4.2. Whether the sprinkler is on or off, and whether it is raining or not, are causes of whether the grass is wet, but knowing that the sprinkler is off won't help you predict whether it's raining. In other words, the state of the sprinkler and whether it's raining are independent. But when you know the grass is wet, also knowing that the sprinkler is off tells you it *must* be raining. So while the state of the sprinkler and the presence or absence of rain are independent, they become conditionally dependent, given the state of the grass.

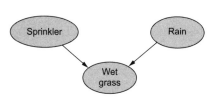

**Figure 4.2   The sprinkler being on or off and whether or not it rains causes the grass to be wet or not. Knowing that the sprinkler is off won't help you predict whether it's raining—the sprinkler state and rain state are independent. But given that the grass is wet, knowing the sprinkler is off tells you it must be raining—the sprinkler state and rain state are conditionally dependent, given the state of the grass.**

In this case "wet grass" is a *collider*: an effect with at least two independent causes. Colliders are interesting because they illustrate how causal variables can be independent but then become dependent if we condition on a shared effect variable. In conditional independence terms, the parent causes are independent (sprinkler ⊥ rain) but become dependent after we observe (condition on) the child (sprinkler ⊥̸ rain | wet grass).

For another example, let's look at blood type again, as shown in figure 4.3.

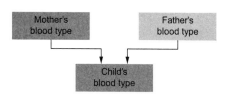

**Figure 4.3   Mothers and fathers are usually unrelated, so knowing mother's blood type can't help predict the father's blood type. But if we know the mother's blood type and the child's blood type, it narrows down the possible blood types of the father.**

If we assume the mother and father are unrelated, the mother's blood type tells us nothing about the father's blood type—(mother's blood type ⊥ father's blood type). But suppose we know the child's blood type is B. Does that help us use the mother's blood type to predict the father's blood type?

To answer this, examine the standard blood type table in figure 4.4. We see that if mother has blood type A and the child has blood type B, then possibly blood types for the father are B and AB.

| | | Child's blood type | | | | |
|---|---|---|---|---|---|---|
| | | A | B | AB | O | |
| Mother's blood type | A | A, B, AB, O | B, AB | B, AB | A, B, O | Possible blood types for father |
| | B | A, AB | A, B, AB, O | A, AB | A, B, O | |
| | AB | A, B, AB, O | A, B, AB, O | B, AB | Not Possible | |
| | O | A, AB | B, AB | Not Possible | A, B, O | |

**Figure 4.4 Knowing the mother's blood type can help you narrow down the father's blood type if you know the child's blood type.**

Knowing the mother's blood type alone doesn't tell us anything about the father's blood type. But if we add information about the child's blood type (the collider), we can narrow down the father's blood type from four to two possibilities. In other words, (mother's blood type ⊥ father's blood type), but the mother's and father's blood type become dependent once we condition on the child's blood type.

Colliders show up in various parts of causal inference. In section 4.6, we'll see that colliders are important in the task of causal discovery, where we try to learn a causal DAG from data. When we look at causal effects in chapters 7 and 11, we'll see how accidentally "adjusting for" colliders can introduce unwanted "collider bias" when inferring causal effects.

For now, we'll note that colliders can be at odds with our statistical intuition, because they describe how causal logic leads to situations where two things are independent but "suddenly" become dependent when you condition on a third or more variables.

### 4.1.2 *Abstracting independence with a causal graph*

In the previous section, we used the basic rules of blood type heredity to show how causality induces conditional independence. If we want to write code that can help us make causal inferences across different domains, we'll need an abstraction for mapping causal relationships to conditional independence that doesn't rely on the rules of a particular domain. "D-separation" solves this problem.

*D-separation* and *d-connection* refer to how we use graphs to reason about conditional independence. The concepts are novel at first glance, but they will be some of your most important tools for graph-based causal reasoning. As a bit of a spoiler for chapter 7, consider the problem of causal effect inference, illustrated in figure 4.5. In causal inference, you are interested in statistically quantifying how much a cause (often called a "treatment") affects an effect (an "outcome").

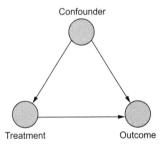

**Figure 4.5 In causal effect inference, we are interested in statistically quantifying how much a cause (treatment) affects an effect (outcome). *Confounders* are common causes that are a source of non-causal correlation between treatment and outcome. Causal effect inference requires "adjusting" for confounders. D-separation is the backbone of the theory that tells us how.**

As you saw in chapter 3, you can describe variables in a DAG in terms of their role in a causal inference task. One role in the task of causal effect inference is the *confounder*. Confounders are common causes that are a source of non-causal correlation between the treatment and the effect. To estimate the causal effect of the treatment on the outcome, we have to "adjust" for the confounder. The theoretical justification for doing so is based on "d-separating" the path {treatment ← confounder → outcome} and zooming in on the path {treatment → outcome}.

## 4.2     D-separation and conditional independence

Recall the following ideas from previous chapters:

- A causal DAG is a model of the data generating process (DGP).
- The DGP entails a joint probability distribution.
- Causal relationships induce independence and conditional independence between variables in the joint probability distribution.

D-separation and d-connection are graphical abstractions for reasoning about the conditional independence in the joint probability distribution that a causal DAG models. The concept refers to nodes and paths between nodes in the causal DAG; the nodes and paths are "d-connected" or "d-separated," where the "d" stands for "directional." The idea is for a statement like "these nodes are d-separated in the graph" to correspond to a statement like "these variables are conditionally independent." D-separation is not about stating what causes what; it is about whether paths between variables in the DAG indicate the absence or presence of dependence between those variables in the joint probability distribution.

We want to make this correspondence because reasoning about graphs is easier than reasoning about probability distributions directly; tracing paths between nodes is easier than taking graduate-level classes in probability theory. Also, recall from chapter 2 that graphs are fundamental to algorithms and data structures, and that statistical modeling benefits from making conditional independence assumptions.

### 4.2.1     D-separation: A gateway to simplified causal analysis

Suppose we have a statement that $U$ and $V$ are conditionally independent given $Z$ (i.e., $U \perp V | Z$). Our task is to define a corresponding statement purely in graphical terms. We'll write this statement as $U \perp_G V | Z$ and read it as "$U$ and $V$ are d-separated by $Z$ in graph $G$."

Let $Z$ represent a set of nodes called the d-separating set or "blockers." In terms of conditional independence, $Z$ corresponds to a set of variables we condition on. Our goal is to define d-separation such that the nodes in $Z$ in some sense "block" the dependence between $U$ and $V$ that is implied by the causal structure of our DAG.

Next, let $P$ be a *path*, meaning a series of connected edges (and nodes) between two nodes. It does not matter if the nodes on the paths are observed or not in your data (we'll see how the data factors in later). Our definition of "path" does not depend on the orientation of the edges; for example, $\{x \to y \to z\}$, $\{x \leftarrow y \to z\}$, $\{x \leftarrow y \leftarrow z\}$, and $\{x \to y \leftarrow z\}$ are all paths between $x$ and $z$.

Finally, let's revisit the collider. A collider structure refers to a motif like $x \rightarrow y \leftarrow z$ where the middle node $y$ (the collider) has incoming edges.

We'll define d-separation now. First, two nodes $u$ and $v$ are said to be d-separated (blocked) by $Z$ if all *paths* between them are d-separated by $Z$. If any of those paths between $u$ and $v$ are not d-separated, then $u$ and $v$ are d-connected.

Let's define d-separation for a path. A path $P$ is d-separated by node set $Z$ if any of four criteria are met.

1. $P$ contains a chain, $i \rightarrow m \rightarrow j$, such that the middle node $m$ is in $Z$.
2. $P$ contains a chain, $i \leftarrow m \leftarrow j$, such that the middle node $m$ is in $Z$.
3. $P$ contains a child-parent-child structure $i \leftarrow m \rightarrow j$, such that the middle (parent) node $m$ is in $Z$.

Let's pause. Criteria 1–3 are just walking through the ways we can orient edges between three nodes. If this keeps up, then $P$ is always d-separated if a node on $P$ is in set $Z$. That would be nice, because it would mean that two nodes are d-connected (i.e., dependent) if there are any paths between them in the DAG, and they are d-separated if all those paths are blocked by nodes in set $Z$.

Unfortunately, colliders make the fourth criterion contrary to the others:

4. $P$ contains a *collider structure*, $i \rightarrow m \leftarrow j$, such that the middle node $m$ is not in $Z$, and no descendant of $m$ is in $Z$.

This fourth criterion is how d-separation captures the way two independent (d-separated) items can become dependent when conditioning on a collider.

Many writers conflate d-separation and conditional independence. Keep the distinction clear in your mind: $\perp_G$ speaks of graphs, whereas $\perp$ speaks of distributions. It matters because, as you'll see later in this chapter, we'll use d-separation to test our causal assumptions against statistical evidence of conditional independence in the data.

Let's work through a few examples.

### EXAMPLE WITH CHAIN I → M → J

Consider the DAG in figure 4.6, where $P$ is $u \rightarrow i \rightarrow m \rightarrow j \rightarrow v$. This path is d-connected by default. Now let $Z$ be the set $\{m, k\}$. $P$ contains a chain $i \rightarrow m \rightarrow j$, and $m$ is in $Z$. If we block on $Z$, the first criterion is satisfied, and $u$ and $v$ are d-separated.

For some (but not all), a helpful analogy for understanding d-separation is an electronic circuit. Paths without colliders are d-connected and are like closed circuits, where electrical current flows uninhibited. "Blocking" on a node on that path d-separates the path and will "break the circuit" so current can't flow.

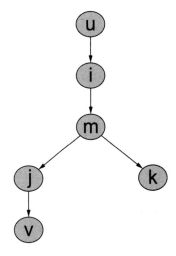

**Figure 4.6   Does the set {m, k} d-separate path $u \rightarrow i \rightarrow m \rightarrow j \rightarrow v$?**

Blocking on $Z$ (specifically, blocking on $m$, which is in $Z$) "breaks the circuit" as shown in figure 4.7.

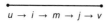

**Circuit is closed by default (d-connected)**

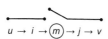

**Blocking on $m$ breaks the circuit (d-separated)**

**Figure 4.7   The path is d-connected by default, but blocking on m ∈ Z d-separates the path and figuratively breaks the circuit ("∈" means "in").**

### EXAMPLE WITH CHAIN I ← M → J

Now consider the DAG in figure 4.8, where $P$ is $u \leftarrow i \leftarrow m \rightarrow j \rightarrow v$. This path is also d-connected by default. Note that d-connection can go against the grain of causality. In figure 4.7, the d-connected path from $u$ to $v$ takes steps in the direction of causality: $u$ to $i$ ($u \leftarrow i$), then $i$ to $m$ ($i \leftarrow m$), then $m$ to $j$ ($m \rightarrow j$), and then $j$ to $v$ ($j \rightarrow v$). But here, we have two *anticausal* (meaning against the direction of causality) steps, namely the step from $u$ to $i$ ($u \leftarrow i$) and $i$ to $m$ ($i \leftarrow m$).

Suppose we block on set $Z$, and $Z$ contains only the node $m$. Then condition 3 is satisfied and the path is d-separated, as illustrated in figure 4.9.

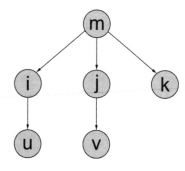

**Figure 4.8   Does the set {m} d-separate path u ← I ← m → j → v?**

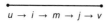

**Circuit is closed by default (d-connected)**

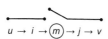

**Blocking on $m$ breaks the circuit (d-separated)**

**Figure 4.9   This path from u to v is also d-connected by default, even though it has some steps (u to I and I to m) that go against the direction of causality. Again, blocking on m ∈ Z d-separates the path and figuratively breaks the circuit.**

### COLLIDERS MAKE D-SEPARATION WEIRD

The fourth criterion focuses on the collider motif $i \rightarrow m \leftarrow j$: $P$ contains a *collider structure*, $i \rightarrow m \leftarrow j$, such that the middle node $m$ is not in $Z$, and no descendant of $m$ is in $Z$.

Let's relate this back to our blood type example. Here $i$ and $j$ are the parents' blood types and $m$ is the child's blood type. We saw that colliders are a bit odd, because conditioning on the collider (the child's blood type) induces dependence between two independent things (like the parents' blood types). This oddness makes d-separation a bit tricky to understand at first glance. Figure 4.10 illustrates how colliders affect d-separation.

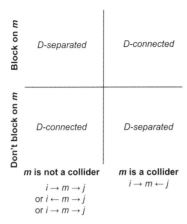

**Figure 4.10  Colliders make d-connection tricky. Given a node *m* on a path, if *m* is not a collider, the path is d-connected by default and d-separated when you block on *m*. If *m* is a collider, the path is d-separated by default and d-connected when you block on *m*.**

The following is true of colliders:

- All paths between two nodes d-connect by default *unless that path has a collider motif.* A path with a collider is d-separated by default.
- Blocking with any node on a d-connected path will d-separate that path *unless that node is a collider.* Blocking on a collider will d-connect a path by default, as will blocking with a descendant of that collider.

In terms of the circuit analogy, colliders are like an open switch, which prevents current flow in an electronic circuit. When a path has a collider, the collider stops all current from passing through it. Colliders break the circuit. Blocking on a collider is like closing the switch, and the current that couldn't pass through before now can pass through (d-connection).

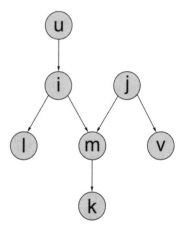

In the DAG in figure 4.11, is the path $u \rightarrow i \rightarrow m \leftarrow j \rightarrow v$ d-connected by default? No, because the path contains a collider structure $m$ $(i \rightarrow m \leftarrow j)$. Now consider what would happen if the blocking set $Z$ included $m$. In this case, condition 4 is violated and the path *becomes d-connected*, as in figure 4.12.

**Figure 4.11  Does the set {*m*} (or {*k*} or {*m, k*}) d-separate path $u \rightarrow i \rightarrow m \leftarrow j \rightarrow v$?**

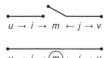

Collider opens circuit by default (d-separated)

Blocking on *m* closes the circuit (d-connected)

**Figure 4.12  This path from *u* to *v* is d-separated by default because it contains a collider *m*. The collider is analogous to an open circuit. Blocking on *m* or any of its descendants d-connects the path and figuratively closes the circuit.**

The path would also become d-connected if $Z$ didn't have $m$ but just had $k$ (or if $Z$ included both $m$ and $k$). Blocking on a descendant of a collider d-connects in the same manner as blocking on a collider.

Can you guess why? It's because the collider's descendant is *d-connected to the collider*. In causal terms, we saw how, given a mother's blood type, observing the child's blood type (the collider) might reveal the father's blood type. Suppose that if instead of observing the child's blood type, we observed the child's child's blood type (call it the grandchild's blood type). That grandchild's blood type could help narrow down the child's blood type and thus narrow down the father's blood type. In other words, if the mother's and father's blood types are dependent, given the child's blood type, and the grandchild's blood type gives you information about the child's blood type, then the mother's and father's blood types are dependent given the grandchild's blood type.

### D-SEPARATION AND SETS OF NODES

D-separation doesn't just apply to pairs of nodes, it applies to pairs of sets of nodes. In the notation $u \perp v | Z$, $Z$ can be a set of blockers, and $u$ and $v$ can be sets as well. We d-separate two sets by blocking all d-connected paths between members of each set. Other graph-based causal ideas, such as the do-calculus, also generalize to sets of nodes. If you remember that fact, we can build intuition on individual nodes, and that intuition will generalize to sets.

When the blocking set $Z$ is the singleton set $\{m\}$, this set is sufficient to block the paths $u \to i \to m \to j \to v$ in figure 4.7 and $u \leftarrow i \leftarrow m \to j \to v$ in figure 4.8. Altogether, the sets $\{i\}$, $\{m\}$, $\{j\}$, $\{i, m\}$, $\{i, j\}$, $\{m, j\}$, and $\{i, m, j\}$ all d-separate $u$ and $v$ on these two paths. However, $\{i\}$, $\{m\}$, and $\{j\}$ are the *minimal d-separating sets*, meaning that all the other d-separating sets include at least one of these sets. The minimal d-separation sets are sufficient to d-separate the two nodes. When reasoning about d-separation and when implementing it in algorithms, we want to focus on finding minimal d-separating sets; if $U \perp V | Z$ and $U \perp V | Z, W$ are both true, we don't want to waste effort on $U \perp V | Z, W$.

### 4.2.2   *Examples of d-separating multiple paths*

Suppose we want to d-separate two nodes. Often there are multiple d-connected paths between those nodes. To d-separate those nodes, we need to find blockers that d-separate each of those paths. Let's walk through some examples.

### FINDING A MINIMAL D-SEPARATING SET

In a bigger graph with more edges, the number of paths between two nodes can be quite large. But often longer paths often get blocked as a side-effect of blocking shorter paths. So we can start with shorter paths, and work our way to longer paths that haven't been blocked yet, until no unblocked paths remain.

For example, $U$ and $V$ are d-connected in figure 4.13. What sets of nodes are fully required to d-separate them?

In figure 4.13, *U* and *V* are d-connected through these paths:

- $U \to I \to V$
- $U \to J \to V$
- $U \to J \to I \to V$

First, we can d-separate $U \to I \to V$ by blocking on *I*. Then, we d-separate $U \to J \to V$ by blocking on *J*. At this point, we see that our blocking set {*I*, *J*} already d-separates $U \to J \to I \to V$, so we are done.

In another example, how do we d-separate *U* and *V* in figure 4.14?

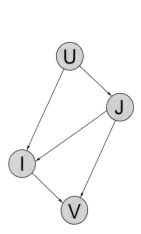

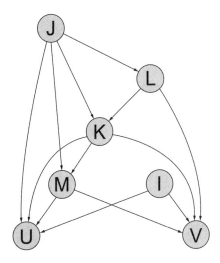

**Figure 4.13   We can d-separate *U* and *V* with {*I*, *J*}.**

**Figure 4.14   We can d-separate *U* and *V* with sets {*I*, *M*, *K*, *J*} or {*I*, *M*, *K*, *L*}.**

There are many paths between *U* and *V*. Let's first enumerate three of the shortest paths:

- $U \leftarrow I \to V$
- $U \leftarrow M \to V$
- $U \leftarrow K \to V$

We'll need to block on at least on {*I*, *M*, *K*} to d-separate these three paths. Note that *U* has another parent *J*, and there are several paths from *U* to *V* through *J*, but there are only two paths we haven't already d-separated; $U \leftarrow J \to L \to V$ and $U \leftarrow J \to K \leftarrow L \to V$. Both *J* and *L* will block these paths, so we could d-separate *U* and V with minimal sets {*I*, *M*, *K*, *J*} or {*I*, *M*, *K*, *L*}. Note that $U \leftarrow J \to K \leftarrow L \to V$ was d-connected because we initially added *K*, a collider on this path, to our blocking set. Next, we look at another example of this phenomenon.

### WHEN D-SEPARATING ONE PATH D-CONNECTS ANOTHER

When you attempt to d-separate a path between *U* and *V* by blocking on a node that is a collider on another path, you potentially d-connect that other path. That is fine, as long as you take additional steps to d-separate that path as well. To illustrate, consider

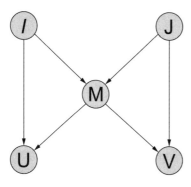

**Figure 4.15   Blocking with *M* will block the path *U* ← *M* → *V* but would d-connect the path *U* ← *I* → *M* ← *J* → *V* because *M* is a collider between *I* and *J*. So we need to additionally block on either *I* or *J* to d-separate *U* ← *I* → *M* ← *J* → *V*.**

the graph in figure 4.15. This graph is simple enough that we can enumerate all of the paths.

Let's start with the three d-connecting paths:

- $U \leftarrow M \rightarrow V$
- $U \leftarrow I \rightarrow M \rightarrow V$
- $U \leftarrow M \leftarrow J \rightarrow V$

We also have a path $U \leftarrow I \rightarrow M \leftarrow J \rightarrow V$, but that is not a d-connecting path because *M* is a collider on that path.

The easiest way to block all three of these d-connected paths with one node is to block on *M*. However, if we block on that collider, the path $U \leftarrow I \rightarrow M \leftarrow J \rightarrow V$ d-connects. So we need to additionally block on *I* or *J*. In other words, our minimal d-separating sets are {*I*, *M*} and {*J*, *M*}.

### 4.2.3   D-separation in code

Don't fret if you are still hazy on d-separation. We've defined four criteria for describing paths between nodes on a graph, which is just the sort of thing we can implement in a graph library. In Python, the graph library NetworkX already has a utility that checks for d-separation. You can experiment with these tools to build an intuition for d-separation on different graphs.

---

**Setting up your environment**

This code was written with pgmpy version 0.1.24. The pandas version was 2.0.3.

---

Let's verify our d-separation analysis of the causal DAG shown previously in figure 4.15.

**Listing 4.1   D-separation analysis of the DAG in figure 4.15**

```
from networkx import is_d_separator
from pgmpy.base import DAG
dag = DAG([
    ('I', 'U'),
    ('I', 'M'),
    ('M', 'U'),
    ('J', 'V'),
    ('J', 'M'),
    ('M', 'V')
])
print(is_d_separator(dag, {"U"}, {"V"}, {"M"}))
```

The graph library NetworkX implements the d-separation algorithm for NetworkX graph objects, such as DiGraph (directed graph).

DAG is a base class for the BayesianNetwork class. The base class for DAG is NetworkX's DiGraph. So is_d_separator will work on objects of the class DAG (and BayesianNetwork).

Build the graph in figure 4.11. Blocking on a collider M blocks the path $U \leftarrow M \rightarrow V$ but will d-connect the path $U \leftarrow I \rightarrow M \leftarrow J \rightarrow V$, so this will print False.

```
print(is_d_separator(dag, {"U"}, {"V"}, {"M", "I", "J"}))
print(is_d_separator(dag, {"U"}, {"V"}, {"M", "I"}))
print(is_d_separator(dag, {"U"}, {"V"}, {"M", "J"}))
```

Blocking on M will block U ← M → V and open (d-connect) U ← I → M ← J → V, but we can block that path with I and J, so this evaluates to True.

Blocking on both I and J is overkill. The minimal d-separating sets are {"M", "I"} and {"M", "J"}.

pgmpy also has a `get_independencies` method in the DAG class that enumerates minimal d-separating states that are true given a graph.

**Listing 4.2   Enumerating d-separations in pgmpy**

```
from pgmpy.base import DAG
dag = DAG([
    ('I', 'U'),
    ('I', 'M'),
    ('M', 'U'),
    ('J', 'V'),
    ('J', 'M'),
    ('M', 'V')
])
dag.get_independencies()
```

Obtain all the minimal d-separation statements that are true in the DAG.

The `get_independencies` method returns the following results. (You might see a slight difference in the ordering of the output depending on your environment.)

```
(I ⊥ J)
(I ⊥ V | J, M)
(I ⊥ V | J, U, M)
(V ⊥ I, U | J, M)
(V ⊥ U | I, M)
(V ⊥ I | J, U, M)
(V ⊥ U | J, M, I)
(J ⊥ I)
(J ⊥ U | I, M)
(J ⊥ U | I, M, V)
(U ⊥ V | J, M)
(U ⊥ J, V | I, M)
(U ⊥ V | J, M, I)
(U ⊥ J | I, M, V)
```

Note that the `get_independencies` function name is a misnomer; it does not "get independencies"; it gets d-separations. Again, don't conflate d-separation in the causal graph with conditional independence in the joint probability distribution entailed by the DGP the graph is meant to model. Keeping this distinction in your mind will help you with the next task: using d-separation to test a DAG against evidence of conditional independence in the data.

## 4.3    Refuting a causal DAG

We have seen how to build a causal DAG. Of course, we want to find a causal model that fits the data well, so now we'll evaluate the causal DAG against the data. We could use standard goodness-of-fit and predictive statistics to evaluate fit, but here we're going to focus on *refuting* our causal DAG, using data to show that our model is wrong.

Statistical models fit curves and patterns in the data. There is no "right" statistical model; there are just models that fit the data well. In contrast, causal models go beyond the data to make causal assertions about the DGP, and those assertions are either true or false. As modelers of causality, we try to find a model that fits well, but we also try to *refute* our model's causal assertions.

---

### Refutation and Popper

The approach to building DAGs by refutation aligns with Karl Popper's falsifiable theories framework. Karl Popper was a 20th-century philosopher known for his contributions to the philosophy of science, particularly his theory of falsification. Popper argued that scientific theories cannot be proven true, but they can be tested and potentially falsified, or in other words, *refuted*.

We take a "Popperesque" approach to model building, meaning that we don't merely want to find a model that fits the evidence. Rather, we actively search for evidence that refutes our model. When we find it, we reject our model, build a better one, and repeat.

---

D-separation is our first tool for refutation. Suppose you build a causal DAG and it implies conditional independence. You then look for evidence in the data of dependence, where your DAG says there should be conditional independence. If you find that evidence, you have refuted your DAG. You then go back and iterate on the causal DAG, until you can no longer refute it, given your data.

Once you've done that, you move on to your downstream causal inference workflow. But keep this refutation mentality in mind. If you work with the same causal DAG repeatedly, you should always be seeking new ways to refute and iterate upon it. Practically, your goal is not getting the true DAG, but getting a hard-to-refute DAG.

### 4.3.1    Revisiting the causal Markov property

Recall that we saw two aspects of the causal Markov property:

- *Local Markov property*—A node is conditionally independent of its non-descendants, given its parents.
- *Markov factorization property*—The joint probability distribution factorizes into conditional distributions of variables, given their direct parents in the causal DAG.

Now we'll introduce a third face of this property called the *global Markov property*. This property states that d-separation in the causal DAG implies conditional independence in the joint probability distribution. In notation, we write

$$U \perp_G V \mid Z \Rightarrow U \perp V \mid Z$$

In plain words, that notation reads as "If $U$ and $V$ are d-separated by $Z$ in graph $G$, they are conditionally independent given $Z$." Note that if any of the three facets of the causal Markov property are true, they are all true.

The global Markov property gives us a straightforward way to refute our causal model. We can use d-separations to specify statistical tests for the presence of conditional independence. Failing tests refute the model.

### 4.3.2 Refutation using conditional independence tests

There are multiple ways to statistically evaluate conditional independence, and the most obvious is with a statistical test for conditional independence. pgmpy and other libraries make it relatively easy to run conditional independence tests. Let's revisit the transportation model, shown again in figure 4.16.

Recall that for our transportation model we were able to collect the following observations:

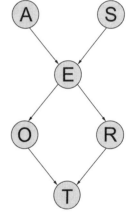

- *Age (A)*—Recorded as young ("young") for individuals up to and including 29 years, adult ("adult") for individuals from 30 to 60 years old (inclusive), and old ("old") for people 61 and over.
- *Gender (S)*—The self-reported gender of an individual, recorded as male ("M"), female ("F"), or other ("O").

**Figure 4.16** The transportation model. Age (*A*) and gender (*S*) determine education (*E*). Education causes occupation (*O*) and residence (*R*). Occupation and residence cause transportation (*T*).

- *Education (E)*—The highest level of education or training completed by the individual, recorded as either high school ("high") or university degree ("uni").
- *Occupation (O)*—Employee ("emp") or a self-employed worker ("self").
- *Residence (R)*—The population size of the city the individual lives in, recorded as small ("small") or big ("big").
- *Travel (T)*—The means of transport favored by the individual, recorded as car ("car"), train ("train"), or other ("other").

In the graph, $E \perp_G T \mid O, R$. So let's test the conditional independence statement $E \perp T \mid O, R$. Statistical hypothesis tests have a *null hypothesis* (denoted $H_0$) and an *alternative hypothesis* (denoted $H_a$). For statistical hypothesis tests of conditional independence, it is standard that the null hypothesis $H_0$ is the hypothesis of conditional independence, and $H_a$ is the hypothesis that the variables are not conditionally independent.

A statistical hypothesis test uses the $N$ data points of observed values of $U$, $V$, and $Z$ (from an exploratory dataset) to calculate a statistic. The following code loads the transportation data. After loading, it creates two DataFrames, one with all the data and one with just the first 30 rows so we can see how sample size affects the significance test.

#### Listing 4.3   Loading the transportation data

```
import pandas as pd
survey_url = "https://raw.githubusercontent.com/altdeep/causalML/master
[CA] /datasets/transportation_survey.csv"
fulldata = pd.read_csv(survey_url)

data = fulldata[0:30]          ◁──┐ Subsetting the data to only 30
print(data[0:5])                   │ datapoints for explanation
```

The line `print(data[0:5])` prints the first five rows of the DataFrame.

```
      A   S    E    O      R      T
0  adult  F  high  emp  small  train
1  young  M  high  emp    big    car
2  adult  M   uni  emp    big  other
3    old  F   uni  emp    big    car
4  young  F   uni  emp    big    car
```

Most conditional independence testing libraries will implement frequentist hypothesis tests. These tests will conclude in favor of $H_0$ or $H_a$ depending on whether a given statistic falls above or below a certain threshold. "Frequentist," in this context, means that the statistic produced by the test is called a *p*-value, and the threshold is called a significance level, which by convention is usually .05 or .01.

The test favors the null hypothesis $H_0$ of conditional independence if the *p*-value falls above the significance threshold and the alternative hypothesis $H_a$ if it falls below the threshold. This frequentist approach is an optimization that guarantees the significance level is an upper bound on the chances of concluding in favor of dependence when $E$ and $T$ are actually conditionally independent.

Most software libraries provide conditional independence testing utilities that make specific mathematical assumptions when calculating a *p*-value. For example, we can run a specific conditional independence test that derives a test statistic that theoretically follows the chi-squared probability distribution, and then use this assumption to derive a *p*-value. The following code runs the test.

#### Listing 4.4   Chi-squared test of conditional independence

```
from pgmpy.estimators.CITests import chi_square    ◁──┐ Import the chi_square
significance = .05                                     │ test function.
```
                            ◁──┐ Set the significance
                                │ level to .05.

```
result = chi_square(
    X="E", Y="T", Z=["O", "R"],
    data=data,
    boolean=False,
    significance_level=significance
)
print(result)
```

> When the boolean argument is set to False, the test returns a tuple of three elements. The first two are the chi-square statistic and the corresponding p-value of 0.56. The last element is a chi-squares distribution parameter called degrees of freedom, which is needed to calculate the p-value.

This prints the tuple (1.1611111111111112, 0.5595873983053805, 2), where the values are chi-squared test statistic, *p*-value, and degrees of freedom respectively. The *p*-value is greater than the significance level, so this test favors the null hypothesis of conditional independence. In other words, this particular test did not offer falsifying evidence against our model.

We can jump directly to the result of the test by setting the `chi_square` function's `boolean` argument to `True`. The function will then return `True` if the *p*-value is greater than the significance value (favoring conditional independence) and `False` otherwise (favoring dependence).

**Listing 4.5  Chi-squared test with Boolean outcome**

```
from pgmpy.estimators.CITests import chi_square
significance = .05
result = chi_square(
    X="E", Y="T", Z=["O", "R"],
    data=data,
    boolean=True,
    significance_level=significance
)
print(result)
```

> Import the chi_square test function.

> Set the significance level to .05.

> When the boolean argument is set to True, the test returns a simple True or False outcome. It will return True if the p-value is greater than the significance value, which favors conditional independence. It returns False otherwise, favoring dependence.

This prints the result `True`. Now let's iterate through all the d-separation statements we can derive from the transportation graph, and test them one by one. The following script will print each d-separation statement along with the outcome of the corresponding conditional independence test.

**Listing 4.6  Run a chi-squared test for each d-separation statement**

```
from pprint import pprint
from pgmpy.base import DAG
from pgmpy.independencies import IndependenceAssertion

dag = DAG([
    ('A', 'E'),
    ('S', 'E'),
    ('E', 'O'),
    ('E', 'R'),
    ('O', 'T'),
    ('R', 'T')
])
dseps = dag.get_independencies()
```

```
def test_dsep(dsep):
    test_outputs = []
    for X in list(dsep.get_assertion()[0]):
        for Y in list(dsep.get_assertion()[1]):
            Z = list(dsep.get_assertion()[2])
            test_result = chi_square(
                X=X, Y=Y, Z=Z,
                data=data,
                boolean=True,
                significance_level=significance
            )
            assertion = IndependenceAssertion(X, Y, Z)
            test_outputs.append((assertion, test_result))
    return test_outputs

results = [test_dsep(dsep) for dsep in dseps.get_assertions()]
results = dict([item for sublist in results for item in sublist])
pprint(results)
```

The result is a list of d-separation statements and whether the evidence in the data supports (or fails to refute) that statement.

```
{(O ⊥ A | R, E, T, S): True,
 (S ⊥ R | E, T, A): True,
 (S ⊥ O | E, T, A): True,
 (T ⊥ S | R, O, A): True,
 (S ⊥ O | R, E): True,
 (R ⊥ O | E): False,
 (S ⊥ O | E, A): True,
 (S ⊥ R | E, A): True,
 (S ⊥ R | E, T, O, A): True,
 (S ⊥ R | E, O, A): True,
 (O ⊥ A | E, T): True,
 (S ⊥ O | R, E, T): True,
 (R ⊥ O | E, S): False,
 ...
 (T ⊥ A | E, S): True}
```

We can count the number of tests that pass.

**Listing 4.7    Calculate the proportion of d-separations with passing tests**

```
num_pass = sum(results.values())
num_dseps = len(dseps.independencies)
num_fail = num_dseps - num_pass
print(num_fail / num_dseps)
```

Here we get `0.2875`. This implies that 29% of the d-separations lack corresponding evidence of conditional independence in the data.

This number seems high, but as we'll see in section 4.4, this statistic depends on the size of the data and other factors. We'll want to compare it to the result for other candidate DAGs. For now, the next step is to inspect these cases of apparent dependence where our DAG says there should be conditional independence. If the evidence of dependence is strong, we need to think about how to improve our causal DAG to explain it.

Earlier, I used the `chi_square` function, which constructs a specific test statistic with a chi-squared test distribution—the distribution used to calculate the *p*-value. The chi-squared distribution is just another canonical distribution, like the normal or Bernoulli distributions. The chi-squared distribution comes up frequently for discrete variables, because there are several test statistics in the discrete setting that either have a chi-squared distribution or get closer to one as the size of the data increases. Overall, independence tests have a variety of test statistics with different test distributions. pgmpy provides several options by way of calls to SciPy's stats library.

One common concern is that the test makes strong assumptions. For example, some conditional independence tests between continuous variables assume any dependence between the variables would be *linear*. An alternative approach is to use a *permutation* test, which is an algorithm that constructs the *p*-value without relying on a canonical test distribution. Permutation tests make fewer assumptions but are computationally expensive.

### 4.3.3 *Some tests are more important than others*

The previous analysis tested all the d-separations implied by a causal DAG. But some d-separations might be more important to you than others. Some dependence relations and conditional independence relations are pivotal to a downstream causal inference analysis, while others don't affect that analysis at all.

For example, consider figure 4.17, which we looked at earlier in section 3.3. We added the variable *Z* to the graph because we might want to use it as an "instrumental variable" in the estimation of the causal effect.

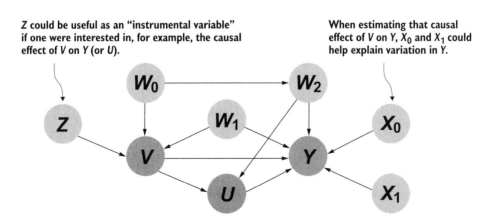

**Figure 4.17** *Z*, $X_0$, and $X_1$ were included in the DAG because they play a useful role in analyzing the causal effect of *U* on *Y*. Their role depends on conditional independence, and it is important to test that they can indeed serve those roles.

We'll discuss instrumental variables in depth in chapter 11. For now, suffice it to say that for $Z$ to be an instrument, it must be independent of $W_0$, $W_1$, and $W_2$. So we'd pay special attention to testing that assumption.

## 4.4 Caveats with conditional independence testing

As I mentioned, conditional independence tests are perhaps the most obvious way to test the conditional independence constraints implied by your proposed causal DAG. However, there are several caveats with using statistical tests to test a causal DAG. In my experience, these issues can distract analysts from their ultimate goal of answering a causal question. In this section, I'll highlight some of these caveats and propose some alternatives to conditional independence testing. The main takeaway is that statistical testing is an important tool for building your DAG, but as with any statistical methodology, it is not a panacea (and that's fine).

### 4.4.1 Statistical tests always have some chance of error

I mentioned that with d-separation, we should not "confuse the map for the terrain"; d-separation is not the same thing as conditional independence. Rather, if your model is a good representation of causality, d-separation *implies* conditional independence.

Similarly, conditional independence is not the same as *statistical evidence* of conditional independence. The causal structure of the DGP imposes conditional independence constraints on the joint probability distribution. But you can't "see" the joint distribution and the independencies it contains; you can only "see" (and run statistical tests on) the data sampled from that distribution.

Just like with prediction, classification, or any other statistical pattern recognition procedure, the procedure for detecting these independencies in data can get it wrong. You can get false negatives, where a pair of variables are truly conditionally independent but the statistical independence test concludes they are dependent. You can have false positives, where a statistical independence test finds a pair of variables to be conditionally independent when they are not.

### 4.4.2 Testing causal DAGs with traditional CI tests is flawed

I say that the proposed conditional independence tests for refutation are "flawed" because they violate the spirit of statistical hypothesis testing in science. Suppose you think you have discovered some pattern in stock prices. You are biased to think the pattern is more than coincidence because, if it is, you can make money. To be rigorous and not fall prey to your biases, your alternative hypothesis says the pattern is real and exploitable, whereas the null hypothesis is that it is just random noise. The frequentist test assumes the null hypothesis is true and gives you a $p$-value, which quantifies the chances that random noise could form a pattern at least as strong as the one you found. The test forces you to reject the pattern as real unless that $p$-value is really small. Most mainstream statistical testing libraries are designed for this use case.

When you propose a causal model, you are also biased to believe it is true. But causal models induce conditional independences, which by definition are the *absences* of patterns. In this case the null and alternative hypotheses should switch; the alternative should be that your model is right and there isn't a pattern (and any evidence of patterns in the data is just spurious correlation), and the null should be that there is a pattern. It is possible to implement such a hypothesis test, but it is not mathematically trivial, and most mainstream statistical libraries like SciPy do not support this use case.

The compromise is using the traditional tests, where the null hypothesis specifies conditional independence less as a theoretically rigorous analysis and more as a *heuristic*—an empirical problem solving technique that can be suboptimal but sufficient to reach a good enough solution.

### 4.4.3 *p-values vary with the size of the data*

The conclusion of a traditional conditional independence test depends on a significance threshold. If the *p*-value falls below this threshold, you favor dependence, and if it falls above, you favor conditional independence. The choice of threshold is a bit arbitrary; people tend to go with commonly selected values like .1 or .05 or .01.

The problem is that the *p*-value statistic varies with the size of the data. All else equal, as the size of the data increases, the *p*-value decreases. In other words, the larger the data, the more that things start to look dependent. If you have a large dataset, it is more likely that *p*-values will fall below that arbitrary threshold, and the data will look like it's refuting the conditional independence implied by your DAG, even when that conditional independence is true.

To illustrate, the test of $E \perp T \mid O, R$ in section 4.3.2 had 30 data points and produced a *p*-value of 0.56. In our data, $E \perp T \mid O, R$ is ground truth (via simulation), so if a test concludes against $E \perp T \mid O, R$, it is because of statistical issues with the test, not the quality of the data. The following bootstrap statistical analysis will show how the estimate of the *p*-value falls as the size of the data increases.

First, we'll write a `sample_p_value` function that samples a *p*-value for a given data size. The next function, `estimate_p_value`, will do this sampling repeatedly and calculate a mean *p*-value, a 90% confidence interval, and the probability that the *p*-value falls below the significance threshold, which is the probability of rejecting the correct conclusion that $E \perp T \mid O, R$.

---

**Listing 4.8  Bootstrap analysis of sensitivity of test of $E \perp T \mid O, R$ to sample size**

```
from numpy import mean, quantile

def sample_p_val(data_size, data, alpha):
    bootstrap_data = data.sample(n=data_size, replace=True)
    result = chi_square(
        X="E", Y="T", Z=["O", "R"],
        data=bootstrap_data,
        boolean=False,
        significance_level = alpha
    )
    p_val = result[1]
    return p_val
```

**Given a certain data size, this function randomly samples that number of rows from the full dataset. It then runs the chi-squared independence test and returns the p-value.**

Calculate the probability of a
test concluding in favor of
conditional independence.

This function conducts a "bootstrap"
procedure that samples 1,000 p-values for a
given data size and calculates the mean p-
value and 90% p-value confidence interval.

```
def estimate_p_val(data_size, data=fulldata, boot_size=1000, α=.05):
    samples = [
        sample_p_val(data_size, data=fulldata, alpha=α)
        for _ in range(boot_size)
    ]
    positive_tests = [p_val > significance for p_val in samples]
    prob_conclude = mean(positive_tests)
    p_estimate = mean(samples)
    quantile_05, quantile_95 = quantile(samples, [.05, .95])
    lower_error = p_estimate - quantile_05
    higher_error = quantile_95 - p_estimate
    return p_estimate, lower_error, higher_error, prob_conclude

data_size = range(30, 1000, 20)
result = list(zip(*[estimate_p_val(size) for size in data_size]))
```

Calculate the mean of
the p-values to get
the bootstrap mean.

Run the
bootstrap
analysis.

Calculate the 5th and 95th percentiles to
get a 90% bootstrap confidence interval.

Finally, we'll visualize the results. We'll plot the size of the data against the mean and 90% confidence intervals for the *p*-values we get for that given data size. We'll also plot how the probability of concluding in favor of the true hypothesis ($E \perp T \mid O, R$) for a significance level of .05 depends on data size.

**Listing 4.9   Visualize dependence of conditional independence testing on data size**

```
import numpy as np
import matplotlib.pyplot as plt

p_vals, lower_bars, higher_bars, probs_conclude_indep = result
plt.title('Data size vs. p-value (Ind. of E & T | O & R)')
plt.xlabel("Number of examples in data")
plt.ylabel("Expected p-value")
error_bars = np.array([lower_bars, higher_bars])
plt.errorbar(
    data_size,
    p_vals,
    yerr=error_bars,
    ecolor="grey",
    elinewidth=.5
)
plt.hlines(significance, 0, 1000, linestyles="dashed")
plt.show()
plt.title('Probability of favoring independence given data size')
plt.xlabel("Number of examples in data")
plt.ylabel("Probability of test favoring conditional independence")
plt.plot(data_size, probs_conclude_indep)
```

Run the bootstrap analysis to get
quantiles of p-values and probability of
concluding in favor of independence.

Plot the data size vs.
p-value. At larger
data sizes, the
expected p-value
falls below a
threshold.

Plot data size vs. the probability of
concluding in favor of independence,
given .05 significance.

Figure 4.18 shows the first plot. The descending curve is the expected *p*-values at different data sizes, the vertical lines are error bars showing a 90% bootstrap confidence interval. By the time we get to a dataset of size 1,000, the expected *p*-value is below the threshold, meaning that the test favors the conclusion that $E \perp T \mid O, R$ is false.

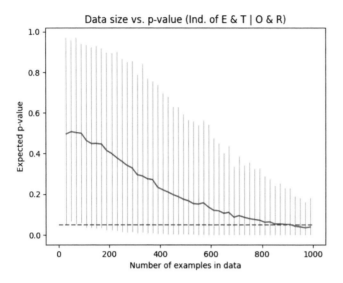

Figure 4.18 Sample size vs. expected *p*-value of the conditional independence test for $E \perp T \mid O, R$ (solid line). The vertical lines are the error bars; they show the 90% bootstrap confidence intervals. The horizontal dashed line is a .05 significance level, above which we favor the null hypothesis of conditional independence and below which we reject it. As the sample size increases, we eventually cross the line. Thus, the result of our refutation analysis depends on the size of the data.

Note that the lower bound of the confidence interval crosses the significance threshold well before 1,000, suggesting that at even lower data sizes, we have a good chance of rejecting the true conclusion of $E \perp T \mid O, R$. This becomes clearer in figure 4.19, where the probability of concluding in favor of the true conclusion decreases as the size of the data increases.

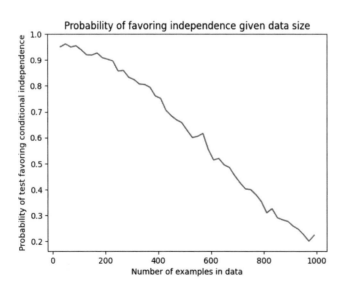

Figure 4.19 As the size of the data increases, the probability of concluding in favor of this (true) instance of the conditional independence relation $E \perp T \mid O, R$ decreases.

You might think that as the size of the data increases, the algorithm is detecting subtle dependencies between $E$ and $T$ that were undetectable with less data. Not so, for this transportation data is simulated in such a way that $E \perp T \mid O, R$ is definitely true. This is a case where more data leads us to rejecting independence because more data leads to more spurious correlations—patterns that aren't really there.

A causal model is either right or wrong about causality in the DGP it describes. The conditional independence the model implies is either there or it's not. Yet if that conditional independence is there, the test can still conclude in favor of dependence when the data is arbitrarily large.

Again, if we view conditional independence testing as a heuristic for refuting our DAG, then this sensitivity to the size of the data shouldn't upset us. Regardless of the data size and the significance thresholds, the *relative* differences between *p*-values when there is no conditional independence and when there is will be large and obvious.

### 4.4.4   *The problem of multiple comparisons*

In statistical hypothesis testing, the more tests you run, the more testing errors you rack up. The same is true when running a test for each d-separation implied by a causal DAG. In statistics, this problem is called the *multiple comparisons problem*. There are solutions to dealing with multiple comparisons problems, such as using *false discovery rates*. If you are familiar with such methods, applying them won't hurt. If you want to learn more, see the chapter's notes at www.altdeep.ai/causalAIbook for references to false discovery rates in the context of causal modeling. But again, I encourage you to view traditional conditional independence testing as a heuristic that helps with the ultimate goal of building a good causal DAG. Focus on this goal and on the subsequent causal inference analysis you will conduct using your DAG, and avoid rabbit holes of statistical testing rigor.

### 4.4.5   *Conditional independence testing struggles in machine learning settings*

Commonly used libraries for conditional independence testing are generally limited to one-dimensional variables with fairly simple patterns of correlation between them. pgmpy's conditional independence tests, which are imported from SciPy, are no exception. In recent years, several nonparametric tests have been developed for more nuanced distributions, such as kernel-based conditional independence tests. Tests in the PyWhy library PyWhy-Stats are a good place to start if you are interested in such tests.

However, in machine learning, it is common for variables to have more than one dimension such as vectors, matrices, and tensors. For example, one variable in a causal DAG might represent a matrix of pixels constituting an image. Further, the statistical associations between these variables can be nonlinear.

One solution is to focus on prediction. If two things are independent, they have no ability to predict one another. Suppose we have two predictive models $M_1$ and $M_2$. $M_1$ predicts $Y$ using $Z$ as a predictor. $M_2$ predicts $Y$ using $X$ and $Z$ as a predictor. Predictors can have dimensions greater than one. If $X \perp Y \mid Z$, then any $X$ has no predictive information about $Y$ beyond what is already provided by $Z$. So you can test $X \perp Y \mid Z$ by comparing the model predictive accuracy of $M_2$ to $M_1$. When the models perform similarly, we have evidence of conditional independence. Note that you'd want to prevent $M_2$ from "cheating" on its predictive accuracy by taking steps to avoid overfitting—yet another way spurious correlation can creep into our analysis.

### 4.4.6 Final thoughts

Conditional independence testing is an extensive and nuanced subject. Your goal with this testing is to refute your causal DAG, not to create the Platonic ideal of a conditional independence testing suite. I recommend getting a testing workflow that is *good enough*, and then focusing on building your DAG and using that DAG in downstream causal inferences. For example, if I had a mix of continuous and discrete variables, then rather than implementing a test that could accommodate my different data types, I would discretize my continuous variables (for example, turning age as time since birth into age brackets) and use a vanilla chi-squared test, to keep things moving along.

## 4.5 Refuting a causal DAG given latent variables

The method of testing DAGs with conditional independence has a latent variable problem. If a variable in our causal DAG is latent (not observed in the data), we can't run any conditional independence tests involving that variable. That is a major problem; if a variable is an important part of the DGP, we can't exclude it from our DAG simply because we can't test independence assertions with that variable.

To illustrate, consider the causal DAG in figure 4.20. This figure represents how smoking behavior ($S$) is influenced both by the cost of cigarettes ($C$) as well as genetic factors (denoted $D$ as in "DNA") that make one more or less prone to nicotine addiction. Those same genetic factors influence one's likelihood of getting lung cancer ($L$). In this model, smoking's effect on cancer is *mediated* through tar buildup ($T$) in the lungs.

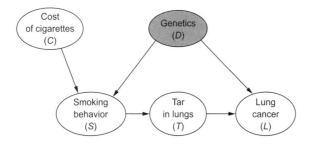

**Figure 4.20   A causal DAG representing smoking's effect on cancer. The variable for genetics (*D*) is gray because it is unobserved in the data, so we can't run tests for conditional independencies involving *D*. However, we can test other types of constraints.**

If we have data observing all these variables, we can run conditional independence tests targeting the following d-separations: $(C \perp_G T \mid S)$, $(C \perp_G L \mid D, T)$, $(C \perp_G L \mid D, S)$, $(C \perp_G D)$, $(S \perp_G L \mid D, T)$, and $(T \perp_G D \mid S)$. But suppose we don't have data on the genetics variable $(D)$. For example, perhaps measuring this genetics feature requires an infeasibly expensive and invasive laboratory test. Of all the d-separations we listed, the only one not involving $D$ is $(C \perp_G T \mid S)$. We are down from six to one feasible conditional independence test with which to test our DAG.

In general, a proposed causal model can have various implications for the joint probability distributions that are testable with data. The conditional independence implied by the graph structure is one type of testable implication. But some of the model's implications are testable in cases of latent variables. In this section, we're going to look at how we can test a DAG with one of these latent variable–related constraints.

### 4.5.1   *An example of a testable implication that works with latent variables*

The causal Markov assumption says d-separations imply conditional independence in the data. So far, we've explored direct conditional independence between variables, but when some variables are latent, the graph can imply conditional independence *between functions of observed variables*. These implications are called "Verma constraints" in the literature, though I will use the less jargony "functional constraints."

To illustrate, the DAG in figure 4.20 with latent variable $D$ has the following functional constraint (for now, don't worry about how its derived):

$$C \perp_G h(L, C, T)$$
$$h(l, c, t) = \sum_s P(l \mid c, s, t) P(s \mid c)$$

Just as the d-separation $(C \perp_G T \mid S)$ implies that the conditional independence statement $(C \perp T \mid S)$ should hold for the observational joint distribution, the functional constraint $(C \perp_G h(L, C, T))$ implies that $C$ is independent of some function $h(.)$ of variables $L$, $C$, and $T$ in the observational joint distribution. Both implications are testable since they don't involve $D$. We now have two tests we can run instead of one.

$h(.)$ has two components:

- $P(l \mid c, s, t)$ is a function that returns the probability that $L = l$ (suppose $l$ is "true" for "has lung cancer" and "false" for "no lung cancer"), given $C = c$, $S = s$, and $T = t$.
- $P(s \mid c)$ is a function that returns the probability that $S = s$ (suppose $s$ is "low," "medium," or "high" depending on how heavily a smoker smokes) given the cost of cigarettes $C = c$.

$h(.)$ then sums over all values of $S$. The function's output is a random variable that, according to the DAG, should be independent of $C$. $h(l, c, t)$ is a function of $P(l \mid c, s, t)$ and $P(s \mid c)$, and it may feel odd thinking about independence in terms of probability functions. Remember that the independence relation is itself just a function of joint probability distributions.

Next, we'll fit models of $P(l|c, s, t)$ and $P(s|c)$ from data and test this independence relation. But first, we'll look at libraries that let us enumerate functional constraints like $(C \perp_G h(L, C, T))$ from a DAG just like we could enumerate d-separations with pgmpy's `get_independencies`.

### 4.5.2 Libraries and perspectives on testing functional constraints

How do we derive functional constraints like $C \perp_G h(L, C, T)$? Like d-separation, we can derive this type of constraint algorithmically from the graph. One implementation is in the `verma.constraints` function in the causaleffect R library. This function takes in the DAG with nodes labeled as latent and returns a set of testable constraints just like pgmpy's `get_independencies`. For Python, the library Y0 (pronounced "why-not") has a `r_get_verma_constraints` function (as of version 0.2.10), which is a wrapper that calls causaleffect's R code. I'll omit the Python code here because it requires installing R, but visit www.altdeep.ai/causalAIbook for links to libraries and references.

---

### Mathematical intuition for functional constraints, and some advice

Our goal for this section is only to show that there are ways to test your causal model even when there are latent variables. Functional constraints are one way to do this, but we don't want to over-index on this particular flavor of testable implication. It is more important to avoid the dangerous mindset of limiting ourselves only to DAGs that are fully observed in the data.

That said, for the curious, I'll offer a very high-level intuition for the math. Recall that the local Markov property says that *a node is conditionally independent of its non-descendants, given its parents*. From there, we derive graphical criteria called d-separation that lets us find sets of nodes where this applies, we write a graph algorithm that uses those criteria to enumerate d-separations, and we use that algorithm to enumerate some conditional independence tests we can run.

For a given node $X$, let's say "orphaned cousins" means non-descendants of $X$ that share a latent ancestor of $X$. Here is, in informal terms, a latent variable analog to the local Markov property: *A node is conditionally independent of its non-descendants given its nearest observed ancestors, its orphaned cousins, and other nearest observed ancestors of those cousins*. Just as with d-separations, we can derive graphical criteria to identify individual cases where this applies.

Recall that we can factorize the joint probability distribution such that each factor is the conditional probability of a node's outcome, given its parents. The probability functions in the functional constraint (like the $P(l|c, s, t)$ and $P(s|c)$ terms in $h(l,c,t)$) come into the picture once we start marginalizing that factorization over the latent variables and doing subsequent probability math.

See the references listed at www.altdeep.ai/causalAIbook if you want to deep dive. But my warning from the previous section holds here—*our goal is to falsify our DAG and move on to our target causal inference.* Beware of falling down statistical, mathematical, and theoretical rabbit holes on the way to that goal.

Now that we have a new testable implication in the form of $C \perp_G h(L, C, T)$, let's test it out.

### 4.5.3  *Testing a functional constraint*

To test $(C \perp_G h(L, C, T))$, we have to calculate $h(l, c, t) = \Sigma_S P(l|c, s, t) P(s|c)$ for each item in our data. That requires us to model $P(l| c, s, t)$ and $P(s|c)$. There are several modeling approaches we could go with, but we'll use a naive Bayes classifier for this example so we can stick with using the pgmpy and pandas libraries. We'll take the following steps:

1  Discretize cost $(C)$ so we can treat it as a discrete variable.
2  Use pgmpy to fit a naive Bayes classifier to $P(l| c, s, t)$ and $P(s|c)$.
3  Write a function that takes in values of $L$, $C$, $T$ and calculates $h(L, C, T)$.
4  Apply that function to each row in the data to get a new column of $h(L, C, T)$ values.
5  Run an independence test between that column and the $C$ column.

> **Setting up your environment**
>
> The following code uses pgmpy version 0.1.19 because versions up to 0.1.24 (current at the time of writing) have a bug (already reported) that can cause issues with some of the naive Bayes classifier inference code. You don't need to do this if you use another method of calculating $P(l|c, s, t)$ and $P(s|c)$. For stability, we'll also use pandas version 1.4.3, which was the version when pgmpy 0.1.19 was current. Note that if you have installed later versions of pgmpy and pandas, you might have to uninstall those versions before installing these, or you could just spin up a new Python environment. Visit www.altdeep.ai/causalaibook for links to the Jupyter notebooks with the code and notes on setting up a working environment.

First, we'll import the data. We'll also discretize the cost of cigarettes ($C$) so it is more amenable to modeling with pgmpy.

#### Listing 4.10  Importing and formatting cigarette and cancer data

```
from functools import partial
import numpy as np                                    Load the CSV file into
import pandas as pd                                   a pandas DataFrame.

data_url = "https://raw.githubusercontent.com/altdeep/causalML/master
[CA] /datasets/cigs_and_cancer.csv"
data = pd.read_csv(data_url)                           ◁
cost_lower = np.quantile(data["C"], 1/3)
cost_upper = np.quantile(data["C"], 2/3)
def discretize_three(val, lower, upper):               Discretize cost (C) into a discrete
    if val < lower:                                    variable with three levels to facilitate
        return "Low"                                   conditional impendence tests.
    if val < upper:
```

```
        return "Med"
    return "High"

data_disc = data.assign(
    C = lambda df: df['C'].map(
        partial(
            discretize_three,
            lower=cost_lower,
            upper=cost_upper
        )
    )
)
data_disc = data_disc.assign(
    L = lambda df: df['L'].map(str),
)
print(data_disc)
```

**Discretize cost (C) into a discrete variable with three levels to facilitate conditional impendence tests.**

**Turn lung cancer (L) from a Boolean to a string, so the conditional independence test will treat it as a discrete variable.**

The `print(data_disc)` line prints out the elements of the `data_disc` DataFrame.

```
        C      S      T      L
0    High    Med    Low   True
1     Med   High   High  False
2     Med   High   High   True
3     Med   High   High   True
4     Med   High   High   True
..   ...    ...    ...    ...
95    Low   High   High   True
96   High   High   High  False
97    Low    Low    Low  False
98   High    Low    Low  False
99    Low   High   High   True

[100 rows x 4 columns]
```

Now we need to model $P(l|\ c, s, t)$ and $P(s|c)$. We'll opt for a naive Bayes classifier, a probabilistic model that "naively" assumes that, in the case of $P(l|\ c, s, t)$, cost $(C)$, smoking $(S)$, and tar $(T)$ are conditionally independent given lung cancer status $(L)$. According to our causal DAG, that is clearly not true, but that doesn't matter if all we want is a good way to calculate probability values for $L$ given $C$, $S$, and $T$. A naive Bayes classifier will do that well enough.

---

**Listing 4.11  Fit naive Bayes classifier of *P(l| c, s, t)***

```
from pgmpy.inference import VariableElimination
from pgmpy.models import NaiveBayes

model_L_given_CST = NaiveBayes()
model_L_given_CST.fit(data_disc, 'L')
infer_L_given_CST = VariableElimination(model_L_given_CST)

def p_L_given_CST(L_val, C_val, S_val, T_val):
    result_out = infer_L_given_CST.query(
        variables=["L"],
```

**We'll use a naive Bayes classifier in pgmpy to calculate the probability value for a given value of L given values of C, S, and T. In this case, we'll use variable elimination.**

```
        evidence={'C': C_val, 'S': S_val, 'T': T_val},
        show_progress=False
    )
    var_outcomes = result_out.state_names["L"]
    var_values = result_out.values
    prob = dict(zip(var_outcomes, var_values))
    return prob[L_val]
```

> We'll use a naive Bayes
> classifier in pgmpy to calculate
> the probability value for a
> given value of L given values of
> C, S, and T. In this case, we'll
> use variable elimination.

Now we'll do the same for $P(s|c)$.

**Listing 4.12   Fit naive Bayes classifier of $P(s|c)$**

```
model_S_given_C = NaiveBayes()
model_S_given_C.fit(data_disc, 'S')
infer_S_given_C = VariableElimination(model_S_given_C)
def p_S_given_C(S_val, C_val):
    result_out = infer_S_given_C.query(
        variables=['S'],
        evidence={'C': C_val},
        show_progress=False
    )
    var_names = result_out.state_names["S"]
    var_values = result_out.values
    prob = dict(zip(var_names, var_values))
    return prob[S_val]
```

Now we'll bring these together to implement the $h(L, T, C)$ function. The following code uses a `for` loop to do the summation over *S*.

**Listing 4.13   Combine models to create $h(L, T, C)$**

```
def h_function(L, C, T):        ◁—┤ Implement h(L, C, T).
    summ = 0
    for s in ["Low", "Med", "High"]:
        summ += p_L_given_CST(L, C, s, T) * p_S_given_C(s, C)
    return summ
```

> Implement the
> summation of
> P(l|c,s,t) * P(s|c)
> over s.

Now, we'll calculate the full set of outcomes for set {*C, T, L*}. Given these outcomes, we can calculate the $h(L, C, T)$ for each of these combinations using the preceding function.

**Listing 4.14   Calculate the outcome combinations of *C*, *T*, and *L***

```
ctl_outcomes = pd.DataFrame(
    [
        (C, T, L)
        for C in ["Low", "Med", "High"]
        for T in ["Low", "High"]
        for L in ["False", "True"]
    ],
    columns = ['C', 'T', 'L']
)
```

> Calculate these values for each possible
> combination of outcomes of L, C, and T.
> First, we use list comprehensions to make a
> DataFrame containing all the combinations.

Printing this shows all combinations of outcomes for *C*, *T*, and *L*.

```
        C      T      L
0     Low    Low  False
1     Low    Low   True
2     Low   High  False
3     Low   High   True
4     Med    Low  False
5     Med    Low   True
6     Med   High  False
7     Med   High   True
8    High    Low  False
9    High    Low   True
10   High   High  False
11   High   High   True
```

For each of these outcomes, we'll apply $h(L, C, T)$.

**Listing 4.15   Calculate $h(L, C, T)$ for each outcome of C, T, L**

```
h_dist = ctl_outcomes.assign(
    h_func = ctl_outcomes.apply(
        lambda row: h_function(
            row['L'], row['C'], row['T']), axis = 1
    )
)
print(h_dist)
```

Now for each joint outcome of *C*, *T*, and *L*, we have a value of $h(L, C, T)$.

```
        C      T      L    h_func
0     Low    Low  False  0.392395
1     Low    Low   True  0.607605
2     Low   High  False  0.255435
3     Low   High   True  0.744565
4     Med    Low  False  0.522868
5     Med    Low   True  0.477132
6     Med   High  False  0.369767
7     Med   High   True  0.630233
8    High    Low  False  0.495525
9    High    Low   True  0.504475
10   High   High  False  0.344616
11   High   High   True  0.655384
```

Finally, we'll merge this `h_func` distribution into the dataset such that for each row of our data, we get a value of $h(L, C, T)$.

**Listing 4.16   Merge to get a value of $h(L, C, T)$ for each row in the data**

```
df_mod = data_disc.merge(h_dist, on=['C', 'T', 'L'], how='left')    ◁
print(df_mod)
```

**Add a column representing
the variable h(L, C, T).**

We see the result with `print(df_mod)`:

```
       C      S      T      L   h_func
0    High    Med    Low   True  0.504475
1     Med   High   High  False  0.369767
2     Med   High   High   True  0.630233
3     Med   High   High   True  0.630233
4     Med   High   High   True  0.630233
..   ...    ...    ...    ...       ...
95    Low   High   High   True  0.744565
96   High   High   High  False  0.344616
97    Low    Low    Low  False  0.392395
98   High    Low    Low  False  0.495525
99    Low   High   High   True  0.744565

[100 rows x 5 columns]
```

The functional constraint says that $C$ and $h(L, C, T)$ should be independent, so we can look at the evidence of independence between the `h_func` column and the $C$ column. Since we discretized $C$, our calculated outcomes for $h(L, C, T)$ are technically discrete, so we could use a chi-squared test. But $h(L, C, T)$ is continuous in theory, so instead we'll use a box plot to visualize dependence between the two variables. The functional constraint says $C$ and $h(L, C, T)$ should be independent, so we'll use a box plot that plots values of $h(L, C, T)$ against values of $C$ to visually inspect whether $C$ and $h(L, C, T)$ look independent.

Listing 4.17   Box plot visualizing independence between C and h(L, C, T)

```
df_mod.boxplot("h_func", "C")
```

This produces figure 4.21.

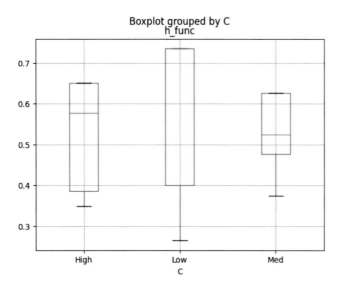

Figure 4.21   A box plot visualization of cost (C) on the x-axis and the function h(L, C, T) on the y-axis (labeled "Sum product"). The overlap of the distributions of the sum product for each value of C supports the functional constraints assertion that these two quantities are independent.

The *x*-axis in figure 4.21 is different levels of cost (low, medium, and high). The *y*-axis represents values of the sum. Figure 4.21 is a box wand whiskers plot; each box is a representation of the distribution of the sum product for a given value of *C*. The top and bottom of the boxes are the quartiles of the distribution, the lines in the middle of the boxes are the median, and the shorter horizonal lines are the max and min values (for low cost, the median, upper quartile, and max are quite close). In summary, it looks as though the distributions of the sum product don't change much across the different levels of cost; that's what independence is supposed to look like.

   We can also derive a *p*-value using an *analysis of variance* (ANOVA) approach, this time using an F-test rather than a chi-squared test. The following code uses the statsmodels library to run an ANOVA test.

**NOTE**   "PR( >F)" means the probability of seeing an F-statistic for a given variable (in our case, *C*) is at least as large as the F-statistic calculated from the data, assuming that the variable is independent of sum_product (i.e., the *p*-value).

**Listing 4.18   Using ANOVA to evaluate independence**

```
from statsmodels.formula.api import ols
import statsmodels.api as sm

model = ols('h_func ~ C', data=df_mod).fit()
aov_table = sm.stats.anova_lm(model, typ=2)
print(aov_table["PR(>F)"]["C"])

model = ols('h_func ~ T', data=df_mod).fit()
aov_table = sm.stats.anova_lm(model, typ=2)
print(aov_table["PR(>F)"]["T"])

model = ols('h_func ~ L', data=df_mod).fit()
aov_table = sm.stats.anova_lm(model, typ=2)
print(aov_table["PR(>F)"]["L"])
```

A recipe for doing ANOVA using the statmodels library

Returns a high p-value, which supports (fails to falsify) the assertion that h(L, C, T) and C are independent

Just as a sanity check, we run the same test to see whether h(L, C, T) looks independent of T and L. Unlike C, T and L should not be independent of h(L, C, T) and as expected, these tests return much smaller p-values, indicating dependence.

We print the *p*-value for *C* with `print(aov_table["PR(>F)"]["C"])` and get ~0.1876. That *p*-value indicates we can't reject the null hypothesis of independence, so it looks like the data supports the constraint. We also run the same test for *T* and *L* and, as expected, these are much smaller, indicating evidence of dependence. They are lower, both falling below the common .1 threshold where a standard hypothesis test would reject the hypothesis that *h*(*L*, *C*, *T*) is independent of *T* and *L*.

### 4.5.4   *Final thoughts on testable implications*

A DAG's d-separation and functional constraints imply that certain conditional independencies should hold in the joint probability distribution *if* the DAG is a good causal model of the DGP. We can falsify the DAG by running statistical tests for conditional independence.

More generally, a causal model can have different mathematical implications for the underlying joint probability distribution, and some of these can be tested. For example, if your model assumed the relationship between a cause and effect was linear, you could look for evidence of nonlinearity in the data (we'll see more about functional causal assumptions in chapter 6). And, of course, you can falsify your model's implications with experiments (as we'll see in chapter 7).

The better we get at causal modeling, the better we get at testing and falsifying our causal models. But remember, don't let the statistical and mathematical nuances of testing distract you from your goal of getting a good enough model and moving on to your target causal inference.

## 4.6    *Primer on (the perils of) causal discovery*

In the previous workflow, we proposed a causal DAG, considered what implications (like conditional independence) the DAG had for the observational joint distribution, and then tested those implications with the data. What if we went in the other direction? What if we analyzed the data for statistical evidence of causality induced constraints, and then constructed a causal DAG that is consistent with those constraints?

This describes the task of *causal discovery*: statistical learning of causal DAGs from data. In this section, I'll provide a brief primer on causal discovery and cover what you need to know to make use of this class of algorithms.

> ### Beware the false promises of causal discovery
>
> Causal discovery algorithms are often presented as magical tools that convert any dataset, no matter how limited in quality, into a causal DAG. That false promise discourages the mindset of modeling the DGP (rather than the data) and falsifying candidate models. It is also why it is hard to find consistent use cases for discovery in practice. This section takes the approach of framing how discovery algorithms work and where they fail, rather than going through a list of algorithms. I'll conclude with advice about how to effectively incorporate these algorithms into your analysis workflow.

We'll start with an overview of key ideas that underpin discovery algorithms.

### 4.6.1    *Approaches to causal discovery*

There are several approaches to causal discovery. Some algorithms (often called *constraint-based* algorithms) do what I just suggested—reverse engineer a graph from evidence of conditional independence in the data. Other algorithms (often called *score-based* algorithms) turn the causal DAG into an explanatory model of the data and find causal DAGs that have a high goodness-of-fit score. Yet another approach is to assume additional constraints on the functional relationships between parents and children in the causal DAG, as we'll see with structural causal models in chapter 6.

The space of possible DAGs is a discrete space. One class of approaches tries to soften this space into a continuous space and use continuous optimization techniques. The popularity of automatic differentiation libraries for deep learning have accelerated this trend.

Because the space of DAGs can be quite large, it is useful to incorporate prior knowledge to constrain the size of that space. This often takes the form of specifying what edges must be present or what must be absent, or of using Bayesian priors on graph structure.

Some causal discovery algorithms can work with experimental data. This requires telling the algorithm which variables were set by the experimenter (or as we'll say starting in chapter 7, which were "intervened upon").

To get started with causal discovery using Python, I recommend the PyWhy libraries for causal discovery such as causal-learn and DoDiscover.

### 4.6.2 *Causal discovery, causal faithfulness, and latent variable assumptions*

The causal Markov property assumes that if our DAG is true, d-separations in that DAG imply conditional independence statements in the joint probability of the variables:

$$U \perp_G V | Z \Rightarrow U \perp V | Z$$

*Causal faithfulness* (or just "faithfulness") is the converse statement—conditional independence in the joint distribution implies d-separation in the graph:

$$U \perp V | Z \Rightarrow U \perp_G V | Z$$

Many causal discovery algorithms rely on an assumption that faithfulness holds. It may not.

#### DISCOVERY AND FAITHFULNESS VIOLATIONS

In section 4.4, we used the Markov property to test a candidate DAG; given a d-separation statement that held for the DAG, we ran a statistical test to check for empirical evidence of the conditional independence implied by that d-separation.

Imagine you wanted to build your graph by going in reverse. You detect evidence of an instance of conditional independence in your data, and then you limit your space of candidate DAGs to those consistent with the implied d-separation. You do this iteratively until you've narrowed down the space of candidate DAGs. Some discovery algorithms do some version of this procedure, and those that do are relying on a faithfulness assumption.

> **NOTE** Algorithms that match evidence of conditional independence to d-separation are often called "constraint-based" discovery algorithms. A well-known example is the PC algorithm. Constraint-based algorithms find DAGs that are *constrained* to be consistent with the empirical evidence of causality.

The trouble comes from "faithfulness violations"—special cases where conditional independence in a joint probability distribution does not map to d-separation statements in a ground truth DAG. A simple example of a faithfulness violation is the case of a three-variable system that can decompose as follows: $P(x, y, z) = P(x, y)P(y, z)P(x, z)$. That is, for any value of one variable, the association between the other two variables is always the same. You could detect this peculiar form of independence in data, but you can't represent it with d-separation in a DAG. (If you don't believe me, try.)

Researchers worry about these special cases because they mean a discovery algorithm that relies on faithfulness doesn't generalize to all distributions. When you use these algorithms, you are assuming faithfulness holds for you problem domain, and that's not something you can test. However, violations of causal faithfulness are not typically the biggest source of headaches in practical causal discovery. That honor is reserved for latent variables.

#### THE CHALLENGE OF LATENT VARIABLES

The bigger pain is that most causal discovery algorithms, yet again, have a latent variable problem. To illustrate, suppose the true causal DAG was the DAG in figure 4.22.

In this DAG, variables $B$, $C$, and $D$ are conditionally independent of one another, given $A$. Now suppose that $A$ were not observed in the data. With $A$ as a latent variable, the discovery algorithm can't run tests like $B \perp C \mid A$. The algorithm will detect a dependence between $B$, $C$, and $D$ but will not find conditional independence between the three given $A$, and it might possibly return a DAG like figure 4.23, which reflects these results.

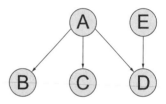

**Figure 4.22  Assume this is the true causal DAG. Here, *B*, *C*, and *D* are conditionally independent, given *A*.**

The remedy for this problem is to provide strong domain-specific assumptions about the latent variable structure in the discovery algorithm. A few generic discovery algorithms provide some accommodation for latent variable assumptions (the causal-learn library has a few). But this is rare, because it is hard to make it easy for users to specify domain-specific assumptions while still generalizing across domains.

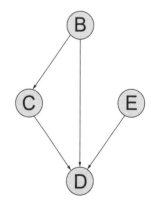

### 4.6.3   *Equivalence classes and PDAGs*

Let's suppose our algorithm were to correctly recover all the true conditional independence statements from data and map them back to a true set of d-separation statements (causal faithfulness holds). The problem we face now is that multiple causal DAGs may have the same set of d-separation statements. This set

**Figure 4.23  If *A* is latent, conditional independence tests that condition on *A* can't be run. The algorithm would detect dependence between *B*, *C*, and *D* but no conditional independence given *A*, and it might possibly return a graph such as this.**

of candidate DAGs is called a *Markov equivalence class.* The true causal DAG would be one of a possibly large set of members of this class.

For example, suppose the DAG on the left of figure 4.24 were the ground truth DAG. The DAG on the right of the graph differs from the correct graph in the edge between *A* and *T*. The two graphs have the same set of d-separation. In fact, we can also change the directions of the edges between {*L*, *S*} and {*B*, *S*} and still be in the same equivalence class, except for introducing a collider {*L* → *S* ← *B*}, because a new collider would change the set of d-separations.

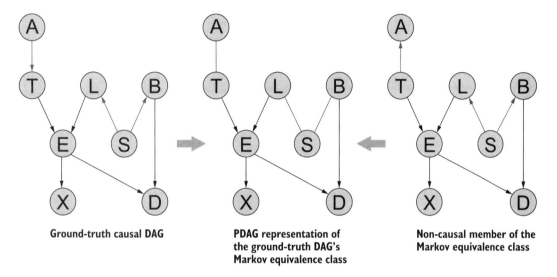

**Ground-truth causal DAG**        **PDAG representation of the ground-truth DAG's Markov equivalence class**        **Non-causal member of the Markov equivalence class**

**Figure 4.24   Supposing the DAG on the left is the ground truth DAG, the (wrong) DAG on the right is in the same Markov equivalence class. The PDAG in the middle represents the equivalence class, where undirected edges represent edges where members disagree on direction.**

Some discovery algorithms will return a partially directed acyclic graph (PDAG), such as the DAG in the center of figure 4.24. In the PDAG, undirected edges correspond to edges where there is disagreement on the edge's direction between members of the Markov equivalence class. This is nice, because we get a graphical representation of the equivalence class, and the algorithm can potentially search through the space of PDAGs instead of the larger space of DAGs.

## Colliders and discovery

Colliders feature prominently in causal discovery because they allow us to orient edges in the DAG from evidence of statistical dependence alone. Suppose we are using data to attempt to construct the ground-truth DAG in figure 4.24. We find evidence of

*(continued)*

dependence in the data of an edge between *A* and *T*. The idea of Markov equivalence means that evidence is not enough to determine the direction of that edge. Generally, evidence of dependence and independence in the data can imply the presence of edges but not their direction.

Colliders are the exception. It is possible to detect colliders like {$T \rightarrow E \leftarrow L$} from evidence of independence and dependence alone; if the data suggests *T* and *L* are independent, but become dependent when conditioning on *E*, you have evidence of a collider with directed edges {$T \rightarrow E \leftarrow L$}.

Colliders can also force orientation of edges outside of the collider. For example, consider the edge between *E* and *X* in the ground-truth DAG in figure 4.23. We might infer the existence of that edge from the following evidence in the data:

- *E* and *X* are dependent.
- *T* and *X* are dependent.
- *T* and *X* are independent, given *E*.

An edge between *E* and *X* is consistent with that evidence, but should we go with $E \rightarrow X$ or $E \leftarrow X$? Here, the collider {$T \rightarrow E \leftarrow L$} helps; it already oriented the edge $T \rightarrow E$, so adding $E \leftarrow X$ would induce another collider {$T \rightarrow E \leftarrow X$}. That collider would suggest *T* and *X* are independent but become dependent when conditioning on *E*, which violates the second and third observed items of evidence. So we conclude the edge is oriented as $E \rightarrow X$ by process of elimination.

Some causal discovery algorithms essentially algorithmicize this kind of logic. But remember, this logic breaks down when latent variables induce dependence between observed variables.

That said, PDAGs and Markov equivalence classes only capture equivalence between DAGs encoding the same set of conditional independence constraints. If you want to find all graphs that satisfy an additional layer of constraining assumptions, such as all graphs that have the same posterior probability given a certain prior, then the PDAG might not be sufficient.

If we go only on conditional independence, data can't distinguish between members of the Markov equivalence class, because having the same set of d-separations means having the same evidence of conditional independence in the data. This is an example of a *lack of causal identification*—when our data and a set of causal assumptions are not sufficient to disambiguate between possible answers to a causal question (in this case "what is the right causal DAG?"). We'll explore causal identification in depth in chapter 10.

### 4.6.4   *How to think about causal discovery*

In section 4.3, I argued that testing for causality induced constraints like conditional independence using off-the-shelf hypothesis testing libraries should be viewed more as a heuristic approach to refuting your causal DAG than a rigorous statistical procedure for validating the DAG. Similarly, I argued that for the practical user, off-the-shelf causal discovery algorithms should be viewed as a tool for exploratory data analysis during a human-driven causal DAG building process. The more you can input various types of domain knowledge and knowledge of latent variables into these algorithms, the better. But even then, they will produce obvious errors. Just as with the hypothesis testing case, avoid rabbit holes of trying to "fix" the discovery algorithm so it doesn't make these errors. Use causal discovery as one imperfect tool in your broader project of building a good causal DAG and running the subsequent causal inference analysis.

## Summary

- Causal modeling induces conditional independence constraints on the joint probability distribution. D-separation provides a graphical representation of conditional independence constraints.

- Building an intuition for d-separation is important for reasoning about causal effect inference and other queries.

- The colliders might make d-separation confusing, but you can build intuition by using d-separation functions in NetworkX and pgmpy.

- Using traditional conditional independence testing libraries to test d-separation has its challenges. The tests are sensitive to sample size, they don't work well in many machine learning settings, and their hypotheses are misaligned.

- Because of these challenges, it is best to view the attempts to falsify the DAG using off-the-shelf conditional independence testing libraries as more of a heuristic. Focus on the overall goal of building a good (i.e., hard to refute) causal DAG and moving on to your downstream causal inference task. Avoid fixating on theoretical rigor in statistical hypothesis testing.

- When there are latent variables, a causal DAG may still have testable implications for functions of the observed variables.

- Causal discovery refers to the use of statistical algorithms to recover a causal DAG from data.

- The causal faithfulness property assumes conditional independence in the joint probability distribution maps to a true set of d-separations that hold in the ground truth causal DAG.

- A Markov equivalence class of DAGs is a set of DAGs with the same set of d-separations. Assuming you have the true set of d-separations, the ground truth causal DAG generally shares that set with other (wrong) DAGs.

- Causal discovery is especially vulnerable to latent variables.

- The more you can constrain causal inference with prior assumptions, such as latent structure and which edges cannot possibly exist and which must exist, the better.

- Causal discovery algorithms are useful exploratory data analysis tools in the process of building a causal DAG, but they are not reliable replacements for that process. Again, focus on the overall goal of building a good causal DAG and moving on to the downstream causal inference analysis. Avoid trying to "fix" causal discovery algorithms so they don't produce obvious errors in your domain.

# Connecting causality and deep learning

The title of this book is *Causal AI*, but how exactly does causality connect to AI? More specifically, how does causality connect with deep learning, the dominant paradigm in AI? In this chapter, I look at this question from two perspectives:

- *How to incorporate deep learning into a causal model*—We'll look at a causal model of a computer vision problem (section 5.1) and then train the deep causal image model (section 5.2).
- *How to use causal reasoning to do better deep learning*—We'll look at a case study on independence of mechanism and semi-supervised learning (section 5.3.1 and 5.3.2), and we'll demystify deep learning with causality (section 5.3.3).

The term *deep learning* broadly refers to applications of deep neural networks. It's a machine learning approach that stacks many nonlinear models together in sequential layers, emulating the connections of neurons in brains. "Deep" refers to stacking many layers to achieve more modeling power, particularly in terms of modeling high-dimensional and nonlinear data, such as visual media and natural language text. Neural nets have been around for a while, but relatively recent advancements in hardware and automatic differentiation have made it possible to scale deep neural networks to extremely large sizes. That scaling is why, in recent years, there have been multiple cases of deep learning outperforming humans on many advanced inference and decision-making tasks, such as image recognition, natural language processing, game playing, medical diagnosis, autonomous driving, and generating lifelike text, images, and video.

But asking how deep learning connects to causality can elicit frustrating answers. AI company CEOs and leaders in big tech fuel hype about the power of deep learning models and even claim they can learn the causal structure of the world. On the other hand, some leading researchers claim these models are merely "stochastic parrots" that can echo patterns of correlation that, while nuanced and complex, still fall short of true causal understanding.

Our goal in this chapter is to reconcile these perspectives. But skipping ahead, the main takeaway is that deep learning architecture can be integrated into a causal model and we can train the model using deep learning training techniques. But also, we can use causal reasoning to build better deep learning models and improve how we train them.

We'll anchor this idea in two case studies:

- Building a causal DAG for computer vision using a variational autoencoder
- Implementing better semi-supervised learning using independence of mechanism

Other examples of the interplay of causality and AI that you'll see in the rest of the book will build on the intuition we get from these case studies. For example, chapter 9 will illustrate counterfactual reasoning using a variational autoencoder like the one we'll build in this chapter. In chapter 11, we'll explore machine learning and probabilistic deep learning approaches for causal effect inference. Chapter 13 will show how to combine large language models and causal reasoning.

We'll start by considering how to incorporate deep learning into a causal model.

## 5.1    *A causal model of a computer vision problem*

Let's look at a computer vision problem that we can approach with a causal DAG. Recall the MNIST data from chapter 1, composed of images of digits and their labels, illustrated in figure 5.1.

There is a related dataset called Typeface MNIST (TMNIST) that also features digit images and their digit labels. However, instead of handwritten digits, the images

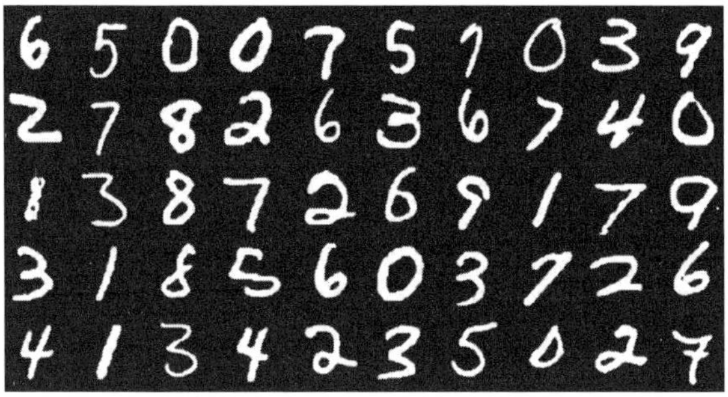

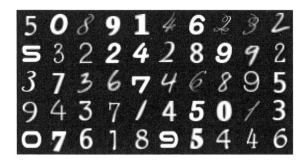

**Figure 5.1   MNIST data featuring images of handwritten digits and their digit labels**

are digits rendered in 2,990 different fonts, illustrated in figure 5.2. For each image, in addition to a digit label, there is a font label. Examples of the font labels include "GrandHotel-Regular," "KulimPark-Regular," and "Gorditas-Bold."

**Figure 5.2   Examples from the Typeface MNIST, which is composed of typed digits with different typefaces. In addition to a digit label for each digit, there is a label for one of 2,990 different typefaces (fonts).**

In this analysis, we'll combine these datasets into one and build a simple deep causal generative model on that data. We'll simplify the "fonts" label into a sample binary label that indicates "handwritten" for MNIST images and "typed" for the TMNIST images.

We have seen how to build a causal generative model on top of a DAG. We factorized the joint distribution into a product of *causal Markov kernels* representing the conditional probability distributions for each node, conditional on their parents in the DAG. In our previous examples in pgmpy, we fit a conditional probability table for each of these kernels.

You can imagine how hard it would be to use a conditional probability table to represent the conditional probability distribution of pixels in an image. But there is nothing stopping us from modeling the causal Markov kernel with a deep neural net, which we know is flexible enough to work with high-dimensional features like pixels. In this section, I'll demonstrate how to use deep neural nets to model the causal Markov kernels defined by a causal DAG.

### 5.1.1    *Leveraging the universal function approximator*

Deep learning is a highly effective universal function approximator. Let's imagine there is a function that maps some set of inputs to some set of outputs, but we either don't know the function or it's too hard to write down in math or code. Given enough examples of those inputs and outputs, deep learning can approximate that function with high precision. Even if that function is nonlinear and high-dimensional, with enough data, deep learning will learn a good approximation.

We regularly work with functions in causal modeling and inference, and sometimes it makes sense to approximate them, so long as the approximations preserve the causal information we care about. For example, the causal Markov property makes us interested in functions that map values of a node's parents in the causal DAG to values (or probability values) of that node.

In this section, we'll do this mapping between a node and its parents with the variational autoencoder (VAE) framework. We'll train two deep neural nets in the VAE, one of which maps parent cause variables to a distribution of the outcome variable, and another that maps the outcome variable to a distribution of the cause variables. This example will showcase the use of deep learning when causality is nonlinear and high-dimensional; the effect variable will be an image represented as a high-dimensional array, and the cause variables will represent the contents of the image.

### 5.1.2    *Causal abstraction and plate models*

But what does it mean to build a causal model of an image? Images are comprised of pixels arranged in a grid. As data, we can represent that pixel grid as a matrix of numerical values corresponding to color. In the case of both MNIST and TMNIST, the image is a $28 \times 28$ matrix of grayscale values, as illustrated in figure 5.3.

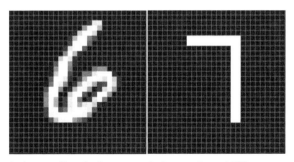

**An image of handwritten "6" (as in MNIST)**

**An image of typed "7" (as in Typeface MNIST)**

Figure 5.3   An MNIST image of "6" (left) and a TMNIST image of "7". In their raw form, these are $28 \times 28$ matrices of numeric values corresponding to grayscale values.

A typical machine learning model looks at this $28 \times 28$ matrix of pixels as $28 \times 28 = 784$ features. The machine learning algorithm learns statistical patterns connecting the pixels to one another and their labels. Based on this fact, one might be tempted to treat each individual pixel as a node in the naive causal DAG, as in figure 5.4, where for visual simplicity I've drawn 16 pixels (an arbitrary number) instead of all 784.

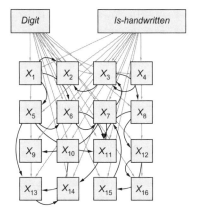

In figure 5.4, there are edges from the *digit* and *is-handwritten* variables to each pixel. Further, there are examples of edges representing possible causal relationships *between* pixels. Causal edges between pixels imply the color of one pixel is a cause of another. Perhaps most of these relationships are between nodes that are close, with a few far-reaching edges. But how would we know if one pixel causes another? If two pixels are connected, how would we know the direction of causality?

**Figure 5.4   What a naive causal DAG might look like for an image represented by a 4 × 4 matrix**

### WORKING AT THE RIGHT LEVEL OF ABSTRACTION

With these connections among only 16 pixels, the naive DAG in figure 5.4 is already quite unwieldy. It would be much worse with 784 pixels. Aside from the unwieldiness of a DAG, the problem with a pixel-level model is that our causal questions are generally not at the pixel level—we'd probably never ask "what is the causal effect of this pixel on that pixel?" In other words, the pixel is too low a level of abstraction, which is why thinking about causal relationships between individual pixels feels a bit absurd.

In applied statistics domains, such as econometrics, social science, public health, and business, our data has variables like per capita income, revenue, location, age, etc. These variables are typically already at the level of abstraction we want to think about when we get the data. But modern machine learning focuses on many perception problems from raw media, such as images, video, text, and sensor data. We don't generally want to do causal reasoning at the low level of these features. Our causal questions are usually about the high-level abstractions behind these low-level features. We need to model at these higher abstraction levels.

Instead of thinking about individual pixels, we'll think about the entire image. We'll define a variable $X$ to represent how the image appears; i.e., $X$ is a matrix random variable representing pixels. Figure 5.5 illustrates a causal DAG for the TMNIST case. Simply put, the identity of the digits (0–9) and the font (2,990 possible values) are the causes, and the image is the effect.

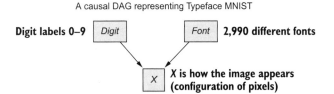

**Figure 5.5   A simple causal DAG that represents the implied DGP behind Typeface MNIST**

In this case, we are using the causal DAG to make an assertion that the label causes the image. That is not always the case, as we'll discuss in our case study on semi-supervised learning in section 5.3. As with all causal models, it depends on the data generating process (DGP) within a domain.

## Why say that the digit *causes* the image?

Plato's allegory of the cave describes a group of people who have lived in a cave all their lives, without seeing the world. They face a blank cave wall and watch shadows projected on the wall from objects passing in front of a fire behind them. The shadows are simplified and sometimes distorted representations of the true objects passing in front of the fire. In this case, we can think of the form of the objects as being the cause of the shadow.

Analogously, the true form of the digit label causes the representation in the image. The MNIST images were written by people, and they have some *Platonic ideal* of the digit in their head that they want to render onto paper. In the process, that ideal is distorted by motor variation in the hand, the angle of the paper, the friction of the pen on the paper, and other factors—the rendered image is a "shadow" caused by that "ideal."

This idea is related to a concept called "vision as inverse graphics" in computer vision (see www.altdeep.ai/causalAIbook for sources with more information). In causal terms, the takeaway is that when we are analyzing images rendered from raw signals from the environment, and the task is to infer the actual objects or events that resulted in those signals, causality flows from those objects or events to the signals. The inference task is to use the observed signals (shadows on the cave wall) to infer the nature of the causes (objects in front of the fire).

That said, images can be causes too. For example, if you were modeling how people behave *after* seeing an image in a mobile app (e.g., whether they "click", "like", or "swipe left"), you could model the image as a cause of the behavior.

### PLATE MODELING

Modeling 2,990 fonts in our TMNIST data is overkill for our purposes here. Instead, I combined these datasets into one—half from MNIST and half from Typeface MNIST. Along with the "digit" label, I'm just going to have a simple binary label called "is-handwritten", which is 1 (true) for images of handwritten digits from MNIST and 0 (false) for images of "typed" digits from TMNIST. We can modify our causal DAG to get figure 5.6.

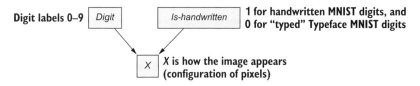

**Figure 5.6  A causal DAG representing the combined MNIST and TMNIST data, where "is-handwritten" is 1 (MNIST images) or 0 (TMNIST images)**

Plate modeling is a visualizing technique used in probabilistic machine learning that provides an excellent way to visualize the higher-level abstractions while preserving the lower-level dimensional detail. Plate notation is a method of visually representing variables that repeat in a DAG (e.g., $X_1$ to $X_{16}$ in figure 5.4)—in our case, we have repetition of the pixels.

Instead of drawing each of the 784 pixels as an individual node, we use a rectangle or "plate" to group repeating variables into subgraphs. We then write a number on the plate to represent the number of repetitions of the entities on the plate. Plates can nest within one another to indicate repeated entities nested within repeated entities. Each plate gets a letter subscript indexing the elements on that plate. The causal DAG in figure 5.7 represents one image.

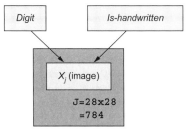

**Figure 5.7   A plate model representation of the causal DAG. Plates represent repeating variables, in this case 28 × 28 = 784 pixels. $X_j$ is the $j^{th}$ pixel.**

During training, we'll have a large set of training images. Next, we'll modify the DAG to capture all the images in the training data.

## 5.2   Training a neural causal model

To train our neural causal model, we need to load and prepare the training data, create the architecture of our model, write a training procedure, and implement some tools for evaluating how well training is progressing. We'll start by loading and preparing the data.

### 5.2.1   Setting up the training data

Our training data has $N$ example images, so we need our plate model to represent all $N$ images in the training data, half handwritten and half typed. We'll add another plate corresponding to repeating $N$ sets of images and labels, as in figure 5.8.

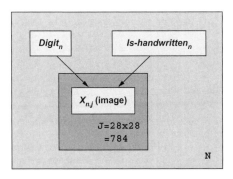

**Figure 5.8   The causal model with an additional plate for the $N$ images in the data**

Now we have a causal DAG that illustrates both our desired level of causal abstraction as well as the dimensional information we need to start training the neural nets in the model.

Let's first load Pyro and some other libraries and set some hyperparameters.

---

**Setting up your environment**

This code was written using Python version 3.10.12 and tested in Google Colab. The versions of the main libraries include Pyro (pyro-ppl) version 1.8.4, torch version 2.2.1, torchvision version 0.18.0+cu121, and pandas version 2.0.3. We'll also use matplotlib for plotting.

Visit www.altdeep.ai/causalAIbook for links to a notebook that will load in Google Colab.

---

If GPUs are available on your device, it will be faster to train the neural nets with CUDA (a platform for parallel computing on GPUs). We'll run a bit of code that lets us toggle it on. If you don't have GPUs or aren't sure if you do, leave USE_CUDA set to False.

**Listing 5.1   Setting up for GPU training**

```
import torch
USE_CUDA = False                                          ⟵───  Use CUDA if it is available.
DEVICE_TYPE = torch.device("cuda" if USE_CUDA else "cpu")
```

First, we'll make a subclass of the Dataset class (a class for loading and preprocessing data) that will let us combine the MNIST and TMNIST datasets.

**Listing 5.2   Combining the data**

```
from torch.utils.data import Dataset

import numpy as np
import pandas as pd
from torchvision import transforms              This class loads and processes a dataset that
                                                combines MNIST and Typeface MNIST. The
class CombinedDataset(Dataset):      ⟵───       output is a torch.utils.data.Dataset object.
    def __init__(self, csv_file):
        self.dataset = pd.read_csv(csv_file)

    def __len__(self):
        return len(self.dataset)

    def __getitem__(self, idx):
        images = self.dataset.iloc[idx, 3:]
        images = np.array(images, dtype='float32')/255.    Load, normalize, and
        images = images.reshape(28, 28)                    reshape the images to
        transform = transforms.ToTensor()                  28 × 28 pixels.
        images = transform(images)
        digits = self.dataset.iloc[idx, 2]           Get and process the
        digits = np.array([digits], dtype='int')     digit labels, 0–9.
```

```
            is_handwritten = self.dataset.iloc[idx, 1]
            is_handwritten = np.array([is_handwritten], dtype='float32')
            return images, digits, is_handwritten
```

1 for handwritten digits
(MNIST), and 0 for "typed"
digits (TMNIST)

Return a tuple of the image,
the digit label, and the
is_handwritten label.

Next, we'll use the `DataLoader` class (which allows for efficient data iteration and batching during training) to load the data from a CSV file in GitHub and split it into training and test sets.

---

**Listing 5.3   Downloading, splitting, and loading the data**

```
from torch.utils.data import DataLoader
from torch.utils.data import random_split

def setup_dataloaders(batch_size=64, use_cuda=USE_CUDA):
    combined_dataset = CombinedDataset(
"https://raw.githubusercontent.com/altdeep/causalML/master/datasets
/combined_mnist_tmnist_data.csv"
    )
    n = len(combined_dataset)
    train_size = int(0.8 * n)
    test_size = n - train_size
    train_dataset, test_dataset = random_split(
        combined_dataset,
        [train_size, test_size],
        generator=torch.Generator().manual_seed(42)
    )
    kwargs = {'num_workers': 1, 'pin_memory': use_cuda}
    train_loader = DataLoader(
        train_dataset,
        batch_size=batch_size,
        shuffle=True,
        **kwargs
    )
    test_loader = DataLoader(
        test_dataset,
        batch_size=batch_size,
        shuffle=True,
        **kwargs
    )
    return train_loader, test_loader
```

Set up the data loader that
loads the data and splits it
into training and test sets.

Allot 80% of the data
to training data and
the remaining 20%
to test data.

Create training
and test loaders.

Next, we'll set up the full variational autoencoder.

## 5.2.2   *Setting up the variational autoencoder*

The variational autoencoder (VAE) is perhaps the simplest deep probabilistic machine learning modeling approach. In the typical setup for applying VAE to images, we introduce a latent continuous variable $Z$ that has a smaller dimension than the image data. Here, *dimensionality* refers to the number of elements in a vector representation of the data. For instance, our image is a 28 × 28 matrix of pixels, or alternatively a vector with dimension 28 × 28 = 784. By having a much smaller dimension than the image dimension, the latent variable $Z$ represents a compressed encoding of the image information. For each image in the dataset, there is a corresponding latent $Z$ value that represents an encoding of that image. This setup is illustrated in figure 5.9.

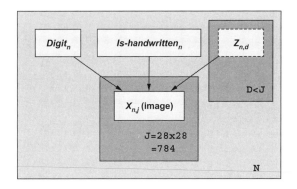

**Figure 5.9    The causal DAG plate model, extended to include an "encoding" variable $Z$. During training, the variable is latent, indicated by the dashed line. (After the model is deployed, *digit* and *is-handwritten* are also latent).**

$Z$ appears as a new parent in the causal DAG, but it's important to note that the classical VAE framework does not define $Z$ as causal. Now that we are thinking causally, we'll give $Z$ a causal interpretation. Specifically, as parents of the image node in the DAG, we view *digit* and *is-handwritten* as causal drivers of what we see in the image. Yet there are other elements of the image (e.g., the stroke thickness of a handwritten character, or the font of a typed character) that are also causes of what we see in the image. We'll think of $Z$ as a continuous latent *stand-in* for all of these other causes of the image that we are not explicitly modeling, like *digit* and *is-handwritten*. Examples of these causes include the nuance of the various fonts in the TMNIST labels and all of the variations in the handwritten digits due to different writers and motor movements as they wrote. With that in mind, we can view $P(X|\ digit,\ is\text{-}handwritten,\ Z)$ as the causal Markov kernel of $X$. That said, it is important to remember that the representation we learn for $Z$ is a stand-in for latent causes and is not the same as learning the actual latent causes.

The VAE setup will train two deep neural networks: One called an "encoder", which encodes an image into a value for $Z$. The other neural network, called the "decoder," will align with our DAG. The decoder generates an image from the *digit* label, the *is-handwritten* label, and a $Z$ value, as in figure 5.10.

The decoder acts like a rendering engine; given a $Z$ encoding value and the values for *digit* and *is-handwritten*, it renders an image.

**Decoder**

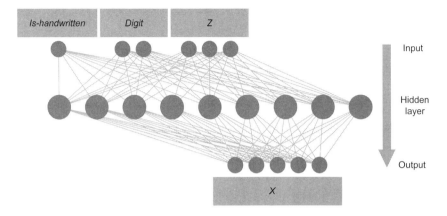

**Figure 5.10   The decoder neural network generates as output an image *X* from inputs *Z*
and the labels *is-handwritten* and *digit*. As with any neural net, the inputs are processed
through one or more "hidden layers."**

### Key VAE concepts so far

*Variational autoencoder (VAE)*—A popular framework in deep generative modeling.
We're using it to model a causal Markov kernel in a causal model.

*Decoder*—We use the decoder as the model of the causal Markov kernel. It maps the
observed causes *is-handwritten* and *digit*, and the latent variable *Z*, to our image outcome variable *X*.

This VAE approach allows us to use a neural net, a la the decoder, to capture the complex and nonlinear relations needed to model the image as an effect caused by *digit*
and *is-handwritten*. Modeling images would be difficult with the conditional probability
tables and other simple parameterizations of causal Markov kernels we've discussed
previously.

First, let's implement the decoder. We'll pass in arguments `z_dim` for the dimension
of *Z* and `hidden_dim` for the dimension (width) of the hidden layers. We'll specify
these variables when we instantiate the full VAE. The decoder combines the latent vector *Z* with additional inputs—the variable representing the *digit*, and *is-handwritten* (a
binary indicator of whether the digit is handwritten). It will produce a 784-dimensional
output vector representing an image of size $28 \times 28$ pixels. This output vector contains
the parameters for a Bernoulli distribution for each pixel, essentially modeling the
likelihood of each pixel being "on." The class uses two fully connected layers (`fc1` and
`fc2`), and employs `Softplus` and `Sigmoid` "activation functions," which are the hall-
marks of how neural nets emulate neurons.

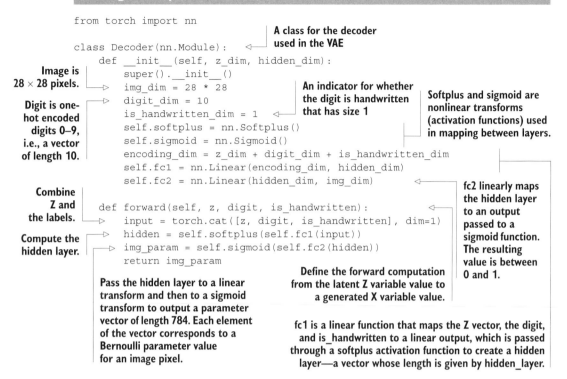

##### Listing 5.4   Implement the decoder

```
from torch import nn

class Decoder(nn.Module):
    def __init__(self, z_dim, hidden_dim):
        super().__init__()
        img_dim = 28 * 28
        digit_dim = 10
        is_handwritten_dim = 1
        self.softplus = nn.Softplus()
        self.sigmoid = nn.Sigmoid()
        encoding_dim = z_dim + digit_dim + is_handwritten_dim
        self.fc1 = nn.Linear(encoding_dim, hidden_dim)
        self.fc2 = nn.Linear(hidden_dim, img_dim)

    def forward(self, z, digit, is_handwritten):
        input = torch.cat([z, digit, is_handwritten], dim=1)
        hidden = self.softplus(self.fc1(input))
        img_param = self.sigmoid(self.fc2(hidden))
        return img_param
```

**A class for the decoder used in the VAE**

**Image is 28 × 28 pixels.**

**Digit is one-hot encoded digits 0–9, i.e., a vector of length 10.**

**An indicator for whether the digit is handwritten that has size 1**

**Softplus and sigmoid are nonlinear transforms (activation functions) used in mapping between layers.**

**fc2 linearly maps the hidden layer to an output passed to a sigmoid function. The resulting value is between 0 and 1.**

**Combine Z and the labels.**

**Compute the hidden layer.**

**Pass the hidden layer to a linear transform and then to a sigmoid transform to output a parameter vector of length 784. Each element of the vector corresponds to a Bernoulli parameter value for an image pixel.**

**Define the forward computation from the latent Z variable value to a generated X variable value.**

**fc1 is a linear function that maps the Z vector, the digit, and is_handwritten to a linear output, which is passed through a softplus activation function to create a hidden layer—a vector whose length is given by hidden_layer.**

We use the decoder in the causal model. Our causal DAG acts as the scaffold for a causal probabilistic machine learning model that, with the help of the decoder, defines a joint probability distribution on {*is-handwritten, digit, X, Z*}, where *Z* is latent. We can use the model to calculate the likelihood of the training data for a given value of *Z*.

The latent variable z, the digit identity represented as a one-hot vector digit, and a binary indicator is_handwritten are modeled as samples from standard distributions. These variables are then fed into the decoder to produce parameters (img_param) for a Bernoulli distribution representing individual pixel probabilities of an image.

Note, using the Bernoulli distribution to model the pixels is a bit of a hack. The pixels are not binary black and white outcomes—they have grayscale values. The line dist.enable_validation(False) lets us cheat by getting Bernoulli log likelihoods for the images given a decoder's img_param output.

The following model code is a class method for a PyTorch neural network module. We'll see the entire class later.

##### Listing 5.5   The causal model

```
import pyro
import pyro.distributions as dist
```

Disabling distribution validation lets Pyro calculate log likelihoods for pixels even though the pixels are not binary values.

The model of a single image. Within the method, we register the decoder, a PyTorch module, with Pyro. This lets Pyro know about the parameters inside of the decoder network.

We model the joint probability of Z, digit, and is_handwritten, sampling each from canonical distributions. We sample Z from a multivariate normal with location parameter z_loc (all zeros) and scale parameter z_scale (all ones).

```
dist.enable_validation(False)
def model(self, data_size=1):
    pyro.module("decoder", self.decoder)
    options = dict(dtype=torch.float32, device=DEVICE_TYPE)
    z_loc = torch.zeros(data_size, self.z_dim, **options)
    z_scale = torch.ones(data_size, self.z_dim, **options)
    z = pyro.sample("Z", dist.Normal(z_loc, z_scale).to_event(1))
    p_digit = torch.ones(data_size, 10, **options)/10
    digit = pyro.sample(
        "digit",
        dist.OneHotCategorical(p_digit)
    )
    p_is_handwritten = torch.ones(data_size, 1, **options)/2
    is_handwritten = pyro.sample(
        "is_handwritten",
        dist.Bernoulli(p_is_handwritten).to_event(1)
    )
    img_param = self.decoder(z, digit, is_handwritten)
    img = pyro.sample("img", dist.Bernoulli(img_param).to_event(1))
    return img, digit, is_handwritten
```

We also sample the digit from a one-hot categorical distribution. Equal probability is assigned to each digit.

We similarly sample the is_handwritten variable from a Bernoulli distribution.

The decoder maps digit, is_handwritten, and Z to a probability parameter vector.

The parameter vector is passed to the Bernoulli distribution, which models the pixel values in the data. The pixels are not technically Bernoulli binary variables, but we'll relax this assumption.

The preceding `model` method represents the DGP for one image. The `training_model` method in the following listing applies that `model` method to the $N$ images in the training data.

**Listing 5.6  Method for applying `model` to N images in data**

```
def training_model(self, img, digit, is_handwritten, batch_size):
    conditioned_on_data = pyro.condition(
        self.model,
        data={
            "digit": digit,
            "is_handwritten": is_handwritten,
            "img": img
        }
    )
    with pyro.plate("data", batch_size):
        img, digit, is_handwritten = conditioned_on_data(batch_size)
    return img, digit, is_handwritten
```

Now we condition the model on the evidence in the training data.

The model represents the DGP for one image. The training_model applies that model to the N images in the training data.

This context manager represents the N-size plate representing repeating IID examples in the data in figure 5.9. In this case, N is the batch size. It works like a for loop, iterating over each data unit in the batch.

Our probabilistic machine learning model models the joint distribution of {*Z, X, digit, is-handwritten*}. But since *Z* is latent, the model will need to learn *P*(*Z*|*X, digit, is-handwritten*). Given that we use the decoder neural net to go from *Z* and the labels to *X*, the distribution of *Z*, given *X* and the labels will be complex. We will use *variational inference*, a technique where we first define an approximating distribution *Q*(*Z*|*X, digit, is-handwritten*), and try to make that distribution as close to *P*(*Z*|*X, digit, is-handwritten*) as we can.

The main ingredient of the approximating distribution is the second neural net in the VAE framework, the encoder, illustrated in figure 5.11. The encoder maps an observed image and its labels in the training data to a latent *Z* variable.

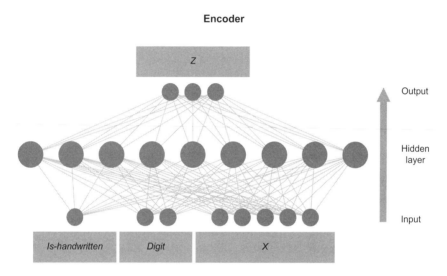

**Figure 5.11**   **The encoder maps actual images as input to the latent *Z* variable as output.**

The encoder does the work of compressing the information in the image into a lower-dimensional encoding.

### Key VAE concepts so far

*Variational autoencoder (VAE)*—A popular framework in deep generative modeling. We're using it to model a causal Markov kernel in our causal model.

*Decoder*—We use the decoder as the model of the causal Markov kernel. It maps observed causes *is-handwritten* and *digit*, and the latent variable *Z*, to our image outcome variable *X*.

*Encoder*—The encoder maps the image, *digit*, and *is-handwritten* indicator to the parameters of a distribution where we can draw samples of *Z*.

In the following code, the encoder takes as input an image, a digit label, and the *is-handwritten* indicator. These inputs are concatenated and passed through a series of fully connected layers with Softplus activation functions. The final output of the encoder consists of two vectors representing the location (z_loc) and scale (z_scale) parameters of the latent space distribution on *Z*, given observed values for *image* (img), *digit* (digit), and *is-handwritten* (is_handwritten).

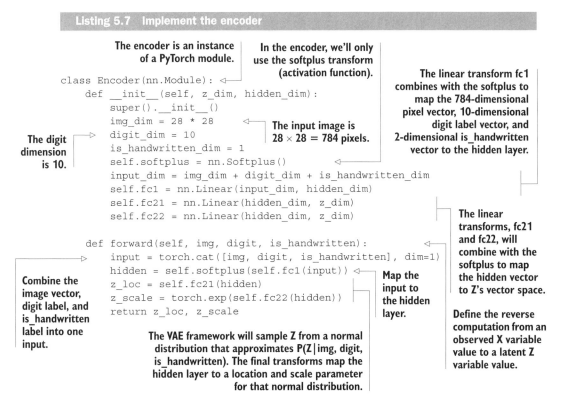

Listing 5.7   Implement the encoder

The encoder is an instance of a PyTorch module.

In the encoder, we'll only use the softplus transform (activation function).

The linear transform fc1 combines with the softplus to map the 784-dimensional pixel vector, 10-dimensional digit label vector, and 2-dimensional is_handwritten vector to the hidden layer.

```
class Encoder(nn.Module):
    def __init__(self, z_dim, hidden_dim):
        super().__init__()
        img_dim = 28 * 28
        digit_dim = 10
        is_handwritten_dim = 1
        self.softplus = nn.Softplus()
        input_dim = img_dim + digit_dim + is_handwritten_dim
        self.fc1 = nn.Linear(input_dim, hidden_dim)
        self.fc21 = nn.Linear(hidden_dim, z_dim)
        self.fc22 = nn.Linear(hidden_dim, z_dim)

    def forward(self, img, digit, is_handwritten):
        input = torch.cat([img, digit, is_handwritten], dim=1)
        hidden = self.softplus(self.fc1(input))
        z_loc = self.fc21(hidden)
        z_scale = torch.exp(self.fc22(hidden))
        return z_loc, z_scale
```

The digit dimension is 10.

The input image is 28 × 28 = 784 pixels.

Combine the image vector, digit label, and is_handwritten label into one input.

Map the input to the hidden layer.

The linear transforms, fc21 and fc22, will combine with the softplus to map the hidden vector to Z's vector space.

Define the reverse computation from an observed X variable value to a latent Z variable value.

The VAE framework will sample Z from a normal distribution that approximates P(Z|img, digit, is_handwritten). The final transforms map the hidden layer to a location and scale parameter for that normal distribution.

The output of the encoder produces the parameters of a distribution on *Z*. During training, given an image and its labels (*is-handwritten* and *digit*), we want to get a good value of *Z*, so we write a *guide function* that will use the encoder to sample values of *Z*.

Listing 5.8   The guide function

```
def training_guide(self, img, digit, is_handwritten, batch_size):
    pyro.module("encoder", self.encoder)
    options = dict(dtype=torch.float32, device=DEVICE_TYPE)
    with pyro.plate("data", batch_size):
```

training_guide is a method of the VAE that will use the encoder.

This is the same plate context manager for iterating over the batch data that we see in the training_model.

Register the encoder so Pyro is aware of its weight parameters.

```
z_loc, z_scale = self.encoder(img, digit, is_handwritten)
normal_dist = dist.Normal(z_loc, z_scale).to_event(1)
z = pyro.sample("Z", normal_dist)
```

**Sample Z from that normal distribution**

**Use the encoder to map an image and its labels to parameters of a normal distribution.**

We combine these elements into one PyTorch neural network module representing the VAE. We'll initialize the latent dimension of $Z$ to be 50. We'll set our hidden layer dimension to 400 in both the encoder and decoder. That means that given a dimension of $28 \times 28$ for the image, 1 for the binary *is-handwritten*, and 10 for the one-hot-encoded *digit* variable, we'll take a $28 \times 28 + 1 + 10 = 795$-dimensional feature vector and compress it down to a 400-dimensional hidden layer, and then compress that down to a 50-dimensional location and scale parameter for $Z$'s multivariate normal (Gaussian) distribution. The decoder takes as input the values of *digit, is-handwritten*, and $Z$ and maps these to a 400-dimensional hidden layer and to the $28 \times 28$–dimensional image. These architectural choices of latent variable dimension, number of layers, activation functions, and hidden layer dimensions depend on the problem and are typically selected by convention or by experimenting with different values.

Now we'll put these pieces together into the full VAE class.

**Listing 5.9 Full VAE class**

```
class VAE(nn.Module):
    def __init__(
        self,
        z_dim=50,
        hidden_dim=400,
        use_cuda=USE_CUDA,
    ):
        super().__init__()
        self.use_cuda = use_cuda
        self.z_dim = z_dim
        self.hidden_dim = hidden_dim
        self.setup_networks()

    def setup_networks(self):
        self.encoder = Encoder(self.z_dim, self.hidden_dim)
        self.decoder = Decoder(self.z_dim, self.hidden_dim)
        if self.use_cuda:
            self.cuda()

    model = model
    training_model = training_model
    training_guide = training_guide
```

**Set the latent dimension to 50.**

**Set the hidden layers to have a dimension of 400.**

**Set up the encoder and decoder.**

**Add in the methods for model, training_model, and training_guide.**

Having specified the VAE, we can now move on to training.

### 5.2.3 The training procedure

We know we have a good generative model when the encoder can encode an image into a latent value of $Z$, and then decode it into a *reconstructed* version of the image. We can minimize the *reconstruction error*—the difference between original and reconstructed images—in the training data.

---

### A bit of perspective on the "variational inference" training algorithm

In this section, you'll see a bunch of jargon relating to variational inference, which is the algorithm we'll use for training. It helps to zoom out and examine why we're using this algorithm. There are many statistical estimators and algorithms both for fitting neural net weights and other parameters and for causal inference. One of these is variational inference.

To be clear, variational inference is not a "causal" idea. It is just another probabilistic inference algorithm. In this book, I favor this inference algorithm more than others because it scales well even when variables in the DAG are latent in the training data, and it works with deep neural nets and leverages deep learning frameworks like PyTorch. This opens the door to reasoning causally about richer modalities such as text, images, video, etc., whereas traditional causal inference estimators were developed for numerical data. Further, we can tailor the method to different problems (see the discussion of "commodification of inference" in chapter 1) and leverage domain knowledge during inference (such as by using knowledge of conditional independence in the guide). Finally, the core concepts of variational inference show up across many deep generative modeling approaches (such as latent diffusion models).

---

In practice, solely minimizing reconstruction error leads to overfitting and other issues, so we'll opt for a probabilistic approach: given an image, we'll use our guide function to sample a value of $Z$ from $P(Z|image, is\text{-}handwritten, digit)$. Then we'll plug that value into our model's decoder, and the output parameterizes $P(image|is\text{-}handwritten, digit, Z)$. Our probabilistic approach to minimizing reconstruction error optimizes the encoder and decoder such that we'll maximize the likelihood of $Z$ with respect to $P(Z|image, is\text{-}handwritten, digit)$ and the likelihood of the original image with respect to $P(image|is\text{-}handwritten, digit, Z)$.

But typically we can't directly sample from or get likelihoods from the distribution $P(Z|image, is\text{-}handwritten, digit)$. So, instead, our guide function attempts to approximate it. The guide represents a *variational distribution*, denoted $Q(Z|X, is\text{-}handwritten, digit)$. A change in the weights of the encoder represents a shifting of the variational distribution. Training will optimize the weights of the encoder such that the variational distribution shifts toward $P(Z|image, is\text{-}handwritten, digit)$. That training approach is called *variational inference*, and it works by minimizing the *Kullback–Leibler divergence* (KL divergence) between the two distributions; KL divergence is a way of quantifying how two distributions differ.

Our variational inference procedure optimizes a quantity called *ELBO*, which means *expected lower bound on the log-likelihood of the data*. Minimizing negative ELBO loss indirectly minimizes reconstruction error and KL divergence between $Q(Z|...)$ and $P(Z|...)$. Pyro implements ELBO in a utility called `Trace_ELBO`.

Our procedure will use *stochastic* variational inference (SVI), which simply means doing variational inference with a training procedure that works with randomly selected subsets of the data, or "batches", rather than the full dataset, which reduces memory use and helps scale to larger data.

---

### Key VAE concepts so far

*Variational autoencoder (VAE)*—A popular framework in deep generative modeling. We're using it to model a causal Markov kernel in our causal model.

*Decoder*—We use the decoder as the model of the causal Markov kernel. It maps the observed causes *is-handwritten* and *digit*, and the latent variable *Z*, to our image outcome variable *X*.

*Encoder*—The encoder maps the *image*, *digit*, and *is-handwritten* to the parameters of a distribution where we can draw samples of *Z*.

*Guide function*—During training, we want values of *Z* that represent an image, given *is-handwritten* and *digit*; i.e., we want to generate *Z*s from *P(Z|image, is-handwritten, digit)*. But we can't sample from this distribution directly. So we write a *guide function* that uses the encoder and convenient canonical distributions like the multivariate normal to sample values of *Z*.

*Variational distribution*—The guide function represents a distribution called *the variational distribution*, denoted *Q(Z|image, is-handwritten, digit)*. During inference, we want to sample from *Q(Z|...)* in a way that is representative of *P(Z|image, is-handwritten, digit)*.

*Variational inference*—This is the training procedure that seeks to maximize the closeness between *Q(Z|...)* and *P(Z|...)* so sampling from *Q(Z|...)* produces samples representative of *P(Z|...)* (e.g., by minimizing KL divergence).

*Stochastic variational inference (SVI)*—Variational inference where training relies on randomly selected subsets of the data, rather than on the full data, in order to make training faster and more scalable.

---

Before we get started, we'll make a helper function for plotting images so we can see how we are doing during training.

**Listing 5.10  Helper function for plotting images**

```
def plot_image(img, title=None):          ◁─┐  Helper function for plotting an image
    fig = plt.figure()
    plt.imshow(img.cpu(), cmap='Greys_r', interpolation='nearest')
    if title is not None:
        plt.title(title)
    plt.show()
```

Next, we'll create a `reconstruct_img` helper function that will *reconstruct* an image, given its labels, where "reconstruct" means encoding the image into a latent representation and then decoding the latent representation back into an image. We can then compare the original image and its reconstruction to see how well the encoder and decoder have been trained. We'll create a `compare_images` function to do that comparison.

**Listing 5.11 Define a helper function for reconstructing and viewing the images**

```python
import matplotlib.pyplot as plt

def reconstruct_img(vae, img, digit, is_hw, use_cuda=USE_CUDA):
    img = img.reshape(-1, 28 * 28)
    digit = F.one_hot(torch.tensor(digit), 10)
    is_hw = torch.tensor(is_hw).unsqueeze(0)
    if use_cuda:
        img = img.cuda()
        digit = digit.cuda()
        is_hw = is_hw.cuda()
    z_loc, z_scale = vae.encoder(img, digit, is_hw)
    z = dist.Normal(z_loc, z_scale).sample()
    img_expectation = vae.decoder(z, digit, is_hw)
    return img_expectation.squeeze().view(28, 28).detach()
```

**Given an input image, this function reconstructs the image by passing it through the encoder and then through the decoder.**

```python
def compare_images(img1, img2):
    fig = plt.figure()
    ax0 = fig.add_subplot(121)
    plt.imshow(img1.cpu(), cmap='Greys_r', interpolation='nearest')
    plt.axis('off')
    plt.title('original')
    ax1 = fig.add_subplot(122)
    plt.imshow(img2.cpu(), cmap='Greys_r', interpolation='nearest')
    plt.axis('off')
    plt.title('reconstruction')
    plt.show()
```

**Plots the two images side by side for comparison**

Next, we'll create some helper functions for handling the data. We'll use `get_random_example` to grab random images from the dataset. The `reshape_data` function will convert an image and its labels into input for the encoder. And we'll use `generate_data` and `generate_coded_data` to simulate an image from the model.

**Listing 5.12 Data processing helper functions for training**

```python
import torch.nn.functional as F

def get_random_example(loader):
    random_idx = np.random.randint(0, len(loader.dataset))
    img, digit, is_handwritten = loader.dataset[random_idx]
    return img.squeeze(), digit, is_handwritten
```

**Choose a random example from the dataset.**

```python
def reshape_data(img, digit, is_handwritten):
    digit = F.one_hot(digit, 10).squeeze()
    img = img.reshape(-1, 28*28)
    return img, digit, is_handwritten
```

**Reshape the data.**

```
def generate_coded_data(vae, use_cuda=USE_CUDA):
    z_loc = torch.zeros(1, vae.z_dim)
    z_scale = torch.ones(1, vae.z_dim)
    z = dist.Normal(z_loc, z_scale).to_event(1).sample()
    p_digit = torch.ones(1, 10)/10
    digit = dist.OneHotCategorical(p_digit).sample()
    p_is_handwritten = torch.ones(1, 1)/2
    is_handwritten = dist.Bernoulli(p_is_handwritten).sample()
    if use_cuda:
        z = z.cuda()
        digit = digit.cuda()
        is_handwritten = is_handwritten.cuda()
    img = vae.decoder(z, digit, is_handwritten)
    return img, digit, is_handwritten

def generate_data(vae, use_cuda=USE_CUDA):
    img, digit, is_handwritten = generate_coded_data(vae, use_cuda)
    img = img.squeeze().view(28, 28).detach()
    digit = torch.argmax(digit, 1)
    is_handwritten = torch.argmax(is_handwritten, 1)
    return img, digit, is_handwritten
```

Generate data that is encoded.

Generate (unencoded) data.

Finally, we can run the training procedure. First, we'll set up stochastic variational inference. We'll first set up an instance of the Adam optimizer, which will handle optimization of the parameters in `training_guide`. Then we'll pass `training_model`, `training_guide`, the optimizer, and the ELBO loss function to the SVI constructor to get an SVI instance.

#### Listing 5.13   Set up the training procedure

```
from pyro.infer import SVI, Trace_ELBO
from pyro.optim import Adam

pyro.clear_param_store()
vae = VAE()
train_loader, test_loader = setup_dataloaders(batch_size=256)
svi_adam = Adam({"lr": 1.0e-3})
model = vae.training_model
guide = vae.training_guide
svi = SVI(model, guide, svi_adam, loss=Trace_ELBO())
```

Clear any values of the parameters in the guide memory.

Initialize the VAE.

Load the data.

Initialize the optimizer.

Initialize the SVI loss calculator. Loss negative "expected lower bound" (ELBO).

When training generative models, it is useful to set up a procedure that uses test data to evaluate how well training is progressing. You can include anything you think is useful to monitor during training. Here, I calculate and print the loss function on the test data, just to make sure the test loss is progressively decreasing along with training loss (a flattening of test loss while training loss continues to decrease would indicate overfitting).

A more direct way of determining how well our model is training is to generate and view images. In my test evaluation procedure, I produce two visualizations. First, I inspect how well it can reconstruct a random image from the test data. I pass the image through the encoder and then through the decoder, creating a "reconstruction" of the image. Then I plot the original and reconstructed images side by side and compare them visually, looking to see that they are close to identical.

Next, I visualize how well it is performing as an overall generative model by generating and plotting an image from scratch. I run this code once each time a certain number of epochs are run.

**Listing 5.14  Setting up a test evaluation procedure**

```
def test_epoch(vae, test_loader):
    epoch_loss_test = 0
    for img, digit, is_hw in test_loader:
        batch_size = img.shape[0]
        if USE_CUDA:
            img = img.cuda()
            digit = digit.cuda()
            is_hw = is_hw.cuda()                              Calculate
        img, digit, is_hw = reshape_data(                    and print
            img, digit, is_hw                                test loss.
        )
        epoch_loss_test += svi.evaluate_loss(
            img, digit, is_hw, batch_size
        )
    test_size = len(test_loader.dataset)
    avg_loss = epoch_loss_test/test_size
    print("Epoch: {} avg. test loss: {}".format(epoch, avg_loss))
    print("Comparing a random test image to its reconstruction:")    Compare a
    random_example = get_random_example(test_loader)                 random test
    img_r, digit_r, is_hw_r = random_example                         image to its
    img_recon = reconstruct_img(vae, img_r, digit_r, is_hw_r)        reconstruction.
    compare_images(img_r, img_recon)
    print("Generate a random image from the model:")
    img_gen, digit_gen, is_hw_gen = generate_data(vae)               Generate a
    plot_image(img_gen, "Generated Image")                           random image
    print("Intended digit: ", int(digit_gen))                       from the model.
    print("Intended as handwritten: ", bool(is_hw_gen == 1))
```

Now we'll run the training. For a single epoch, we'll iteratively get a batch of data from the training data loader and pass it to the step method and run a training step. After a certain number of epochs (a number set by TEST_FREQUENCY), we'll use our helper functions to compare a random image to its reconstruction, as well as simulate an image from scratch and plot it.

**Listing 5.15  Running training and plotting progress**

```
NUM_EPOCHS = 2500
TEST_FREQUENCY = 10

train_loss = []
train_size = len(train_loader.dataset)
```

```
for epoch in range(0, NUM_EPOCHS+1):          ◁─┐ Run the training procedure for
    loss = 0                                       a certain number of epochs.
    for img, digit, is_handwritten in train_loader:
        batch_size = img.shape[0]
        if USE_CUDA:
            img = img.cuda()
            digit = digit.cuda()
            is_handwritten = is_handwritten.cuda()
        img, digit, is_handwritten = reshape_data(
            img, digit, is_handwritten
        )
        loss += svi.step(
            img, digit, is_handwritten, batch_size   Run a training step on
        )                                            one batch in one epoch.
    avg_loss = loss / train_size
    print("Epoch: {} avgs training loss: {}".format(epoch, loss))
    train_loss.append(avg_loss)
    if epoch % TEST_FREQUENCY == 0:    The test data evaluation procedure
        test_epoch(vae, test_loader)   runs every 10 epochs.
```

Again, see www.altdeep.ai/causalAIbook for a link to a Jupyter notebook with the full VAE, encoder/decoder, and training code, including a link for running it in Google Colab.

### 5.2.4 *Evaluating training*

At certain points during training, we randomly choose an image and "reconstruct" it by passing the image through the encoder to get a latent value of $Z$, and passing that value back through the decoder. In one run, the first image I see is a non-handwritten number 6. Figure 5.12 shows this image and its reconstruction.

During training, we also simulate random images from the generative model and plot it. Figure 5.13 shows the first simulated image in one run—in this case, the number 3.

Comparing a random test image to its reconstruction:

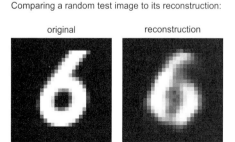

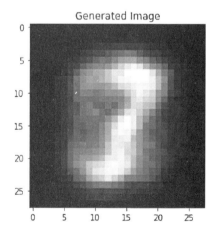

Figure 5.12   The first attempt to reconstruct an image during training shows the model has learned something but still has much progress to make.

Figure 5.13   The first instance of an image generated from the generative model during training

But the model learns quickly. By 130 epochs, we get the results in figure 5.14.

After training is complete, we can see a visualization of loss over training (negative ELBO) in figure 5.15.

The code will train the parameters of the encoder that maps images and the labels to the latent variable. It will also train the decoder that maps the latent variable and the labels to the image. That latent variable is a fundamental feature of the VAE, but we should take a closer look at how to interpret the latent variable in causal terms.

Comparing a random test image to its reconstruction:

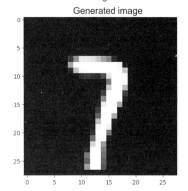

Generate a random image from the model:

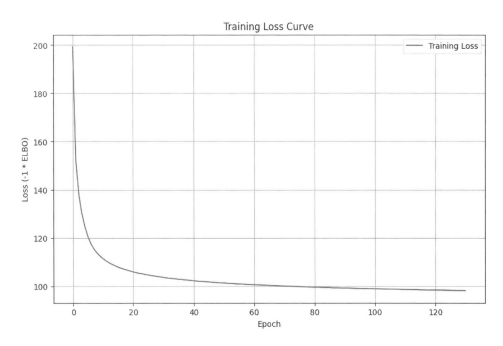

Intended digit: 7
Intended as handwritten: False

**Figure 5.14   Reconstructed and randomly generated images from the model after 130 epochs of training look much better.**

**Figure 5.15   Test loss as training progresses. The *X*-axis is the epoch.**

### 5.2.5   *How should we causally interpret Z?*

I said we can view $Z$ as a "stand-in" for all the independent latent causes of the object in the image. $Z$ is a representation we learn from the pixels in the images. It is tempting to treat that representation like a higher-level causal abstraction of those latent causes, but it is probably not doing a great job as a causal abstraction. The autoencoder paradigm trains an encoder that can take an image and embed it into a low-dimensional representation $Z$. It tries to do so in a way that enables it to reconstruct the original image as well as possible. In order to reconstruct the image with little loss, the framework tries to encode as much information from the original image as it can in that lower dimensional representation.

A good *causal* representation, however, shouldn't try to capture as much information as possible. Rather, it should strive to capture only the *causal* information in the images and ignore everything else. Indeed, the task of "disentangling" the causal and non-causal factors in $Z$ is generally impossible when $Z$ is unsupervised (meaning we lack labels for $Z$). However, domain knowledge, interventions, and semi-supervision can help. See www.altdeep.ai/causalAIbook for references on *causal representation learning* and *disentanglement of causal factors*. As we progress through the book, we'll develop intuition for what the "causal information" in such a representation should look like.

### 5.2.6   *Advantages of this causal interpretation*

There is nothing inherently causal about our VAE's setup and training procedure; it is typical of a vanilla supervised VAE you'd see in many machine learning settings. The only causal element of our approach was our interpretation. We say that the *digit* and *is-handwritten* are causes, and $Z$ is a stand-in for latent causes, and the image is the outcome. Applying the causal Markov property, our causal model factorizes the joint distribution into $P(Z)$, $P(\textit{is-handwritten})$, $P(\textit{digit})$, and $P(\textit{image}|Z, \textit{is-handwritten}, \textit{digit})$, where the latter factor is the causal Markov kernel of the image.

What can we do with this causal interpretation? First, we can use it to improve deep learning and general machine learning workflows and tasks. We'll see an example of this with *semi-supervised learning* in the next section.

---

**Incorporating generative AI in causal models is not limited to VAEs**

I demonstrated how to use a VAE framework to fit a causal Markov kernel entailed by a causal DAG, but a VAE was just one approach to achieving this end. We could have used another deep probabilistic machine learning framework, such as a generative adversarial network (GAN) or a diffusion model.

---

In this section, we incorporated deep learning into a causal graphical model. Next, we investigate how to use causal ideas to enhance deep learning.

## 5.3    Using causal inference to enhance deep learning

We can use causal insights to improve how we set up and train deep learning models. These insights tend to lead to benefits such as improved sample efficiency (i.e., doing more with less data), the ability to do transfer learning (using what a model learned in solving one task to improve performance on another), data fusion (combining different datasets), and enabling more robust predictions.

Much of the work of deep learning is trial and error. For example, when training a VAE or other deep learning models, you typically experiment with different approaches (VAE vs. another framework), architectural choices (latent variable and hidden layer dimension, activation functions, number of layers, etc.), and training approaches (choice of loss function, learning rate, optimizer, etc.) before you get a good result. These experiments cost time, effort, and resources. In some cases, causal modeling can help you make better choices about what might work and what is unlikely to work, leading to cost savings. In this section, we'll look at a particular example of this case in the context of semi-supervised learning.

### 5.3.1    Independence of mechanism as an inductive bias

Suppose we had a DAG with two variables: "cause" $C$ and "outcome" $O$. The DAG is simply $C \rightarrow O$. Our causal Markov kernels are $P(C)$ and $P(O|C)$. Recall the idea of *independence of mechanism* from chapter 3—the causal Markov kernel $P(O|C)$ represents a mechanism of how the cause $C$ drives the outcome $O$. That mechanism is distinct from other mechanisms in the system, such that changes to those mechanisms have no effect on $P(O|C)$. Thus, knowing about $P(O|C)$ tells you nothing about the distribution of the cause $P(C)$ and vice versa. However, knowing something about the distribution of the outcome $P(O)$ might tell you something about the distribution of the cause given the outcome $P(C|O)$, and vice versa.

To illustrate, consider a scenario where $C$ represents sunscreen usage and $O$ indicates whether someone has sunburn. You understand the *mechanism* by which sunscreen protects against sunburn (UV rays, SPF levels, regular application, the perils of sweat and swimming, etc.), and by extension, the chances of getting sunburn given how one uses sunscreen, captured by $P(O|C)$. However, this understanding of the mechanism doesn't provide any information about how *common* sunscreen use is, denoted by $P(C)$.

Now, suppose you're trying to guess whether a sunburned person used sunscreen, i.e., you're mentally modeling $P(C|O)$. In this case, knowing the prevalence of sunburns, $P(O)$, could help. Consider whether the sunburned individual was a case of someone who did use sunscreen but got a sunburn anyway. That case would be more likely if sunburns were a common problem than if sunburns were rare—if sunburns are common, sunscreen use is probably common, but if sunburns were uncommon, people would be less cautious about prevention.

Similarly, suppose $C$ represents study effort and $O$ represents test scores. You know the causal mechanism behind how studying more causes higher test scores, captured by $P(O|C)$. But this doesn't tell you how common it is for students to study hard, captured by $P(C)$. Suppose a student got a low test score, and you are trying to infer whether they studied hard—you are mentally modeling $P(C|O)$. Again, knowing the typical distribution of test scores $P(O)$ can help. If low scores are rare, students might be complacent, and thus more likely not to study hard. You can use that insight as an *inductive bias*—a way to constrain your mental model of $P(C|O)$.

---

### Causal inductive bias

"Inductive bias" refers to the assumptions (explicit or implicit) that lead an inference algorithm to prefer certain inferences or predictions over others. Examples of inductive bias include Occam's Razor and the assumption in forecasting that trends in the past will continue into the future.

Modern deep learning relies on using neural network architectures and training objectives to encode inductive bias. For example, "convolutions" and "max pooling" are architectural elements in convolutional neural networks for computer vision that encode an inductive bias called "translation invariance"; i.e., a kitten is still a kitten regardless of whether it appears on the left or right of an image.

Causal models provide inductive biases in the form of causal assumptions about the DGP (such as a causal DAG). Deep learning can leverage these causal inductive biases to attain better results just as it does with other types of inductive biases. For example, independence of mechanism suggests that knowing $P(O)$ could provide a useful inductive bias in learning $P(C|O)$.

---

Now consider two variables $X$ and $Y$ (which can be vectors) with joint distribution $P(X, Y)$. We want to design an algorithm that solves a task by learning from data observed from $P(X, Y)$. The chain rule of probability tells us that $P(X=x, Y=y) = P(X=x|Y=y)P(Y=y) = P(Y=y|X=x)P(X=x)$. So, from that basic probabilistic perspective, modeling the set $\{P(X|Y), P(Y)\}$ is equivalent to modeling the set $\{P(Y|X), P(X)\}$. But consider the cases where either $X$ is a cause of $Y$ or where $Y$ is a cause of $X$. Under these circumstances, the independence of mechanism gives us an asymmetry between sets $\{P(X|Y), P(Y)\}$ and $\{P(Y|X), P(X)\}$ (specifically, $\{P(Y|X), P(X)\}$ represents the independent mechanism behind $X$'s causal influence on $Y$, and $\{P(X|Y), P(Y)\}$ does not) that we can possibly leverage as an inductive bias in these algorithms. Semi-supervised learning is a good example.

### 5.3.2   *Case study: Semi-supervised learning*

Returning to our TMNIST-MNIST VAE-based causal model, suppose we had, in addition to our original data, a large set of images of digits that were unlabeled (i.e., *digit* and *is-handwritten* are not observed). Our causal interpretation of our model suggests we can leverage this data during training using semi-supervised learning.

Independence of mechanism can help you determine when semi-supervised learning will be effective. In *supervised learning*, the training data consists of $N$ samples of $X$,

*Y* pairs; $(x_1, y_1)$, $(x_2, y_2)$, ..., $(x_N, y_N)$. *X* is the *feature data* used to predict the *labels Y*. The data is "supervised" because every *x* is paired with a *y*. We can use these pairs to learn $P(Y|X)$. In *unsupervised learning*, the data *X* is unsupervised, meaning we have no labels, no observed value of *Y*. Our data looks like $(x_1)$, $(x_2)$, ..., $(x_N)$. With this data alone, we can't directly learn anything about $P(Y|X)$; we can only learn about $P(X)$. Semi-supervised learning asks the question, suppose we had a combination of supervised and unsupervised data. Could these two sets of data be combined in a way such that our ability to predict *Y* was better than if we only used the supervised data? In other words, can learning more about $P(X)$ from the unsupervised data somehow augment our learning of $P(Y|X)$ from the supervised data?

The semi-supervised question is quite practical. It is common to have abundant unsupervised examples if labeling those examples is costly. For example, suppose you worked at a social media site and were tasked with building an algorithm that classified whether an uploaded image depicted gratuitous violence. The first step is to create supervised data by having humans manually label images as gratuitously violent or not. Not only does this cost many people-hours, but it is mentally stressful for the labelers. A successful semi-supervised approach would mean you could minimize the amount of labeling work you need to do.

Our task is to learn a representation of $P(X, Y)$ and use it to predict from $P(Y|X)$. For semi-supervised learning to work, the unlabeled values of *X* must update the representation of $P(X, Y)$ in a way that provides information about $P(Y|X)$. However, independence of mechanism means the task of learning $P(X, Y)$ decomposes into learning distinct representations of the causal Markov kernels, where the parameter vector of each representation is orthogonal to the others. That parameter modularity (see section 3.2) can block flow of parameter updating information from the unlabeled observations of *X* to the learned representation of $P(Y|X)$. To illustrate, let's consider two possibilities, one where *Y* is a cause of *X*, and one where *X* is a cause of *Y*. If *Y* is a cause of *X*, such as in our MNIST-TMNIST example (*Y* is the is-handwritten and digit variables, and *X* is the image), then our learning task decomposes into learning distinct representations of $P(X|Y)$ and P(Y). Unlabeled observations of *X* can give us a better

representation of $P(X)$, we can use to flip $P(X|Y)$ into $P(Y|X)$ by way of Bayes rule. However, when *X* is a cause of *Y*, our learning task decomposes into learning distinct representations of $P(X)$ and $P(Y|X)$. That parameter modularity means those unlabeled values of *X* will help us update $P(X)$'s representation but not that of $P(Y|X)$.

The case where the feature causes the label is sometimes called *causal learning* because the direction of the prediction is from the cause to the effect. *Anti-causal learning* refers to the case when the label causes the feature. The two cases are illustrated in figure 5.16.

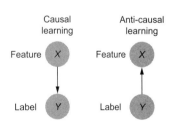

**Figure 5.16  In causal learning, the features cause the label. In anti-causal learning, the label causes the features.**

Independence of mechanism suggests semi-supervised learning can achieve performance gains (relative to a baseline of supervised learning on only the labeled data) only in the anti-causal case. See the chapter notes at www.altdeep.ai/causalAIbook for a more detailed explanation and references. But intuitively, we can see that this mirrors the the sunscreen and sunburn example—knowing the prevalence of sunburns $P(O)$ helped in learning how to guess sunscreen use when you know if someone has a sunburn $P(C|O)$. In this same anti-causal learning case, having only observations from $P(X)$ can still be helpful in learning a good model of $P(Y|X)$. But in the causal learning case, it would be a waste of effort and resources.

In practice, the causal structure between $X$ and $Y$ could be more nuanced and complicated than these simple $X{\rightarrow}Y$ and $X{\leftarrow}Y$ cases. For example, there could be unobserved common causes of $X$ and $Y$. The takeaway here is that when you know something about the causal relationships between the variables in your machine learning problem, you can leverage that knowledge to model more effectively, even if the task is not a causal inference task (e.g., simply predicting $Y$ given $X$). This could help you avoid spending time and resources on an approach that is not likely to work, as in the semi-supervised case. Or it could enable more efficient, robust, or better performing inferences.

### 5.3.3  *Demystifying deep learning with causality*

Our semi-supervised learning example highlights how a causal perspective can explain when we'd expect semi-supervised learning to work and when to fail. In other words, it somewhat *demystifies* semi-supervised learning.

That mystery around the effectiveness of deep learning methods led AI researcher Ali Rahimi to compare modern machine learning to alchemy.

> *Alchemy worked. Alchemists invented metallurgy, ways to dye textiles, modern glassmaking processes, and medications. Then again, alchemists also believed they could cure diseases with leeches and transmute base metals into gold.*

In other words, alchemy works, but alchemists lacked an understanding of the underlying scientific principles that made it work when it did. That *mystery* made it hard to know when it would fail. As a result, alchemists wasted considerable effort on dead ends (philosopher's stones, immortality elixirs, etc.).

---

### Chapter checkpoint

Incorporating deep learning into a causal model:

✓ A causal model of a computer vision problem

✓ Training the deep causal image model

Using causal reasoning to enhance machine learning:

✓ Case study on independence of mechanism and semi-supervised learning

☞ Demystifying deep learning with causality

Similarly, deep learning "works" in that it achieves good performance on a wide variety of prediction and inference tasks. But we often have an incomplete understanding of why and when it works. That *mystery* has led to problems with reproducibility, robustness, and safety. It also leads to irresponsible applications of AI, such as published work that attempts to predict behavior (e.g., criminality) from profile photos. Such efforts are the machine learning analog of the alchemical immortality elixirs that contained toxins like mercury; they don't work *and* they cause harm.

We often hear about the "superhuman" performance of deep learning. Speaking of superhuman ability, imagine an alternative telling of Superman's origin story. Imagine if, when Superman made his first public appearance, his superhuman abilities were unreliable? Suppose he demonstrated astounding superhuman feats like flight, super strength, and laser vision, but sometimes his flight ability failed and his super strength faltered. Sometimes his laser vision was dangerously unfocused, resulting in terrible collateral damage. The public would be impressed and hopeful that he could do some good, but unsure if it would be safe to rely on him when the stakes were high.

Now imagine that his adoptive Midwestern parents, experts in causal inference, used causal analysis to model the *how* and *why* of his powers. Having demystified the mechanisms underlying his superpowers, they were able to engineer a pill that stabilized those powers. The pill wouldn't so much give Superman new powers; it would just make his existing powers more reliable. The work of developing that pill would get fewer headlines than flight and laser vision, but it would be the difference between merely having superpowers and being Superman.

This analogy helps us understand the impact of using causal methods to demystify deep learning and other machine learning methods. Less mystery leads to more robust methods and helps us avoid wasteful or harmful applications.

## *Summary*

- Deep learning can be used to enhance causal modeling and inference. Causal reasoning can enhance the setup, training, and performance of deep learning models.
- Causal models can leverage the ability of deep learning to scale and work with high-dimensional nonlinear relationships.
- You can use generative AI frameworks like the variational autoencoder to build a causal generative model on a DAG just as we did with pgmpy.
- The decoder maps the outcomes of direct parents (the labels of an image) to the outcomes of the child (the image).
- In other words, the decoder gives us a nonlinear high-dimensional representation of the causal Markov kernel for the image.
- The encoder maps the image variable and the causes (labels) back to the latent variable $Z$.
- We can view the learned representation of the latent variable as a stand-in for unmodeled causes, but it still lacks the qualities we'd expect from an ideal

causal representation. Learning latent causal representations is an active area of research.

- Causality often enhances deep learning and other machine learning methods by helping elucidate the underlying principles that make it work. For example, causal analysis shows semi-supervised learning should work in the case of *anti-causal learning* (when the features are *caused by* the label) but not in the case of *causal learning* (when the features cause the label).

- Such causal insights can help the modeler avoid spending time, compute, person-hours, and other resources on a given algorithm when it is not likely to work in a given problem setting.

- Causal insights can demystify elements of building and training deep learning models, such that they become more robust, efficient, and safe.

# Part 3

## The causal hierarchy

Part 3 takes a code-first deep dive into the core concepts of causal inference. Readers will explore structural causal models, interventions, multi-world counterfactual reasoning, and causal identification—where we determine what kinds of causal questions you can answer with your model and your data. This part will prepare you to take on the more challenging but rewarding aspects of causal inference, providing practical code-based tools for reasoning about "what if" scenarios. By the end, you'll be ready to use causal inference techniques in real-world decision-making scenarios, leveraging both generative modeling frameworks and deep learning tools.

# Structural causal models

**This chapter covers**

- Converting a general causal graphical model to a structural causal model
- Mastering the key elements of SCMs
- Implementing SCMs for rule-based systems
- Building an SCM from scratch using additive models
- Combining SCMs with deep learning

In this chapter, I'll introduce a fundamental causal modeling approach called the structural causal model (SCM). An SCM is a special case of a causal generative model that can encode causal assumptions beyond those we can capture with a DAG. If a DAG tells us *what* causes what, an SCM tells us both *what* causes what and *how* the causes affect the effects. We can use that extra "how" information to make better causal inferences.

In this chapter, we'll focus on defining and building an intuition for SCMs using examples in code. In later chapters, we'll see examples of causal inferences that we can't make with a DAG alone but we can make with an SCM.

## 6.1 *From a general causal graphical model to an SCM*

In the causal generative models we've built so far, we defined, for each node, a conditional probability distribution given the node's direct parents, which we called a *causal Markov kernel*. We then *fit* these kernels using data. Specifically, we made a practical choice to use some parametric function class to fit these kernels. For example, we fit the parameters of a probability table using pgmpy's `TabularCPD` because it let us work with pgmpy's convenient d-separation and inference utilities. And we used a neural decoder in a VAE architecture because it solved the problem of modeling a high-dimensional variable like an image. These practical reasons have nothing to do with causality; our causal assumptions stopped at the causal DAG.

Now, with SCMs, we'll use the parametric function class to capture additional causal assumptions beyond the causal DAG. As I said, the SCM lets us represent additional assumptions of *how* causes affect their effects; for example, that a change in the cause always leads to a proportional change in the effect. Indeed, a probability table or a neural network can be *too flexible* to capture assumptions about the "how" of causality; with enough data they can fit anything and thus don't imply strong assumptions. More causal assumptions enable more causal inferences, at the cost of additional risk of modeling error.

SCMs are a special case of causal graphical models (CGMs)—one with more constraints than the CGMs we've built so far. For clarity, I'll use CGM to refer to the broader set of causal graphical models that are not SCMs. To make the distinction clear, let's start by looking at how we might modify a CGM so it satisfies the constraints of an SCM.

### 6.1.1 *Forensics case study*

Imagine you are a forensic scientist working for the police. The police discover decomposed human remains consisting of a skull, pelvic bone, several ribs, and a femur. An apparent blunt force trauma injury to the skull leads the police to open a murder investigation. First, they need you to help identify the victim.

When the remains arrive in your lab, you measure and catalog the bones. From the shape of the pelvis, you can quickly tell that the remains most likely belong to an adult male. You note that the femur is 45 centimeters long. As you might suspect, there is a strong predictive relationship between femur length and an individual's overall height. Moreover, that relationship is causal. Femur length is a cause of height. Simply put, having a long femur makes you taller, and having a short femur makes you shorter.

Indeed, when you consult your forensic text, it says that height is a *linear function* of femur length. It provides the following probabilistic model of height, given femur length (in males):

$$n_y \sim N(0, 3.3)$$
$$y = 25 + 3x + n_y$$

Here, *x* is femur length in centimeters, and *y* is height in centimeters. Of course, exact height will vary with other causal factors, and $n_y$ represents variations in height from those factors. $N_y$ has a normal distribution with mean 0 and scale parameter 3.3 cm.

This is an example of an SCM. We'll expand this example as we go, but the key element to focus on here is that our model is assuming the causal mechanism underpinning height (*Y*) is linear. Height (*Y*) is a linear function of its causes, femur length (*X*) and $N_y$, which represents other causal determinants of height.

Linear modeling is an attractive choice because it is simple, stands on centuries of theory, and is supported by countless statistical and linear algebra software libraries. But from a causal perspective, that's beside the point. Our SCM is not using this linear function because it is convenient. Rather, we are intentionally asserting that the relationship between the cause and the effect is linear—that for a change in femur length, there is a proportional change in height.

Let's drill down on this example to highlight the differences between a CGM and an SCM.

### 6.1.2 Converting to an SCM via reparameterization

In this section, we will start by converting the type of CGM we've become familiar with into an SCM. Our conversion exercise will highlight those properties and make clear the technical structure of the SCM and how it differs relative to the CGMs we've seen so far. Note, however, that this "conversion" is intended to build intuition; in general, you should build your SCM from scratch rather than try to shoehorn non-SCMs into SCMs, for reasons we'll see in section 6.2.

Let's suppose our forensic SCM were a CGM. We might implement it as in figure 6.1.

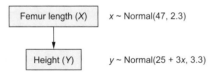

$x \sim \text{Normal}(47, 2.3)$

$y \sim \text{Normal}(25 + 3x, 3.3)$

**Figure 6.1   A simple two-node CGM. Femur length (*X*) is a cause of height (*Y*). *X* has a normal distribution with a mean of 47 centimeters and a standard deviation of 2.3 centimeters. *Y* has a distribution with a mean of 25 + 3x centimeters and a standard deviation of 3.3 centimeters.**

Recall from chapter 2 that $x \sim P(X)$ and $y \sim P(Y|X=x)$ means we generate from the probability distribution of *X* and conditional probability distribution of *Y* given *X*. In this case, $P(X)$, the distribution of femur length, represented as a normal distribution with a mean of 47 centimeters and a standard deviation of 2.3 centimeters. $P(Y|X=x)$ is the distribution on height given the femur length, given as a normal distribution with a mean of 25 + *x* centimeters and a standard deviation of 3.3 centimeters. We would implement this model in Pyro as follows in listing 6.1.

**Setting up your environment**

The code in this chapter was written using Python version 3.10, Pyro version 1.9.0, pgmpy version 0.1.25, and torch 2.3.0. See www.altdeep.ai/causalAIbook for links to the notebooks that run the code. We are also using MATLAB for some plotting; this code was tested with version 3.7.

**Listing 6.1  Pyro pseudocode of the CGM in figure 6.1**

```
from pyro.distributions import Normal
from pyro import sample

def cgm_model():
    x = sample("x", Normal(47., 2.3))        x and y are sampled from their
    y = sample("y", Normal(25. + 3*x, 3.3))  causal Markov kernels, in this
    return x, y                              case normal distributions.
                          ◁
                            Repeatedly calling cgm_model will
                            return samples from P(X, Y).
```

We are going to convert this model to an SCM using the following algorithm:

1  Introduce a new latent causal parent for $X$ called $N_x$ and a new latent causal parent for $Y$ called $N_y$ with distributions $P(N_x)$ and $P(N_y)$.

2  Make $X$ and $Y$ deterministic functions of $N_x$ and $N_y$ such that $P(X, Y)$ in this new model is the same as in the old model.

Following these instructions and adding in two new variables, we get figure 6.2.

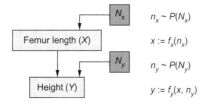

$n_x \sim P(N_x)$

$x := f_x(n_x)$

$n_y \sim P(N_y)$

$y := f_y(x, n_y)$

**Figure 6.2   To convert the CGM to an SCM, we introduce latent "exogenous" parents, $N_x$ for $X$ and $N_y$ for $Y$, and probability distributions $P(N_x)$ and $P(N_y)$ for these latents. We then set $X$ and $Y$ deterministically, given their parents, via functions $f_x$ and $f_y$.**

We have two new latent variables $N_x$ and $N_y$ with distributions $P(N_x)$ and $P(N_y)$. $X$ and $Y$ each have their own functions $f_x$ and $f_y$ that that deterministically set $X$ and $Y$, given their parents in the graph. This difference is key; $X$ and $Y$ are generated in the model described in figure 6.1 but set deterministically in this new model. To emphasize this, I use the assignment operator ":=" instead of the equal sign "=" to emphasize that $f_x$ and $f_y$ assign the values of $X$ and $Y$.

To meet our goal of converting our CGM to an SCM, we want $P(X)$ and $P(Y|X=x)$ to be the same across both models. To achieve this, we have to choose $P(N_x)$, $P(N_y)$, $f_x$, and $f_y$ such that $P(X)$ is still Normal(47, 2.3) and $P(Y|X=x)$ is still Normal(25 + 3.3x, 3.3). One option is to do a simple reparameterization. Linear functions of normally distributed random variables are also normally distributed. We can implement the model in figure 6.3.

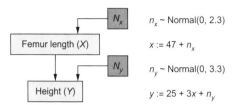

$n_x \sim \text{Normal}(0, 2.3)$

$x := 47 + n_x$

$n_y \sim \text{Normal}(0, 3.3)$

$y := 25 + 3x + n_y$

**Figure 6.3   A simple reparameterization of the original CGM produces a new SCM model with the same $P(X)$ and $P(Y|X)$ as the original.**

In code, we rewrite this as follows.

**Listing 6.2   CGM rewritten as an SCM**

```
from pyro.distributions import Normal
from pyro import sample

def scm_model():
    n_x = sample("n_x", Normal(0., 2.3))
    n_y = sample("n_y", Normal(0., 3.3))
    x = 47. + n_x
    y = 25. + 3.*x + n_y
    return x, y
```

We sample these new latent variables from a standard normal distribution.

X and Y are calculated deterministically as linear transformations of n_x and n_y.

The returned samples of P(X, Y) match the first model.

With this introduction of new exogenous variables $N_x$ and $N_y$, some linear functions $f_x$ and $f_y$, and a reparameterization, we converted the CGM to an SCM that encodes the same distribution $P(X, Y)$. Next, let's look more closely at the elements we introduced.

### 6.1.3   *Formalizing the new model*

To build an SCM, we're going to assume we've already built a causal DAG, as in figure 6.1. In figures 6.2 and 6.3, we see two kinds of variables: exogenous and endogenous. The *endogenous variables* are the original variables $X$ and $Y$—we'll define them as the variables we are modeling explicitly. These are the variables we included in our causal DAG.

The *exogenous variables* (also called *noise* variables) are our new nodes $N_x$ and $N_y$. These variables represent all unmodeled causes of our endogenous variables. In our formulation, we pair each of the endogenous variable with its own exogenous variable parent; $X$ gets new exogenous causal parent $N_x$, and $Y$ gets exogenous parent $N_y$. We add these to our DAG for completeness as in figures 6.2 and 6.3.

In our formulation, we'll assume exogenous variables have no parents and have no edges between one another. In other words, they are root nodes in the graph, and they are independent relative to other exogenous variables. Further, we'll treat the exogenous variables as latent variables.

Each endogenous variable also gets its own *assignment function* (also called a *structural assignment*) $f_x$, and $f_y$. The assignment function *deterministically* sets the value of the endogenous variables $X$ and $Y$ given values of their parents in the causal DAG.

Assignment functions are how we capture assumptions about the "how" of causality. For instance, to say that the causal relationship between height ($Y$) and femur length ($X$) is linear, we specify that $f_x$ is a linear function.

While the endogenous variables are set deterministically, the SCM generates the values of the exogenous variables from probability distributions. In our femur example, we generate values $n_x$ and $n_y$ of exogenous variables $N_x$ and $N_y$ from distributions $P(N_x)$ and $P(N_y)$, which are $N(0, 2.3)$ and $N(0, 3.3)$, as seen in figure 6.3.

---

**Elements of the generative SCM**

- *A set of endogenous variables (e.g., X, Y)*—These are the variables we want to model explicitly. They are the models we build into our causal DAG.
- *A set of exogenous variables (e.g., $N_x$ and $N_y$)*—These variables stand in for unmodeled causes of the endogenous variables. In our formulation, each endogenous variable has one corresponding latent exogenous variable.
- *A set of assignment functions (e.g., $f_x$ and $f_y$)*—Each endogenous variable has an assignment function that sets its value deterministically given its parents (its corresponding exogenous variable and other endogenous variables).
- *A set of exogenous variable probability distributions (e.g., $P(N_x)$ and $P(N_y)$)*—The SCM becomes a generative model with a set of distributions on the exogenous variables. Given values generated from these distributions, the endogenous variables are set deterministically.

---

Let's look at another example of an SCM, this time using discrete variables.

### 6.1.4   *A discrete, imperative example of an SCM*

Our femur example dealt with continuous variables like height and length. Let's now return to our rock-throwing example from chapter 2 and consider a discrete case of an SCM. In this example, either Jenny or Brian or both throw a rock at window if they are inclined to do so. The window breaks depending on whether either or both Jenny and Brian throw and the strength of the windowpane.

How might we convert this model to an SCM? In fact, this model is *already* an SCM. We captured this with the following code.

**Listing 6.3   The rock-throwing example from chapter 2 is an SCM**

```
import pandas as pd
import random

def true_dgp(
    jenny_inclination,
    brian_inclination,
    window_strength):
```

The input values are instances of exogenous variables.

Jenny and Brian throw the rock if so inclined.
jenny_throws_rock and brian_throws_rock
are endogenous variables.

```
jenny_throws_rock = jenny_inclination > 0.5
brian_throws_rock = brian_inclination > 0.5
if jenny_throws_rock and brian_throws_rock:
    strength_of_impact = 0.8
elif jenny_throws_rock or brian_throws_rock:
    strength_of_impact = 0.6
else:
    strength_of_impact = 0.0
window_breaks = window_strength < strength_of_impact
return jenny_throws_rock, brian_throws_rock, window_breaks

generated_outcome = true_dgp(
    jenny_inclination=random.uniform(0, 1),
    brian_inclination=random.uniform(0, 1),
    window_strength=random.uniform(0, 1)
)
```

strength_of_impact is an
endogenous variable. This entire
if-then expression is the assignment
function for strength of impact.

window_breaks is an endogenous
variable. The assignment function is
lambda strength_of_impact,
window_strength:
strength_of_impact >
window_strength.

Each exogenous variable has
a Uniform(0, 1) distribution.

You'll see that it satisfies the requirements of an SCM. The arguments to the `true_dgp` function (namely `jenny_inclination`, `brian_inclination`, `window_strength`) are the exogenous variables. The named variables inside the function are the endogenous variables, which are set deterministically by the exogenous variables.

Most SCMs you'll encounter in papers and textbooks are written down as math. However, this rock-throwing example shows us the power of reasoning causally with an imperative scripting language like Python. Some causal processes are easier to write in code than in math. It is only recently that tools such as Pyro have allowed us to make sophisticated code-based SCMs.

### 6.1.5   *Why use SCMs?*

More causal assumptions mean more ability to make causal inferences. The question of whether to use an SCM instead of a regular CGM is equivalent to asking whether the additional causal assumptions encoded in the functional assignments will serve your causal inference goal.

In our femur example, our DAG says femur length causes height. Our SCM goes further and says that for every unit increase in femur length, there is a proportional increase in height. The question is whether that additional information helps us answer a causal question. One example where such a linear assumption helps make a causal inference is the use of *instrumental variable estimation* of causal effects, which I'll discuss in chapter 11. This approach relies on linearity assumptions to infer causal effects in cases where the assumptions in the DAG alone are not sufficient to make the inference. Another example is where an SCM can enable us to answer *counterfactual queries* using an algorithm discussed in chapter 9.

Of course, if your causal inference is relying on an assumption, and that assumption is incorrect, your inference will probably be incorrect. The "what" assumptions in a DAG are simpler than the additional "how" assumptions in an SCM. An edge in a DAG is a true or false statement that $X$ causes $Y$. An assignment function in an SCM model is a statement about *how* $X$ causes $Y$. The latter assumption is more nuanced and quite hard to validate, so it's easier to get incorrect. Consider the fact that there are longstanding drugs on the market that we know work, but we don't fully understand their mechanism of action—*how* they work.

### 6.1.6   *Differences from related approaches*

SCMs have a rich history across different fields. You may have seen formulations that are similar to but nonetheless different from what we've laid out here. Here, we'll highlight the differentiating elements of this formulation and why they matter to us.

#### GENERATIVE SCMS WITH LATENT EXOGENOUS VARIABLES

We want to use our SCMs as generative models. To that end, we treat exogenous variables (variables we don't want to model explicitly) as latent proxies for unmodeled causes of the endogenous variables. We just need to specify probability distributions of the exogenous variables and we get a generative latent variable model.

#### FLEXIBLE SELECTION OF ASSIGNMENT FUNCTIONS

You'll find that the most common applications of SCMs use linear functions as assignment functions, like we did in the femur example. However, in a generative AI setting, we certainly don't want to constrain ourselves to linear models. We want to work with rich function classes we can write as code, optimize with automatic differentiation, and apply to high-dimensional nonlinear problems, like images. These function classes can do just as well in representing the "how" of causality.

#### CONNECTION TO THE DAG

We contextualize the SCM within the DAG-based view of causality. First, we build a causal DAG as in chapters 3 and 4. Each variable in the DAG becomes an endogenous variable (a variable we want to model explicitly) in the SCM. For each endogenous variable, we add a single latent exogenous parent node to the DAG. Next, we define "assignment function" as a function that assigns a given endogenous variable a value, given the values of its parents in the DAG. All of our DAG-based theory still applies, such as the causal Markov property and independence of mechanism.

Note that not all formulations of the SCM adhere so closely to the DAG. Some practitioners who don't adopt a graphical view of causality still use SCM-like models (e.g., structural equation modeling in econometrics). And some variations of graphical SCMs allow us to relax acyclicity and work with cycles and feedback loops.

#### INDEPENDENT EXOGENOUS VARIABLES

Introducing one exogenous variable for every endogenous variable can be a nuisance; sometimes it is easier to treat a node with no parents in the original DAG as exogenous, or have the same exogenous parent for two endogenous nodes. But this approach lets us add exogenous variables in a way that maintains the d-separations entailed by the original DAG. It also allows us to make a distinction between *endogenous* variables we care to model explicitly, and all the *exogenous* causes we don't want to model explicitly. This comes in handy when, for example, you're building a causal image model like in chapter 5, and you don't want to explicitly represent *all* the many causes of the appearance of an image.

### 6.1.7  *Causal determinism and implications to how we model*

The defining element of the SCM is that endogenous variables are set deterministically by assignment functions instead of probabilistically by drawing randomly from a distribution conditioned on causal parents. This deterministic assignment reflects the philosophical view of *causal determinism,* which argues that if you knew all the causal factors of an outcome, you would know the outcome with complete certainty.

The SCM stands on this philosophical foundation. Consider again our femur-height example, shown in figure 6.4.

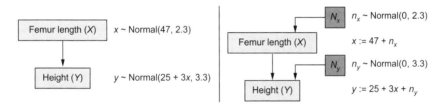

**Figure 6.4   The original CGM samples endogenous variables from causal Markov kernels. The new model sets the endogenous variables deterministically.**

In the original CGM on the left of figure 6.4, we generate values of $X$ and $Y$ from models of their causal Markov kernels. In the corresponding SCM on the right, the endogenous variables are set deterministically, no longer drawn from distributions. The SCM is saying that given femur length and all the other unmodeled causes of height represented by $N_y$, height is a certainty.

Note that despite this deterministic view, the SCM is still a probabilistic model of the joint probability distribution of the endogenous variables $P(X, Y)$. But in comparison to the CGM on the left of figure 6.4, the SCM on the right shunts all the randomness of the model to the exogenous variable distributions. $X$ and $Y$ are still random variables in the SCM, because they are functions of $N_x$ and $N_y$, and a function of a random variable is a random variable. But conditional on the exogenous variables, the endogenous variables are fully determined (*degenerate*).

The causal determinism leads to eye-opening conclusions for us as causal modelers. First, when we apply a DAG-based view of causality to a given problem, we implicitly assume *the ground-truth data generating process* (DGP) is an SCM. We already assumed that the ground-truth DGP had an underlying ground-truth DAG. Going a step further and assuming that each variable in that DAG is set deterministically, given all its causes (both those in and outside the DAG), is equivalent to assuming the ground-truth DGP is an SCM. The SCM might be a black box, or we might not be able to easily write it down in math or code, but it is an SCM nonetheless. That means, whether we're using a traditional CGM or an SCM, we are *modeling a ground-truth SCM*.

Second, it suggests that if we were to generate from the ground-truth SCM, all the random variation in those samples would be *entirely due to exogenous causes*. It would *not be due to an irreducible source of stochasticity* like, for example, Heisenberg's uncertainty principle or butterfly effects. If such concepts drive the outcomes in your modeling domain, CGMs might not be the best choice.

Now that we know we want to model a ground-truth SCM, let's explore why we can't simply learn it from data.

## 6.2   *Equivalence between SCMs*

A key thing to understand about SCMs is that we can't fully learn them from data. To see why, let's revisit the case where we turned a CGM into an SCM. Let's see why, in general, this can't give us the ground-truth SCM.

### 6.2.1   *Reparameterization is not enough*

When we converted the generic CGM to the SCM, we used the fact that a linear transformation of a normally distributed random variable produces a normally distributed random variable. This ensured that the joint probability distribution of the endogenous variables was unchanged.

We could use this "reparameterization trick" (as this technique is called in generative AI) with other distributions. When we apply the reparameterization trick, we are shunting all the uncertainty in those conditional probability distributions to the distributions of the newly introduced exogenous variables. The problem is that different "reparameterization tricks" can lead to different SCMs with different causal assumptions, leading to different causal inferences.

#### REPARAMETERIZATION TRICK FOR A BERNOULLI DISTRIBUTION

As an example, let $X$ represent the choice of a weighted coin and $Y$ represent the outcome of a flip of the chosen coin. $Y$ is 1 if we flip heads and 0 if we flip tails. $X$ takes two values, "coin A" or "coin B". Coin A has a .8 chance of flipping heads, and coin B has a .4 chance of flipping heads, as shown in figure 6.5.

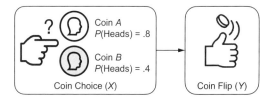

**Figure 6.5   A simple CGM. $X$ is a choice of one of two coins with different weights on heads and tails. $Y$ is the outcome of the coin flip (heads or tails).**

We can simulate an outcome of the flip with a variable $Y$ sampled from a Bernoulli distribution with parameter $p_x$, where $p_x$ is .8 or .4, depending on the value of $x$.

$$y \sim \text{Bernoulli}(p_x)$$

How could we apply the reparameterization trick here to make the outcome $Y$ be the result of a deterministic process?

Imagine that we have a stick that's one meter long (figure 6.6).

**Figure 6.6   To turn the coin flip model into an SCM, first imagine a one meter long stick.**

Imagine using a pocket knife to carve a mark that partitions the stick into two regions: one corresponding to "tails" and one for "heads." We cut the mark at a point that makes the length of each region proportional to the probability of the corresponding outcome; the length of the heads region is $p_x$ meters, and the length of the tails region is $1 - p_x$ meters. For coin $A$, this would be .8 meters (80 centimeters) for the heads region and .2 meters for the tails region (figure 6.7).

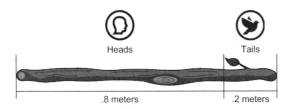

**Figure 6.7   Divide the stick into two regions corresponding to each outcome. The length of the region is proportional to the probability of the outcome.**

After marking the partition, we will now randomly select a point on the stick's length where we will break the stick. The probability that the break will occur in a given region is equal to the probability of that region's associated outcome (figure 6.8). The equality comes from having the length of the region correspond to the probability of the outcome. If the break point is to the left of the partition we cut with our pocket knife, $y$ is assigned 0 ("heads"), and if the break point is to the right, $y$ is assigned 1 ("tails").

To randomly select a point to break the stick, we can generate from a uniform distribution. Suppose we sample .15 from a uniform$(0, 1)$ and thus break the stick at a point .15 meters along its length, as shown in figure 6.8. The .15 falls into the "heads" region, so we return heads. If we repeat this stick-breaking procedure many times, we'll get samples from our target Bernoulli distribution.

In math, we can write this new model as follows:

$$n_y \sim \text{Uniform}(0, 1)$$
$$y := I(n_y \leq p_x)$$

where $p_x$ is .8 if $X$ is coin $A$, or .4 if $X$ is coin $B$. Here, $I(.)$ is the indicator function that returns 1 if $n_y < p_x$ and 0 otherwise.

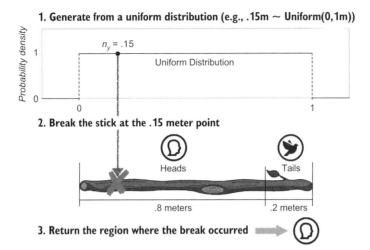

**1. Generate from a uniform distribution (e.g., .15m ~ Uniform(0,1m))**

$n_y = .15$

Uniform Distribution

Probability density

1

0

0

1

**2. Break the stick at the .15 meter point**

Heads

Tails

.8 meters

.2 meters

**3. Return the region where the break occurred**

**Figure 6.8   Generate from a uniform distribution on 0 to 1 meters, break the stick at that point, and return the outcome associated with the region where the break occurred. Repeated generation of uniform variates will cause breaks in the "heads" region 80% of the time, because its length is 80% of the full stick length.**

This new model is technically an SCM, because instead of *Y* being generated from a Bernoulli distribution, it is set deterministically by an indicator "assignment" function. We did a reparameterization that shunted all the randomness to an exogenous variable with a uniform distribution, and that variable is passed to the assignment function.

### DIFFERENT "REPARAMETERIZATION TRICKS" LEAD TO DIFFERENT SCMS

The main reason to use SCM modeling is to have the functional assignments represent causal assumptions beyond those captured by the causal DAG. The problem with the reparameterization trick is that different reparameterization tricks applied to the same CGM will create SCMs with different assignment functions, implying different causal assumptions.

To illustrate, suppose that instead of a coin flip, *Y* was a three-sided die, like we saw in chapter 2 (figure 6.9). *X* determines which die we'll throw; die A or die B (figure 6.10). Each die is weighted differently, so they have different probabilities of rolling a 1, 2, or 3.

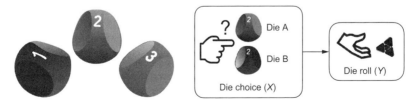

**Figure 6.9   Three-sided dice**

**Figure 6.10   Suppose we switch the model from choosing a coin (two outcomes) to choosing a three-sided die (three outcomes).**

We can extend the original model from a Bernoulli distribution (which is the same as a categorical distribution with two outcomes) to a categorical distribution with three outcomes:

$$y \sim \text{Categorical}([p_{x1}, p_{x2}, p_{x3}])$$

where $p_{x1}$, $p_{x2}$, and $p_{x3}$ are the probabilities of rolling a 1, 2, and 3 respectively (note that one of these is redundant, since $p_{x1} = 1 - p_{x2} - p_{x3}$).

We can use the stick-based reparameterization trick here as well; we just need to extend the stick to have one more region. Suppose for die $A$, the probability of rolling a 1 is $p_{x1}=.1$, rolling a 2 is $p_{x2}=.3$, and rolling a 3 is $p_{x3}=.6$. We'll mark our stick as in figure 6.11.

**Figure 6.11   Divide the stick into three regions corresponding to outcomes of the three-sided die.**

We'll then use the same selection of a remote region using a generated uniform variate as before (figure 6.12).

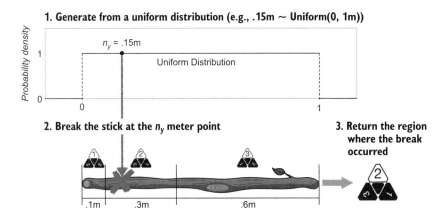

**Figure 6.12   The conversion to the stick-breaking SCM when $Y$ has three outcomes**

In math we'll write this as follows:

$$n_y \sim Uniform\,(0,\ 1)$$

$$y := \begin{cases} 1, & p_{x1} \\ 2, & p_{x1} < n_y \leq p_{x1} + p_{x2} \\ 3, & p_{x1} + p_{x2} < n_y \leq 1 \end{cases}$$

But what if we mark the stick differently, such that we change the ordering of the regions on the stick? In the second stick, the region order is 3, 1, and then 2 (figure 6.13).

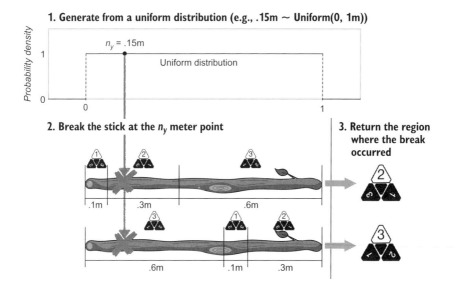

**Figure 6.13   Two different ways of reparameterizing a causal generative model yield two different SCMs. They encode the same joint probability distribution but different endogenous values given the same exogenous value.**

In terms of the probability of each outcome (1, 2, or 3), the two sticks are equivalent—the size of the stick regions assigned to each die-roll outcome are the same on both sticks. But our causal mechanism has changed! These two sticks can return *different* outcomes for a given value of $n_y$. If we randomly draw .15 and thereby break the sticks at the .15 meter point, the first stick will break in region 2, returning a 2, and the second stick will break in region 3, returning a 3.

In math, the second stick-breaking SCM has this form:

$$n_y \sim Uniform\,(0,\ 1)$$

$$y := \begin{cases} 3, & n_y \leq p_{x3} \\ 1, & p_{x3} < n_y \leq p_{x3} + p_{x1} \\ 2, & p_{x3} + p_{x1} < n_y \leq 1 \end{cases}$$

Metaphorically speaking, imagine that in your modeling domain, the sticks are always marked a certain way, with the regions ordered in a certain way. Then there is no guarantee that a simple reparameterization trick will give you the ground-truth marking.

To drive the point home, let's look back at the reparameterization trick we performed to convert our femur-height model to an SCM (figure 6.14).

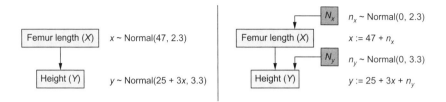

**Figure 6.14   Revisiting the femur-height SCM**

Suppose we create a new SCM that is the same, except that the assignment function for $y$ now looks like this:

$$y := 25 + 3x - n_y$$

Now we have a second SCM that subtracts $n_y$ instead of adding $n_y$. A normal distribution is symmetric around its mean, so since $n_y$ has a normal distribution with mean 0, the probability values of $n_y$ and $-n_y$ are the same, so the probability distribution of $Y$ is the same in both models. But for the same values of $n_y$ and $x$, the actual assigned values of $y$ will be different. Next, we'll examine this idea in formal detail.

### 6.2.2   *Uniqueness and equivalence of SCMs*

Given a causal DAG and a joint probability distribution on endogenous variables, there can generally be multiple SCMs consistent with that DAG and joint probability distribution. This means that we can't rely on data alone to learn the ground-truth SCM. We'll explore this problem of *causal identifiability* in depth in chapter 10. For now, let's break this idea down using concepts we've seen so far.

#### MANY SCMs ARE CONSISTENT WITH A DAG AND CORRESPONDING DISTRIBUTIONS

Recall the many-to-one relationships we outlined in figure 2.24, shown again here in figure 6.15.

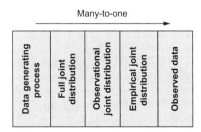

**Figure 6.15   We have many-to-one relationships as we move from the DGP to observed data.**

If we can represent the underlying DGP as a ground-truth SCM, figure 6.15 becomes as shown in figure 6.16.

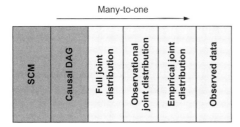

**Figure 6.16    Different SCMs can entail the same DAG structure and distributions. The SCMs can differ in assignment functions (and/or exogenous distributions).**

In other words, given a joint distribution on a set of variables, there can be multiple causal DAGs consistent with that distribution—in chapter 4 we called these DAGs a *Markov equivalence class*. Further, we can have *equivalence classes of SCMs*—given a causal DAG and a joint distribution, there can be multiple SCMs consistent with that DAG and distribution. We saw this with how the two variants of the stick-breaking die-roll SCM are both consistent with the DAG $X$ (die choice) $\rightarrow Y$ (die roll) and with the distributions $P(X)$ (probability distribution on die selection) and $P(Y|X)$ (probability of die roll).

### THE GROUND-TRUTH SCM CAN'T BE LEARNED FROM DATA (WITHOUT CAUSAL ASSUMPTIONS)

When we were working to build a causal DAG in previous chapters, our implied objective was to reproduce the ground-truth causal DAG. Now we seek to reproduce the ground-truth SCM, as in figure 6.16.

In chapter 4, we saw that data cannot distinguish between causal DAGs in an equivalence class of DAGs. Similarly, data alone is not sufficient to recover the ground-truth SCM. Again, consider the stick-breaking SCMs we derived. We derived two marked sticks, with two different orderings of regions. Of course, there are $3 \times 2 \times 1 = 6$ ways of ordering the three outcomes: ({1, 2, 3}, {1, 3, 2}, {2, 1, 3}, {2, 3, 2}, {3, 1, 2}, {3, 2, 1}). That's six ways of marking the stick and thus six different possible SCMs consistent with the distributions $P(X)$ and $P(Y|X)$ (probability of die roll).

Suppose one of these marked sticks was the ground-truth SCM, and it was hidden from us in a black box, as in figure 6.17. Suppose we repeatedly ran the SCM to generate some die rolls. Based on those die rolls, could we figure out how the ground-truth stick was marked? In other words, which of the six orderings was the black box ordering?

**Repeatedly generate $n_y$ from Uniform(0, 1). Each time, break the stick at the $n_y$ meter point.**

**Return die outcomes according to regions where the breaks occurred.**

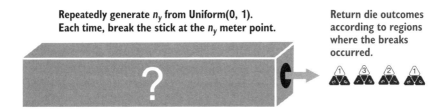

**Figure 6.17    Suppose we didn't know which "marked stick" was generating the observed die rolls. There would be no way of inferring the correct marked stick from the die rolls alone. More generally, SCMs cannot be learned from statistical information in the data alone.**

The answer is no. More generally, because of the many-to-one relationship between SCMs and data, you cannot learn the ground-truth SCM from statistical information in the data alone.

Let that sink in for a second. I'm telling you that even with infinite data, the most cutting-edge deep learning architecture, and a bottomless compute budget, you cannot figure out the true SCM even in this trivial three-outcome stick-breaking example. In terms of statistical likelihood, each SCM is equally likely, given the data. To prefer one SCM to another in the equivalence class, you would need additional assumptions, such as that {1, 2, 3} is the most likely marking because the person marking the stick would probably mark the regions in order. That's a fine assumption to make, as long as you are *aware* you are making it.

In the practice of machine learning, we are often unaware that we are making such assumptions. To illustrate, suppose you ran the following experiment. You created a bunch of stick-breaking SCMs and then simulated data from those SCMs. Then you vectorized the SCMs and used them as labels, and the simulated data as features, in a deep supervised learning training procedure focused on predicting the "true" SCM from simulated data, as illustrated in figure 6.18.

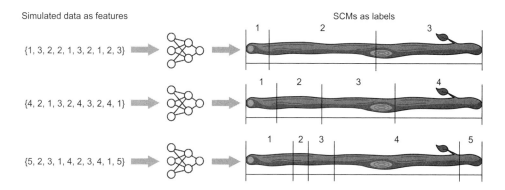

**Figure 6.18** You create many SCMs and simulate data from each of them. You could then do supervised learning of a deep net that predicted the ground-truth SCM from the simulated data. Given two SCMs of the same equivalence class, this approach would favor the SCM with attributes that appeared more often in the training data.

Suppose then you fed the trained model data actual samples of three-sided die rolls, with the goal of predicting the ground-truth SCM. That predictive model's prediction might favor a stick with the {1, 2, 3} ordering over the equivalent {2, 3, 1} ordering. But it would only do so if the {1, 2, 3} ordering was more common in the training data.

### Analogy to program induction

The problem of learning an SCM from data is related to the challenge of program induction in computer science. Suppose a program took "foo" and "bar" as inputs

**(continued)**

and returned "foobar" as the output. What is the program? You might think that the program simply concatenates the inputs. But it could be anything, including one that concatenates the inputs along with the word "aardvark", then deletes the "aardvark" characters, and returns the result. The "data" (many examples of inputs to and outputs of the program) are not enough distinguish which program of all the possible programs is the correct one. For that you need additional assumptions or constraints, such as an Occam's razor type of inductive bias that prefers the simplest program (e.g., the program with the *minimum description length*).

Trying to learn an SCM from data is a special case of this problem. The program's inputs are the exogenous variable values, and the outputs are the endogenous variable values. Suppose you have the causal DAG, just not the assignment functions. The problem is that an infinite number of assignment functions could produce those outputs, given the inputs. Learning an SCM from data requires additional assumptions to constrain the assignment functions, such as constraining the function class and using Occam's razor (e.g., model selection criterion).

Next, we'll dive into implementing an SCM in a discrete rule-based setting.

## 6.3    *Implementing SCMs for rule-based systems*

A particularly useful application for SCMs is modeling rule-based systems. By "rule-based," I mean that known rules, often set by humans, determine the "how" of causality. Games are a good example.

To illustrate, consider the *Monty Hall problem*—a probability-based brain teaser named after the host of a 1960's game show with a similar setup.

### 6.3.1    *Case study: The Monty Hall problem*

A contestant on a game show is asked to choose between three closed doors. Behind one door is a car; behind the others, goats. The player picks the first door. Then the host, who knows what's behind the doors, opens another door, for example the third door, which has a goat. The host then asks the contestant, "Do you want to switch to the second door, or do you want to stay with your original choice?" The question is which is the better strategy, switching doors or staying?

The correct answer is to switch doors. This question appeared in a column in *Parade* magazine in 1990, with the correct answer. Thousands of readers mailed in, including many with graduate-level mathematical training, to refute the answer and say that there is no advantage to switching, that staying or switching have the same probability of winning.

Figure 6.19 illustrates the intuition behind why switching is better. Switching doors is the correct answer because under the standard assumptions, the "switch" strategy has a probability of two-thirds of winning the car, while the "stay" strategy has only a one-third probability. It seems counterintuitive because each door has an equal chance of having the car when the game starts. It seems as if, once the host eliminates one door, each remaining door should have a 50-50 chance. This logic is false, because the host doesn't eliminate a door at random. He only eliminates a door that isn't the player's initial selection *and* that doesn't have the car. A third of the times, those are the same door, and two-thirds of the time they are different doors; that one-third to two-thirds asymmetry is why the remaining doors don't each have a 50-50 chance of having the car.

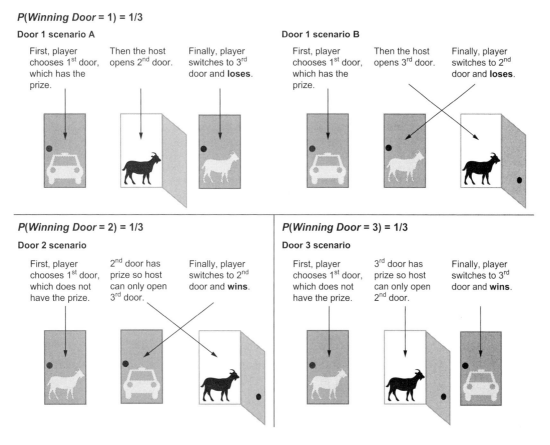

**Figure 6.19   The Monty Hall problem. Each door has an equal probability of concealing a prize. The player chooses a door initially, the host reveals a losing door, and the player has the option to switch their initial choice. Contrary to intuition, the player should switch; if they switch, they will win two out of three times. This illustration assumes door 1 is chosen, but the results are the same regardless of the initial choice of door.**

### 6.3.2   A causal DAG for the Monty Hall problem

Causal modeling makes the Monty Hall problem much more intuitive. We can represent this game with the causal DAG in figure 6.20.

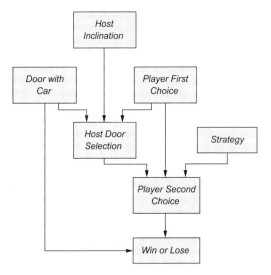

**Figure 6.20   A causal DAG for the Monty Hall problem**

The possible outcomes for each variable are as follows:

- *Door with Car*—Indicates the door that has the car behind it. $1^{st}$ for the first door, $2^{nd}$ for the second door, or $3^{rd}$ for the third door.
- *Player First Choice*—Indicates which door the player chooses first. $1^{st}$ for the first door, $2^{nd}$ for the second door, or $3^{rd}$ for the third door.
- *Host Inclination*—Suppose the host is facing the doors, such that from left to right they are ordered $1^{st}$, $2^{nd}$, and $3^{rd}$. This *Host Inclination* variable has two outcomes, Left and Right. When the outcome is Left, the host is inclined to choose the left-most available door; otherwise the host will be inclined to choose the right-most available door.
- *Host Door Selection*—The outcomes are again $1^{st}$, $2^{nd}$, and $3^{rd}$.
- *Strategy*—The outcomes are Switch if the strategy is to switch doors from the first choice, or Stay if the strategy is to stay with the first choice.
- *Player Second Choice*—Indicates which door the player chooses after being asked by the host whether they want to switch or not. The outcomes again are $1^{st}$, $2^{nd}$, and $3^{rd}$.
- *Win or Lose*—Indicates whether the player wins; the outcomes are Win or Lose. Winning occurs when *Player Second Choice == Door with Car*.

Next, we'll see how to implement this as an SCM in pgmpy.

### 6.3.3   *Implementing Monty Hall as an SCM with pgmpy*

The rules of the game give us clear logic for the assignment functions. For example, we can represent the assignment function for *Host Door Selection* with table 6.1.

**Table 6.1**   A lookup table for *Host Door Selection*, given *Player First Choice, Door with Car,* and *Host Inclination*. It shows which door the host selects, given the player's first choice, which door has the car, and the *Host Inclination*, which refers to whether the host will choose the left-most or right-most door in cases when the host has two doors to choose from.

| Host Inclination | Left | | | | | | | | | Right | | | | | | | | |
|---|---|---|---|---|---|---|---|---|---|---|---|---|---|---|---|---|---|---|
| Door with Car | 1st | | | 2nd | | | 3rd | | | 1st | | | 2nd | | | 3rd | | |
| Player First Choice | 1st | 2nd | 3rd | 1st | 2nd | 3rd | 1st | 2nd | 3rd | 1st | 2nd | 3rd | 1st | 2nd | 3rd | 1st | 2nd | 3rd |
| Host Door Selection | 2nd | 3rd | 2nd | 3rd | 1st | 1st | 2nd | 1st | 1st | 3rd | 3rd | 2nd | 3rd | 3rd | 1st | 2nd | 1st | 2nd |

When the door with the car and the player's first choice are different doors, the host can only choose the remaining door. But if the door with the car and the player's first choice are the same door, the host has two doors to choose from. He will choose the left-most door if *Host Inclination* is Left. For example, if *Door with Car* and *Player First Choice* are both 1st, the host must choose between the 2nd and 3rd doors. He will choose the 2nd door if *Host Inclination* == Left and the 3rd if *Host Inclination* == Right.

This logic would be straightforward to write using if-then logic with a library like Pyro. But since the rules are simple, we can use the far more constrained pgmpy library to write this function as a conditional probability table (table 6.2).

**Table 6.2**   We can convert the *Host Door Selection* lookup table (table 6.1) to a conditional probability table that we can implement as a `TabularCPD` object in pgmpy, where the probability of a given outcome is 0 or 1, and thus, deterministic.

| Host Inclination | | Left | | | | | | | | | Right | | | | | | | | |
|---|---|---|---|---|---|---|---|---|---|---|---|---|---|---|---|---|---|---|---|
| Door with Car | | 1st | | | 2nd | | | 3rd | | | 1st | | | 2nd | | | 3rd | | |
| Player First Choice | | 1st | 2nd | 3rd | 1st | 2nd | 3rd | 1st | 2nd | 3rd | 1st | 2nd | 3rd | 1st | 2nd | 3rd | 1st | 2nd | 3rd |
| Host Door Selection | 1st | 0 | 0 | 0 | 0 | 1 | 1 | 0 | 1 | 1 | 0 | 0 | 0 | 0 | 0 | 1 | 0 | 1 | 0 |
| | 2nd | 1 | 0 | 1 | 0 | 0 | 0 | 1 | 0 | 0 | 0 | 0 | 1 | 0 | 0 | 0 | 1 | 0 | 1 |
| | 3rd | 0 | 1 | 0 | 1 | 0 | 0 | 0 | 0 | 0 | 1 | 1 | 0 | 1 | 1 | 0 | 0 | 0 | 0 |

The entries in the table correspond to the probability of the *Host Door Selection* outcome given the values of the causes. Each probability outcome is either 0 or 1, given the causal parents, so the outcome is completely deterministic given the parents. Therefore, we can use this as our assignment function, and since it is a conditional probability table, we can implement it using the `TabularCPD` class in pgmpy.

**Listing 6.4   Implementation of *Host Door Selection* assignment function in pgmpy**

```python
from pgmpy.factors.discrete.CPD import TabularCPD
f_host_door_selection = TabularCPD(
    variable='Host Door Selection',
    variable_card=3,
    values=[
        [0,0,0,0,1,1,0,1,1,0,0,0,0,0,1,0,1,0],
        [1,0,1,0,0,0,1,0,0,0,0,1,0,0,0,1,0,1],
        [0,1,0,1,0,0,0,0,0,1,1,0,1,1,0,0,0,0]
    ],
    evidence=[
        'Host Inclination',
        'Door with Car',
        'Player First Choice'
    ],
    evidence_card=[2, 3, 3],
    state_names={
        'Host Door Selection':['1st', '2nd', '3rd'],
        'Host Inclination': ['left', 'right'],
        'Door with Car': ['1st', '2nd', '3rd'],
        'Player First Choice': ['1st', '2nd', '3rd']
    }
)
```

The name of the variable

The cardinality (number of outcomes)

The probability table. The values match the value in table 6.2, as long as the ordering of the causal variables in the evidence argument matches the top-down ordering of causal variable names in the table.

The conditioning (causal) variables

The cardinality (number of outcomes) for each conditioning (causal) variable

The state names of each the variables

This code produces `f_host_door_selection`, a `TabularCPD` object we can add to a model of the class `BayesianNetwork`. We can then use this in a CGM as we would a more typical `TabularCPD` object.

Similarly, we can create a look-up table for *Player Second Choice*, as shown in table 6.3.

**Table 6.3   A lookup table for *Player Second Choice*, conditional on *Player First Choice*, *Host Door Selection*, and *Strategy*. *Player Second Choice* cells are empty in the impossible cases where *Player First Choice* and *Host Door Selection* are the same.**

| Strategy | Stay | | | | | | | | | Switch | | | | | | | | |
|---|---|---|---|---|---|---|---|---|---|---|---|---|---|---|---|---|---|---|
| Host Door Selection | 1st | | | 2nd | | | 3rd | | | 1st | | | 2nd | | | 3rd | | |
| Player First Choice | 1st | 2nd | 3rd | 1st | 2nd | 3rd | 1st | 2nd | 3rd | 1st | 2nd | 3rd | 1st | 2nd | 3rd | 1st | 2nd | 3rd |
| Player Second Choice | | 2nd | 3rd | 1st | | 3rd | 1st | 2nd | | | 3rd | 2nd | 3rd | | 1st | 2nd | 1st | |

The host will never choose the same door as the player's first choice, so *Host Door Selection* and *Player First Choice* can never have the same value. The entries of *Player Second Choice* are not defined in these cases.

Expanding this to a conditional probability table gives us table 6.4. Again, the cells with impossible outcomes are left blank.

**Table 6.4** The result of converting the lookup table for *Player Second Choice* (table 6.3) to a conditional probability table that we can implement as a `TabularCPD` object

| Strategy | | Stay | | | | | | | | | Switch | | | | | | | | |
|---|---|---|---|---|---|---|---|---|---|---|---|---|---|---|---|---|---|---|---|
| Host Door Selection | | 1st | | | 2nd | | | 3rd | | | 1st | | | 2nd | | | 3rd | | |
| Player First Choice | | 1st | 2nd | 3rd | 1st | 2nd | 3rd | 1st | 2nd | 3rd | 1st | 2nd | 3rd | 1st | 2nd | 3rd | 1st | 2nd | 3rd |
| Player Second Choice | 1st | | 0 | 0 | 1 | | 0 | 1 | 0 | | | 0 | 0 | 0 | | 1 | 0 | 1 | |
| | 2nd | | 1 | 0 | 0 | | 0 | 0 | 1 | | | 0 | 1 | 0 | | 0 | 1 | 0 | |
| | 3rd | | 0 | 1 | 0 | | 1 | 0 | 0 | | | 1 | 0 | 1 | | 0 | 0 | 0 | |

Unfortunately, we can't leave the impossible values blank when we specify a `Tabular-CPD`, so in the following code, we'll need to assign arbitrary values to these elements.

**Listing 6.5 Implementation of *Player Second Choice* assignment function in pgmpy**

```python
from pgmpy.factors.discrete.CPD import TabularCPD
f_second_choice = TabularCPD(
    variable='Player Second Choice',
    variable_card=3,
    values=[
        [1,0,0,1,0,0,1,0,0,0,0,0,0,1,0,1,0],
        [0,1,0,0,1,0,0,1,0,1,0,1,0,1,0,1,0,1],
        [0,0,1,0,0,1,0,0,1,0,1,0,1,0,0,0,0,0]
    ],
    evidence=[
        'Strategy',
        'Host Door Selection',
        'Player First Choice'
    ],
    evidence_card=[2, 3, 3],
    state_names={
        'Player Second Choice': ['1st', '2nd', '3rd'],
        'Strategy': ['stay', 'switch'],
        'Host Door Selection': ['1st', '2nd', '3rd'],
        'Player First Choice': ['1st', '2nd', '3rd']
    }
)
```

> The probability values are 0 or 1, so the assignment function is deterministic. In cases where the parent combinations are impossible, we still have to assign a value.

That gives us a second `TabularCPD` object. We'll create one for each node.

First, let's set up the causal DAG.

**Listing 6.6 Implementing the full Monty Hall SCM**

```python
from pgmpy.models import BayesianNetwork
from pgmpy.factors.discrete.CPD import TabularCPD
```

```
monty_hall_model = BayesianNetwork([
    ('Host Inclination', 'Host Door Selection'),
    ('Door with Car', 'Host Door Selection'),
    ('Player First Choice', 'Host Door Selection'),
    ('Player First Choice', 'Player Second Choice'),
    ('Host Door Selection', 'Player Second Choice'),
    ('Strategy', 'Player Second Choice'),
    ('Player Second Choice', 'Win or Lose'),
    ('Door with Car', 'Win or Lose')
])
```

**Build the causal DAG.**

`monty_hall_model` is now a causal DAG. It will become an SCM after we add the exogenous variable distributions and assignment functions.

The following listing adds the exogenous variable distribution.

**Listing 6.7   Create the exogenous variable distributions**

**A CPD for the Host Inclination variable. In cases when the player chooses the door with the car, the host has a choice between the two other doors. This variable is "left" when the host is inclined to choose the left-most door, and "right" if the host is inclined to choose the right-most door.**

```
p_host_inclination = TabularCPD(
    variable='Host Inclination',
    variable_card=2,
    values=[[.5], [.5]],
    state_names={'Host Inclination': ['left', 'right']}
)
```

```
p_door_with_car = TabularCPD(
    variable='Door with Car',
    variable_card=3,
    values=[[1/3], [1/3], [1/3]],
    state_names={'Door with Car': ['1st', '2nd', '3rd']}
)
```

**A CPD for the variable representing which door has the prize car. Assume each door has an equal probability of having the car.**

```
p_player_first_choice = TabularCPD(
    variable='Player First Choice',
    variable_card=3,
    values=[[1/3], [1/3], [1/3]],
    state_names={'Player First Choice': ['1st', '2nd', '3rd']}
)
```

**A CPD for the variable representing the player's first door choice. Each door has an equal probability of being chosen.**

```
p_host_strategy = TabularCPD(
    variable='Strategy',
    variable_card=2,
    values=[[.5], [.5]],
    state_names={'Strategy': ['stay', 'switch']}
)
```

**A CPD for the variable representing the player's strategy. "Stay" is the strategy of staying with the first choice, and "switch" is the strategy of switching doors.**

Having created the exogenous distributions, we'll now create the assignment functions. We've already created `f_host_door_selection` and `f_second_choice`, so we'll add `f_win_or_lose`—the assignment function determining whether the player wins or loses.

### Listing 6.8  Create the assignment functions

```
f_win_or_lose = TabularCPD(
    variable='Win or Lose',
    variable_card=2,
    values=[
        [1,0,0,0,1,0,0,0,1],
        [0,1,1,1,0,1,1,1,0],
    ],
    evidence=['Player Second Choice', 'Door with Car'],
    evidence_card=[3, 3],
    state_names={
        'Win or Lose': ['win', 'lose'],
        'Player Second Choice': ['1st', '2nd', '3rd'],
        'Door with Car': ['1st', '2nd', '3rd']
    }
)
```

Finally, we'll add the exogenous distribution and the assignment functions to `monty_hall_model` and create the SCM.

### Listing 6.9  Create the SCM for the Monty Hall problem

```
monty_hall_model.add_cpds(
    p_host_inclination,
    p_door_with_car,
    p_player_first_choice,
    p_host_strategy,
    f_host_door_selection,
    f_second_choice,
    f_win_or_lose
)
```

We can run the variable elimination inference algorithm to verify the results of the algorithm. Let's query the probability of winning, given that the player takes the "stay" strategy.

### Listing 6.10  Inferring the winning strategy

We'll use the inference algorithm called "variable elimination."

Print the probabilities of winning and losing when the player uses the "stay" strategy.

```
from pgmpy.inference import VariableElimination   ◁─┘

infer = VariableElimination(monty_hall_model)
q1 = infer.query(['Win or Lose'], evidence={'Strategy': 'stay'})
print(q1)
q2 = infer.query(['Win or Lose'], evidence={'Strategy': 'switch'})
print(q2)
q3 = infer.query(['Strategy'], evidence={'Win or Lose': 'win'})
print(q3)
```

Print the probabilities that the player used a stay strategy versus a switch strategy, given that the player won.

Print the probabilities of winning and losing when the player uses the "switch" strategy.

This inference produces the following output:

```
+-------------------+--------------------+
| Win or Lose       |  phi(Win or Lose)  |
+===================+====================+
| Win or Lose(win)  |             0.3333 |
+-------------------+--------------------+
| Win or Lose(lose) |             0.6667 |
+-------------------+--------------------+
```

The probability of winning and losing under the "stay" strategy is $1/3$ and $2/3$, respectively. In contrast, here's the output for the "switch" strategy:

```
+-------------------+--------------------+
| Win or Lose       |  phi(Win or Lose)  |
+===================+====================+
| Win or Lose(win)  |             0.6667 |
+-------------------+--------------------+
| Win or Lose(lose) |             0.3333 |
+-------------------+--------------------+
```

The probability of winning and losing under the "switch" strategy is $2/3$ and $1/3$, respectively. We can also condition on a winning outcome and infer the probability that each strategy leads to that outcome.

```
+-----------------+-----------------+
| Strategy        |  phi(Strategy)  |
+=================+=================+
| Strategy(stay)  |          0.3333 |
+-----------------+-----------------+
| Strategy(switch)|          0.6667 |
+-----------------+-----------------+
```

These are plain vanilla non-causal probabilistic inferences—we were just validating that our SCM is capable of produce these inferences. In chapter 9, we'll demonstrate how this SCM enables causal *counterfactual* inferences that simpler models can't answer, such as "What would have happened had the losing player used a different strategy?"

### 6.3.4 *Exogenous variables in the rule-based system*

In this Monty Hall SCM, the root nodes (nodes with no incoming edges) in the causal DAG function as the exogenous variables. This is slightly different from our formal definition of an SCM, which states that exogenous variables represent causal factors outside the system. *Host Inclination* meets that definition, as this was not part of the original description. *Door with Car*, *Player First Choice*, and *Strategy* are another matter. To remedy this, we could introduce exogenous parents to these variables, and set these variables deterministically, given these parents, as we do elsewhere in this chapter. But while modeling this in pgmpy, that's a bit redundant.

### 6.3.5 *Applications of SCM-modeling of rule-based systems*

While the Monty Hall game is simple, do not underestimate the expressive power of incorporating rules into assignment functions. Some of the biggest achievements in

AI in previous decades have been at beating expert humans in board games with simple rules. Simulation software, often based on simple rules for how a system transitions from one state to another, can model highly complex behavior. Often, we want to apply causal analysis to rule-based systems engineered by humans (who know and can rewrite those rules), such as an automated manufacturing system.

## 6.4 Training an SCM on data

Given a DAG, we make a choice of whether to use a CGM or an SCM. Let's suppose we want to go with the SCM, and we want to "fit" or "train" this SCM on data. To do this, we choose some *parameterized function class* (e.g., linear functions, logistic functions, etc.) for each assignment function. That function class becomes a specific function once we've fit its parameters on data. Similarly, for each exogenous variable, we want to specify a canonical probability distribution, possibly with parameters we can fit on data.

In our femur-height example, all the assignment functions were linear functions and the exogenous variables were normal distributions. But with tools like Pyro, you can specify each assignment function and exogenous distribution one by one. Then you can train the parameters just as you would with a CGM. For example, instead of taking this femur-height model from the forensic textbook:

$$n_y \sim N(0, 3.3)$$
$$y = 25 + 3x + n_y$$

you can just fit the parameters $\alpha$, $\beta$, and $\delta$ of a linear model on actual forensic data:

$$n_y \sim N(0, \delta)$$
$$y = \alpha + \beta x + n_y$$

In this forensics example, we use a linear assignment function because height is proportional to femur length. Let's consider other ways to capture how causes influence their effects.

### 6.4.1 What assignment functions should I choose?

The most important choice in an SCM model is your choice of *function classes* for the assignment functions, because these choices represent your assumptions about the "how" of causality. You can use function classes common in math, such as linear models. You can also use code (complete with if-then statements, loops, recursion, etc.) like we did with the rock-throwing example.

Remember, you are modeling a ground-truth SCM. You are probably going to specify your assignment functions differently from those in the ground-truth SCM, but that's fine. You don't need your SCM to match the ground truth exactly; you just need your model to be right about the "how" assumptions it is relying on for your causal inferences.

> ### SCMs without "how" assumptions are just CGMs
>
> Suppose you built an SCM where every assignment function is a linear function. You are using a linear Gaussian assumption because your library of choice requires it (e.g., `LinearGaussianCPD` is pretty much your only choice for modeling continuous variables in pgmpy). However, you are not planning on relying on that linear assumption for your causal inference. In this case, while your model checks the boxes of an SCM, it is effectively a CGM with linear models of the causal Markov kernels.

Suppose, for example, that instead of a linear relationship between $X$ and $Y$, $X$ and $Y$ followed a nonlinear S-curve, and your causal inference was sensitive to this S-curve. Imagine that the ground-truth SCM captured this with an assignment function in the form of the Hill equation (a function that arises in biochemistry and that can capture S-curves). But your SCM instead uses a logistic function fit on data. Your model, though wrong, will be sufficient to make a good causal inference if your logistic assignment function captured everything it needed to about the S-curve for your inference to work.

### 6.4.2    *How should I model the exogenous variable distributions?*

In section 6.1.3, we formulated our generative SCM in a particular way, where every node gets its own exogenous variable representing its unmodeled causes. Under that formulation, the role of the exogenous variable distribution is simply to provide sufficient variation for the SCM to model the joint distribution. This means that, assuming you have selected your assignment function classes, you can choose canonical distributions for the exogenous variables based on how well they would fit the data after parameter estimation. Some canonical distributions may fit better than others. You can contrast different choices using standard techniques for model comparison and cross-validation.

These canonical distributions can be parameterized, such as $N(0, \delta)$ in

$$n_y \sim N(0, \delta)$$
$$y = \alpha + \beta x + n_y$$

A more common approach in generative AI is to use constants in the canonical distribution and only train the parameters of the assignment function:

$$n_y \sim N(0, 1)$$
$$y = \alpha + \beta x + \delta n_y$$

Either is fine, as long as your choice captures your "how" assumptions.

### 6.4.3    *Additive models: A popular choice for SCM modeling*

Additive models are SCM templates that use popular trainable function classes for assignment functions. They can be a great place to start in SCM modeling. We'll look at three common types of additive models: linear Gaussian additive model (LiGAM), linear non-Gaussian additive model (LiNGAM), and the nonlinear additive noise model (ANM). These models each encapsulate a pair of constraints: one on the structure of the assignment functions, and one on the distribution of the additive exogenous variables.

Additivity makes this approach easier because there are typically unique solutions to algorithms that learn the parameters of these additive models from data. In some cases, those parameters have a direct causal interpretation. There are also myriad software libraries for training additive models on data.

Let's demonstrate the usefulness of additive models with an example. Suppose you were a biochemist studying the synthesis of a certain protein in a biological sample. The sample has some amount of an enzyme that reacts with some precursors in the sample and synthesizes the protein you are interested in. You measure the quantity of the protein you're interested in. Let $X$ be the amount of enzyme, and let $Y$ be the measured amount of the protein of interest. We'll model this system with an SCM, which has the DAG in figure 6.21.

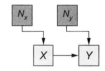

We have qualitative knowledge of how causes affect effects, but we have to turn that knowledge into explicit choices of function classes for assignment functions and exogenous variable distributions. Additive models are a good place to start.

**Figure 6.21   The amount of enzyme ($X$) is a cause the measured quantity of protein ($Y$).**

To illustrate, we'll focus on the assignment function and exogenous variable distribution for $Y$, the amount of the target protein in our example. Generating from the exogenous variable, and setting $Y$ via the assignment function, has the following notation:

$$n_y \sim P(N_y)$$
$$y := f_y(x, n_y)$$

$f_y(.)$ denotes the assignment function for $y$, which takes a value of the endogenous parent $X$ and exogenous parent $N_y$ as inputs.

In an *additive* assignment function, the exogenous variable is always added to some function of endogenous parents. In our example, this means that the assignment function for $Y$ has the following form:

$$y := f_y(x, n_y) = g(x) + n_y$$

Here, $g(.)$ is some trainable function of the endogenous parent(s), and $n_y$ is added to the results of that function.

For our protein $Y$, these models say that the measured amount of protein $Y$ is equal to some function of the enzyme amount $g(X)$ plus some exogenous factors, such as noise in the measurement device. This assumption is attractive, because it lets us think of unmodeled exogenous causes as additive "noise." In terms of statistical signal processing, it is relatively easy to disentangle some core signal (e.g., $g(x)$) from additive noise.

In general, let $V$ represent an endogenous variable in the model, $V_{PA}$ represent the endogenous parents of $V$, and $N_v$ represent an exogenous variable.

$$v := f_v(V_{PA}, n_v) = g(V_{PA}) + n_v$$

Additive SCMs have several benefits, but here we'll focus on their benefit as a template for building SCMs. We'll start with the simplest additive model, the linear Gaussian additive model.

### 6.4.4  *Linear Gaussian additive model*

In a linear Gaussian additive model, the assignment functions are linear functions of the parents, and the exogenous variables have a normal distribution.

In our enzyme example, $N_y$ and $Y$ are given as follows:

$$n_y \sim N(0, \sigma_y)$$
$$y := \beta_0 + \beta_x x + n_y$$

Here, $\beta_0$ is an intercept term, and $\beta_x$ is a coefficient for $X$. We are assuming that for every unit increase in the amount of enzyme $X$, there is a $\beta_x$ increase in the expected amount of the measured protein. $N_y$ accounts for variation around that expected amount due to exogenous causal factors, and we assume it has a normal distribution with a mean of 0 and scale parameter $\sigma_y$. For example, we might assume that $N_y$ is composed mostly of technical noise from the measurement device, such as dust particles that interfere with the sensors. We might know from experience with this device that this noise has a normal distribution.

In general, for variable $V$ with a set of $K$ parents, $V_{PA} = \{V_{pa,1}, \ldots, V_{pa,K}\}$:

$$n_y \sim N(0, \sigma y)$$
$$v := \beta_0 + \sum_j \beta_x v_{pa,j} + n_y$$

This model defines parameters: $\beta_0$ is an intercept term, $\beta_j$ is the coefficient attached to the $j^{\text{th}}$ parent, and $\sigma_v$ is the scale parameter of $N_v$'s normal distribution.

Let's see an example of a LiNGAM model in Pyro.

**Listing 6.11  Pyro example of a linear Gaussian model**

```
from pyro import sample
from pyro.distributions import Normal

def linear_gaussian():
    n_x = sample("N_x", Normal(9., 3.))
    n_y = sample("N_y", Normal(9., 3.))
```

```
x = 10. + n_x
y = 2. * x + n_y
return x, y
```

The functional
assignments are linear.

The distributions of the exogenous
variables are normal (Gaussian).

Linear Gaussian SCMs are especially popular in econometric methods used in the social sciences because the model assumptions have many attractive statistical properties. Further, in linear models, we can interpret a parent causal regressor variable's coefficient as the causal effect (average treatment effect) of that parent on the effect (response) variable.

### 6.4.5 Linear non-Gaussian additive models

Linear non-Gaussian additive models (LiNGAM) are useful when the Gaussian assumption on exogenous variables is not appropriate. In our example, the amount of protein $Y$ cannot be negative, but that can easily occur in a linear model if $\beta_0$, $x$, or $n_x$ have low values. LiNGAM models remedy this by allowing the exogenous variable to have a non-normal distribution.

**Listing 6.12  Pyro example of a LiNGAM model**

```
from pyro import sample
from pyro.distributions import Gamma

def LiNGAM():
    n_x = sample("N_x", Gamma(9., 1.))
    n_y = sample("N_y", Gamma(9., 1.))
    x = 10. + n_x
    y = 2. * x + n_y
    return x, y
```

Instead of a normal (Gaussian)
distribution, the exogenous variables
have a gamma distribution with the
same mean and variance.

These are the same
assignment functions as in
the linear Gaussian model.

In the preceding model, we use a gamma distribution. The lowest possible value in a gamma distribution is 0, so $y$ cannot be negative.

### 6.4.6 Nonlinear additive noise models

As I've mentioned, the power of the SCM is the ability to choose functional assignments that reflect *how* causes affect their direct effects. In our hypothetical example, you are a biochemist. Could you import knowledge from biochemistry to design the assignment function? Here is what that reasoning might look like. (You don't need to understand the biology or the math, in this example, just the logic).

There is a common mathematical assumption in enzyme modeling called *mass action kinetics*. In this model, $T$ is the maximum possible amount of the target protein. The biochemical reactions happen in real time, and during that time, the amount of the target protein fluctuates before stabilizing at some equilibrium value $Y$. Let $Y(t)$ and $X(t)$ be the amount of the target protein and enzyme at a given time point. Mass action kinetics give us the following ordinary differential equation:

$$\frac{dY(t)}{d(t)} = \nu X(t)(T - Y(t)) - \alpha Y(t)$$

Here, $v$ and $\alpha$ are *rate parameters* that characterize the rates at which different biochemical reactions occur in time. This differential equation has the following equilibrium solution,

$$Y = T \times \frac{\beta X}{1 + \beta X}$$

where $Y$ and $X$ are equilibrium values of $Y(t)$ and $X(t)$, and $\beta = v/\alpha$.

As an enzyme biologist, you know that this equation captures something of the actual mechanism underpinning the biochemistry of this system, like physics equations such as Ohm's law and SIR models in epidemiology. You elect to use this as your assignment function for $Y$:

$$Y := T \times \frac{\beta X}{1 + \beta X} + N_y$$

This is a nonlinear additive noise model (ANM). In general, ANMs have the following structure:

$$V = g(V_{pa}) + N_v$$

In our example $g(X) = T \times \beta X / (1 + \beta X)$. $N_y$ can be normal (Gaussian) or non-Gaussian.

> ### Connecting dynamic modeling and simulation to SCMs
>
> Dynamic models describe how a system's behavior evolves in time. The use of dynamic modeling, as you saw in the enzyme modeling example, is one approach to addressing this knowledge elicitation problem for SCMs.
>
> In this section, I illustrated how an enzyme biologist could use a domain-specific dynamic model, specifically an ODE, to construct an SCM. An ODE is just one type of dynamic model. Another example is computer simulator models, such as the simulators used in climate modeling, power-grid modeling, and manufacturing. Simulators can also model complex social processes, such as financial markets and epidemics. Simulator software is a growing multibillion dollar market.
>
> In simulators and other dynamic models, specifying the "how" of causality can be easier than in SCMs. SCMs require assignment functions to explicitly capture the global behavior of the system. Dynamic models only require you to specify the rules for how things change from instant to instant. You can then see global behavior by running the simulation. The trade-off is that dynamic models can be computationally expensive to run, and it is generally difficult to train parameters of dynamic models on data or perform inferences given data as evidence. This has motivated interesting research in combining the knowledge elicitation convenience of dynamic models with the statistical and computational conveniences of SCMs.

Next, we'll examine using regression tools to train these additive models.

### 6.4.7   *Training additive model SCMs with regression tools*

In statistics, regression modeling finds parameter values that minimize the difference between a parameterized function of a set of predictors and a response variable. Regression modeling libraries are ubiquitous, and one advantage of additive SCM models is that they can use those libraries to fit an SCM's parameters on data. For example, parameters of additive models can be fit with standard linear and nonlinear regression parameter fitting techniques (e.g., generalized least squares). We can also leverage these tools' regression goodness-of-fit statistics to evaluate how well the model explains the data.

Note that the predictors in a general regression model can be anything you like. Most regression modeling pedagogy encourages you to keep adding predictors that increase goodness-of-fit (e.g., adjusted R-squared) or reduce predictive error. But in an SCM, your predictors are limited to direct endogenous causes.

---

### Can I use generalized linear models as SCMs?

In statistical modeling, a generalized linear model (GLM) is a flexible generalization of linear regression. In a GLM, the response variable is related to a linear function of the predictors with a *link function*. Further, variance of the response variable can be a function of the predictors. Examples include logistic regression, Poisson regression, and gamma regression. GLMs are a fundamental statistical toolset for data scientists.

In a CGM (non-SCM), GLMs are good choices as models of causal Markov kernels. But a common question is whether GLMs can be used as assignment functions in an SCM.

Several GLMs align with the structure of additive SCMs, but it's generally best not to think of GLMs as templates for SCMs. The functional form of assignment functions in an SCM is meant to reflect the nature of the causal relationship between a variable and its causal parents. The functional form of a GLM applies a (in some cases nonlinear) link function to a linear function of the predictors. The link function is designed to map that linear function of the predictors to the mean of a canonical distribution (e.g., normal, Poisson, gamma). It is not designed to reflect causal assumptions.

---

### 6.4.8   *Beyond the additive model*

If the "how" of an assignment function requires more nuance than you can capture with an additive model, don't constrain yourself to an additive model. Using biochemistry as an example, it is not hard to come up with scenarios where interactions between endogenous and exogenous causes would motivate a multiplicative model.

For these more complex scenarios, it starts making sense to move toward using probabilistic deep learning tools to implement an SCM.

## 6.5    *Combining SCMs with deep learning*

Let's revisit the enzyme kinetic model, where the amount of an enzyme $X$ is a cause of the amount of a target protein $Y$, as in figure 6.22.

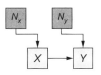

**Figure 6.22    The amount of enzyme ($X$) is a cause of the measured quantity of protein ($Y$).**

I said previously that, based on a dynamic mathematical model popular in the study of enzyme biology, a good candidate for an additive assignment function for $Y$ is

$$Y := T \times \frac{\beta X}{1 + \beta X} + N_y$$

Further, suppose that we knew from experiments that $T$ was 100 and $\beta$ was .08.

Ideally, we would want to be able to reproduce these parameter values from data. Better yet, we should like to leverage the automatic differentiation-based frameworks that power modern deep learning.

### 6.5.1    *Implementing and training an SCM with basic PyTorch*

First, let's create a PyTorch version of the enzyme model.

**Listing 6.13    Implement the PyTorch enzyme model**

```
from torch import nn

class EnzymeModel(nn.Module):          ◁─── Create the
    def __init__(self):                     enzyme model.
        super().__init__()
        self.β = nn.Parameter(torch.randn(1, 1))    ◁─── Initialize the
                                                         parameter β.

    def forward(self, x):                   Calculate the product of
        x = torch.mul(x, self.β)       ◁─── enzyme amount X and β.
        x = x.log().sigmoid()          ◁───
        x = torch.mul(x, 100.)    ◁──┐            Implement the function
        return x                     │ Multiply by │ u / (u + 1) as sigmoid(log(u)), since
                                     │ T = 100.    │ the sigmoid and log functions are
                                                   │ native PyTorch transforms.
```

Suppose we observed the data from this system, visualized in figure 6.23.

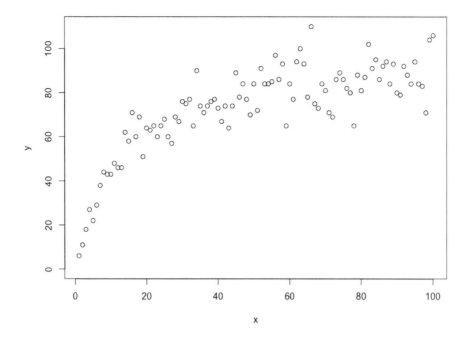

**Figure 6.23   Exampled enzyme data. *X* is the amount of enzyme, and *Y* is the amount of target protein.**

Let's try to learn $\beta$ from this data using a basic PyTorch workflow.

**Listing 6.14   Fitting enzyme data with PyTorch**

```
import pandas as pd
from torch import tensor
import torch

df = pd.read_csv("https://raw.githubusercontent.com/altdeep      Load the enzyme
    /causalML/master/datasets/enzyme-data.csv")                  data from GitHub.
X = torch.tensor(df['x'].values).unsqueeze(1).float()
Y = torch.tensor(df['y'].values).unsqueeze(1).float()            Convert the data to tensors.

def train(X, Y, model, loss_function, optim, num_epochs):
    loss_history = []
    for epoch in range(num_epochs):
        Y_pred = model(X)                                        Create the
        loss = loss_function(Y_pred, Y)                          training
        loss.backward()                                          algorithm.
        optim.step()
        optim.zero_grad()
        if epoch % 1000 == 0:
            print(round(loss.data.item(), 6))                    Print out losses during training.

torch.manual_seed(1)                    Set a random seed
enzyme_model = EnzymeModel()             for reproducibility.
```

```
optim = torch.optim.Adam(enzyme_model.parameters(), lr=0.00001)
loss_function = nn.MSELoss()

train(X, Y, enzyme_model, loss_function, optim, num_epochs=60000)
```

Using mean squared loss error is equivalent to assuming Ny is additive and symmetric.

Initialize an instance of the Adam optimizer. Use a low value for the learning rate because loss is very sensitive to small changes in $\beta$.

When I run this code with the given random seed, it produces a value of 0.1079 (you can access the value by printing `enzyme_model.`$\beta$ `.data`), which only differs slightly from the ground-truth value of .08. This implementation did not represent the exogenous variable $N_y$ explicitly, but statistics theory tells us that using the mean squared error loss function is equivalent to assuming $N_y$ was additive and had a normal distribution. However, it also assumes that the normal distribution had constant variance, while the funnel shape in the scatterplot indicates the variance of $N_y$ might increase with the value of $X$.

### 6.5.2    *Training an SCM with probabilistic PyTorch*

The problem with this basic parameter optimization approach is that the SCM should encode a distribution $P(X, Y)$. So we can turn to a probabilistic modeling approach to fit this model.

---

Listing 6.15    Bayesian estimation $\beta$ in a probabilistic enzyme model

```
import pyro
from pyro.distributions import Beta, Normal, Uniform
from pyro.infer.mcmc import NUTS, MCMC

def g(u):
    return u / (1 + u)

def model(N):
    β = pyro.sample("β", Beta(0.5, 5.0))
    with pyro.plate("data", N):
        x = pyro.sample("X", Uniform(0.0, 101.0))
        y = pyro.sample("Y", Normal(100.0 * g(β * x), x**.5))
    return x, y

conditioned_model = pyro.condition(
    model,
    data={"X": X.squeeze(1), "Y":  Y.squeeze(1)}
)

N = X.shape[0]
pyro.set_rng_seed(526)
```

The simple transform used in the assignment function for Y (amount of target protein)

A "plate" for the N = 100 identical and independently distributed values of X and Y

The probabilistic model

A prior on the parameter $\beta$ that we mean to fit with this model

Condition the model on the observed evidence.

Get the number of examples in the data (100).

Set a random seed for reproducibility.

The marginal probability of the enzyme P(X) is a uniform distribution between 0 and 101.

P(Y|X) is the conditional distribution of Y (protein concentration) given X (and $\beta$). I model P(Y|X) with a normal distribution with both a mean and variance that depends on Y.

```
nuts_kernel = NUTS(conditioned_model, adapt_step_size=True)
mcmc = MCMC(nuts_kernel, num_samples=1500, warmup_steps=500)
mcmc.run(N)
```

**To learn $\beta$, I use a gradient-based MCMC algorithm called a No-U-Turn Sampler (NUTS). This algorithm is one of many probabilistic approaches for parameter learning, and this choice is independent of the causal elements of your model.**

The problem with this approach is that it doesn't have an explicit representation of the exogenous variables. If we want to use a probabilistic machine learning framework to build an SCM, we need to make exogenous variables explicit. That is challenging with the preceding approach for one very nuanced reason: When I write the following statement in Pyro code, `y = pyro.sample("Y", Normal(…, …))`, Pyro knows to use that normal distribution to calculate the probability value (in more precise terms, the *likelihood*) of each value of *Y* in the training data. Those values are used in probabilistic inference algorithms like MCMC. But if I write a statement that represents an assignment function, like `y = f(x, ny)`, Pyro doesn't automatically know how to calculate probability values for *Y*, especially since as far as Pyro is concerned, *f(.)* can be anything.

But there is another problem that is more important than this issue with inference. So far, we've been assuming that we conveniently know a domain-based mathematical functional form for *Y*'s assignment function. It would be nice to use deep learning to fit the assignment functions, but this is problematic.

### 6.5.3   Neural SCMs and normalizing flows

Suppose we used a neural network to model `y = f(x, ny)`. Indeed for a given SCM, we could use a multilayer neural network to model each variable, given its parents—call this a "neural SCM." The problem is that we want the trainable function class we use for our assignment functions to represent our assumptions about the "how" of causality. Neural networks, as universal function approximators, are, by definition, as assumption-free as curve-fitting functions get. Therefore, to use a neural SCM, we need ways to constrain the neural assignment function to remain faithful to our "how" assumptions. This could be done with constraints on the training feature, loss function, and elements of the neural network architecture. Normalizing flows are an example of the latter.

Returning to the enzyme modeling example, let's start by enumerating some basic biological assumptions about the relationships between enzymes and the proteins they help synthesize:

- The process by which the protein leaves the system is independent of the amount of enzyme. So we expect the amount of target protein to *monotonically increase*, given the amount of enzyme.
- However, systems tend to saturate, such that there are diminishing returns in adding more enzyme.

We need a neural network approach that *only* allows for monotonic functions with diminishing returns. For this, we'll use a deep generative modeling approach called *normalizing flows*.

Normalizing flows model a complex probability density as an invertible transformation of a simple base density. I'm going to use flows to model the distribution of endogenous variables as invertible transformations of exogenous variable distributions. There are many different transformations, but I'm going to use *neural splines.*[1] Splines are a decades-old approach to curve-fitting using piece-wise polynomials; a neural spline is the neural network version of a spline.

> **Listing 6.16    Initializing splines for assignment functions**

```
from pyro.distributions.transforms import conditional_spline
print(conditional_spline(input_dim=1, context_dim=1))
```
◁— **A neural spline transform is a type of invertible PyTorch neural network module.**

We get a three-layer neural network with ReLU activation functions:

```
ConditionalSpline(
  (nn): DenseNN(
    (layers): ModuleList(
      (0): Linear(in_features=1, out_features=10, bias=True)
      (1): Linear(in_features=10, out_features=10, bias=True)
      (2): Linear(in_features=10, out_features=31, bias=True)
    )
    (f): ReLU()
  )
)
```

Normalizing flows solve our problem of not having a likelihood value for `y = f(x, ny)`. Like other probabilistic machine learning models, they allow us to connect an input random variable (like an exogenous variable) to an output variable (like an endogenous variable) using layers of transformations. The key difference is that normalizing flow models automatically calculate the probability values of instances of the output variable in the data (using the *change-of-variable formula* from probability theory). That automatic calculation relies on monotonicity; our causal "how" assumption is that the relationship between enzyme concentration and protein abundance is monotonic, and normalizing flows give us monotonicity.

For example, in the following code, `NxDist` is the distribution of exogenous variable $N_x$. We set the distribution as a Uniform$(0, 1)$. `f_x` is the assignment function for $X$, implemented as an `AffineTransformation` that maps this distribution to Uniform$(1, 101)$.

> **Listing 6.17    Transforming a distribution of *Nx* to a distribution of *X***

```
from pyro.distributions import TransformedDistribution
from pyro.distributions.transforms import AffineTransform
```

---

[1] For more information on neural splines, see C. Durkan, A. Bekasov, I. Murray, and G. Papamakarios, "Neural spline flows," in *Advances in neural information processing systems, 32 (NeurIPS 2019).*

```
NxDist = Uniform(torch.zeros(1), torch.ones(1))
f_x = AffineTransform(loc=1., scale=100.0)
XDist = TransformedDistribution(NxDist, [f_x])
```

**The exogenous distribution of X is Uniform(0, 1).**

**XDist is an explicit representation of P(X). Multiplying by 100 and adding 1 gives you a Uniform(1, 101).**

**The assignment function for f_x. The AffineTransform multiplies Nx by 100 and adds 1.**

So XDist allows us to calculate the probability value of *X* even when its value is set deterministically by an assignment function. You can calculate the log-probability value of 50 with XDist.log_prob(torch.tensor([50.0])), which under the Uniform(1, 101) distribution will be log(1/100).

Let's first specify the model.

**Listing 6.18   Specify the flow-based SCM**

```
import pyro
from pyro.distributions import (
    ConditionalTransformedDistribution,
    Normal, Uniform,
    TransformedDistribution
)
from pyro.distributions.transforms import (
    conditional_spline, spline
)
import torch
from torch.distributions.transforms import AffineTransform

pyro.set_rng_seed(348)

NxDist = Uniform(torch.zeros(1), torch.ones(1))
f_x = AffineTransform(loc=1., scale=100.0)
XDist = TransformedDistribution(NxDist, [f_x])

NyDist = Normal(torch.zeros(1), torch.ones(1))
f_y = conditional_spline(input_dim=1, context_dim=1)
YDist = ConditionalTransformedDistribution(NyDist, [f_y])
```

**The assignment function for f_x. The AffineTransform multiplies Nx by 100 and adds 1.**

**The exogenous distribution of X is Uniform(0, 1).**

**XDist is an explicit representation of P(X). Multiplying by 100 and adding 1 gives you a Uniform(1, 101).**

**The exogenous distribution of Y is Normal(0, 1).**

**We implement the assignment function for f_y with a neural spline. Optimization will optimize the parameters of this spline.**

**YDist is an explicit representation of P(Y|X).**

Now we run the training.

**Listing 6.19   Train the SCM**

```
import matplotlib.pyplot as plt

modules = torch.nn.ModuleList([f_y])
optimizer = torch.optim.Adam(modules.parameters(), lr=3e-3)
losses = []
maxY = max(Y)
Ynorm = Y / maxY
```

**Register the neural spline functional assignment function for Y.**

**Initialize the optimizer.**

**Normalize Y, since the assignment function is working with neural networks.**

```
for step in range(800):
    optimizer.zero_grad()          ◁──┤ Set all gradients to 0.
    log_prob_x = XDist.log_prob(X)                        ◁──┤ Use P(X) to calculate a log likelihood
    log_prob_y = YDist.condition(X).log_prob(Ynorm)          value for each value of X.
    loss = -(log_prob_x + log_prob_y).mean()            ◁──┐ Use P(Y|X) to calculate a
    loss.backward()                                          log likelihood value for
    optimizer.step()                                         each value of Y, given X.
    XDist.clear_cache()
    YDist.clear_cache()            Fit the parameters of the neural
    losses.append(loss.item())     network modules using maximum
                                    likelihood as an objective.

plt.plot(losses[1:])
plt.title("Loss")              Visualize losses
plt.xlabel("step")             during training.
plt.ylabel("loss")
```

Figure 6.24 shows the training loss over training.

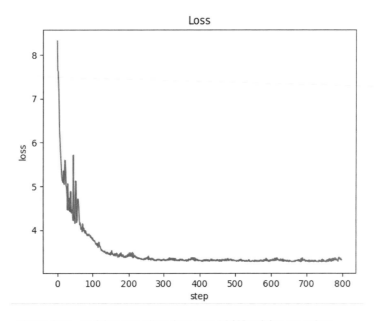

**Figure 6.24   Training loss of the flow-based SCM-training procedure**

Now we can generate samples from the model and compare them to the training data.

---

**Listing 6.20   Generate from the trained model**

```
x_flow = XDist.sample(torch.Size([100,]))
y_flow = YDist.condition(x_flow).sample(torch.Size([100,])) * maxY

plt.title("""                                    Generate synthetic examples
Observed values of enzyme concentration X\n         from the trained model.
```

```
and protein concentration Y""")
plt.xlabel('X')
plt.ylabel('Y')
plt.xlim(0, 105)
plt.ylim(0, 120)
plt.scatter(
    X.squeeze(1), Y.squeeze(1), color='firebrick',
    label='Actual Data',
    alpha=0.5
)
plt.scatter(
    x_flow.squeeze(1), y_flow.squeeze(),
    label='Generated values from trained model',
    alpha=0.5
)
plt.legend()
plt.show()
```

**Visualize the synthetic examples over the examples in the training data to validate model fit.**

Figure 6.25 overlays generated samples with the actual examples in the training data.

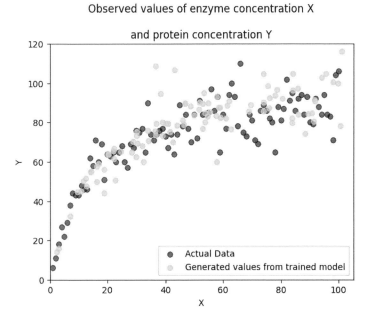

**Figure 6.25   Generated examples from the trained model overlaid upon actual examples in the training data**

The ability to have multilayered flows as in other neural network frameworks makes this an extremely flexible modeling class. But this is not a mere curve-fitting exercise. With the variational autoencoder example in chapter 5, you saw that you can use neural networks to map causal parents to their child effects in the general class of CGMs.

But that is not sufficient for SCMs, even if you set endogenous variables deterministically. Again, SCMs reflect causal assumptions about the "how" of causality in the form of assignment functions. In this enzyme example, we are asserting that the monotonic relationship between the enzyme and protein abundance is important in the causal inferences we want to make, and so we're constraining the neural nets (and other transforms) in my assignment functions to those that preserve monotonicity.

## *Summary*

- Structural causal models (SCMs) are a type of causal graphical model (CGM) that encode causal assumptions beyond the assumptions encoded in the causal DAG. The causal DAG assumptions capture *what* causes *what*. The SCM additionally captures *how* the causes affect the effects.
- SCMs are composed of exogenous variables, probability distributions on those exogenous variables, endogenous variables, and functional assignments.
- Exogenous variables represent unmodeled causes.
- Endogenous variables are the variables explicitly included in the model, corresponding to the nodes we've seen in previous causal DAGs.
- The functional assignments set each endogenous variable deterministically, given its causal parents.
- The SCM's additional assumptions represent the "how" of causality in the form of functional assignments.
- SCMs represent a deterministic view of causality, where an outcome is known for certain if all the causes are known.
- You can derive an SCM from a more general (non-SCM) CGM. But given a general CGM, there are potentially multiple SCMs that entail the same DAG and joint probability distribution as that CGM.
- You can't learn the functional assignments of an SCM from statistical information in the data alone.
- SCMs are an ideal choice for representing well-defined systems with simple, deterministic rules, such as games.
- Additive noise models provide a useful template for building SCMs from scratch.
- Normalizing flows are a useful probabilistic machine learning framework for modeling SCMs when your causal "how" assumption is monotonicity.

# Interventions and causal effects

## This chapter covers

- Case studies of interventions in machine learning engineering contexts
- How interventions relate to A/B tests and randomized experiments
- Implementing interventions on causal models with intervention operators
- Using a causal model to represent many interventional distributions
- Causal effects as natural extensions of an intervention distribution

An intervention is something an agent *does* to cause other things to happen. Interventions *change* the data generating process (DGP).

Interventions are the most fundamental concept in how we define causality. For example, the concept of intervention, written in terms of "manipulation" and "varying" a factor, is central to this definition from an influential 1979 textbook on experimental design:

*The paradigmatic assertion in causal relationships is that manipulation of a cause will result in the manipulation of an effect . . . . Causation implies that by varying one factor I can make another vary.*[1]

Interventions are how we go from correlation to causality. Correlation is symmetric; the statements "Amazon's laptop sales correlate with Amazon's laptop bag sales" and "Amazon's laptop bag sales correlate with Amazon's laptop sales" are equivalent. But interventions make causality a one-way street: if Amazon recommends the sale of laptops, laptop bag sales will increase, but if Amazon promotes the sale of laptop bags, we wouldn't expect people to respond by buying new laptops to fill them.

A model must have a way of reasoning about intervention to be admitted to the club of causal models. Any model that lets you reason about how interventions change the DGP is, by definition, a causal model.

You are probably already familiar with interventions in the form of experiments, such as A/B tests or randomized clinical trials. Such experiments focus on inferring causal effects. Put simply, a causal effect is just a comparison of the expected results of different interventions (e.g., a treatment and a control, or "A" and "B" in an A/B test).

In this chapter, you'll learn how to model an intervention and causal effects even if, indeed *especially* if, we do not or cannot do the intervention in real life. We'll start this chapter with case studies that motivate modeling interventions. All the datasets and notebooks for executing them are available at www.altdeep.ai/causalAIbook.

## 7.1    Case studies of interventions

A machine learning model can drive decisions to make "interventions." Those interventions can, in turn, create conditions different from those that occurred during model training. This mismatch in training conditions and deployment conditions can lead to problems.

### 7.1.1    Case study: Predicting the weather vs. business performance

Every day you wake up, look out the window, and guess whether or not it will rain. Based on that guess, you decide whether to take an umbrella on your morning walk to work. Several times you guess and choose incorrectly; you either take an umbrella and it doesn't rain, making you look like a fop, or you don't take the umbrella, and it rains, making you look wet. You decide to train a machine learning model that will take detailed atmospheric readings in the morning and produce a prediction of whether or not it will rain. By leveraging machine learning to get more accurate predictions, you expect fewer mistakes in deciding whether to bring the umbrella.

You start by collecting daily atmospheric readings as features, and record whether it rained as labels. After enough days, you have your first block of training data. Next,

---

[1] D.T. Campbell and T.D. Cook, *Quasi-experimentation: Design & Analysis Issues for Field Settings* (Rand McNally, 1979), p36.

you train the model on that training data and validate its accuracy on hold-out data. Finally, you deploy the trained model, meaning that you use it daily to decide whether to take or leave your umbrella. As you use the deployed model, you continue to log features and labels daily. Eventually, you have enough additional data for a second training block, and you retrain your model to benefit from both blocks of data, leading to higher accuracy than you had after training on just the first block. You continue to iteratively train the model as you collect more blocks of data. Figure 7.1 illustrates the workflow.

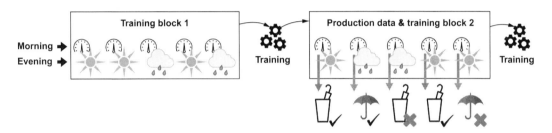

**Figure 7.1   Example of a machine learning training workflow where the sensor data is the features, weather is the label, and bringing an umbrella is the decision. After each training block, the new data is used to update the old model, and a new model is deployed. In this case, the decision does not affect future data.**

Now let's consider a parallel example in business. You are a data scientist at a company. Instead of atmospheric readings, you have economic and industry data. Instead of predicting whether the day will be rainy, you are predicting whether the quarter will end with low revenues. Instead of deciding whether to bring an umbrella, you are deciding whether to advertise. Figure 7.2 illustrates the workflow, which mirrors the weather example in figure 7.1 exactly; sunny and rainy days in figure 7.1 map to good and bad quarters in figure 7.2, and the decision to bring or leave the umbrella maps to the decision to advertise or not.

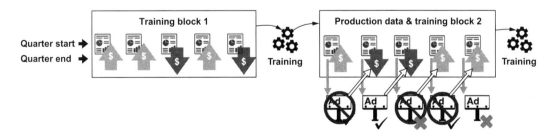

**Figure 7.2   This is a mirror example of the workflow in figure 7.1. Business indicators are the features, quarterly performance is the label, and advertising is the decision. In this case, the decision affects future data.**

Even though the labels and decisions in the two examples mirror one another, the causal structure of the business example is fundamentally different; the act of bringing an umbrella will not affect the weather in future days, but the act of advertising will affect business in future quarters. As a result, training block 2 represents a different DGP than training block 1 because revenue in training block 2 was affected by advertising. During training, a naive predictive model might go so far as to associate signs of a lousy quarter with *high* revenue, since, in the past, signs of bad quarters led your company to advertise, which consequently boosted revenue.

We deploy machine learning models to drive or automate decisions. Those decisions do not impact the data in domains like meteorology, geology, and astronomy. But in many, if not most, domains where we want to use machine learning, those model-driven decisions are interventions—actions that change the DGP. That can lead to a mismatch between the model's training and deployment conditions, leading to problems in the model's reliability.

Another real-world example of this problem occurs in anomaly detection.

### 7.1.2    *Case study: Credit fraud detection*

Anomaly detection seeks to predict when an abnormal event is occurring. One example is detecting a fraudulent transaction on a credit card. Credit card companies do supervised training of predictive models of fraud using transaction data, where attributes of credit card transactions (buying patterns, location, cost of the item, etc.) are the features, and whether the customer later reports the transaction as fraudulent is the label.

As in the weather and business examples, you train a model on an initial training block. After training, you can deploy the algorithm to predict fraud in real time. When a transaction is initiated, the algorithm is run, and a prediction is generated. If the algorithm predicts fraud, the transaction is rejected.

While this system is in deployment, a second training set is being compiled. Some fraud still gets through and is later reported as fraudulent by the customers. Those transactions are labeled fraudulent in this new block of data, but the DGP has changed from the initial training set. The deployed version 1.0 predictive model is rejecting transactions that it predicted were fraudulent, but because they were rejected, you don't know if they were actual cases of fraud. These rejected transactions are excluded from the next training set because they lack labels.

If the model is retrained on the second block, it may develop a bias toward fraud that slipped past the fraud rejection system and against the cases of fraud that were rejected. This bias can become more severe over several iterations. This process is analogous to a homicide detective who, over time, does well in solving cases involving uncommon weapons but poorly in cases involving guns.

The filtering of fraudulent transactions in deployment is an intervention. In practice, anomaly detection algorithms address this problem by accounting for interventions in some way.

### 7.1.3    Case study: Statistical analysis for an online role-playing game

Suppose you are a data scientist at an online role-playing game company. Your leadership wants to know if side-quest engagement (mini-objectives that are tangential to the game's primary objectives) is a driver of in-game purchases of virtual artifacts. If the answer is yes, the company will intervene in the game dynamics such that players engage in more side-quests.

You do an analysis. You query the database and pull records for a thousand players, the first five of which are shown in table 7.1. This is observational data (in contrast to experimental data) because the data is logged observations of the natural behavior of players as they log in and play. (The full dataset is available in the notebooks for the chapter: www.altdeep.ai/causalAIbook.)

**Table 7.1    Example rows from observational data on *Side-Quest Engagement* and *In-Game Purchases***

| User ID | Side-Quest Engagement | In-Game Purchases |
|---------|----------------------|-------------------|
| 71d44ad5 | high | 156.77 |
| e6397485 | low | 34.89 |
| 87a5eaf7 | high | 172.86 |
| c5d78ca4 | low | 215.74 |
| d3b2a8ed | high | 201.07 |
| dc85d847 | low | 12.93 |

The standard data science analysis would involve running a statistical test of the hypothesis that there is a difference between the *In-Game Purchases* of players highly engaged in side-quests and those with low *Side-Quest Engagement*. The test calculates the mathematical difference between the sample means of *In-Game Purchases* for both groups. In statistical terms, this difference estimates an *effect size*. The test will examine whether this estimated effect size is significantly different from zero.

> **Setting up your environment**
>
> The code for this chapter was written with Pyro version 1.9.0, pandas version 2.2.1, and pgmpy version 0.1.25. Using Pyro's `render` function to visualize a Pyro model as a DAG will require Graphviz. Visit www.altdeep.ai/causalAIbook for a link to a notebook that contains the code.

We'll perform this hypothesis test with the pandas library. First, we'll pull the data and get the sample means and standard deviations within each group.

```
import pandas as pd
data_url = (
    "https://raw.githubusercontent.com/altdeep/causalML/master/"
    "datasets/sidequests_and_purchases_obs.csv"
)
df = pd.read_csv(data_url)
summary = df.drop('User ID', axis=1).groupby(
    ["Side-quest Engagement"]
).agg(
    ['count', 'mean', 'std']
)
summary
```

Load the data from the database query into a pandas DataFrame.

For each level of Side-Quest Engagement ("low", "high"), calculate the sample count (number of players), the sample mean In-Game Purchases amount, and the standard deviation.

This produces the summary in table 7.2.

**Table 7.2  Summary statistics from the online game data**

| Side-Quest Engagement | mean purchases | std | n |
| --- | --- | --- | --- |
| low | 73.10 | 75.95 | 518 |
| high | 111.61 | 55.56 | 482 |

This database query pulled 1,000 players, where 482 of them were highly engaged in side-quests and 518 were not. The mean *In-Game Purchases* amount for highly engaged players is around $112 for high *Side-Quest Engagement* and $73 for low *Side-Quest Engagement*. Generalizing beyond this data, we conclude that players who are highly engaged in side-quests spend, on average 112 − 73 = $39 dollars more than those who aren't. We can run a two-sample *Z*-test to make sure this difference is significant.

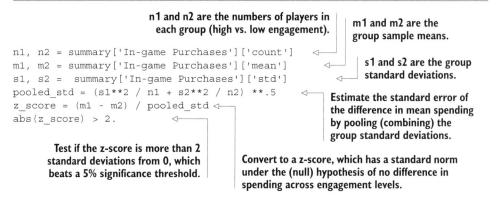

Running this code shows that the difference in means is significant. Great, you did some data science that showed you have a statistically significant effect size: *In-Game*

*Purchases* are significantly higher for players who are highly engaged in side-quests relative to those who are not. Based on your findings, leadership decides to modify the game dynamics to draw players into more side-quests. As a result, *In-Game Purchases decline.* How could this happen?

### 7.1.4   *From randomized experiments to interventions*

By now you've probably recognized that the result from listing 7.2 is a textbook example of how correlation doesn't imply causation. If management wanted to know if intervening on game dynamics would lead to an increase in *In-Game Purchases*, they should have relied on analysis from a randomized experiment, not simple observational data. We'll use the randomized experiment to build more intuition for a formal model of intervention and see how that intervention model could simulate a randomized experiment.

### 7.1.5   *From observations to experiments*

Suppose that instead of running an observational study, you run an experiment. Rather than pull data from a SQL query, you randomly select a set of 1,000 players and randomly assign them to one of two groups of 500. In one group, the game dynamics are modified such that *Side-Quest Engagement* is artificially fixed at "low," and in the other group it is fixed to "high." We'll then observe their level of *In-Game Purchases.*

This will create experimental data that is the same size and has roughly the same split between engaged and unengaged players as the observational data in section 7.1.3. Similarly, we'll run the same downstream analysis. This will let us make an apples-to-apples comparison of using observational versus experimental data.

Table 7.3 shows examples from the experimental data. You can find links to the data in www.altdeep.ai/causalAIbook.

Table 7.3   Example rows from the experimental data evaluating the effect of *Side-Quest Engagement* on *In-Game Purchases*

| User ID | Side-Quest Engagement | In-Game Purchases |
|---------|------------------------|-------------------|
| 2828924d | low | 224.39 |
| 7e7c2452 | low | 19.89 |
| 3ddf2915 | low | 221.26 |
| 10c3d883 | high | 93.21 |
| c5080957 | high | 61.82 |
| 241c8fcf | high | 188.76 |

Again, we summarize the data with the following code.

**Listing 7.3  Load experimental data and summarize**

```
import pandas as pd
exp_data_url = (
    "https://raw.githubusercontent.com/altdeep/causalML/master/"
    "datasets/sidequests_and_purchases_exp.csv"
)
df = pd.read_csv(exp_data_url)
summary = df.drop('User ID', axis=1).groupby(
    ["Side-quest Engagement"]
).agg(
    ['count', 'mean', 'std']
)
print(summary)
```

Load the experimental data from the database query into a pandas DataFrame.

For each level of Side-Quest Engagement ("low", "high"), calculate the sample count (number of players), the sample mean in-game purchase amount, and the standard deviation.

Table 7.4 shows the same summary statistics for the experimental data as table 7.2 does for the observational data.

**Table 7.4  Summary statistics from the online game experimental data**

| Side-Quest Engagement | mean purchases | std | n |
|---|---|---|---|
| low | 92.99 | 51.67 | 500 |
| high | 131.38 | 94.84 | 500 |

The experiment reflects what happened when the company intervened to increase *Side-Quest Engagement*. The sign of the effect size is negative relative to our first analysis; we got −38.39, meaning the mean purchases went down $38.39. When we rerun the test of significance in listing 7.4, we see the difference is significant for the experimental data, just as it was for the observational data.

**Listing 7.4  Conduct significance test on (experimental) difference in mean purchases**

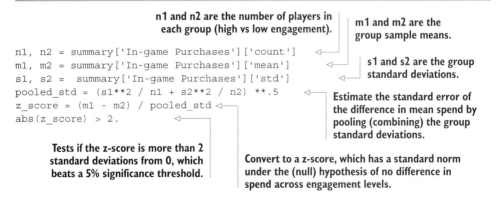

n1 and n2 are the number of players in each group (high vs low engagement).

m1 and m2 are the group sample means.

```
n1, n2 = summary['In-game Purchases']['count']
m1, m2 = summary['In-game Purchases']['mean']
s1, s2 =  summary['In-game Purchases']['std']
pooled_std = (s1**2 / n1 + s2**2 / n2) **.5
z_score = (m1 - m2) / pooled_std
abs(z_score) > 2.
```

s1 and s2 are the group standard deviations.

Estimate the standard error of the difference in mean spend by pooling (combining) the group standard deviations.

Tests if the z-score is more than 2 standard deviations from 0, which beats a 5% significance threshold.

Convert to a z-score, which has a standard norm under the (null) hypothesis of no difference in spend across engagement levels.

The result shows the difference in group means is again significant. If you had reported the results of this experiment instead of the results of the observational study, you would have correctly concluded that a policy of encouraging higher *Side-Quest Engagement* would lead to a drop in average *In-Game Purchases* (and you wouldn't have recommended doing so).

This experiment had a cost. Many of those 1,000 players who were included in the experiment would have spent more on *In-Game Purchases* had they not been included in the experiment, and this is especially true for the 500 players assigned to the high side-quests group. That amounts to lost revenue that would have been realized had you not run the experiment. Moreover, the experiment created a suboptimal gaming experience for players who were assigned a level of *Side-Quest Engagement* that was different from their preferred level. These players are paying the company for a certain experience, and the experiment degraded that experience.

The least ideal outcome is reporting based on our simple two-sample analysis of the observational data; this had no cost, but it gave the wrong answer. A better outcome is running the experiment and getting the correct answer, though this comes at a cost. The ideal outcome is getting the right answer on the observational data for free. To do that, we need a causal model.

### 7.1.6   *From experiments to interventions*

Let's see how we can use a causal model to simulate the results of the experiment from the observational data. First, let's assume the causal DAG in figure 7.3.

In our online game, many players are members of guilds. Guilds are groups of players who pool resources and coordinate their gameplay, such as working together on side-quests. Our model assumes that the amount of *In-Game Purchases* a player makes also depends on whether they are in a guild;

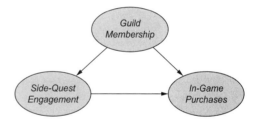

**Figure 7.3   A simple DAG showing the causal relationship between *Side-Quest Engagement* and *In-Game Purchases*. *Guild Membership* is a common cause of both.**

members of the same guild pool resources, and many resources are virtual items they must purchase.

Suppose you run a modified version of that initial database query. The query produces the same exact observational data seen in table 7.1, except this time it includes an additional column indicating *Guild Membership*. Again, we see six players in table 7.5 (the same six as players shown in table 7.1).

**Table 7.5   The same observational data as in table 7.1, but with a *Guild Membership* column**

| User ID | Side-Quest Engagement | Guild Membership | In-Game Purchases |
|---------|----------------------|------------------|-------------------|
| 71d44ad5 | high | member | 156.77 |
| e6397485 | low | nonmember | 34.89 |

**Table 7.5   The same observational data as in table 7.1, but with a *Guild Membership* column *(continued)***

| User ID | Side-Quest Engagement | Guild Membership | In-Game Purchases |
|---------|----------------------|------------------|-------------------|
| 87a5eaf7 | high | member | 172.86 |
| c5d78ca4 | low | member | 215.74 |
| d3b2a8ed | high | member | 201.07 |
| dc85d847 | low | nonmember | 12.93 |

We are going to build a causal graphical model on this observational data using Pyro. To do this, we'll need to model the causal Markov kernels: the probability distributions of *Guild Membership, Side-Quest Engagement* given *Guild Membership,* and *In-Game Purchases* given *Guild Membership* and *Side-Quest Engagement.* In our Pyro model, we'll need to specify some canonical distributions for these variables and estimate their parameters.

### ESTIMATING PARAMETERS AND BUILDING THE MODEL

Pyro can jointly estimate the parameters of each of our causal Markov kernels just as it could the parameters across a complex neural network architecture. But it will make our lives easier to estimate the parameters of each kernel one at a time using everyday data science analysis, leveraging the concept of *parameter modularity* discussed in chapter 2. Let's start with *Guild Membership.*

**Listing 7.5   Estimate the probability distribution of *Guild Membership***

```
import pandas as pd
full_obs_url = (                                                    Load the data
    "https://raw.githubusercontent.com/altdeep/causalML/master/"     from the
    "datasets/sidequests_and_purchases_full_obs.csv"                 database query
)                                                                    into a pandas
df = pd.read_csv(full_obs_url)                                       DataFrame.
membership_counts = df['Guild Membership'].value_counts()
dist_guild_membership = membership_counts / sum(membership_counts)
print(dist_guild_membership)
```

Calculate the proportions of
members vs. nonmembers.

This prints out the following result:

```
nonmember    0.515
member       0.485
Name: Guild Membership, dtype: float64
```

These are the proportions of guild members vs. nonmembers in the data. We can use these as estimates of the probability that a player is a member or a nonmember. If we took these proportions as is, they would be maximum likelihood estimates of the probabilities, but for simplicity, we'll just put it at 50/50 (the probability of being a member is .5).

Next, we'll do the same for the conditional probability distribution (CPD) of *Side-Quest Engagement* level given *Guild Membership*.

**Listing 7.6   Estimate the CPD of *Side-Quest Engagement* given *Guild Membership***

```
member_subset = df[(df['Guild Membership'] == 'member')]
member_engagement_counts = (
    member_subset['Side-quest Engagement'].value_counts()
)
dist_engagement_member = (
    member_engagement_counts / sum(member_engagement_counts)
)
print(dist_engagement_member)

nonmember_subset = df[(df['Guild Membership'] == 'nonmember')]
nonmember_engagement_counts = (
    nonmember_subset['Side-quest Engagement'].value_counts()
)
dist_engagement_nonmember = (
    nonmember_engagement_counts /
    sum(nonmember_engagement_counts)
)
print(dist_engagement_nonmember)
```

**Calculate the probability distribution of Side-Quest Engagement level ("high" vs. "low") given that a player is a member of a guild.**

**Calculate the probability distribution of Side-Quest Engagement level ("high" vs. "low") given that a player is not a member of a guild.**

Listing 7.6 prints the following output proportions of *Side-Quest Engagement* levels for guild members:

```
high    0.797938
low     0.202062
```

The following proportions are for non-guild-members:

```
high    0.184466
low     0.815534
```

Again, we'll round these results. Guild members have an 80% chance of being highly engaged in side-quests, while nonmembers have only a 20% chance of being highly engaged.

Finally, for each combination of *Guild Membership* and *Side-Quest Engagement*, we'll calculate the sample mean and standard deviation of *In-Game Purchases*. We'll use these sample statistics as estimates for mean and location parameters in a canonical distribution when we code the causal Markov kernel for *In-Game Purchases* in the causal model.

**Listing 7.7   Calculate purchase stats across levels of engagement and *Guild Membership***

```
purchase_dist_nonmember_low_engagement = df[
    (df['Guild Membership'] == 'nonmember') &
    (df['Side-quest Engagement'] == 'low')
].drop(
    ['User ID', 'Side-quest Engagement', 'Guild Membership'], axis=1
).agg(['mean', 'std'])
print(round(purchase_dist_nonmember_low_engagement, 2))
```

**Estimate the sample mean and standard deviation of In-Game Purchases for non-guild-members with low Side-Quest Engagement.**

```
purchase_dist_nonmember_high_engagement = df[
    (df['Guild Membership'] == 'nonmember') &
    (df['Side-quest Engagement'] == 'high')
].drop(
  ['User ID', 'Side-quest Engagement', 'Guild Membership'], axis=1
).agg(['mean', 'std'])
print(round(purchase_dist_nonmember_high_engagement, 2))
```
**Estimate the sample mean and standard deviation of In-Game Purchases for non-guild-members with high Side-Quest Engagement.**

```
purchase_dist_member_low_engagement = df[
    (df['Guild Membership'] == 'member') &
    (df['Side-quest Engagement'] == 'low')
].drop(
  ['User ID', 'Side-quest Engagement', 'Guild Membership'], axis=1
).agg(['mean', 'std'])
print(round(purchase_dist_member_low_engagement, 2))
```
**Estimate the sample mean and standard deviation of In-Game Purchases for guild members with low Side-Quest Engagement.**

```
purchase_dist_member_high_engagement = df[
    (df['Guild Membership'] == 'member') &
    (df['Side-quest Engagement'] == 'high')
].drop(
  ['User ID', 'Side-quest Engagement', 'Guild Membership'], axis=1
).agg(['mean', 'std'])
print(round(purchase_dist_member_high_engagement, 2))
```

**Estimate the sample mean and standard deviation of In-Game Purchases for guild members with high Side-Quest Engagement.**

For non-guild-members with low *Side-Quest Engagement*, we have these results:

```
       In-game Purchases
mean               37.95
std                23.80
```

For non-guild-members with high *Side-Quest Engagement*, we have

```
       In-game Purchases
mean               54.92
std                 4.92
```

For guild members with low *Side-Quest Engagement*, we have

```
       In-game Purchases
mean              223.71
std                 5.30
```

For guild members with high *Side-Quest Engagement*, we have

```
       In-game Purchases
mean              125.53
std                53.44
```

Finally, in listing 7.8, we use these various statistics as parameter estimates in a causal graphical model built in Pyro.

**Listing 7.8   Building a causal model of *In-Game Purchases* in Pyro**

```python
import pyro
from torch import tensor
from pyro.distributions import Bernoulli, Normal

def model():
    p_member = tensor(0.5)
    is_guild_member = pyro.sample(
        "Guild Membership",
        Bernoulli(p_member)
    )
    p_engaged = (tensor(0.8)*is_guild_member +
                tensor(.2)*(1-is_guild_member))
    is_highly_engaged = pyro.sample(
        "Side-quest Engagement",
        Bernoulli(p_engaged)
    )
    get_purchase_param = lambda param1, param2, param3, param4: (
        param1 * (1-is_guild_member) * (1-is_highly_engaged) +
        param2 * (1-is_guild_member) * (is_highly_engaged) +
        param3 * (is_guild_member)   * (1-is_highly_engaged) +
        param4 * (is_guild_member)   * (is_highly_engaged)
    )
    μ = get_purchase_param(37.95, 54.92, 223.71, 125.50)
    σ = get_purchase_param(23.80, 4.92, 5.30, 53.49)
    in_game_purchases = pyro.sample(
        "In-game Purchases",
        Normal(μ, σ)
    )
    guild_membership = "member" if is_guild_member else "nonmember"
    engagement = "high" if is_highly_engaged else "low"
    in_game_purchases = float(in_game_purchases)
    return guild_membership, engagement, in_game_purchases
```

Probability of being a guild member vs. a nonmember is .5. Using this probability, we generate a Guild Membership value (1 for member, 0 for nonmember) from a Bernoulli distribution.

We generate a value for Side-Quest Engagement from a Bernoulli distribution (1 for high, 0 for low) with a parameter that depends on Guild Membership.

Helper function for calculating parameters for In-Game Purchases

We specify the location parameter of a normal distribution on In-Game Purchases using the sample means we found in the observational data.

As with the mean parameters, we specify the scale parameters for a canonical distribution on In-Game Purchases using the standard deviations we found in the data.

To confirm that the Pyro model encodes a causal DAG, we can run `pyro.render_model(model)`, which produces figure 7.4.

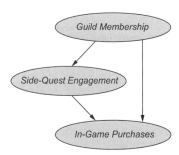

**Figure 7.4   Result of calling `pyro.render_model` with the causal model**

## Leveraging the parametric flexibility of probabilistic programming

Note the flexibility of our choices for modeling the variables in the Pyro model. For example, in modeling the distribution of *In-Game Purchases*, we used the normal distribution, but we could have used other distributions. For example, *In-Game Purchases* cannot be a negative number, so we could have selected a canonical distribution that is only defined for positive numbers, rather than a normal distribution, which is defined for negative and positive numbers. This would be especially useful for non-guild-members with low *Side-Quest Engagement*, because generation from a normal distribution with a mean of 37.95 and a scale parameter of 23.80 will have about a 5.5% chance of generating a negative value. However, we're choosing to be a bit lazy and use the normal distribution in this case, since a few negative numbers for *In-Game Purchases* won't have much impact on the results of our analysis.

The point is that probabilistic programming tools like Pyro provide us with parametric flexibility, unlike tools like pgmpy. It is good practice to leverage that flexibility to reflect your assumptions about the DGP.

### PYRO'S INTERVENTION ABSTRACTION

Pyro has an abstraction for representing an intervention in `pyro.do`. It takes a model and returns a new model that reflects the intervention. Listing 7.9 shows how we can use `pyro.do` to change the previous model into one that reflects an intervention that sets *Side-Quest Engagement* to "high" and to "low."

#### Listing 7.9  Representing interventions with `pyro.do`

```
int_engaged_model = pyro.do(
    model,
    {"Side-quest Engagement": tensor(1.)}
)
int_unengaged_model = pyro.do(
    model,
    {"Side-quest Engagement": tensor(0.)}
)
```

> An intervention that sets Side-Quest Engagement to 1.0 (i.e., "high"). This returns a new model.

> An intervention that sets Side-Quest Engagement to 0.0 (i.e., "low"). This returns a new model.

Now we have two new models: one with an intervention that sets *Side-Quest Engagement* to "high" and one that sets it to "low." If our original model is correct, generating 500 examples from each of these new intervened-upon models, and combining them into 1000 examples, effectively *simulates* the experiment. Remember, we estimated the parameters of this causal model using only the observational data illustrated in table 7.4. If we can train a model on observational data and use it to accurately simulate the results of an experiment, that saves us from actually having to run the experiment.

Listing 7.10 uses `int_engaged_model` and `int_unengaged_model` to simulate experimental data. We can confirm that the simulation was effective by comparing the summary statistics of this simulated data to the summary statistics of the actual experimental data.

Listing 7.10 Simulating experimental data with `pyro.do` interventions

```
pyro.util.set_rng_seed(123)                          ◁──────── Set a random seed
simulated_experimental_data = [                               for reproducibility.
    int_engaged_model() for _ in range(500)
] + [
    int_unengaged_model() for _ in range(500)
]
simulated_experimental_data = pd.DataFrame(     Simulate 500 rows from each
    simulated_experimental_data,                intervention model, and
    columns=[                                   combine them to create
        "Guild Membership",                     simulated experimental data.
        "Side-quest Engagement",
        "In-Game Purchases"
    ]
)
sim_exp_df = simulated_experimental_data.drop(
    "Guild Membership", axis=1)                      The simulated data will
summary = sim_exp_df.groupby(                         include a Guild Membership
        ["Side-quest Engagement"]    Recreate the statistical   column. We can drop it to
    ).agg(                           summaries of In-Game        get simulated data that
        ['count', 'mean', 'std']     Purchases for each level    looks like the original
    )                                of engagement.              experiment.
print(summary)
```

This code simulates the experiment, providing the summaries in table 7.6. Again, these are sample statistics from a simulated experiment we created by first estimating some parameters on observational data, second, building a causal generative model with those parameters, and third, using `pyro.do` to simulate the results of an intervention. Contrast these with the statistics in table 7.7 that we obtained from the *actual* experimental data.

Table 7.6 Summary statistics from the simulated experiment

| Side-Quest Engagement | count | mean | std |
|---|---|---|---|
| high | 500 | 89.897309 | 52.696709 |
| low | 500 | 130.674021 | 93.921543 |

Table 7.7 Summary statistics from the actual experiment

| Side-Quest Engagement | count | mean | std |
|---|---|---|---|
| high | 500 | 92.99054 | 51.673631 |
| low | 500 | 131.38228 | 94.840705 |

The two sets of summaries are similar enough that we can say that we've successfully replicated the experimental results from the observational data.

### 7.1.7  Recap

Let's recap. A causal DAG combined with a Pyro abstraction for an intervention allowed us to do an analysis on an observational dataset that produced the same results as an analysis on an experimental dataset. Had you run this analysis on the initial observational data instead of the simple two-sample statistical test, you would have provided the correct answer to leadership, and they would not have changed the dynamics to increase *Side-Quest Engagement*.

Note that this wasn't a free lunch. This analysis required causal assumptions in the form of a causal DAG. Errors in specifying the causal DAG can lead to errors in the output of the analysis. But assuming your causal DAG was correct (or close enough), it would have saved you the actual costs and opportunity costs of running that experiment.

So how exactly does `pyro.do` work? How does it modify the model to represent an intervention? We'll answer these questions with the ideas of *ideal interventions* and *intervention operators*.

## 7.2    The ideal intervention and intervention operator

To understand how our simulated experiment worked, we need a concrete definition of intervention. We'll use a specific definition, called the *ideal intervention*, and also known as the *atomic intervention, structural intervention, surgical intervention,* and *independent intervention.*

The definition of an ideal intervention breaks down into three parts:

- The ideal intervention targets a specific variable or set of variables in the DGP.
- The operation sets those variables to a fixed value.
- By setting the variable to a fixed value, the intervention blocks the influence from the target's causes, such that the target is now statistically independent of its causes.

We'll use the notation do($X=x$) to represent an ideal intervention that sets $X$ to $x$. Note that we can have interventions on sets of variables, as in do($X = x$, $Y = y$, $Z = z$).

### 7.2.1  Intervention operators

A causal model represents relationships in the DGP. The preceding definition of the ideal intervention describes how it *changes* the DGP. Now it remains to us to define how our causal models will reflect that change.

An *intervention operator* is some way of *changing* our causal model to reflect an intervention. One of the first tasks of creating *any* novel computational representation of causality is to define an intervention operator for the ideal intervention.

Intervention operators can implement ideal interventions, stochastic interventions (discussed in section 7.5), and other types of interventions. Unless I indicate otherwise, you can assume that "intervention operator" means "intervention operator for ideal interventions."

Fortunately, structural causal models and general causal graphical models have well-defined intervention operators. We'll explore those, as well as look at intervention operators designed for causal programs like `pyro.do`.

### 7.2.2 Ideal interventions in structural causal models

We'll start with the structural causal model. Let $M$ represent a structural causal model of the online game. We'd write $M$ as follows:

$$M = \{n_G \sim P(N_G); n_E \sim P(N_E); n_I \sim P(N_I);$$
$$g := f_G(n_g); e := f_E(g, n_e); i := f_I(g, e, n_i)\}$$

$f_G$, $f_E$, and $f_I$ are the assignment functions for $G$ (*Guild Membership*), $E$ (*Side-Quest Engagement*), and $I$ (*In-Game Purchases*), respectively.

An ideal intervention do($E$="high") transforms the model as follows:

$$M^{\text{do}(E:=\text{"high"})} = \{n_G \sim P(N_G); n_E \sim P(N_E); n_I \sim P(N_I);$$
$$g := f_G(n_g); e := \text{"high"}; i := f_I(g, e, n_i)\}$$

The intervention operator for the SCM replaces the intervention target $E$'s assignment function with the intervention value "high."

Suppose you have an SCM with a variable (or set of variables) $X$. You want to apply an intervention do($X=x$). The intervention operator replaces the intervention target's assignment function with the intervention value.

Consider how this meets the three elements of our definition of an ideal intervention:

- The intervention do($X=x$) only directly affects the assignment function for $X$. No other assignment function is affected.
- The intervention explicitly sets $X$ to a specific value.
- Since the value of $X$ is set to a constant, it no longer depends on its direct causal parents.

### 7.2.3 Graph surgery: The ideal intervention in causal DAGs and causal graphical models

Now we'll consider how to think graphically about the ideal intervention. First, let's reexamine the online game's causal DAG in figure 7.5.

According to our graph, *Guild Membership* is the causal parent of *Side-Quest Engagement*. That parent-child relationship determines a causal Markov

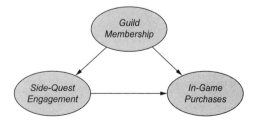

**Figure 7.5  The causal DAG for the online game**

kernel—the conditional probability distribution of *Side-Quest Engagement*, given *Guild Membership*. Recall our model of this causal Markov kernel, shown in table 7.8.

**Table 7.8   Conditional probability table for causal Markov kernel of *Side-Quest Engagement***

|  |  | Guild Membership | |
| --- | --- | --- | --- |
|  |  | nonmember | member |
| Side-Quest Engagement | low | .8 | .2 |
|  | high | .2 | .8 |

Imagine the mechanics of our experiment. Players log on, and the digital experimentation platform selects some players for participation in the experiment. Some of those players are guild members, and some are not.

Consider a player named Jojo, who is not a guild member, who is logging on. Given this information only, he will have a 20% chance of engaging highly in side-quests during this session of gameplay, according to our model.

But the experimentation platform selects him for the experiment. It randomly assigns him to the high *Side-Quest Engagement* group. Once he is in that group, what is the probability that Jojo will engage highly in side-quests? The answer is 100%. In experimental terms, what is the probability that someone assigned to the treatment group will be exposed to the treatment? 100%. For data scientists familiar with the jargon of A/B testing, what is the probability that someone assigned to group A will be exposed to variant A? 100%.

Indeed, supposing instead of Jojo, the subject was Ngozi, who is a guild member. While originally Ngozi had an 80% chance of being highly engaged in side-quests, upon being assigned to the high *Side-Quest Engagement* group in the experiment, she changes to having a 100% chance of being highly engaged.

We need to rewrite our conditional probability distribution of *Side-Quest Engagement* to reflect these new probabilities, as in table 7.9.

**Table 7.9   Rewriting the conditional probability table of *Side-Quest Engagement* to reflect the certainty of engagement level upon being assigned to the high-engagement group in the experiment**

|  |  | Guild Membership | |
| --- | --- | --- | --- |
|  |  | nonmember | member |
| Side-Quest Engagement | low | 0.0 | 0.0 |
|  | high | 1.0 | 1.0 |

Now we see that this modified distribution of *Side-Quest Engagement* is the same regardless of *Guild Membership*. That is the definition of probabilistic independence, so we should simplify this conditional probability table to reflect that; we can reduce table 7.9 to table 7.10.

**Table 7.10** Rewriting the conditional probability table of *Side-Quest Engagement* to reflect the fact that engagement level no longer depends on *Guild Membership*

|  | | |
| --- | --- | --- |
| **Side-Quest Engagement** | low | 0.0 |
|  | high | 1.0 |

When we simplify the distribution in this way, we have to recall that this is a model of a causal Markov kernel, which is defined by the graph. Our initial graph says *Side-Quest Engagement* is caused by *Guild Membership*. But it seems that after the experiment randomly allocates players either to the high engagement or low engagement group, that causal dependency is broken; a player's engagement level is solely determined by the group they are assigned to.

We need an intervention operator that changes our causal graph to reflect this broken causal dependency. This intervention operator is called *graph surgery* (also known as *graph mutlitation*), and it's illustrated in figure 7.6.

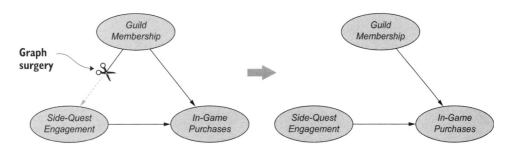

**Figure 7.6**  Graph surgery removes an incoming edge to the intervention target *Side-Quest Engagement*.

While *Guild Membership* is a cause of *Side-Quest Engagement* in normal settings, the experiment's intervention on *Side-Quest Engagement* broke that variable's causal dependence on *Guild Membership*. Since that causal dependence is gone, graph surgery changes the graph to one where the edge from *Guild Membership* to *Side-Quest Engagement* is snipped.

In general, suppose you have a causal graph with node *X*. You want to apply an intervention do(*X=x*). Then you represent that intervention on the causal DAG by "surgery" removing all incoming edges to *X*. Graph surgery is available in libraries such as pgmpy. For example, here is how we would use pgmpy to apply graph surgery to the online gaming DAG.

---

**Listing 7.11   Graph surgery on a DAG in pgmpy**

```
from pgmpy.base import DAG

G = DAG([
    ('Guild Membership', 'Side-quest Engagement'),
    ('Side-quest Engagement', 'In-game Purchases'),
    ('Guild Membership', 'In-game Purchases')
])
G_int = G.do('Side-quest Engagement')
```

Build the
causal DAG.

The do method in the DAG
class applies graph surgery.

We can now plot both the original DAG and the transformed DAG and compare them.

---

**Listing 7.12   Plot the transformed DAG**

```
import pylab as plt
import networkx as nx

pos = {
    'Guild Membership': [0.0, 1.0],
    'Side-quest Engagement': [-1.0, 0.0],
    'In-game Purchases': [1.0, -0.5]
}

ax = plt.subplot()
ax.margins(0.3)
nx.draw(G, ax=ax, pos=pos, node_size=3000,
        node_color='w', with_labels=True)
plt.show()

ax = plt.subplot()
ax.margins(0.3)
nx.draw(G_int, ax=ax, pos=pos,
        node_size=3000, node_color='w', with_labels=True)
plt.show()
```

Create a dictionary of node
positions that we can use to
visualize both graphs.

Visualize the
original graph.

Visualize the
transformed
graph.

These visualizations produce the same DAG as in figure 7.6.

Next, we'll look at the effect of graph surgery on d-separation and its implications for conditional independence.

### 7.2.4   Graph surgery and d-separation

Consider how graph surgery affects reasoning with d-separation, as in figure 7.7. Initially, we have two d-connecting paths between *Side-Quest Engagement* and *In-Game Purchases*: one path was the direct cause path, and the other was through the common cause of *Guild Membership*. After graph surgery, only the direct causal path remains.

Recall that each d-connected path between two variables is a source of statistical dependence between those variables. When we represent an intervention with graph surgery that removes incoming edges to the intervention target(s), we remove any paths to other nodes that go through that variable's causes. Only outgoing paths to other nodes remain. As a result, the remaining paths from that variable reflect

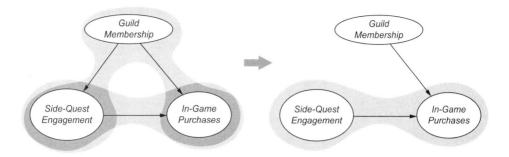

**Figure 7.7  In the original DAG on the left, there are two d-connected paths between *Side-Quest Engagement* and *In-Game Purchases*. These paths equate to two sources of statistical dependence between the two variables. After graph surgery, only the causal path remains, reflecting causal dependence.**

dependence due to that variable's causal influence on other variables. The ideal intervention removes the causal influence the target variable receives from its direct parents. Thus, it removes any dependence on other variables that flows through those parents.

### 7.2.5  Ideal interventions and causal Markov kernels

Graph surgery on the causal DAG removes the incoming edges to the target node(s). However, for a causal graphical model, we need an intervention operator that changes the graph *and* goes one step farther to rewrite the causal Markov kernel of the intervention target, as we did when we collapsed table 7.9 into table 7.10.

Initially, our online gaming model has causal Markov kernels $\{P(G), P(E|G),$ and $P(I|E, G)\}$. In table 7.9 we saw the conditional probability table representation of $P(E|G)$ and how an intervention reduced it to table 7.10, where 100% of the probability is placed on the outcome "high."

Generally, the intervention operator for causal graphical models replaces the causal Markov kernel(s) of the intervention target(s) with a degenerate distribution, meaning a distribution that puts 100% of the probability on one value, namely the intervention value.

When we combine graph surgery with this replacement of the target node's causal Markov kernel with a degenerate distribution, we have an intervention operator on a causal graphical model that meets the three elements of the definition of ideal intervention:

- You only remove incoming edges for the nodes targeted by the intervention.
- 100% of the probability is assigned to a fixed value.
- Removing the incoming edges to the intervention target means that the variable is no longer causally dependent on its parents.

In listing 7.11, graph surgery is implemented in the do method in the DAG class. The BayesianNetwork class, our default for building causal graphical models, also has a do method. Like the DAG method, it takes an intervention target. At the time of writing, the method does not take an intervention value and thus does not satisfy the second element of the definition of ideal intervention.

pgmpy uses objects from subclasses of the `BaseFactor` class (e.g., the `TabularCPD` class) to represent causal Markov kernels. The `do` method in the `BayesianNetwork` class first does graph surgery and then replaces the factor object representing the intervention target's causal Markov kernel. However, that replacement factor object is not degenerate; it does not assign all the probability value to one outcome. Rather, it returns an object representing the probability distribution of the target variable after marginalizing over its parents in the original unmodified graph. Technically, this is an intervention operator for a stochastic intervention, which I'll discuss in section 7.5. To build an intervention operator for the ideal intervention, you need to write additional code to modify the factor to assign all probability to the intervention value.

### 7.2.6   *Ideal interventions in a causal program*

Recall that in listing 7.10 we simulated an experiment where players were assigned to high-engagement and low-engagement groups using the `pyro.do` operator. Specifically, we called `pyro.do` as in following listing.

#### Listing 7.13   Revisiting `pyro.do`

```
int_engaged_model = pyro.do(
    model,
    {"Side-quest Engagement": tensor(1.)}
)
int_unengaged_model = pyro.do(
    model,
    {"Side-quest Engagement": tensor(0.)}
)
```

**An intervention that sets Side-Quest Engagement to 1.0 (i.e., "high"). This returns a new model.**

**An intervention that sets Side-Quest Engagement to 0.0 (i.e., "low"). This returns a new model.**

What exactly does `pyro.do` *do*? `pyro.do` is Pyro's intervention operator. We saw, by using `pyro.render_model` to generate figure 7.4, that our online gaming model in Pyro has an underlying causal DAG, and therefore is a causal graphical model.

But a deep probabilistic machine learning framework like Pyro allows you to do things that we can't easily represent with a causal DAG, such as recursion, conditional control flow, or having a random number of variables not realized until runtime. As an intervention operator, `pyro.do` must work in these cases as well.

The intervention operator in Pyro works by finding calls to `pyro.sample`, and replacing those calls with an assignment to the intervention value. For example, the online game model had the following line:

```
is_highly_engaged = pyro.sample("Side-quest Engagement",
    Bernoulli(p_engaged))
```

This `pyro.sample` call generates a value for *Side-Quest Engagement*. `pyro.do(model, {"Side-quest Engagement": tensor(1.)})` *essentially* replaces that line with this:

```
is_highly_engaged = tensor(1.)
```

(I say "essentially" because `pyro.do` does a few other things too, which I'll discuss in chapter 10).

This replacement is much like the replacement of the assignment function in the SCM, or a causal Markov kernel with a degenerate kernel in a causal graphical model. As an intervention operator, it meets the criteria for an ideal intervention. It targets a specific variable, and it assigns it a specific value. It eliminates its dependence on its causes by removing *flow dependence* (dependence on results of executing preceding statements in the program).

Using a flexible deep probabilistic machine learning tool like Pyro to build a causal model allows you to construct causal representations beyond DAGs and simple ideal interventions. Doing so puts you in underdeveloped territory in terms of theoretical grounding, but it could lead to interesting new applications.

In the next section, we'll consider how interventions affect probability distributions.

## 7.3 *Intervention variables and distributions*

An ideal intervention fixes the random variable it targets, essentially turning it into a constant. But the intervention indirectly affects all the random variables causally downstream of the target variable. As a result, their probability distributions (joint, conditional, or marginal) change from what they were.

### 7.3.1 *"Do" and counterfactual notation*

Causal modeling uses special notation to help reason about how interventions affect random variables and their distributions. One common approach is to use the *"do"-notation*. Using our online game as an example, $P(I)$ is the probability distribution of *In-Game Purchases* across all players, $P(I|E=$"high") is the probability distribution of *In-Game Purchases* given players with "high" engagement, and $P(I|$do$(E=$ "high")) is the probability distribution of *In-Game Purchases* given an intervention that sets a player's engagement level to "high." The second column of table 7.11 illustrates extensions of this notation to joint distributions, multiple interventions, and mixing interventions with observations.

**Table 7.11  Examples of do-notation and counterfactual notation**

| Literal | Do-notation | Counterfactual notation |
|---|---|---|
| The probability distribution of *In-Game Purchases* across all players | $P(I)$ | $P(I)$ |
| The probability distribution of *In-Game Purchases* for players with "high" engagement | $P(I|E=$"high") | $P(I|E=$"high") |
| The probability distribution of *In-Game Purchases* when a player's engagement level is set (by intervention) to "high" | $P(I|$do$(E=$ "high")) | $P(I_{E=\text{"high"}})$ |

**Table 7.11    Examples of do-notation and counterfactual notation** *(continued)*

| Literal | Do-notation | Counterfactual notation |
|---|---|---|
| The joint probability distribution of *In-Game Purchases* and *Guild Membership* when engagement is set to "high" | $P(I, G \vert do(E = \text{"high"}))$ | $P(I_{E = \text{"high"}}, G_{E = \text{"high"}})$ |
| The probability distribution of In-Game Purchases when engagement is set to "high" and membership is set to "nonmember" | $P(I \vert do(E = \text{"high"}, G = \text{"nonmember"}))$ | $P(I_{E = \text{"high"}, G = \text{"nonmember"}})$ |
| The probability distribution of *In-Game Purchases* for guild members when engagement is set to "high" | $P(I \vert do(E = \text{"high"}), G = \text{"member"})$ | $P(I_{E = \text{"high"}} \vert G = \text{"member"})$ |

An alternative is to use counterfactual notation, which uses subscripts to represent a new version of a variable after the system has been exposed to intervention. For example, if $I$ is a variable that represents *In-Game Purchases*, $I_{E = \text{"high"}}$ represents *In-Game Purchases* under an intervention that sets *Side-Quest Engagement* to "high." If $P(I)$ is the probability distribution of *In-Game Purchases*, then $P(I_{E = \text{"high"}})$ is the probability distribution. Again, table 7.11 contrasts do-notation with counterfactual notation in the third column. Going forward, I'll mostly use counterfactual notation.

## From causal language to symbols

In many cases in statistics and machine learning, notation only serves to add formalism and rigor to something just as easily explained in plain language. However, notation is important in causality, because it makes a clear distinction between when we are talking about something causal and when we are not. It is important because making the distinction is harder in plain English. For example, consider the following two questions:

"What would *In-Game Purchases* be for a player who was highly engaged in side-quests?"

"What would *In-Game Purchases* be if a player was highly engaged in side-quests?"

Is it obvious to you that the first question corresponds to $P(I \vert E = \text{"high"})$ and the second to $P(I_{E = \text{"high"}})$? The first question corresponds to a subset of players who are highly engaged. The traditional conditional probability notation is fine when we want to zoom in on a subset of a distribution or population. The second question asks *what if* someone were highly engaged. In the next chapter, we'll see that "what if" hypothetical questions imply an intervention. But because of the ambiguity of language, someone could ask one question while really meaning the other. The notation gives us an unambiguous way of constructing our causal queries.

Again, in chapter 8, we'll investigate more examples of mapping language to counterfactual notation.

### 7.3.2   *When causal notation reduces to traditional notation*

It is crucial to recognize when a variable and that same variable under intervention are the same. Consider the intervention on engagement, as in figure 7.8.

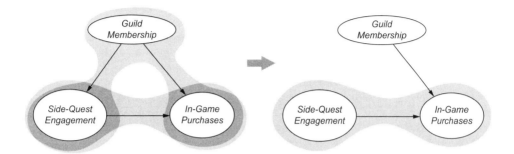

**Figure 7.8   In the original DAG (left), there are two d-connected paths between *Side-Quest Engagement* and *In-Game Purchases*. These paths equate to two sources of statistical dependence between the two variables. After graph surgery, only the causal path remains, reflecting causal dependence.**

Is $P(G|E=\text{“high”})$ (the probability distribution of *Guild Membership* given high *Side-Quest Engagement*) the same as $P(G)$? No. In graphical terms, $G$ and $E$ are d-connected. In probabilistic terms, we can reason that knowing a player's level of *Side-Quest Engagement* is predictive of whether they are in a guild.

But is $P(G_{E=\text{“high”}})$ the same as $P(G)$? Yes. *Guild Membership* is not affected by the intervention on *Side-Quest Engagement* because it can only affect variables causally downstream of *Side-Quest Engagement*. Thus $P(G_{E=\text{“high”}})$ is equivalent to $P(G)$.

In general terms, empirically learning a distribution for a variable $Y_{X=x}$ requires doing the intervention $do(X=x)$ in real life. However, that real-life intervention, at best, has a cost and, at worst, is infeasible or impossible. So if we can equate $Y_{X=x}$ to some distribution involving $Y$ that we can learn from observational data, that's a win. That's going from correlation to causation. In trivial cases, we can do this by looking at the graph, as we did with $G$ and $G_{E=\text{“high”}}$. But usually, we'll need to do some mathematical derivation, either by hand or using algorithms.

This task of deriving equality between variables that are and aren't subject to intervention is called *identification*, and it is the heart of causal inference theory. We'll examine identification at length in chapter 10.

### 7.3.3   *Causal models represent all intervention distributions*

As generative models, the causal models we've worked with encode a joint probability distribution of components of the DGP. Inference algorithms enable those models to represent (e.g., through Monte Carlo sampling) the conditional distribution of some subset of those components, given the state of the other components.

We've now introduced the ideal intervention and how it changes the DGP and, consequently, the joint probability distribution of the variables. Figure 7.9 illustrates how the generative causal model captures the original DGP (and corresponding probability distributions) and any new DGP (and corresponding probability distributions) created by intervening in the original process.

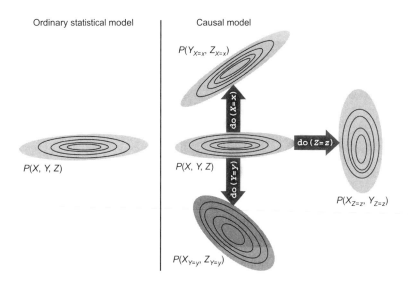

**Figure 7.9   Suppose our DGP has variables *X*, *Y*, and *Z*. A traditional generative model (left) uses observations of *X*, *Y*, and *Z* to statistically learn a representation of *P(X, Y, Z)*. A generative causal model (right) encodes a representation *P(X, Y, Z)* and distributions derived by interventions on *X*, *Y*, and *Z*. In that way, the generative causal model represents a broad family of distributions.**

Consider the statistical implications of this idea. Given data, an ordinary generative model learns a representation of the joint probability distribution. But a generative causal model learns not only that distribution but any new distribution that would be derived by applying some set of ideal interventions. That's how our causal model of the online game was able to reproduce the outcome of an experiment from observational data alone.

## 7.4   *Interventions and causal effects*

The most common use case for our formal model of an intervention will be to model *causal effects.* Now that we've defined and formalized interventions, causal effects are easy to think about; they are simply comparisons between the outcomes of interventions.

### 7.4.1 Average treatment effects with binary causes

The most common causal effect query is the average treatment effect (ATE). Here, we'll focus on the case where we are interested in the causal effect of $X$ on $Y$, and $X$ is binary, meaning it has two outcomes: 1 and 0. Binary causes entail experiments where the cause has a "treatment" value and a "control" value, such as "A/B tests." Using do-notation, the ATE is $E(Y|do(X=1)) - E(Y|do(X=0))$ (recall $E(\ldots)$ means "the expectation of …"). Using counterfactual notation, the ATE is $E(Y_{X=1}) - E(Y_{X=0})$. The advantage of the counterfactual notation is that we can collapse this into one expectation term, $E(Y_{X=1} - Y_{X=0})$.

### 7.4.2 Average treatment effect with categorical causes

When the cause is categorical, the ATE requires choosing which levels of the cause you want to compare. For example, if $X$ has possible outcomes {a, b, c}, you might select "a" to be a baseline, and work with two ATEs, $E(Y_{X=b} - Y_{X=a})$ and $E(Y_{X=c} - Y_{X=a})$. Alternatively, you may choose to work with all pairwise comparisons of levels of $X$, or just convert $X$ to a binary variable with outcomes "a" and "not a" The choice depends on which ATE is most meaningful to you.

### 7.4.3 Average treatment effect for continuous causes

If we want to generalize $E(Y_{X=1} - Y_{X=0})$ to the case where $X$ is continuous, we arrive at derivative calculus. For some baseline $do(X=x)$, imagine changing the intervention value $x$ by some small amount $\Delta$, i.e., $do(X=x+\Delta)$. Taking the difference between the two outcomes, we get $E(Y_{X=x+\Delta} - Y_{X=x})$. Then we can ask, what is the rate of change of $E(Y_X)$ as we make $\Delta$ infinitesimally smaller. This brings us to the definition of the derivative:

$$\lim_{\Delta \to 0} \frac{E(Y_{X=x+\Delta}) - E(Y_{X=x})}{\Delta} = d\frac{E(Y_{X=x})}{dx}$$

Note that this is a function, rather than a point value; when you plug in a value of $x$, you get the rate of change of $Y_{X=x}$ of the $X$ versus $Y_x$ curve.

As a practical example, consider the case of pharmacology, where we want to establish the ATE of a drug dose on a health outcome. The drug dose is continuous, and it usually follows a nonlinear S-curve-like shape; we get more effect as we increase the dose, but eventually the effect gets diminishing returns at higher doses. The derivative gives us the rate of change of the average response for a given dose on the dose-response curve.

### 7.4.4 Conditional average treatment effect

The conditional average treatment effect (CATE) is an ATE conditioned on other covariates. For example, in our online game example, $E(I_{E=\text{"high"}} - I_{E=\text{"low"}})$ is the ATE on *In-Game Purchases* for *Side-Quest Engagement*. If we wished to understand the ATE for guild members, we'd want $E(I_{E=\text{"high"}} - I_{E=\text{"low"}} | G=\text{"member"})$.

In practical settings, it is often important to work with CATEs instead of ATEs, because CATEs can have big differences with ATEs and other CATEs with different conditions. In other words, CATEs better reflect the *heterogeneity* of treatment effects across a population. For example, it is possible that the ATE of a drug on a health outcome is positive across the overall population, but the CATE conditioned on a specific subpopulation (e.g., people with a certain allergy) could be negative. Similarly, in advertising, certain ad copy might drive your customers to purchase more on average, but cause some segment of your customers to purchase less. You can optimize the return on investment for your ad campaign by understanding the CATEs for each segment, or to use CATE-based reasoning to do customer segmentation.

Experts often emphasize the importance of measuring *heterogenous treatment effects* with CATEs, lest one think a point value estimate of an ATE tells the full picture. But in our probabilistic modeling approach, heterogeneity is front and center. If we have a causal graphical model and a model of ideal intervention, then we can model $P(Y_{X=x})$. If we can model $P(Y_{X=x})$, then we can model $P(Y_{X=1} - Y_{X=0})$. We can then use that model to inspect all the variation within $P(Y_{X=1} - Y_{X=0})$, including who in the target population falls above or below 0 or some other threshold.

### 7.4.5   *Statistical measures of association and causality*

In statistics, an effect size is a value that measures the strength or intensity of the relationship between two variables or groups. For example, in our observational analysis of the online gaming data, we quantified the relationship between *Side-Quest Engagement E* and *In-Game Purchases I* as $E(I|E=\text{"high"}) - E(I|E=\text{"low"})$. Our statistical procedure estimated this *true* effect size with a difference in sample averages between both groups. We then conducted a hypothesis test. We specified a null hypothesis $E(I|E=\text{"high"}) - E(I|E=\text{"low"}) = 0$, and then tested if this effect size estimate was statistically different from 0 using a *p*-value calculated under some null hypothesis distribution (usually a normal or t-distribution).

A causal effect is just an *interventional* effect size; in our example, it was $E(I|\text{do}(E=\text{"high"})) - E(I|\text{do}(E=\text{"low"})) = E(I_{E=\text{"high"}} - I_{E=\text{"low"}})$, which is the ATE. The statistical hypothesis testing procedure is the same as before. Indeed, we still need to test if sample-based estimates of ATEs and CATEs are statistically significant. When you conduct a statistical significance test with data from an experiment with a treatment and control, you are testing an estimate of the ATE by definition.

### 7.4.6   *Causality and regression models*

Suppose $X$ is continuous, but its relationship with $Y_X$ is linear. Then the ATE $d E(Y_{X=x})/dx$ is a point value because the derivative of a linear function is a constant. Therefore, if you use a linear model of $E(Y_X)$, then the coefficient for $X$ in that model corresponds to the ATE for $X$.

$$\text{If } E(Y_X) = \beta_0 + \beta \times X, \text{ then ATE } = \beta$$

For this reason, linear regression modeling is a popular approach to modeling causal effects (even when people don't really believe the causal relationship is linear).

This convenience extends to other generalized linear models. Suppose Poisson regression or logistic regression are better models of $E(Y_X)$ than linear regression. These models capture measures of association between two variables not as a difference in means, but as ratios. For example, we can read relative risk (RR) directly from a Poisson regression model and odds ratios (OR) directly from a logistic regression model. In general, these measures of association have no causal interpretation, but we give them a causal interpretation once we use them with interventional variables. For example, if we are modeling $E(Y_X)$, and $Y_X$ is binary, the relative risk and odds ratios are as follows:

$$RR = \frac{P(Y_{X=1} = 1)}{P(Y_{X=0} = 1)} = \frac{E(Y_{X=1})}{E(Y_{X=0})}$$

$$OR = \frac{\frac{E(Y_{X=1})}{1 - E(Y_{X=1})}}{\frac{E(Y_{X=0})}{1 - E(Y_{X=0})}}$$

Thus, traditional non-causal ways of quantifying statistical association become measures of *causal* association once we use them in an interventional context. And when we fit these regression models to data, we can still use all the traditional regression methods for significance testing (Wald tests, F-tests, likelihood ratio tests, etc.).

## 7.5   Stochastic interventions

Stochastic interventions are an important generalization of ideal interventions. The second rule of the ideal intervention is that the intervention is set to a fixed value. In the stochastic intervention, that value is the outcome of a random process; i.e., it is itself a random variable. Most texts treat stochastic interventions as an advanced topic beyond the scope of an introduction to causal modeling, but I make special mention of them as they are important in machine learning, where we often seek data-driven automation. Stochastic interventions are important for automatic selection of interventions.

### 7.5.1   Random assignment in an experiment is a stochastic intervention

For example, the digital experimentation platform in our online gaming experiment automatically assigned players to high- and low-engagement groups. It did so *randomly*. Random assignment is a stochastic intervention; it targets the *Side-Quest Engagement* variable and sets its value by digitally flipping a coin.

Note that randomization is more than what we need to arrive at the right answer. Indeed, in our simulation of the experiment, there was no randomization, only ideal interventions. Those ideal interventions were sufficient to d-separate the path *Side-Quest Engagement* ← *Guild Membership* → *In-Game Purchases*, removing the statistical dependence that comes from that path. If randomization is not necessary to quantify the causal relationship, why is it called "the gold standard of causal inference?" The answer is that randomization works when your causal DAG is *wrong*.

For example, suppose that when we did the experiment, rather than randomizing players into the high versus low *Side-Quest Engagement* group, the digital experimentation platform automatically assigned the first 500 players who logged on to the group with high *Side-Quest Engagement* and the next 500 players to the group with low *Side-Quest Engagement*. This intervention would be sufficient to d-separate the path *Side-Quest Engagement ← Guild Membership → In-Game Purchases*. But what if our DAG was wrong, and there are other paths between *Side-Quest Engagement* and *In-Game Purchases* through unknown common causes?

Figure 7.10 considers what happens when our DAG is wrong—our model is the DAG on the right. Consider what would happen if, instead, the true DAG were the DAG on the left. For the DAG on the left, the time of day when the player logs on drives both the *Side-Quest Engagement* and *In-Game Purchases*.

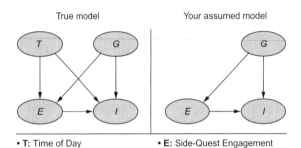

• T: Time of Day
• G: Guild Membership
• E: Side-Quest Engagement
• I: In-Game Purchases

**Figure 7.10   Left: the true causal relationships. Right: your (incorrect) causal DAG.**

Suppose, for example, people who log on earlier tend not to be logging on with friends. They tend to engage more in side-quests because side-quests are amenable to solo gameplay. People who plan missions with friends tend to log on later, since some friends have real-world appointments during the day. Friends playing together focus more on the game's primary narrative and avoid side-quests. Also, players tend to spend more money on *In-Game Purchases* later in the day, corresponding to the broader trend of late-day spending in e-commerce.

When we intervene on a player to assign them to one group or another based on their login, that intervention value now depends on the time of day, as shown in figure 7.11.

The left side of figure 7.11 illustrates the result of an intervention on *Side-Quest Engagement* that depends on the time of day. As we expected, the intervention performs graph surgery, removing the incoming edges to *Side-Quest Engagement* E: T→E and G→E. However, the value set by the intervention is now determined by time of day T, via a `time_select` function. The `time_select` function assigns "high" engage-

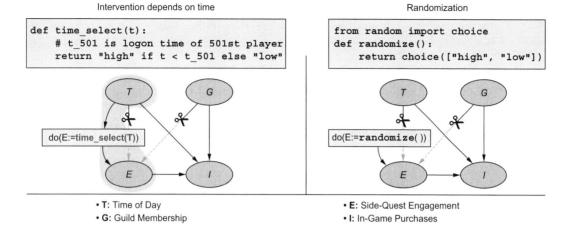

**Figure 7.11   An intervention that sets the level of *Side-Quest Engagement* based on login time changes, but doesn't eliminate, the causal relationship T→E. In contrast, randomization eliminates incoming edges to E.**

ment to every player whose login time is before that of the 501$^{st}$ player to log on and "low" for those who logged in after. After graph surgery, we add back a new causal edge $T{\to}E$ whose mechanism is time_select. Thus, there is still a noncausal statistical association that biases the experiment via the d-connected path $I{\leftarrow}T{\to}E$.

In contrast, randomization on the right side of figure 7.11 did what we hoped, removing all the incoming edges to $E$. It removed the edge from $T{\to}E$ even though our assumed DAG did not know that $T{\to}E$ existed. Indeed, if there are other unknown common causes between $E$ and $I$, randomization will remove those incoming edges to $E$, as in figure 7.12.

The ability of randomization to eliminate statistical bias from common causes we failed to account for in our assumptions is why it is considered "the gold standard of causal inference." But to understand stochastic interventions, note that both assignment mechanisms: one based on login time and the other using randomization, are sto-

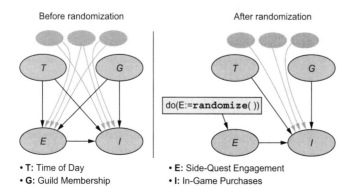

**Figure 7.12   Randomization eliminates incoming edges from unknown common causes.**

chastic interventions. Both set the *Side-Quest Engagement* level of a player using a random process; one depends on when someone logs in, and the other depends on a coin flip.

### 7.5.2    *Intervention policies*

Stochastic interventions are closely related to policies in automated decision-making domains, such as bandit algorithms and reinforcement learning. In these domains, an agent (e.g., a robot, a recommender algorithm) operates in some environment. A *policy* is an algorithm that takes as input the state of some variables in the environment and returns an action for the agent to execute. If there are elements of randomness in the selection of that action, it is a stochastic intervention.

In our previous example, randomization is a *policy* that selects interventions at random. But in automated decision-making, most policies choose interventions based on the state of other variables in the system, much like the biased experiment that intervenes based on the *time of day* variable. Of course, policies in automated decision-making are typically trying to optimize some utility function rather than bias an experiment. We'll focus on causality in automated decision-making in chapter 12.

## 7.6    *Practical considerations in modeling interventions*

I'll close this chapter with some practical considerations for modeling interventions. We'll consider how ideal (and stochastic) interventions allow us to model the impossible. Then we'll make sure we ground that modeling in pragmatism.

### 7.6.1    *Reasoning about interventions that we can't do in reality*

In our online gaming example, we used an intervention operator on a causal model to replicate the results of an experiment. I presented a choice between actually running an experiment and simulating the experiment. Simulation avoids the costs of running the experiment, but running the experiment is more robust to errors in causal assumptions, especially with tools like randomization.

However, there are many times when we can't run an experiment, because doing so is either infeasible, unethical, or impossible.

- *Example of an infeasible experiment*—A randomized experiment that tests the effect of interest rates on intergenerational wealth.
- *Example of an unethical experiment*—A randomized experiment that tests the effect of caffeine on miscarriages.
- *Example of an impossible experiment*—A randomized experiment that tests the effects of black hole size on spectroscopic redshift.

In these scenarios, simulation with a causal model is our only choice.

### 7.6.2    *Refutation and real-world interventions*

Suppose your causal model predicts the outcome of an intervention. You then do that intervention in the real world, such as with a controlled experiment. If your predicted intervention outcome conflicts with your actual intervention outcome, your causal model is wrong.

In chapter 4, we discussed the concept of validating, or rather, *refuting*, a causal model by checking data for evidence of dependence that violates the conditional independence implications of the model's DAG. In chapter 11, we'll extend refutation from the causal DAG all the way to a causal inference of interest (e.g., estimating a causal effect). However, comparing predicted and actual intervention outcomes gives us a stronger refutation standard than the methods in chapters 4 and 11. The catch, of course, is that doing these real-world interventions must be feasible.

Assuming they are, comparing predicted and real-world intervention outcomes provides a nice iterative framework for building a causal model. First, enumerate a set of interventions you can apply in the real world. Select one of those interventions, use your model to predict its outcome, and then do the intervention in the real world. If the outcomes don't match, update your model so that it does. Repeat until you have exhausted your ability to run real-world interventions.

Doing a real-world intervention usually costs resources and time. To save on costs, use your causal model to predict all the interventions you can run, rank the predicted outcomes according to which are more interesting or surprising, and then prioritize running real-world interventions according to this ranking. Interesting or surprising intervention predictions are likely a sign your model is wrong, so prioritizing them means you'll make big updates to your model sooner and at less cost. And if your model turns out to be right, you will have spent less to arrive at some important insights into your DGP.

### 7.6.3 *"No causation without manipulation"*

The idea behind "no causation without manipulation" is that one should define the variables in the causal model such that the mechanics of *how* one might intervene in it is clear. Clarity here means you could run a real-world experiment that implemented the intervention, or, if the experiment were infeasible, unethical, or impossible, you could at least clearly articulate how the hypothetical experiment would work. "No causation without manipulation" is essentially trying to tether a causal model's abstractions to experimental semantics.

For example, proponents of this idea might object to having "race" as a cause in a causal model, because the concept of race is nebulous from the standpoint of an intervention applied in an experiment—how would you change somebody's race while holding constant everything about that person not caused by their race? They would prefer defining the variable in terms precise enough to be theoretically intervenable, such as "racial bias of loan officer" or "racial indicators on application form." Of course, we have important questions to ask about fuzzy abstractions like "race," so we don't want to add so much precision that we can't generalize the results of our analyses in ways that help answer those questions.

One strategy for establishing this tether to experimentation is to include variables in our model that we can manipulate in a hypothetical experiment. For example, if we are interested in the causal relationship wealth $\rightarrow$ anxiety, we could add a "cash subsidy" variable and cash subsidy $\rightarrow$ wealth edge. Cash subsidy represents direct payments to an individual, which is easier to do in an experiment than directly manipulating an individual's wealth.

### 7.6.4  *Modeling "non-ideal" interventions*

Often the types of interventions we use in practical settings can be challenging to map to ideal interventions. For example, a biologist might be studying the causal relationships between the expression of different genes in a cell, with causal relationships like gene A → gene B → gene C. The biologist might want to know how a stressor in the cellular environment (e.g., a toxin or hypoxia) affects gene expression. The stressor is an intervention; it changes the DGP. However, modeling it as an ideal intervention is challenging because it will likely be unclear which genes those stressors affect directly or what specific amount of gene expression is set by the stressor. A practical solution for these interventions is to model them explicitly as root nodes in the causal DAG, such as the hypoxia node in figure 7.13.

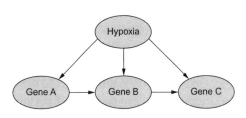

Figure 7.13  **"Hypoxia" is an intervention that has no specific target. Include it as a root node with edges to all variables that are possibly affected.**

Explicit representation of interventions as part of the DGP is less expressive than the ideal (or stochastic) intervention, which captures how an arbitrary intervention can *change* the DGP.

### Summary

- An intervention is an action that changes the data generating process (DGP). Interventions are fundamental to defining causality and causal models.
- Many, if not most, machine learning–driven decisions are interventions that can render the model's deployment environment different from its training environment.
- The ability to model an intervention allows one to simulate the outcome of experiments.
- Simulating experiments with an intervention model can save costs or enable simulated experiments when running an actual experiment is infeasible, unethical, or impossible.
- An ideal intervention targets specific variables, fixes them to a specific value, and renders the target independent of its causal parents.
- Causal effects are simple extensions of intervention distributions. For example, the average treatment effect (ATE) of $X$ on $Y$ is $E(Y_{X=1}) - E(Y_{X=0})$, the difference in means between two intervention distributions for $Y$. Conditional average treatment effects (CATEs) are simply differences in conditional expectations for intervention distributions on $Y$.

- Stochastic interventions are like ideal interventions, but they fix the intervention targets at a value determined by some random process. That value could depend on the states of other variables in the system. In this way, they are related to policies in automated decision-making domains such as bandit algorithms and reinforcement learning.
- An intervention operator describes how a causal model is altered to reflect an ideal (or stochastic) intervention.
- The intervention operator for a structural causal model replaces the target variables assignment function with the intervention value.
- Graph surgery is the intervention operator for causal DAGs.
- The intervention operator for causal graphical models applies graph surgery and replaces the causal Markov kernel for the target with a degenerate distribution that places all probability on the intervention value.
- Causal models can use observational data to statistically learn the observational distribution and any interventional distribution that can be derived through the intervention operator.
- Randomization is a stochastic intervention that eliminates causal influence on the intervention target from unknown causes.
- "No causation without manipulation" suggests defining your causal model so that interventions are tethered to hypothetical experiments.
- You can model interventions that don't meet the ideal intervention standard as root nodes with outgoing edges to variables they may affect.

# Counterfactuals and parallel worlds

## This chapter covers

- Motivating examples for counterfactual reasoning
- Turning counterfactual questions into symbolic form
- Building parallel world graphs for counterfactual reasoning
- Implementing the counterfactual inference algorithm
- Building counterfactual deep generative models of images

Marjani, a good friend of mine, once had to choose between two dating prospects at the same time. She had something of a mental score card for an ideal long-term match. She had good chemistry with one guy, but he didn't rank well on the score card. In contrast, the second guy checked all the boxes, so she chose him. But after some time, despite him meeting all her criteria, she couldn't muster any feelings for him. It was like a failed ritual summoning; the stars were perfectly aligned, but the summoned spirit never showed up. And so, as any of us would in that situation, she posed the *counterfactual question*:

*I chose a partner based on my criteria and it's not working out. Would it have worked out if I chose based on chemistry?*

Counterfactual queries like this describe hypothetical events that did not occur but could have occurred if something had been different. Counterfactuals are fundamental to how we define causality; if the answer to Marjani's question is yes, it implies that choosing based on her score card *caused* her love life to be unsuccessful.

Counterfactuals are core to the bread-and-butter question of causal effect inference, where we compare observed outcomes to "potential outcomes" that didn't happen, like the outcome of Marjani's love life if she chose a partner based on chemistry. More broadly, answering counterfactual questions is useful in learning policies for better decision-making. When some action leads to some outcome, and you ask how a different action might have led to a different outcome, a good answer can help you select better actions in the future. For example, after this experience, Marjani revised her score card to factor in chemistry when considering later romantic prospects.

We'll look at practical examples in this chapter, but I led with this love and romance example because it is universally relatable. It illustrates how fundamental counterfactual reasoning is to human cognition—our judgments about the world are fueled by our imagination of what could have been.

Note that Marjani's counterfactual reasoning involves a type of prediction. Like a Marvel superhero film, she is imagining a *parallel world* where she chose based on chemistry, and she's *predicting* the outcome of her love life in that world. But statistical machine learning algorithms are better at making predictions than humans. That insight leads us to the prospect of building AI that automates human-like counterfactual reasoning with statistical machine learning tools.

In this chapter, we'll pursue that goal by learning to formalize counterfactual questions with probability. In the next chapter, we'll implement a probabilistic counterfactual inference algorithm that can answer these questions. Let's start by exploring some practical case studies that motivate algorithmic counterfactual reasoning.

## 8.1  Motivating counterfactual reasoning

Here, I'll introduce some case studies demonstrating the business value of answering counterfactual questions. I'll then argue how they are useful for enhancing decision-making.

### 8.1.1  Online gaming

Recall the online gaming example from chapter 7, where the amount of in-game purchases a player made was driven by their level of engagement in side-quests and whether they were in a guild. Suppose we observed an individual player who was highly engaged in side-quests and had many in-game purchases. A counterfactual question of interest might be, "What would their amount of in-game purchases be if their engagement was low?"

### 8.1.2   *The streaming wars*

The intense competition amongst subscription streaming companies for a finite market of subscribers has been dubbed "the streaming wars." Netflix is a dominant player with long experience in the space. It has learned to attract new subscribers by building blockbuster franchises from scratch, such as *House of Cards, Stranger Things,* and *Squid Game.*

However, Netflix competes with Amazon, Apple, and Disney—companies with extremely deep pockets. They can compete with Netflix's ability to build franchises from scratch by simply buying existing successful franchises (e.g., *Star Wars*) and making novel content within that franchise (e.g., *The Mandalorian*).

Suppose that Disney is in talks to buy *James Bond,* the most valuable spy thriller franchise ever, and Netflix believes that a successful Bond deal may cause it to lose subscribers to Disney. Netflix hopes to prevent this by striking a deal with a famous showrunner to create a new spy-thriller franchise called *Dead Drop.* This new franchise would combine tried and true spy thriller tropes (e.g., gadgetry, exotic backdrops, car chases, over-the-top action sequences) with the complex characters, diverse representation, and emotionally compelling storylines characteristic of Netflix-produced shows. There is uncertainty about whether Netflix executives can close a deal with the candidate showrunner, as both parties would have to agree on creative control, budget, royalties, etc.

Suppose the Bond deal succeeded, and Disney Plus now runs new series and films set in the "Bond-verse." However, the *Dead Drop* deal fell through. Netflix then acquires data that identifies some subscribers who subsequently left Netflix, subscribed to Disney Plus, and went on to watch the new Bond content.

A Netflix executive would be inclined to ask the following counterfactual: "Would those lost subscribers have stayed, had the *Dead Drop* deal succeeded?" Suppose the answer is "no," because the Bond content was so strong an attraction that the *Dead Drop* deal outcome didn't matter. In this case, the employees who failed to close the deal should not be blamed for losing subscribers.

Or, suppose the *Dead Drop* deal succeeded, and Netflix subscribers can now watch the new *Dead Drop* franchise. "Would those subscribers who watch *Dead Drop* have left for the new Bond series on Disney, had the deal failed?" Again, if the answer is "no," the employees who successfully closed the deal shouldn't get credit for keeping all those subscribers.

In both cases, answering these questions would help inform future deal-making decisions.

### 8.1.3   *Counterfactuals analysis of machine learning models*

In this chapter, we are focusing on using a causal model to reason counterfactually about some data generating process. In machine learning, often the goal is a counterfactual analysis of a machine learning model itself; i.e., given some input features and some output predictions, how would the predictions have differed if the inputs were different? This counterfactual analysis supports explainable AI (XAI), AI fairness, and other tasks.

### COUNTERFACTUAL ANALYSIS IN CLASSIFICATION

Consider the task of classification—a trained algorithm takes as input some set of features for a given example and produces a predicted class for that example. For example, given the details of a loan application, an algorithm classifies the application as "reject" or "approve."

Given a rejected application, a counterfactual question naturally arises: "Would the application have been approved if *some elements* of the application were different?" Often, the goal of the counterfactual analysis is to find a minimal change to the feature vector that corresponds to a change in the classification. Figure 8.1 illustrates this idea.

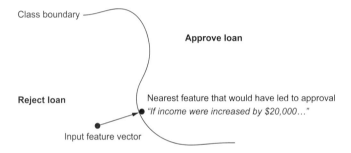

**Figure 8.1   What is the minimal change to the input feature that would have led to approval? In this case, the loan would have been approved if income were $20,000 higher.**

Finding the minimal change that would have led to approval requires defining a distance metric in the feature space and then finding the feature value on the other side of the class boundary. In this example, the hypothetical condition "if the applicant had $20,000 more a year in income . . ." corresponds to the smallest change to the feature vector (in terms of distance on the decision surface) that would have led to approval. This type of analysis is useful for XAI; i.e., for understanding how features drive classification on a case-by-case basis.

### COUNTERFACTUAL ALGORITHMIC RECOURSE

Increasing salary by $20,000 is unrealistic for most loan applicants. That's where counterfactual-based algorithmic recourse can be useful. *Algorithmic recourse* looks for the nearest hypothetical condition that would have led to a different classification. It operates under the constraint that the hypothetical condition was *achievable* or *actionable* by the applicant. Figure 8.2 shows how this works.

In this example, the assumption is that increasing income by $5,000 *and* improving one's credit score was achievable, according to some criteria (while increasing income by $20,000 was not).

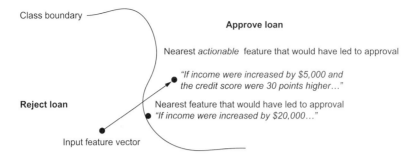

**Figure 8.2**   **In algorithmic recourse, we're often interested in the nearest *actionable* feature vector on the other side of the decision boundary.**

Algorithmic recourse aims to give individuals subjected to machine learning–based decisions information that they can work with. If one fails an exam and asks why, an explanation of "because you are not a genius" is less useful than "because you didn't review the practice exam," even though both may be true.

### COUNTERFACTUAL FAIRNESS

Counterfactual fairness analysis is a similar analysis that applies in cases where some of the input features correspond to attributes of a person. The idea is that certain attributes of an individual person should not, on ethical grounds, impact the classification. For example, it is unethical to use one's ethnicity or gender in the decision to offer a loan. Even if such "protected attributes" are not explicitly coded into the input features, the classification algorithm may have learned proxies for protected attributes, such as the neighborhood where one lives, one's social network, shopping habits, etc. It may make sense to have such features in the model, and it may not be obvious when those features behave as proxies for protected attributes.

Figure 8.3 uses the loan algorithm example to illustrate how a counterfactual fairness analysis would ask counterfactual questions. In this case, the counterfactual question is "Would this person have been approved if they were of a different ethnicity?" The analyst would find features that are proxies for ethnicity and then see if a change to those proxies corresponding to a change in ethnicity would result in a classification

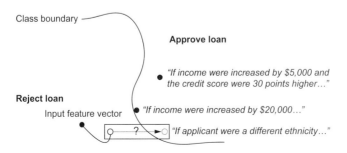

**Figure 8.3   For counterfactual fairness, suppose we want to test whether the algorithm has a bias against certain ethnicities. For a given feature vector, an ethnicity element, and a corresponding "reject" outcome, we test if the outcome would change if the ethnicity element changed.**

of "approve." Some techniques attempt to use this analysis during training to produce fairer algorithms.

While counterfactual fairness analysis is not enough to solve the broad problem of AI fairness, it is an essential element in the AI fairness toolkit.

### 8.1.4   Regret and why do we care about what "would have happened?"

Traditional machine learning is usually forward-looking. Given data, you make a prediction, that prediction drives some decision to be made in the present, and that decision brings about some future cost or benefit. We want good predictions so we can get more future benefits. Imagine, for example, a machine learning algorithm that could accurately forecast the performance of a stock portfolio—that would obviously be quite valuable.

Now, imagine a different algorithm that could accurately tell you how your portfolio would perform today if you had bought different stocks; that would certainly be less valuable than predicting the future. This contrast highlights a common criticism that modeling counterfactuals is backward-looking. For example, the counterfactual questions in our motivating case studies focus on decisions and outcomes that happened in the past. What's done is done; getting the answers to such questions won't change the past.

But, first, not all counterfactuals are retrospective. In section 8.3 we'll model questions like "What are the chances the subscriber would churn if you don't send them a promotion and would not churn if you did send a promotion?" ("Churn" means to stop using a product or service within a certain time period.) That question has no past tense, does have business value, and is something we can model.

Second, *retrospective counterfactuals help you understand how to make better decisions in the future.* Indeed, analyzing how your portfolio would have performed given different allocations—what investors call "backtesting"—is ideal for comparing various investment strategies. Similarly, the counterfactual insights from a failed *Dead Drop* deal might help Netflix executives make a deal with another famous showrunner.

When we consider retrospective reasoning about things that *would have* or *could have* been, we arrive at the notion of *regret*. Regret is about retrospective counterfactual contrasts; given a choice, regret is a comparison between an outcome of the option you chose and an imagined counterfactual outcome of an option you rejected. In colloquial terms, regret is the bad feeling you get when the counterfactual outcome of an option you rejected is better than the option you chose. But cognitive science calls this *negative regret*; there is also *positive regret*, which is the good feeling you get when, upon comparing to imagined counterfactual outcomes, you realize you chose the better option (as in, "whew, I really dodged a bullet").

Regret can be useful for learning to make better decisions. Suppose you make a choice, you pay a cost (time, effort, resources, etc.), and it leads to an outcome. That gives you a baseline single point of data for learning. Now, suppose that, with the benefit of hindsight, you could imagine with 100% accuracy the outcome that would have occurred had you made a different choice. Now you have two comparable points of data for learning, and you only had to pay a cost for one of them.

Usually your ability to imagine the counterfactual outcome of the rejected option is not 100% accurate. Even with the benefit of hindsight, there is still some uncertainty about the counterfactual outcome. But that's no problem—we can model that uncertainty with probability. As long as hindsight knowledge provides you with some information about counterfactual outcomes, you can do better than the baseline of learning from a single point of data.

In reinforcement learning and other automated decision-making, we often call our decision-making criteria "policies." We can incorporate counterfactual analysis and regret in *evaluating* and *updating policies.*

### 8.1.5    *Reinforcement learning and automated decision-making*

In automated decision-making, a "policy" is a function that takes in information about a decision problem and automatically selects some course of action. Reinforcement learning algorithms aim to find policies that optimize good outcomes over time.

Automated counterfactual reasoning can credit good outcomes to the appropriate actions. In the investing example, we can imagine an algorithm that periodically backtests different portfolio allocation policies as more recent prices enter the data. Similarly, imagine we were writing a reinforcement learning (RL) algorithm to learn to play a game. We could have the algorithm use saved game instances to simulate how that game instance would have turned out differently if it had used a different policy. The algorithm can quantify the concept of regret by comparing those simulated outcomes to actual outcomes and using the results to learn a better policy. This would reduce the number of games the AI needed to learn a good policy, as well as enable it to learn from simulated conditions that don't occur normally in the game. We'll focus more on automated decision-making, bandits, and reinforcement learning in chapter 12.

### 8.1.6    *Steps to answering a counterfactual query*

Across each of these applications, we can answer these counterfactual inference questions with the following workflow:

1    *Pose the counterfactual question*—Clearly articulate the counterfactual question(s) we want to pose in the simplest terms.

2    *Convert to a mathematical query*—Convert the query to mathematical symbols so it is formal enough to apply mathematical or algorithmic analysis.

3    *Do inference*—Run an inference algorithm that will generate an answer to the question.

In the following sections, we'll focus on steps 1 and 2. In chapter 9, we'll handle step 3 with an SCM-based algorithm for inferring the query we create in step 2. In chapter 10, we'll see ways to do step 3 without an SCM but only data and a DAG.

## 8.2 Symbolic representation of counterfactuals

In chapter 7, we saw the "counterfactual notation," which uses subscripts to represent interventions. Now we are going to use this notation for counterfactual expressions. The trick is remembering, as we'll see, that counterfactual queries are just a special type of *interventional* queries. We'll see how interventional queries flow into counterfactual queries by revisiting our online gaming example.

### 8.2.1 Hypothetical statements and questions

Consider our online gaming case study. When considering how much a player makes, we might say something like this:

> *The level of in-game purchases for a typical player would be more than $50.*

We'll call this a *hypothetical statement*. In grammatical terms, I am using a *modal verb* (e.g., "would", "could", "should" in "would be more") to intentionally mark *hypothetical language* rather than using *declarative language* (e.g., "is more" or "will be more"), which we use to make statements about objective facts.

We want to formalize this statement in probability notation. For this statement, we'll write $P(I > 50)$—recall that we used the random variable $I$ to represent *In-Game Purchases*, $E$ to represent *Side-Quest Engagement*, and $G$ to represent *Guild Membership*.

We'll use hypothetical language in our open questions as well, like this:

> *What would be the amount of in-game purchases for a typical player?*

I am inquiring about the range of values the variable $I$ could take, and I represent that with $P(I)$.

---

**Declarative vs. hypothetical language and probability**

Declarative language express certainty, as in "amount of in-game purchases is more than $50." In contrast, hypothetical language is used for statements that convey conjecture, imagination, and supposition, as in "amount of in-game purchases *would be* more than $50."

Many of us learn to associate probability notation with declarative language, because of probability theory's connection to propositional logic: $P(I > 50)$ quantifies the probability that the declarative statement "amount of in-game purchases is more than $50" is true. But we are going to lean into the hypothetical language.

Hypothetical language has an implicit lack of certainty—we are talking of things that *could be*, rather than things that *are*. Lack of certainty is equivalent to uncertainty, and the Bayesian philosophy we adopt in this book nudges us toward using probability to model uncertainty, so using hypothetical language will make it easier for us to formalize the question in probability notation. We'll find this will help us formalize causal statements and questions.

Note that the tense of the question or statement doesn't matter when we map it to probabilistic notation. For example, we could have used this phrasing:

> *What would have been the amount of in-game purchases for a typical player?*

Regardless of tense, we use the notation $P(I)$ to represent our uncertainty about a variable of interest in our question.

### 8.2.2    *Facts filter hypotheticals to a subpopulation*

Suppose my statement was as follows:

> *The level of in-game purchases for a player with high side-quest engagement would be more than $50. P(I>50|E="high")*

Here, I am making a statement about a subset of players (those with high side-quest engagement) rather than all players. I'm doing the same when I ask this question:

> *What would be the level of in-game purchases for players with high side-quest engagement? P(I|E="high")*

The fact that *Side-Quest Engagement* is high serves to filter the population of players down to those for whom that fact is true. As discussed in chapter 2, we use conditional probability to zoom in on a subpopulation. In this example, we use $P(I>50|E="high")$ for the statement, and $P(I|E="high")$ for the question.

I'll use "factual conditions" to refer to facts, events, and evidence like $E="high"$ that narrow down the target population. These factual conditions appear on the right side of "|" in the conditional probability notation $P(.|.)$. We might normally call them "conditions," but I want to avoid confusion with "conditional hypothetical," which I'll introduce next.

### 8.2.3    *Conditional hypotheticals, interventions, and simulation*

Now, suppose I made the following statement:

> *If a player's side-quest engagement was high, they would spend more than $50 on in-game purchases. $P(I_{E="high"}>50)$*

We'll call this a *conditional hypothetical* statement. We'll call the "If side-quest engagement was high" part the *hypothetical condition*, and "they would spend more than $50 on in-game purchases" is the *hypothetical outcome*.

The hypothetical conditions in conditional hypothetical questions often follow a similar "what if" style of phrasing:

> *What would be the amount of in-game purchases for a player if their side-quest engagement was high? $P(I_{E="high"})$*

We will use the intervention notation (i.e., the subscripts in counterfactual notation) to represent these conditions. For the statement, we will use $P(I_{E="high"}>50)$, and for the question, $P(I_{E="high"})$.

**IMAGINATION, CONDITIONS, AND INTERVENTIONS**

Using the ideal intervention to model hypothetical conditions in conditional hypothetical statements is a philosophical keystone of our causal modeling approach. The idea is that when we pose hypothetical conditionals, *we only attend to the causal consequences of the hypothetical conditional.*

---

### Refresher: Ideal intervention

An ideal intervention is a change to the data generating process that does the following:

1. Targets a fixed variable (e.g., $X$)
2. Sets that variable to a specific value (e.g., $x$)
3. In so doing, severs the causal influence of that variable's parents

This definition generalizes to a *set* of variables.

We sometimes write interventions with *do-notation*, as in do($X=x$). In counterfactual notation, for a variable $Y$, we write $Y_{X=x}$ to indicate that the variable $Y$ is under the influence of an intervention on $X$. In a DAG, we represent ideal intervention with graph surgery, meaning we cut the incoming edges to the target variable. In an SCM, we represent an ideal intervention by replacing the target variable's assignment function with the intervention value. Causal libraries often implement these operations for us, often with a function or method called "do".

---

Let me illustrate by counterexample. Suppose we ask this:

> *What would be the amount of in-game purchases for a player if their side-quest engagement were high?*

Suppose we then modeled this with $P(I|E=\text{"high"})$. Then inference on this query would use not just the causal impact that high engagement has on *In-Game Purchases* but also the non-causal association through the path $E \leftarrow G \rightarrow I$; you can infer whether a player is in a guild from their level of *Side-Quest Engagement*, and *Guild Membership* also drives *In-Game Purchases*. But this question is not about *Guild Membership*; we're just interested in how *Side-Quest Engagement* drives *In-Game Purchases*.

"What if" hypotheticals use the ideal intervention because they attend only to the causal consequences of the condition. To illustrate, let's rephrase the previous question to make that implied ideal intervention explicit:

> *What would be the amount of In-Game Purchases for a player if their side-quest engagement were **set to** high?* $P(I_{E=\text{"high"}})$

The verb "set" connotes the action of intervening. Modeling hypothetical conditions with ideal interventions argues that the original phrasing and this phrasing mean the same thing (going forward, I'll use the original phrasing).

As humans, we answer "what if" questions like the preceding $P(I_{E=\text{"high"}})$ question (either the original or rephrased version) by imagining a world where the hypothetical condition is true and then imagining how the hypothetical scenario plays out as a consequence. The variables in our hypothetical condition may have their own causal drivers in the data-generating process (e.g., *Guild Membership* is a cause of *Side-Quest Engagement*), but we ignore those drivers because we are only interested in the consequences of the hypothetical condition. We isolate the variables in a hypothetical condition in our imaginations just as we would in an experiment. The ideal intervention is the right tool for setting a variable independently of its causes.

### AVOIDING CONFUSION BETWEEN FACTUAL AND HYPOTHETICAL CONDITIONS

It is particularly easy to confuse "factual conditions" with "hypothetical conditions." To reiterate in general terms, in the question "What would $Y$ be if $X$ were $x$", $X = x$ is a hypothetical condition and we use the notation $P(Y_{X=x})$. In contrast, factual conditions serve to narrow down the population we are asking about. For example, in the question "What would $Y$ be for cases where $X$ is $x$?" $X = x$ is an actual condition used to filter down to cases where $X = x$. Here, we use notation $P(Y|X=x)$.

Keep in mind that we can combine factual and hypothetical conditions, as in the following question:

> *What would be the amount of in-game purchases for a player in a guild if their side-quest engagement was high?* $P(I_{E=\text{"high"}}|G=g)$

Here, we are asking a conditional hypothetical on a subset of players who are guild members. This query is different from the following:

> *What would be the amount of in-game purchases for a player if their side-quest engagement was high and they were in a guild?* $P(I_{E=\text{"high"}, \, G=\text{"member"}})$

That said, with the ambiguity of natural language, someone might ask the second question when what they really want is the answer to the first question. It is up to the modeler to dispel confusion, clarify meaning, and write down the correct notation.

## 8.2.4   *Counterfactual statements*

In natural language, a *counterfactual statement* is a conditional hypothetical statement where there is some conflict between factual conditions and hypothetical conditions or outcomes. In other words, it is a conditional hypothetical statement that is "counter to the facts."

In everyday language, those conflicting factual conditions could be stated before the statement or implied by context. For our purposes, we'll require counterfactual statements to state the conflicting factual conditions explicitly:

> *For a player with low side-quest engagement and an amount of in-game purchases less than $50, if the player's side-quest engagement were high, they would spend more than $50 on in-game purchases.* $P(I_{E=\text{"high"}}>50|E=\text{"low"}, \, I\leq50)$

As a question, we might ask:

*What would be the amount of in-game purchases for a player with low side-quest engagement and in-game purchases less than $50 if their side-quest engagement was high? $P(I_{E=\text{"high"}} \mid E=\text{"low"}, I \leq 50)$*

In both the statement and the question, the factual condition of low engagement conflicts with the hypothetical condition of high engagement. In the statement, the hypothetical outcome where in-game purchases is more than 50 conflicts with the factual condition where it is less than or equal to 50. Similarly, the question considers all possible hypothetical outcomes for in-game purchases, most of which conflict with the factual condition of being less than or equal to 50. We use counterfactual notation to write these queries just as we would other conditional hypotheticals..

## Overview of terminology in formalizing counterfactuals

*Hypothetical language*—Used to express hypotheses, conjecture, supposition, and imagined possibilities. In English, it often involves "would" or "could" and contrasts with the declarative language. It is arguably easier to formalize causal statements and questions phrased in hypothetical language.

*Hypothetical statement*—A statement about the world phrased in hypothetical language, such as "Y would be y," which we'd write in math as $P(Y=y)$.

*Factual conditions*—Refer to facts, events, and evidence that narrow down the scope of what's being talked about (the target population). Used as the conditions in conditional probability. For example, we'd write "Where Z is z, Y would be y" as $P(Y=y|Z=z)$.

*Hypothetical conditions*—Conditions that frame a hypothetical scenario, as in "what if X were x?" or "If X were x ..." We model hypothetical conditions with the ideal intervention and subscript $_{X=x}$ in counterfactual notation.

*Conditional hypothetical statement*—A hypothetical statement with hypothetical conditions, such as "If X were x, Y would be y," which becomes $P(Y_{X=x}=y)$. We can add factual conditions like "Where Z is z, if X were x, Y would be y" becomes $P(Y_{X=x}=y|Z=z)$.

*Counterfactual statement*—A counterfactual statement is a conditional hypothetical statement where the variables in the factual conditions overlap with those in the hypothetical conditions or hypothetical outcomes. For example, in "Where X is x, if X were x', Y would be y" ($P(Y_{X=x'}=y|X=x)$), the factual condition "Where X is x" overlaps with the hypothetical condition "if X were x'". In "Where Y is y, if X were x', Y would be y'" ($P(Y_{X=x'}=y'|Y=y)$), the factual condition "Where Y is y" overlaps with the hypothetical outcome "Y would be y."

*Consistency rule*—You can drop a hypothetical condition in the subscript if a factual condition and a hypothetical condition overlap but don't conflict. For example, $P(Y_{X=x}|X=x) = P(Y|X=x)$.

Note that many texts will use the word "counterfactual" to describe formal causal queries that don't necessarily condition on factual conditions, such as $Y_{X=x}$ or $P(Y_{X=x}=y)$ or $P(Y_{X=x}=1, Y_{X=x'}=0)$. I'm using "counterfactual statement" and other phrases above to describe common hypothetical and counterfactual natural language and to aid in the task of converting to formal counterfactual notation.

Note that we can combine conflicting factual conditions with other non-conflicting factual conditions, such as being a member of the guild in this example:

> *What would be the amount of in-game purchases for a player in a guild with low side-quest engagement and in-game purchases less than $50 if their side-quest engagement was high?* $P(I_{E=\text{"high"}} \mid E=\text{"low"}, I \leq 50, G=\text{"member"})$

Figure 8.4 diagrams the elements of a formalized counterfactual query.

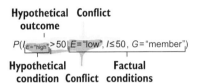

**Figure 8.4   Elements of a conditional counterfactual hypothetical formalized in counterfactual notation**

### Formalizing counterfactuals with large language models

Formalizing a counterfactual question into counterfactual notation is an excellent task for a large language model (LLM). State-of-the-art LLMs perform quite well at benchmarks where a natural language query is converted to a symbolic query, such as an SQL statement, and formalizing a counterfactual question is an example of this task. We'll look more at LLMs and causality in chapter 13, but for now you can experiment with prompting your favorite LLM to convert questions to counterfactual notation.

### 8.2.5   *The consistency rule*

Consider the distribution $P(I_{E=\text{"high"}}|E=\text{"low"})$. Suppose that instead of the subscript $_{E=\text{"high"}}$ we had $_{E=\text{"low"}}$, so the distribution is $P(I_{E=\text{"low"}} \mid E=\text{"low"})$. The *consistency rule* states that this distribution is equivalent to the simpler $P(I|E=\text{"low"})$. More generally, $P(Y_{X=x}|X=x, Z=z) = P(Y|X=x, Z=z)$ for any $z$.

Intuitively, $P(I_{E=\text{"low"}}|E=\text{"low"})$ corresponds to the rather odd question, "What would be the amount of in-game purchases for a player with low side-quest engagement if their side-quest engagement was low?" In this question, the factual condition and the hypothetical condition overlap but don't conflict. The *consistency rule* says that, in this case, we drop the hypothetical condition, saying that this is equivalent to asking "What would be the amount of in-game purchases for a player with low side-quest engagement?"

Now consider a version of this counterfactual where we observe an actual outcome for in-game purchases. Specifically, consider $P(I_{E=\text{"high"}}|E=\text{"low"}, I=75)$. This is the corresponding counterfactual question:

*What would be the amount of in-game purchases for a player with low side-quest engagement and in-game purchases equal to $75 if their side-quest engagement was high?*

Now, instead, suppose we changed it to $P(I_{E=\text{``low''}}|E=\text{``low''}, I=75)$. By the consistency rule, this collapses to $P(I|E=\text{``low''}, I=75)$:

*What would be the amount of in-game purchases for a player with low side-quest engagement and in-game purchases equal to $75?*

The answer, of course, is $75. If we ask about the distribution of $I$ conditional on $I=75$, then we have a distribution with all the probability value concentrated on 75.

In counterfactual reasoning, we often want to know about hypothetical outcomes for the same variables we observe in the factual conditions. The consistency rule states that if the hypothetical conditions are the same as what actually happened, the hypothetical outcome must be the same as what actually happened.

Recall that we use an intervention to model the hypothetical condition. The rule assures us that if a player had low *Side-Quest Engagement* and a certain amount of *In-Game Purchases*, they would have the exact same amount of *In-Game Purchases* if they were selected for an experiment that randomly selected them for the low *Side-Quest Engagement* group. That's important if we expect our causal inferences to predict the outcomes of experiments.

### 8.2.6 More examples

Table 8.1 presents several additional examples of mapping counterfactual questions to counterfactual notation.

**Table 8.1   Examples of counterfactual notation**

| Question | Type | Distribution in counterfactual notation |
|---|---|---|
| What would be the amount of in-game purchases for a typical player? | Hypothetical | $P(I)$ |
| What would be the amount of in-game purchases for a player with high side-quest engagement? | Hypothetical focused on highly engaged players | $P(I|E=\text{``high''})$ |
| What would be the amount of in-game purchases for a player if they had high side-quest engagement? | Conditional hypothetical | $P(I_{E=\text{``high''}})$ |
| What would be the level of engagement *and* amount of in-game purchases if the player were a guild member? | Conditional hypothetical on two outcomes of interest | $P(E_{G=\text{``member''}}, I_{G=\text{``member''}})$ |

**Table 8.1  Examples of counterfactual notation** *(continued)*

| Question | Type | Distribution in counterfactual notation |
|---|---|---|
| What would be the level of in-game purchases for a player if they had high side-quest engagement and they were not a guild member? | Conditional hypothetical with two hypothetical conditions | $P(I_{E=\text{"high"}, \, G=\text{"nonmember"}})$ |
| What would be the level of in-game purchases for a player in a guild if they had high side-quest engagement? | Conditional hypothetical focused on guild members | $P(I_{E=\text{"high"}} \mid G=\text{"member"})$ |
| For a player with low engagement, what would their level of in-game purchases be if their level of engagement was high? | Counterfactual. Factual condition conflicts with hypothetical condition. | $P(I_{E=\text{"high"}} \mid E=\text{"low"})$ |
| For a player who had at most \$50 of in-game purchases, what would their level of in-game purchases be if their level of engagement was high? | Counterfactual. Factual condition (in-game purchases of ≤\$50) conflicts with possible hypothetical outcomes (in-game purchases possibly >\$50). | $P(I_{E=\text{"high"}} \mid I \leq 50)$ |
| For a player who had low engagement and at most \$50 of in-game purchases, what would their level of in-game purchases be if their level of engagement was high? | Counterfactual. Factual conditions conflict with a hypothetical condition and possible hypothetical outcomes. | $P(I_{E=\text{"high"}} \mid E=\text{"low"}, \, I \leq 50)$ |
| For a player in a guild who had low engagement, what would their level of in-game purchases be if their engagement were high and they weren't a guild member? | Counterfactual. Factual conditions conflict with hypothetical conditions. | $P(I_{E=\text{"high"}, \, G=\text{"nonmember"}} \mid E=\text{"low"}, \, G=\text{"member"})$ |
| What would be the level of engagement if the player were a guild member? Moreover, what would be their level of in-game purchases if they were *not* a guild member? | Counterfactual. Involves two conflicting hypothetical conditions on two different outcomes. | $P(E_{G=\text{"member"}}, \, I_{G=\text{"nonmember"}})$ |

The last case in table 8.1 is a special case, more common in theory than practice, that does not involve a factual condition but has conflicting hypothetical conditions.

Next, we'll look at a particular class of counterfactuals that involve binary causes and outcomes.

## 8.3  *Binary counterfactuals*

An important subclass of counterfactual query is one we'll call *binary counterfactuals*. These are counterfactuals involving binary hypothetical conditions and outcome variables. Binary variables, especially binary causes, arise when we think in terms of observational and experimental studies, where we have "exposed" and "unexposed" groups, or "treatments" and "control" groups. But binary variables are also useful in reasoning about the occurrence of events; an event either happens or does not.

Binary counterfactual queries deserve special mention because they are often simpler to think about, have simplifying mathematical properties that queries on nonbinary variables lack, and have several practical applications that we'll cover in this section. Further, you can often word the question you want to answer in binary terms, such that you can convert nonbinary variables to binary variables when formalizing your query. To illustrate, in our online gaming example, suppose a player made $152.34 in online purchases, and we ask "Why did this player pay so much?" We are not interested in why they paid exactly that specific amount but why they paid such a high amount, where "such a high amount" is defined as, for example, more than $120. So our binary indicator variable is $X = \{1$ if $I \geq 120$ else $0\}$.

### 8.3.1   *Probabilities of causation*

The probabilities of causation are an especially useful class of binary counterfactuals. Their utility lies in helping us answer "why" questions. They are foundational concepts in practical applications, including attribution in marketing, credit assignment in reinforcement learning, root cause analysis in engineering, and personalized medicine.

Let's demonstrate the usefulness of the probabilities of causation in the context of a churn attribution problem. In a subscription business model, churn is the rate at which your service loses subscribers, and it has a major impact on the value of a business or business unit. Typically, a company deploys a predictive algorithm that rates subscribers as having some degree of churn risk. The company wants to discourage subscribers with a high risk of churn from actually doing so. In our example, the company will send a promotion that will entice the subscriber to stay (not churn). The probabilities of causation can help us understand why a user would churn or stay.

Given a binary (true/false) cause $X$ and outcome $Y$, we'll define the following probabilities of causation: probability of necessity, of sufficiency, of necessity *and* sufficiency, of enablement, and of disablement.

#### PROBABILITY OF NECESSITY

For a binary cause $X$ and binary outcome $Y$, the *probability of necessity* (PN) is the query $P(Y_{X=0}=0|X=1, Y=1)$. In plain language, the question underlying PN is "For cases where $X$ happened, and $Y$ happened, if $X$ had not happened, would $Y$ not have happened?" In other words, did $X$ *need* to happen for $Y$ to happen?

Let's consider our churn problem. Let $X$ represent whether we sent a promotion and $Y$ represent whether the user stayed (didn't churn). In this example, $P(Y_{X=0}=0|X=1, Y=1)$ represents the query "For a subscriber who received the promotion and stayed, what are the chances they would have churned if they had not received the promotion?" In other words, was the promotional offer necessary to maintain the subscriber?

## PROBABILITY OF SUFFICIENCY

The *probability of sufficiency* (PS) is $P(Y_{X=1}=1|X=0, Y=0)$. A common plain language articulation of PS is "For cases where neither $X$ nor $Y$ happened, if $X$ had happened, would $Y$ have happened?" In other words, is $X$ happening sufficient to cause $Y$ to happen? For example, "for users who did not receive a promotion and didn't stay (churned), would they have stayed had they received the promotion?" In other words, would a promotion have been enough (sufficient) to keep them?

The plain language interpretation of sufficiency can be confusing. The factual conditions of the counterfactual query zoom in on cases where $X=0$ and $Y=0$ (cases where neither $X$ nor $Y$ happened). However, we're often interested in looking at cases where $X=1$ and $Y=1$ and asking if $X$ was sufficient by itself to cause $Y=1$. In other words, given that $X$ happened and $Y$ happened, would $Y$ still have happened even if the various other events that influenced $Y$ had turned out different? But $P(Y_{X=1}=1|X=0, Y=0)$ entails this interpretation without requiring us to enumerate all the "various other events that influenced $Y$" in the query. See the chapter notes at www.altdeep.ai/causalAIbook for pointers to deeper research discussions on sufficiency.

### Probabilities of causation and the law

The probabilities of causation are closely related to legal concepts in the law. It is helpful to know this relationship, since practical applications often intersect with the law, and many stakeholders we work with in practical settings have legal training.

- *But-for causation and the probability of necessity*—The but-for test is one test for determining causation in tort and criminal law. The way we phrase the probability of necessity is the probabilistic equivalent to the but-for test, rephrasing "if $X$ had not happened, would $Y$ not have happened?" as "but for $X$ happening, would $Y$ have happened?"
- *Proximal causality and the probability of sufficiency*—In law, proximate cause refers to the primacy that a cause $X$ had in the chain of events that directly brings about an outcome (e.g., injury or damage). There is indeed a connection with sufficiency, though not an equivalency. Proximal causality indeed considers whether a causal event was sufficient to cause the outcome, but legal theories of proximal cause often go beyond sufficiency to invoke moral judgments as well.

## PROBABILITY OF NECESSITY AND SUFFICIENCY

The *probability of necessity and sufficiency* (PNS) is $P(Y_{X=1}=1, Y_{X=0}=0)$. In plain language, $P(Y_{X=1}=1, Y_{X=0}=0)$ reads, "$Y$ would be 0 if $X$ were 0 *and* $Y$ would be 1 if $X$ were 1." For example, "What are the chances that a given user would churn if they didn't receive a promotion and would stay if they did receive a promotion?" PNS decomposes as follows:

$$PNS = P(X = 1, Y = 1)PN + P(X = 0, Y = 0)PS$$

**PROBABILITY OF DISABLEMENT AND ENABLEMENT**

The *probabilities of disablement* (PD) and *enablement* (PE) are similar to PN and PS, except they do not condition on the cause *X*.

PD is the query $P(Y_{X=0}=0|Y=1)$, meaning "For cases where *Y* happened, if *X* had not happened would *Y* not have happened?" For the churn problem, PD asks the question "What is the overall chance of churn if we don't send promotions? exclusively in reference to the subpopulation of users who didn't churn (regardless of whether they received a promotion).

PE is the query $P(Y_{X=1}=1|Y=0)$, or "For cases where *Y* didn't happen, if *X* had happened, would *Y* have happened?" In our churn problem, PE asks, "What is the overall chance of staying if we send promotions?" exclusively in reference to the subpopulation of users who churned (regardless of whether they received a promotion).

The probabilities of causation can work as basic counterfactual primitives in advanced applications of counterfactual analysis. Next, I'll give an example in the context of attribution.

### 8.3.2  *Probabilities of causation and attribution*

The probabilities of causation are the core ingredients for methods that quantify why a given outcome happens. For example, suppose that a company's network has a faulty server, such that accessing the server can cause the network to crash. Suppose the network crashes, and you're tasked with analyzing the logs to find the root cause. You find that your colleague Lazlo has accessed the faulty server. Is Lazlo to blame?

To answer that, you might quantify the chances that Lazlo was a sufficient cause of the crash; i.e., the chance that Lazlo accessing the server was enough to tip the domino that ultimately led to the network to crash. Second, what are the chances that Lazlo was a necessary cause? For example, perhaps Lazlo wasn't a necessary cause because if he hadn't accessed the server, someone else would have eventually.

The probabilities of causation need to be combined with other elements to provide a complete view of attribution. One example is the concept of abnormality. The abnormality of a causal event describes whether that event, in some sense, violated expectations. For example, Lazlo might get more blame for crashing the network if it was highly unusual for employees to access that server. We can quantify the abnormality of a causal event with probability; if event *X*=1 was abnormal, then it was unlikely to have occurred, so we assign a low value to $P(X=1)$. One attribution measure, called actual causal strength (ACS), combines abnormality with probabilities of causation as follows:

$$ACS = P(X = 0) \times PN + P(X = 1) \times PS$$

In other words, this approach views attribution as a trade-off between being an *abnormal* necessary cause and a *normal* sufficient cause.

There is also a growing body of methods that combine attribution methods from the field of explainable AI (e.g., Shapley and SHAP values) with concepts of abnormality and causal concepts, such as the probabilities of causation. See the book notes at www.altdeep.ai/causalAIbook for a list of references, including actual causal strength and explainable AI methods.

### 8.3.3    *Binary counterfactuals and uplift modeling*

Statistical analysis of campaigns to influence human behavior is common in business, politics, and research. For instance, in our churn example, the goal of offering a promotion is to convince people not to churn. Similarly, businesses advertise to convince people to buy their products, and politicians reach out to voters to get them to vote or donate to a campaign.

One of the challenges of campaigns to influence behavior is identifying who is likely to respond favorably to your attempt to influence so you only spend your limited resources influencing those people. John Wanamaker, a pioneer of the field of marketing, put it best:

> *Half the money I spend on advertising is wasted; the trouble is I don't know which half.*

*Uplift modeling* refers to a class of statistical techniques that seek to answer this question with data. However, a data scientist approaching this problem space for the first time will find various statistical approaches, varying in terminology, presumptive data types, modeling assumptions, and modeling approaches, leading to confusion. Binary counterfactuals are quite useful in understanding the problem at a high level and how various solutions succeed or fail at addressing it.

#### SEGMENTING USERS INTO PERSUADABLES, SURE THINGS, LOST CAUSES, AND SLEEPING DOGS

In our churn example, we can assume there are two kinds of subscribers. For some subscribers, a promotion will influence their decision to churn. Others are non-responders, meaning people for whom the promotion will have no influence. We can break up the latter non-responders into two groups:

- *Lost causes*—People who will churn regardless of whether they receive a promotion
- *Sure things*—People who will stay regardless of whether they receive a promotion

Of the people who do respond to the promotion, we have two groups:

- *Persuadables*—Subscribers who could be persuaded by a promotion not to leave the service
- *Sleeping dogs*—Subscribers who would not churn if you didn't send a promotion, and people who would churn if you did

Sleeping dogs are named for the expression "let sleeping dogs lie" (last they wake up and bite you). These people will do what you want if you leave them alone, but they'll behave against your wishes if you don't. Have you ever received a marketing email from a subscription service and thought, "These people send me too much spam! I'm going to cancel." You were a "sleeping dog"—the company's email was the kick that woke you up, and you bit them for it. Figure 8.5 shows how our subscribers break down into these four segments.

**Segments of the target population**

|  | Responders | Non-responders |
|---|---|---|
| **Behave favorably** | *Persuadables* ◎ | *Sure things* |
| **Behave unfavorably** | *Sleeping dogs* | *Lost causes* |

**Figure 8.5  In attempts to influence behavior, we break down the target population into these four segments. Given limited resources, we want to target our influence efforts on the persuadables and avoid the others, especially the sleeping dogs.**

Promotions have a cost in terms of the additional value you give to the subscriber. You want to avoid spending that cost on subscribers who weren't going to churn (sure things) and subscribers who were always going to churn (lost causes). And you definitely want to avoid spending that cost only to cause someone to churn (sleeping dogs). So, of these four groups, you want to send your promotions *only* to the persuadables. The task of statistical analysis is to segment our users into these four groups.

This is where counterfactuals can help us; we can define each segment in probabilistic counterfactual terms:

- *Lost causes*—People who probably would churn if we send a promotion and still churn if we did not send a promotion; i.e., $P(Y_{X=1}=0, Y_{X=0}=0)$ is high.
- *Sure things*—People who probably would stay if we send a promotion and stay if we did not send a promotion; i.e., $P(Y_{X=1}=1, Y_{X=0}=1)$ is high.
- *Persuadables*—People who probably would stay if we send a promotion and churn if we did not send a promotion; i.e., $P(Y_{X=1}=1, Y_{X=0}=0)$ is high. In other words, PNS is high.
- *Sleeping dogs*—People who probably would churn if we send a promotion and would stay if we did not send a promotion; i.e., $P(Y_{X=1}=0, Y_{X=0}=1)$ is high.

You can see, in figure 8.6, how the population can be segmented.

**Segments of the target population**

|  | Responders | Non-responders |
|---|---|---|
| **Behave favorably** | $P(Y_{X=1}=1, Y_{X=0}=0)$ ◎ | $P(Y_{X=1}=1, Y_{X=0}=1)$ |
| **Behave unfavorably** | $P(Y_{X=1}=0, Y_{X=0}=1)$ | $P(Y_{X=1}=0, Y_{X=0}=0)$ |

**Figure 8.6  We can segment the population in counterfactual terms.**

Each subscriber has some set of attributes (demographics, usage habits, content preferences, etc.). Our goal is to convert these attributes to predict whether a subscriber is a persuadable, sleeping dog, lost cause, or sure thing.

Let $C$ represent a set of subscriber attributes. Given a subscriber with attributes $C=c$, our causal query of interest is $P(Y_{X=1}, Y_{X=0}|C=c)$. Various statistical segmentation methods seek to define $C$ such that users fall into groups that have high probability for one of the four outcomes of $P(Y_{X=1}, Y_{X=0}|C=c)$, but before we apply the stats, our first task will be to ensure we can estimate this query using sufficient assumptions and data. We'll cover how to estimate counterfactuals with SCMs in chapter 9 and how to use identification with broader estimation techniques in chapter 10.

Now that we've learned to pose our causal query and formalize it into math, let's revisit the steps of making the counterfactual inference, in figure 8.7.

**Figure 8.7   The counterfactual inference workflow**

In the next section, we'll study the idea of possible worlds and parallel world graphs. These ideas are important to both identification (determining whether we can answer the question) and the inference algorithm.

## 8.4 *Possible worlds and parallel world graphs*

In this section, I'll introduce the notion of possible worlds and parallel world graphs, an extension of a causal DAG for an SCM that supports counterfactual reasoning across possible worlds.

### 8.4.1 *Potential outcomes in possible worlds*

Counterfactual reasoning involves reasoning over *possible worlds*. A possible world is a way the world is or could be. The *actual world* is the possible world with the event outcomes we observed. All other possible worlds are *hypothetical worlds*.

In terms of the data generating process (DGP), the actual world is how the DGP unrolled to produce our data. Other possible worlds are defined by all the ways the DGP could have produced different data.

*Potential outcomes* are a fundamental concept in causal effect inference. "Potential outcomes" refers to outcomes of the same variable across differing possible worlds. If you have a headache and take an aspirin, you might say there are two potential outcomes in two possible worlds: one where your headache gets better and one where it doesn't.

## Review of possible world terminology

*Possible world*—A way the world is or could be

*Actual world*—A possible world with observed event outcomes

*Hypothetical world*—A possible world with no observed event outcomes

*Potential outcomes*—Outcomes of the same variable across differing possible worlds

*Parallel worlds*—A set of possible worlds being reasoned over, sharing both common and differing attributes

*Parallel world graph*—A graphical representation of parallel worlds used both for identifying counterfactual queries and in counterfactual inference algorithms

### 8.4.2   *The parallel world graph*

A parallel world graph is a simple extension of a causal DAG that captures causality across possible worlds. Continuing with the online gaming example, suppose we are interested in the question, "For a player who had low engagement and less than $50 of in-game purchases, what would their level of in-game purchases be if their level of engagement was high?" I.e., $P(I_{E=\text{"high"}}|E=\text{"low"}, I<50)$. For this counterfactual query, we can visualize both the actual and the hypothetical worlds in figure 8.8

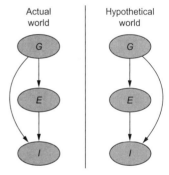

**Figure 8.8   To answer the counterfactual query for the online gaming example, we start by duplicating the causal DAG across possible worlds.**

We duplicate the causal DAG for the online gaming example across both possible worlds. Having one DAG for each world reflects that the causal structure of the DGP is the same in each world. But we'll need to connect these DAGs in some way to reason *across* worlds.

We'll connect the two worlds using an SCM defined on the causal DAG. We'll suppose that the original nodes of the DAG are the endogenous variables of the SCM and expand the DAG visualization by adding the exogenous variables. Further, the two causal DAGs will use the same exogenous nodes. We call the resulting graph a *parallel world graph* (or, for this typical case of two possible worlds, a "twin-world graph"). Figure 8.9 visualizes the parallel world graph.

**Figure 8.9   In the parallel world graph, we use the exogenous variables in an SCM to unite the duplicate causal DAGs across worlds. The result is a single SCM with duplicate endogenous variables.**

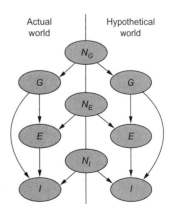

## Refresher: The structural causal model (SCM)

An SCM is a causal model with the following components:

- *Endogenous variables*—Endogenous variables are the variables we specifically want to model.
- *Exogenous variables*—A set of exogenous variables. Exogenous variables are proxies for all the causes of our endogenous variables we don't wish to model explicitly. In our formulation, we pair each endogenous variable $X$ with a single exogenous variable $N_X$ (there are more general formulations).
- *Exogenous distributions*—To use the SCM as a generative model, we need a set of marginal probability distributions for each exogenous variable, such as $P(N_X)$, which represents the modeler's uncertainty about the values $N_X$.
- *Functional assignments*—Each endogenous variable has a functional assignment that sets its value deterministically, given its parents.

For example, written as a generative model, an SCM for our online game model would look as follows.

$$n_G \sim P(N_G)$$
$$n_E \sim P(N_E)$$
$$n_I \sim P(N_I)$$
$$g = f(n_G)$$
$$e = f(g, n_E)$$
$$i = f(e, g, n_I)$$

The assignment functions induce the causal DAG; each variable is a node, the exogenous variables are root nodes, and the inputs of a variable's assignment function correspond to its parents in the DAG. The SCM is a particular case of a causal graphical model where endogenous variables are set by deterministic functions rather than sampled from causal Markov kernels.

The result is a single SCM with one shared set of exogenous variables and duplicate sets of endogenous variables—one set for each possible world. Note that in an SCM, the endogenous variables are set deterministically, given the exogenous variables. So upon observing that $E$="low" and $I<50$ in the actual world, we know that the hypothetical outcomes of $E$ and $I$ must be the same. Indeed, even though *Guild Membership* ($G$) is a latent variable in the actual world, we know that whatever value $G$ takes in the actual world must be the same as in the hypothetical world. In other words, our SCM upholds the consistency rule, as illustrated in figure 8.10. In figure 8.10, the $E$ and $I$ in the actual world are observed variables because we condition on them in the query $P(I_{E=\text{"high"}}|E=\text{"low"}, I < 50)$.

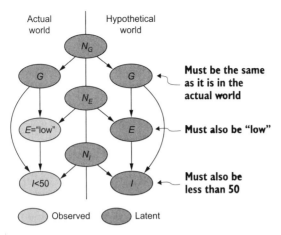

Figure 8.10  In an SCM, the endogenous variables are set deterministically, given the exogenous variables. In this model, the endogenous variables are duplicated across worlds. Therefore, upon observing low engagement and less than $50 of in-game purchases in the actual world, we know that those values must be the same in the hypothetical world unless we change something in the hypothetical world.

### 8.4.3  Applying the hypothetical condition via graph surgery

The hypothetical world will, typically, differ from the actual world by the hypothetical condition. For example, in $P(I_{E=\text{"high"}}|E=\text{"low"}, I < 50)$, "if engagement were high" $(_{E=\text{"high"}})$ differs from the factual condition "engagement was low" ($E=\text{"low"}$). As we've discussed, we model the hypothetical condition with the ideal intervention—we intervene on $E$, setting it to "high" in the hypothetical world. We model the ideal intervention on the graph with graph surgery—we'll remove incoming edges to the $E$ variable in the hypothetical world as in figure 8.11.

Now the outcome for *In-Game Purchases* ($I$) in the hypothetical world can take a different outcome than the actual world's outcome of $I=50$ because its causal parent $E$ has different outcomes in each world.

### 8.4.4  Reasoning across more than two possible worlds

The counterfactual notation and the parallel worlds graph formalism support counterfactual reasoning that extends across more than two possible worlds. To illustrate, let's refer back to the Netflix example at the beginning of the chapter. Summarizing the story, the key variables in that narrative are as follows:

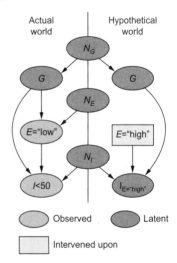

Figure 8.11  The ideal intervention and graph surgery represents the hypothetical condition in the hypothetical world. In this setting, the outcome for *I* in the hypothetical world can now take a different outcome than it has in the actual world because its parent *E* has a different outcome than it has in the actual world.

- Disney is trying to close a deal to buy the Bond franchise. Let $B$ = "success" if the deal closes. Otherwise, $B$ = "fail".
- Netflix is trying to close a deal to start a new spy franchise called *Dead Drop*. $D$ = "success" if the *Dead Drop* deal closes and "fail" otherwise. If the Bond deal closes, it will affect the terms of this deal. Therefore, $B$ causes $D$.
- If the *Dead Drop* deal closes, it will affect engagement in spy-thriller-related content on Netflix. Let $E$ = "high" if a subscriber's engagement in Netflix's spy-thriller content is high and "low" otherwise.
- The outcome of the Bond deal and the *Dead Drop* deal will both affect the attrition of spy-thriller fans to Disney. Let $A$ be the rate of attrition to Disney.

With this case study, the following multi-world counterfactual is plausible. Suppose the Bond deal was successful ($B$ = "success"), but Netflix's *Dead Drop* deal failed, and as a result, engagement was low ($E$ = "low") and Netflix attrition to Disney is 10 percent. Figure 8.12 illustrates this actual world outcome.

As a Netflix executive, you start wondering about attribution. You assume that engagement would have been high if the Dead Drop deal had been successful. You ask the following counterfactual question:

> *Disney's Bond deal succeeded, the Dead Drop deal failed, and as a result, Netflix's spy thriller engagement was low, and attrition to Disney was 10%. I assume that had the Dead Drop deal been successful, engagement would have been high. In that case, how much attribution would there have been?*

We can implement this assumption with world 2 in the parallel world graph in figure 8.13.

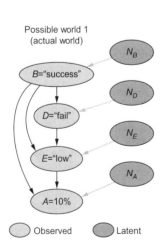

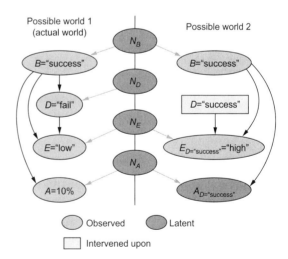

Observed     Latent     Intervened upon

**Figure 8.12   A causal DAG representing the Netflix case study. The light gray nodes are observed outcomes in the actual world. The dark nodes are latent variables.**

**Figure 8.13   The second possible world represents the assumption that if the *Dead Drop* deal was successful (via intervention $D$="success") engagement would have been high ($E_{D=\text{"success"}}$="high").**

Finally, you wonder what the level of Netflix attrition would be *if the Bond deal had failed.* But you wonder this based on your second-world assumption that engagement would be high if the *Dead Drop* deal had been successful. Since the Bond deal failing is a hypothetical condition that conflicts with the Bond deal success condition in the second world, you need a third world, as illustrated in figure 8.14.

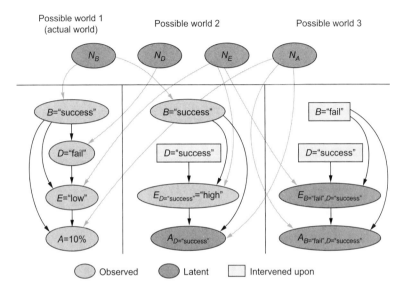

**Figure 8.14   Given the actual outcomes in world 1, the hypothetical conditions and outcomes in world 2, you pose conditions in world 3 and reason about attrition in world 3.**

In summary, this is the counterfactual question:

> *Disney's Bond deal succeeded, the Dead Drop deal failed, and as a result, Netflix's spy thriller engagement was low, and attrition to Disney was 10%. I assume that had the Dead Drop deal been successful, engagement would have been high. In that case, how much attribution would there have been if the Bond deal had failed?*

Note that the preceding reasoning is different from the following:

> *Disney's Bond deal succeeded, the Dead Drop deal failed, and as a result, Netflix's spy thriller engagement was low, and attrition to Disney was 10%. I assume that had the Dead Drop deal been successful and the Bond deal failed, engagement would have been high. In that case, how much attribution would there have been?*

Figure 8.15 illustrates the latter question.

The latter question assumes engagement would be high if the Bond deal failed *and* the *Dead Drop* deal was successful ($E_{B=\text{"fail"}, \, D=\text{"success"}}=\text{"high"}$). In contrast, the former "three world" question assumes engagement would be high if both deals were success-

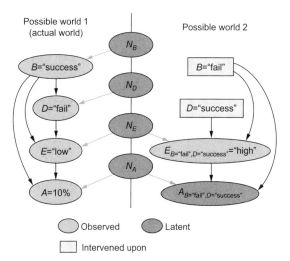

Figure 8.15   In the case of assuming $E_{B="fail",D="success"}$, only two worlds are needed.

ful. Then, in the third world, It allows for different possible levels of engagement in the hypothetical scenario where the Bond deal failed. For example, perhaps engagement would be high since Netflix would have its spy-thriller franchise and Disney wouldn't. Or perhaps, without a Bond reboot there would be less overall interest in spy-thrillers, resulting in low engagement in *Dead Drop*.

### 8.4.5   Rule of thumb: Hypothetical worlds should be simpler

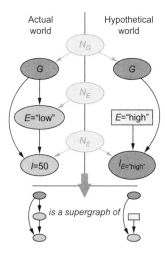

Figure 8.16   The graph representing the possible world with the hypothetical conditional is simpler than the graph representing the actual world.

Consider again the endogenous nodes in our online gaming example in figure 8.16. Notice that, in this example, the two worlds have the same sets of endogenous nodes, and the edges in the hypothetical world are a subset of the edges of those in the actual world. In other words, the possible world where we do intervene is simpler than the possible world where we condition on evidence.

Similarly, in the three-world graph for the Netflix case study, world 3 is a subgraph of world 2, which is a subgraph of world 1. As an algorithmic rule of thumb, it is useful to have this descending ordering on possible worlds. This rule of thumb reduces the risk of algorithmic instability.

That said, there are use cases for having more complicated hypothetical worlds. For example, a modeler could introduce new nodes as conditions in the hypothetical world. Or they could use stochastic interventions that randomly introduce new edges in the hypothetical world. Indeed, human counterfactual reasoning can be quite imaginative. Exploring such approaches could lead to interesting new algorithms for causal AI.

In the next chapter, we'll dive into using parallel world graphs in an algorithm for general counterfactual inference.

## *Summary*

- Counterfactual statements describe hypothetical events that potentially conflict with actual events. They are fundamental to defining causality.

- Counterfactual reasoning supports learning policies for better decision-making.

- Counterfactual reasoning involves reasoning over possible worlds. A *possible world* is a way the world is or could be. The *actual world* is a possible world with event outcomes we observed. Other possible worlds are hypothetical worlds.

- In machine learning, often the goal is counterfactual analysis of a machine learning model itself. Here, we reason about how a prediction would have been different if elements of the input feature vector were different.

- Counterfactual analysis in classification can help find the minimal change in features that would have led to a different classification.

- Counterfactual analysis supports explainable AI by helping identify changes to features that would have changed the prediction outcome on a case-by-case basis.

- Counterfactual analysis supports algorithmic recourse by identifying *actionable* changes to features that would change the prediction outcome.

- Counterfactual analysis supports AI fairness by identifying features corresponding to protected attributes where changes to said features would change the prediction outcome.

- "Potential outcomes" is a commonly used term that refers to outcomes for a given variable from across possible worlds.

- We can use the ideal intervention and parallel world graphs to model hypothetical conditions in natural language counterfactual statements and questions.

- Counterfactual notation helps represent hypothetical statements and questions in the language of probability. Probability can be used to quantify uncertainty about the truth of hypothetical statements and questions, including counterfactuals.

- Using hypothetical language rather than declarative language helps with formalizing a counterfactual statement or question into counterfactual notation. Using hypothetical language implies imagined possibility, and thus uncertainty, which invites us to think about the probability of a hypothetical statement being true.

- Binary counterfactual queries refer to queries on variables (hypothetical conditions and outcomes) that are binary.

- The *probabilities of causation*, such as the *probability of necessity* (PN), *probability of sufficiency* (PS), and *probability of necessity and sufficiency* (PNS), are binary counterfactual queries that are useful as primitives in causal attribution methods and other types of advanced causal queries.
- Binary counterfactual queries are also useful for distinguishing between "persuadables," "sure things," "lost causes," and "sleeping dogs" in uplift modeling problems.
- A parallel world graph is a simple extension of a causal DAG that captures causality across possible worlds. It represents an SCM over possible worlds that share a common set of exogenous variables and duplicate sets of endogenous variables.

# The general counterfactual inference algorithm

**This chapter covers**

- Implementing the general counterfactual inference algorithm
- Directly implementing a parallel world DAG as a causal graphical model
- Using a variational inference to implement the algorithm
- Building counterfactual deep generative models of images

The previous chapter taught you how to formalize counterfactuals and use the parallel world graph to reason across possible worlds. In this chapter, I'll introduce an algorithm for inferring counterfactual queries. Then I'll present three case studies showing implementations of the algorithm using different probabilistic ML approaches.

I call the algorithm we'll discuss in this chapter the "general" algorithm for probabilistic counterfactual inference because you can infer any counterfactual query with this algorithm. The catch is that you need an SCM. Moreover, differences between your SCM and the ground-truth SCM can lead to inaccuracies in your counterfactual inferences. We'll look more closely at this issue when we discuss identification in chapter 10, where you'll also learn ways of inferring counterfactuals without knowing the ground-truth SCM. In this chapter, you'll see the power of this SCM-based approach, especially in machine learning.

## 9.1    Algorithm walkthrough

In this section, we'll do a high-level walkthrough of the general algorithm probabilistic counterfactual inference. The algorithm has three steps commonly called *abduction*, *action*, and *prediction*:

1  *Abduction*—Infer the distribution of the exogenous variables given the factual conditions.
2  *Action*—Implement the hypothetical condition as an ideal intervention (graph surgery) in the hypothetical world.
3  *Prediction*—Use the conditional distribution on the exogenous variables from step 1 to derive the distributions of the hypothetical outcomes.

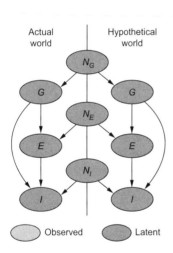

Actual world    Hypothetical world

Observed    Latent

**Figure 9.1    A parallel world graph for the online gaming example**

I'll illustrate how we can perform these steps using the parallel world graph for our online gaming example, shown again as a parallel world graph in figure 9.1.

Recall that in this example, guild member $G$ is a cause of side-quest engagement $E$ and in-game purchases $I$. Side-quest engagement is also a cause of in-game purchases.

**NOTE** This example changes the condition $I < \$50$ used in chapter 8 to $I = \$50$ in order to make the explanations a bit less verbose. Either condition would work with the algorithm we're discussing.

Let's suppose our counterfactual question is "For a player with low side-quest engagement and $50 of in-game purchases, what would their level of in-game purchases be if their side-quest engagement were high?" The corresponding query is $P(I_E=\text{"high"}|E=\text{"low"}, I=50)$. Let's examine how to apply the algorithm to this query.

### 9.1.1    Abduction: Infer the exogenous variables given the observed endogenous variables

The term "abduction" refers to doing *abductive inference*, meaning we're inferring causes from observed outcomes. In our online gaming SCM, we want to infer the latent exogenous variables ($N_G$, $N_E$, and $N_I$) from the factual conditions ($E$="low" and $I$=50).

In our probabilistic modeling approach, we treat the exogenous variables as latent variables and target them with probabilistic inference. In our example, we infer $N_E$ from observing $E$="low". Figures 9.2 and 9.3 illustrate the d-connected paths to inference of $N_G$ and $N_I$, respectively.

As you can see in figure 9.2, we have a path from $E$ to $N_G$ through the path $E{\leftarrow}G{\leftarrow}N_G$. Further, observing both $E$ and $I$ opens a collider path to $N_G$: $E{\rightarrow}I{\leftarrow}G{\leftarrow}N_G$. Similarly, in figure 9.3, observing $E$ and $I$ also opens a collider path to $N_I$ via $E{\rightarrow}I{\leftarrow}N_I$.

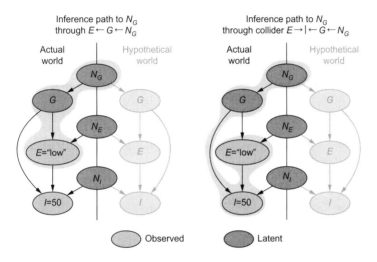

**Figure 9.2** To infer the counterfactual outcomes, we infer the exogenous variables conditional on observed outcomes in the actual world. There is a path from $E$ to $N_G$ through the path $E{\leftarrow}G{\leftarrow}N_G$. Also, observing $E$ and $I$ opens a collider path $E{\rightarrow}I{\leftarrow}G{\leftarrow}N_G$.

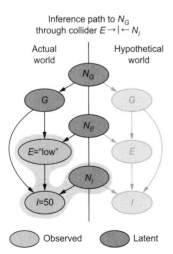

**Figure 9.3** Observing $E$ and $I$ opens a collider path to $N_I$ via $E{\rightarrow}I{\leftarrow}N_I$.

Finally, observing *E* has a directly connecting path to $N_E$, as shown in figure 9.4.

Our SCM is a probabilistic model. In the abduction step, we use this model to infer $P(N_G, N_E, N_I|$ *E*="low", *I*=50). That inference will follow these paths of dependence.

### 9.1.2   Action: Implementing the hypothetical causes

Recall from chapter 8 that we use the ideal intervention to implement hypothetical conditions. Our hypothetical condition is "if their side-quest engagement were high," and we implement this with an ideal intervention that sets *E* to "high" in the hypothetical world. Since we're using a graph, we implement the intervention with graph surgery as in figure 9.5.

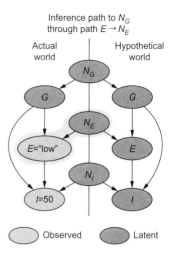

**Figure 9.4   E is a direct child of $N_E$, so observing E gives direct information about $N_E$.**

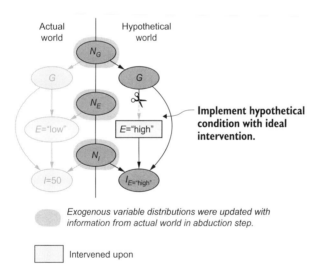

**Figure 9.5   Implement the hypothetical condition as an ideal intervention (via graph surgery) in the hypothetical world.**

Now the parallel worlds differ. Note that the probability distributions on the exogenous variables have been updated with information from the actual world during the abduction step. In the final step, we'll propagate this information through this modified hypothetical world.

### 9.1.3   *Prediction: Inferring hypothetical outcomes*

We're working with an SCM, so the values of the variables in the hypothetical world are set deterministically by the exogenous variables. Having updated the exogenous variable distributions conditional on observations in the actual world, we'll now propagate that actual world information from the exogenous variables to the endogenous variables in the hypothetical world. If we hadn't applied the intervention in the hypothetical world, the hypothetical world would mirror everything we observed in the actual world by the law of consistency (see the definition in chapter 8). However, since we applied an intervention in the hypothetical world, the hypothetical variable distributions downstream of that intervention can differ from those in the actual world.

In our gaming example, our query $P(I_{E=\text{"high"}}|E=\text{"low"}, I = 50)$ targets the hypothetical value of $I_{E=\text{"high"}}$. Figure 9.6 illustrates the path of inference from the exogenous variables to the hypothetical value of $I_{E=\text{"high"}}$. Note that in this example, the paths of influence only come from $N_G$ and $N_I$, since the intervention on $E$ cut $N_E$'s bridge to the hypothetical world.

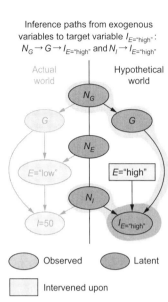

Inference paths from exogenous variables to target variable $I_{E=\text{"high"}}$:
$N_G \rightarrow G \rightarrow I_{E=\text{"high"}}$ and $N_I \rightarrow I_{E=\text{"high"}}$

**Figure 9.6   Paths for inferring the hypothetical distribution of *I* from the conditional distribution $P(N_G, N_E, N_I| E=\text{"low"}, I=50)$ on the exogenous variables, given the observed actual world outcomes**

---

### Be careful about d-connection and d-separation on parallel world graphs

Recall that with a causal DAG, we can use a graphical criterion called d-separation/d-connection to reason about conditional independence in the data generating process using a causal DAG. Indeed, this is what I do when I highlight paths of inference to $I_{E=\text{"high"}}$ given *E* and *I* via $N_I$ and $N_G$. I do this to explain the abduction and prediction steps of the algorithm. However, in general, one cannot rely on d-separation and d-connection to reason about the dependence between endogenous variables across worlds. That's because the law of consistency requires that the same endogenous variables across worlds must have the same value (unless one of the pairs is impacted by an intervention). Two variables always having the same value is a *perfect* dependence; the rules of d-separation do not capture that dependence on the parallel world graph.

In the next chapter, I'll introduce *counterfactual graphs*, a causal DAG derived from a parallel world graph where the connections between d-separation and independence hold across worlds.

We can see how information flows during inference from factual conditions $E=$"low" and $I=50$ in the actual world, through the exogenous variables, to our target variable $I_{E=\text{"high"}}$ in the hypothetical world. How we implement the inference depends on our preference for inference algorithms. For example, suppose $f_G$, and $f_I$ represent the SCM's assignment functions for $G$ and $I$. We could use a simple forward-sampling algorithm:

1   Draw a sample of exogenous values $n_G$, $n_E$, and $n_I$ from $P(N_G, N_E, N_I | E=$"low", $I=50)$.
2   Derive a sample of the hypothetical value of guild membership $g^* = f_G(n_G)$.
3   Derive a sample of the hypothetical value of in-game purchases $i^* = f_I(E=$"high", $g^*, n_I)$.
4   Repeat many times to get samples from the distribution $P(I_{E=\text{"high"}}|E=$"low", $I=50)$.
5   This would give us samples from our target $P(I_{E=\text{"high"}}|E=$"low", $I=50)$.

### 9.1.4   *Counterfactual Monte Carlo*

The output of the general probabilistic counterfactual inference algorithm produces samples from a distribution. Recall from chapter 2 that once you can sample from a distribution, you can apply the Monte Carlo techniques to make inferences based on that distribution. That same is true with counterfactual distributions.

For example, in chapter 8, I introduced the idea of regret, where we compare counterfactual outcomes. For our player who had low engagement and only spent $50, we might ask how much *more* their in-game purchases would have been had engagement been high. Given the gamer spent $50, we can define a regret variable as $R_{E=e} = I_{E=e} - 50$. By taking our samples from $P(I_{E=\text{"high"}}|E=$"low", $I=50)$ and subtracting 50, we get samples from $P(R_{E=\text{"high"}}|E=$"low", $I=50)$. We can also take the average of those differences to estimate expected regret $E(R_{E=\text{"high"}}|E=$"low", $I=50)$. Note that $E(\dots)$ here refers to the expectation operator, not to side-quest engagement.

When we want to use these counterfactual Monte Carlo techniques in automated decision-making algorithms, we are typically posing counterfactual questions about *policies*. Suppose, for example, a recommendation algorithm recommends certain content to a player based on their profile. We can contrast the amount of in-game purchases they made under one recommendation policy to the amount they would have made under a different policy. We can then adjust the recommendation algorithm in a way that would have minimized cumulative regret across players. We'll look at automated decision-making more closely in chapter 12.

Next, we'll explore a few case studies of various ways to implement this algorithm in code.

### 9.1.5   *Introduction to the case studies*

There are several ways we can implement this algorithm using modern probabilistic ML tools. In sections 9.2–9.4, we'll explore three case studies.

MONTY HALL PROBLEM

The first case study will focus on the Monty Hall problem discussed earlier in section 6.3. We'll use the pgmpy library to implement a full parallel-world graphical SCM. We'll use pgmpy's `TabularCPD` to implement SCM assignment functions, something it wasn't designed to do. In exchange for this awkwardness, we'll be able to leverage pgmpy's graph-based inference algorithm (`VariableElimination`) to collapse the abduction and prediction steps into one inference step. Using graph-based inference will save us from implementing an inference algorithm for abduction; we only have to build the model, apply the action step, and run inference.

FEMUR LENGTH AND HEIGHT

Next, we'll revisit the forensics example from section 6.1, where we have an SCM in which femur length is a cause of height. This example will show us how to do the abduction step with variational inference, a modern and popular probabilistic inference technique that works well with cutting-edge deep learning frameworks.

In this example, we'll implement the SCM in Pyro, a PyTorch-based library for probabilistic ML. Using Pyro will feel less awkward than pgmpy because Pyro modeling abstractions are more flexible. The trade-off is that we must write explicit inference code for the abduction step.

The example is simple: the data is small, each variable has only one dimension, and the relationships are linear. However, we can use the same variational inference-based abduction technique with the large, high-dimensional, and nonlinear data settings where variational inference shines.

SEMANTIC IMAGE EDITING WITH COUNTERFACTUALS

In the final case study, we'll examine how we'd apply the counterfactual inference algorithm using a pretrained generative image model in PyTorch. While the Monty Hall and femur length problems are simple problems with simple math, this case study demonstrates the use of the algorithm on a modern problem with image generation in deep generative AI.

## 9.2 Case study 1: Monty Hall problem

We'll start by revisiting the SCM for the Monty Hall problem. Summarizing again, there is a game show where the player starts with a choice of three doors. Behind one door is a car. The player picks a door, say the first door, and the host, who knows what's behind the doors, opens another door, say the third, which does not have the car. The host gives the player the opportunity to switch doors. In this case, since the player picked the first door and the host revealed that the car is not behind the third door, the player can switch to the second door. The question is whether a strategy of staying with the original choice or switching doors is better.

The answer is, counterintuitively to many, that a switching strategy is better—two times out of three, the switching strategy leads to a win. Figure 9.7 illustrates the possible outcomes of switching.

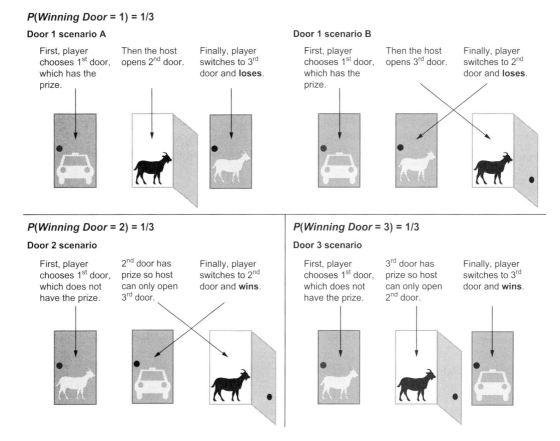

**Figure 9.7    The Monty Hall problem. Assuming the player initially chooses the first door, two out of three times the switching strategy will lead to a win. This illustration assumes the first door is chosen, but the results are the same regardless of the initial choice of door.**

We'll explore two counterfactual questions:

- For a player who stayed with their first door and lost, what is the probability that they would have won if they switched doors?
- For a player who lost, what is the probability that they would have won if they switched doors?

We'll answer these questions with the following steps:

1. Build the parallel world model as a generative graphical model in pgmpy.
2. Condition on evidence in one world to do inference of outcomes in the other.

Before we start, we'll download some tools to help us with the analysis. Listing 9.1 downloads some helper functions for working with pgmpy: the do function for implementing ideal interventions and clone for duplicating a TabularCPD object. Also, to generate the visualizations, you'll need to install the Graphviz visualization library.

**Setting up your environment**

The code in this chapter was tested with pgmpy version 0.1.25 and Pyro version 1.9.1. I use Matplotlib 3.7 for plotting. Plotting of the DAGs relies on Graphviz.

Graphviz installation depends on your environment. Using Ubuntu 22.04, I installed graphvizl via libgraphviz-dev, and then I installed the Python libraries Graphviz version 0.20.3, PyGraphviz version 1.13, and NetworkX version 3.3.

Depending on your environment, you may need to install pydot version 3.0. Graphviz and pydot are for plotting only, so if you get stuck, you could forgo plotting in the rest of the code.

**Listing 9.1  Installing Graphviz and helper functions**

```
import graphviz
import networkx as nx
from networkx.drawing.nx_agraph import write_dot
def plot_graph(G):
    dot_format = nx.nx_pydot.to_pydot(G).to_string()
    return graphviz.Source(dot_format)
```
Install Graphviz libraries for visualization, and create a helper function for plotting graphs. This was tested in Ubuntu 22.04.3 but may depend on your environment. If you have trouble, you can forgo graph plotting and run the rest of the code.

```
import requests
def download_code(url):
    response = requests.get(url)
    if response.status_code == 200:
        code_content = response.text
        print("Code fetched successfully.")
        return code_content
    else:
        print("Failed to fetch code.")
        return None
```
Helper function for downloading some utilities from GitHub

```
url_do = (
    "https://raw.githubusercontent.com/altdeep/"
    "causalML/master/book/pgmpy_do.py"
)
code_do = download_code(url_do)
```
Download code for a "do" function for applying ideal interventions.

```
url_clone = (
    "https://raw.githubusercontent.com/altdeep/"
    "causalML/master/book/chapter%209/hyp_function.py"
)
code_clone = download_code(url_clone)
```
Download code for a "clone" helper function for cloning assignment functions across worlds.

```
print(code_do)
print(code_clone)
#exec(code_do)
#exec(code_clone)
```
It's good security practice to inspect the downloaded code before executing. Uncomment the "exec" calls to execute the downloaded code.

Next, we'll build the full parallel world model as a graphical model. Our first step is to specify the exogenous variable distributions.

### 9.2.1   *Specifying the exogenous variables*

We want to implement the model as an SCM, so we'll create exogenous variables with distributions that entail all the random elements of the game. In other words, given the outcomes of these random elements and the host's and player's choices, the outcome of the game will be deterministic.

Specifically, we'll introduce two rolls of three-sided dice and a coin flip. We'll call the first die roll *Car Door Die Roll*; it selects a door for placement of the car. The player rolls the second die, a variable we'll call *1st Choice Die Roll*, to select the player's first door selection. Both dice rolls assign a 1/3 probability to each outcome. Next, we have a coin flip, which we'll just call *Coin Flip*, which I'll explain shortly.

---

**Listing 9.2   Model building: Specify distributions for exogenous variables**

```
from pgmpy.factors.discrete.CPD import TabularCPD

p_door_with_car = TabularCPD(
    variable='Car Door Die Roll',
    variable_card=3,
    values=[[1/3], [1/3], [1/3]],
    state_names={'Car Door Die Roll': ['1st', '2nd', '3rd']}
)
```

Prior distribution on exogenous variable for the three-sided die roll that selects which door gets the car

```
p_player_first_choice = TabularCPD(
    variable='1st Choice Die Roll',
    variable_card=3,
    values=[[1/3], [1/3], [1/3]],
    state_names={'1st Choice Die Roll': ['1st', '2nd', '3rd']}
)
```

Prior distribution on the exogenous variable for the three-sided die roll that selects the player's first choice of door

```
p_coin_flip = TabularCPD(
    variable='Coin Flip',
    variable_card=2,
    values=[[.5], [.5]],
    state_names={'Coin Flip': ['tails', 'heads']}
)
```

**Prior distribution on the exogenous variable for the coin flip. The host flips a coin that determines which door the host chooses to reveal as carless and whether the player chooses a stay or switch strategy.**

---

Next, we'll build assignment functions for our endogenous variables.

### 9.2.2   *Specifying the assignment functions for the endogenous variables*

Our endogenous variables will be *Host Door Selection*, *Strategy* (whether taking a switch or stay strategy), *2nd Choice* (choosing door 1, 2, 3 based on one's strategy), and *Win or Lose* (the outcome of the game).

Our definition of the SCM in chapter 6 assumes a one-to-one pairing between endogenous and exogenous variables—we typically make that assumption of independent exogenous variables because if we knew of a common cause, we'd usually model it explicitly. Here, we'll relax that assumption and match each exogenous variable to two endogenous variables:

- *1st Choice Die Roll* will drive *Host Door Selection* and *2nd Choice*
- *Coin Flip* will drive *Host Door Selection* and *Strategy*
- *Car Door Die Roll* will drive *Host Door Selection* and *Win or Lose*

We'll use this simplified approach of matching one exogenous variable to two endogenous variables because it will require less code. This shortcut works well in this case because the exogenous variables precisely encode all the exogenous random elements of the game—these elements completely determine the game's outcome. We could use the traditional formulation (where each endogenous variable has a unique exogenous variable) and get the same results.

Let's walk through the steps of the game and then construct the DAG.

### STRATEGY

The player will use *Coin Flip* as the basis of their *Strategy* decision—if the host flips heads, the player will adopt a switch door strategy. Otherwise, they'll adopt a strategy of keeping their original choice.

**Listing 9.3   Create the assignment function for *Strategy***

```
f_strategy = TabularCPD(
    variable='Strategy',
    variable_card=2,
    values=[[1, 0], [0, 1]],
    evidence=['Coin Flip'],
    evidence_card=[2],
    state_names={
        'Strategy': ['stay', 'switch'],
        'Coin Flip': ['tails', 'heads']}
)
```

### HOST DOOR SELECTION

*Host Door Selection* depends on which door has the car (*Car Door Die Roll*) and the player's initial choice of door (*1st Choice Die Roll*). The host will use *Coin Flip* to select a door from two available doors in the event that the winning door and the first choice door are the same. If *Coin Flip* is heads, they'll choose the right-most door, otherwise the left-most.

**Listing 9.4   Create the assignment function for *Host Door Selection***

```
f_host_door_selection = TabularCPD(
    variable='Host Door Selection',
    variable_card=3,
    values=[
        [0,0,0,0,1,1,0,1,1,0,0,0,0,0,1,0,1,0],
        [1,0,1,0,0,0,1,0,0,0,0,1,0,0,0,1,0,1],
        [0,1,0,1,0,0,0,0,0,1,1,0,1,1,0,0,0,0]
    ],
    evidence=['Coin Flip',
              'Car Door Die Roll',
              '1st Choice Die Roll'],
```

```
        evidence_card=[2, 3, 3],
        state_names={
            'Host Door Selection':['1st', '2nd', '3rd'],
            'Coin Flip': ['tails', 'heads'],
            'Car Door Die Roll': ['1st', '2nd', '3rd'],
            '1st Choice Die Roll': ['1st', '2nd', '3rd']
        }
)
```

## 2ND CHOICE

*2nd Choice*, the player's choice of which door to pick in the second round, depends on *Strategy*, *Host Door Selection* (the player can't switch to the door the host opened), and *1st Choice Die Roll* (the player must stay with or switch from the door selected in the first round).

**Listing 9.5  Create an assignment function for *2nd Choice***

```
f_second_choice = TabularCPD(
    variable='2nd Choice',
    variable_card=3,
    values=[
        [1,0,0,1,0,0,1,0,0,0,0,0,0,0,1,0,1,0],
        [0,1,0,0,1,0,0,1,0,1,0,1,0,1,0,1,0,1],
        [0,0,1,0,0,1,0,0,1,0,1,0,1,0,0,0,0,0]
    ],
    evidence=['Strategy', 'Host Door Selection',
              '1st Choice Die Roll'],
    evidence_card=[2, 3, 3],
    state_names={
        '2nd Choice': ['1st', '2nd', '3rd'],
        'Strategy': ['stay', 'switch'],
        'Host Door Selection': ['1st', '2nd', '3rd'],
        '1st Choice Die Roll': ['1st', '2nd', '3rd']
    }
)
```

## WIN OR LOSE

*Win or Lose* depends on which door the player picked in *2nd Choice* and whether that door is the winning door (*Car Door Die Roll*).

**Listing 9.6  Create an assignment function for *Win or Lose***

```
f_win_or_lose = TabularCPD(
    variable='Win or Lose',
    variable_card=2,
    values=[
        [1,0,0,0,1,0,0,0,1],
        [0,1,1,1,0,1,1,1,0],
    ],
    evidence=['2nd Choice', 'Car Door Die Roll'],
    evidence_card=[3, 3],
    state_names={
```

```
        'Win or Lose': ['win', 'lose'],
        '2nd Choice': ['1st', '2nd', '3rd'],
        'Car Door Die Roll': ['1st', '2nd', '3rd']
    }
)
```

With the exogenous variable distributions and the assignment functions complete, we can build the full parallel world graphical model.

### 9.2.3  *Building the parallel world graphical model*

We can now begin building the full parallel world model. First we'll add the edges that are in the graph.

**Listing 9.7   Build the parallel world graphical model**

```
exogenous_vars = ["Car Door Die Roll",
                  "Coin Flip",
                  "1st Choice Die Roll"]
endogenous_vars = ["Host Door Selection",
                   "Strategy",
                   "2nd Choice", "Win or Lose"]
```
**Specify lists of the exogenous and endogenous variables in the causal DAG.**

```
actual_world_edges = [
    ('Coin Flip', 'Host Door Selection'),
    ('Coin Flip', 'Strategy'),
    ('Car Door Die Roll', 'Host Door Selection'),
    ('1st Choice Die Roll', 'Host Door Selection'),
    ('1st Choice Die Roll', '2nd Choice'),
    ('Host Door Selection', '2nd Choice'),
    ('Strategy', '2nd Choice'),
    ('2nd Choice', 'Win or Lose'),
    ('Car Door Die Roll', 'Win or Lose')
]
```
**Specify the edges of the SCM.**

```
possible_world_edges = [
    (a + " Hyp" if a in endogenous_vars else a,
     b + " Hyp" if b in endogenous_vars else b)
    for a, b in actual_world_edges
]
```
**Clone the edges for the hypothetical world.**

Next, we'll compile and plot the graph.

**Listing 9.8   Compiling and visualizing the parallel world graph**

```
from pgmpy.models import BayesianNetwork

twin_world_graph = BayesianNetwork(
    actual_world_edges +
    possible_world_edges
)
```
**Create the parallel world graph.**

```
twin_world_graph.add_cpds(
    p_door_with_car,
    p_player_first_choice,
    p_coin_flip,
    f_strategy,
    f_host_door_selection,
    f_second_choice,
    f_win_or_lose,
    clone(f_strategy),
    clone(f_host_door_selection),
    clone(f_second_choice),
    clone(f_win_or_lose),
)
```

**Plot the parallel world graph.**

**Add probability distributions on exogenous variables.**

**Add assignment functions from the SCM.**

**Clone the assignment functions.**

```
plot_graph(twin_world_graph)
```

The preceding code prints the parallel world graph in figure 9.8.

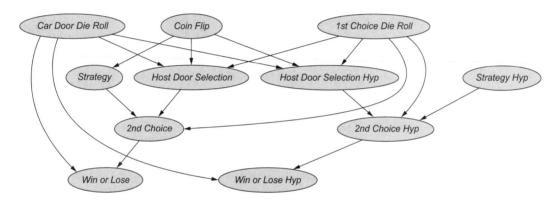

**Figure 9.8   The full parallel world graph for our counterfactual question. Hypothetical world variables have the suffix "Hyp."**

Before we answer our counterfactual questions, we'll do a quick sanity check to confirm that our model can generate the result that the switching strategy leads to a win two-thirds of the time.

> **Listing 9.9   Confirm correct probability of winning given a switch strategy**

```
from pgmpy.inference import VariableElimination
infer = VariableElimination(twin_world_graph)
strategy_outcome = infer.query(
    ['Win or Lose'],
    evidence={"Strategy": "switch"}
)
print(strategy_outcome)
```

**Infer the probability distribution of "Win or Lose" given that the player uses a switch strategy.**

**Instantiate the inference algorithm with variable elimination.**

This prints the following table.

```
+-------------------+---------------------+
| Win or Lose       |   phi(Win or Lose) |
+===================+=====================+
| Win or Lose(win)  |              0.6667 |
+-------------------+---------------------+
| Win or Lose(lose) |              0.3333 |
+-------------------+---------------------+
```

As we expect, we win two-thirds of the time when we adopt a strategy of switching doors.

### 9.2.4   *Running the counterfactual inference algorithm*

Finally, we'll use inference to answer our counterfactual questions:

- For a player who stayed with their first door and lost, what is the probability that they would have won if they switched doors?
- For a player who lost, what is the probability that they would have won if they switched doors?

Again, we use variable elimination as our choice of inference algorithm. We'll use the do function to do the action step and implement the hypothetical condition of switching. Then we'll use the `VariableElimination` inference algorithm to do the abduction and prediction steps all in one go.

---

**Listing 9.10   Infer the counterfactual distributions**

Action step: Set "Strategy Hyp" to 'switch' using "do", an implementation of an ideal intervention.

```
cf_model = do(twin_world_graph, {'Strategy Hyp': 'switch'})    <─┘
infer = VariableElimination(cf_model)    <─┐
                                            └─ Apply variable elimination as our inference
                                               algorithm on the parallel world graph.

cf_dist1 = infer.query(
    ['Win or Lose Hyp'],
    evidence={'Strategy': 'stay', 'Win or Lose': 'lose'}
)
print(cf_dist1)

cf_dist2 = infer.query(
    ['Win or Lose Hyp'],
    evidence={'Win or Lose': 'lose'}
)
print(cf_dist2)
```

This inference query answers "For a player who used the stay strategy and lost, would they have won if they used the switch strategy?" Conditional on "Strategy == stay" and "Win or Lose == lose," we infer the probability distribution of "Win or Lose Hyp" on the parallel world graph.

This inference query answers "For a player who lost, would they have won if they used the switch strategy?" Conditional on "Win or Lose == lose," we infer the probability distribution of "Win or Lose Hyp" on the parallel world graph.

For the question "For a player who stayed with their first door and lost, what is the probability that they would have won if they switched doors?" we have the following probability table:

```
+----------------------+--------------------------+
| Win or Lose Hyp      |  phi(Win or Lose Hyp) |
+======================+==========================+
| Win or Lose Hyp(win) |                   1.0000 |
+----------------------+--------------------------+
| Win or Lose Hyp(lose) |                  0.0000 |
+----------------------+--------------------------+
```

The result of the first question is obvious. If the player lost on a stay strategy, their first choice did not have the car. Therefore, one of the other two doors must have had the car. Of those two, the host would have had to open the one without the car. The remaining door would then have had the car. That is the only door the player could switch to on a switch strategy. So, conditional on losing with a stay strategy, the chances they would have won with a switch strategy are 100%.

For the question "For a player who lost, what is the probability that they would have won if they switched doors?" we have the following probability table:

```
+----------------------+--------------------------+
| Win or Lose Hyp      |  phi(Win or Lose Hyp) |
+======================+==========================+
| Win or Lose Hyp(win) |                   0.6667 |
+----------------------+--------------------------+
| Win or Lose Hyp(lose) |                  0.3333 |
+----------------------+--------------------------+
```

The answer to the second question extends from the first. We know from the original results of the model that if a player lost, there is a 2/3 chance they used a stay strategy. As we saw from the first question, in this case, flipping to a switch strategy has a 100% chance of winning. There is a 1/3 chance it was a stay strategy, in which case, by the consistency rule, there is 100% chance of losing.

Using pgmpy's graphical model inference algorithms enables counterfactual reasoning for discrete variable problems like the Monty Hall problem. In the next case study, we will solve the abduction step with variational inference, which generalizes to a broader class of problems and leverages modern deep learning.

## 9.3   *Case study 2: Counterfactual variational inference*

In this next case study, we'll implement the counterfactual inference algorithm using a generative model in the PyTorch-based probabilistic modeling library Pyro. Here we'll focus on the example of a forensic SCM where femur length is a cause of human height (discussed earlier in section 6.1).

In the Monty Hall example, all the variables were discrete, and the exogenous causes completely captured the game's random elements. That allowed us to implement the SCM (albeit awkwardly) using `TabularCPD` for assignment functions in pgmpy, and then explicitly create a parallel world graphical model. Once that was accomplished, the graphical modeling inference algorithm `VariableElimination` handled the abduction and prediction steps for us.

In contrast, our second case study presents an approach that generalizes to more types of problems. We'll use the PyTorch-based deep probabilistic modeling library Pyro. We'll handle the abduction step using variational inference, a popular inference algorithm in the deep learning era.

In this example, we'll use this modeling approach to contrast two questions:

- A conditional hypothetical: "What would an individual's height be if their femur length was 46 cm?" $P(H_{F=46})$
- A parallel-world counterfactual: "An individual's femur is 44 cm, and their height is 165 cm. What would their height be if femur length was 46 cm?" $P(H_{F=46}|F=44, H=165)$

In both cases, we infer a distribution on $H_{F=46}$ (where $H$ is height and $F$ is femur length), but in the counterfactual case, we condition on having observed $F=44$ and $H=165$. Implementing code that contrasts these two distributions on $H_{F=46}$ will help us understand what makes counterfactual queries unique.

### 9.3.1   Building the model

To make things more interesting, we'll modify the model by adding a variable for biological sex, which drives both femur length and height. Figure 9.9 illustrates the new causal DAG. Notice that our questions do not mention anything about sex, so we'll expect to see sex-related variance in our distributions $P(H_{F=46})$ and $P(H_{F=46}|F=44, H=165)$.

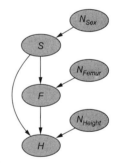

$S$ = Sex
$F$ = Femur length
$H$ = Height

The following code below implements the model in Pyro. Note the creation and use of a `PseudoDelta` distribution function. Endogenous variables are deterministic functions of the exogenous variables, but for variational inference to work, we must assign the endogenous variables a distribution using `pyro.sample`. We could use the Dirac delta distribution, which would assign all probability value to the output of a variable's assignment function. But gradient-based optimization

**Figure 9.9   The causal DAG for the relationship between femur length and height. Both are driven by biological sex.**

won't work in this case. Instead, we'll approximate inference with a "pseudo-delta" distribution—a normal distribution with a very small scale parameter.

**Listing 9.11   Implement the femur SCM in Pyro**

```
from torch import tensor
from pyro.distributions import Bernoulli, Normal
from pyro import sample
```

```
from functools import partial
PseudoDelta = partial(Normal, scale=.01)
```

Enable approximate inference with a "pseudo-delta" distribution to emulate a deterministic delta distribution.

```
def f_sex(N_sex):
    return sample("sex", Bernoulli(N_sex))
```

**The assignment function for biological sex**

```
def f_femur(sex, N_femur):
    if sex == tensor(1.0):
        μ = 43.7 + 2.3 * N_femur
    else:
        μ = 40.238 + 1.9 * N_femur
    return sample("femur", PseudoDelta(μ))
```

The assignment function for femur length in cm. The assignment uses two linear functions, one for each sex.

```
def f_height(femur, sex, N_height):
    if sex == tensor(1.0):
        μ = 61.41 + 2.21 * femur + 7.62 * N_height
    else:
        μ = 54.1 + 2.47 * femur + 7 * N_height
    return sample("height", PseudoDelta(μ))
```

The assignment function for height. Again, it uses two linear functions, one for each sex.

```
def model(exogenous):
    N_sex = sample("N_sex", exogenous['N_sex'])
    N_femur = sample("N_femur", exogenous['N_femur'])
    N_height = sample("N_height", exogenous['N_height'])
    sex = f_sex(N_sex)
    femur = f_femur(sex, N_femur)
    height = f_height(femur, sex, N_height)
    return sex, femur, height
```

Sample from the exogenous variable prior distributions

Obtain the endogenous variables given the exogenous variables.

```
exogenous = {
    'N_sex': Bernoulli(.5),
    'N_femur': Normal(0., 1.),
    'N_height': Normal(0., 1.),
}
```

Specify the prior distributions for the exogenous variables.

Again, there are three steps to our counterfactual inference algorithm:

1  Abduction

2  Action

3  Prediction

Unlike our pgmpy model, we won't need to clone all the variables for the parallel world. We'll just use the intervention operator `pyro.do` to apply the intervention and get an intervention model. For $P(H_{F=46})$, we'll generate from the intervention model based on samples from $P(N_{Sex}, N_{Femur}, N_{Height})$. For the counterfactual distribution, we'll do the abduction step using a variational inference algorithm to learn $P(N_{Sex}, N_{Femur}, N_{Height}|F=44, H=165)$. Then we'll generate from the intervention model again, but this time based on samples from $P(N_{Sex}, N_{Femur}, N_{Height}|F=44, H=165)$.

### Dealing with intractable likelihoods

We use variational inference to do the abduction step, inferring the exogenous variables given observed endogenous variables. Variational inference is a likelihood-based technique. Typically, we get likelihoods by sampling from a distribution and then getting the probability value for that sampled value using the distribution's probability mass/density function. But we can't do that for SCMs because endogenous variable values are set by the assignment functions rather than being sampled. The code in this forensic example uses sampling from a "pseudo"-Dirac delta distribution, meaning a normal distribution with a very small scale parameter. This approach, which provides likelihood values from a normal distribution, falls into a class of methods called *approximate Bayesian computation,* and it shares some of the trade-offs with other members of that class.

One alternative is to use *amortized inference.* In this method, you sample many exogenous variable values and use these to calculate many endogenous variable values. Finally, you use these samples to train a model that predicts the exogenous variable value, given the endogenous variable value. You then use this trained model during the abduction step.

Dealing with intractable likelihoods is a broader challenge in probabilistic machine learning, which is beyond the scope of this book. See the chapter notes at http://www.altdeep.ai/causalAIbook for links to additional references and resources.

### 9.3.2 *Implementing an intervention with pyro.do*

Now let's pose the conditional hypothetical, "What would height be if femur length was 46 cm?" Figure 9.10 illustrates the modified DAG representing the ideal intervention that sets femur length to 46.

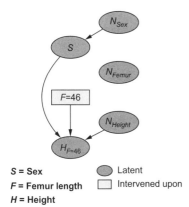

S = Sex
F = Femur length
H = Height

⬭ Latent
▢ Intervened upon

**Figure 9.10  We represent the hypothetical condition with an ideal intervention and graph surgery on the causal DAG.**

In Pyro, we'll apply `pyro.do` to the original model and get an intervention model. We'll then repeatedly call the algorithm with the prior on the exogenous variable distribution and return generated endogenous values. We'll repeat this several times and visualize the intervention distribution on height with a histogram.

```
import matplotlib.pyplot as plt
import pyro
```
Implement the hypothetical condition "...if femur length were 46 cm" with pyro.do, which returns a new model that implements the intervention.

```
int_model = pyro.do(model, data={"femur": tensor(46.0)})   ◁
int_samples = []
for _ in range(10000):
    _, _, int_height = int_model(exogenous)
    int_samples.append(float(int_height))
```
Sample from the intervention distribution.

```
plt.hist(
    int_samples,
    bins=20,
    alpha=0.5,
    label="Intervention Samples",
    density=True
)
plt.ylim(0., .35)
plt.legend()
plt.xlabel("Height")
plt.show()
```
Visualize the intervention distribution with a histogram of samples.

Figure 9.11 shows the resulting histogram of samples from $P(H_{F=46})$. We'll contrast this with the histogram from $P(H_{F=46}|F=44, H=165)$.

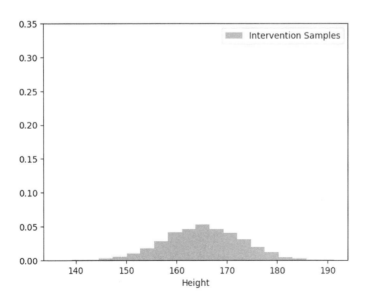

Figure 9.11   This histogram of samples visualizes the interventional distribution—the x-axis corresponds to different ranges of height values, and the y-axis is proportions of the sampled heights that fall within each range.

Now we'll do the counterfactual inference.

### 9.3.3   Implementing the abduction step with variational inference

Our conditional hypothetical question was, "What would an individual's height be if their femur length was 46 cm?" Now we want to answer the counterfactual: "An individual's femur is 44 cm, and their height is 165 cm. What would their height be if their femur length was 46 cm?" In other words, we want to extend $P(H_{F=46})$ to $P(H_{F=46}|F=44, H=165)$. Figure 9.12 illustrates the corresponding parallel world graph.

Following the counterfactual inference algorithm, we need to do the abduction step and infer $P(N_{Sex}, N_{Femur}, N_{Height}|F=44, H=165)$. We'll use variational inference, where we'll specify a *guide function*—a function with trainable parameters representing a distribution $Q(N_{Sex},$

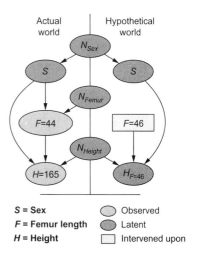

**Figure 9.12   The parallel world graph for the femur length counterfactual**

$N_{Femur}, N_{Height})$. The training procedure optimizes the parameters of the guide such that $Q(N_{Sex}, N_{Femur}, N_{Height})$ closely approximates $P(N_{Sex}, N_{Femur}, N_{Height}|F=44, H=165)$.

---

### Refresher: Proposal distributions and Pyro's guide function

Pyro's use of "guide functions" enables the developer to write their own proposal distributions that "propose" values for variables in the target distributions. Sampling-based inference algorithms (e.g., importance sampling or MCMC) use the proposal to generate samples and then operate on the samples so they represent the target distribution. Variational inference optimizes the parameters of the proposal distribution such that it becomes close to (or "approximates") the target distribution. In contrast to pgmpy's automatic inference algorithms, guide functions let the developer "guide" inference as they see fit.

---

**Listing 9.13   Specifying the guide function for variational inference**

```
import torch.distributions.constraints as constraints
from pyro.primitives import param
from pyro.distributions import Delta

def guide(exogenous):
    p = param("p", tensor(.5),
              constraint=constraints.unit_interval)
    n_sex = sample("N_sex", Bernoulli(p))
    sex = sample("sex", Bernoulli(n_sex))
```

The exogenous prior distribution is passed to the guide function. The function won't use this argument, but the signatures of the guide and the model functions must match.

The guide function tries to approximate P(N_sex|femur, height) from a Bernoulli distribution. Optimization targets the parameter of this Bernoulli distribution.

n_sex is either 0 or 1. When passed as a parameter to a Bernoulli, the outcome is deterministic.

```
n_femur_loc = param("n_femur_loc", tensor(0.0))
n_femur_scale = param(
    "n_femur_scale",
    tensor(1.0),
    constraint=constraints.positive
)
femur_dist = Normal(n_femur_loc, n_femur_scale)
n_femur = sample("N_femur", femur_dist)
n_height_loc = param("n_height_loc", tensor(0.0))
n_height_scale = param(
    "n_height_scale",
    tensor(1.0),
    constraint=constraints.positive
)
height_dist = Normal(n_height_loc, n_height_scale)
n_height = sample("N_height", height_dist)
femur = sample("femur", Delta(n_femur))
height = sample("height", Delta(n_height))
```

**The guide function tries to approximate P(N_femur|femur, height) from a normal distribution. Optimization targets the location and scale parameters of this normal distribution.**

**The guide function tries to approximate P(N_height|femur, height), also from a normal distribution.**

**Since we condition on femur and height, they are not needed in the guide function. But it is useful to have them in case we want to condition on different outcomes in a new analysis.**

## Deterministic abduction

A special case of the abduction step is when both of the following are true:

1  You observe all the endogenous variables.

2  The SCM assignment functions are invertible.

In that case, given observations of all the endogenous variables, you can calculate exact point values for the exogenous variables with the inverted assignment functions. Consequently, you apply the assignment functions in the hypothetical world to get point values of the hypothetical outcomes. However, most practical examples fall in the following general case:

1  You only condition on some endogenous variables.

2  The SCM assignment functions are not invertible.

In our abduction step, we first condition the model on observed values of femur and height.

**Listing 9.14   Conditioning on actual values of femur and height**

```
conditioned_model = pyro.condition(
    model,
    data={"femur": tensor(44.0), "height": tensor(165.0)}
)
```

Next, we infer the exogenous variable, given femur and height, using variational inference.

```
from pyro.infer import SVI, Trace_ELBO
from pyro.optim import Adam

pyro.util.set_rng_seed(123)          ◁──┘  Set a seed for
pyro.clear_param_store()                    reproducibility.      Clear any current
svi = SVI(                           ◁──            parameter values.
          model=conditioned_model,      Initialize the stochastic variational
          guide=guide,                   inference algorithm.
          optim=Adam({"lr": 0.003}),  ◁──
          loss=Trace_ELBO()  ◁──             Optimize the parameters
      )                                       with a learning rate of .003.

                                          Use (negative) evidence lower
losses = []                               bound (ELBO) as the loss function.
num_steps = 5000
for t in range(num_steps):
      losses.append(svi.step(exogenous))      Run the optimization for 5,000 steps. The
                                               SVI's step object has the same signature as
                                               the model and the guide, so any model/
plt.plot(losses)                               guide arguments must be passed in here.
plt.title("Loss During Training")   Plot the
plt.xlabel("step")                  loss during
plt.ylabel("loss")                  training.
```

Annotations: "Set a seed for reproducibility." · "Clear any current parameter values." · "Initialize the stochastic variational inference algorithm." · "Initialize a list to store loss values for plotting." · "Optimize the parameters with a learning rate of .003." · "Use (negative) evidence lower bound (ELBO) as the loss function." · "Run the optimization for 5,000 steps. The SVI's step object has the same signature as the model and the guide, so any model/guide arguments must be passed in here." · "Plot the loss during training."

Figure 9.13 shows loss during training indicating variational inference converged.

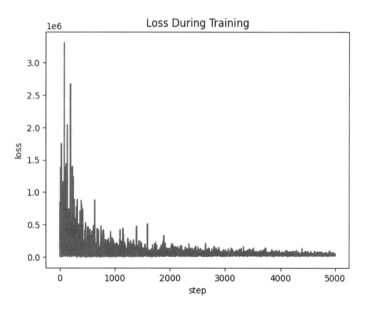

Figure 9.13   Loss during optimization of the parameters of the distribution approximating $P(N_{Sex}, N_{Femur}, N_{Height}|F=44, H=165)$

After training is completed, we extract the optimized parameters for our updated exogenous variable distribution.

**Listing 9.16   Extract parameters of updated exogenous distribution**

```
n_sex_p = param("p").item()
n_femur_loc = param("n_femur_loc").item()
n_femur_scale = param("n_femur_scale").item()      Extract the
n_height_loc = param("n_height_loc").item()        parameter values.
n_height_scale = param("n_height_scale").item()

exogenous_posterior = {                            Do the abduction by using the
    'N_sex': Bernoulli(n_sex_p),                   optimized parameters to create
    'N_femur': Normal(n_femur_loc, n_femur_scale), new "posterior" exogenous
    'N_height': Normal(n_height_loc, n_height_scale), variable distributions.
}
```

One thing to note is that while we typically specify independent prior distributions for exogenous variables in an SCM, exogenous variables are generally conditionally dependent given endogenous variables (because of collider paths!). However, I wrote a guide function that samples the exogenous variables independently, ignoring this conditional dependence. Writing a guide that treats dependent variables as independent is convenient and is common practice, but doing so will add some bias to the results. You can avoid this by doing the extra work of writing a guide function that maintains the dependencies implied by the graph.

### Counterfactual modeling with ChiRho

ChiRho is a causal extension of Pyro that seeks to more seamlessly blend the probabilistic modeling approach of Pyro with causal inference. ChiRho has parallel world abstractions and abstractions for implementing counterfactual inference with normalizing flows and the variational inference approach discussed in this example. As an extension to Pyro, the modeling techniques discussed in this case study will also work with ChiRho.

### 9.3.4   *Implementing the action and prediction steps*

In the Monty Hall example, we built the parallel world model explicitly. In this example, we can just perform the action step by using `pyro.do` to get the hypothetical world model, and sample from this model using the updated exogenous variable distribution.

We'll repeat the procedure of generating samples from the intervention model that set femur length to 46 cm. Recall that we already created the intervention model in listing 9.11 with this line:

```
int_model = pyro.do(model, data={"femur": tensor(46.0)})
```

To sample from the intervention distribution, we called `int_model` on our original `exogenous` variable distribution. Now, for the prediction step, we'll call it again, this time with `exogenous_posterior` instead of `exogenous`, because `exogenous_posterior` encodes all the information from the actual world.

**Listing 9.17   Sampling from the counterfactual distribution**

```
cf_samples = []
for _ in range(10000):
    _, _, cf_height = int_model(exogenous_posterior)
    cf_samples.append(float(cf_height))
```

Finally, we overlay a histogram of samples from the counterfactual distribution against the interventional distribution histogram in figure 9.14, and we can see the clear differences between these distributions.

**Listing 9.18   Comparing the interventional and counterfactual distributions**

```
plt.hist(
    int_samples,
    bins=20,
    alpha=0.5,
    label="Intervention Samples",
    density=True
)
plt.hist(
    cf_samples,
    bins=20,
    alpha=0.5,
    label="Counterfactual Samples",
    density=True
)
plt.ylim(0., .35)
plt.legend()
plt.xlabel("Height")
plt.show()
```

The resulting plot, shown in figure 9.14, contrasts histograms of the interventional and counterfactual samples.

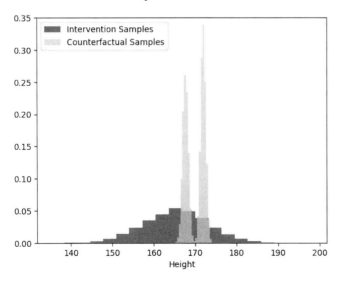

**Figure 9.14   Histograms of generated samples from the interventional and counterfactual distributions encoded by the causal model**

Figure 9.14 illustrates how the counterfactual distribution generally has much less spread than an interventional distribution representing the same hypothetical conditions. The counterfactual distribution essentially filters the interventional distribution down to cases where the conditions observed in the actual world are true. In this case, we have two height bell curves corresponding to two sexes. Those bell curves have a stronger overlap in the interventional distribution.

In a final example, we'll evaluate how to run the counterfactual inference algorithm in the context of a generative AI image model.

## 9.4    Case study 3: Counterfactual image generation with a deep generative model

**Figure 9.15   The output of a generative AI image model, given the natural language input prompt "What would Harriet Tubman look like as a pirate captain?"**

In generative AI, the user provides an input, and the algorithm generates some output. For example, suppose I wanted to write a script for an alternative history where Harriet Tubman was a pirate captain. I turned to a generative image model for some concept art, posing the text question, "What would Harriet Tubman look like as a pirate captain?" The model generated the image in figure 9.15.

The question itself is a counterfactual—Harriet Tubman was not a pirate. We'll explore natural language counterfactuals with large language models in chapter 13. Here, we'll reason counterfactually about the image in figure 9.15.

Suppose I like this image, but I want to make an edit—I want to change this image to remove the glasses. One way of doing this is to use a tool like "in-fill," where I select the pixels with the glasses and indicate that I want whatever is in the pixels to go away. This would be directly editing the form of the image.

An alternative approach would be *semantic editing*, where rather than manipulating the pixels in the image, I manipulate some latent representation of the image corresponding to "glasses." In effect, I pose the counterfactual question, "what would this image look like if the subject were not wearing glasses?" Figure 9.16 contrasts the original and "counterfactual" versions of the image.

This is an attractive use case, as manipulating underlying concepts is often preferable to manipulating form, especially when the edits you want to make aren't all located in the same specific area of pixels. This is especially attractive if our conceptual model is a causal model, so the downstream causal consequences of changing a

**Figure 9.16** Given the generated image on the left, the user might prompt the generative AI with the counterfactual question, "What would this image look like without the glasses?" They would expect something like the image on the right, where conceptual elements of the image not causally downstream of glasses removal should be unaffected.

concept are reflected in the image, while the law of consistency prevents change in the parts of the image that should be unaffected by the change in concept.

With this use case in mind, this section will use our counterfactual algorithm to implement a form of semantic editing. We'll start with the actual image. In the abduction step, we'll infer some latent representation of the image. In the action step, we'll propose the desired edit, and in the prediction step, we'll generate the new image.

In this example, we'll use an SCM built with a variational autoencoder in PyTorch. We'll also use a simple dataset called dSprites for proof of concept. The dSprites data demonstrates the idea and is simple enough to train a model quickly on an ordinary laptop. See the chapter notes at www.altdeep.ai/causalAIbook for references with more practical counterfactual image modeling examples.

### 9.4.1 The dSprites data

The dSprites dataset consists of 2D shapes, each rendered in 8 possible positions, 6 possible scales, and 40 possible rotations. The shapes are composed of 5 independent factors: shape, scale, rotation, $x$-position, and $y$-position. Figure 9.17 demonstrates samples from the dataset.

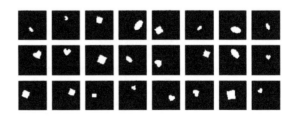

**Figure 9.17** The dSprites data features images causally determined by five independent causal factors: shape, scale, rotation, $x$-position, and $y$-position.

We'll treat each of these factors as causes of an image variable, as illustrated in the causal DAG in figure 9.18.

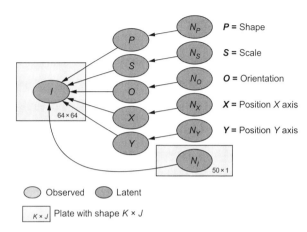

Figure 9.18  The causal DAG for a dSprites image, displayed as a plate model to highlight the shape of $N_I$ and $I$. $N_I$ is the exogenous variable for the image. The model is trained with an encoder-decoder framework that uses a 50 × 1 dimensional image encoding to represent $N_I$.

In the following code, we load a specific image from the dSprites dataset.

**Listing 9.19   Load a dSprites image**

```
import torch
from matplotlib import pyplot as plt

import io
import urllib.request
import numpy as np
url = ('https://github.com/altdeep/causalML/blob/master/'
       'book/chapter%209/sprites_example.npz?raw=true')
with urllib.request.urlopen(url) as response:
    data = response.read()
file = io.BytesIO(data)
npzfile = np.load(file)
img_dict = dict(npzfile)
img = torch.tensor(img_dict['image'].astype(np.float32) )
plt.imshow(img, cmap='Greys_r', interpolation='nearest')
plt.axis('off')
plt.title('original')
plt.show()
causal_factor = torch.from_numpy(img_dict['label']).unsqueeze(0)
print(causal_factor)
```

**Download dSprites example from GitHub and load it.**

**Plot the dSprites image.**

The causal factors of the example are [0 0 1 13 26 14], the first element is always 0, and the second element corresponds to "square" and is represented by 0. The remaining elements correspond to scale, orientation, and X and Y positions.

This plots the image in figure 9.19.

Printing `causal_factor` produces `tensor` (`[[ 0, 0, 1, 13, 26, 14]]`). The first element is 0 for all examples in the data. The second element of the causal factor vector corresponds to shape. Square, ellipse, and heart are represented by 0, 1, and 2, respectively. The image contains a square ($P=0$) with scale $S=1$, orientation $O=13$, and position $X=26$ and $Y=14$.

In this case study, we'll ask, "What would this image look like if the shape were a heart instead of a square?" This suggests the parallel-world network in figure 9.20.

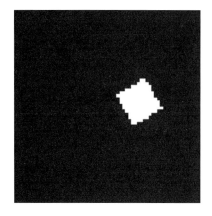

**Figure 9.19   A single example from the dSprites data**

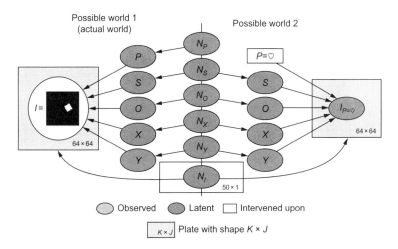

**Figure 9.20   The parallel world graph implied by the question "Given the image, what would it look like if the shape were a heart?"**

First, we'll load a pretrained encoder to map from the image to the exogenous variable for the causal factors. In this simple model, we'll assume the assignment functions for the exogenous variables of the causal factors are identity functions, i.e., the causal factors and their exogenous variables will have the same values. Let's start by initializing the encoder.

**Listing 9.20   Load the encoder of causal factors**

```
import requests
import torch.nn as nn

CARDINALITY = [1, 3, 6, 40, 32, 32]
```
← **Cardinality in each dimensionality of the causal factors**

```
class EncoderCausalFactors(nn.Module):
    def __init__(self, image_dim, factor_dim):
        super(EncoderCausalFactors, self).__init__()
        self.image_dim = image_dim
        self.factor_dim = factor_dim
        hidden_dim = 1000
        self.fc1 = nn.Linear(image_dim, hidden_dim)
        self.fc2 = nn.Linear(hidden_dim, hidden_dim)
        self.fc3 = nn.Linear(hidden_dim, factor_dim)
        self.softplus = nn.Softplus()
        self.sigmoid = nn.Sigmoid()

    def forward(self, img):
        img = img.reshape(-1, self.image_dim)
        hidden1 = self.softplus(self.fc1(img))
        hidden2 = self.softplus(self.fc2(hidden1))
        p_loc = self.sigmoid(self.fc3(hidden2))
        return p_loc

encoder_n_causal_factors = EncoderCausalFactors(
    image_dim=64*64,
    factor_dim=sum(CARDINALITY)
)
```

- **Encoder for the vector of exogenous parents of the causal factors**
- **The hidden layers have a length of 1,000.**
- **Using linear transforms passed through Softplus activation functions**
- **The final activation is a sigmoid function.**
- **Flatten the image.**
- **Calculate the hidden layers.**
- **The output layer generates a probability vector that Is used as the parameter of a OneHotCategorical distribution.**
- **Initialize the encoder. The image dimension is 64 × 64 pixels, and the six elements of the causal factor vector are one-hot encoded into a vector of length 1 + 3 + 6 + 40 + 32 + 32 = 114.**

Next, we'll download and load pretrained weights into this encoder from the book's GitHub repo.

**Listing 9.21   Download and load pretrained weights into the encoder of causal factors**

```
url = ('https://github.com/altdeep/causalML/raw/master/'
       'book/chapter%209/sprites-model-encoder-causal-factors.pt')
response = requests.get(url)
response.raise_for_status()
with open('temp_weights.pt', 'wb') as f:
    f.write(response.content)
state_dict = torch.load(
    'temp_weights.pt',
    map_location=torch.device('cpu')
)
encoder_n_causal_factors.load_state_dict(state_dict)
```

First, we'll test that the encoder can recover the causal factors from the image.

**Listing 9.22   Generate examples of causal exogenous factors**

```
from pyro import distributions as dist

def decode_one_hot(factor_encoded, cardinality=CARDINALITY):
    split = [
```

```
        torch.split(element, cardinality)
        for element in factor_encoded
    ]
    labels = [[int(torch.argmax(vec)) for vec in item]
            for item in split]
    return torch.tensor(labels)
```

Helper function that
decodes the one-hot
encoded output of
the encoder

```
def sample_one_hot(p_encoded, cardinality=CARDINALITY):
    split = [torch.split(element, cardinality)
            for element in p_encoded]
    sample_list = [
        [
            dist.OneHotCategorical(p_vec).sample()
            for p_vec in item
        ] for item in split
    ]
    sample = torch.stack([
        torch.cat(samples, -1)
        for samples in sample_list
    ])
    return sample
```

Samples from the output
probability vector of
encoder_causal_factors

```
inferred_cause_p = encoder_n_causal_factors.forward(img)
sampled_factors = sample_one_hot(
    inferred_cause_p
)
print(decode_one_hot(sampled_factors))
```

Use the encoder to
predict causal factors.

Encoding the sampled image prints the causal factors: `[ 0,  0,  1, 13, 26, 14]`. The encoder accurately recovers the causal factors from the image.

Next, we'll initialize an encoder that we'll use for inference of $N_I$, the exogenous variable for the image. This encoder takes an image and an instance of the causal factor vector as an input.

**Listing 9.23  An encoder for inference of $N_I$**

```
class EncoderNImage(nn.Module):
    def __init__(self, image_dim, factor_dim, n_image_dim):
        super(EncoderNImage, self).__init__()
        self.image_dim = image_dim
        self.factor_dim = factor_dim
        self.n_image_dim = n_image_dim
        hidden_dim = 1000
        self.fc1 = nn.Linear(
            self.image_dim + self.factor_dim, hidden_dim
        )
        self.fc2 = nn.Linear(hidden_dim, hidden_dim)
        self.fc31 = nn.Linear(hidden_dim, n_image_dim)
        self.fc32 = nn.Linear(hidden_dim, n_image_dim)
        self.softplus = nn.Softplus()

    def forward(self, img, factor):
        img = img.reshape(-1, self.image_dim)
```

Encoder used for inference of $N_I$, which
serves as both the exogenous variable for
the image in causal terms, and the
encoding of the image in VAE terms

Using linear transforms
passed into a Softplus
activation function

Flatten
the image.

**Concatenate the image and the causal factor vector.**

```
inputs = torch.cat((img, factor), -1)
hidden1 = self.softplus(self.fc1(inputs))
hidden2 = self.softplus(self.fc2(hidden1))
n_image_loc = self.fc31(hidden2)
n_image_scale = torch.exp(self.fc32(hidden2))
return n_image_loc, n_image_scale
```

**Calculate the hidden layers.**

**Calculate the location and scale parameter of multivariate normal distribution on $N_I$.**

```
encoder_n_image = EncoderNImage(
    image_dim=64*64,
    factor_dim=sum(CARDINALITY),
    n_image_dim=50
)
```

**Initialize the encoder.**

The encoder of the noise variable requires the causal factors to be one-hot encoded, so we'll create a helper function to do just that.

**Listing 9.24   Create a function for one-hot encoding**

```
def encode_one_hot(factor, cardinality=CARDINALITY):
    new_factor = []
    for i, factor_length in enumerate(cardinality):
        new_factor.append(
            torch.nn.functional.one_hot(
                factor[:,i].to(torch.int64), int(factor_length)
            )
        )
    new_factor = torch.cat(new_factor, -1)
    return new_factor.to(torch.float32)
```

Again, we'll download and load pretrained weights for the encoder.

**Listing 9.25   Load pretrained weights for encoder for inference of $N_I$**

```
weight_url = ("https://github.com/altdeep/causalML/raw/master/"
             "book/chapter%209/sprites-model-encoder-n-image.pt")
response = requests.get(weight_url)
response.raise_for_status()
with open('temp_weights.pt', 'wb') as f:
    f.write(response.content)
state_dict = torch.load(
    'temp_weights.pt',
    map_location=torch.device('cpu')
)
encoder_n_image.load_state_dict(state_dict)
n_image_loc, n_image_scale = encoder_n_image.forward(
    img,
    encode_one_hot(causal_factor)
)
n_image = torch.normal(n_image_loc, n_image_scale)
```

**Load the pretrained weights.**

**Pass the image and causal factors into the encoder, and obtain $N_I$ location and scale parameters.**

**Generate from the posterior distribution on $N_I$.**

Finally, we'll load a decoder that maps from $N_I$ and a causal factor back to an image. In causal terms, the decoder is part of the assignment function for the image.

**Listing 9.26  Load and initialize the decoder that maps causes and $N_I$ to images**

The decoder maps from causal factors and N_image to generate a parameter for a multivariate Bernoulli distribution on images.

The model uses linear transforms, a Softplus activate for hidden layers, and sigmoid activate on the output layer.

```python
class Decoder(nn.Module):
    def __init__(self, image_dim, factor_dim, n_image_dim):
        super(Decoder, self).__init__()
        hidden_dim = 1000
        self.fc1 = nn.Linear(n_image_dim + factor_dim, hidden_dim)
        self.fc2 = nn.Linear(hidden_dim, hidden_dim)
        self.fc3 = nn.Linear(hidden_dim, hidden_dim)
        self.fc4 = nn.Linear(hidden_dim, image_dim)
        self.softplus = nn.Softplus()
        self.sigmoid = nn.Sigmoid()

    def forward(self, n_image, factor):
        inputs = torch.cat((n_image, factor), -1)
        hidden1 = self.softplus(self.fc1(inputs))
        hidden2 = self.softplus(self.fc2(hidden1))
        hidden3 = self.softplus(self.fc3(hidden2))
        p_img = self.sigmoid(self.fc4(hidden3))
        return p_img

decoder = Decoder(
    image_dim=64*64,
    factor_dim=sum(CARDINALITY),
    n_image_dim=50
)
```

The network concatenates n_image and factors in the input layer.

The input is passed through three hidden layers with Softplus activation functions.

The output is a probability parameter passed to a multivariate Bernoulli distribution on image pixels.

Initialize the encoder.

Again, we'll download and load pretrained weights into the decoder.

**Listing 9.27  Download and load the decoder weights**

```python
dcdr_url = ("https://github.com/altdeep/causalML/raw/master/"
        "book/chapter%209/sprites-model-decoder.pt")
response = requests.get(dcdr_url)
response.raise_for_status()
with open('temp_weights.pt', 'wb') as f:
    f.write(response.content)
state_dict = torch.load(
    'temp_weights.pt',
    map_location=torch.device('cpu')
)
decoder.load_state_dict(state_dict)
```

Before we generate the counterfactual image, we'll create a helper function to plot it.

**Listing 9.28   Helper function for plotting the counterfactual image**

```
def compare_reconstruction(original, generated):
    fig = plt.figure()
    ax0 = fig.add_subplot(121)
    plt.imshow(
        original.cpu().reshape(64, 64),
        cmap='Greys_r',
        interpolation='nearest'
    )
    plt.axis('off')
    plt.title('actual')
    ax1 = fig.add_subplot(122)
    plt.imshow(
        generated.reshape(64, 64),
        cmap='Greys_r', interpolation='nearest')
    plt.axis('off')
    plt.title('counterfactual')
    plt.show()
```

Now, we'll specify the SCM. We'll write a `p_n_image` function that generates from $P(N_{image})$ and an `f_image` assignment function for the image.

**Listing 9.29   Create an exogenous distribution and assignment function for the image**

A function that generates a variate from the N_image exogenous distribution

The parameters of N_image's distribution include location and scale parameters for a normal distribution and the upper bound of a uniform distribution.

```
def p_n_image(n_image_params):
    n_image_loc, n_image_scale, n_unif_upper = n_image_params
    n_image_norm = dist.Normal(
        n_image_loc, n_image_scale
    ).to_event(1).sample()
    n_image_unif = dist.Uniform(0, n_unif_upper).expand(
        torch.Size([1, 64*64])
    ).sample()
    n_image = n_image_norm, n_image_unif
    return n_image
```

Sample a normal random variate from the normal distribution.

Sample a uniform random variate from a uniform distribution.

Combine these into a single n_image object.

```
def f_image(factor, n_image):
    n_image_norm, n_image_unif = n_image
    p_output = decoder.forward(
        n_image_norm,
        encode_one_hot(factor)
    )    #H
    sim_img = (n_image_unif <= p_output).int()
    return sim_img
```

Assignment function for the image

The normal random variate is passed through the decoder to get a probability vector for the pixels.

The exogenous noise variable decomposes into one normal and one uniform random variate.

Each pixel is set deterministically with an indicator function that returns 1 if an element of the uniform variate is less than the corresponding element of the probability vector, or otherwise returns 0.

Finally, we can run through the steps of the counterfactual inference algorithm to answer the question, "What would this image look like if it was a heart?"

---

**Listing 9.30 Generate a counterfactual image**

Abduction step: infer the exogenous variable given the image.

Infer the parameters of N_I. First, this includes two parameters of a normal distribution.

```
def abduct(img, factor, smoother=1e-3):
    n_image_loc, n_image_scale = encoder_n_image.forward(
        img, encode_one_hot(factor)
    )
    n_unif_upper = decoder.forward(
        n_image_loc,
        encode_one_hot(factor)
    )
    n_unif_upper = n_unif_upper * (1 - 2 * smoother) + smoother
    p_image_params = n_image_loc, n_image_scale, n_unif_upper
    return p_image_params

def do_action(factor, element=1, val=2):
    intervened_factor = factor.clone()
    intervened_factor[0][element] = val
    return intervened_factor

def predict(intervened_factor, n_image_params):
    n_image = p_n_image(n_image_params)
    sim_img = f_image(intervened_factor, n_image)
    return sim_img

def counterfactual(img, factor):
    p_image_params = abduct(img, factor)
    intervened_factor = do_action(factor)
    pred_recon = predict(intervened_factor, p_image_params)
    compare_reconstruction(img, pred_recon)

counterfactual(img, causal_factor)
```

Second, we infer the upper bound of a uniform distribution and apply smoothing so it is not exactly 1 or 0.

Combine these together into one inferred parameter set.

Action step: Apply the intervention that sets the shape element to "heart" (represented by the integer 2).

Prediction step: Generate n_image from P(N_image), and pass this through an assignment function to generate an image.

Apply all three steps: abduct the n_image, apply the intervention, and forward generate the counterfactual image.

Plot the result.

Figure 9.21 shows the results.

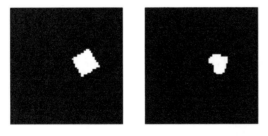

**Figure 9.21** The original (left) and counterfactually generated image (right)

This is a proof of concept—there is additional nuance in counterfactual image generation. I'm cheating a bit with this dSprites example. The counterfactual generation works because the causal factors are independent and because the data is quite simple. For counterfactual image generation to work in general, we need to understand and satisfy certain assumptions.

### 9.4.2   Assumptions needed for counterfactual image generation

In the next chapter, we'll tackle the problem of identification. Identification is determining what causal questions we can answer, given our modeling assumptions and the data available to us. The counterfactual inference algorithm assumes you have the ground-truth SCM. If you can make that assumption, you can use the algorithm to answer any counterfactual (or interventional) query.

In most cases, we can't practically assume we have the ground-truth SCM. At best, you'll have an SCM that acts as an approximation of the ground truth. For example, the true process that generated the dSprites images certainly didn't involve a decoder neural network—we used deep learning with this decoder architecture to approximate that process. As you'll see in the next chapter, such learned approximations are not guaranteed to produce counterfactuals faithful to the ground-truth data generating process.

But there is something special about the counterfactual generation of images and other media modalities (e.g., text, audio, video). In these cases, mathematical guarantees are less critical when we can simply *look* (read, listen, etc.) at the generated counterfactual media and evaluate whether it aligns with what we imagine it *should* be. Does the image in figure 9.21 look like what you imagined replacing the square with a heart would look like? Does the image of pirate captain Harriet Tubman without the spectacles align with your expectations? If so, the tool is quite useful, even without identification guarantees. Here, utility is in terms of aligning with human counterfactual imagination rather than ground-truth accuracy. I have the concept image of Captain Tubman that I wanted, and I can move on to my next creative task.

### Summary

- The counterfactual inference algorithm requires an SCM and involves three steps: abduction, action, and prediction.
- In the abduction step, we infer the exogenous variables, given observed endogenous variables.
- In the action step, we use an ideal intervention to implement the hypothetical condition in the counterfactual query.
- In the prediction step, we predict the hypothetical outcomes given the hypothetical condition and the distribution of the exogenous variables learned in the abduction step.
- We can implement the counterfactual inference algorithm using different probabilistic machine learning frameworks.
- We can use a causal graphical modeling library like pgmpy to directly implement a generative SCM on a parallel world graph, and use graphical model inference algorithms with graph surgery to infer the counterfactual query.

- We can use modern probabilistic deep learning techniques such as variational inference and normalizing flows to do the abduction step of the counterfactual inference algorithm.
- Deep generative models can often be modified to enable counterfactual generation of media (text, images, audio, video, etc.). While there may be identification questions, you can typically examine the generated counterfactual artifact and validate that it matches your expectations.

# 10
# *Identification and the causal hierarchy*

**This chapter covers**

- Motivating examples for identification
- Using y0 for identification and deriving estimands
- How to derive counterfactual graphs in y0
- Deriving SWIGs for graph-based counterfactual identification

The practice of advancing machine learning often relies on a blind confidence that more data and the right architecture can solve any task. For tasks with causal elements, *causal identification* can make that less of a matter of faith and more of a science. It can tell us when more data won't help, and what types of inductive biases are needed for the algorithm to work.

Causal identification is the task of determining when we can make a causal inference from purely observational data or a counterfactual inference from observational or experimental data. In statistics and data science, it is the theory that allows us to distill causation from correlation and estimate causal effects in the presence of confounders. But causal identification has applications in AI. For example, suppose a deep learning algorithm achieves high performance on a particular causal reasoning benchmark. The ideas behind causal identification tell us that certain causal inductive biases must be baked into the model architecture, training data, training procedure, hyperparameters (e.g., prompts), and/or benchmark data. By tracking down that causal information, we can make sure the algorithm can consistently achieve that benchmark performance in new scenarios.

Identification is a theory-heavy part of causal inference. Fortunately, we can rely on libraries to do the theoretical heavy lifting for us and focus on skill-building with these libraries. In this chapter, we'll focus on a library called y0 (pronounced why-not), which implements algorithms for identification using graphs. By the end of the chapter, we'll have demystified causal identification and you'll know how to apply y0's identification algorithms.

## 10.1   The causal hierarchy

The *causal hierarchy*, also known as *Pearl's hierarchy* or the *ladder of causation*, is a three-level hierarchy over the types of causal questions we ask, models we build, data we acquire, and causal inferences we make.

The causal hierarchy consists of three levels:

1  Association
2  Intervention
3  Counterfactual

When we do a statistical or causal analysis, we are reasoning at one of these three levels. When we know at what level we are reasoning, we can determine what kind of assumptions and data we need to rely on to do that reasoning correctly.

### 10.1.1   Where questions and queries fall on the hierarchy

The questions we ask of our causal model, and the causal queries we formalize from those questions, fall at different levels of the hierarchy. First, level 1 (the association level) is concerned with "What is...?" questions. Let's illustrate with the online gaming example, shown again in figure 10.1.

An example level 1 question and associated query is

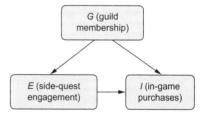

**Figure 10.1   The DAG for the online gaming example**

"*What are in-game purchase amounts for players highly engaged in side-quests?*" $P(I|E=\text{"high"})$

Reasoning at this level aims to describe, model, or detect dependence between variables. At this level, we're not reasoning about any causal relationships between the variables.

Questions at level 2 (the intervention level) involve non-counterfactual hypothetical conditions, such as

*"What would in-game purchases be for a player if side-quest engagement were high?"*
$P(I_{E=\text{"high"}})$

At level 2, we formalize such questions with the ideal intervention. Note that any query derived from a level 2 query is also a level 2 query, such as ATEs, (e.g., $E(I_{E=\text{"high"}} - I_{E=\text{"low"}})$) and CATEs.

Finally, counterfactual questions and queries fall at level 3 (the counterfactual level):

*"Given this player had low side-quest engagement and low purchases, what would their level of purchases have been if they were more engaged?"* $P(I_{E=\text{"high"}}|E=\text{"low"},$
$I=\text{"low"})$

As with level 2 queries, any query we derive from a level 3 query also falls at level 3. For example, a causal attribution query designed to answer "Why did this player have low purchases" would be a level 3 query if it were a function of level 3 queries like the probabilities of causation described in section 8.3.

In identification, we work directly with queries. The y0 library in Python gives us a domain specific language for representing queries. The following code implements the query $P(I_{E=e})$.

---

**Listing 10.1  Creating a query in y0**

```
!pip install git+https://github.com/y0-causal-inference/y0.git@v0.2.0
from y0.dsl import P, Variable
E = Variable("E")
I = Variable("I")
query = P[E](I)
query
```

"P" is for probability distributions, and "Variable" is for defining.

Define variables G (guild membership), E (side-quest engagement), and I (in-game purchases).

Define the distributional query $P(I_E)$.

If running in a notebook environment, this will show a rendered image of $P(I_E)$.

---

### Setting up your environment

In this chapter, I rely on version 0.2.0 of the y0 library. As it is a relatively new library, the library's API is in development and recent versions will deviate slightly from what is shown here. Check out the library's tutorials for recent developments.

Again, we rely on Graphviz and some custom utilities for plotting DAGs. The Graphviz installation depends on your environment. I am using Ubuntu 22.04 and install Graphviz via libgraphviz-dev. Then I install Python libraries graphviz version 0.20.3, and PyGraphviz version 1.13. The Graphviz code is for plotting only, so if you get stuck, you could forgo plotting for the rest of the code.

The `query` object is an object of the class `Probability`. The class's `__repr__` method (which tells Python what to return in the terminal when you call it directly) is implemented such that when we evaluate the object in the last line of the preceding code in a Jupyter notebook, it will display rendered LaTeX (a typesetting/ markup language with a focus on math notation), as in figure 10.2.

$$P(I_E)$$

**Figure 10.2 The rendered math image returned when you evaluate the `query` object in listing 10.1**

The causal hierarchy applies to models and data as well.

### 10.1.2 Where models and assumptions fall on the hierarchy

A "model" is a set of assumptions about the data generating process (DGP). Those assumptions live at various levels of the hierarchy.

#### LEVEL 1 ASSUMPTIONS

Models at the associational level have statistical but non-causal assumptions. For example, suppose we're interested in $P(I|E=e)$, for either value ("low", "high") that $e$ might take. We might fit a linear model to regress in-game purchases $I$ against side-quest engagement $E$. Or we might train a neural network that maps $E$ to $I$. These are two statistical models with different parameterizations. In other words, they differ in non-causal, statistical assumptions placed on $P(I|E)$. Once we add causal assumptions, we move to a higher level of the hierarchy.

#### LEVEL 2 ASSUMPTIONS

Assumptions that we can represent with a causal DAG are level 2 (interventional) assumptions. An example of a level 2 model would be a causal graphical model (aka, a causal Bayesian network)—a probabilistic model trained on a causal DAG. A causal DAG by itself is a level 2 set of assumptions; assumptions about what causes what. Generally, assumptions that let you deduce the consequences of an intervention are level 2 assumptions.

#### LEVEL 3 ASSUMPTIONS

The canonical example of a level 3 model is a structural causal model. But more generally, assumptions about mechanism—*how* variables affect one another—are level 3 (counterfactual) assumptions.

One way to think about this is that any causal assumption you cannot represent in the structure of the DAG is, by process of elimination, a level 3 assumption. For example, suppose your DAG has the edge $X{\rightarrow}Y$. Further, you believe the causal relationship between $X$ and $Y$ is naturally linear. You can't "see" linearity on the DAG structure, so linearity is a level 3 assumption.

### 10.1.3 Where data falls on the hierarchy

Recall the differences between observational data and interventional data. Observational data is passively observed; as a result, it captures statistical associations resulting from dependence between variables in the DGP.

LEVEL **1** DATA

In our online gaming example, the level 1 data was logged examples of side-quest engagement and in-game purchases pulled by a database query. Observational data lives at level 1 of the causal hierarchy.

LEVEL **2** DATA

Interventional data is generated as the result of applying an intervention, such as data collected from a randomized experiment. In the gaming example, this was the data created because of an A/B test that randomly assigned players to different groups where they are coerced into different fixed side-quest engagement levels. Intervention data lives at level 2 of the hierarchy.

LEVEL **3** DATA

Counterfactual data, which lives at level 3 of the hierarchy, is the odd case. Counterfactual data would contain data from across possible worlds. In most domains, we only have data from one world—one *potential outcome* for each unit of observation in the data.

However, there are special cases where counterfactual data exists. For example, cloud service providers use complex but deterministic policies for allocating resources in the cloud, given various constraints. For one example with a given allocation outcome in the log, we could generate a counterfactual outcome for that example by applying a different allocation policy to that example. Similarly, given data produced by simulation software, we could generate counterfactual data by changing the simulation to reflect a *hypothetical condition* and then rerunning it with the same initial conditions as the original data.

### 10.1.4   *The causal hierarchy theorem*

The causal hierarchy offers us a key insight from something called the *causal hierarchy theorem*. That insight is this: "You cannot answer a level $k$ question without level $k$ assumptions." For example, if you want a causal effect, you need a DAG or some other level 2 (or level 3) assumptions. If you want to answer a counterfactual question, you need level 3 assumptions. And even the most cutting-edge of deep learning models can't answer level $k$ questions reliably unless they encode a representation of level $k$ assumptions.

More formally, the causal hierarchy theorem establishes that the three layers of the causal hierarchy are, in mathematical jargon, "almost always separate." Roughly speaking, "separate" means that data from a lower level of the hierarchy is insufficient to infer a query from a higher level of the hierarchy. And "almost always" means this statement is true except in cases so rare that we can dismiss them as practically unimportant.

Aside from this insight, the causal hierarchy makes understanding identification—perhaps the hardest topic in all causal inference—much easier, as we'll see in the rest of the chapter.

## 10.2   Identification and the causal inference workflow

In this section, we'll look at the workflow for posing and answering causal questions and the role that identification plays in that workflow. We'll use the online gaming DAG introduced in chapter 7 as an example. Let's start by building the DAG with y0.

**Listing 10.2   Building the online gaming DAG in y0**

```
import requests
def download_code(url):
    response = requests.get(url)
    if response.status_code == 200:
        code_content = response.text
        print("Code fetched successfully.")
        return code_content
    else:
        print("Failed to fetch code.")
        return None
url = (
    "https://raw.githubusercontent.com/altdeep/"
    "causalML/master/book/chapter%2010/id_utilities.py"
)
utilities_code = download_code(url)
print(utilities_code)
# After checking, uncomment the exec call to load utilities
#exec(utilities_code)

from y0.graph import NxMixedGraph as Y0Graph
from y0.dsl import P, Variable
G = Variable("G")
E = Variable("E")
I = Variable("I")
dag = Y0Graph.from_edges(
    directed=[
        (G, E),
        (G, I),
        (E, I)
    ]
)
gv_draw(dag)
```

Install Graphviz for DAG visualization. Download some helper functions for identification and visualization that convert some y0 abstractions into abstractions we're familiar with.

Inspect the downloaded code before executing as a matter of good security practice. Then uncomment the last line and execute.

Build the graph.

y0 works with a custom graph class called NxMixedGraph. To avoid confusion, we'll call it a Y0Graph and use it to implement DAGs.

Draw the graph with a Graphviz helper function.

This produces the graph in figure 10.3.

Our goal in chapter 7 was to use our model of $P(G, E, I)$ to simulate from $P(I_{E="high"})$ using the intervention operator. In sections 7.1.6 and 7.2.6, we did this simulation and saw empirical evidence that it works for this online game example. Identification means showing that it works in general, based on your model and assumptions. Formally, we want to be sure that level 1 distribution $P(G, E, I)$, or data from that distribution, combined with our DAG,

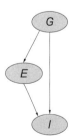

**Figure 10.3   Drawing the online gaming graph with y0**

is enough to simulate from level 2 distribution $P(I_{E=\text{"high"}})$. Identification with y0 confirms that this is indeed possible.

---

**Listing 10.3   Checking identification of $P(I_{E=\text{"high"}})$ from $P(G, E, I)$**

```
e = E
check_identifiable(
    dag,
    query=P(I @ e),
    distribution=P(G, E, I)
)
```

> Check identifiability given the DAG, a distribution, and a target query. Y0 represents ideal interventions with @, so we write $P(I_{E=e}$ as P(I @ e).

> Make a lowercase "e" to represent an intervention value.

---

This will return `True`, but what if we didn't have any observations of guild membership $G$? We can use y0 to test if we have identification for $P(I_{E=\text{"high"}})$ from $P(E, I)$. In other words, test if it is possible to infer $P(I_{E=\text{"high"}})$ from observations of $E$ and $I$ only.

---

**Listing 10.4   Checking identification of $P(I_{E=\text{"high"}})$ from $P(E, I)$**

```
check_identifiable(
    dag,
    query=P(I @ e),
    distribution=P(E, I)
)
```

---

This will return `False`, because we don't have identification for $P(I_{E=e})$ from the DAG and $P(E, I)$ given our graphical assumptions.

---

### Lack of identification and misguided probabilistic ML

Y0 shows us that $P(I_{E=e})$ is not identified from $P(E, I)$ given our online game DAG. Consider the implications of this result from the perspective of probabilistic machine learning (ML). As experts in probabilistic ML, given G is unmeasured, we might be inclined to train a latent variable model on $P(E, I)$ where G is the latent variable. Once we've learned that model, we could implement the intervention with graph surgery setting $E=e$, and then sampling $I$ from the transformed model.

This algorithm would *run*; it would generate samples. But the lack of identification result from y0 proves that, given only the assumptions in our DAG, we could not consider these to be valid samples from $P(I_{E=e})$. And training on more data wouldn't help. The only way this could work is if there were additional causal assumptions constraining inference beyond the assumptions encoded by the DAG.

---

Given this introduction, let's define identification.

### 10.2.1  Defining identification

Suppose I were to randomly choose a pair of numbers, $X$ and $Y$, and add them together to get $Z$. Then, I tell you what $Z$ was and ask you to infer the values of $X$ and $Y$. Could you do it? Not without more information. So, what if I gave you millions of examples of feature $Z$ and label $\{X, Y\}$. Could you train a deep learning model to predict label $\{X, Y\}$ from input feature $Z$? Again, no, at least not without strong assumptions on the possible values of $\{X, Y\}$. What if, instead of millions, I gave you billions of examples? No; more data would not help. In statistics, we would say the prediction target $\{X, Y\}$ is not *identified*.

In other words, you want to infer something, and you have an algorithm (e.g., a deep net) that takes in data and produces an answer. That answer will usually be a bit different than the true value because of statistical variation in the input data. If your inference objective is identified, then the more data you input to the algorithm, the more that variance will shrink and your algorithm's answer will converge to the true answer. If your inference objective is not identified, then more data will not reduce your algorithm's errors.

*Causal identification* is just statistical identification across levels of the causal hierarchy. A causal query is identified when your causal assumptions enable you to infer that query using data from a lower level on the hierarchy.

### 10.2.2   *The causal inference workflow*

Now that we have defined identification, we can define a full workflow for causal inference. Figure 10.4 shows the full workflow.

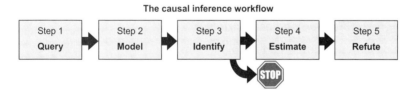

**Figure 10.4   The causal inference workflow. The identification step is an essential step in the workflow.**

Identification is a key step in the workflow. Let's walk through each of the steps.

#### STEP 1: POSE YOUR QUERY

First, we pose our causal question as a query. For example, given our question "What would in-game purchases be for a player if side-quest engagement was high?" our query is $P(I_{E=\text{"high"}})$.

#### STEP 2: BUILD YOUR MODEL

Next, build a causal model that captures your basic causal assumptions. Our model will be the online game causal DAG, shown again in figure 10.5.

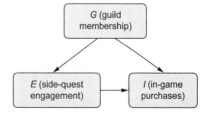

**Figure 10.5   Step 2: Build the model to capture your causal assumptions relative to your query. For the query $P(I_{E=\text{"high"}})$, this is our online gaming DAG.**

Your model's assumptions should at least match the level of your query in the causal hierarchy. For example, the query $P(I_{E=\text{"high"}})$ is a level 2 query, so we need at least some level 2 assumptions. The causal DAG is a level 2 causal model, so in our analysis, the DAG provides the necessary level 2 assumptions.

### STEP 3: CHECK IDENTIFICATION

Evaluate whether you have identification for your query, given your model assumptions and your available data. If you don't have identification, you must either observe additional variables in your data or change your assumptions. For example, we could modify our online gaming DAG (changing level 2 assumptions). Or simply stop and conclude you can't answer the question given your data and knowledge about the problem, and devote your attention elsewhere.

### STEP 4: ESTIMATE YOUR QUERY

Once you know you have identification for your query, you can run statistical inference on, or "estimate," your query. There are a variety of estimation methods and algorithms, from Bayesian inference to linear regression to propensity scores to double machine learning. We'll review some estimation methods in the next chapter.

### STEP 5: REFUTE YOUR CAUSAL INFERENCE

Refutation is a final step where we conduct sensitivity analysis to evaluate how sensitive our results from step 4 are to violations of our assumptions, including the assumptions that enabled identification. We'll see examples of this in chapter 11.

### 10.2.3 Separating identification and estimation

In many texts, identification and estimation are combined in one step by matching the estimators and practical scenarios where those estimators will work. In this book, we'll highlight the separation of identification and estimation for several reasons:

- The separation lets us shunt all the causal considerations into the identification step. This helps us be explicit about what causal assumptions we are relying on for estimation to work and builds intuition for when our analysis might fail.
- The estimation step thus simplifies to purely statistical questions, where we consider the usual statistical trade-offs (bias vs. variance, uncertainty quantification, how well it scales, etc.).
- The separation also allows us to handle estimation with the automatic differentiation capabilities that power cutting-edge deep learning libraries without worrying whether these learning procedures will get the causality wrong.

Next, we'll dive into the most common identification strategy: backdoor adjustment.

## 10.3   Identification with backdoor adjustment

Suppose we want to determine the causal effect of engagement on in-game purchases, i.e., $E(I_{E=\text{"high"}} - I_{E=\text{"low"}})$. We can derive this expectation from the query $E(I_{E=e}=i)$, so we focus on $P(I_{E=e}=i)$. We can use the online gaming DAG to prove the following is true:

$$P(I_{E=\text{"high"}} = i) = \sum_g P(I = i | E = \text{"high"}, G = g) P(G = g)$$

We'll see how to derive this equation in the next section. The right side of this equation is a level 1 quantity called an *estimand* that we can derive from the joint distribution $P(I, E, G)$.

## Queries, estimands, and estimators

In statistics, the *estimand* is the thing the statistical algorithm (the *estimator*) estimates. The task of identification is finding (identifying) an estimand for your query. In terms of the causal hierarchy, causal identification is about finding a lower-level estimand for a higher-level query.

In the online gaming backdoor identification example, $P(I_{E=\text{"high"}}=i)$ is a level 2 query, and $\Sigma_g P(I=i|E=\text{"high"}, G=g)P(G=g)$ is the level 1 estimand called the *backdoor adjustment estimand*. Backdoor adjustment is an operation we apply to $P(E, I, G)$, where we sum out (or integrate out in the continuous case) the common cause G. In some cases, we'll see we don't need to know the estimand explicitly, only that it exists.

We passed our DAG and the intervention-level query $P(I_{E=\text{"high"}})$ to y0, and it told us it identified an estimand, an operation applied to $P(E, I, G)$ that is equivalent to $P(I_{E=\text{"high"}})$. Let's have y0 display that estimand.

### Listing 10.5   Deriving the estimand to get $P(I_{E=\text{"high"}})$ from $P(E, I, G)$

```
from y0.graph import NxMixedGraph as Y0Graph
from y0.dsl import P, Variable
from y0.algorithm.identify import Identification, identify

query = P(I @ e)
base_distribution = P(I, E, G)

identification_task = Identification.from_expression(
    graph=dag,
    query=query,
    estimand=base_distribution)

identify(identification_task)
```

This returns the expression in figure 10.6.

In our notation, this is $\Sigma_g P(I=i|E=\text{"high"}, G=g)$ $\Sigma_{\varepsilon,t} P(E=\varepsilon, G=g, I=i)$, which simplifies to $\Sigma_g P(I=i|E=\text{"high"}, G=g)$ $P(G=g)$. This is the *backdoor adjustment estimand*. We'll see at a high level how y0 derives this estimand. But first, let's look a bit more closely at this estimand.

$$\sum_G P(I|E, G) \sum \sum_{E,I} P(E, G, I)$$

**Figure 10.6   Output of y0's identify function**

### 10.3.1  *The backdoor adjustment formula*

In general terms, suppose *X* is a cause of *Y*, and we are interested in the intervention-level query $P(Y_{X=x})$. In that case, the *backdoor adjustment estimand* is $\Sigma_g P(X=x, Z=z)$ $P(Z=z)$. The *backdoor adjustment formula* equates the causal query $P(X_{X=x})$ with its estimand:

$$P\left(Y_{X=x} = y\right) = \sum_{z} P\left(Y = y | X = x, Z = z\right) P\left(Z = z\right)$$

Here, *Z* is a set of variables called the adjustment set. The summation is shorthand for summation and integration—you sum over discrete variables in the adjustment set and integrate over continuous variables. The adjustment set is defined as fa set of variables that satisfies the *backdoor criterion*—(1) the set collectively *d*-separates all *backdoor paths* from *X* to *Y*, and (2) it contains no descendants of *X*.

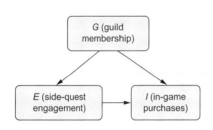

**Figure 10.7   The online gaming DAG**

To understand why we want to d-separate backdoor paths between *X* and *Y*, consider again our DAG for our online gaming example in figure 10.7.

What is the difference between $P(I|E=\text{"high"})$ and $P(I_{E=\text{"high"}})$? Consider the two paths between *E* and *I* in figure 10.8. In the case of $P(I|E=\text{"high"})$, observing *E*="high" gives us information about *I* by way of its direct causal impact on *I*, i.e., through path *E→I*. But observing *E* ="high" also gives us information about *G*, and subsequently about *I* through the *backdoor path E←G→I*. A *backdoor path* between two variables is a *d*-connected path between a common cause. In the case of $P(I_{E=\text{"high"}})$, we only want the impact on *I* through the direct path *E→I*.

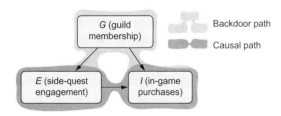

Backdoor path

Causal path

**Figure 10.8   *E←G→I* is a backdoor path where *G* is a "confounder" that is a common cause of *E* and *I*. We are interested in the statistical signal flowing along the causal path from *E* to *I*, but that signal is "confounded" by the noncausal noise from additional statistical information through *G* on the backdoor path *E←G→I*.**

We call *G* a *confounder*, because the statistical "signal" flowing along the causal path from *E* to *I* is "confounded" by the noncausal "noise" from additional statistical information through *G* on the *backdoor path E←G→I*. To address this problem, we seek to d-separate this backdoor path by blocking on *G*.

We want to identify a backdoor estimand for the query $P(I_{E=\text{"high"}})$. So we substitute $I$ for $Y$, and $E$ for $X$ in the backdoor adjustment formula. $G$ blocks the backdoor path $E$ $G\,I$, so the set $G$ becomes our adjustment set:

$$P(I_{E=e}=i) = \Sigma_g P(I=i|E=e,\,G=g)\,P(G=g)$$

The backdoor adjustment formula d-separates the backdoor paths by summing out/ integrating over, or in other words, "adjusting for" the backdoor statistical signal, leaving only the signal derived from the direct causal relationship.

> **NOTE**   Some texts refer to the G-formula instead of backdoor adjustment formula. The backdoor adjustment formula is just the G-formula where the adjustment set is defined in terms of the backdoor criterion.

While an adjustment set can include non-confounders, in practice, excluding all but a minimal set of backdoor-blocking confounders cuts down on complexity and statistical variation. We dive into the statistical considerations of backdoor adjustment in chapter 11.

### 10.3.2   Demystifying the back door

So where does the backdoor adjustment estimand come from? Let's consider our online gaming example again. The query is $P(I_{E=e})$ where $e$ is "high" or "low." In counterfactual terms, let's consider two possible worlds, one with our original DAG, and one where we apply the intervention to side-quest engagement ($E$). Let's view the parallel world graph in figure 10.9.

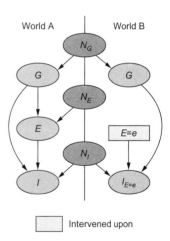

**Figure 10.9   We have two parallel worlds: world A where $E$ is not intervened upon, and world B where $E$ is intervened upon.**

If you squint hard enough at this graph, you'll notice that it implies that $E$ is conditionally independent from $I_{E=e}$ given $G$. We'll use some d-separation–based reasoning to see this. Remember that, in general, we can't use d-separation to reason across worlds on a parallel world graph because the d-separation rules don't account for nodes that are equivalent across worlds (like $G$). But we'll use a trick where we reason about conditional independence between $E$ and $I_{E=e}$ by looking at a d-connected path from $E$ to $G$ in world A, and then extend that d-connected path *from* the equivalent $G$ in world B to $I_{E=e}$.

First, consider that paths from $E$ in world A to world B have to cross one of two bridges between worlds, $N_G$ and $N_I$. But the two paths to $N_I$ ($E \rightarrow I \leftarrow N_I$, $E \leftarrow G \rightarrow I \leftarrow N_I$) are both d-separated due to the collider on $I$.

So we have one d-connected path to world B ($E \leftarrow G \leftarrow N_G$). Now suppose we look at $G$ in world B; from world B's $G$, it is one step to $I_{E=e}$. But we know that, by the law of consistency, the value of $G$ in both worlds must be the same; both $G$s are the same

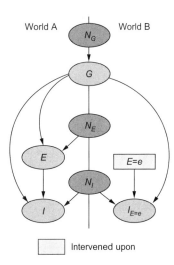

**Figure 10.10  Collapsing G across worlds reveals G d-separates E and $I_{E=e}$.**

deterministic function of $N_G$, and neither $G$ is affected by an intervention. So, for convenience, we'll collapse the two $G$s into one node in the parallel world graph (figure 10.10). Looking now at the path $E \leftarrow G \rightarrow I_{E=e}$, we can see this path is d-separated by $G$. Hence, we can conclude $E \perp I_{E=e} \mid G$.

In causal inference jargon, this simplification is called *ignorability*. *Ignorability* means the causal variable $E$ and the counterfactual potential outcomes like $I_{E=e}$ are conditionally independent given confounders. Ignorability is a common assumption made in causal inference. We can use this ignorability assumption in deriving the backdoor estimand.

Before we start, let's recall a key definitional fact of conditional independence: if two variables $U$ and $V$ are conditionally independent given $Z$, then $P(U|Z=z, V=v) = P(U|Z=z)$. Flipping that around, $P(U|Z=z) = P(U|Z=z, V=v)$. In other words, $P(U|Z=z) = P(U|Z=z, V=\text{``apples''}) = P(U|Z=z, V=\text{``oranges''})$; it doesn't matter what value $V$ takes because, since $Z$ rendered it independent from $U$, its value has no bearing on $U$. Introducing $V$ and giving it whatever value we want is the trick that makes the derivation work. Also, recall the *law of total probability* says that we can marginalize a variable out of a joint distribution by summing (or integrating) over that variable, as in $P(U=u) = \Sigma_v P(U=u, V=v)$. The same is true when the joint distribution is subject to intervention, as in $P(U_{W=w}=u) = \Sigma_v P(U_{W=w}=u, V_{W=w}=v)$.

Now let's start with the causal query $P(I_{E=e})$ and see how to equate it with the backdoor estimand $\Sigma_g P(I|E=e, G=g)P(G=g)$.

1   For some value of in-game purchases $i$, $P(I_{E=e}=i) = \Sigma_g P(I_{E=e}=i, G_{E=e}=g)$ by the law of total probability.

2   $\Sigma_g P(I_{E=e}=i, G_{E=e}=g) = \Sigma_g P(I_{E=e}=i, G=g)$, because we know from our original DAG that $G$ is not affected by the intervention on $E$.

3   Next we use the chain rule to factorize $P(I_{E=e}=i, G=g)$: $\Sigma_g P(I_{E=e}=i, G=g) = \Sigma_g P(I_{E=e}=i| G=g)P(G=g)$.

4   Now we come to the trick—$P(I_{E=e}=i|G=g) = P(I_{E=e}=i|E=e, G=g)$ for any value of $e$, because once we condition on $G=g$, $E=e$ and $I_{E=e}$ are independent. So in our derivation, we can replace $P(I_{E=e}=i|G=g)$ with $P(I_{E=e}=i|E=e, G=g)$.

5   Once we condition that $E=e$, we can use the law of consistency to drop the subscript: $\Sigma_g P(I_{E=e}=i|E=e, G=g)P(G=g) = \Sigma_g P(I=i|E=e, G=g)P(G=g)$.

Let's explain steps 4 and 5. Our ignorability result shows that $I_{E=e}$ and $E$ are conditionally independent given $G$. So in step 4 we apply the independence trick that lets us introduce $E$. Further, we set the value of $E$ to be $e$ so it matches the subscript $_{E=e}$. This allows us to apply the law of consistency from chapter 8 and drop the subscript $_{E=e}$.

Voila, we've identified a backdoor estimand, an estimand from level 1 of the causal hierarchy, for a level 2 causal query $P(I_{E=e})$ using level 2 assumptions encoded in a DAG. Causal identification is just coming up with derivations like this. Much, if not most, of traditional causal inference research boils down to doing this kind of math, or writing algorithms that do it for you.

Next, we'll look at the do-calculus, which provides simple graph-based rules for identification that we can use in identification algorithms.

## 10.4   Graphical identification with the do-calculus

*Graphical identification* (sometimes called *nonparametric identification*) refers to identification techniques that rely on reasoning over the DAG. One of the most well-known approaches to graphical identification is the *do-calculus*, a set of three rules used for identification with causal graphs. The rules use graph surgery and d-separation to determine cases when you can replace causal terms like $I_{E=e}$ with non-causal terms like $I|E=e$. Starting with a query on a higher level of the causal hierarchy, we can apply these rules in sequence to derive a lower-level estimand.

### 10.4.1   Demystifying the do-calculus

Recall high school geometry, where you saw if-then statements like this:

*If the shape is a square, then all the sides are equal.*

When you were trying to solve a geometry problem, you used facts like this in the steps of your solution.

Similarly, the do-calculus consists of three rules (if-then statements) of the following form:

*If certain variables are d-separated after applying graph surgery to the DAG, then probability query A equals probability query B.*

#### THE RULES OF THE DO-CALCULUS ARE NOT INTUITIVE

The three rules of the do-calculus are not intuitive upon reading them, just as geometric rules like $\cos^2 x + \sin^2 x = 1$ were not intuitive when you first saw them in high school. But like those geometric rules, we derive the rules of the do-calculus from simpler familiar concepts, namely d-separation, ideal interventions, and the rules of probability. And like the rules of geometry, we can use the rules of the do-calculus to prove that a causal query from one level of the hierarchy is equivalent to one from another level.

Practically speaking, we can rely either on software libraries that implement the do-calculus in graphical identification algorithms (like y0) or simply hard-code well-known identification results like the backdoor adjustment estimand. To take away some of the mystery, I'll introduce the rules and show how they can derive the backdoor estimand. The goal here is not to memorize these rules, but rather to see how they work in a derivation of the backdoor estimand that contrasts with the derivation in the previous section.

In defining these rules, we'll focus on the target distribution *Y* under an intervention on *X*. We want to generalize to all DAGs, so we'll name two other nodes, *Z* and *W*. *Z* and *W* will allow us to cover cases where we have another potential intervention target *Z* and any node *W* we'd like to condition upon. Further, while I'll often refer to individual variables, keep in mind that the rules apply when *X*, *Y*, *Z*, and *W* are sets of variables.

### RULE 1: INSERTION OR REMOVAL OF OBSERVATIONS

*If Y and Z are d-separated in your DAG by X and W after the incoming edges to X are removed . . .*

*Then $P(Y_{X=x}=y \mid Z=z, W=w) = P(Y_{X=x}=y \mid W=w)$.*

This is called "insertion or removal" because we can remove *Z=z* from $P(Y_{X=x}=y|Z=z, W=w)$ to get $P(Y_{X=x}=y \mid W=w)$ and vice versa.

### RULE 2: EXCHANGE OF AN INTERVENTION FOR AN OBSERVATION

*If Y and Z are d-separated in your DAG by X and W after incoming edges in X and outgoing edges from Z have been removed . . .*

*then $P(Y_{X=x, Z=z}=y \mid W=w) = P(Y_{X=x}=y \mid Z=z, W=w)$.*

Here we can either *exchange* the intervention $_{Z=z}$ in $P(Y_{X=x, Z=z}=y \mid W=w)$ for conditioning on the observation *Z=z* to get $P(Y_{X=x}=y \mid Z=z, W=w)$, or vice versa.

### RULE 3: INSERTION OR REMOVAL OF INTERVENTIONS

For rule 3, we are going to define *Z* as a set of nodes, and *Z(W)* as the subset of *Z* that are not ancestors of *W*.

*If Y and Z are d-separated in your DAG by X and W after you remove all incoming edges to X and Z(W) . . .*

*then $P(Y_{X=x, Z=z}=y \mid W=w) = P(Y_{X=x}=y \mid W=w)$.*

This rule allows you to insert $_{Z=z}$ into $P(Y_{X=x}=y \mid W=w)$ to get $P(Y_{X=x, Z=z}=y \mid W=w)$ or remove $_{Z=z}$ from $P(Y_{X=x, Z=z}=y \mid W=w)$ to get $P(Y_{X=x}=y \mid W=w)$.

### *10.4.2   Using the do-calculus for backdoor identification*

Now we'll use the do-calculus to provide an alternative derivation of the backdoor estimand that differs from our "ignorability"-based definition. Again, I include this derivation to demystify the application of the do-calculus. Don't worry if you don't completely follow each step:

1. $P(I_{E=e}=i) = \Sigma_g P(I_{E=e}=i, G_{E=e}=g)$ by the law of total probability.
2. $\Sigma_g P(I_{E=e}=i, G_{E=e}=g) = \Sigma_g P(I_{E=e, G=g}=i) P(G_{E=e, I=i}=g)$ by way of *c-component factorization*.
3. $P(I_{E=e, G=g}=i) = P(I=i|E=e, G=g)$ by rule 2 of the do-calculus.
4. $P(G_{E=e, I=i}=g) = P(G=g)$ by rule 3 of the do-calculus.
5. Therefore, $P(I_{E=e}=i) = \Sigma_g P(I=i|E=e, G=g) P(G=g)$ by plugging 3 and 4 into 2.

The do-calculus rules are applied in steps 3 and 4.

**NOTE** Step 2 uses a factorization rule called *c-component factorization*. A c-component (confounded component) is a set of nodes in a DAG where each pair of observable nodes is connected by a path with edges that always point toward, never away from, the observable nodes (these are the "orphaned cousins" mentioned in chapter 4). The joint probability of the observed variables can be factorized into c-components, and this fact enabled step 2. Factorizing over c-components is common in identification algorithms. See the references in the chapter notes at www.altdeep.ai/causalAIbook.

This do-calculus-based derivation is far less intuitive than our "ignorability"-based derivation. There are two advantages we get in exchange for that of intuition. First, the do-calculus is *complete*, meaning that if a query has an identifiable estimand using graphical assumptions alone, it can be derived using the do-calculus. Second, we have algorithms that leverage the do-calculus to automate graphical identification.

## 10.5   Graphical identification algorithms

Graphical identification algorithms, often called *ID algorithms*, automate the application of graph-based identification systems like the do-calculus. When we used y0 to check for identification of $P(I_{E=e})$ and to derive the backdoor estimand, it was using its implementation of graphical identification algorithms. In this section, we'll see how we can use these algorithms to identify another useful estimand called the *front-door estimand*.

### 10.5.1   Case study: The front-door estimand

In our online gaming example, suppose we were not able to observe guild membership. Then we would not have backdoor identification of $P(I_{E=e})$. However, suppose we had a *mediator* between side-quest engagement ($E$) and in-game purchases ($I$)—a node on the graph between $E$ and $I$. Specifically, our mediator represents *won items* ($W$), as seen in figure 10.11.

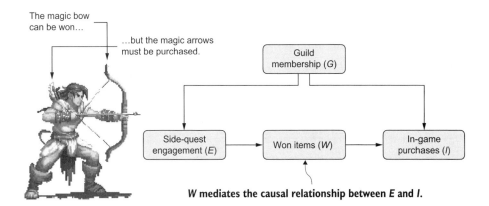

**Figure 10.11   Side-quest engagement leads to winning virtual items like this magic bow. Won items drive more in-game purchases, such as magic arrows for the magic bow, so we introduce a mediator "won items" on the causal path between side-quest engagement and in-game purchases.**

The idea of won items is as follows. When a player successfully completes a side-quest, they win a virtual item. The more side-quests they finish, the more items they earn. Those *won* virtual items and *purchased* virtual items can complement one another. For example, winning a magic bow motivates purchases of magical arrows. Thus, the amount of won items a player has influences the amount of virtual items they purchase.

Given this graph, we can use y0's implementation of graphical identification algorithms to derive the front-door estimand.

### Listing 10.6    Deriving the front-door estimand in y0

```
from y0.graph import NxMixedGraph as Y0Graph
from y0.dsl import P, Variable
G = Variable("G")
E = Variable("E")
I = Variable("I")
W = Variable("W")
e = E
dag = Y0Graph.from_edges(          Build a new graph with
    directed=[                     the mediator variable.
        (G, E),
        (G, I),
        (E, W),
        (W, I)
    ]
)

query=P(I @ e)          ◁───   Still the same query as in
                               listing 10.5, P(I_{E=e})      But now we observe
base_distribution = P(I, E, W)                      ◁──┘     I, E, and W

identification_task = Identification.from_expression(
    graph=dag,                                Finally, we check if the query is
    query=query,                              identified given the DAG and
    estimand=base_distribution)               observational distribution.
identify(identification_task)
```

This code will return the output in figure 10.12.

$$\sum_{G,W} P(I|E,G,W) \sum \sum_{E,I,W} P(E,I,W)P(W|E,G)$$

**Figure 10.12    Y0 renders a math figure as output of identification.**

Rearranging the output, and in our notation, this is the result:

$$P = \sum_{g,w} P(W=w|E=e,G=g) \sum_{\varepsilon,\iota,\omega} P(I=i|E=\varepsilon,G=g,W=w)P(E=\varepsilon,W=\omega,I=\iota)$$

Simplifying as before, we get the front-door estimand:

$$P(I_{E=e} = i) = \sum_w P(W = w | E = e) \sum_\varepsilon P(I = i | E = \varepsilon, W = w) P(E = \varepsilon)$$

Note that there is an outer summation over $W$ and an inner summation over all values of $E$ (with each value of $E$ denoted as $\varepsilon$, distinct from the intervention value $e$).

### 10.5.2 Demystifying the front door

Like the backdoor estimand, the do-calculus derivation of the front-door estimand involves repeated substitutions using rules 2 and 3. The rough intuition behind the front-door estimand is that the statistical association between side-quest engagement and in-game purchases comes from both the direct causal path and the path through the backdoor confounder guild membership ($G$). The front-door estimand uses the mediator to determine how much of that association is due to the direct causal path; the mediator acts as a gauge of the flow of statistical information through that direct causal path.

A key benefit of the estimand is that it does not require observing a set of confounders that block all possible backdoor paths. Avoiding backdoor adjustment is useful when you have many confounders, are unable to adjust due to latent confounders, or are concerned that there might be some unknown confounders.

Next, we'll examine how to identify counterfactuals.

## 10.6 General counterfactual identification

The causal DAG is a level 2 modeling assumption. The causal hierarchy theorem tells us that the graph in general is not sufficient to identify level 3 counterfactual queries. For counterfactual identification from level 1 or level 2 distributions, you need level 3 assumptions. In simple terms, a level 3 assumption is any causal assumption that you can't represent with a simple causal DAG.

In chapter 9, I introduced the general algorithm for counterfactual inference. The algorithm requires a structural causal model (SCM), which is a level 3 model; it encapsulates level 3 assumptions. With an SCM, the algorithm can infer *all* counterfactual queries that can be defined on its underlying variables. The cost of this ability is that the SCM must encapsulate *all* the assumptions needed to answer all those queries. Many of these assumptions cannot be validated with level 1 or level 2 data.

The more assumptions you make, the more vulnerable your inferences are to violations of these assumptions. For this reason, we seek identification techniques that target specific counterfactual queries (rather than every counterfactual query) with the minimal set of level 3 assumptions possible.

### 10.6.1 The problem with the general algorithm for counterfactual inference

We can see the problem with the general algorithm for counterfactual inference when we apply it to two similar SCMs. Let's suppose there is a ground-truth SCM that differs from the SCM you are using to run the algorithm. Suppose both SCMs have the exact same underlying DAG and the same statistical fit on observational and experimental data; in other words, the SCMs provide the same inferences for all level 1 and level 2 queries. Your SCM could still produce different (inaccurate) counterfactual inferences relative to the ground-truth SCM.

To see why, recall the stick-breaking example from chapter 6. I posed two similar but different SCMs. This was the first:

$$n_y \sim \text{Uniform}(0, 1)$$

$$y := \begin{cases} 1, & n_y \le p_{x1} \\ 2, & p_{x1} < n_y \le p_{x1} + p_{x2} \\ 3, & p_{x1} + p_{x2} < n_y \le 1 \end{cases}$$

And this was the second:

$$n_y \sim \text{Uniform}(0, 1)$$

$$y := \begin{cases} 3, & n_y \le p_{x3} \\ 1, & p_{x3} < n_y \le p_{x3} + p_{x1} \\ 2, & p_{x3} + p_{x1} < n_y \le 1 \end{cases}$$

Figure 10.13 visualizes sampling a single value from these models.

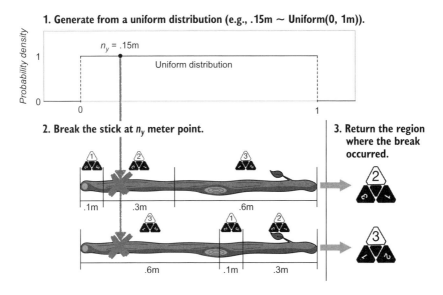

**Figure 10.13   Two different SCMs encode the exact same observational and interventional distributions, but given the same exogenous variable value, you can get two different values of the corresponding endogenous variable in each model.**

Figure 10.13 shows how, given a value of $n_y$ = .15, the sticks break at the .15 meters point, but the first stick will break in region 2, returning a value of 2, while the second stick will break in region 3, returning a 3. They produce different outcomes given the same random input because they differ in a level 3 assumption, i.e., *how* they process the input.

For this reason, when we go in the opposite direction and apply the abduction step in the general counterfactual inference algorithm, we can get different results across these models. For a given value of the endogenous variable, we can get different posterior distributions on the exogenous variable.

Figure 10.14 illustrates how the two models, for an observed outcome of 3, would produce different inferences on $N_y$. For the first SCM, a value of $y$=3 means $P(N_y|Y=3)$ is a continuous uniform distribution on the range $(p_{x1} + p_{x2})$ to 1, and for the second SCM, it is a continuous uniform distribution on the range 0 to $p_{x3}$. These different distributions of $P(N_y|Y=3)$ would lead to different results from the counterfactual inference algorithm. Now suppose SCM 2 is right and SCM 1 is wrong. If we choose SCM 1, our counterfactual inferences will be inaccurate.

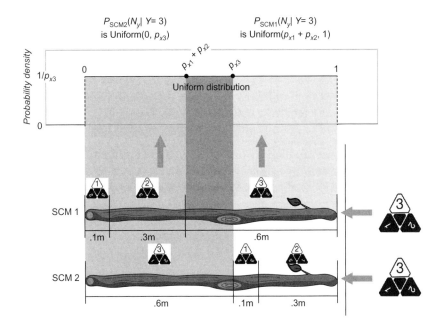

**Figure 10.14   The two SCMs, despite encoding the same set of observational and interventional distributions, would produce two different posteriors of $N_y$ given Y=3 in the abduction step. Therefore, they encode different counterfactual distributions and can produce different counterfactual inferences.**

The general case is even harder; there can be many SCMs entailing the same level 1 and 2 assumptions but have different level 3 assumptions. You might learn one of those SCMs by, for example, using a deep neural network-based approach to learn a deep SCM from level 1 and level 2 data. But the deep SCM might not be the *right* SCM with respect to the counterfactual inferences you want to make.

The general algorithm for counterfactual inference is ideal if you are confident in the ground-truth SCM. But in cases where you aren't, you can look toward counterfactual identification, where you specify a *minimal* set of level 3 assumptions that enable you to identify a target counterfactual query.

### 10.6.2   *Example: Monotonicity and the probabilities of causation*

Monotonicity is an example of a powerful level 3 assumption. Monotonicity is the simple assumption that the relationship between a cause $X$ and an outcome $Y$ is monotonic: $E(Y|X=x)$ either never increases or never decreases as $x$ increases. Note that linearity is a special case of monotonicity.

An intuitive example of monotonicity and non-monotonicity is in the dosage of medicine. In a monotonic dose-response relationship, taking more of the medicine either helps or does nothing. In a non-monotonic dose-response relationship, taking the medicine might help at a normal dose, but taking an overdose might cause the problem to get worse. Monotinicity helps identification by eliminating counterfactual possibilities; if the dose-response relationship is monotonic, when you imagine what would have happened if you took a stronger dose, you can eliminate the possiblity that you would have gotten worse.

Recall the probabilities of causation we saw in chapter 8:

- Probability of necessity (PN): $P(Y_{X=0}=0|X=1, Y=1)$
- Probability of sufficiency (PS): $P(Y_{X=1}=1|X=0, Y=0)$
- Probability of necessity and sufficiency (PNS): $P(Y_{X=1}=1, Y_{X=0}=0)$

Given monotonicity, we can identify the following level 2 estimands for the probabilities of causation.

- PN = $(P(Y=1) - P(Y_{X=0}=1))/P(X=1, Y=1)$
- PS = $(P(Y_{X=1}=1) - P(Y=1))/P(X=0, Y=0)$
- PNS = $P(Y_{X=1}=1) - P(Y_{X=0}=1)$

We can estimate these level 2 estimands from level 2 data, such as a randomized experiment. And, of course, if we only have observational data, we can use backdoor or front-door adjustment or another identification strategy to infer $P(Y_{X=0}=1)$ and $P(Y_{X=1}=1)$ from that data.

We could derive these estimands by hand again, but instead, let's think about the monotonicity enabled this identification by eliminating counterfactual possibilities. To see this, consider our uplift modeling question in chapter 8. There, $X$ was whether we sent a promotion, and $Y$ was whether the customer remained a paying subscriber ($Y=1$) or "churned" (unsubscribed; $Y=0$). We segmented the subscribers as follows:

- *Persuadables*—Subscribers whose chance of remaining increases when you send a promotion
- *Sure things*—Subscribers who have a high chance of remaining regardless of whether you send a promotion

- *Lost causes*—Subscribers who have a low chance of remaining regardless of whether you send a promotion
- *Sleeping dogs*: Subscribers whose chances of remaining *go down* when you send a promotion

If you assume monotonicity, you are assuming that sending the promotion either does nothing or increases the chances of remaining. It assumes there are no users who will respond poorly to the promotion. In other words, assuming monotonicity means you assume there are no sleeping dogs.

Now let's consider how this narrows things down. Suppose you have the following question:

> *I failed to send a promotion to a customer and they churned. Would they have remained had I sent the promotion?* $P(Y_{X=1} = 1 | X = 0, Y = 0)$

This counterfactual query is the probability of sufficiency. We want to know if sending the promotion would have increased the chances of their remaining. Thinking through the question,

- If the customer was a persuadable, sending the promotion would have increased their chances of remaining.
- If the customer was a lost cause, sending the promotion would have had no effect.
- If the customer was a sleeping dog, sending the promotion would have made them *even less* likely to remain.

It's hard to determine if we should have sent the promotion if being a persuadable and being a sleeping dog were both possible for this customer, in one case the promotion would have helped and in the other it would have made churning even more certain. But if we assume monotonicity, we eliminate the possibility that they were a sleeping dog, and can conclude sending the promotion would have helped or, at least, not have hurt their chances of staying.

## Bayesian modeling and counterfactual identification

Although the graphical identification algorithms will work with some counterfactual queries, we don't have general algorithms for counterfactual identification. But given our focus on the tools of probabilistic ML, we can look to Bayesian modeling for a path forward.

Identification is fundamentally about uncertainty. For example, in the counterfactual case, a lack of identification means that even with infinite level 1 and level 2 data, you can't be certain about the true value of the level 3 query. From a Bayesian perspective, we can use probability to handle that uncertainty.

Suppose you have a set of causal assumptions, including non-graphical assumptions, and some level 1 and 2 data. You can take the following Bayesian approach to test whether your assumptions and data are sufficient to identify your counterfactual query:

*(continued)*

1 Specify a set of SCMs that are diverse yet all consistent with your causal assumptions.

2 Place a prior distribution over this set, such that more plausible models get higher prior probability values.

3 Obtain a posterior distribution on the SCMs given observational (level 1) and interventional (level 2) data.

4 Sample SCMs from the posterior distribution, and for each sample SCM, you apply the general algorithm for counterfactual inference for a specific counterfactual query.

The result would constitute the posterior distribution over this counterfactual inference. If your causal assumptions and your data are enough to identify the counterfactual query, the posterior on the counterfactual inference will converge to the true value as the size of your data increases. (Successful convergence assumes typical "regularity" conditions for Bayesian estimation. Results will depend on the quality of the prior.) But even if it doesn't converge to the true value, your assumptions might still enable convergence to a ballpark region around the true value that is small enough to be useful (this is called partial identification, as described in section 10.9).

The Pyro library, and its causality-focused extension ChiRho, facilitate combining Bayesian and causal ideas in this way.

There are generalizations of monotonicity from binary actions (like sending or not sending a promotion) to multiple actions as in a decision or reinforcement learning problem, see the course notes at www.altdeep.ai/causalAIbook for references.

## 10.7 *Graphical counterfactual identification*

A conventional causal DAG only encodes level 2 assumptions, but there are graphical techniques for reasoning about counterfactuals. Graphical counterfactual inference only works in special cases, but these cases are quite practical. Further, working with graphs enables us to automate identification with algorithms. To illustrate graphical counterfactual identification, we'll introduce a new case study.

When you open Netflix, you see the Netflix dashboard, which shows several forms of recommended content. Two of these are "Top Picks For You," which is a personalized selection of shows and movies that Netflix's algorithms predict you will enjoy based on your past viewing behavior and ratings, and "Because You Watched," which recommends content based on things you watched recently. The model of this system includes the following variables:

- $T$—A variable for the recommendation policy that selects a subscriber's "Top Picks for You" content. For simplicity, we'll consider a policy, "$+t$", that is currently in production. We'll use "$-t$", meaning "not $t$", to represent alternative policies.

- $B$—A variable for the recommendation policy that selects a subscriber's "Because You Watched" content. Again, we'll simplify this to a binary variable with policy "+$b$", representing the policy in production, and all alternative policies "−$b$", as in "not $b$."

- $V$—The amount of engagement that a subscriber has with the content recommended by "Because You Watched."
- $W$—The amount of engagement that a subscriber has with the content recommended by "Top Picks for You."
- $A$—Attrition, meaning whether a subscriber eventually leaves Netflix.
- $C$—Subscriber context, meaning the type of subscriber (location, demographics, preferences, etc.) we are dealing with.

Recommendation algorithms always take the profile of the subscriber into account, along with the viewership history, so subscriber profile $C$ is a cause of both recommendation policy variables $T$ and $B$.

In this section, we'll use y0 to analyze this problem at various levels of the hierarchy. We'll start by visualizing the graph.

---

**Listing 10.7  Plot the recommendation DAG**

```
T = Variable("T")                       Define variables
W = Variable("W")                       for the model.
B = Variable("B")
V = Variable("V")
C = Variable("C")
A = Variable("A")
t, a, w, v, b = T, A, W, V, B
dag = Y0Graph.from_edges(directed=[
    (T, W),
    (W, A),
    (B, V),                             Create the
    (V, A),                             graph.
    (C, T),
    (C, A),
    (C, B)
])
gv_draw(dag)      ◁——| Plot the graph.
```

---

This generates the DAG in figure 10.15.

As a preliminary investigation, you might look at the average treatment effect (ATE, a level 2 query) of the "Top Picks for You" content on attrition $E(A_{T=+t} − A_{T=-t})$. Given that attrition $A$ has a binary outcome, we can write this as $P(A_{T=+t}=+a) − P(A_{T=-t}=+a)$. Focusing on $P(A_{T=-t}=+a)$, we know right away that we can identify this via both the (level 2) backdoor and the front door. So let's move on to an interesting (level 3) counterfactual query called *effect of treatment on the treated* (ETT).

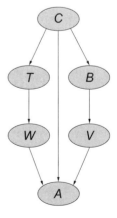

**Figure 10.15  Causal DAG for the recommendation algorithm problem**

### 10.7.1  *Effect of treatment on the treated*

Recall that you get the ATE directly (without needing to identify and estimate a level 1 estimand) from a randomized experiment. Suppose you ran such an experiment on a cohort of users, and it showed a favorable ATE, such as that $+t$ has a favorable impact on $W$ and $A$ relative to $-t$. So your team deploys the policy.

Suppose the $+t$ policy works best with users who have watched a lot of movies and thus have more viewing data. For this reason, when the policy is deployed to production, such users are more likely to get assigned the policy. But since they are so highly engaged, they are unlikely to leave, regardless of whether they are assigned the $+t$ or $-t$ policy. We could have a situation where the $+t$ policy looks effective in an experiment where people are assigned policies randomly, regardless of their level of engagement, but in production the assignment is biased to highly engaged people who are indifferent to the policy.

The level 3 query that addresses this is a counterfactual version of the ATE called effect of treatment on the treated (ETT, or sometimes ATT, as in *average treatment effect on the treated*). We write this as counterfactual query $E(A_{T=+t} - A_{T=-t} | T=+t)$, as in "for people who saw policy $+t$, how much more attrition do they have relative to what they would have if they had seen $-t$?" Decomposing for binary $A$ as we did with the ATE, we can write this as $P(A_{T=+t}=+a | T=+t) - P(A_{T=-t}=+a | T=+t)$. $P(A_{T=+t}=+a | T=+t)$ simplifies to $P(A=+a | T=+t)$ by the law of consistency. So we can focus on the second term, $P(A_{T=-t}=+a | T=+t)$.

In this special case of binary $A$, we can identify the ETT using graphical identification (for non-binary $A$, more level 3 assumptions are needed). To do graphical identification for counterfactuals, we can use graphical identification algorithms with counterfactual graphs.

### 10.7.2  *Identification over the counterfactual graph*

Y0 can derive an estimand for ETT using a graphical identification algorithm called "IDC*" (pronounced I-D-C-star).

---

#### Graph ID algorithms, ID, IDC, ID*, IDC*, in y0

Some of the core graphical identification algorithms implemented in y0 are ID, ID*, IDC, and IDC*. ID identifies interventional (level 2) queries from a DAG and observational (level 1) data. ID* identifies counterfactual (level 3) queries from observational and experimental (level 1 and level 2) data. IDC and IDC* extend ID and ID* to work on queries that condition on evidence, such as ETT.

The algorithms use the structure of the causal graph to recursively simplify the identification problem by removing irrelevant variables and decomposing the graph into c-component subgraphs. They apply the rules of do-calculus to reduce intervention terms, block confounding backdoor paths, and factorize the query into simpler subqueries. If no further simplification is possible due to the graph's structure, the algorithms return a 'non-identifiable' result.

This chapter's code relies on Y0's implementations of these algorithms, though Y0 implements other graphical identification algorithms as well.

**Listing 10.8  Identifying ETT with a graphical identification algorithm**

```
from y0.algorithm.identify.idc_star import idc_star

idc_star(
    dag,
    outcomes={A @ -t: +a},
    conditions={T: +t}
)
```

Hypothetical outcome
$A_{T=-t} = +a$

Factual condition
$T = +t$

This will produce a rather verbose level 2 estimand. We can then apply level 2 graphical identification algorithms to get a level 1 estimand, which will simplify to the following:

$$P(A_{T=-t} = +a|T = +t) = \sum_c P(A = +a|C = c, T = -t)P(C = c|T = +t)$$

I'll show a simple derivation in the next section.

For now, the intuition is that we are applying graphical identification algorithms over something called a counterfactual graph. Up until now, our graph of choice for counterfactual reasoning was the parallel world graph. Indeed, we can have y0 make a parallel world graph for us.

**Listing 10.9  Plotting the parallel world graph with y0**

```
from y0.algorithm.identify.cg import make_parallel_worlds_graph
parallel_world_graph = make_parallel_worlds_graph(
    dag,
    {frozenset([+t])}
)
gv_draw(parallel_world_graph)
```

The make_parallel_worlds_graph method takes an input DAG and sets of interventions. It constructs a new world for each set.

The helper function visualizes the graph in a familiar way.

This graph differs slightly from the ones I've drawn because the algorithm applies the subscript for an intervention to every node in the world where the intervention occurred; the subscript indexes all the variables in a world. It's up to us to reason that $C$ from one world and $C_{+t}$ from another must have the same outcomes, since $C_{+t}$ is not affected by its world's intervention $do(T=+t)$.

Now recall that the problem with the parallel world graph is that d-separation won't work with it. For example, in figure 10.16, d-separation suggests that $C$ and $C_{+t}$ are conditionally independent given their common exogenous parent $N_C$, but we just articulated that $C$ and $C_{+t}$ must be the same; if C has a value, $C_{+t}$ must have the same value, so they are perfectly dependent.

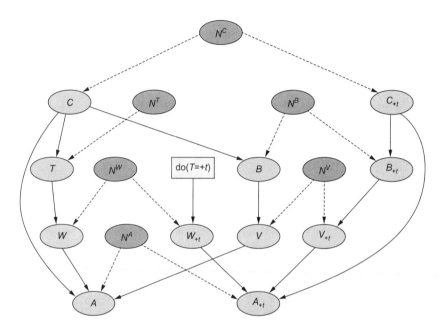

**Figure 10.16   A parallel world graph drawn by y0 (and Graphviz). In this version of the parallel world graph, the subscripts indicate a world. For example, +t indicates the world where the intervention do(T=+t) is applied. To prevent confusion, the exogenous variables use superscripts instead of subscripts to indicate their child endogenous variables (e.g., $N^C$ is the parent of C (and $C_{+t}$).**

We can remedy this with the *counterfactual graph*. A counterfactual graph is created by using a parallel world graph and the counterfactual query to understand which nodes across worlds in the parallel world graph are equivalent, and then collapsing equivalent nodes into one. The resulting graph contains nodes across parallel worlds that are relevant to the events in the query. Unlike parallel world graphs, you can use d-separation to reason about counterfactual graphs. We can use y0 to create a counterfactual graph for events $A_{T=-t}=+a$ and $T=+t$.

**Listing 10.10   Listing 10.10 Counterfactual graph events $A_{T=-t}=+a$ and $T=+t$**

```
from y0.algorithm.identify.cg import make_counterfactual_graph
```

```
events = {A @ -t: +a, T: +t}
cf_graph, _ = make_counterfactual_graph(dag, events)
gv_draw(cf_graph)
```

◁─┐ **Counterfactual graphs work with event outcomes in the query. For $P(A_{T=-t}=+a | T=+t)$, we want events $A_{T=-t}=+a$ and $T=+t$.**

This creates the counterfactual graph in figure 10.17.

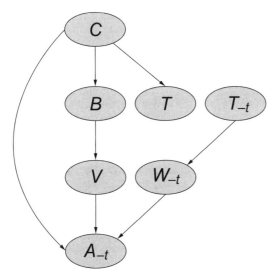

**Figure 10.17 Counterfactual graph for events, produced by y0 (and Graphviz). $T_{-t}$ corresponds to the intervention do($T=-t$).**

At a high level, graphical identification algorithms in y0 do counterfactual identification by working with counterfactual graphs in lieu of conventional DAGs. First, it finds a level 2 estimand for a level 3 query. From there, you can use experimental data to answer the level 2 terms in the estimand, or you can attempt to further derive them to level 1 estimands from the level 2 terms.

### Graphs alone won't work when you condition on outcome!

Suppose that instead of the ETT term $P(A_{T=-t}=+a|T=+t)$, you were interested in $P(A_{T=-t}=+a|T=+t, A=+a)$, answering the question "Given a subscriber exposed to policy $+t$ and later unsubscribed, would they still have unsubscribed had they not been exposed to that policy?" Or you could be interested in $E(A_{T=-t} - A_{T=+t}|T=+t, A=+a)$ sometimes called *counterfactual regret*, which captures the amount the policy $+t$ contributed to an unsubscribed individual's decision to unsubscribe.

$P(A_{T=-t}=+a|T=+t, A=+a)$ is an example of a query where the hypothetical outcomes and factual conditions are in conflict. In this case, the factual conditions contain an outcome for $A$, and the hypothetical condition contains an interventional outcome for $A$. The graphical counterfactual identification techniques mentioned in this section will not work for this type of query. Identification in this case requires additional level 3 assumptions.

This is unfortunate, because this type of counterfactual is precisely the kind of "how might things have turned out differently?" counterfactual questions that are the most interesting, and the most central to how humans reason and make decisions.

We can also use graphical identification for more advanced queries. For example, suppose you want to isolate how $T$ affects $A$ from how $B$ affects $A$. You want to focus on users where $B$ was $-b$. You find the data from a past experiment where "Because you watched . . ." policy $B$ was randomized. You take that data and zoom in on participants in the experiment who were assigned $-b$. The outcome of interest in that experiment was $V$, the amount of engagement with the content recommended in the "Because you Watched" box. So you have the outcomes of $V_{B=-b}$ for those subscribers of interest. With this new data, you expand your query from $P(A_{T=-t}=+a|T=+t)$ to $P(A_{T=-t}=+a|T=+t, B=-b, V_{B=-b}=v)$, including $V_{B=-b}=v$ because it is helpful in predicting attrition. Now you have three parallel worlds to reason over: the actual world, the world with $\text{do}(T=+t)$, and the world with $\text{do}(B=-b)$.

---

**Listing 10.11   Create a parallel world graph for do($T=+t$) and do($B=-b$)**

```
parallel_world_graph = make_parallel_worlds_graph(
    dag,
    {frozenset([-t]), frozenset([-b])}  ◁──  The second argument enumerates
)                                              the hypothetical conditions.
gv_draw(parallel_world_graph)
```

This code creates this three-world parallel world graph seen in figure 10.18.

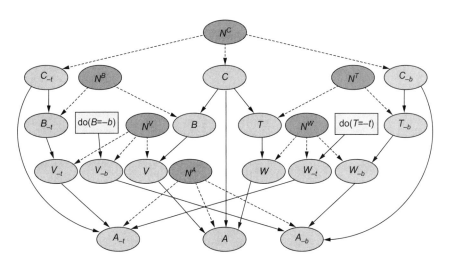

**Figure 10.18   A parallel world graph with the actual world *T*=+*t* and hypothetical worlds do(*T*=−*t*) and do(*B*=−*b*). The dashed lines are edges from exogenous variables (dark gray).**

Notably, the query $P(A_{T=-t}=+a|T=+t, B=-b, V_{B=-b}=v)$ collapses the parallel world graph to the same counterfactual graph as $P(A_{T=-t}=+a|T=+t)$.

**Listing 10.12   Counterfactual graph for expanded expression**

```
joint_query = {A @ -t: +a, T: +t, B: -b, V @ -b: +v}
cf_graph, _ = make_counterfactual_graph(dag, joint_query)
gv_draw(cf_graph)
```

This gives us the counterfactual graph in figure 10.19, which is the same as the graph in figure 10.17.

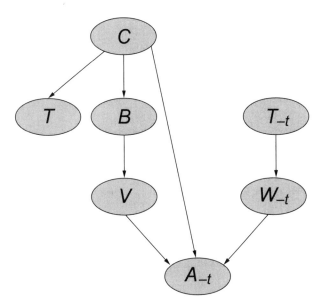

**Figure 10.19   The counterfactual graph for $P(A_{T_{=-t}}=+a|T=+t, B=-b, V_{B=-b}=v)$ is the same as for $P(A_{T_{=-t}}=+a|T=+t)$.**

Next, we'll look at another graph-based approach called single-world intervention graphs.

### 10.7.3 *Counterfactual identification with single-world intervention graphs*

Single-world intervention graphs (SWIGs) provide an alternative to counterfactual identification with counterfactual graphs. Like a counterfactual graph, we construct a SWIG using the original causal DAG and the causal query. We'll use the Netflix recommendation example to construct a SWIG for the interventions do($T=-t$) and do($B=-b$). Let's construct a SWIG from a causal DAG.

#### NODE-SPLITTING OPERATION

We have the intervention that targets do($T=+t$), and we can implement it with a special kind of graph surgery called a *node-splitting operation*. We split a new node off the intervention target $T$, as in figure 10.20. $T$ still represents the same variable as in the original graph, but the new node represents a constant, the intervention value $+t$. $T$ keeps its parents (in this case $C$) but loses its children (in this case $W$) to the new node.

### SUBSCRIPT INHERITANCE

Next, every node downstream of the new node inherits the new node's values as a subscript. For example, in figure 10.21, $W$ and $A$ are downstream of the intervention, so the subscript $T=-t$ is appended to these nodes, so they become $W_{T=-t}$ and $A_{T=-t}$.

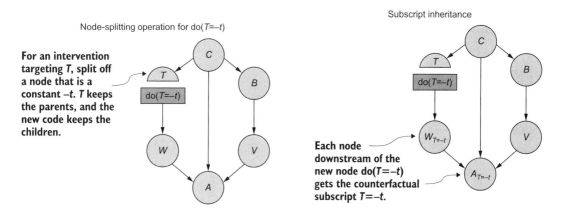

**Figure 10.20**   The intervention operator for a SWIG is the node-splitting operation.

**Figure 10.21**   Every node downstream of the intervention gets the intervention subscript.

### REPEAT FOR EACH INTERVENTION

We repeat this process for each intervention. In figure 10.22, we apply $do(B=-b)$, and split $B$ and we convert $V$ to $V_{B=-b}$ and $A_{T=-t}$ to $A_{T=-t,B=-b}$.

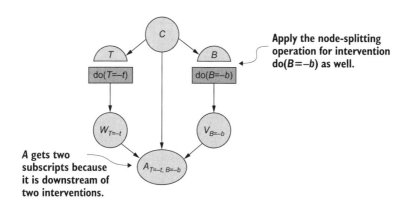

**Figure 10.22**   A node takes the subscript of all its upstream interventions.

Like the counterfactual graph, the SWIG contains counterfactual variables and admits d-separation. With these properties, we can do identification.

### 10.7.4 Identification with SWIGs

Suppose we are interested in ETT and want to identify $P(A_{T=-t}=+a|T=+t)$. We derive the SWIG in figure 10.23.

With this graph, we can identify $P(A_{T=-t}=+a|T=+t)$ using the ignorability trick I introduced in section 10.4:

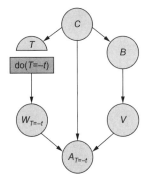

1. $P(A_{T=-t}=+a|T=+t) = \Sigma_c\, P(A_{T=-t}=+a,\, C_{T=-t}=c|T=+t)$ by the law of total probability.

2. $\Sigma_c\ P(A_{T=-t}=+a,\ C_{T=-t}=c|T=+t) = \Sigma_c\ P(A_{T=-t}=+a,\ C=c|T=+t)$, since $C$ is not affected by interventions on $T$.

3. $\Sigma_c P(A_{T=-t}=+a,\ C=c|T=+t)$ factorizes into $\Sigma_c P(A_{T=-t}=+a|C=c,\ T=+t)\ P(C=c\ |\ T=+t)$ by the chain rule of probability.

4. $P(A_{T=-t}=+a|C=c,\ T=+t) = P(A_{T=-t}=+a|C=c,\ T=-t)$, again by the ignorability trick.

5. And as before, $P(A_{T=-t}=+a|C=c,\ T=-t) = P(A=+a|C=c,\ T=-t)$ by the law of consistency. Thus, $P(A_{T=-t}=+a|T=+t) = \Sigma_c P(A=+a|C=c,\ T=-t)\ P(C=c\ |\ T=+t)$

**Figure 10.23  We can use the SWIG to derive ETT using the ignorability trick.**

The magic happens in the ignorability trick in step 4, where $C$'s d-separation of $A_{T=-t}$ and $T$ lets us change $T=+t$ to $T=-t$. Notice that the same d-separation exists in the counterfactual graph we derived for $P(A_{T=-t}=+a|T=+t)$, shown in figure 10.17. The difference is that deriving the SWIG is easy, while deriving the counterfactual graph is nuanced, and one generally uses an algorithm like `make_counterfactual_grap` in y0.

### 10.7.5 The single-world assumption

The node-splitting operation relies on a new level 3 assumption. If you are going to node-split a variable $X$, then you are assuming it is possible to know what value $X$ would naturally take without the intervention and that it would be possible for you intervene before it realized that value. Imagine in our Netflix example that, given a subscriber had profile $C=c$, the recommendation algorithm was about to assign the subscriber a policy $+t$ for recommending "Top picks for you," but before that policy went into effect, you intervened and artificially changed it to $-t$. It's possible that the way you forced the policy to be $-t$ had some side effects that changed the recommendation system in some fundamental way, such that in this new system, $T$ would not have been $+t$, in the first place. With the single-world assumption, you assume you can know T's natural value would have been $+t$, and that your intervention wouldn't change the system in a way that would affect $T$ taking that natural value. You are implicitly making this assumption when you reason with SWIGs.

That assumption allows you to avoid the need to create additional worlds to reason over. You can condition on outcome $T=+t$ and intervene $do(T=-t)$ in a "single world." You can also run experiments, where you apply the intervention $do(T=-t)$ and test if $T$ (where you know T's "natural values") is conditionally independent of

$A(T=-t)$ given $C$. This reduces the number of counterfactual queries you can answer, but proponents of SWIGs suggest this is a strength, because it limits you to counterfactuals that can be validated by experiments.

---

### Contrasting counterfactual graphs and SWIGs

Counterfactual graphs and SWIGs are similar in function, but they are distinctly different artifacts.

- *Counterfactual graphs*—The counterfactual graph works by collapsing equivalent parallel world graph nodes over possible worlds. They only contain nodes relevant to the specific query. They are defined for binary events like {$T=+t$} and {$T=-t$}—this works well even with continuous variables, because counterfactual language typically compares one *hypothetical condition* to one *factual condition* (e.g., "We invested 1 million; what if we had invested {2/more/half/ ...}?").
- *Single-world intervention graphs (SWIGs)*—The SWIG works by applying a node-splitting type of graph surgery. Unlike counterfactual graphs, they work with general variables (rather than just binary events) and are not query-specific (all original nodes are present). However, they rely on a single-world assumption—that it is possible to know with certainty what value a variable would have taken had it not been intervened upon.

The primary use case for both graphs is identification. Neither counterfactual graphs nor SWIGs enable identification from level 1 or 2 data of counterfactual queries such as $P(A_{T=-t}=+a|T=+t, A=+a)$ where the same variable appears in the hypothetical outcome and the factual condition. But you can still *derive* the counterfactual graph for such queries; this is not true for SWIGs. That is useful if you want to reason about independence across worlds in cases of queries such as $P(A_{T=-t}=+a|T=+t, A=+a)$.

---

## 10.8   *Identification and probabilistic inference*

We've seen that a core part of the identification task is deriving an estimand. How does that estimand mesh with a probabilistic machine learning approach?

Consider, for example, our online game model, where ETT $= E(I_{E=\text{"high"}} - I_{E=\text{"low"}}|E=\text{"high"}) = E(I_{E=\text{"high"}}|E=\text{"high"}) - E(I_{E=\text{"low"}}|E=\text{"high"})$. We need to identify $P(I_{E=\text{"high"}}|E=\text{"high"})$ and $P(I_{E=\text{"low"}}|E=\text{"high"})$. Recall that $P(I_{E=\text{"high"}}|E=\text{"high"})$ simplifies to the level 1 query $P(I|E=\text{"high"})$ by the law of consistency, so the challenge lies with identifying the counterfactual distribution $P(I_{E=\text{"low"}}|E=\text{"high"})$.

Using a probabilistic machine learning approach with Pyro, we know we can infer $P(I|E=\text{"high"})$ by using `pyro.condition` to condition on $E=\text{"high"}$ and then running inference. The question is how we'll infer the counterfactual distribution $P(I_{E=\text{"low"}}|E=\text{"high"})$.

In the previous section, we saw that we can identify this query with a SWIG (assuming the single-world assumption holds). We used the SWIG to derive the following estimand for $P(I_{E=0}=i|E=\text{"high"})$:

$$\sum_g P(I = i|G = g, E = \text{low})P(G = g|E = \text{high})$$

But what do we do with this estimand with respect to building a model in Pyro? We could construct two Pyro models, one for $P(G|E)$ and one for $P(I|G, E)$, infer $P(I=i| G=g, E=\text{"low"})$ and $P(G=g| E=\text{"high"})$ and then do the summation. But this is inelegant relative to our regular approach to probabilistic inference with a causal generative model:

1. Implement the full causal generative model.
2. Train its parameters on data.
3. Apply the intervention operator to simulate an intervention.
4. Run an inference algorithm.

In this approach, we build one causal model—we don't build separate models for the estimand's components $P(G|E)$ and $P(I|G, E)$. Nonetheless, our regular approach to probabilistic inference with a causal generative model does work if we have identification, given the causal assumptions we implement in step 1 and the data we train on in step 2. We don't even need to know the estimand explicitly; it is enough to know it exists—in other words, that the query is identified (e.g., by using Y0's `check_identifiable` function). With identification, steps 2–4 collectively become just another estimator for that estimand.

To illustrate, let's consider how we'd sample from $P(I_{E=\text{"low"}}|E=\text{"high"})$ using a Pyro model of our online gaming example. For simplicity, let's replace $E=\text{"high"}$ and $E=\text{"low"}$ with $E=1$ and $E=0$ respectively. We know $P(I_{E=0}|E=1)$ is identified given our causal DAG and the single-word assumption. Fortunately, Pyro's (and ChiRho's) `do` intervention operator implements the SWIG's node-splitting operation by default (if you used `pyro.render_model` to visualize an intervention and didn't get what you expected, this is why). For ordinary interventional queries on a causal DAG, there is no difference between this and the ordinary graph surgery approach to interventions. But when we want to condition on $E=1$ and intervene to set $E=0$, Pyro will accommodate us. We'll use this approach to sample from $P(I_{E=0}|E=1)$. As a sanity check, we'll also sample from the plain vanilla intervention distribution $P(I_{E=0})$ and contrast those samples with samples from $P(I_{E=0}|E=1)$.

**Setting up your environment**
As a change in pace, I'll illustrate this example using NumPyro instead of Pyro, though the code will work in Pyro with small tweaks. We'll use NumPyro version 0.15.0. We'll also use an inference library meant to complement NumPyro and Pyro called Funsor, version 0.4.5. We'll also use Matplotlib for plotting.

First, let's build the model.

### NumPyro vs. Pyro

Pyro extends PyTorch, while NumPyro extends NumPy and automatic differentiation with JAX. The user interfaces are quite similar. If you are less comfortable with PyTorch abstractions and debugging PyTorch errors, or you prefer MCMC-based inference with the Bayesian programming patterns one uses in Stan or PyMC, then you might prefer NumPyro.

---

**Listing 10.13    Generating from $P(I_{E=0})$ vs. $P(I_{E=0}|E=1)$ in Pyro**

```python
import jax.numpy as np
from jax import random
from numpyro import sample
from numpyro.handlers import condition, do
from numpyro.distributions import Bernoulli, Normal
from numpyro.infer import MCMC, NUTS
import matplotlib.pyplot as plt

rng = random.PRNGKey(1)

def model():
    p_member = 0.5
    is_guild_member = sample(
        "Guild Membership",
        Bernoulli(p_member)
    )
    p_engaged = (0.8*is_guild_member + 0.2*(1-is_guild_member))
    is_highly_engaged = sample(
        "Side-quest Engagement",
        Bernoulli(p_engaged)
    )
    p_won_engaged = (.9*is_highly_engaged + .1*(1-is_highly_engaged))
    high_won_items = sample("Won Items", Bernoulli(p_won_engaged))
    mu = (
        37.95*(1-is_guild_member)*(1-high_won_items) +
        54.92*(1-is_guild_member)*high_won_items +
        223.71*(is_guild_member)*(1-high_won_items) +
        125.50*(is_guild_member)*high_won_items
    )
    sigma = (
        23.80*(1-is_guild_member)*(1-high_won_items) +
        4.92*(1-is_guild_member)*high_won_items +
        5.30*(is_guild_member)*(1-high_won_items) +
        53.49*(is_guild_member)*high_won_items
    )
    norm_dist = Normal(mu, sigma)
    in_game_purchases = sample("In-game Purchases", norm_dist)
```

A version of the online gaming model.
The weights are estimates from the data
(learning procedure not shown here).

Next, we'll apply the intervention and run inference to sample from $P(I_{E=0})$.

**Listing 10.14 Apply intervention do($E$=0) and infer from $P(I_{E=0})$**

```
intervention_model = do(                          Apply the do operator
    model,                                        to the model.
    {"Side-quest Engagement": np.array(0.)})
intervention_kernel = NUTS(intervention_model)
intervention_model_sampler = MCMC(
    intervention_kernel,
    num_samples=5000,                             Apply inference
    num_warmup=200                                to sample from
)                                                 P(I_{E=0}).
intervention_model_sampler.run(rng)
intervention_samples = intervention_model_sampler.get_samples()
int_purchases_samples = intervention_samples["In-game Purchases"]
```

We'll contrast these samples from $P(I_{E=0})$ with samples we'll draw from $P(I_{E=0}|E=1)$. To infer $P(I_{E=0}|E=1)$, we'll condition `intervention_model` on the factual condition $E=1$. Then we'll run inference again on this conditioned-upon intervened-upon model.

**Listing 10.15 Condition intervention model and infer $P(I_{E=0}|E=1)$**

```
cond_and_int_model = condition(                   Now apply the condition
    intervention_model,                           operator to sample from
    {"Side-quest Engagement": np.array(1.)}       P(I_{E=0}|E=1).
)
int_cond_kernel = NUTS(cond_and_int_model)
int_cond_model_sampler = MCMC(
    int_cond_kernel,
    num_samples=5000,                             Apply inference
    num_warmup=200                                to sample from
)                                                 P(I_{E=0}|E=1).
int_cond_model_sampler.run(rng)
int_cond_samples = int_cond_model_sampler.get_samples()
int_cond_purchases_samples = int_cond_samples["In-game Purchases"]
```

Note that Pyro's `do` and `condition` subroutines mutually compose; i.e., for a model with a variable $X$, `do(condition(model, {"X": 1.}), {"X": 0.})` is equivalent to `condition(do(model, {"X": 0.}), {"X": 1.})`.

Finally, we'll plot samples from $P(I_{E=0})$ and $P(I_{E=0}|E=1)$ and evaluate the difference in these distributions.

**Listing 10.16 Plot samples from $P(I_{E=0})$ and $P(I_{E=0}|E=1)$**

```
plt.hist(
    int_purchases_samples,                        Plot a histogram
    bins=30,                                      of samples
    alpha=0.5,                                    from P(I_{E=0}).
    label='$P(I_{E=0})$'
)
```

```
plt.hist(
    int_cond_purchases_samples,
    bins=30,
    alpha=0.5,
    label='$P(I_{E=0}|E=1)$'
)
plt.legend(loc='upper left')
plt.show()
```

**Plot a histogram of samples from $P(I_{E=0}|E=1)$.**

This code generates the histograms in figure 10.24.

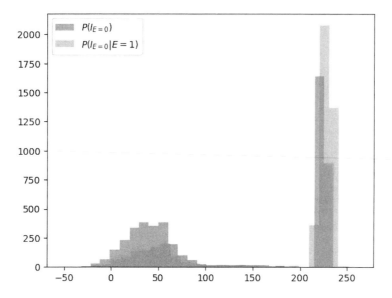

**Figure 10.24**   **Histograms of samples from $P(I_{E=0})$ and $P(I_{E=0}|E=1)$ generated in Pyro**

In this example, the parameters were given. In chapter 11, where we'll look at estimation, we'll seamlessly combine this query inference with Bayesian parameter inference from data.

## 10.9   *Partial identification*

We'll close this chapter with a quick note on partial identification. Sometimes a query is not identified, given your assumptions, but it may be *partially identifiable*. Partial identifiability means you can identify estimands for an upper and lower bound of your query. Partial identification is highly relevant to causal AI because machine learning algorithms often rely on finding and optimizing bounds on objective functions. Let's walk through a few examples.

### MCMC vs. SVI

Here we used Markov chain Monte Carlo (MCMC), but both Pyro and NumPyro have abstractions for stochastic variational inference (SVI). In this example, the parameters (`p_member`, `p_engaged`, etc.) of the model are specified. We could also make the parameters unknown variables with Bayesian priors and do the inference on these causal queries $P(I_{E=0})$ and $P(I_{E=0}|E=1)$; in this case, we'd be doing Bayesian inference of these queries.

But for this we'd need $N$ IID samples from an observational distribution where we had graphical identification ($P(G, E, W, I)$, $P(G, E, I)$, or $P(E, W, I)$). In the case of $P(G, E, W, I)$, where all the variables in the DAG are observed, the number of unknown variables is just the number of parameters. But in the latter two cases, of $P(G, E, I)$ or $P(E, W, I)$, where there is a latent $G$ or $W$ of size $N$, the number of unknowns grows with $N$. In this case, SVI will scale better with large $N$. We'll see an example in chapter 11.

Suppose in our online gaming example you ran an experiment where you randomly assigned players to a treatment or control group. Players in the treatment group are exposed to a policy that encourages more side-quest engagement. You reason that since you can't actually force players to engage in side-quests, it's better to have this randomized treatment/control variable as a parent of our side-quest engagement variable, as seen in the DAG in figure 10.25.

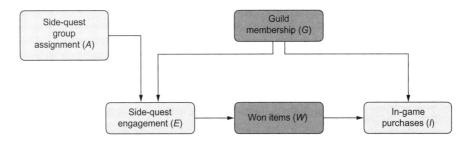

**Figure 10.25** **We don't have identification for the ATE of *E* on *I* because *G* and *W* are unobserved. But we have partial identification given variable *A*, representing gamers' assignments in a randomized experiment.**

For this new variable $A$, let $A=1$ refer to the treatment group and $A=0$ refer to the control group. We have this new variable $A$, and the average treatment effect of the policy on in-game purchases $E(I_{A=1} - I_{A=0})$ is an interesting query. But suppose we're still ultimately interested in knowing the average treatment effect of side-quest engagement *itself* on purchases, i.e., $E(I_{E=\text{“high”}} - I_{E=\text{“low”}})$.

If guild membership ($G$) were observed, we'd have identification through backdoor adjustment. If won items ($W$) were observed, we could use front-door adjustment. But suppose that in this scenario you observe neither. In this case, observing the side-quest group assignment variable would give you partial identification. Suppose that the in-game purchases variable was a binary 1 for "high" and 0 for "low" instead of a continuous value. Then the bounds on $E(I_{E=\text{"high"}} - I_{E=\text{"low"}})$ are

$$
\begin{aligned}
LB = {} & P(I = \text{high}|A = 1) - P(I = \text{high}|A = 0) \\
& - P(I = \text{high}, E = \text{low}|A = 1) - P(I = \text{low}, E = \text{high}|A = 0) \\
UB = {} & P(I = \text{high}|A = 1) - P(I = \text{high}|A = 0) \\
& - P(I = \text{low}, E = \text{low}|A = 1) - P(I = \text{high}, E = \text{high}|A = 0)
\end{aligned}
$$

These bounds can be the next best thing to having full identification, especially if the bounds are tight. Alternatively, perhaps it is enough to know that the lower bound on the ATE for side-quest engagement is significantly greater than 0.

Similarly, general bounds exist for common counterfactual queries, such as probabilities of causation. For example, suppose you wanted to know if high side-quest engagement was a necessary and sufficient condition of high in-game purchases. You can construct the following bounds on the probability of necessity and sufficiency (PNS):

$$
\max\left(0, P\left(I_{E=\text{high}} = \text{high}\right) - P\left(I_{E=\text{low}} = \text{high}\right)\right) < PNS
$$
$$
< \min\left(P\left(I_{E=\text{high}} = \text{high}\right), P\left(I_{E=\text{low}} = \text{low}\right)\right)
$$

These bounds consist of level 2 quantities like $P(I_{E=e}=i)$, and you can go on to identify level 1 estimands if possible given your assumptions.

Remember that partial identification bounds are highly specific to your causal assumptions (like the DAG) and the parameterization of the variables; for example, the preceding examples are specific to binary variables. See the chapter notes at www.altdeep.ai/causalAIbook for links to papers that derived these bounds as well as bounds for other practical sets of assumptions.

## Summary

- The importance of causal identification has increased in the AI era as we seek to understand the causal inductive bias in deep learning architectures.
- Libraries like y0 implement strategies for algorithmic identification.
- The causal hierarchy is a three-tiered structure that categorizes the causal questions we pose, the models we develop, and the causal inferences we draw. These levels are association, intervention, and counterfactual.
- Association-level reasoning addresses "what is" questions and models that answer these questions with basic statistical assumptions.

- Interventional or counterfactual queries fall on their corresponding level of the hierarchy.

- Observational data falls on the associational level, and experimental data falls on the interventional level of the hierarchy. Counterfactual data arises in situations where the modeler can control a deterministic data generating process (DGP).

- Causal identification is the procedure of discerning when causal inferences can be drawn from experimental or observational data. It is done by determining if data at a lower level of the hierarchy can be used to infer a query at a higher level of the hierarchy.

- An example of a causal identification result is the backdoor formula, which equates intervention level query $P(Y_{X=x})$ to association level quantity $\Sigma_z P(Y|X=x, Z=z) P(Z=z)$, where $Z$ is a set of common causes.

- The causal hierarchy theorem shows how lower-level data is insufficient to infer a distribution at a higher level without higher-level modeling assumptions.

- The do-calculus has three rules that can be used for graph-based identification.

- A counterfactual graph is a DAG that includes variables across counterfactual worlds on one graph. Unlike the parallel world graph, it admits d-separation. We derive the counterfactual graph from the parallel world graph and the target query.

- Graphical identification algorithms automate identification with graphs using rules such as the do-calculus.

- Nonparametric identification is identification with non-graphical assumptions, such as assumptions about the functional relationships between variables in the model.

- The ignorability assumption is that the causal variable and the potential outcomes are conditionally independent given confounders.

- Effect of treatment on the treated (ETT) evaluates the effect of a cause on the subset of the population that was exposed to the cause.

- Single world intervention graphs (SWIGs) provide an intuitive alternative to counterfactual identification with do-calculus and counterfactual graphs. They are constructed by applying a node-splitting operation to the original causal DAG. SWIGs use a "single-world" assumption, which assumes it's possible to know a variable's natural value while also intervening on it before it realizes that value without any side-effects that would affect that natural value.

- SWIGs work with variables and a narrow set of counterfactuals under the single-world assumption, while counterfactual graphs can accommodate queries that cannot be graphically identified.

- Pyro implements the SWIG's node-splitting model of intervention, which enables probabilistic inference of SWIG-identified quantities.

- Inference of causal queries using a causal graphical model and probabilistic inference algorithms is possible as long as the query is identified, given the model's assumptions and training data.
- Partial identification means you can at least identify estimands for bounds on a target query. This can be quite useful if you lack full identification, especially since machine learning often works by optimizing bounds on objective functions.

# Part 4

# Applications of causal inference

In part 4, we'll turn our attention to the application of causal inference methods to practical problems. You will gain hands-on experience with causal effect estimation workflows, automated decision-making, and the integration of causality with large language models and other foundation models. By this end of this part, you'll be able to use machine learning–based methods for causal effect estimation, as well as use causal inference methods to enhance modern machine learning applications from reinforcement learning to cutting-edge generative AI.

# 11

# *Building a causal*
# *inference workflow*

**This chapter covers**

- Building a causal analysis workflow
- Estimating causal effects with DoWhy
- Estimating causal effects using machine learning methods
- Causal inference with causal latent variable models

In chapter 10, I introduced a causal inference workflow, and in this chapter we'll focus on building out this workflow in full. We'll focus on one type of query in particular—causal effects—but the workflow generalizes to all causal queries.

We'll focus on causal effect inference, namely estimation of average treatment effects (ATEs) and conditional average treatment effects (CATEs) because they are the most popular causal queries.

In chapter 1, I mentioned "the commodification of inference"—how modern software libraries enable us to abstract away the statistical and computational details of the inference algorithm. The first thing you'll see in this chapter is how the DoWhy library "commodifies" causal inference, enabling us to focus at a high level on the causal assumptions of the algorithms and whether they are appropriate for our problem.

We'll see the phenomenon at play again in an example that uses probabilistic machine learning to do causal effect inference on a causal generative model with latent variables. Here, we'll see how deep learning with PyTorch provides another way to commodify inference.

## 11.1 Step 1: Select the query

Recall the causal inference workflow from chapter 10, shown again in figure 11.1.

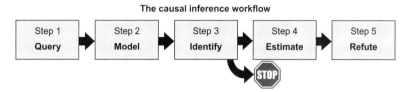

Figure 11.1    A workflow for a causal inference analysis

Let's return to our online gaming example and use this workflow to answer a simple question:

*How much does side-quest engagement drive in-game purchases?*

We'll call the cause of interest, *Side-Quest Engagement (E)*, the "treatment" variable; *In-Game Purchases (I)* will be the "outcome" variable. Our query of interest is the average treatment effect (ATE):

$$E(I_{E=\text{"high"}} - I_{E=\text{"low"}})$$

---

**Refresher: Why ATEs and CATEs dominate**

Estimating ATEs and CATEs is the most popular causal effect inference task for several reasons, including the following:

- We can rely on causal effect inference techniques when randomized experiments are not feasible, ethical, or possible.
- We can use causal effect inference techniques to address practical issues with real-world experiments (e.g., post-randomization confounding, attrition, spillover, missing data, etc.).
- In an era when companies can run many different digital experiments in online applications and stores, causal effect inference techniques can help prioritize experiments, reducing opportunity costs.

---

Further, as we investigate our gaming data, we find data from a past experiment designed to test the effect of *encouraging* side-quest engagement on in-game purchases. In this experiment, all players were randomly assigned either to the treatment group or a control group. In the treatment group, the game mechanics were modified to tempt players into engaging in more side-quests, while the control group played the unmodified version of the game. We'll define the *Side-Quest Group Assignment (A)* variable as whether the player was assigned to the treatment group in this experiment or the control group.

Why not just go with the estimate of the ATE produced by this experiment? This would be an estimate of $E(I_{A=\text{"treatment"}} - I_{A=\text{"control"}})$.

This is the causal effect of the modification of game mechanics on in-game purchases. While this drives side-quest engagement, we know side-quest engagement is also driven by other potentially confounding factors. So we'll focus on $E(I_{E=\text{"high"}} - I_{E=\text{"low"}})$.

## 11.2  Step 2: Build the model

Next, we'll build our causal model. Since we are targeting an ATE, we can stick with a DAG. Let's suppose we build a more detailed version of our online gaming example and produce the causal DAG in figure 11.2.

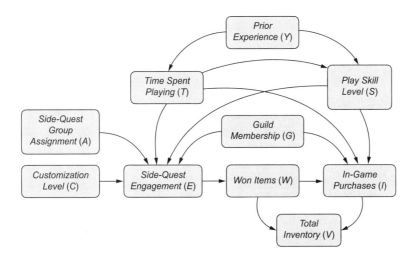

**Figure 11.2  An expanded version of the online gaming DAG. With respect to the causal effect of side-quest engagement on in-game purchases, we add two additional confounders and two instruments.**

The expanded model adds some new variables:

- *Side-Quest Group Assignment (A)*—Assigned a value of 1 if a player was exposed to the mechanics that encouraged more side-quest engagement in the randomized experiment; 0 otherwise.
- *Customization Level (C)*—A score quantifying the player's customizations of their character and the game environment.
- *Time Spent Playing (T)*—How much time the player has spent playing.

- *Prior Experience (Y)*—How much experience the player had prior to when they started playing the game.
- *Player Skill Level (S)*—A score of how well the player performs in game tasks.
- *Total Inventory (V)*—The amount of game items the player has accumulated.

We are interested in the ATE of *Side-Quest Engagement* on *In-Game Purchases*, so we know, based on causal sufficiency (chapter 3), that we need to add common causes for these variables. We've already seen *Guild Membership* (*G*), but now we add additional common causes: *Prior Experience*, *Time Spent Playing*, and *Player Skill Level*. We also add *Side-Quest Group Assignment* and *Customization Level* because these might be useful *instrumental variables*—variables that are causes of the treatment of interest, and where the only path of causality from the variable to the outcome is via the treatment. I'll say more about instrumental variables in the next section.

Finally, we'll add *Total Inventory*. This is a collider between *In-Game Purchases* and *Won Items*. Perhaps it is common for data scientists in our company to use this as a predictor of the *In-Game Purchases*. But as you'll see, we'll want to avoid adding collider bias to causal effect estimation.

## Setting up your environment

The following code was written with DoWhy 0.11 and EconML 0.15, which expects a version of NumPy before version 2.0. The specific pandas version was 1.5.3. Again, we use Graphviz for visualization, with python PyGraphviz library version 1.12. The code should work, save for visualization, if you skip the PyGraphviz installation.

First, let's build the DAG and visualize the graph with the PyGraphviz library.

#### Listing 11.1  Build the causal DAG

```
import pygraphviz as pgv                              ◁┐ Download PyGraphviz
from IPython.display import Image          ◁┐          and related libraries.
                                            
causal_graph = """                                     Optional import for visualizing
digraph {                                              the DAG in a Jupyter notebook
    "Prior Experience" -> "Player Skill Level";
    "Prior Experience" -> "Time Spent Playing";
    "Time Spent Playing" -> "Player Skill Level";
    "Guild Membership" -> "Side-quest Engagement";
    "Guild Membership" -> "In-game Purchases";
    "Player Skill Level" -> "Side-quest Engagement";
    "Player Skill Level" -> "In-game Purchases";
    "Time Spent Playing" -> "Side-quest Engagement";
    "Time Spent Playing" -> "In-game Purchases";
    "Side-quest Group Assignment" -> "Side-quest Engagement";
    "Customization Level" -> "Side-quest Engagement";
    "Side-quest Engagement" -> "Won Items";
    "Won Items" -> "In-game Purchases";
```

```
    "Won Items" -> "Total Inventory";
    "In-game Purchases" -> "Total Inventory";
}
"""
G = pgv.AGraph(string=causal_graph)
G.draw('/tmp/causal_graph.png', prog='dot')
Image('/tmp/causal_graph.png')
```

**Specify the DAG as a DOT language string, and load a PyGraphviz AGraph object from the string.**

**Render the graph to a PNG file.**

**Display the graph.**

This returns the graph in figure 11.3.

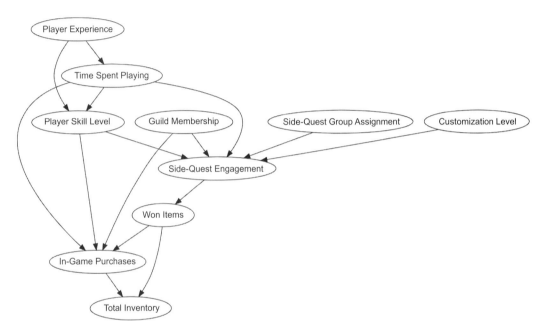

**Figure 11.3   Visualizing our model with the PyGraphviz library**

At this stage, we can validate our model using the conditional independence testing techniques outlined in chapter 4. But keep in mind that we can also focus on the subset of assumptions we rely on for causal effect estimation to work in the "refutation" (step 5) part of the workflow.

## 11.3   Step 3: Identify the estimand

Next, we'll run identification. Our causal query is

$$E(I_{E=\text{"high"}} - I_{E=\text{"low"}})$$

For simplicity, let's recode "high" as 1 and "low" as 0.

$$E(I_{E=1} - I_{E=0})$$

This query is on level 2 of the causal hierarchy. We are not running an experiment; we only have observational data—samples from a level 1 distribution. Our identification task is to use our level 2 query and our causal model and identify a level 1 estimand, an operation we can apply to the distribution of the variables in our data.

First, let's download our data and see what variables are in our observational distribution.

#### Listing 11.2   Download and display the data

```
import pandas as pd
data = pd.read_csv(
    "https://raw.githubusercontent.com/altdeep/causalML/master/datasets
    /online_game_example_do_why.csv"                    ◁─┐ Download an online
)                                                           gaming dataset.
print(data.columns)    ◁─┐ Print the
                          variables.
```

This prints out the following set of variables:

```
Index(['Guild Membership', 'Player Skill Level', 'Time Spent Playing',
       'Side-quest Group Assignment', 'Customization Level',
       'Side-quest Engagement', 'Won Items', 'In-game Purchases',
       'Total Inventory'],
     dtype='object')
```

Our level 1 observational distribution includes all the variables in the DAG except *Prior Experience*. Thus, *Prior Experience* is a latent variable (figure 11.4).

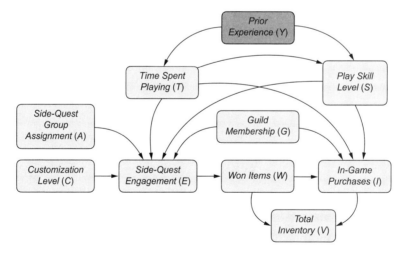

**Figure 11.4**  *Prior Experience* **is not observed in the data; it is a latent (unobserved) variable with respect to our DAG.**

We specified the base distribution for the estimand using y0's domain-specific language for probabilistic expressions:

```
Identification.from_expression(
    graph=dag,
    query=query,
    estimand=observational_distribution
)
```

Here, we'll use DoWhy. With DoWhy, we specify the observational distribution by just passing in the pandas DataFrame, along with the DAG and the causal query, to the constructor of the `CausalModel` class.

**Listing 11.3   Instantiate an instance of DoWhy's `CausalModel`**

```
from dowhy import CausalModel          ◁─┐ Install DoWhy and load
                                          │ the CausalModel class.
model = CausalModel(
    data=data,                          ◁─┐ Instantiate the CausalModel object with the
    treatment='Side-quest Engagement',  │ data, which represents the level 1 observational
    outcome='In-game Purchases',        │ distribution from which we derive the estimands.
    graph=causal_graph   ◁─┐ Provide the
)                          │ causal DAG.   Specify the target causal query we wish
                                          to estimate, namely the causal effect of
                                          the treatment on the outcome.
```

Next, the `identify_effect` methods will show us possible estimands we can target, given our causal model and observed variables.

**Listing 11.4   Run identification in DoWhy**

```
identified_estimand = model.identify_effect()  ◁─┐ The identify_effect method
print(identified_estimand)                        │ of the CausalModel class
                                                  │ lists identified estimands.
```

The `identified_estimand` object is an object of the class `IdentifiedEstimand`. Printing it will list the estimands, if any, and the assumptions they entail. In our case, we have three estimands we can target:

- The backdoor adjustment estimand through the adjustment set *Player Skill Level, Guild Membership*, and *Time Spent Playing*
- The front-door adjustment estimand through the mediator *Won Items*
- Instrumental variable estimands through *Side-Quest Group Assignment* and *Customization Level*

### Graphical identification in DoWhy

At the time of writing, DoWhy does implement graphical identification algorithms like y0, but these are experimental and are not the default identification approach. The default approach looks for commonly used estimands (e.g., backdoor, front door, instrumental variables) based on the structure of your graph. There may be identifiable estimands that the default approach misses, but these would be estimands that are not commonly used.

Let's examine these estimands more closely.

### 11.3.1  *The backdoor adjustment estimand*

Let's look at the printed summary for the first estimand, the backdoor adjustment estimand:

```
Estimand type: EstimandType.NONPARAMETRIC_ATE
### Estimand : 1
Estimand name: backdoor
Estimand expression:
        d
───────────────────────────(E[In-game Purchases|Time Spent Playing,Guild
d[Side-quest Engagement]

Membership, Player Skill Level])

Estimand assumption 1, Unconfoundedness: If U→{Side-quest Engagement} and
    U→In-game Purchases then P(In-game Purchases|Side-quest Engagement,Time
    Spent Playing,Guild Membership,Player Skill Level,U) = P(In-game
    Purchases|Side-quest Engagement,Time Spent Playing,Guild
    Membership,Player Skill Level)
```

This printout tells us a few things:

- `EstimandType.NONPARAMETRIC_ATE`—This means the estimand can be identified with graphical or "nonparametric" methods, such as the do-calculus.
- `Estimand name: backdoor`—This is the backdoor adjustment estimand.
- `Estimand expression`—The mathematical expression of the estimand. Since we want the ATE, we modify the backdoor estimand to target the ATE.
- `Estimand assumption 1`—The causal assumptions underlying the estimand.

The last item is the most important. For each estimand, DoWhy lists the causal assumptions that must hold for valid estimation of the target causal query. In this case, the assumption is that there are no hidden (unmeasured) confounders, which DoWhy refers to as U. Estimation of a backdoor adjustment estimand assumes that all confounders are adjusted for.

Note that we do not need to observe *Prior Experience* to obtain a backdoor adjustment estimand. We just need to observe an adjustment set of common causes that d-separates or "blocks" all backdoor paths.

The next estimand in the printout is an instrumental variable estimand.

### 11.3.2  *The instrumental variable estimand*

The printed summary for the second estimand, the instrumental variable estimand, is as follows (note, I shortened the variable names to acronyms so the summary fits this page):

```
### Estimand : 2
Estimand name: iv
```

Estimand expression:

$$E\left[\frac{d}{d[\text{SQGA CL}]}(\text{IGP}) \cdot \left(\frac{d}{d[\text{SQGA CL}]}([\text{SQE}])\right)^{-1}\right]$$

Estimand assumption 1, As-if-random:
    If U⇸IGP then ¬(U ⇸{SQGA,CL})
Estimand assumption 2, Exclusion:
    If we remove {SQGA,CL}→{SQE} then ¬({SQGA,CL}→IGP)

There are two level 2 definitional requirements for a variable to be a valid instrument:

1  *As-if-random*—Any backdoor paths between the instrument and the outcome can be blocked.

2  *Exclusion*—The instrument is a cause of the outcome only indirectly through the treatment.

The variables in our model that satisfy these constraints are *Side-Quest Group Assignment* and *Customization Level*, as shown in figure 11.5.

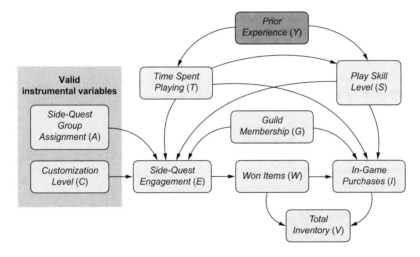

**Figure 11.5**  *Side-Quest Group Assignment* and *Customization Level* are valid instrumental variables.

The printout of identified_estimand shows the two constraints:

1  Estimand assumption 1, As-if-random—DoWhy assumes that none of the other causes of the outcome (*In-Game Purchases*) are also causes of either instrument. In other words, there are no backdoor paths between the instruments and the outcome.

2  Estimand assumption 2, Exclusion—This says that if we remove the causal path from the instruments to the treatment (*Side-quest Engagement*), there would

be no causal paths from the instruments to the outcome (*In-Game Purchases*). In other words, there are no causal paths between the instruments and the outcome that are not mediated by the treatment.

Note that DoWhy's constraints are relatively restrictive; DoWhy prohibits the *existence* of backdoor paths and non-treatment-mediated causal paths between the instrument and the outcome. In practice, it would be possible to block these paths with backdoor adjustment. DoWhy is making a trade-off that favors a simpler interface.

> ### Parametric assumptions for instrumental variable estimation
> The level 2 graphical assumptions are not sufficient for instrumental variable identification; additional parametric assumptions are needed. DoWhy, by default, makes a linearity assumption. With a linear assumption, you can derive the ATE as a simple function of the coefficients of linear models of outcome and the treatment given the instrument. DoWhy does this by fitting linear regression models.

Next, we'll look at the third estimand identified by DoWhy—the front door estimand.

### 11.3.3  *The front-door adjustment estimand*

Let's move on to the assumptions in the third estimand, the front-door estimand. DoWhy's printed summary is as follows (again, I shortened the variable names to acronyms in the printout so it fits the page):

```
### Estimand : 3
Estimand name: frontdoor
Estimand expression:
 ⎡      d                d            ⎤
E⎢───────────(IGP)·──────────([WI])⎥
 ⎣d[WI]        d[SQE]              ⎦
Estimand assumption 1, Full-mediation:
    WI intercepts (blocks) all directed paths from SQE to IGP.
Estimand assumption 2, First-stage-unconfoundedness:
    If U→{SQE} and U→{WI}
    then P(WI|SQE,U) = P(WI|SQE)
Estimand assumption 3, Second-stage-unconfoundedness:
    If U→{WI} and U→IGP
    then P(IGP|WI, SQE, U) = P(IGP|WI, SQE)
```

As we saw in chapter 10, the front-door estimand requires a mediator on the path from the treatment to the outcome—in our DAG, this is *Won Items*. The printout for `identified_estimand` lists three key assumptions for the front-door estimand:

1  `Full-mediation`—The mediator (*Won-Items*) intercepts all directed paths from the treatment (*Side-Quest Engagement*) to the outcome (*In-Game Purchases*). In other words, conditioning on *Won-Items* would d-separate (block) all the paths of causal influence from the treatment to the outcome.

2  `First-stage-unconfoundedness`—There are no hidden confounders between the treatment and the mediator.

   **3**  `Second-stage-unconfoundedness`—There are no hidden confounders between the outcome and the mediator.

With our DAG and the variables observed in the data, DoWhy has identified three estimands for the ATE of *Side-Quest Engagement* on *In-Game Purchases*. Remember, the estimand is the thing we estimate, so which estimand should we estimate?

### 11.3.4   *Choosing estimands and reducing "DAG anxiety"*

In step 2 of the causal inference workflow, we specified our causal assumptions about the domain as a DAG (or SCM or other causal model). The subsequent steps all rely on the assumptions we make in step 2.

    Errors in step 2 can lead to errors in the results of the analysis, and while we can empirically test these assumptions to some extent (e.g., using the methods in chapter 4), we cannot verify all our causal assumptions with observational data alone. This dependence on our subjective and unverified causal assumptions leads to what I call "DAG anxiety"—a fear that if one gets any part of the causal assumptions wrong, then the output of the analysis becomes wrong. Fortunately, we don't need to get all the assumptions right; we only need to rely on the assumptions required *to identify our selected estimand.*

    This is what makes DoWhy's `identify_effect` method so powerful. By showing us the assumptions required for each estimand it lists, we can compare these assumptions and target the estimand where we are most confident about those assumptions.

    For example, the key assumption behind the backdoor adjustment estimand is that we can adjust for all sources of confounding from common causes. In our original DAG, we have an edge from *Time Spent Playing* to *Player Skill Level*. What if you weren't sure about the direction of this edge, as illustrated in figure 11.6.

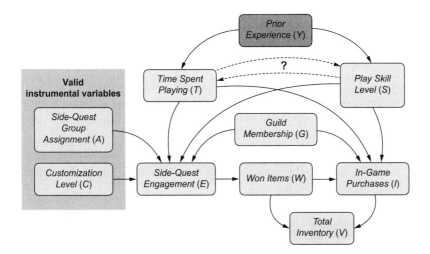

**Figure 11.6   Uncertainty about the edge between *Time Spent Playing* and *Player Skill Level* doesn't matter with respect to the backdoor adjustment estimand of the ATE of interest.**

When we initially built the DAG, you might have been thinking that playing more causes skill level to increase. But now you may worry that perhaps the relationship is the other way around—that being more skilled causes you to want to spend more time playing. It doesn't matter! At least, not with respect to the backdoor estimand for the target query—the ATE of *Side-Quest Engagement* on *In-Game Purchases*.

Suppose that instead you were worried that the model might have omitted edges that reflect direct influence that *Prior Experience* has on *Side-Quest Engagement* and *In-Game Purchases*. You worry that players might bring their habits in side-quest playing and virtual item purchasing from previous games they've played to the game environment you are modeling, as in figure 11.7.

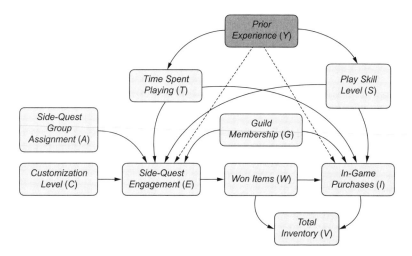

**Figure 11.7   Direct influence of a latent variable on the treatment and outcome would violate the assumption underpinning the backdoor adjustment estimand. If you are not confident in an estimand's assumptions, target another.**

If this is true, your backdoor adjustment estimand assumption would be violated—you would have a confounder you couldn't adjust for, a backdoor path you couldn't block. In this case, you'll need to consider whether the backdoor adjustment estimand is the right estimand to target.

Fortunately, in this example, we still have two other estimands to choose from. Neither the instrumental variable estimand nor the front-door adjustment estimand rely on our ability to adjust for all common causes. As long as we're comfortable with the assumptions for either of these estimands, we can continue.

### 11.3.5  *When you don't have identification*

The stop sign in the causal inference workflow, shown again in figure 11.8, warns against proceeding with estimation when you don't have identification.

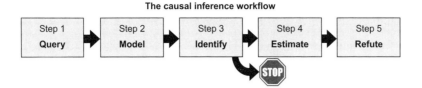

**Figure 11.8  If you lack identification, do not proceed to estimation. Rather, consider how to acquire data that enables identification.**

Let's consider what happens if our observational distribution only contains a subset of our initial variables, as in figure 11.9.

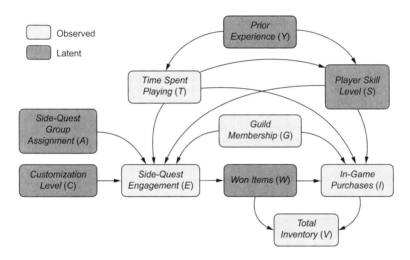

**Figure 11.9  *Player Skill Level, Won Items, Prior Experience, Side-Quest Group Assignment, and Customization Level become latent variables.***

In this case, we have some problems:

- If *Player Skill Level* is latent, we can't adjust for confounding from *Player Skill Level* and thus have no backdoor estimand.
- If *Won Items* is latent, we can't identify a front-door estimand.
- If the instrumental variables are latent, we can't target an instrumental variable estimand.

When you lack identification, you should not proceed with the next step of estimation. Rather, use the results from identification to determine what additional variables to collect—consider how you can collect new data with

- Additional confounders that would enable backdoor identification

- A mediator that would enable front-door identification
- Variables you can use as instruments

Avoid the temptation to change the DAG to get identification with your current data—you are modeling the data generating process (DGP), not the data.

However, if you do have an identified estimand, you can move on to step 4— estimation.

## 11.4   Step 4: Estimate the estimand

In step 4 of the causal inference workflow, we select an estimation method for whichever estimand we wish to target. In this section, we'll walk through several estimators for each of our three estimands. Note that your results for estimation may vary slightly from those in the text, depending on modifications to the dataset and to random elements of the estimator.

In DoWhy, we do estimation using a method in the `CausalModel` class called `estimate_effect`, as in the following example.

---

**Listing 11.5    Estimating the backdoor estimand with linear regression**

```
causal_estimate_reg = model.estimate_effect(
    identified_estimand,
    method_name="backdoor.linear_regression",
    confidence_intervals=True
)
```

The estimate_effect method takes the output of the identify_effect method as input.

Return confidence intervals

method_name is of the form "[estimand].[estimator]". Here we use the linear regression estimator to estimate the backdoor estimand.

---

The first argument is the `identified_estimand` object. The second argument `method_name` is a string of the form `"[estimand].[estimator]"`, where `"[estimand]"` is the estimand we want to target, and `"[estimator]"` is the estimation method we want to use. Thus, `method_name="backdoor.linear_regression"` means we want to use linear regression to estimate the backdoor estimand.

In this section, we'll see the benefits of distinguishing identification from estimation. In step 3 of the causal inference workflow, we compared identified estimands and selected an estimand with assumptions in which we are confident. That step frees us to focus on the statistical and computational trade-offs common across data science and machine learning when we choose an estimation method in step 4. We'll walk through these trade-offs in this section. Let's start by looking at the linear regression estimation of the backdoor estimand.

### 11.4.1   Linear regression estimation of the backdoor estimand

In many causal inference texts, particularly from econometrics, the default approach to causal inference is regression—specifically, regressing the outcome on the treatment and any confounders we wish to adjust for or "control for." What we are doing in this case is using linear regression to estimate the backdoor estimand.

Recall that in the case where *Side-Quest Engagement* is continuous, the ATE would be

$$\frac{dE(I_{E=x})}{dx}$$

This is a function of x, not a point value. However, it becomes a point value when $E(I_{E=x})$ is linear—the derivative of a linear function is a constant.

So we turn to regression. The backdoor adjustment estimand identifies *Guild Membership* ($G$), *Time Spent Playing* ($T$), and *Player Skill Level* ($S$) as the confounders we have to adjust for. In general, we have to sum or integrate over these variables in the backdoor adjustment estimand. But in the linear regression case, this simplifies to simply regressing $I$ on the treatment $E$ and the confounders $G$, $T$, and $S$. The coefficient estimate for $E$ is the ATE. In the case of a binary treatment like our target ATE,

$$E(I_{E=1} - I_{E=0})$$

we simply treat $E$ as a regression dummy variable. The coefficient estimates for the confounders are *nuisance parameters*—meaning they are necessary to estimate the ATE, but we can discard them once we have it.

To illustrate, let's print the results of our call to `estimate_method`.

**Listing 11.6 Print the linear regression estimation results**

```
print(causal_estimate_reg)
```

This prints a bunch of stuff, including the following:

```
## Realized estimand
b: In-game Purchases~Side-quest Engagement+Guild Membership+Time Spent
    Playing+Player Skill Level
Target units: ate


## Estimate
Mean value: 178.08617115757784
95.0% confidence interval: [[168.68114922 187.4911931 ]]
```

`Realized estimand` shows the regression formula. `Estimate` shows the estimation results, the point value, and the 95% confidence interval.

Here we see why linear regression is so popular as an estimator:

- The coefficient estimate of the treatment is a point estimate of the ATE.
- We adjust for backdoor confounders by simply including them in the regression model (no summation, no integration).
- The statistical properties of the estimator (confidence intervals, *p*-values, etc.) are well established.
- Many people are familiar with regression and how to evaluate a regression fit.

Once we have backdoor identification, the question of whether we should use a linear regression estimator in this case involves the same considerations of whether a linear regression model is appropriate in non-causal explanatory modeling settings (e.g., is the relationship linear?).

---

### Valid backdoor adjustment sets: What you can and can't adjust for

You do not need to adjust for *all* confounding from common causes. Any valid backdoor adjustment set of common causes will do. As discussed in chapter 10, a valid backdoor adjustment set any set that satisfies the backdoor criterion, meaning that it d-separates *all* backdoor paths. For example, *Guild Membership*, *Time Spent Playing*, and *Player Skill Level* are a valid adjustment set. You don't need *Prior Experience* because *Time Spent Playing* and *Player Skill Level* are sufficient to d-separate the backdoor path through *Prior Experience*. This is fortunate for us, since *Prior Experience* is unobserved. Though, if it were observed, we could add it to the adjustment set—this superset would also be a valid set.

DoWhy selects a valid adjustment set when it identifies a backdoor estimand. If you write your own estimator, you'll select your own adjustment set.

Some applied regression texts argue that you should try to adjust for or "control for" any covariates in your data because they could be potential confounders. This is bad advice. Doing so only makes sense if you are sure the covariate is not a mediator or a collider between the treatment and outcome variables. Adjusting for a mediator will d-separate the causal path you mean to quantify with the ATE. Adjusting for a collider will add collider bias. This is a painfully common error in social science, one committed even by experts.

---

### 11.4.2 *Propensity score estimators of the backdoor estimand*

Propensity score methods are a collection of estimation methods for the backdoor estimand that use a quantity called the *propensity score*. The traditional definition of a propensity score is the probability of being exposed to the treatment conditional on the confounders. In the context of the online gaming example, this is the probability that a player has high *Side-Quest Engagement* given their *Guild Membership*, *Time Spent Playing*, and *Player Skill Level*, i.e., $P(E=1|T=t, G=g, S=s)$ where $t$, $g$, and $s$ are that player's values for $T$, $G$, and $S$. In other words, it quantifies the player's "propensity" of being exposed to the treatment ($E=1$). Typically $P(E=1|T=t, G=g, S=s)$ is fit by logistic regression.

But we can take a more expansive, machine learning–friendly view of the propensity score. We can learn a propensity score function $\lambda(...)$ of the backdoor adjustment set of confounders that renders those confounders conditionally independent of the treatment, as in figure 11.10.

Here, we learn a function $\lambda(T, S, G)$ such that it effectively compresses the explanatory influence that $T$, $S$, and $G$ have on $E$. The traditional function of $P(E=1|G, S, T)$ compresses this influence into a probability value, but other approaches can work as well.

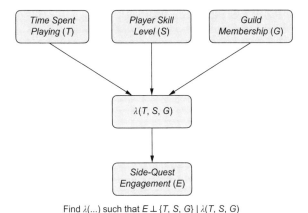

Find λ(...) such that $E \perp \{T, S, G\} \mid \lambda(T, S, G)$

**Figure 11.10   The propensity score is a compression of the causal influence of the common causes in the backdoor adjustment set.**

The utility of propensity score modeling is dimensionality reduction; now we only need to adjust for the score instead of all the confounders in the adjustment set. There are three common propensity score methods:

- Propensity score stratification
- Propensity score matching
- Propensity score weighting

These methods make different trade-offs in how they go about backdoor adjustment. Let's examine their use in DoWhy.

**PROPENSITY SCORE STRATIFICATION**

Propensity score stratification tries to break the data up into subsets ("strata") according to propensity scores and then adjust over the strata. Note that this algorithm may take some time to run.

**Listing 11.7   Propensity score stratification**

```
causal_estimate_strat = model.estimate_effect(
    identified_estimand,
    method_name="backdoor.propensity_score_stratification",    ◁─┐ Propensity score
    target_units="ate",                                          │ stratification
    confidence_intervals=True
)

print(causal_estimate_strat)
```

This produces the following results:

```
## Estimate
Mean value: 187.2931023294184
95.0% confidence interval: (180.3291962554186, 196.4556029137768)
```

The propensity score estimator gives us an estimate and confidence interval that differ slightly from that of the regression estimator.

**PROPENSITY SCORE MATCHING**

*Propensity score matching* tries to match individuals where treatment = 1 with individuals that have a similar propensity score but where treatment = 0 and then compare outcomes across matched pairs.

**Listing 11.8   Propensity score matching**

```
causal_estimate_match = model.estimate_effect(
    identified_estimand,
    method_name="backdoor.propensity_score_matching",       ◁─────┐ Propensity score
    target_units="ate",                                            matching
    confidence_intervals=True
)
print(causal_estimate_match)
```

This returns the following results:

```
## Estimate
Mean value: 199.8110290000004
95.0% confidence interval: (183.23361900000054, 210.5281390000008)
```

Propensity score matching, despite also being a propensity score method, returns an estimate and confidence interval different from that of propensity score stratification.

**PROPENSITY SCORE WEIGHTING**

*Propensity score weighting* methods use the propensity score to calculate a weight in a class of inference algorithms called *inverse probability weighting*. We implement this method in DoWhy as follows.

**Listing 11.9   Propensity score weighting**

```
causal_estimate_ipw = model.estimate_effect(                    Inverse probability
    identified_estimand,                                        weighting with the
    method_name="backdoor.propensity_score_weighting",    ◁──── propensity score
    target_units = "ate",
    method_params={"weighting_scheme":"ips_weight"},      ◁──── Parameters used to
    confidence_intervals=True                                   set the IPS algorithm
)
print(causal_estimate_ipw)
```

This returns the following:

```
## Estimate
Mean value: 437.79246624944926
95.0% confidence interval: (358.10472302821745, 515.2480572854872)
```

The fact that this estimator's result differs so dramatically from the others suggest that it is relying on statistical assumptions that don't hold in this data.

Next, we'll move on to a popular class of backdoor estimators that implement machine learning.

### 11.4.3  *Backdoor estimation with machine learning*

Recent developments in causal effect estimation focus on leveraging machine learning models, and most of these target the backdoor estimand. These approaches to causal effect estimation scale to large datasets and allow us to relax parametric assumptions, such as linearity. The following DoWhy code uses the sklearn and EconML libraries for these machine learning methods. DoWhy's `estimate_effects` provides a wrapper to the EconML implementation of these methods.

#### DOUBLE MACHINE LEARNING

Double machine learning (double ML) is a backdoor estimator that uses machine learning methods to fit two predictive models: a model of the outcome, given the adjustment set of confounders, and a model of the treatment, given the adjustment set. The approach then combines these two predictive models in a final-stage estimation to create a model of the target causal effect query.

The following code performs double ML using a gradient boosting model and regularized regression model (`LassoCV`) from sklearn.

**Listing 11.10   Double ML with DoWhy, EconML, and sklearn**

```
from sklearn.preprocessing import PolynomialFeatures
from sklearn.linear_model import LassoCV
from sklearn.ensemble import GradientBoostingRegressor

featurizer = PolynomialFeatures(degree=1, include_bias=False)
gb_estimate = model.estimate_effect(
    identified_estimand,
    method_name = "backdoor.econml.dml.DML",        Select the double
    control_value = 0,                              ML estimator.
    treatment_value = 1,
    method_params={                                 Use a gradient boosting
        "init_params":{                             model to model the outcome
            'model_y': GradientBoostingRegressor(),  given the confounders.
            'model_t': GradientBoostingRegressor(),    Use a gradient
            'model_final': LassoCV(fit_intercept=False),  boosting model to
            'featurizer': featurizer                   model the treatment
        },                                             given the confounders.
        "fit_params":{}       Use linear regression with
    }                         L1 regularization (LASSO)
)                             as the final model.
print(gb_estimate)
```

This produces the following output:

```
## Estimate
Mean value: 175.7229947190752
```

This gives us an estimate in the ballpark of some of the other estimators.

#### META LEARNERS

Meta learners are another ML method for backdoor estimation. Broadly speaking, meta learners train a model (or models) of the outcome given the treatment variable and the confounders, and then account for the difference in prediction across treatment and control values of the treatment variable. They are particularly focused on highlighting heterogeneity of treatment effects across the data. The following code shows a meta learner example called a T-learner that uses a random forest predictor.

Listing 11.11   Backdoor estimation with a meta learner

```
from sklearn.ensemble import RandomForestRegressor
metalearner_estimate = model.estimate_effect(
    identified_estimand,
    method_name="backdoor.econml.metalearners.TLearner",
    method_params={
        "init_params": {'models': RandomForestRegressor()},
        "fit_params": {}
    }
)

print(metalearner_estimate)
```

> Meta learner estimation of the backdoor estimand. This uses a T-learner with a random forest predictor.

This returns the following output:

```
## Estimate
Mean value: 197.20665049459512
Effect estimates: [[ 192.6234]
 [  -5.3165]
 [ 133.2457]
 ...
 [  17.2561]
 [-152.1482]
 [ 264.887 ]]
```

The values under "Effect estimates" are the estimate of the CATE for each row of the data, conditional on the confounder values in the columns of that row.

#### CONFIDENCE INTERVALS WITH MACHINE LEARNING METHODS

DoWhy and EconML provide support for estimating confidence intervals for ML methods using a statistical method called nonparametric bootstrap, but this is computationally costly for large data. Cheap confidence interval estimation is one thing you give up for the flexibility and scalability of using ML methods for backdoor estimation.

### 11.4.4   *Front-door estimation*

Recall from chapter 10 that the front-door estimator for our ATE, given our *Won Items* mediator, is

$$P(I_{E=e} = i) = \sum_{w} P(W = w|E = e) \sum_{\varepsilon} P(I = i|E = \varepsilon, W = w)P(E = \varepsilon)$$

We can estimate this by fitting two statistical models, one that predicts *W* given *E*, and one that predicts *I* given *E* and *W*. DoWhy does this with linear regression by default, but you also have the option of selecting different predictive models.

> **Listing 11.12  Front door estimation with DoWhy**

```
causal_estimate_fd = model.estimate_effect(        Select two-stage
    identified_estimand,                           regression for the
    method_name="frontdoor.two_stage_regression",  front-door estimand.
    target_units = "ate",
    method_params={"weighting_scheme": "ips_weight"},  Specify estimator
    confidence_intervals=True                          hyperparameters.
)
print(causal_estimate_fd)
```

This produces the following output:

```
## Estimate
Mean value: 170.20560581290403
95.0% confidence interval: (141.53468188231938, 202.97221450388332)
```

The front-door estimate is similar to some of the backdoor estimators, but note that the confidence interval is skewed left.

### 11.4.5  *Instrumental variable methods*

Instrumental variable-based estimation of the ATE is straightforward in DoWhy.

> **Listing 11.13  Instrumental variable estimation in DoWhy**

```
causal_estimate_iv = model.estimate_effect(
    identified_estimand,                           Select instrumental
    method_name="iv.instrumental_variable",        variable estimation.
    method_params = {
        "iv_instrument_name": "Side-quest Group Assignment"   Select side-quest
    },                                                        engagement as
    confidence_intervals=True                                 the instrument.
)
print(causal_estimate_iv)
```

This prints the following output:

```
## Estimate
Mean value: 205.82297621514252
95.0% confidence interval: (-369.04011492007703, 923.6814756173349)
```

Note how large the confidence interval is despite the size of the data. This indicates that this estimator, with its default assumptions, might have too much variance to be useful.

**Good instrumental variables should be "strong"**

One requirement for good instrumental variable estimation is that the instrument is strong, meaning it has a strong causal effect on the treatment variable. If you explore this data, you'll find *Side-Quest Group Assignment* is a weak instrument. Weak instruments can lead to high variance estimates of the ATE. Keep this in mind when selecting an instrument.

**REGRESSION DISCONTINUITY**

Regression discontinuity is an estimation method popular in econometrics. It uses a continuously valued variable related to the treatment variable, and it defines a threshold (a "discontinuity") in the values of that variable that partition the data into "treatment" and "control" groups. It then compares observations lying closely on either side of the threshold, because those data points tend to have similar values for the confounders.

DoWhy treats regression discontinuity as an instrumental variable approach that uses continuous instruments. The `rd_variable_name` argument names a continuous instrument to use for thresholding, and `rd_threshold_value` is the threshold value. `rd_bandwidth` is the distance from the threshold within which confounders can be considered the same between treatment and control.

**Listing 11.14   Regression discontinuity estimation with DoWhy**

```
causal_estimate_regdist = model.estimate_effect(        DoWhy treats regression
    identified_estimand,                                discontinuity as a special
    method_name="iv.regression_discontinuity",   ◁──┘   type of IV estimator.
    method_params={
        'rd_variable_name':'Customization Level',   ◁──┐   Use Customization Level
        'rd_threshold_value':0.5,              ◁──┐         as our instrument.
        'rd_bandwidth': 0.15   ◁──┐
    },                                         The threshold value for the
    confidence_intervals=True,                 split ("discontinuity")
)
                                   The distance from the threshold within
                                   which confounders are considered the
                                   same between treatment and control
                                   values of the treatment variable
```

This returns the following results:

```
Mean value: 156.85691281931338
95.0% confidence interval: (-463.32687612531663, 940.698188663685)
```

Again, the variance is too large for us to rely on this estimator. The instrument is likely weak, or we need to tune the arguments passed to the estimator.

### Conditional average treatment effect estimation and segmentation

The conditional average treatment effect (CATE) is the ATE for a subset of the target population; i.e., we condition the ATE on specific values of covariates. DoWhy enables you to estimate the CATE as easily as the ATE.

Sometimes the goal of CATE estimation is *segmentation*—breaking the population down into segments that have a distinct CATE from other segments. A good tool for segmentation is EconML, which enables CATE-segmentation using regression trees. EconML can segment data into groups that respond similarly to intervention on the treatment variable, and find an optimal intervention value for each group in the leaf nodes of the regression tree.

### 11.4.6   Comparing and selecting estimators

In chapter 1, I mentioned a phenomenon called *the commodification of inference*. The way DoWhy reduces estimation to merely a set of arguments passed to the `estimate_effect` method is an example of this phenomenon. You don't need a detailed understanding of the estimator to get going. Once you've selected the estimand you wish to target, you can switch out different estimators.

### Advice: Start with synthetic data

One excellent practice is to build your workflow on synthetic data, rather than real data. Simulate a synthetic dataset that matches the size and correlation structure of your data, as well as your causal and statistical assumptions about your data. For example, you can write a causal generative model of your data, and use your data to train its parameters. Using this model as ground truth, simulate some data and derive a ground truth ATE.

You can then see if DoWhy's estimates get close to the ground truth ATE, and if its confidence intervals contain it. You can also see how well the estimators perform under the ideal conditions where all your assumptions are true—even in these conditions, the estimates will have biases and uncertainty.

Once you debug any problems that arise in these ideal conditions, you can switch out the synthetic data for real data. Then, the problems that arise are likely due to incorrect assumptions, and you can treat these by revisiting your assumptions.

My suggestion is to compare estimators after adding the next step, *refutation*, to the workflow. Refutation will help you stress test both the causal assumptions in the estimand and the statistical assumptions in the estimator. This enables you to make empirical comparisons of different estimators. Then, once you know what estimator you want and have seen how it performs on your data, you can do a deep dive into the statistical nuts and bolts of your chosen estimator.

## 11.5   *Step 5: Refutation*

We know that the result of our causal inference depends on our initial causal assumptions in step 2, or more specifically, the subset of those assumptions we rely on for identification in step 3. In step 4, we select an estimator that makes its own statistical assumptions. What if those causal and statistical assumptions are wrong?

We can address this in step 5 with *refutation*, where we actively search for evidence that our analysis is faulty. We first saw this concept in chapter 4, when we saw how to refute the causal DAG by finding statistical evidence of dependence in the data that conflicts with the conditional independence implications of the causal DAG. In section 7.6.2, we saw how to refute a model by finding cases where its predicted intervention outcomes clash with real-world intervention outcomes. Here, we implement refutation as a type of *sensitivity analysis* that tries to refute the various assumptions underpinning an estimate by simulating violations to those assumptions.

The `CausalModel` class in DoWhy has a `refute_estimate` method that provides a suite of refuters we can run. Each refuter provides a different attack vector for our assumptions. The refuters we run with `refute_estimate` perform a simulation-based statistical test; the null hypothesis is that the assumptions are not refuted, and the alternative hypothesis is that the assumptions are refuted. The tests return a *p*-value. If we take a standard significance threshold of .05 and the p-value falls below this threshold, we conclude that our assumptions are refuted.

In this section, we'll investigate a few of DoWhy's refuters with various estimands and estimators.

### 11.5.1   *Data size reduction*

One way to test the robustness of the analysis is to reduce the size of the data and see if we obtain similar results. We are assuming our analysis has more than enough data to achieve a stable estimation. We can refute this assumption by slightly reducing the size of the data and testing whether we get a similar estimate. Let's try this with the estimator of the front-door estimand.

##### Listing 11.15   Refuting the assumption of sufficient data

```
identified_estimand.set_identifier_method("frontdoor")
res_subset = model.refute_estimate(
    identified_estimand,
    causal_estimate_fd,
    method_name="data_subset_refuter",
    subset_fraction=0.8,
    num_simulations=100
)
print(res_subset)
```

Not always necessary, but clarifying the estimand targeted by the estimator we want to test can help avoid errors.

The refute_estimate function takes in the identified estimand and the estimator that targets the estimand.

Set the size of the subset to 80% the size of the original data.

Select data_subset_refuter, which tests if the causal estimate is different when we run the analysis on a subset of the data.

This produces the following output (this is a random process so your results will differ slightly):

```
Refute: Use a subset of data
Estimated effect:170.20560581290403
New effect:169.14858189323638
p value:0.82
```

The `Estimated effect` is the effect from our original analysis. `New effect` is the average ATE across the simulations. We want these two effects to be similar, because otherwise it would mean that our analysis is sensitive to the amount of data we have. The *p*-value here is above the threshold, so we failed to refute this assumption.

### 11.5.2  Adding a dummy confounder

One way to test our models is to add dummy common-cause confounders. If a variable is not a confounder, it has no bearing on the true ATE, so we assume that our causal effect estimation workflow will be unaffected by these variables. In truth, additional variables might add statistical noise that throws off our estimator.

The following listing attempts to refute the assumption that such noise does not affect the double ML estimator of the backdoor estimand.

**Listing 11.16  Adding a dummy confounder**

```
identified_estimand.set_identifier_method("backdoor")
res_random = model.refute_estimate(
    identified_estimand,
    gb_estimate,                              Runs 100 simulations of
    method_name="random_common_cause",       the addition of a dummy
    num_simulations=100,                      confounder to the model
)
print(res_random)
```

This returns output such as the following:

```
Refute: Add a random common cause
Estimated effect:175.2192519976428
New effect:176.59119763647792
p value:0.30000000000000004
```

Again, `Estimated effect` is the original causal effect estimate, and `New effect` is the new causal effect estimate obtained after adding a random common cause to the data and re-running the analysis. The dummy variable has no real effect, so we expect the ATE to be the same. Again, the *p*-value is above the significance threshold, so we failed to refute our assumptions.

### 11.5.3  Replacing treatment with a dummy

We can also experiment with replacing the treatment variable with a dummy variable. This is analogous to giving our causal effect inference workflow a "placebo," and seeing how much causality it ascribes to this fake treatment. Since this dummy variable will have no effect on the treatment, we expect the ATE to be 0.

Let's try this with our inverse probability weighting estimator.

**Listing 11.17 Replacing the treatment variable with a dummy variable**

```
identified_estimand.set_identifier_method("backdoor")
res_placebo = model.refute_estimate(
identified_estimand,
    causal_estimate_ipw,                              This refuter replaces the
    method_name="placebo_treatment_refuter",         treatment variable with a
    placebo_type="permute",                           dummy (placebo) variable.
    num_simulations=100
)

print(res_placebo)
```

This produces the following output:

```
Refute: Use a Placebo Treatment
Estimated effect:437.79246624944926
New effect:-531.2490111208127
p value:0.0
```

In this case, the *p*-value is calculated under the null hypothesis that `New effect` is equal to 0. Again, a low *p*-value would refute our assumptions.

In this case, it would seem that our inverse probability weighting estimator was thrown off by this refuter. This result indicates that there is an issue somewhere in the joint assumptions made by the backdoor estimand and this estimator. If we then used this refuter with other backdoor estimators and they were not refuted, we would have narrowed down the source of the issue to the statistical assumptions made by this estimator.

### 11.5.4 Replacing outcome with a dummy outcome

We can substitute the outcome variable with a dummy variable. The ATE in this case should be 0, because the treatment has no effect on this dummy. We'll simulate it as a linear function of some of the confounders so the outcome still has a meaningful relationship with some of the covariates.

Let's try this with the front door estimator.

**Listing 11.18 Replacing the outcome variable with a dummy variable**

```
import numpy as np                                          Create a function
                                                            that generates a new
coefficients = np.array([100.0, 50.0])                      dummy outcome
bias = 50.0                                                 variable as a linear
def linear_gen(df):                                         function of the
    subset = df[['guild_membership','player_skill_level']]  covariates.
    y_new = np.dot(subset.values, coefficients) + bias
    return y_new
```

```
ref = model.refute_estimate(
    identified_estimand,
    causal_estimate_fd,
    method_name="dummy_outcome_refuter",
    outcome_function=linear_gen
)
```
**Runs refute_estimate with a dummy outcome refuter**

```
res_dummy_outcome = ref[0]
print(res_dummy_outcome)


Refute: Use a Dummy Outcome
Estimated effect:0
New effect:-0.024480394297227835
p value:0.86
```

Again, the *p*-value is calculated under the null hypothesis that `New effect` equals 0, and a low *p*-value refutes our assumptions. In this case, our assumptions are not refuted.

Next, we'll evaluate the sensitivity of the analysis to unobserved confounding.

### 11.5.5   *Testing robustness to unmodeled confounders*

Our backdoor adjustment estimand assumes that the adjustment set blocks all backdoor paths. If there were a confounder that we failed to adjust for, that assumption is violated, and our estimate would have a confounder bias. That is not necessarily the worst thing; if we adjust for all the *major* confounders, bias from unknown confounders might be small and not impact our results by much. On the other hand, missing a major confounder could lead us to conclude that there is a nonzero ATE when one doesn't exist, or conclude a positive ATE when the true ATE is negative, or vice versa. We can therefore test how robust our analysis is to the introduction of latent confounders that our model failed to capture. The hope is that the new estimate does not change drastically when we introduce some modest influence from a newly introduced confounder.

**Listing 11.19   Adding an unobserved confounder**

```
identified_estimand.set_identifier_method("backdoor")
res_unobserved = model.refute_estimate(
    identified_estimand,
    causal_estimate_fd,
    method_name="add_unobserved_common_cause"
)
```
**Setting up a refuter that adds an unobserved common cause**

```
print(res_unobserved)
```

This code does not return a *p*-value. It produces the heatmap we see in figure 11.11, showing how quickly the estimate changes when the unobserved confounder assumption is violated. The horizontal axis shows the various levels of influence the unobserved confounder has on the outcome, and the vertical axis shows the various levels of influence the confounder can have on the treatment. The color corresponds to the new effect estimates that result at different levels of influence.

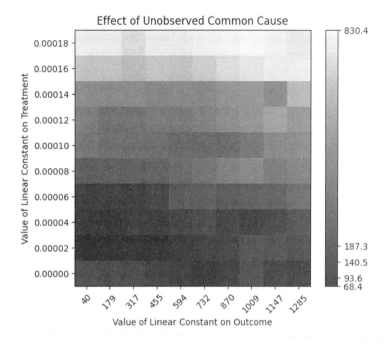

**Figure 11.11    A heatmap illustrating the effects of adding an unobserved confounder on the ATE estimate**

The code also prints out the following.

```
Refute: Add an Unobserved Common Cause
Estimated effect:187.2931023294184
New effect:(-181.5795321684548, 398.98672237350416)
```

Here, we see that the ATE is quite sensitive to the effect the confounder has on the treatment. Note that you can change the default parameters of the refuter to experiment with different impacts the confounder could have on the treatment and outcome.

Now that we've run through a full workflow in DoWhy, let's explore how we'd build a similar workflow using the tools of probabilistic machine learning.

## 11.6  *Causal inference with causal generative models*

At the end of chapter 10, we calculated an ATE using the `do` intervention operator and a probabilistic inference algorithm. This is a powerful universal approach to doing causal inference that leverages cutting-edge probabilistic machine learning. But this wasn't *estimation*. Estimation requires data. It would be *estimation* if we estimated the model parameters from data *before* running that workflow with the `do` function and probabilistic inference.

In this section, we'll run through a full ATE estimation workflow that uses the `do` intervention operator and probabilistic inference. We used MCMC for the probabilistic inference step in chapter 10, but here we'll use variational inference with a variational autoencoder to handle latent variables in the data. Further, we'll use a Bayesian estimation approach, meaning we'll assign prior probabilistic distributions to the parameters. The ATE inference step with the intervention operator will depend on sampling from the posterior distribution on parameters.

The advantage of this approach relative to using DoWhy is being able to use modern deep learning tools to work with latent variables as well as use Bayesian modeling to address uncertainty. Further, this approach will work in cases of causal identification that are not covered by DoWhy (e.g., edge cases of graphical identification, identification derived from assignment functions or prior distributions, partial identification, etc.).

This approach to ATE estimation is a specific case of a general approach to causal inference where we train a causal graphical model, *transform* the model in some way that reflects the causal query (e.g., with an intervention operator), and then run a probabilistic inference algorithm. Let's review various ways we can transform a model for causal inference.

### 11.6.1  *Transformations for causal inference*

We have seen several ways of modifying a causal model such that it can readily infer a causal query. We'll call these "transformations": we transform our model into a new model that targets a causal inference query. Let's review the transformations we've seen so far.

#### GRAPH SURGERY

One of the transformations was basic *graph surgery*, illustrated in figure 11.12. This operation implements an *ideal intervention*, setting the intervention target to a constant and severing the causal influence from the parents. This operation allows us to use our model to infer $P(I_{E=1})$, the ATE, and similar level 2 queries, and it's how we have been implementing interventions in pgmpy.

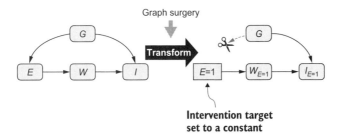

Figure 11.12   Graph surgery is a transformation that implements an ideal intervention by removing incoming causal influence on the target node and setting the target node to a constant.

We implemented graph surgery in pgmpy by using the `do` method on the `Bayesian-Network` class, and then we added a hack that modified the `TabularCPD` object assigned to the intervention project so that the intervention value had a probability of 1.

PyMC is a probabilistic programming language similar to Pyro. It does implicit graph surgery by transforming the logic of the model. For example, PyMC might specify $E$, a function of $G$, as `E = Bernoulli("E", p=f(G))`. PyMC uses a `do` function to implement the intervention, as in `do(model, {"E": 1.0})`. Under the hood, this function does implicit graph surgery by effectively replacing `E = Bernoulli("E", p=f(G))` with `E = 1.0`.

### NODE-SPLITTING

In chapter 10, we discussed a slightly nuanced version of graph surgery called a node-splitting operation, illustrated in figure 11.13. Node-splitting converts the graph to a *single world intervention graph*, allowing us to infer level 2 queries just as graph surgery does. It also allows us to infer level 3 queries where the factual conditions and hypothetical outcome don't overlap, such as $P(I_{E=0}|E=1)$ (though doing so relies on an additional "single world assumption," as discussed in chapter 10).

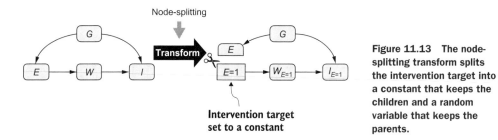

Figure 11.13    The node-splitting transform splits the intervention target into a constant that keeps the children and a random variable that keeps the parents.

Pyro's `do` function implements node-splitting (though it behaves just like PyMC's `do` function if you don't target level 3 queries).

### MULTI-WORLD TRANSFORMATION

We also saw how to transform a structural causal model into a parallel world graph. Let's call this a multi-world transformation, illustrated in figure 11.14.

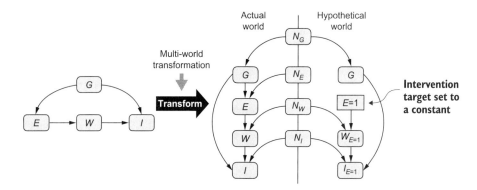

Figure 11.14    Yet another transform converts the model into a parallel-world model.

We created parallel-world models by hand in chapter 9 with pgmpy and Pyro. The y0 library produces parallel world graphs from DAGs. ChiRho, the causal library that extends Pyro, has a `TwinWorldCounterfactual` handler that does the multi-world transformation.

#### TRANSFORMATION TO A COUNTERFACTUAL GRAPH

Recall that we can also transform the causal DAG to a counterfactual graph (which, in the case of a level 2 query like $P(I_{E=1})$, will simplify to the result of graph surgery). Y0 creates a counterfactual graph from your DAG and a given query. Future versions of causal probabilistic ML libraries may provide the same transformation for a Pyro/PyMC/ChiRho type model.

### 11.6.2   Steps for inferring a causal query with a causal generative model

Given a causal generative model and a target causal query, we have two steps to infer the target query: first, apply the transformation, and then run probabilistic inference.

   We did this with the online gaming example at the end of chapter 10. We targeted $P(I_{E=0})$ and $P(I_{E=0}|E=1)$. For each of these queries, we used the `do` function in Pyro to modify the model to represent the intervention $E=0$. In the case of $P(I_{E=0}|E=1)$, we also conditioned on $E=1$. Then we ran an MCMC algorithm to generate samples from these distributions. We also used the probabilistic inference with parallel-world graphs to implement level 3 counterfactual inferences in chapter 9.

### 11.6.3   Extending inference to estimation

To extend this workflow to estimation, like the DoWhy methods in this chapter, we simply need to add a parameter estimation step to our causal graphical inference workflow:

1   Estimate model parameters.
2   Apply the transformation.
3   Run probabilistic inference on the transformed model.

Let's look at how to do this with the online game data. For simplicity, we'll work with a reduced model that drops the instruments and the collider, since we won't be using them.

   We'll model the causal Markov kernels of each node with some unique parameter vector. We can estimate the parameters any way we like, but to stay on brand with probabilistic reasoning, let's use a Bayesian setup, treating each parameter vector as its own random variable with its own prior probability distribution. Figure 11.15 illustrates a plate model representation of the causal DAG (we discussed plate model visualizations in chapter 2), drawing these random variables as new nodes, using Greek letters to highlight the fact that they are parameters, rather than causal components of the real world DGP.

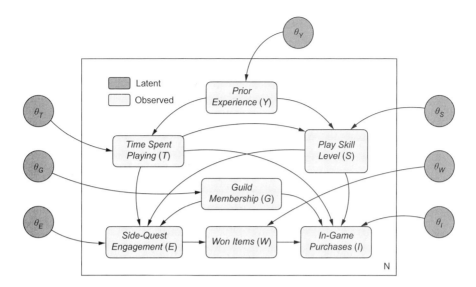

**Figure 11.15   A plate model of the causal DAG with new nodes representing parameters associated with each causal Markov kernel. There is a single plate with *N* identical and independent observations in the training data. $\theta$ corresponds to parameters, which are outside the plate, because the parameters are the same for each of the *N* data points.**

In this case, Bayesian estimation will target the posterior distribution:

$$P\left(\theta_Y, \theta_T, \theta_S, \; \theta_G, \theta_E, \theta_W, \theta_I \middle| \vec{E}, \; \vec{Y}, \vec{T}, \vec{S}, \vec{G}, \vec{W}, \vec{I}\right)$$

where $\vec{E}, \vec{Y}, \vec{T}, \vec{S}, \vec{G}, \vec{W}, \vec{I}$ each represent the *N* examples of *E, Y, T, G, S, W, I* in the data.

Estimating the $\theta$s in this case is easy. For example, in pgmpy we just run `model.fit(data, estimator= BayesianEstimator, ...)`, where "..." contains arguments that specify the type of prior to assign the $\theta$s. Pgmpy uses the posterior to give us point estimates of the $\theta$s. In Pyro, we just write sample statements for the $\theta$s and use one of Pyro's various inference algorithms to get samples from the posterior.

But the causal effect methods in DoWhy highlight the ability to do causal inferences when some causal variables are *latent*, such as confounders:

- Backdoor adjustment with some latent confounders is possible (e.g., *Prior Experience*) if you have a valid adjustment set (*Time Spent Playing, Guild Membership,* and *Player Skill Level*).
- If too many confounders are latent, such that you do not have backdoor adjustment, you can use other techniques, such as using instrumental variables and front-door adjustment.

So for causal generative modeling to compete with DoWhy, it needs to accommodate latent variables. Let's consider the case where the backdoor adjustment estimand is not identified. Next, we'll explore how we can train a latent causal generative model and then apply the transformation and probabilistic inference.

In this model, we'll assume that *Guild Membership* is the only observed confounder, as in figure 11.16. In this case, we no longer have backdoor identification.

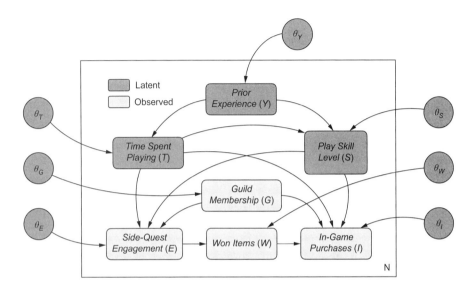

**Figure 11.16** *Guild Membership* **is the only observed confounder, so the backdoor estimand is not identified.**

## SETTING UP YOUR ENVIRONMENT
The following code is written with torch 2.2, pandas 1.5, and pyro-ppl 1.9. We'll use matplotlib and seaborn for plotting.

Let's first reload and modify the data to reflect this paucity of observed variables.

**Listing 11.20  Load and reduce data to a subset of observed variables**

```
import pandas as pd
import torch

url = ("https://raw.githubusercontent.com/altdeep/"
       "causalML/master/datasets/online_game_ate.csv")    Load the data.
df = pd.read_csv(url)
df = df[["Guild Membership", "Side-quest Engagement",
         "Won Items", "In-game Purchases"]]
```

Load the data.

Drop everything but Guild Membership, Side-Quest Engagement, Won Items, and In-Game Purchases.

```
device = torch.device("cuda" if torch.cuda.is_available() else "cpu")
data = {
    col: torch.tensor(df[col].values, dtype=torch.float32).to(device)
    for col in df.columns
}
```

**Convert the data to tensors and dynamically set the device for performing tensor computations depending on the availability of a CUDA-enabled GPU.**

Now we are targeting the following posterior:

$$P\left(\theta_Y, \theta_T, \theta_S, \theta_G, \theta_E, \theta_W, \theta_I, \ \vec{Y}, \vec{T}, \vec{S} \middle| \vec{E}, \vec{G}, \vec{W}, \vec{I}\right)$$

Targeting this posterior is harder because, since the observations of $\vec{Y}, \vec{T}, \vec{S}$ are not observed, they are not available to help in inferring $\theta_Y$, $\theta_T$, and $\theta_S$. In fact, in general, $\theta_Y$, $\theta_T$, and $\theta_S$ are *underdetermined*, meaning multiple configurations of $\{\theta_Y, \theta_T, \theta_S\}$ would be equally likely given the data. Further, we'll have trouble estimating with $\theta_E$ and $\theta_I$ because it will be hard to disentangle them from the other latent variables.

But it doesn't matter! At least, not in terms of our goal of inferring $P(I_{E=e})$, because we know we have identified the front-door estimand of $P(I_{E=e})$. In other words, the existence of a front-door estimand proves we can infer $P(I_{E=e})$ from the observed variables regardless of the lack of identifiability of some of the parameters.

### 11.6.4 *A VAE-inspired model for causal inference*

We'll make our modeling easier by creating proxy variables $\vec{Z}$ and $\theta_Z$ to stand in for $\{\vec{Y}, \vec{T}, \vec{S}\}$ and $\{\theta_Y, \theta_T, \theta_S\}$ respectively. Collapsing the latent confounders into these proxies reduces the dimensionality of the estimation problem, and any loss of information that occurs from collapsing these variables won't matter because we are ultimately relying on information flowing through the front door. We'll create a causal generative model inspired by the variational autoencoder, where $\vec{Z}$ is a latent encoding and $\theta_E$ and $\theta_I$ become weights in decoders. This is visualized in figure 11.17. Now our inference will target the posterior:

$$P\left(\theta_Z, \theta_G, \theta_E, \theta_W, \theta_I, \ \vec{Z} \middle| \vec{E}, \ \vec{G}, \vec{W}, \vec{I}\right)$$

Our model will have two decoders. One decoder maps $\vec{Z}$ and $G$ to $E$, returning a derived parameter ρ_engagement that acts as the probability that *Side-Quest Engagement* is high. Let's call this network Confounders2Engagement. As shown in figure 11.17, $\vec{Z}$ is a vector with $K$ elements, but we'll set $K=1$ for simplicity.

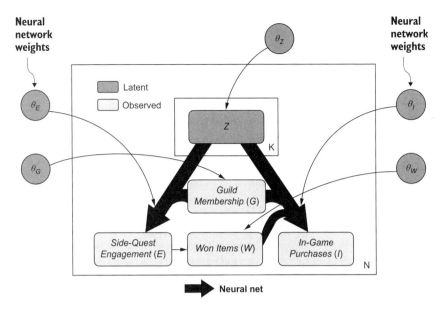

**Figure 11.17   VAE-inspired model where latent vector *Z* of length *K* proxies for the latent confounders in figure 11.16**

---

**Listing 11.21   Specify** `Confounders2Engagement` **neural network**

```python
import torch.nn as nn

class Confounders2Engagement(nn.Module):
    def __init__(
        self,
        input_dim=1+1,          # Input is confounder proxy Z
                                # concatenated with Guild Membership.
        hidden_dim=5            # Choose a hidden
    ):                          # dimension of width 5.
        super().__init__()
        self.fc1 = nn.Linear(input_dim, hidden_dim)    # Linear map from input
                                                       # to hidden dimension
        self.f_engagement_ρ = nn.Linear(hidden_dim, 1)
        self.softplus = nn.Softplus()                  # Linear map from
        self.sigmoid = nn.Sigmoid()                    # hidden dimension to
                                                       # In-Game Purchases
                                                       # location parameter
    def forward(self, input):                          # Activation function
        input = input.t()                              # for Side-Quest
        hidden = self.softplus(self.fc1(input))        # Engagement parameter
        ρ_engagement = self.sigmoid(self.f_engagement_ρ(hidden))
        ρ_engagement = ρ_engagement.t().squeeze(0)
        return ρ_engagement                            # From hidden layer
                                                       # to ρ_engagement
```

Annotations in left margin: **Activation function for hidden layer**; **From input to hidden layer**

---

Next, let's specify another neural net decoder that maps *Z*, *W*, and *G* to a location and scale parameter for *I*. Let's call this `PurchasesNetwork`.

Listing 11.22    `PurchasesNetwork` neural network

```
class PurchasesNetwork(nn.Module):
    def __init__(
        self,
        input_dim=1+1+1,
        hidden_dim=5
    ):
        super().__init__()
        self.f_hidden = nn.Linear(input_dim, hidden_dim)
        self.f_purchase_μ = nn.Linear(hidden_dim, 1)
        self.f_purchase_σ = nn.Linear(hidden_dim, 1)
        self.softplus = nn.Softplus()

    def forward(self, input):
        input = input.t()
        hidden = self.softplus(self.f_hidden(input))
        μ_purchases = self.f_purchase_μ(hidden)      H
        σ_purchases = 1e-6 + self.softplus(self.f_purchase_σ(hidden))
        μ_purchases = μ_purchases.t().squeeze(0)
        σ_purchases = σ_purchases.t().squeeze(0)
        return μ_purchases, σ_purchases
```

Input is confounder proxy Z concatenated with Guild Membership and Won Items.

Choose a hidden dimension of width 5.

Linear map from input to hidden dimension

Activation for hidden layer

Linear map from hidden dimension to In-Game Purchases location parameter

Linear map from hidden dimension to In-Game Purchases scale parameter

From input to hidden layer

Mapping from hidden layer to location parameter for purchases

Mapping from hidden layer scale parameter for purchases. The 1e-6 lets us avoid scale values of 0.

Now we use both networks to specify the causal model. The model will take a dictionary of parameters called `params` and use them to sample the variables in the model. The Bernoulli distributions of *Guild Membership* and *Won Items* have parameters passed in a dictionary called `params`, with keys ρ_member representing $\theta_G$, and ρ_won_engaged and ρ_won_not_engaged together representing $\theta_W$. ρ_engagement, which represents the *Side-Quest Engagement* parameter $\theta_E$, is set by the output of `Confounders2Engagement`, and μ_purchases and σ_purchases, which jointly represent the *In-Game Purchases* parameter $\theta_Y$, are the output of `PurchaseNetwork`. The parameter set $\theta_Z$ is a location and scale parameter for a normal distribution. Rather than a learnable $\theta_Z$, I use fixed $\theta_Z = \{0, 1\}$ and let the neural nets handle the linear transform for Z.

Listing 11.23    Specify the causal model

```
from pyro import sample
from pyro.distributions import Bernoulli, Normal
from torch import tensor, stack

def model(params, device=device):
    z_dist = Normal(
        tensor(0.0, device=device),
        tensor(1.0, device=device))
    z = sample("Z", z_dist)
    member_dist = Bernoulli(params['ρ_member'])
    is_guild_member = sample("Guild Membership", member_dist)
    engagement_input = stack((is_guild_member, z)).to(device)
    ρ_engagement = confounders_2_engagement(engagement_input)
```

The causal model

A latent variable that acts as a proxy for other confounders

Whether someone is in a guild

Use confounders_2_engagement to map is_guild_member and z to a parameter for Side-Quest Engagement and In-Game Purchases.

**Modeling
Side-Quest
Engagement**

```
engage_dist = Bernoulli(ρ_engagement)
is_highly_engaged = sample("Side-quest Engagement", engage_dist)
p_won = (
    params['ρ_won_engaged'] * is_highly_engaged +
    params['ρ_won_not_engaged'] * (1 - is_highly_engaged)
)
won_items = sample("Won Items", Bernoulli(p_won))
purchase_input = stack((won_items, is_guild_member, z)).to(device)
μ_purchases, σ_purchases = purchases_network(purchase_input)
purchase_dist = Normal(μ_purchases, σ_purchases)
in_game_purchases = sample("In-game Purchases", purchase_dist)
```

**Modeling amount
of Won Items**

**Use purchases_network to map
is_guild_member, z, and won_items
to in_game_purchases.**

**Model
in_game_purchases.**

This model represents a single data point. Now we need to extend the model to every example data point in the dataset. We'll build a data_model that loads the neural networks, assigns priors to the parameters, and models the data.

> **Listing 11.24   Build a data model**

```
import pyro
from pyro import render_model, plate
from pyro.distributions import Beta
from pyro import render_model

confounders_2_engagement = Confounders2Engagement().to(device)
purchases_network = PurchasesNetwork().to(device)
def data_model(data, device=device):
    pyro.module("confounder_2_engagement", confounders_2_engagement)
    pyro.module("confounder_2_purchases", purchases_network)
    two = tensor(2., device=device)
    five = tensor(5., device=device)
    params = {
        'ρ_member': sample('ρ_member', Beta(five, five)),
        'ρ_won_engaged': sample('ρ_won_engaged', Beta(five, two)),
        'ρ_won_not_engaged': sample('ρ_won_not_engaged', Beta(two, five)),
    }
    N = len(data["In-game Purchases"])
    with plate("N", N):
        model(params)

render_model(data_model, (data, ))
```

**Initialize
the neural
networks.**

**pyro.module lets Pyro know about all
the parameters inside the networks.**

**Sample
from prior
distribution
for ρ_member**

**Sample from prior distribution
for ρ_won_not_engaged**

**The plate context manager
declares N independent
samples (observations)
from the causal variables.**

**Sample from prior
distribution for
ρ_won_engaged**

render_model lets us visualize the resulting plate model, producing figure 11.18. ρ_member, ρ_won_engaged, ρ_won_not_engaged are the parameters we wish to estimate, alongside the weights in the neural nets.

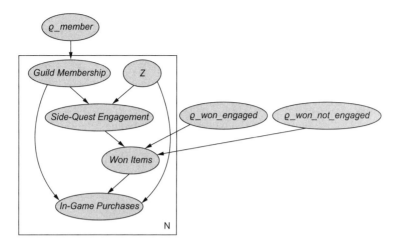

**Figure 11.18    The plate model representation produced by Pyro**

Now that we've specified the model, lets set up inference with SVI.

### 11.6.5  *Setting up posterior inference with SVI*

We have a data model over an underlying causal model, so we can now move on to inference. Using SVI, we need to build a *guide function* that represents a distribution that approximates the posterior—the guide function will have hyperparameters directly optimized during training, which will bring the approximating distribution as close as possible to the posterior.

### Why do inference with SVI and not MCMC?

In chapter 10, we used an MCMC inference algorithm to derive $P(I_{E=0})$ and $P(I_{E=0}|E=1)$ from $P(G, W, I, E)$. The $\theta$ parameters were given. Now the $\theta$ parameters are unknown, and we are using *Bayesian estimation*, meaning we want to infer $I_{E=e}$ conditional on values of those $\theta$ parameters sampled from a posterior distribution derived from training data. We do this by considering variables $\{\vec{E}, \vec{G}, \vec{W}, \vec{I}, \vec{Z}\}$ where $\{\vec{E}, \vec{G}, \vec{W}, \vec{I}\}$ is a set of variables in the training data, $\vec{Z}$ is a latent proxy for our latent confounders, and each of these variables are vectors of length $N$, the size of our training data.

The challenge is the computational complexity of MCMC algorithms generally grows exponentially in the dimension of the posterior. When $\vec{Z}$ is a latent variable, it gets added to the posterior as another unknown along with the $\theta$s, so the shape of the posterior increases by $\vec{Z}$'s dimension, which is at least the size of the training data $N$. This poses a challenge when $N$ is large. We want an inference method that works well with large data so we can leverage all that data to do cool things like use deep neural networks to help us proxy our latent confounders in a causal generative model. So here we use SVI instead of MCMC because SVI shines in high-dimensional large data settings.

The main ingredient of the guide function is an encoder that will map *Side-Quest Engagement*, *Won Items*, and *In-Game Purchases* to *Z*; i.e., it will *impute* the latent values of *Z*.

---

**Listing 11.25   Create an encoder for Z**

Input dimension is 3 because it will combine Side-Quest Engagement, In-Game Purchases, and Guild Membership.

I use a simple univariate Z, but we could give it higher dimension with sufficient data.

The width of the hidden layer is 5.

```
class Encoder(nn.Module):
    def __init__(self, input_dim=3,
                 z_dim=1,
                 hidden_dim=5):
        super().__init__()
        self.f_hidden = nn.Linear(input_dim, hidden_dim)
        self.f_loc = nn.Linear(hidden_dim, z_dim)
        self.f_scale = nn.Linear(hidden_dim, z_dim)
        self.softplus = nn.Softplus()

    def forward(self, input):
        input = input.t()
        hidden = self.softplus(self.f_hidden(input))
        z_loc = self.f_loc(hidden)
        z_scale = 1e-6 + self.softplus(self.f_scale(hidden))
        return z_loc.t().squeeze(0), z_scale.t().squeeze(0)
```

Go from input to hidden layer.

Mapping from hidden layer to location parameter for Z

Mapping from hidden layer scale parameter to Z

---

Now, using the encoder, we build the overall guide function. In the following guide, we'll sample the parameters ρ_member, ρ_won_engaged, and ρ_won_not_engaged from beta distributions parameterized by constants set using `param`. These "hyperparameters" are optimized during training, alongside the weights of the neural networks.

---

**Listing 11.26   Build the guide function (approximating distribution)**

The guide samples ρ_member from a beta distribution where the shape parameters are trainable.

ρ_won_engaged and ρ_won_not_engaged are also sampled from beta distributions with trainable parameters.

```
from pyro import param
from torch.distributions.constraints import positive

encoder = Encoder().to(device)

def guide(data, device=device):
    pyro.module("encoder", encoder)
    α_member = param("α_member", tensor(1.0, device=device),
                     constraint=positive)
    β_member = param("β_member", tensor(1.0, device=device),
                     constraint=positive)
    sample('ρ_member', Beta(α_member, β_member))
    α_won_engaged = param("α_won_engaged", tensor(5.0, device=device),
                          constraint=positive)
    β_won_engaged = param("β_won_engaged", tensor(2.0, device=device),
                          constraint=positive)
    sample('ρ_won_engaged', Beta(α_won_engaged, β_won_engaged))
    α_won_not_engaged = param("α_won_not_engaged",
                              tensor(2.0, device=device),
                              constraint=positive)
```

```
β_won_not_engaged = param("β_won_not_engaged",
                     tensor(5.0, device=device),
                     constraint=positive)
beta_dist = Beta(α_won_not_engaged, β_won_not_engaged)
sample('ρ_won_not_engaged', beta_dist)
N = len(data["In-game Purchases"])
with pyro.plate("N", N):
    z_input = torch.stack(
        (data["Guild Membership"],
         data["Side-quest Engagement"],
         data["In-game Purchases"])
    ).to(device)
    z_loc, z_scale = encoder(z_input)
    pyro.sample("Z", Normal(z_loc, z_scale))
```

△ ρ_**won_engaged** and ρ_**won_not_engaged** are also sampled from beta distributions with trainable parameters.

**Z** is sampled from a normal with parameters returned by the encoder.

Finally, we set up the inference algorithm and run the training loop.

**Listing 11.27  Run the training loop**

```
from pyro.infer import SVI, Trace_ELBO
from pyro.optim import Adam
from pyro import condition

pyro.clear_param_store()
adam_params = {"lr": 0.0001, "betas": (0.90, 0.999)}
optimizer = Adam(adam_params)
training_model = condition(data_model, data)
svi = SVI(training_model, guide, optimizer, loss=Trace_ELBO())
elbo_values = []
N = len(data['In-game Purchases'])
for step in range(500_000):
    loss = svi.step(data) / N
    elbo_values.append(loss)
    if step % 500 == 0:
        print(loss)
```

Reset parameter values in case we restart the training loop.

Set up Adam optimizer. A learning rate ("lr") of 0.001 may work better if using CUDA.

Condition the data_model on the observed data.

Set up SVI.

Run the training loop.

We'll now plot the loss curve to see how training performed.

**Listing 11.28  Plot the losses during training**

```
import math
import matplotlib.pyplot as plt

plt.plot([math.log(item) for item in elbo_values])
plt.xlabel('Step')
plt.ylabel('Log-Loss')
plt.title('Log Training Loss')
plt.show()
```

Plot the log of training loss, since loss is initially large.

The losses shown in figure 11.19 indicate training has converged.

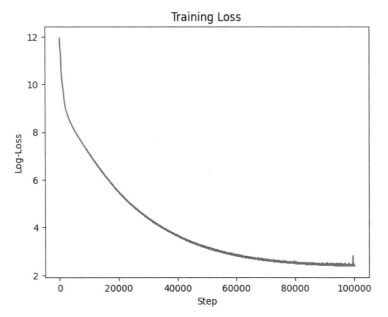

**Figure 11.19
Log of ELBO loss
during training**

We can print the trained values of the hyperparameters ($\alpha$_member, $\beta$_member, $\alpha$_won_engaged, $\beta$_won_engaged, $\alpha$_won_not_engaged, and $\beta$_won_not_engaged).

**Listing 11.29   Print the values of the trained parameters in the guide function**

```
print((
    pyro.param("α_member"),
    pyro.param("β_member"),
    pyro.param("α_won_engaged"),
    pyro.param("β_won_engaged"),
    pyro.param("α_won_not_engaged"),
    pyro.param("β_won_not_engaged")
))
```

This returned the following:

```
(tensor(1.3953, grad_fn=<AddBackward0>), tensor(1.3558,
    grad_fn=<AddBackward0>), tensor(4.3976, grad_fn=<AddBackward0>),
    tensor(3.1667, grad_fn=<AddBackward0>), tensor(0.8065,
    grad_fn=<AddBackward0>), tensor(10.8452, grad_fn=<AddBackward0>))
```

We'll approximate our posterior by sampling $\rho$_member, $\rho$_won_engaged, and $\rho$_won_not_engaged from beta distributions with these values, sampling $Z$ from a normal(0, 1), and then sampling the remaining causal variables based on these values.

### 11.6.6   *Posterior predictive inference of the ATE*

Given a sample of the parameters and a sample vector of $Z$ from the guide (our proxy for the posterior), we can simulate a new data set. A common way of checking how well a Bayesian model fits the data is to compare this simulated data with the original data. This comparison is called a *posterior predictive check*, and it helps us understand if the trained model is a good fit for the data. In the following code, we'll do a posterior predictive check of *In-Game Purchases*; we'll use the guide to generate samples and use those samples to repeatedly simulate *In-Game Purchase* datasets. For each simulated dataset, we'll create a density curve. We'll then plot these curves, along with the density curve of the *In-Game Purchases* in the original data.

---

**Listing 11.30   Posterior predictive check of *In-Game Purchases***

```
import matplotlib.pyplot as plt
import seaborn as sns
from pyro.infer import Predictive

predictive = Predictive(data_model, guide=guide, num_samples=1000)
predictive_samples_all = predictive(data)
predictive_samples = predictive_samples_all["In-game Purchases"]
for i, sample_data in enumerate(predictive_samples):
    if i == 0:
        sns.kdeplot(sample_data,
            color="lightgrey", label="Predictive density")
    else:
        sns.kdeplot(sample_data,
            color="lightgrey", linewidth=0.2, alpha=0.5)

sns.kdeplot(
    data['In-game Purchases'],
    color="black",
    linewidth=1,
    label="Empirical density"
)

plt.legend()
plt.title("Posterior Predictive Check of In-game Purchases")
plt.xlabel("Value")
plt.ylabel("Density")
plt.show()
```

> **Simulate data from the (approximate) posterior predictive distribution.**

> **For each batch of simulated data, create and plot a density curve of In-Game Purchases.**

> **Overlay the empirical density distribution of In-Game Purchases so we can compare it with the predictive plots.**

---

This produces a plot as in figure 11.20. The degree to which the simulated distribution matches the empirical distribution depends on the model, the size of the data, and how well the model is trained.

Our Bayesian estimator of the ATE will be our approach of applying transformation and inference to the posterior distribution represented by our model and guide. Since the ATE is $E(I_{E=1}) - E(I_{E=0})$, we'll do posterior predictive sampling from $P(I_{E=1})$ and $P(I_{E=0})$.

First, we'll use `pyro.do` to transform the model to represent the intervention. Then we'll do forward sampling from the model using the `Predictive` class. This will sample 1,000 simulated datasets, each equal in length to the original data, and each corresponding to a random sample of ρ_member, ρ_won_engaged, ρ_won_unengaged, and a data vector of $Z$ values. Objects from the `Predictive` class do simple forward

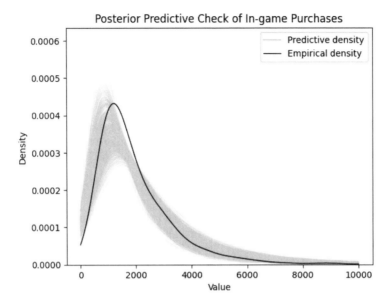

**Figure 11.20   Posterior predictive check of *In-Game Purchases*. Grey lines are density curves calculated on simulations from the posterior predictive distribution. The black line is the empirical density (density curves calculated on the data itself). More overlap indicates the model fits the data well.**

sampling. If we needed to condition on anything (e.g., conditioning on $E=1$ in $P(I_{E=0}|E=1)$), we'd need to use another inference approach (e.g., importance sampling, MCMC, etc.).

**Listing 11.31   Sampling from the posterior predictive distributions $P(I_{E=0})$ and $P(I_{E=1})$**

```
from pyro.infer import Predictive
from pyro import do

data_model_low_engagement = do(
    data_model, {"Side-quest Engagement": 0.})
predictive_low_engagement = Predictive(
    data_model_low_engagement, guide=guide, num_samples=1000)
predictive_low_engagement_samples = predictive_low_engagement(data)

data_model_high_engagement = do(
    data_model, {"Side-quest Engagement": 1.})
predictive_high_engagement = Predictive(
    data_model_high_engagement, guide=guide, num_samples=1000)
predictive_high_engagement_samples = predictive_high_engagement(data)
```

**Apply pyro.do transformation to implement intervention do(E=0).**

**Sample 1,000 samples of datasets from $P(I_{E=0})$.**

**Apply pyro.do transformation to implement intervention do(E=1).**

**Sample 1,000 samples of datasets from $P(I_{E=1})$.**

We can plot these two sets of posterior predictive samples as follows:

**Listing 11.32    Plot density curves of predictive datasets sampled from $P(I_{E=1})$ and $P(I_{E=0})$**

```
low_samples = predictive_low_engagement_samples["In-game Purchases"]
for i, sample_data in enumerate(low_samples):
    if i == 0:
        sns.kdeplot(sample_data,
            clip=(0, 35000), color="darkgrey", label="$P(I_{E=0})$")
    else:
        sns.kdeplot(sample_data,
            clip=(0, 35000), color="darkgrey",
            linewidth=0.2, alpha=0.5)

high_samples = predictive_high_engagement_samples["In-game Purchases"]
for i, sample_data in enumerate(high_samples):
    if i == 0:
        sns.kdeplot(sample_data,
            clip=(0, 35000), color="lightgrey", label="$P(I_{E=1})$")
    else:
        sns.kdeplot(sample_data,
            clip=(0, 35000), color="lightgrey",
            linewidth=0.2, alpha=0.5)
title = ("Posterior predictive sample density "
        "curves of $P(I_{E=1})$ & $P(I_{E=0})$")
plt.title(title)
plt.legend()
plt.xlabel("Value")
plt.ylabel("Density")
plt.ylim((0, .0010))
plt.xlim((0, 4000))
plt.show()
```

> For each sample, use kdeplot to draw a curve. Plot $P(I_{E=0})$ as dark grey and $P(I_{E=1})$ as light gray.

> Plot the density curves.

Whereas figure 11.20 plotted a predictive distribution on $P(I)$, figure 11.21 plots predictive density plots of $P(I_{E=0})$ and $P(I_{E=1})$. We can see that the distributions differ.

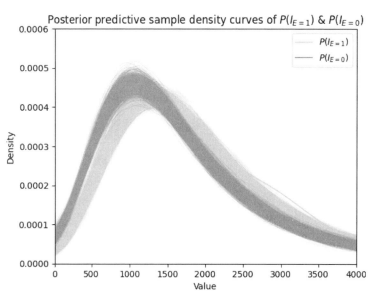

**Figure 11.21 Posterior predictive visualization of density curves calculated from simulated data from $P(I_{E=1})$ (light gray) and $P(I_{E=0})$ (dark gray)**

Finally, to estimate $E(I_{E=1})$ and $E(I_{E=0})$, we just need take the means of each posterior predictive sample dataset simulated from $P(I_{E=1})$ and $P(I_{E=1})$, respectively. This will yield 1,000 samples of posterior predictive values of the ATE. Variation between the samples reflects posterior uncertainty about the ATE.

**Listing 11.33 Estimate the ATE**

```
samp_high = predictive_high_engagement_samples['In-game Purchases']
exp_high = samp_high.mean(1)
samp_low = predictive_low_engagement_samples['In-game Purchases']
exp_low = samp_low.mean(1)
ate_distribution = exp_high - exp_low

sns.kdeplot(ate_distribution)
plt.title("Posterior distribution of the ATE")
plt.xlabel("Value")
plt.ylabel("Density")
plt.show()
```

**Estimate** $E(I_{E=1})$.
**Estimate** $E(I_{E=0})$.

Estimate the **ATE** $= E(I_{E=1}) - E(I_{E=0})$.

Use a density curve to visualize posterior variation in the ATE values.

This prints figure 11.22, a visualization of the posterior predictive distribution of the ATE.

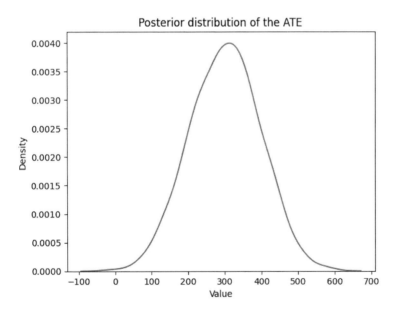

**Figure 11.22  Posterior predictive distribution of the ATE**

With a Bayesian approach, we get a posterior predictive distribution of the ATE. If we want a CATE, we can simply modify the posterior predictive inference to condition on other variables. If we want a point estimate of the ATE, we can take the mean of these predictive samples. More data reduces variance in the ATE distribution (assuming the ATE is identified) as in figure 11.23.

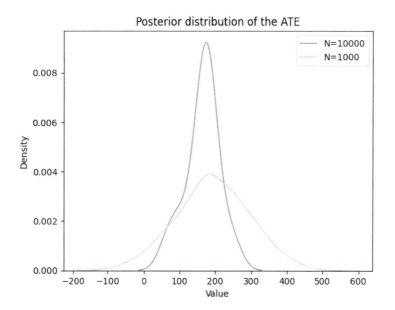

**Figure 11.23  Posterior uncertainty declines with more data.**

We can construct *credible intervals* (the Bayesian analog to confidence intervals) by taking percentiles from this distribution.

### 11.6.7  On the identifiability of the Bayesian causal generative inference

We got these results with a causal latent variable model, where $Z$ was the latent variable. We are no strangers to latent variable models in probabilistic machine learning, but are they safe for causal inference? For example, if we could do causal inference with this latent variable model, what is to stop us from using the model in figure 11.24?

We could train this model, apply the transformations, get samples from the posterior predictive distribution of the ATE, and get an answer. But we lack graphical identification in this case. Our answer would have confounder bias that we couldn't fix with more data, at least not without some strong, non-graphical assumptions (e.g., in the priors or in the functional relationships between variables).

Our model has graphical identification. In our case, we observed a mediator in *Won Items*, so we know we have a front-door estimand. Our causal generative model estimation procedure is just another estimator of that estimand.

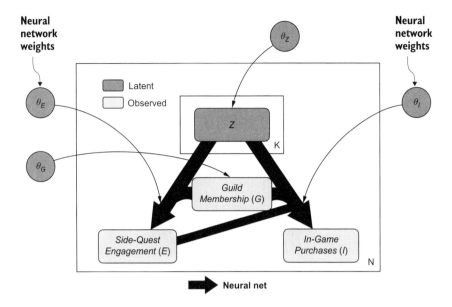

**Figure 11.24** The causal latent variable model with no mediator *W*, and thus no identification. If we had fit this model and used it to infer the ATE, we'd get a result. But without identification, we wouldn't be able to eliminate confounder bias, even with more data.

### 11.6.8 Closing thoughts on causal latent variable models

This approach of combining causal generative models with latent variables and deep learning is not limited to ATEs—it is general to all causal queries. We only need to select the right transformation for the query. This approach "commodifies inference" by relying on auto-differentiation tools to do the statistical and computational heavy lifting, instead of having to understand and implement different estimators like in DoWhy. It also scales to multidimensional causes, outcomes, and other variables in a way DoWhy does not. An additional advantage is that tools like Pyro and PyMC allow you to put Bayesian priors on the causal models themselves. Since the lack of causal identification boils down to model uncertainty, putting priors on models gives us an additional way of encoding domain assumptions that yield additional identification.

## Summary

- DoWhy provides a useful workflow for identifying and estimating causal effects.
- In step 1 of the causal inference workflow, we specify our target query. In this chapter, we focused on causal effects (ATEs and CATEs).
- In step 2 we specify our causal model. We specified a DAG in Graphviz DOT format and loaded it into a `CausalModel` in DoWhy.
- In step 3 we run identification. DoWhy identified backdoor, front-door, and instrumental variable estimands.

- Each estimand relies on a different set of causal assumptions. If you are more confident in the causal assumptions of one estimand than others, you should target that estimand.
- We targeted the backdoor estimand with linear regression, propensity score methods, and machine learning (ML) methods.
- The backdoor adjustment set is the set of backdoor variables we adjust for in the backdoor adjustment estimand. A valid adjustment set d-separates all backdoor paths. There could be more than one valid set.
- In step 4 we estimate our selected estimand. DoWhy makes it easy to try different estimators.
- Linear regression is a popular estimand because it is simple, familiar, and gives a point estimate of the ATE even for continuous causes.
- A propensity score is traditionally the probability a subject in the data is exposed to the treatment value of the binary cause (treatment) variable, conditional on the confounders in the adjustment set. It is often modeled using logistic regression.
- However, a propensity score can be any variable you construct that renders the treatment variable conditionally independent of the adjustment set.
- Propensity score methods include matching, stratification, and inverse probability weighting.
- ML methods targeting the backdoor estimand include double ML and meta learners. DoWhy provides a wrapper to EconML that implements several ML methods.
- Generally, ML methods are a good choice when you have larger datasets. They allow you to rely on fewer statistical assumptions. However, calculating confidence intervals on the estimates is computationally expensive.
- Instrumental variable estimation and front-door estimation don't rely on having a valid backdoor adjustment set, but they rely on different causal assumptions.
- In step 5, we run refutation analysis. Refutation is a sensitivity analysis that attempts to refute the causal and statistical assumptions we rely on in estimating our target query.
- Causal generative models combine model transformations, such as graph mutilation, node-splitting, and multi-world transforms, with probabilistic inference to do causal inference.
- This approach becomes an estimator of an identified estimand when the model parameters are learned from data.
- When there are latent variables, such as latent confounders, you can train the causal generative model as a latent variable model.
- The causal inference with the latent variable model will work if you have graphical identification. If not, you'll need to rely on other identifying assumptions.

# 12

# Causal decisions and reinforcement learning

---

**This chapter covers**

- Using causal models to automate decisions
- Setting up causal bandit algorithms
- How to incorporate causality into reinforcement learning

When we apply methods from statistics and machine learning, it is typically in service of making a decision or automating decision-making. Algorithms for automated decision-making, such as *bandit* and *reinforcement learning* (RL) algorithms, involve agents that *learn* how to make good decisions. In both cases, decision-making is fundamentally a causal problem: a decision to take some course of action leads to consequences, and the objective is to choose the action that leads to consequences favorable to the decision-maker. That motivates a causal framing.

Often, the path from action to consequences has a degree of randomness. For example, your choice of how to play a hand of poker may be optimal, but you still might lose due to chance. That motivates a probabilistic modeling approach.

The causal probabilistic modeling approach we've used so far in this book is a stone that hits both these birds. This chapter will provide a *causality-first* introduction to basic ideas in statistical decision theory, sequential decision-making, bandits, and RL. By "causality-first," I mean I'll use the foundation we've built in previous chapters to introduce these ideas in a causal light. I'll also present the ideas in a way that is compatible with our probabilistic ML framing. Even if you are already familiar with these decision-making and RL concepts, I encourage you to read on and see them again through a causal lens. Once we do that, we'll see cases where the causal approach to RL gets a better result than the noncausal approach.

## 12.1 A causal primer on decision theory

Decision theory is concerned with the reasoning underlying an agent's choice of some course of action. An "agent" here is an entity that chooses an action.

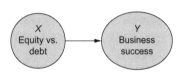

**Figure 12.1   A simple causal DAG where action X causes some outcome Y. Decision theory is a causal problem because if deciding on an action didn't have causal consequences, what would be the point of making decisions?**

For example, suppose you were deciding whether to invest in a company by purchasing equity or purchasing debt (i.e., loaning money to the company and receiving interest payments). We'll call this variable $X$. Whether the company is successful ($Y$) depends on the type of investment it receives.

Since $X$ causally drives $Y$, we can immediately introduce a causal DAG, as in figure 12.1.

We'll use this example to illustrate basic concepts in decision theory from a causal point of view.

### 12.1.1 Utility, reward, loss, and cost

The agent generally chooses actions that will cause them to gain some utility (or minimize some loss). In decision modeling, you can define a utility function (aka a reward function) that quantifies the desirability of various outcomes of a decision. Suppose you invest at $1,000:

- If the company becomes successful, you get $100,000. Your utility is 100,000 – 1,000 = $99,000.
- If the company fails, you get $0 and lose your investment. Your utility is –1,000.

We can add this utility as a node on the graph, as in figure 12.2.

Figure 12.2   A utility node can represent utility/reward, loss/cost.

Note that utility is a deterministic function of $Y$ in this model, which we'll denote $U(Y)$.

$$U(y) = \begin{cases} 99000; & y = \text{success} \\ -1000; & y = \text{failure} \end{cases}$$

Instead of a utility/reward function, we could define a loss function (aka, a cost function), which is simply –1 times the utility/reward function. For example, in the second scenario, where you purchase stock and the company fails, your utility is –$1,000 and your loss is $1,000.

While the agent's goal is to decide on a course of action that will maximize utility, doing so is challenging because there is typically some uncertainty in whether an action will lead to the desired result. In our example, it may seem obvious to invest in equity because equity will lead to business success, and business success will definitely lead to more utility. But there is some uncertainty in whether an equity investment will lead to business success. In other words we don't assume $P(Y=\text{success}|X=\text{equity}) = 1$. Both success and failure have nonzero probability in $P(Y|X=\text{equity})$.

### 12.1.2  Uncertainty comes from other causes

In causal terms, given action $X$, there is still some uncertainty in the outcome $Y$ because there are other causal factors driving that outcome. For example, suppose the success of the business depends on economic conditions, as in figure 12.3.

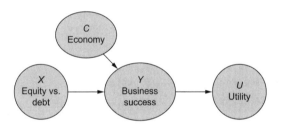

**Figure 12.3   We typically have uncertainty in our decision-making. From a causal perspective, uncertainty is because of other causal factors out of our control that affect variables downstream of our actions.**

Alternatively, those other causal factors could affect utility directly. For example, rather than the two discrete scenarios of profit or loss I outlined for our business investment, the amount of utility (or loss) could depend on how well or how poorly the economy fares, as in figure 12.4. We can leverage statistical and probability modeling to address this uncertainty.

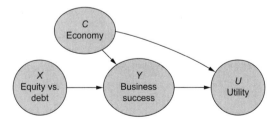

**Figure 12.4   Causal factors outside of our control can impact utility (or loss) directly.**

Suppose you are thinking about whether to invest in this business. You want your decision to be data-driven, so you research what other investors in this market have done before. You consider the causal DAG in figure 12.5.

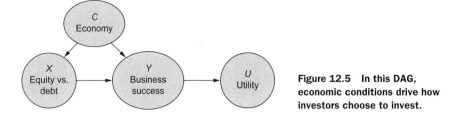

Figure 12.5   **In this DAG, economic conditions drive how investors choose to invest.**

Based on your research, you conclude that past investors' equity vs. debt choice also depends on the economic conditions. $P(X|C)$ represents an action distribution—the distribution of actions that the population of investors you are studying take.

However, the goal of your analysis centers on yourself, not other investors. You want to answer questions like "what if *I* bought equity?" That question puts us in causal territory. We are not reasoning about observational investment trends; we are reasoning about conditional hypotheticals. That is an indicator that we need to introduce intervention-based reasoning and counterfactual notation.

## 12.2    Causal decision theory

In this section, we'll highlight decision-making as a causal query and examine what that means for modeling decision-making.

### 12.2.1    Decisions as a level 2 query

A major source of confusion for causal decision modeling is the difference between actions and interventions. In many decision contexts, especially in RL, the action is a thing that the agent *does* that changes their environment. Yet, the action is also a variable *driven by* the environment. We see this when we look at the investment example, shown again in figure 12.6.

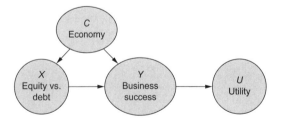

Figure 12.6   **In this version of the investment DAG, the choice of action is caused by external factors.**

The action of selecting equity or debt is a variable causally driven by the economy. What does that mean? Is an action a variable with causes, or is it an intervention?

The answer is *both*, depending on context. When it is which depends on the question we are asking and where that question sits in the causal hierarchy (discussed in chapter 10). When we are talking about what actions usually happen, such as when we are observing the actions of other agents (or even when reflecting on our own past actions) and what results those actions led to, we are reflecting on trends in population, and we are on level 1 of the causal hierarchy. In the case of our investment example, we're reasoning about $P(C, X, Y, U)$. But if we're asking questions like "what would happen if I made an equity investment?" then we're asking a level 2 question, and we need the proposed action as an intervention.

Next, we'll characterize common decision rules using our causal notation.

### 12.2.2 Causal characterization of decision rules and policies

A decision rule is a rule for choosing an action based on the utility distribution $P(U(Y_{X=x}))$. The agent chooses an optimal action according to a decision rule. For example, a common decision rule is choosing the action that minimizes loss or cost or maximizes utility or reward.

In automated decision-making, the decision rule is often called a "policy." In public health settings, decision rules are sometimes called "treatment regimes."

#### MAXIMIZING EXPECTED UTILITY

The most intuitive and commonly seen decision rule is to choose the action that maximizes expected utility. First, we can look at the expectation of the utility distribution. Since utility is a deterministic function of $Y_{X=x}$, this is just the expectation of $U(Y_{X=x})$ over the intervention distribution of $Y$.

$$E(U(Y_{X=x})) = \sum_y U(y)P(Y_{X=x} = y)$$

$$E(U(Y_{X=x})) = \int_y U(y)P(Y_{X=x} = y)dy \text{ (continuous case)}$$

We then choose the action (value of $x$) that maximizes expected utility:

$$\underset{x}{\operatorname{argmax}} E(U(Y_{X=x}))$$

In our investment example, this means choosing the investment approach that is expected to make you the most money.

#### MINIMAX DECISION RULES

To understand the minimax decision rule, recall that the terms "utility" and "loss" are two sides of the same coin; utility == negative loss. Let $L(y) = -U(y)$. Then a minimax decision rule is

$$\underset{x}{\operatorname{argmin}} \underset{Y_{X=x}}{\max} L(Y_{X=x})$$

In plain English, this means "choose the action that minimizes the maximum amount of possible loss." In our investment example, this means choosing the investment approach that will minimize the amount of money you'd lose in the worst case scenario. There are many variants of minimax rules, but they have the same flavor—minimizing loss or maximizing utility during bad times.

### SOFTMAX RULES

A softmax decision rule randomly selects an action with a probability proportional to the resulting utility.

Let's define $C(x)$ as the probability of choosing the action $x$. Then $C(x)$ is defined as a probability value proportional to

$$C(x) \propto e^{\alpha E(U(Y_{X=x}))}$$

The noise parameter $\alpha$ modulates between the two extremes. When $\alpha=0$, we have a uniform distribution on all the choices. As $\alpha$ gets larger, we approach maximizing expected utility.

Sometimes our goal is to model the decision-making of other agents, such as in inverse RL. The softmax decision rule is useful when agents don't always make the utility-optimizing choice. The softmax decision rule provides a simple, analytically tractable, and empirically validated model of suboptimal choice.

Another reason we might want to use the softmax rule is when there is a trade-off between *exploring* and *exploiting*, such as with bandit problems. Suppose the agent is uncertain about the shape of the distibution $P(Y_{X=x})$. The optimal action according to an incorrect model of $P(Y_{X=x})$ might be different from the optimal choice according to the correct model of $P(Y_{X=x})$. The softmax decision rule allows us to choose various actions, get some data on the results, and use that data to update our model of $P(Y_{X=x})$. When this is done in sequence, it's often called *Thompson sampling*.

In our investment analogy, suppose we were to invest in several businesses. Perhaps, according to our current model, equity investment maximizes expected utility, but we're not fully confident in our current model, so we opt to select debt investment even though the current model says its less optimal. The goal is to add diversity to our dataset, so that we can learn a better model.

### OTHER TYPES OF DECISION RULES

There are other types of decision rules, and they can become complicated, especially when they involve statistical estimation. For example, using *p*-values in statistical hypothesis testing involves a nuanced utility function that balances the chances of a false positive (incorrectly choosing the alternative hypothesis) and a false negative (incorrectly choosing the null hypothesis).

Fortunately, when we work with probabilistic causal models, the math tends to be easier, and we get a nice guarantee called *admissibility*.

### 12.2.3 *Causal probabilistic decision-modeling and admissibility*

In this section, I'll provide a short justification for choosing a causal probabilistic modeling approach to decision-making. When you implement an automated decision-making algorithm in a production setting, you might have to explain why your implementation is better than another. In that setting, it is useful if you know if your algorithm is *admissible*.

A decision rule is *admissible* if there are no other rules that dominate it. A decision rule dominates another rule if the performance of the former is sometimes better, and never worse, than that of the other rule with respect to the utility function. For example, the softmax decision rule is dominated by maximizing expected utility (assuming you know the true shape of $P(Y_{X=x})$) because sometimes it will select sub-optimal actions, and it is thus inadmissible. Determining *admissibility* is a key task in decision theory.

The challenge for us occurs when we use data and statistics to deal with unknowns, such as parameters or latent variables. If we want to use data to estimate a parameter or work with latent variables, there are usually a variety of statistical approaches to choose from. If our decision-making algorithm depends on a statistical procedure, the choice of procedure can influence which action is considered optimal. How do we know if our statistical decision-making procedure is admissible?

Probabilistic modeling libraries like Pyro leverage Bayesian inference to estimate parameters or impute latent variables. Bayesian decision theory tells us that *Bayes rules*, (not to be confused with Bayes's rule) decision rules that optimize posterior expected utility, have an admissibility guarantee under mild regularity conditions. This means that if we use Bayesian inference in Pyro or similar libraries to calculate and optimize posterior expected loss, we have an admissibility guarantee (if those mild conditions hold, and they usually do). That means you needn't worry that someone else's decision-making model (that makes the same modeling assumptions, has the same utility function, and uses the same data) will beat yours.

### 12.2.4 *The deceptive alignment of argmax values of causal and non-causal expectations*

Most conventional approaches to decision-making, including in RL, focus on maximizing $E(U(Y)|X=x)$ rather than $E(U(Y_{X=x}))$. Let's implement the model in figure 12.6 with pgmpy and compare the two approaches.

First, we'll build the DAG in the model.

> ### Setting up your environment
> This code was written with pgmpy version 0.1.24. See the chapter notes at www .altdeep.ai/causalAIbook for a link to the notebook that runs this code.

**Listing 12.1  DAG for investment decision model**

```
from pgmpy.models import BayesianNetwork
from pgmpy.factors.discrete import TabularCPD
from pgmpy.inference import VariableElimination
import numpy as np
```

```
model = BayesianNetwork([
    ('C', 'X'),
    ('C', 'Y'),                        Set up the DAG
    ('X', 'Y'),
    ('Y', 'U')
])
```

Next we'll build the causal Markov kernels for *Economy* (*C*), *Debt vs. Equity* (*X*), and *Business Success* (*Y*). The causal Markov kernel for *Economy* (*C*) will take two values: "bear" for bad economic conditions and "bull" for good. The causal Markov kernel for *Debt vs. Equity* (*X*) will depend on *C*, reflecting the fact that investors tend to prefer equity in a bull economy and debt in a bear economy. *Success* (*Y*) depends on the economy and the choice of debt or equity investment.

**Listing 12.2   Create causal Markov kernels for C, X, and Y**

```
cpd_c = TabularCPD(
    variable='C',                         Set up causal Markov kernel
    variable_card=2,                      for C (economy). It takes two
    values=[[0.5], [0.5]],                values: "bull" and "bear".
    state_names={'C': ['bear', 'bull']}
)

cpd_x = TabularCPD(                                          Set up causal
    variable='X',                                           Markov kernel for
    variable_card=2,                                        action X, either
    values=[[0.8, 0.2], [0.2, 0.8]],                        making a debt
    evidence=['C'],                                         investment or
    evidence_card=[2],                                      equity investment
    state_names={'X': ['debt', 'equity'], 'C': ['bear', 'bull']}   depending on the
)                                                           economy.

cpd_y = TabularCPD(
    variable='Y',                                            Set up causal Markov
    variable_card=2,                                         kernel for business
    values= [[0.3, 0.9, 0.7, 0.6], [0.7, 0.1, 0.3, 0.4]],   outcome Y, either
    evidence=['X', 'C'],                                     success or failure,
    evidence_card=[2, 2],                                    depending on the type of
    state_names={                                            investment provided (X)
        'Y': ['failure', 'success'],                         and the economy (C).
        'X': ['debt', 'equity'],
        'C': ['bear', 'bull']
    }
)
```

Finally, we'll add the *Utility* node (*U*). We use probabilities of 1 and 0 to represent a deterministic function of *Y*. We end by adding all the kernels to the model.

**Listing 12.3   Implement the utility node and initialize the model**

```
cpd_u = TabularCPD(
    variable='U',            Set up the utility node.
    variable_card=2,
```

```
    values=[[1., 0.], [0., 1.]],
    evidence=['Y'],
    evidence_card=[2],
    state_names={'U': [-1000, 99000], 'Y': ['failure', 'success']}
)
print(cpd_u)
model.add_cpds(cpd_c, cpd_x, cpd_y, cpd_u)
```

Set up the utility node.

This code prints out the following conditional probability tables for our causal Markov kernels. This one is for the *Utility* variable:

```
+-----------+------------+------------+
| Y         | Y(failure) | Y(success) |
+-----------+------------+------------+
| U(-1000)  | 1.0        | 0.0        |
+-----------+------------+------------+
| U(99000)  | 0.0        | 1.0        |
+-----------+------------+------------+
```

This reflects the investor trends of favoring equity investments in a bull market and debt investments in a bear market.

The following probability table is for the *Business Success* variable Y:

```
+------------+-----------+-----------+------------+------------+
| X          | X(debt)   | X(debt)   | X(equity)  | X(equity)  |
+------------+-----------+-----------+------------+------------+
| C          | C(bear)   | C(bull)   | C(bear)    | C(bull)    |
+------------+-----------+-----------+------------+------------+
| Y(failure) | 0.3       | 0.9       | 0.7        | 0.6        |
+------------+-----------+-----------+------------+------------+
| Y(success) | 0.7       | 0.1       | 0.3        | 0.4        |
+------------+-----------+-----------+------------+------------+
```

This reflects debt being a less preferred source of financing in a bear market when interest rate payments are higher, and equity being preferred in a bull market because equity is cheaper.

Finally, the *Utility* node is a simple deterministic function that maps Y to utility values:

```
+-----------+------------+------------+
| Y         | Y(failure) | Y(success) |
+-----------+------------+------------+
| U(-1000)  | 1.0        | 0.0        |
+-----------+------------+------------+
| U(99000)  | 0.0        | 1.0        |
+-----------+------------+------------+
```

Next, we'll calculate $E(U(Y_{X=x}))$ and $E(U(Y)|X=x)$. Before proceeding, download and load a helper function that implements an ideal intervention. To allay any security concerns of directly executing downloaded code, the code prints the downloaded script and prompts you to confirm before executing the script.

```
import requests

url = "https://raw.githubusercontent.com/altdeep/causalML/master/book/
    pgmpy_do.py"
response = requests.get(url)
content = response.text
```
**Load an implementation of an ideal intervention.**

```
print("Downloaded script content:\n")
print(content)
confirm = input("\nDo you want to execute this script? (yes/no): ")
if confirm.lower() == 'yes':
    exec(content)
else:
    print("Script execution cancelled.")
```
**To allay security concerns, you can inspect the downloaded script and confirm it before running.**

By now, in this book, you should not be surprised that $E(U(Y_{X=x}))$ is different from $E(U(Y)|X=x)$. Let's look at these values.

Listing 12.5   Calculate $E(U(Y)|X=x)$ and $E(U(Y_{X=x}))$

```
def get_expectation(marginal):
    u_values = marginal.state_names["U"]
    probs = marginal.values
    expectation = sum([x * p for x, p in zip(u_values, probs)])
    return expectation
```
**A helper function for calculating the expected utility**

```
infer = VariableElimination(model)
marginal_u_given_debt = infer.query(
    variables=['U'], evidence={'X': 'debt'})
marginal_u_given_equity = infer.query(
    variables=['U'], evidence={'X': 'equity'})
e_u_given_x_debt = get_expectation(marginal_u_given_debt)
e_u_given_x_equity = get_expectation(marginal_u_given_equity)
print("E(U(Y)|X=debt)=", e_u_given_x_debt)
print("E(U(Y)|X=equity)=", e_u_given_x_equity)
```
**Set X by intervention to debt and equity and calculate the expectation of U under each intervention.**

```
int_model_x_debt = do(model, {"X": "debt"})
infer_debt = VariableElimination(int_model_x_debt)
marginal_u_given_debt = infer_debt.query(variables=['U'])
expectation_u_given_debt = get_expectation(marginal_u_given_debt)
print("E(U(Y_{X=debt}))=", expectation_u_given_debt)
int_model_x_equity = do(model, {"X": "equity"})
infer_equity = VariableElimination(int_model_x_equity)
marginal_u_given_equity = infer_equity.query(variables=['U'])
expectation_u_given_equity = get_expectation(marginal_u_given_equity)
print("E(U(Y_{X=equity}))=", expectation_u_given_equity)
```
**Condition on X = debt and X = equity, and calculate the expectation of U.**

This gives us the following conditional expected utilities (I've marked the highest with *):

- $E(U(Y)|X=\text{debt}) = 57000$ *
- $E(U(Y)|X=\text{equity}) = 37000$

It also gives us the following interventional expected utilities:

- $E(U(Y_{X=\text{debt}})) = 39000$ *
- $E(U(Y_{X=\text{equity}})) = 34000$

So $E(U(Y)|X=\text{debt})$ is different from $E(U(Y_{X=\text{debt}}))$, and $E(U(Y)|X=\text{equity})$ is different from $E(U(Y_{X=\text{equity}}))$. However, our goal is to optimize expected utility, and in this case, debt maximizes both $E(U(Y)|X=\text{x})$ and $E(U(Y_{X=x}))$.

$$\underset{x}{\text{argmax}}\, E(U(Y_{X=x}))$$
$$= \underset{x}{\text{argmax}}\, E(U(Y|X=x))$$
$$= \text{``debt''}$$

If "debt" maximizes both queries, what is the point of causal decision theory? What does it matter if $E(U(Y)|X=x)$ and $E(U(Y_{X=x}))$ are different if the optimal action for both is the same?

In decision problems, it is quite common that a causal formulation of the problem provides the same answer as more traditional noncausal formulations. This is especially true in higher dimensional problems common in RL. You might observe this and wonder why the causal formulation is needed at all.

To answer, watch what happens when we make a slight change to the parameters of $Y$ in the model. Specifically, we'll change the parameter for $P(Y=\text{success}|X=\text{equity}, C=\text{bull})$ from .4 to .6. First, we'll rebuild the model with the parameter change.

---

**Listing 12.6   Change a parameter in the causal Markov kernel for Y**

```
model2 = BayesianNetwork([
    ('C', 'X'),              Initialize a
    ('C', 'Y'),              new model.
    ('X', 'Y'),
    ('Y', 'U')
])
                             Create a new conditional
                             probability distribution for Y.
cpd_y2 = TabularCPD(
    variable='Y',
    variable_card=2,
    values=[[0.3, 0.9, 0.7, 0.4],   [0.7, 0.1, 0.3, 0.6]],    Change the parameter
    evidence=['X', 'C'],                                      P(Y=success|X=equity,
    evidence_card=[2, 2],                                     C=bull) = 0.4 (the
    state_names={                                             last parameter in the
        'Y': ['failure', 'success'],                          first list) to 0.6.
        'X': ['debt', 'equity'],
        'C': ['bear', 'bull']
    }
)

model2.add_cpds(cpd_c, cpd_x, cpd_y2, cpd_u)    Add the causal Markov
                                                kernels to the model.
```

Next, we rerun inference.

**Listing 12.7   Compare outcomes with changed parameters**

```
infer = VariableElimination(model2)
marginal_u_given_debt = infer.query(variables=['U'],
    evidence={'X': 'debt'})
marginal_u_given_equity = infer.query(variables=['U'],
    evidence={'X': 'equity'})
e_u_given_x_debt = get_expectation(marginal_u_given_debt)
e_u_given_x_equity = get_expectation(marginal_u_given_equity)
print("E(U(Y)|X=debt)=", e_u_given_x_debt)
print("E(U(Y)|X=equity)=", e_u_given_x_equity)

int_model_x_debt = do(model2, {"X": "debt"})
infer_debt = VariableElimination(int_model_x_debt)
marginal_u_given_debt = infer_debt.query(variables=['U'])
expectation_u_given_debt = get_expectation(marginal_u_given_debt)
print("E(U(Y_{X=debt}))=", expectation_u_given_debt)
int_model_x_equity = do(model2, {"X": "equity"})
infer_equity = VariableElimination(int_model_x_equity)
marginal_u_given_equity = infer_equity.query(variables=['U'])
expectation_u_given_equity = get_expectation(marginal_u_given_equity)
print("E(U(Y_{X=equity}))=", expectation_u_given_equity)
```

Set X by intervention to debt and equity, and calculate the expectation of U under each intervention.

Condition on X = debt and X = equity, and calculate the expectation of U.

This gives us the following conditional expectations (* indicates the optimal choice):

- $E(U(Y)|X=\text{debt}) = 57000$ *
- $E(U(Y)|X=\text{equity}) = 53000$

It also gives us the following interventional expectations:

- $E(U(Y_{X=\text{debt}})) = 39000$
- $E(U(Y_{X=\text{equity}})) = 44000$ *

With that slight change in a single parameter, "debt" is still the optimal value of *x* in $E(U(Y)|X=x)$, but now "equity" is the optimal value of *x* in $E(U(Y_{X=x}))$. This is a case where the causal answer and the answer from conditioning on evidence are different. Since we are trying to answer a level 2 query, the causal approach is the right approach.

This means that while simply optimizing a conditional expectation often gets you the right answer, you are vulnerable to getting the wrong answer in certain circumstances. Compare this to our discussion of semi-supervised learning in chapter 4—often the unlabeled data can help with learning, but, in specific circumstances, the unlabeled data adds no value. Causal analysis helped us characterize those circumstances in precise terms. Similarly, in this case, there are specific scenarios where the causal formulation of the problem will lead to a different and more correct result relative to the traditional noncausal formulation. Even the most popular decision-optimization algorithms, including the deep learning-based approaches used in deep RL, can improve performance by leveraging the causal structure of a decision problem.

Next, we'll see another example with Newcomb's paradox.

### 12.2.5  Newcomb's paradox

A famous thought experiment called Newcomb's paradox contrasts the causal approach to decision theory, maximizing utility under intervention, with the conventional approach of maximizing utility conditional on some action. We'll look at an AI-inspired version of this thought experiment in this section, and the next section will show how to approach it with a formal causal model.

There are two boxes designated A and B as shown in figure 12.7. Box A always contains $1,000. Box B contains either $1,000,000 or $0. The decision-making agent must choose between taking only box B or *both* boxes. The agent does not know what is in box B until they decide. Given this information, it is obvious the agent should take both boxes—choosing both yields either $1,000 or $1,001,000, while choosing only B yields either $0 or $1,000,000.

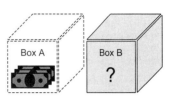

**Figure 12.7   An illustration of the boxes in Newcomb's paradox**

Now, suppose there is an AI that can predict with high accuracy what choice the agent intends to make. If the AI predicts that the agent intends to take both boxes, it will put no money in box B. If the AI is correct and the agent takes both boxes, the agent only gets $1,000. However, if the AI predicts that the agent intends to take only box B, it will put $1,000,000 in box B. If the AI predicts correctly, the agent gets the $1,000,000 in box B but not the $1,000 in box A. The agent does not know for sure what the AI predicted or what box B contains until they make their choice.

The traditional paradox arises as follows. A causality-minded agent reasons that the actions of the AI are out of their control. They only focus on what they can control—the causal consequences of their choice. They can't *cause* the content of box B, so they pick both boxes on the off-chance box B has the million, just as one would if the AI didn't exist. But if the agent knows how the AI works, doesn't it make more sense to choose only box B and get the million with certainty?

Let's dig in further by enumerating the possible outcomes and their probabilities. Let's assume the AI's predictions are 95% accurate. If the agent chooses both boxes, there is a 95% chance the AI will have guessed the agent's choice and put no money in B, in which case the agent only gets the $1,000. There is a 5% chance the algorithm will guess wrong, in which case it puts 1,000,000 in box B, and the agent wins $1,001,000. If the agent chooses only box B, there is a 95% chance the AI will have predicted the choice and placed $1,000,000 in box B, giving the agent $1,000,000 in winnings. There is a 5% chance it will not, and the agent will take home nothing. We see these outcomes in table 12.1. The expected utility calculations are shown in table 12.2.

**Table 12.1   Newcomb's problem outcomes and their probabilities**

| Strategy | AI action | Winnings | Probability |
|---|---|---|---|
| Choose both | Put $0 in box B | $1,000 | .95 |
| Choose both | Put $1,000,000 in box B | $1,001,000 | .05 |

**Table 12.1   Newcomb's problem outcomes and their probabilities *(continued)***

| Strategy | AI action | Winnings | Probability |
|---|---|---|---|
| Choose only box B | Put $1,000,000 in box B | $1,000,000 | .95 |
| Choose only box B | Put $0 in box B | $0 | .05 |

**Table 12.2   Expected utility of each choice in Newcomb's problem**

| Strategy (*X*) | *E*(*U*\|*X*=*x*) |
|---|---|
| Choose both | 1,000 × .95 + 1,001,000 × .05 = $51,000 |
| Choose only box B | 1,000,000 × .05 + 0 × .05 = $950,000 |

The conventional approach suggests choosing box only box B.

When the paradox was created, taking a causal approach to the problem meant only attending to the causal consequences of one's actions. Remember that the AI makes the prediction *before* the agent acts. Since effects cannot precede causes in time, the AI's behavior is not a consequence of the agent's actions, so the agent with the causal view ignores the AI and goes with the original strategy of choosing both boxes.

It would seem that the agent with the causal view is making an error in failing to account for the actions of the AI. But we can resolve this error by having the agent use a formal causal model.

### 12.2.6  *Newcomb's paradox with a causal model*

In the traditional formulation of Newcomb's paradox, the assumption is that the agent using causal decision theory only attends to the consequences of their actions— they are reasoning on the causal DAG in figure 12.8. But the true data generating process (DGP) is better captured by figure 12.9.

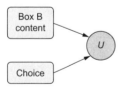

**Figure 12.8   Newcomb's paradox assumes a version of causal decision theory where a naive agent uses this incorrect causal DAG.**

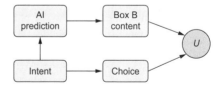

**Figure 12.9   A better causal DAG representing the framing of Newcomb's paradox**

The choice of the agent can't *cause* the AI's prediction, because the prediction happens first. Thus, we assume the AI agent is inferring the agent's *intent*, and thus the intent of the agent is the cause of the AI's prediction.

The causal decision-making agent would prefer the graph in figure 12.9 because it is a better representation of the DGP. The clever agent wouldn't focus on maximizing $E(U_{choice=x})$. The clever agent is aware of its own intention, and knowing that this intention is a cause of the content of box B, it focuses on optimizing $E(U_{choice=x}|intent=i)$, where $i$ is their original intention of which box to pick.

$$\operatorname*{argmax}_x E(U_{\text{choice}=x}|\text{intent} = i)$$

We'll assume the agent's initial intention is an impulse it cannot control. But while they can't control their initial intent, they can do some introspection and become aware of this intent. Further, we'll assume that upon doing so, they have the ability to change their choice to something different from what it initially intended, after the AI has made their prediction and set the contents of box B. Let's model this system in pgmpy and evaluate maximizing $E(U_{choice=x}|intent=i)$.

First, let's build the DAG.

**Listing 12.8   Create the DAG**

```
model = BayesianNetwork(
    [
        ('intent', 'AI prediction'),
        ('intent', 'choice'),
        ('AI prediction', 'box B'),
        ('choice', 'U'),
        ('box B', 'U'),
    ]
)
```

Next, we'll create causal Markov kernels for intent and choice.

**Listing 12.9   Create causal Markov kernels for intent and choice**

```
cpd_intent = TabularCPD(
    'intent', 2, [[0.5], [0.5]],
    state_names={'intent': ['B', 'both']}
)
print(cpd_intent)
```

We assume a 50-50 chance the agent will prefer both boxes vs. box B.

```
cpd_choice = TabularCPD(
    'choice', 2, [[1, 0], [0, 1]],
    evidence=['intent'],
    evidence_card=[2],
    state_names={
        'choice': ['B', 'both'],
        'intent': ['B', 'both']
    }
)
print(cpd_choice)
```

We assume the agent's choice is deterministically driven by their intent.

Similarly, we'll create the causal Markov kernels for the AI's decision and the content of box B.

Listing 12.10    Create causal Markov kernels for AI prediction and box B content

```
cpd_AI = TabularCPD(
    'AI prediction', 2, [[.95, 0.05], [.05, .95]],
    evidence=['intent'],
    evidence_card=[2],
    state_names={
        'AI prediction': ['B', 'both'],
        'intent': ['B', 'both']
    }
)
print(cpd_AI)
```

The AI's prediction is 95% accurate.

```
cpd_box_b_content = TabularCPD(
    'box B', 2, [[0, 1], [1, 0]],
    evidence=['AI prediction'],
    evidence_card=[2],
    state_names={
        'box B': [0, 1000000],
        'AI prediction': ['B', 'both']
    }
)
print(cpd_box_b_content)
```

Box B contents are set deterministically by the AI's prediction.

Finally, we'll create a causal Markov kernel for utility and add all the kernels to the model.

Listing 12.11    Create utility kernel and build the model

```
cpd_u = TabularCPD(
    'U', 4,
    [
        [1, 0, 0, 0],
        [0, 1, 0, 0],
        [0, 0, 1, 0],
        [0, 0, 0, 1],
    ],
    evidence=['box B', 'choice'],
    evidence_card=[2, 2],
    state_names={
        'U': [0, 1000, 1000000, 1001000],
        'box B': [0, 1000000],
        'choice': ['B', 'both']
    }
)
print(cpd_u)

model.add_cpds(cpd_intent, cpd_choice, cpd_AI, cpd_box_b_content, cpd_u)
```

Set up the utility node.

Build the model.

Now we'll evaluate maximizing $E(U_{choice=x}|intent=i)$.

**Listing 12.12   Infer optimal choice using intervention and conditioning on intent**

```
int_model_x_both = do(model, {"choice": "both"})
infer_both = VariableElimination(int_model_x_both)                    Infer
marginal_u_given_both = infer_both.query(               E(U(Y_choice=both|intent=both)).
    variables=['U'], evidence={'intent': 'both'})
expectation_u_given_both = get_expectation(marginal_u_given_both)
print("E(U(Y_{choice=both}|intent=both))=", expectation_u_given_both)
int_model_x_box_B = do(model, {"choice": "B"})
infer_box_B = VariableElimination(int_model_x_box_B)                  Infer
marginal_u_given_box_B = infer_box_B.query(             E(U(Y_choice=box B|intent=both)).
    variables=['U'], evidence={'intent': 'both'})
expectation_u_given_box_B = get_expectation(marginal_u_given_box_B)
print("E(U(Y_{choice=box B}|intent=both))=", expectation_u_given_box_B)
int_model_x_both = do(model, {"choice": "both"})
infer_both = VariableElimination(int_model_x_both)                    Infer
marginal_u_given_both = infer_both.query(               E(U(Y_choice=both|intent=B)).
    variables=['U'], evidence={'intent': 'B'})
expectation_u_given_both = get_expectation(marginal_u_given_both)
print("E(U(Y_{choice=both}|intent=B))=", expectation_u_given_both)
int_model_x_box_B = do(model, {"choice": "B"})
infer_box_B = VariableElimination(int_model_x_box_B)                  Infer
marginal_u_given_box_B = infer_box_B.query(             E(U(Y_choice=box B|intent=B)).
    variables=['U'], evidence={'intent': 'B'})
expectation_u_given_box_B = get_expectation(marginal_u_given_box_B)
print("E(U(Y_{choice=box B}|intent=B))=", expectation_u_given_box_B)
```

This code produces the following results (* indicates the optimal choice for a given intent):

- $E(U(Y_{choice=both}|intent=both)) = 51000$ *
- $E(U(Y_{choice=box\ B}|intent=both)) = 50000$
- $E(U(Y_{choice=both}|intent=B)) = 951000$ *
- $E(U(Y_{choice=box\ B}|intent=B)) = 950000$

When the agent's initial intention is to select both, the best choice is to select both. When the agent intends to choose only box B, the best choice is to ignore those intentions and choose both. Either way, the agent should choose both. Note that when the agent initially intends to choose only box B, switching to both boxes gives them an expected utility of \$951,000 which is greater than the optimal choice utility of \$950,000 in the noncausal approach.

The agent, unfortunately, cannot control their initial intent; if they could, they would deliberately 'intend' to pick box B and then switch at the last minute to choosing both boxes after the AI placed the million in box B. However, they can engage in a form of introspection, factoring their initial intent into their decision and, in so doing, accounting for the AI's behavior rather than ignoring it.

### 12.2.7  *Introspection in causal decision theory*

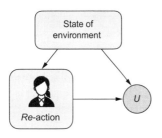

**Figure 12.10   Often our actions are simply reactions to our environment, rather than the result of deliberate decision-making.**

Newcomb's problem illustrates a key capability of causal decision theory—the ability for us to include introspection as part of the DGP.

To illustrate, consider that often our actions are simply *reactions* to our environment, as in figure 12.10.

For example, you might have purchased a chocolate bar *because* you were hungry and it was positioned to tempt you as you waited in the checkout aisle of the grocery store. Rather than go through some deliberative decision-making process, you had a simple, perhaps even unconscious, *reaction* to your craving and an easy way to satisfy it.

However, humans are capable of introspection—observing and thinking about their internal states. A human might consider their normal reactive behavior as part of the DGP. This introspection is illustrated in figure 12.11.

**Figure 12.11   Humans and some other agents can think about a DGP that includes them as a component of that process.**

Through this introspection, the agent can perform level 2 hierarchical reasoning about what would happen if they did not react as usual but acted deliberately (e.g., sticking to their diet and not buying the chocolate bar), as in figure 12.12.

In many cases, the agent may not know the full state of their environment. However, if the agent can disentangle their urge to react a certain way from their action, they can use that "urge" as evidence in deliberative decision-making, as in figure 12.13.

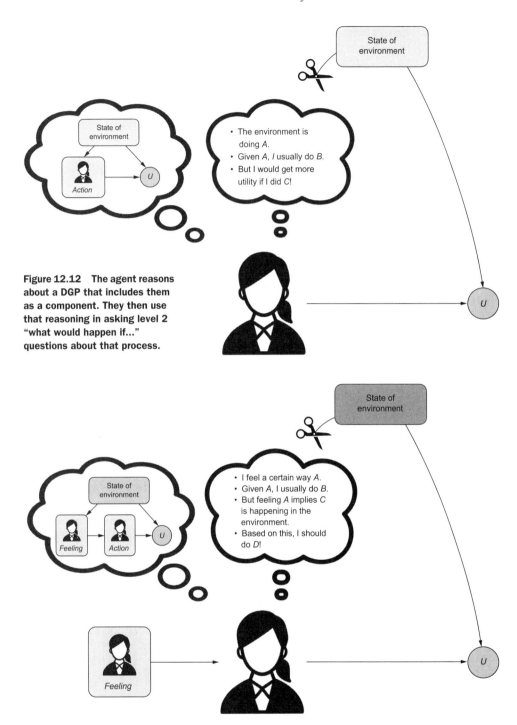

**Figure 12.12   The agent reasons about a DGP that includes them as a component. They then use that reasoning in asking level 2 "what would happen if..." questions about that process.**

**Figure 12.13   The agent may not know the states of other variables in the environment, but through introspection, they may have an intuition about those variables. That intuition can be used as evidence in conditional causal inferences.**

We saw this pattern in the Newcomb example; the agent does not know what the AI has predicted, but, through introspection, they can use their initial intention to choose both boxes as *evidence* of what the AI has chosen.

Was there ever a time where you noticed you had started to make clumsy errors in your work and used that as evidence that you were fatigued, even though you didn't feel so, and you thought, "what if I take a break?" Have you had a gut feeling that something was off, despite not knowing what, and based on this feeling started to make different decisions? Causal modeling, particularly with causal generative models, make it easy to write algorithms that capture this type of self-introspection in decision-making.

Next, we'll look at causal modeling of sequential decision-making.

## 12.3   *Causal DAGs and sequential decisions*

Sequential decision processes are processes of back-to-back decision-making. These processes can involve sequential decisions made by humans or by algorithms and engineered agents.

When I model decision processes in sequence, I use a subscript to indicate a discrete step in the series, such as $Y_1$, $Y_2$, $Y_3$. When I want to indicate an intervention subscript, I'll place it to the right of the time-step subscript, as in $Y_{1,X=x}$, $Y_{2,X=x}$, $Y_{3,X=x}$.

In this section, I'll show causal DAGs for several canonical sequential decision-making processes, but you should view these as templates, not as fixed structures. You can add or remove edges in whatever way you deem appropriate for a given problem.

Let's look at the simplest case, bandit feedback.

### 12.3.1   *Bandit feedback*

*Bandit feedback* refers to cases where, at each step in the sequence, there is an act $X$ that leads to an outcome $Y$, with some utility $U(Y)$. A bandit sequence has two key features. The first is that, at every step, there is instant feedback after an act occurs. The second is independent trials, meaning that the variables at the $t^{\text{th}}$ timestep are independent of variables at other timesteps. The term "bandit" comes from an analogy to "one-armed bandits," which is a slang term for casino slot machines that traditionally have an arm that the player pulls to initiate gameplay. Slot machine gameplay provides bandit feedback—you deposit a token, pull the arm, and instantly find out if you win or lose. That outcome is independent of previous plays.

We can capture bandit feedback with the causal DAG in figure 12.14.

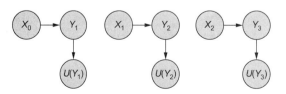

Figure 12.14   A causal DAG illustrating simple bandit feedback

The causal DAG in figure 12.14 captures instant feedback with a utility node at each timestep, and with a lack of edges, reflecting an independence of variables across timesteps.

### 12.3.2 Contextual bandit feedback

In contextual bandit feedback, one or more variables are common causes for both the act and the outcome. In figure 12.15, the context variable $C$ is common to each $\{X, Y\}$ tuple in the sequence. In this case, the context variable $C$ could represent the profile of a particular individual, and the act variable $X$ is that user's behavior.

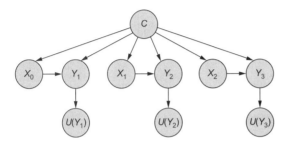

**Figure 12.15   A causal DAG illustrating contextual bandit feedback**

Alternatively, the context variable could change at each step, as in figure 12.16.

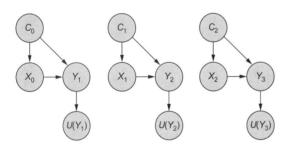

**Figure 12.16   A causal DAG illustrating contextual bandit feedback where the context changes at each timestep**

We can vary this template in different ways. For example, we could have the actions drive the context variables in the next timestep, as in figure 12.17. The choice depends on your specific problem.

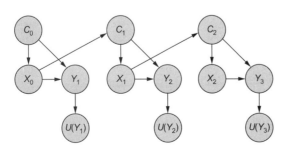

**Figure 12.17   A causal DAG where the action at one timestep influences the context at the next timestep**

### 12.3.3  *Delayed feedback*

In a delayed-feedback setting, the outcome variable and corresponding utility are no longer instant feedback. Instead, they come at the end of a sequence. Let's consider

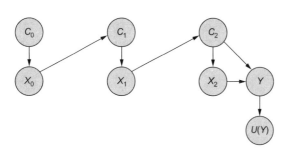

an example where a context variable drives the acts. The acts affect the next instance of the context variable.

Again, figure 12.18 shows an example of this approach based on the previous model. Here the act at time $k$ influences the context variable ($C$) at time $k + 1$, which in turn affects the act at time $k + 1$.

**Figure 12.18   Example of a causal DAG for sequential decision making with delayed feedback**

Consider a case of chronic pain. Here the context variable represents whether a subject is experiencing pain ($C$). The presence of pain drives the act of taking a painkiller ($X$). Taking the painkiller (or not) affects whether there is pain in the next step. Figure 12.19 illustrates this DAG.

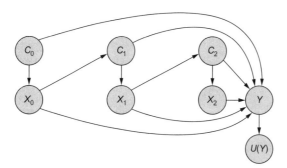

**Figure 12.19   A causal DAG representing the treatment of chronic pain**

$Y$ here is the ultimate health outcome of the subject, and it is driven both by the overall amount of pain over time, and the amount of drugs the subject took (because perhaps overuse of painkillers has a detrimental health effect).

### 12.3.4  *Causal queries on a sequential model*

We may want to calculate some causal query for our sequential decision problem. For example, given the DAG in figure 12.19, we might want to calculate the causal effect of $X_0$ on $U(Y)$:

$$E\left(U(Y_{X_0=x}) - U(Y_{X_0=x'})\right)$$

Or perhaps we might be interested in the causal effect of the full sequence of acts on $U(Y)$:

$$E\left(U\left(Y_{X_0=a,X_1=b,X_2=c}\right) - U\left(Y_{X_0=a',X_1=b',X_2=c'}\right)\right)$$

Either way, now that we have framed the sequential problem as a causal model, we are in familiar territory; we can simply use the causal inference tools we've learned in previous chapters to answer causal queries with this model.

As usual, we must be attentive to the possibility of latent causes that can confound our causal inference. In the case of causal effects, our concern is latent common confounding causes between acts $(X)$ and outcomes $(Y)$, or alternatively between acts $(X)$ and utilities $(U)$. Figure 12.20 is the same as figure 12.15, except it introduces a latent $Z$ confounder.

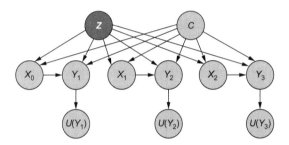

**Figure 12.20   Contextual bandit with a latent confounder**

Similarly, we could have a unique confounder at every timestep, as in figure 12.21.

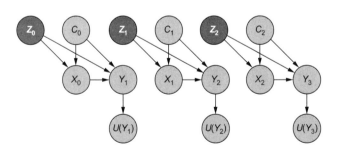

**Figure 12.21   Bandit feedback with a different context and latent confounders at each timestep**

Similarly, figure 12.22 shows a second version of the chronic pain graph where the confounders affect each other and the context variables. This confounder could be some external factor in the subject's environment that triggers the pain and affects well-being.

These confounders become an issue when we want to infer the causal effect of a sequence of actions on $U(Y)$.

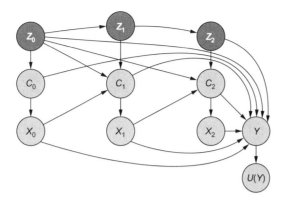

**Figure 12.22    A version of the chronic pain DAG where the confounders affect each other and the context variables**

Next, we'll look at how we can view policies for automatic decision making in sequential decision-making processes as stochastic interventions.

## 12.4    *Policies as stochastic interventions*

In automated sequential decision-making, the term "policy" is preferred to "decision rule." I'll introduce a special notation for a policy: $\pi(.)$. It will be a function that takes in observed outcomes of other variables and returns an action.

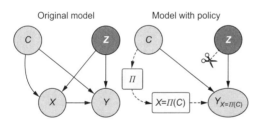

**Figure 12.23    The dashed lines show edges modulated by the policy. The policy breaks the influence of the confounder *Z* like an ideal intervention, but dependence on *C* remains through the policy.**

To consider how a policy affects the model, we'll contrast the DAG before and after a policy is implemented. Figure 12.23 illustrates a simple example with a context variable $C$ and a latent variable $Z$. The policy uses context $C$ to select a value of $X$.

The policy is a type of stochastic intervention; it selects a intervention value for $X$ from some process that depends on $C$. Like an ideal intervention, it changes the graph. The left of figure 12.23 shows the DAG prior to deployment of the policy. On the right is the DAG after the policy is deployed. I add a special policy node to the graph to illustrate how the policy modulates the graph. The dashed edges highlight edges modulated by the policy. Just like an ideal intervention, the policy-generated intervention removes $X$'s original incoming edges $C{\to}X$ and $Z{\to}X$. However, because the policy depends on $C$, the dashed edges illustrate the new flow of influence from $C$ to $X$.

Suppose we are interested in what value $Y$ would have for a policy-selected action $X=\Pi$. In counterfactual notation, we write

$$P(Y_{X=\Pi(C)})$$

In sequence settings, the policy applies a stochastic intervention at multiple steps in the sequence. From a possible worlds perspective, each intervention induces a new hypothetical world. This can stretch the counterfactual notation a bit, so going forward, I'll simplify the counterfactual notation to look like this:

$$Y_{3,\pi_0,\pi_1,\pi_2}$$

This means $Y_3$ ($Y$ at timestep 3) is under influence of the policy's outcomes at times 0, 1, and 2.

### 12.4.1   Examples in sequential decision-making

In the case of bandit feedback, the actions are produced by a *bandit algorithm*, which is a type of policy that incorporates the entire history of actions and utility outcomes in deciding the optimal current action. Though actions and outcomes in the bandit feedback process are independent at each time step, the policy introduces dependence on past actions and outcomes, as shown in figure 12.24.

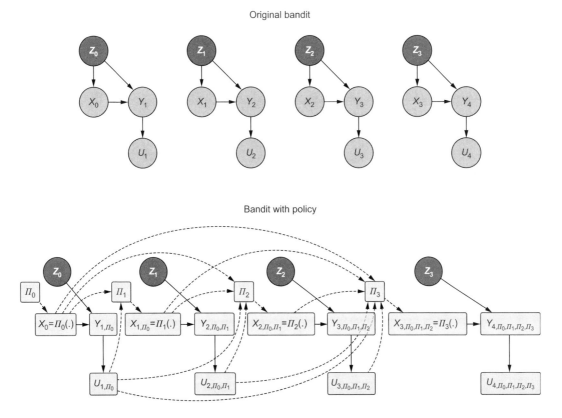

**Figure 12.24   Bandit feedback where a bandit policy algorithm selects the next action based on past actions and reward outcomes**

Recall our previous example of an agent taking pain medication in response to the onset of pain. Figure 12.25 shows how a policy would take in the history of degree of pain and how much medication was provided.

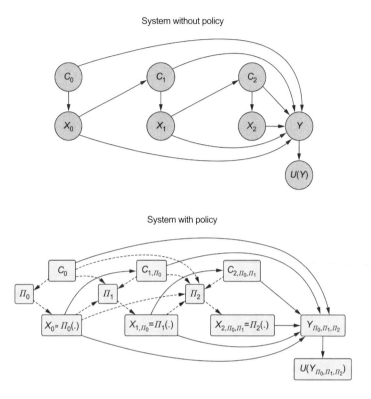

**Figure 12.25   In the pain example, the policy considers the history of recorded levels of pain and corresponding dosages of medication.**

The policy is like a doctor making the rounds on a hospital floor. They come to a patient's bed, and the patient reports some level of pain. The doctor looks at that patient's history of pain reports and the subsequent dosages of medication and uses that information to decide what dosage to provide this time. The doctor's utility function is in terms of pain, risk of overdose, and risk of addiction. They need to consider historic data, not just the current level of pain, to optimize this utility function.

### 12.4.2  *How policies can introduce confounding*

As stochastic interventions, policies introduce interventions conditional on other nodes in the graph. Because of this, there is a possibility that the policy will introduce new backdoor paths that can confound causal inferences. For example, consider again the DAG in figure 12.26.

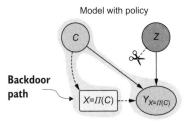

Model with policy

Backdoor path

**Figure 12.26   The policy eliminates the backdoor path through Z but not the backdoor path through C.**

The policy breaks the backdoor path from $X$ to $Y$ through $Z$, but there is still a path from $X$ to $Y$ through $C$. Thus, typical causal queries involving $X$ and $Y$ would have to condition on or adjust for $C$.

In the next section, we'll characterize causal RL in causal terms.

## 12.5    *Causal reinforcement learning*

Reinforcement learning (RL) is a branch of machine learning that generally involves an agent learning policies that maximize cumulative reward (utility). The agent learns from the consequences of its actions, rather than from being explicitly taught, and adjusts its behavior based on the rewards or losses (reinforcements) it receives. Many sequential decision-making problems can be cast as RL problems.

### 12.5.1   *Connecting causality and Markov decision processes*

RL typically casts a decision process as a Markov decision process (MDP). A canonical toy example of an MDP is a grid world, illustrated in figure 12.27.

Figure 12.27 presents a $3 \times 4$ grid world. An agent can act within this grid world with a fixed set of actions, moving up, down, left, and right. The agent wants to execute a set of actions that deliver it to the upper-right corner {0, 3}, where it gains a reward of 100. The agent wants to avoid the middle-right square {1, 3}, where it has a reward of –100 (a *loss* of 100). Position {1, 1} contains an obstacle the agent cannot traverse.

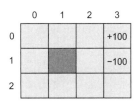

**Figure 12.27   A simple grid world**

We can think of it as a game. When the game starts, the agent "spawns" randomly in one of the squares, except for {0, 3}, {1, 3}, and {1, 1}. When the agent moves into a goal square, the game ends. To win, the agent must navigate around the obstacle in {1, 1}, avoid {1, 3}, and reach {0, 3}.

A Markov decision process models this and much more complicated "worlds" (aka domains, problems, etc.) with abstractions for states, actions, transition functions, and rewards.

#### STATES

States are a set that represents the current situation or context that the agent is in, within its environment. In the grid-world example, a state represents the agent being at a specific cell. In this grid, there are 12 different states (the cell at {1, 1} is an unreachable state). We assume the agent has some way of knowing which state they are in.

We'll denote state as a variable $S$. In a grid world, $S$ is a discrete variable, but in other problems, $S$ could be continuous.

## ACTIONS

Actions are the things the agent can do, and they lead to a change of state. Some actions might not be available when in a particular state. For example, in the grid world, the borders of the grid are constraints on the movements of the agent. If the agent is in the bottom-left square {2, 0}, and they try to move left or down, they will stay in place. Similarly, the cell at {1, 1} is an obstacle the agent must navigate around. We denote actions with the variable $A$, which has four possible outcomes {up, down, right, left}.

## TRANSITION FUNCTION

The transition function is a probability distribution function. It tells us the probability of moving to a specific next state, given the current state and the action taken.

If states are discrete, the transition function looks like this:

$$P(S_{t+1} = s' \mid S_t = s, A_t = a)$$

Here, $S_t = s$ means the agent is currently in state $s$. $A_t = a$ means the agent performs action $a$. $P(S_{t+1} = s' \mid S_t = s, A_t = a)$ is the probability that the agent transitions to a new state s' given it is in state s and performs action $a$. When the action leads to a new state with complete certainty, this probability distribution function becomes degenerate (all probability is concentrated on one value).

## REWARDS

The term "reward" is preferred to "utility" in RL. In the context of MDPs, the reward function will always take a state $s$ as an argument. We will write it as $U(s)$.

In the grid-world example, $U(\{0, 3\}) = 100$, $U(\{1, 3\}) = -100$. The reward of all other states is 0. Note that sometimes in the MDP/RL literature, $U()$ is a function of state and an action, as in $U(s, a)$. We don't lose anything by just having actions be a function of state because you can always fold actions into the definition of a state.

### 12.5.2 *The MDP as a causal DAG*

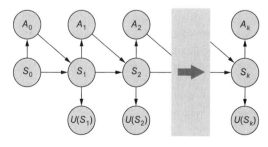

**Figure 12.28   The Markov decision process represented as a DAG**

Figure 12.28 shows the MDP as a causal DAG.

As a causal DAG, the MDP looks like the other sequential decision processes we've outlined, except that we limit ourselves to states, actions, and rewards. In figure 12.28, the process continues until we reach a terminal state ($S_k$), such as getting to the terminal cells in the grid-world example.

### THE CAUSAL MARKOV PROPERTY AND THE MDP

The "Markov" in "Markov decision process" comes from the fact that the current state is independent of the full history of states given the last state. Contrast this with the causal Markov property of causal DAGs: a node in the DAG is independent of indirect "ancestor" causes given its direct causal parents. We can see that when we view the MDP as a causal DAG, this Markovian assumption is equivalent to the causal Markov property. That means we can use our d-separation-based causal reasoning, including the do-calculus, in the MDP graphical setting.

### THE TRANSITION FUNCTION AND THE CAUSAL MARKOV KERNEL

Note that based on this DAG, the parents of a state $S_{(t+1)}$ are the previous state $S_t$ and the action $A_t$ taken when in that previous state. Therefore, the causal Markov kernel is $P(S_{t+1}=s'|S_t=s, A_t=a)$, i.e., the transition function. Thus, the transition function is the causal Markov kernel for a given state.

## 12.5.3  *Partially observable MDPs*

An extension of MDPs is *partially observed MDPs* (POMDPs). In a POMDP, the agent doesn't know with certainty what state they are in, and they must make inferences about that state given incomplete evidence from their environment. This applies to many practical problems where the agent cannot observe the full state of the environment.

A POMDP can entail different causal structures depending on our assumptions about the causal relationships between the unobserved and observed states. For example, suppose a latent state $S$ is a cause of the observed state $X$. The observed state $X$ now drives the act $A$ instead of $S$. Figure 12.29 illustrates this formulation of a POMDP as a causal DAG.

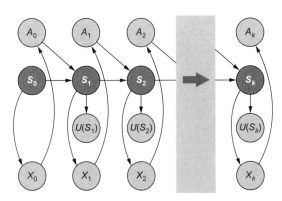

**Figure 12.29   A POMDP where a latent state S causes an observed state X. X drives the actions A.**

In contrast, figure 12.30 illustrates an example where the latent state is a latent common cause (denoted Z) of the observed state (mediated through the agent's action) and the utility (note a slight change of notation from $U(S_i)$ to $U_i$). Here, unobserved factors influence both the agent's behavior and the resulting utility of that behavior.

Again, the basic MDP and POMDP DAGs should be seen as templates for starting our analysis. Once we understand what causal queries we are interested in answering, we can explicitly represent various components of observed and unobserved states as specific nodes in the graph, and then use identification and adjustment techniques to answer our causal queries.

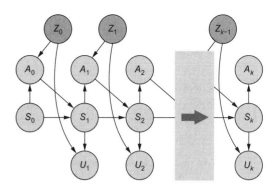

**Figure 12.30    A POMPD formulation where the unobserved states are latent common causes that could act as confounders in causal inferences**

### 12.5.4  *Policy in an MDP*

As before, policies in an MDP act as stochastic interventions. Figure 12.31 illustrates a policy that selects an optimal action based on the current state in a way that disrupts any influence on the action from a confounder.

Original MDP

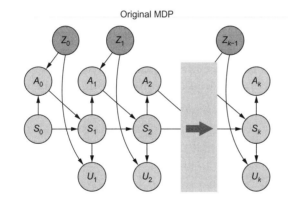

MDP with policy

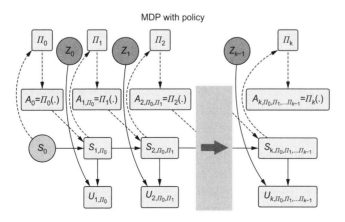

**Figure 12.31    Modification of an MDP DAG by a policy**

Figure 12.31 is simple in that it only selects an action based on the current state. The challenge is in the implementation, because in most RL settings, states can be high-dimensional objects.

### 12.5.5   Causal Bellman equation

RL is about searching for the optimal policy, which is characterized with the Bellman equation, often written as follows:

$$\Pi^* = \underset{\Pi}{\text{argmax}}\, E\left(\sum_{t=0}^{\infty} \gamma^{t+1} U\left(S_{t+1}\right)\middle| A_t = \Pi\left(S_t\right)\right)$$

In plain words, we're looking for a policy $\Pi^*$ maximizes the cumulative reward over time. Here $\gamma$ is a discount rate, a value between 0 and 1, that makes sure the agent values rewards in the near future more than rewards in the far future.

Since we're reasoning about what would happen if we deployed the policy, the causal formulation would be as follows:

$$\Pi^* = \underset{\Pi}{\text{argmax}}\, E\left(\sum_{t=0}^{\infty} \gamma^{t+1} U\left(S_{t+1, A_t = \Pi(S_t)}\right)\right)$$

Note that we could do the same causal rewrite for other variants of the Bellman equation, such as the Q-function used in Q-learning.

The difference between the noncausal and causal formulations of the Bellman equation is the same as the difference between optimizing $E(U(Y)|X{=}x)$ and $E(U(Y_{X=x}))$ in section 12.2.4. The process of solving the causally naive version of the Bellman equation may introduce biases from latent confounders or from conditioning on colliders and mediators. Our causally attuned approach can help avoid these biases. In many cases, the solution of the naive approach will coincide with the causal approach because those biases might not affect the ranking of the top policy relative to others. However, as in the $E(U(Y)|X{=}x)$ versus $E(U(Y_{X=x}))$ example, there will be cases where the solutions to the noncausal and causal formulations differ, and your RL problem might be one of those cases.

## 12.6   Counterfactual reasoning for decision-theory

So far, we've discussed the problem of choosing optimal actions with respect to a utility function as a level 2 query on the causal hierarchy. Is there a use for level 3 counterfactual reasoning in decision theory? In this section, we'll briefly review some applications for level 3 reasoning.

### 12.6.1   Counterfactual policy evaluation

Counterfactual policy evaluation involves taking logged data from a policy in production and asking, "given we used this policy and got this cumulative reward, how much cumulative reward would we have gotten had we used a different policy?" See the chapter notes at www.altdeep.ai/causalAIbook for references to techniques such as *counterfactually guided policy search* and *counterfactual risk minimization.*

### 12.6.2  Counterfactual regret minimization

In chapters 8 and 9, I introduced *regret* as a counterfactual concept. We can further clarify the idea now that we have introduced the language of decision-making; regret is the difference between the utility/reward that was realized given a specific action or set of actions, and the utility/reward that would have been realized had another action or set of actions been taken.

*Counterfactual regret minimization* is an approach to optimizing policies that seeks to minimize regret. To illustrate, suppose we have a policy variable $\Pi$, which can return one of several available policies. The policies take in the context and return an action. The action leads to some reward $U$.

Suppose, for a single instance in our logged data, the policy was $\Pi=\pi$ and the context was $C=c$. We get a certain action $A=\pi(c)$ and reward $U=u$. For some policy $\pi'$, regret is the answer to the counterfactual question, "How much more reward would we have gotten if the policy had been $\pi=\pi'$?" In terms of expectation,

$$E(u - U_{\Pi=\pi'}|C = c, \Pi = \pi, A = \pi(c), U_{A=\pi(c)} = u)$$
$$= u - E(U_{\Pi=\pi'}|C = c, \Pi = \pi, A = \pi(c), U_{A=\pi(c)} = u)$$

Again, this is regret for a single instance in logged data where the context was $C=c$ and the utility was $u$. There are many variations, but the general idea is to find the policy that would have minimized cumulative regret over all the cases of $C=c$ in the logged data, with the goal of favoring that policy in cases of $C=c$ in the future.

### 12.6.3  Making level 3 assumptions in decision problems

The question, of course, is how to make the level 3 assumptions that enable counterfactual inferences. One approach would be to specify an SCM and use the general algorithm for counterfactual reasoning (discussed in chapter 9). For example, in RL, the transition function $P(S_{t+1}=s'|S_t=s, A_t=a)$ captures the rules of state changes in the environment. As I mentioned, $P(S_{t+1}|S_t=s, A_t=a)$ is the causal Markov kernel for a given state $S_{t+1}$. We could specify an SCM with an assignment function that entails that causal Markov kernel, and write that assignment function as

$$s' = f_{S_{t+1}} (s, a, n_{s'})$$

Here, $n_{s'}$ is the value of an exogenous variable for $S_t$.

The challenge is specifying assignment functions that encode the correct counterfactual distributions. This is easier in domains where we know more about the underlying causal mechanisms. A key example is in rule-based games; game rules can provide the level 3 constraints that enable simulation of counterfactuals. Recall how, in chapter 9, the simple rules of the Monte Hall problem enabled us to simulate counterfactual outcomes for stay versus switch strategies. Or consider multiplayer games like poker, where in a round of play each player is dealt a hand of cards and can take certain actions (check, bet, call, raise, or fold) that lead to outcomes (win, lose, tie) based on simple rules, which in turn determine the amount of chips won or lost in that round. A player's counterfactual regret is the difference between the chips they netted and the most they could have netted had they decided on different actions. This is done while accounting for the information available at the time of the decision, not using hindsight about the opponents' cards.

Counterfactual regret minimization algorithms in this domain attempt to find game playing policies that minimize counterfactual regret across multiple players. The concrete rules of the game enable simulation of counterfactual game trajectories. The challenge lies in searching for optimal policies within a space of possible counterfactual trajectories that is quite large because of multiple player interactions over several rounds of play. See the chapter notes on counterfactual regret minimization in multiagent games at www.altdeep.ai/causalAIbook for references.

## Summary

- Decision-making is naturally a causal problem because decisions cause consequences, and our goal is to make the decision that leads to favorable consequences.

- Choosing the optimal decision is a level 2 query as we are asking "what would happen if I made this decision?"

- $E(U(Y|X=x))$ and $E(U(Y_{X=x}))$ are different quantities. Usually, people want to know the value of $X$ that optimizes $E(U(Y_{X=x}))$, but optimizing $E(U(Y|X=x))$ will often yield the same answer without the bother of specifying a causal model.

- This is especially true in reinforcement learning (RL), where the analogs to $E(U(Y|X=x))$ and $E(U(Y_{X=x}))$ are, respectively, the conventional and causal formulations of the Bellman equation. Confounder, mediator, and collider biases may be present in conventional approaches to solving the Bellman equation. But those bias often don't influence the ranking of the top policy relative to other policies.

- Nonetheless, sometimes the value of $X$ that optimizes $E(U(Y|X=x))$ is different from that which optimizes $E(U(Y_{X=x}))$. Similarly, addressing causal nuances when solving the Bellman equation may result in a different policy than ignoring them. If your decision problem falls into this category, causal approaches are the better choice.

- Newcomb's paradox is a thought experiment meant to contrast causal and non-causal approaches to decision theory. The "paradox" is less mysterious once we use a formal causal model.

- Causal decision theory, combined with probabilistic modeling tools like Pyro and pgmpy, is well suited to modeling introspection, where an agent reflects on their internal state (feelings, intuition, urges, intent) and uses that information to predict the "what-if" outcomes of their decisions.

- When we represent a sequential decision process with a causal DAG, we can employ all the tools of graphical causal inference in that decision problem.

- Policies operate like stochastic interventions. They change the graph but still have dependence on observed nodes in the past, and that dependence can introduce backdoor confounding.

- In causal RL, we can represent MDPs and POMDPs as causal DAGs and, again, make use of graphical causal inference theory.

- We can use template DAGs to represent sequential decision processes, but you should tailor these templates for your problem.

- Common use cases for counterfactual reasoning in decision theory are counterfactual policy evaluation and counterfactual regret minimization.

- If you have access to the rules underlying state transitions in your MDP, such as in physical systems or games, you could build an SCM that is counterfactually faithful to those rules, and use it to handle counterfactual use cases in decision-making.

# Causality and large language models

Large language models (LLMs) represent a significant advancement in the field of artificial intelligence. These models are large neural networks designed to generate and understand human-readable text. They are "large" because their scale is truly impressive—cutting-edge LLMs have parameters numbering in the billions and trillions. As generative models, their main function is to generate coherent and contextually relevant natural language. They can also generate structured text, such as programming code, markup languages, mathematical symbols, database queries, and many other useful things in text form.

LLMs are just one example of a broad class of generative AI. For example, we can use the neural network architecture underlying cutting-edge LLMs to model other sequences, such as time-series or DNA. LLMs are a type of *foundation model*,

439

meaning large-scale models that serve as a base or foundation upon which more specialized models or applications can be built. Some LLMs are multimodal, meaning they work with text as well as other content modalities, such as images. In this chapter, we'll focus specifically on LLMs, but much of what we discuss can be generalized to these related ideas.

To start, let's explore some use cases for using LLMs to enhance a causal analysis.

## 13.1  *LLMs as a causal knowledgebase*

As I've mentioned several times in this book, in causal modeling, we don't model the data, we model the data generating process (DGP). In other words, causal modeling requires causal information about the DGP that we can use as assumptions that enable identification of our causal queries. Cutting-edge LLMs are excellent resources for sourcing and validating that causal information. In this section, I'll demonstrate some proven use cases for using LLMs to query causal information that augments a causal analysis.

The following results come from OpenAI's LLM GPT-4 via the ChatGPT interface. Because of the random generation from the model, and OpenAI's periodic updates to the model and ChatGPT software, your results will vary from mine to some degree.

### 13.1.1  *Building a causal DAG*

Let's start with using the LLM to augment the first workflow we discussed in this book: building the causal DAG. Specifying assumptions in the form of a causal DAG can be daunting. What if your DAG is wrong? Modern LLMs are invaluable as a way of leveraging public expert knowledge to build a DAG.

 You are a helpful causal analysis assistant. I'm interested in modeling the relationship between smoking and lung cancer. Provide me a causal DAG that captures this causal relationship.

 Certainly! A Directed Acyclic Graph (DAG) is a powerful tool to represent causal relationships. Here's a basic causal DAG to represent the relationship between smoking and lung cancer:

1  Nodes:
   - **S**: Smoking behavior (e.g., smoker, non-smoker, or frequency of smoking)
   - **LC**: Lung Cancer (presence or absence)
2  Directed Edge:
   - A directed edge from **S** to **LC** represents that smoking behavior can cause or influence the occurrence of lung cancer.
3  Potential Confounders:
   - Other nodes can be introduced into the DAG to account for potential confounders. Some potential confounders might be:
     a  **G**: Genetics (a family history of lung cancer)
     b  **A**: Age (older age might be associated with a higher risk)

   c **E**: Environmental exposure (like asbestos, pollution, etc.)

   d **O**: Other health behaviors (like diet, exercise)

4 Potential Mediators:

- Mediators are intermediate variables through which a cause exerts its effect on an outcome.
- For instance, one could hypothesize that smoking might cause lung damage, which in turn causes lung cancer. In this case:

   a **LD**: Lung Damage

The DAG might look like this with the confounders and the mediator:

1 **S <- G -> LC**
2 **S <- A -> LC**
3 **S <- E -> LC**
4 **S <- O -> LC**
5 **S -> LC**
6 **S -> LD -> LC**

In the process of modeling, it's important to:

- **Identify all potential confounders** to avoid biased results. **Remember that correlation does not imply causation**. Just because two nodes are correlated does not mean one causes the other.
- **Validate your DAG with domain experts**. They can provide insights into relationships you might not have considered.
- **Use data** to test and validate the causal relationships in your DAG, e.g., through controlled experiments or statistical methods like instrumental variables or propensity score matching when experiments are not feasible.
- Bear in mind that this is a simplified DAG for the relationship between smoking and lung cancer. Depending on the granularity and depth of your study, you might need to adjust and expand this framework.

Continuing, I can prompt the LLM to provide potential instrumental variables.

 Suggest two good candidates for instrumental variables. Be brief in your response.

 Certainly. For the relationship between smoking and lung cancer, two potential instrumental variables (IVs) could be:

1 **Cigarette Tax or Price**: If certain regions or periods have higher cigarette prices or taxes, this can influence smoking behavior without directly influencing lung cancer rates except through the effect of reduced smoking. The assumption here is that the only way cigarette prices could affect lung cancer is by influencing smoking behavior.

2 **Anti-Smoking Campaigns or Legislation**: Introduction or intensity of anti-smoking campaigns or legislation in certain regions or times can be used as an instrument. If these campaigns or laws are exogenously determined (not based on current lung cancer rates), they can affect smoking rates without having a direct effect on lung cancer, except through their impact on smoking behavior.

For both IVs, it's crucial to validate the two key assumptions of instrument validity:

1  The instrument is related to the exposure (e.g., cigarette tax affects smoking behavior).

2  The instrument affects the outcome (e.g., lung cancer) only through its effect on the exposure and not through other pathways.

---

**Prompting best practice**

The prompt preface "You are a helpful causal analysis assistant" is an example of what is sometimes called a "system prompt." System prompts provide general context about what is expected from the LLM. System prompting, and other prompt engineering techniques (e.g., chain-of-thought prompting, in-context learning) are best practices for getting good generations from LLMs. For the sake of brevity, I'll use system prompts but omit some of the other prompt engineering best practices in this section—it is smart to include them in practical settings.

---

Continuing to interact with the LLM in this way, perhaps through multiple sessions, you can come up with a candidate DAG that makes sense to you and your stakeholders. Next, you can prompt the LLM to give you code to run an analysis.

### 13.1.2  *Generating code for DAGs, models, and causal analyses*

Modern LLMs are trained on vast corpora of code from a wide variety of programming languages. This greatly speeds up causal analyses, particularly if the libraries you're using are represented in the training data. For example, we can prompt ChatGPT to implement its suggested lung cancer DAG in DoWhy and estimate the causal effect.

 Provide me with code that uses the DoWhy library in Python to implement the causal DAG that you suggested above. Include cigarette price as an instrumental variable and provide code for estimating the causal effect.

 Certainly! Here's a basic example using the DoWhy library in Python for implementing the causal DAG for the relationship between smoking and lung cancer, using cigarette price as an instrumental variable.

---

**Setting up your environment**

The code in this chapter was written with DoWhy version 0.11, Transformers version 4.38.2, Accelerate version 0.28.0, pandas 2.0.3, NumPy 1.25.2, and pyro-ppl (Pyro) version 1.9.0. Visit the chapter notes at www.altdeep.ai/causalAIbook for a link to a notebook containing the chapter's code.

---

Chat GTP then went on to generate the following code.

**Listing 13.1  DoWhy code generated by ChatGPT (verbatim)**

```
import numpy as np
import pandas as pd
import dowhy
from dowhy import CausalModel
from dowhy.datasets import linear_dataset
from dowhy.do_why import CausalModel

# Let's create a sample dataset for illustration purposes
# Normally, you'd import your own dataset: data =
    pd.read_csv('your_dataset.csv')
n_points = 1000
data = pd.DataFrame({
    "S": np.random.binomial(n=1, p=0.5, size=n_points),
    "LC": np.random.binomial(n=1, p=0.5, size=n_points),
    "Price": np.random.normal(loc=5, scale=1, size=n_points),
})

# Create a causal DAG
model=CausalModel(
        data = data,
        treatment='S',
        outcome='LC',
        common_causes=['G', 'A', 'E', 'O'],  # Potential confounders
        instruments=['Price']  # Instrumental Variable
)

# Identify the causal effect
identified_estimand = model.identify_effect(proceed_when_unidentifiable=True)

# Estimate the causal effect using Instrumental Variable method
estimate = model.estimate_effect(identified_estimand,
                                method_name="iv.instrumental_variable",
                                method_params={'iv_instrument_name': 'Price'})

# Print the causal effect estimate
print(estimate)
```

> **This line is wrong, but the code runs if you remove it.** ← (pointing to `from dowhy.do_why import CausalModel`)

> **Simulate smoker status: 0 for non-smoker, 1 for smoker.** ← (pointing to `"S": np.random.binomial(n=1, p=0.5, size=n_points),`)

> **Simulate lung cancer status: 0 for no lung cancer, 1 for lung cancer.** ← (pointing to `"LC": np.random.binomial(n=1, p=0.5, size=n_points),`)

> **Simulate cigarette price with a mean price of 5.** ← (pointing to `"Price": np.random.normal(loc=5, scale=1, size=n_points),`)

 This is a simplified example. In a real-world application:

1. Your data would be imported rather than simulated as above.

2. Ensure that your DAG correctly models the relationships based on domain knowledge.

3. Assumptions behind the instrumental variables need to be rigorously checked.

4. Further analytical steps (e.g., statistical tests, checking robustness) would be necessary.

When you generate code, you may get errors. For example, DoWhy has gone through several iterations, and there is nothing forcing the LLM to keep up with the latest version of the library. In this case, there is an error in the line `from dowhy.do_why import CausalModel`. There is no module called `do_why`, and `CausalModel` is already imported in a previous line. We'll address errors produced by the LLM in section 13.1.7. For now, if you delete that line, the code will run.

ChatGPT will work well with pgmpy and Pyro, the libraries we've worked with extensively in the book. As an exercise, I suggest taking one of the models you built in pgmpy, and prompting the LLM to convert it to a model in Pyro.

Next, we'll look at what the LLM can tell us beyond the structure of the DAG.

### 13.1.3 *Explanations and mechanism*

The advantage of DAGs is that graphs are an intuitive way to represent what causes what. But they do not tell us anything about the nature of the mechanism by which a cause drives an effect.

Structural causal models provide a mathematical way of characterizing the mechanism underlying a causal relationship. Characterizing mechanisms in mathematical terms makes sense in natural sciences, where we have plenty of equations describing natural laws. It is harder in, for example, business domains where we lack equations beyond mere approximations (what is the equation relating ad spending and engagement?).

LLMs leverage common and expert knowledge to provide mechanistic explanations that go beyond the DAG but that are in a form more accessible than formal math.

 You are a helpful causal explanation generator. Provide a characterization of the causal relationship between ad spending and brand awareness. Be concise enough to fit a single slide in a slide deck.

 Causal Relationship Between Ad Spending and Brand Awareness

- **Direct Causality**: As ad spending increases, brand awareness typically rises.
  - a **Mechanism**: Larger ad spends mean more frequent and widespread exposure of the brand to the target audience.
- **Diminishing Returns**: After a certain point, additional ad spending might not lead to proportionally higher brand awareness.
  - a **Reason**: Market saturation, ad fatigue, or redundancy in audience reach.
- **External Factors**: Ad efficiency isn't solely based on spend.
  - a **Influences**: Ad quality, placement, target audience relevancy, competition, and market conditions can affect the outcome.

Consider that some counterfactual queries can be identified, with simple categorical assumptions about the functional relationship between the cause and effect. For example, the probability of necessity is identifiable from intervention data and partially identifiable from observational data if the relationship between $X$ and $Y$ is monotonic:

 Is this a monotonic relationship? Limit your answer to one sentence.

 Yes, the relationship between ad spending and brand awareness is generally monotonic, as increased ad spending will not decrease brand awareness, though the rate of increase might diminish.

We needn't limit ourselves to one explanation; we can use the LLM as a generator of explanatory hypotheses. Consider, for example, *abductive reasoning tasks* where one infers likely causes of a particular observed set of effects (e.g., in science, criminal investigation, and medical diagnosis).

To illustrate, let's pose a modified version of a medical diagnostic question sourced from the US Medical License Exam to ChatGPT. I'll prompt for multiple hypotheses about the cause of the observed symptoms, which is what a doctor would call a *differential diagnosis*:

 You are a causal explanation assistant. Your job is to generate 3 one sentence-long hypotheses that explain the observations. This is a medical diagnosis example.

Observations: A 48-year-old woman presents with diplopia, ocular pain, amenorrhea, hot flashes, weight loss, tachycardia, hypertension, moist palms, enlarged thyroid, prominent eyes, lid retraction, conjunctival injection, and inability to converge eyes. Visual acuity is 20/20 bilaterally.

 1  The patient may have Graves' disease, an autoimmune disorder affecting the thyroid, leading to hyperthyroidism and its associated symptoms, including ocular manifestations.

2  The woman's symptoms, including amenorrhea and hot flashes, suggest a possible concomitant early menopause or another endocrine disorder affecting her reproductive hormones.

3  The ocular symptoms, including diplopia, lid retraction, and inability to converge eyes, hint at a potential thyroid eye disease or orbital myopathy.

One of the challenges of causal modeling is working with domain experts to encode domain assumptions into the structure of the model. These types of generated explanations and hypotheses are valuable assets for communicating with domain experts who might agree with, or better yet, iterate upon these generated explanations.

### 13.1.4   *The causal frame problem and AI alignment*

Given a query of interest, we have to decide what variables are relevant to the problem. Philosoper and AI researcher Clark Glymour does a good job of describing the challenge behind this task: "Given an enormous amount of stuff, and some task to be done using some of the stuff, what is the relevant stuff for the task?"[1]

LLMs are useful at establishing a *causal frame*—the problem of selecting the causal variables relevant to a causal query. In chapter 3's discussion on building the DAG, I mentioned *causal sufficiency* as a d-separation–based criteria for selecting variables for inclusion in the DAG. But when we prompted the LLM to provide a DAG containing variables relevant to smoking's effect on lung cancer, it is highly doubtful that the LLM was using causal sufficiency to select those variables. More likely, it was using

---

[1]   C. Glymour, "Android epistemology and the frame problem," in Z.W. Pylyshyn, ed., *The robot's dilemma: The frame problem in artificial intelligence* (Praeger, 1987), pp. 63–75.

common knowledge found in its training data about this relationship. That knowledge was sufficient to provide a reasonably minimal set of relevant variables.

To illustrate the utility of this ability, consider the following ChatGPT interaction:

 You are a helpful causal reasoning assistant. Consider the following story.

Jake is on an office network. There was an open shared folder on the server. Jake is transferring files across the network and accidentally clicks on the folder, starting a process that consumes a significant amount of bandwidth. This causes the network to slow down. How responsible is Jake for the network slowdown?

 Based on the provided story, let's analyze the situation using causal reasoning:

1 **Direct Cause**: Jake started a process that consumes a significant amount of bandwidth by accidentally clicking on a file.

2 **Effect**: The network slowed down due to the consumed bandwidth.

Given these facts, we can establish that Jake's action was the direct cause of the network slowdown.

However, responsibility can be considered from different dimensions:

1 **Intent**: Jake's action was accidental. He did not intend to slow down the network.

2 **Prevention Mechanisms**: The story does not specify if there were any warnings or user prompts before starting such a process that consumes significant bandwidth. If there were no warnings, one could argue that the system was not designed to prevent such accidental actions.

3 **Knowledge & Training**: Was Jake trained or informed about the implications of transferring large files or about the particular file that consumes a lot of bandwidth? If not, his knowledge gap contributed to the accident.

4 **System Design**: The open shared folder on the server was accessible to Jake. If the file was known to be a bandwidth hog, it's worth asking why such a file was placed in an open shared folder without any warnings or restrictions.

To directly answer the question: Jake is responsible for the network slowdown in the sense that his action was the direct cause. However, the degree of his responsibility might be mitigated if there were systemic design flaws, lack of training, or absence of preventive measures. If other factors, like the ones mentioned above, played a role in the incident, then the responsibility would be shared among Jake and those other factors.

Here, the response includes the systemic design flaws, lack of training, or absence of preventive measures as factors relevant to the causal frame, despite the fact that I made no mention of these factors in the prompt.

More importantly, consider the many factors the LLM could have included but did not: perhaps Jake's mouse had a physical glitch that caused him to click on the file, or perhaps a hacker removed security features on that file, or any other possible mitigating factors. A human would likely exclude these from the causal frame unless explicitly mentioned, and so does the LLM.

If humans are already good at establishing the causal frame, why would we care whether the LLM can do so? Consider the problem of root cause analysis from network logs. Suppose the same story about Jake were rewritten in the form of network logs, such as in the following:

```
Aug 22 14:02:34 User "Jake" logged in from 192.168.0.105.
Aug 22 14:03:12 Shared folder accessed by user "Jake" at //SERVER/shared-
    folder.
Aug 22 14:03:20 File transfer initiated by "Jake" from local: /home/jake/
    documents to remote: //SERVER/shared-folder/documents.
Aug 22 14:03:25 WARNING: Unusual network activity detected. User "Jake"
    launched file "heavy_process.exe" on //SERVER/shared-folder.
Aug 22 14:03:30 Network performance alert: Bandwidth usage spikes at 95%.
Aug 22 14:04:00 Network slowdown detected: Packet loss rate 35%.
```

This is harder for a human to parse than the natural language story, even for an experienced network administrator. Further, there would likely be many other network events unrelated to the events of this narrative that the human would have to read through and disregard. But the LLM has plenty of network logs in its training data, and extracting relevant events from a longer body of text is an established capability of LLMs.

In most of this book, we've focused on using causal models to infer objective causal truth about the world, such as whether smoking causes lung cancer. In this example, the objective truth, that Jake caused the network slowdown, is trivial. The question of how responsible Jake is for the slowdown is highly subjective. But this is still a valuable question to answer, especially if you are trying to find a root cause in a large network log file.

*AI alignment* is the task of making sure an AI system's behaviors are consistent with human goals and preferences. Here, we want a specific type of AI alignment. We want the LLM to go beyond confirming obvious causal facts to aligning with the ways humans tend to make causal judgments. In this case, I asked the LLM an open question about Jake's responsibility, and it gave a response that many humans would agree with. I could also have instructed the LLM to follow certain criteria when generating a judgement. For example, an attorney could prompt the LLM to apply certain legal theories and case law in generating a legal opinion.

Next, we'll look at how to use the LLM to understand and contextualize more nuanced causal concepts.

### 13.1.5  *Understanding and contextualizing causal concepts*

It can be challenging to understand formal causal concepts and apply them within your domain. The LLM can serve as a tool for explaining and contextualizing these concepts. Let's illustrate with the counterfactual concept of *necessary causation*.

 You are a helpful explainer of causal inference topics. Provide a one paragraph explanation of the concept of necessary causation.

Certainly! Necessary causation refers to a causal relationship where the cause is a necessary condition for the effect to occur. In other words, without the presence of the cause, the effect cannot happen. However, the presence of the cause does not guarantee the effect will occur, as there may be other conditions that also need to be met. Think of it like a key to a lock: the key (cause) is necessary to open the lock (effect), but just having the key doesn't mean the lock will open automatically; you still need to insert and turn it. If the lock remains locked without the key, then the key is a necessary cause for unlocking.

A cutting-edge LLM would be trained on a wide variety of theory and research from across domains. It can be useful to contextualize an idea within various domains.

In one paragraph, explain how necessary causation is conceptualized in legal theory.

In legal theory, necessary causation, often termed "but-for causation," is a foundational concept used to establish a direct link between a defendant's actions and the harm suffered by a plaintiff. For an action to be a but-for cause of an outcome, the outcome would not have occurred in the absence of the action. In other words, if one can say "but for the defendant's action, the harm would not have occurred," then necessary causation is established. However, it's worth noting that while but-for causation is a critical component in many legal contexts, it's not always sufficient on its own to establish liability. Other factors, such as foreseeability and proximate cause, often come into play to determine the full scope of legal responsibility.

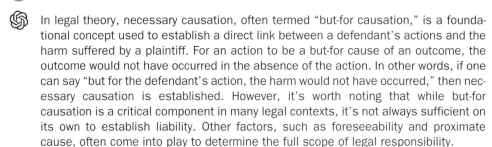

From the perspective of cognitive science, explain in one brief paragraph the role necessary causation plays in human judgments.

From a cognitive science perspective, necessary causation plays a pivotal role in human judgments and decision-making. Our brains are wired to seek patterns and causal relationships in the environment to predict and navigate future events. When we perceive an event as a necessary cause of another, it simplifies our cognitive processing by creating a deterministic link between the two events. This means that when we encounter the cause, we can anticipate the effect, allowing for more efficient planning and response. However, this predisposition can also lead to cognitive biases, where we might mistakenly attribute an effect to a perceived necessary cause, even when other contributing factors are at play.

From the perspective of philosophy, explain in only one sentence how Kant and Hume differed in their beliefs about necessary causation.

Kant believed in the existence of a priori synthetic knowledge and that our minds impose causal order on our experiences, while Hume argued that causation is not a feature of the world itself but a habit of thought based on the regular succession of events.

Now that we've unpacked the concept of necessary causation, let's apply it to a practical problem in our domain of interest. Suppose you are a data scientist at Netflix:

Give me an example of necessary causation that involves a Netflix user unsubscribing from Netflix.

A necessary causation for a Netflix user unsubscribing from Netflix might be the exclusive content that is only available on the platform. If a particular show or movie that the user is deeply interested in is removed from Netflix while remaining available somewhere else, then the removal of that content becomes a necessary cause for that user's decision to unsubscribe. Without the removal of that content, the user might not have unsubscribed.

Now that the LLM has helped us understand necessary causation, we can get its help in formalizing the concept.

### 13.1.6  *Formalization of causal queries*

For humans, natural language is the medium of our causal reasoning. But we need to convert that natural language into formal terms so that we can apply mathematical and algorithmic analysis. This can be a challenge. Fortunately, LLMs can help greatly in this respect.

For example, in chapter 8, I introduced several examples of the language of parallel world counterfactuals and how to convert them into counterfactual notation. Necessary causation, more specifically the *probability of necessity*, was one of these counterfactuals. Let's put this task to the LLM in our Netflix context:

 You are a helpful causal inference assistant. I'm considering a counterfactual inference problem in the context of Netflix. I have the following query: "There is a set of users who unsubscribed after content was removed from the platform. What is the probability a given member of this set of users would not have unsubscribed had the content not been removed?" Write this query as a probabilistic expression with Pearl's counterfactual notation.

 Certainly! Pearl's counterfactual notation offers a concise way to express such queries.

Let's define some variables:

1  $X$ =removal of the content (binary, 1 if removed, 0 if not removed).

2  $Y$ =whether user unsubscribes (binary, 1 if user unsubscribes, 0 if they did not unsubscribe).

Your query is essentially asking for the probability that a user would not have subscribed, had the content not been removed, given that it was removed and they did unsubscribe.

Using Pearl's counterfactual notation, this can be written as:

$$P(Y_{x=0} = 0 | X = 1, Y = 1)$$

Where:

- $Y_{x=0}$ is the counterfactual outcome for $Y$ had $X$ been set to 0 (i.e., the content is not removed).
- $X=1$ denotes that the content was removed.

- $Y=1$ denotes that the user unsubscribed.

So, $P(Y_{x=0} = 0 | X = 1, Y = 1)$ is the probability that a user would not have unsubscribed had the content not been removed, given that it was removed and they did unsubscribe.

The LLM can take us from conceptualization to formalization. But beware, as it can also "hallucinate."

### 13.1.7  *Beware: LLMs hallucinate*

We've seen that LLMs can aid in code generation. Let's ask for code that implements the probability of necessity.

 Provide Python code that, for a given pair of treatment and outcome variables, calculates the counterfactual query "probability of necessity."

 The Probability of Necessity (PN) is the proportion of cases where the treatment is present, and the outcome is achieved ONLY when the treatment is present. In simpler terms, it indicates the probability that the outcome occurs because of the treatment.

Given that definition, you can calculate PN using the following formula:

$$PN = \frac{P(\text{Treatment} \cap \text{Outcome}) - P(\neg\text{Treatment} \cap \text{Outcome})}{P(\text{Treatment} \cap \text{Outcome})}$$

Where:

- $P(Treatment \cap Outcome)$ is the probability of both the treatment and outcome occurring.
- $P(\neg Treatment \cap Outcome)$ is the probability of the outcome occurring but not the treatment.

The response goes on to provide Python code that is well formatted, well commented, and compiles. *But this answer is wrong.* This is what is commonly called a "hallucination," a convincing lie. This example is especially convincing—that formula is true *only* when the relationship between the treatment and outcome is monotonic, when there are no confounders, and when $P(Treatment) = P(Outcome)$. Those assumptions are so strong that we can't forgive ChatGPT for not mentioning them. Other generations from the model were even more off base.

We can use the LLM to augment our causal analysis, particularly with common and expert causal knowledge as well as generated code. But hallucination means this isn't a panacea. We need to rely on our own causal expertise to spot when hallucination occurs and understand when it threatens the quality of our analysis.

To understand why this hallucination occurred, let's first examine how LLMs work.

## 13.2  *A causality-themed LLM primer*

To understand how to deploy LLMs for causal applications, it is important to understand how they work, as well as their limitations. This section provides a quick high-level causality-themed tour of the core ideas.

### 13.2.1  *A probabilistic ML view of LLMs*

In the context of LLMs, a "token" refers to a sequence of characters that the model reads, which can be as short as one character or as long as one word. Tokens are the units into which input text is divided into manageable pieces for the model.

Hugging Face's Transformers library has a publicly available version of GPT-2, which is far inferior to cutting-edge models but has a similar *Transformer* architecture. The Transformer architecture is a type of deep learning model designed to process and understand text and other sequential data, by focusing on the relationships between words in a sentence regardless of their position. Let's tokenize the expression "Can LLMs reason counterfactually?"

**Listing 13.2   Viewing example tokens that an LLM operates upon**

```
from transformers import GPT2Tokenizer          Initialize the
tokenizer = GPT2Tokenizer.from_pretrained('gpt2')   GPT-2 tokenizer.
tokens = tokenizer.tokenize("Can LLMs reason counterfactually?")
print(tokens)        Print out                                Tokenize the
                     the tokens.                               sequence.
```

This prints out the following tokens:

```
['Can', 'ĠLL', 'Ms', 'Ġreason', 'Ġcounter', 'fact', 'ually', '?']
```

The "Ġ" corresponds to a space. Note that punctuation marks are tokens, and that words like "counterfactual" are broken up into multiple tokens. Each token corresponds to an integer indexing the token in a large "vocabulary." GPT-2 has a vocabulary size of 50,257.

**Listing 13.3   Converting tokens to integers**

```
input_ids = tokenizer.encode(
    "Can LLMs reason counterfactually?",      "Encode" the tokens into integers
    return_tensors='pt'                       that index the token in a list of
)                                             tokens called the "vocabulary".
print(input_ids)
```

This *encodes* the tokens into a sequence of integers:

```
tensor([[ 6090, 27140, 10128,  1738,  3753, 22584,   935,    30]])
```

The Transformer architecture works with these numeric values.

LLMs define a joint probability distribution on sequences of tokens. For the phrase "Can LLMs reason counterfactually?" the model defines a probability distribution:

$$P(X_0 = \text{"Can"}, X_1 = \text{"LL"}, X_2 = \text{"Ms"}, X_3 = \text{"reason"}, \dots, X_7 = \text{"?"})$$

The models will also consider the chances that this sequence ended at the question mark, rather than continuing. For that, the LLM's vocabulary includes a special token to mark the end of a sequence. For GPT-2, this is token is `<|endoftext|>`:

$$P(X_0 = \text{"Can"}, X_1 = \text{"LL"}, X_2 = \text{"Ms"}, X_3 = \text{"reason"},$$
$$\ldots, X_7 = \text{"?"}, X_8 = \text{"<|endoftext|>"})$$

Further, autoregressive LLMs, such as the GPT and Llama series of Transformer models, model text in the order of the text sequence, so they factorize this joint probability as follows:

$$P(X_0 = \text{"Can"}) \times P(X_1 = \text{"LL"}|X_0 = \text{"Can"}) \times P(X_2 = \text{"Ms"}|X_0 = \text{"Can"}, X_1 = \text{"LL"})$$
$$\cdots \times P(X_8 = \text{"<|endoftext|>"}|X_0 = \text{"Can"}, X_1 = \text{"LL"}, X_2 = \text{"Ms"}, X_3 = \text{"reason"}, \ldots)$$

We can calculate each of these probabilities on the log scale with the Transformers library. In generating the log probability, we first calculate *logits* for each term in the vocabulary. For a probability value $p$, the corresponding logit is $\log(p \ / \ (1-p))$.

**Listing 13.4   Calculate the log probability of each token in the sequence**

```
import torch
from transformers import GPT2LMHeadModel

model = GPT2LMHeadModel.from_pretrained('gpt2-medium')
model.eval()

input_text = "Can LLMs reason counterfactually?<|endoftext|>"
input_ids = tokenizer.encode(input_text, return_tensors='pt')

with torch.no_grad():
    outputs = model(input_ids)
    logits = outputs.logits

log_probs = torch.nn.functional.log_softmax(logits, dim=-1)
for idx, token in enumerate(input_ids[0]):
    token_log_prob = log_probs[0][idx][token].item()
    print(f"Token: {tokenizer.decode(token)}" +
        " | Log Probability: {token_log_prob}")
```

Initialize the **GPT-2** model and set to evaluation mode.

Tokenize and encode the phrase, including the end-of-sequence token.

Given the phrase, the model produces logits for every element in the vocabulary.

For each position in the sequence, get the log probability corresponding to the token that was actually present in that position.

This prints the following output:

```
Token: Can | Log Probability: -10.451835632324219
Token:  LL | Log Probability: -9.275650978088379
Token: Ms | Log Probability: -14.926365852355957
Token:  reason | Log Probability: -10.416162490844727
Token:  counter | Log Probability: -8.359155554907227
Token: fact | Log Probability: -22.62082290649414
Token: ually | Log Probability: -11.302435874938965
Token: ? | Log Probability: -10.131906509399414
Token: <|endoftext|> | Log Probability: -11.475025177001953
```

Summing these together provides the joint probability of the sequence under the model.

Of course, as a generative model, GPT-2 can generate the next token conditional on the tokens that came before it. The *prompt* the user provides is the beginning of the sequence, and the model's response extends the sequence.

**Listing 13.5  Generation from the LLM**

```
prompt = "Counterfactual reasoning would enable AI to"       Specify and encode
input_ids = tokenizer.encode(prompt, return_tensors='pt')    the prompt.

output = model.generate(                    Generate from the model. The
    input_ids,                              "do_sample=True" argument means
    max_length=25,                          we're doing random selection from the
    do_sample=True,                         probability distribution of the next
    pad_token_id=tokenizer.eos_token_id     token, given all the previous tokens.
)

generated_text = tokenizer.decode(output[0], skip_special_tokens=True)
print(generated_text)
                                                           Decode and print
                                                           the output.
```

This prints out the following:

```
Counterfactual reasoning would enable AI to figure out what people want
    before they ask them. It would also enable self-awareness
```

Again, note that ChatGPT generation has a random element, so this will likely produce something different for you.

> **Note about confusing terminology**
>
> Models like the GPT models are often called "causal language models," but these are not causal models in the way we've discussed in this book. They are not a causal model of a DGP. "Causal" here refers to the autoregressive nature of the model—the model evaluates the probability of a token in a sequence conditional only on the tokens that came before it.

All this is to say that the LLM is at a basic level a probability model of the joint probability of a sequence of tokens. The canonical training procedures for these models attempt to fit the joint probability distribution of the tokens. Models like GPT optimize the model's ability to predict a given token in a training document given the previous tokens. Understanding that the LLM is a probability model over tokens doesn't explain why LLMs can generate *coherent* text (meaning text with logical and consistent interrelation of ideas that forms a comprehensible whole). For that, we need to understand *attention*.

### 13.2.2 The attention mechanism

One of the main drivers behind the success of LLMs is use of *Transformer architectures* and other neural network architectures that rely on a mechanism called *attention*. The attention mechanism allows the model to weigh the importance of different parts of an input sequence differently. That allows the model to learn to "focus" on specific parts of a sequence that are more relevant to a given task, while "ignoring" or assigning lesser weight to less pertinent parts.

Consider, for example, the following conditional counterfactual statement about leaves being a necessary cause of a fire:

> *The Labor Day weekend wildfire started in the forest and spread rapidly due to the dry leaves on the ground. Had there been a controlled burn, the fire wouldn't have spread so rapidly.*

The attention mechanism helps the model recognize that "leaves" refers to foliage, not a departure, by weighing the relevance of surrounding words like "ground," "dry," and "forest."

Modern LLMs have attention mechanisms stacked over many neural network layers. This enables the LLM to attend to concepts at different levels of granularity. For example, while the first layer of attention focuses on immediate word-to-word relationships, such as "leaves" with "ground," the next few layers connect broader phrases, treating "The Labor Day weekend wildfire" as a single entity connected to the phrase "spread rapidly."

Latter layers can represent the overarching theme or subject of the sentence and the broader text, connecting "The Labor Day weekend wildfire" to information about how it spread.

### 13.2.3 From tokens to causal representation

The ability to talk about how attention enables the LLM to learn higher-level abstractions becomes of interest to us from the standpoint of causality. Recall figure 13.1, which first appeared in chapter 5 (as figure 5.4).

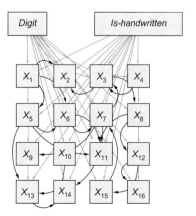

Figure 13.1    Example from chapter 5, where *digit* and *is-handwritten* are high-level causal drivers of low-level $X_i$ pixels

The small squares represent pixels in an image, while the squares *digit* and *is-handwritten* represent the digit depicted in the image and whether it was handwritten, respectively. In that example (section 5.1.2), I suggested that whatever causal relations exist between individual pixels doesn't matter to us; we're interested in reasoning at the level of the objects depicted in the image.

There is a similar thing going on with tokens, as shown in figure 13.2.

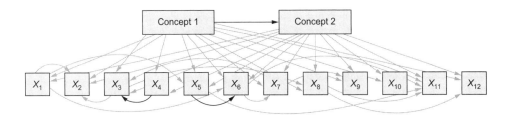

**Figure 13.2**  $X_1$ through $X_{12}$ are a sequence of tokens. Whatever structure (causal or otherwise) exists between the tokens is of passing interest. We are interested in the causal relations between concepts described by the tokens.

In figure 13.2, as with the pixels, there is some structure at the level of the tokens. But that structure is beside the point—we're interested in the causal relationships between the concepts that form the meaning behind the tokens.

The question becomes, under what circumstances could attention, insofar as it can learn higher-level representations, learn a *causal* representation. For example, could an attention-based model, perhaps under some set of architectural or learning constraints, or use of interventions in training data, learn the parallel world structure and abstractions in the Labor Day counterfactual statement?

To consider this, we can revisit LLM hallucinations in our question about the probability of necessity, and connect it to causal identification.

### 13.2.4  *Hallucination, attention, and causal identification*

The hallucination about probability of necessity was generated with GPT-4. The same model got the Netflix question about probability of necessity correct. Indeed, the hallucinated answer would have been right if it merely stated the correct identifying assumptions. I believe future versions of GPT and similar models will likely get this question right on the first try.

But for someone who is unfamiliar with the definition of probability of necessity, how would they know if the model were right or if it were hallucinating? First, the causal hierarchy tells us that in order to be capable of generating a right answer beyond a random guess, the query would need to be identified with level 3 information. Perhaps that information is provided by the user in the prompt. Perhaps the

LLM has somehow learned level 3 representations (such a claim would require hard proof).

If the user were providing that identifying information in the prompt, how would the user know if the model was successfully using that information to respond to the prompt? Suppose instead that the requirements for identification exist and are buried in the learned representations or data, and that they were being successfully leveraged by the model in answering the causal query, how could the user know for sure this was happening?

We need to engineer solutions that answer these and other desiderata to build toward a causal AI future. In the next section, we'll start on this path with a simple causal LLM.

## 13.3   *Forging your own causal LLM*

In this section, we'll sidestep the question of "can cutting-edge LLMs reason causally?" and move on to building a causal LLM that can reason causally. We'll build for causality from the ground up, rather than as an afterthought.

### 13.3.1 *An LLM for script writing*

Often our data has some implicit causal structure. When we make that structure explicit during training, the foundation model can learn better causal representations.

To illustrate, suppose a prolific film production studio has historically insisted their writers use script-writing software that required following a three-act narrative archetype, which is common for romantic comedies: "boy meets girl, boy loses girl, boy gets girl back." For this archetype, they have a corpus of many scripts. In causal terms, the events in act 1 cause the events of act 2, and the events of acts 1 and 2 cause the events of act 3. We can draw the DAG in figure 13.3.

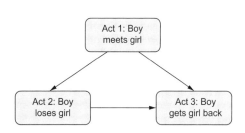

**Figure 13.3   A causal DAG for a three-act archetype**

The studio works with many such archetypes, and the company has many scripts that follow a given archetype template. Suppose that a set of archetypes involve a king acting a certain way in act 1, a prince acting a certain way in act 2, and these two actions having an effect on a kingdom in act 3. For example, one possible archetype is "King declares war, Prince leads army, kingdom experiences prosperity." But there are multiple outcomes for each act:

- King in act 1: {king declares war; king negotiates peace; king falls ill}
- Prince in act 2: {prince leads army; prince abdicates throne; prince marries foreigner}

- Kingdom in act 3: {kingdom wins battle; kingdom falls into poverty; kingdom experiences prosperity}

Figure 13.4 shows this space of archetypes in the form of a causal DAG.

This describes only $3 \times 3 \times 3 = 27$ possible archetypes, but as you might expect, some archetypes are more common and some are less common. We could easily model these archetypes and the joint probability distribu-

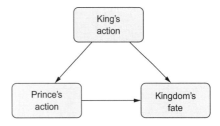

**Figure 13.4   A causal DAG representing various King-Prince-Kingdom archetypes**

tion by explicitly coding causal Markov kernels in pgmpy or Pyro. But that would only be a causal generative model on the archetypes. If we want a script generator, we want a causal generative model on the scripts.

To demonstrate a proof-of-concept for this idea, we'll work with a training dataset of short vignettes, rather than full scripts. Let's load and examine the training data.

**Listing 13.6   Load causal narrative data**

```
import pandas as pd
url = ("https://raw.githubusercontent.com/altdeep/"
       "causalML/master/book/chapter%2013/"
       "king-prince-kingdom-updated.csv")
df = pd.read_csv(url)
print(df.shape[0])
```
The data has 21,000 stories, broken up into three short vignettes.

```
print(df["King"][0] + "\n")
print(df["King"][1] + "\n")
print(df["King"][2])
```
**First, the king acts.**

```
print("----")
print(df["Prince"][0] + "\n")
print(df["Prince"][1] + "\n")
print(df["Prince"][2])
```
**Then the prince acts.**

```
print("----")
print(df["Kingdom"][0] + "\n")
print(df["Kingdom"][1] + "\n")
print(df["Kingdom"][2])
```
**Finally, the kingdom experiences the consequences of the royals' actions.**

This code prints the following:

```
21000
----
King brokers a peace treaty with a rival kingdom, putting an end to years of
    bloody conflict

A wise king successfully negotiates peace with a rival nation

A wise king successfully negotiates peace between his kingdom and a long-time
    enemy
```

```
----
however, his son, the Prince, falls in love and marries a foreigner, causing
      political unrest

Prince falls in love with and marries a foreign princess, forging a strong
      alliance

but when a new threat emerges, the Prince leads the army to defend their
      realm
----
despite efforts, the ongoing war results in both kingdoms falling into
      poverty."

the alliance strengthens their forces, leading the kingdom to a victorious
      battle."

however, a series of misfortunes and disastrous decisions plunge their once
      prosperous kingdom into poverty."
```

There are 21,000 sets of three vignettes. The preceding output shows the first three sets in the dataset.

### 13.3.2 *Using pretrained models for causal Markov kernels*

To train the causal Markov kernels for each node in our DAG, we'll take pretrained models from the Hugging Face Transformers library, and then further train (aka "fine-tune") the models using our vignettes. The pretraining took care of the heavy lifting in terms of learning to generate coherent natural language text. The fine-tuning will align the models toward representing our causal Markov kernels.

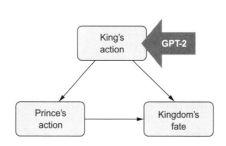

**Figure 13.5   GPT-2 is fine-tuned to represent the distribution of King's action vignettes.**

First, we'll use a GPT-2 variant to model the King's action vignettes. As a text-completion model, it typically takes a prompt as input, but we'll train it to generate with an empty prompt and produce vignettes according to the marginal probabilities of the King's action texts in the training data, as in figure 13.5.

Next, we'll use a BART model for the causal Markov kernel Prince's action. BART is a Transformer model released in 2019 designed specifically to take an input sequence and generate a corresponding output sequence, such as with translation or summarization. Large models like GPT-4 can handle sequence-to-sequence tasks quite well, but we'll use a version of BART with roughly 4,000-times fewer parameters than GPT-4, making it easier for you to load and train on your laptop or basic Python development environment. Given the King's action vignette as input, it will generate a Prince's action vignette, as illustrated in figure 13.6.

We'll also use a BART model to model the causal Markov kernel for the Kingdom's fate, as shown in figure 13.7. The model will map the King's and Prince's actions to the Kingdom's fate.

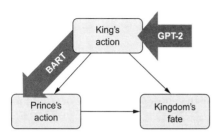

**Figure 13.6 A BART sequence-to-sequence model is fine-tuned to represent the Prince's action given the King's action.**

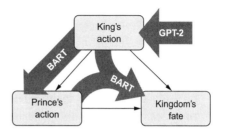

**Figure 13.7 A BART sequence-to-sequence model is also used to model the Kingdom's fate given the King's action and Prince's action.**

Jumping ahead, we're interested in the conditional probability distribution of the Kingdom's fate, given a certain action by the Prince. Since that will require inference of the King's actions given the Prince, we'll additionally train one more BART model that generates a King's action vignette given a Prince's action vignette, as shown in figure 13.8.

Let's run the training procedure. First, we'll set up our imports and our tokenizer. We'll use Bart as the tokenizer for all of our models.

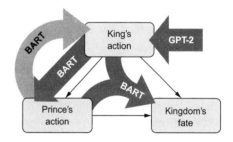

**Figure 13.8 A BART sequence-to-sequence model is also fine-tuned to model the Kingdom's fate, given the King's and Prince's actions.**

#### Listing 13.7 Training the causal LLM

```
import torch
from sklearn.model_selection import train_test_split
from torch.utils.data import Dataset
from transformers import (
    AutoModelForCausalLM, AutoModelForSeq2SeqLM,
    AutoTokenizer, DataCollatorForLanguageModeling,
    Seq2SeqTrainer, Seq2SeqTrainingArguments,
    Trainer, TrainingArguments)
url = ("https://raw.githubusercontent.com/altdeep/"
       "causalML/master/book/chapter%2013/"
       "king-prince-kingdom-updated.csv")
df = pd.read_csv(url)

tokenizer = AutoTokenizer.from_pretrained("facebook/bart-base")
tokenizer.pad_token = tokenizer.eos_token
```

The pad token is used to make all the sequences the same length to facilitate matrix operations. It is common to set it to the "end-of-sequence (EOS)" token.

Set up the tokenizer.

```
def tokenize_phrases(phrases, max_length=40):
    return tokenizer(
        phrases,
        truncation=True,
        padding='max_length',
        max_length=max_length
    )
```

> The max length of the token is set to 40, as all of the vignettes are less than 40 tokens.

Next we'll create a class and a function that tokenizes the King dataset. We'll create a custom subclass of the PyTorch Dataset class called ModelDataset that will store token encodings and their corresponding labels. When accessed by index, it returns a dictionary containing token encodings for that index and the associated label, and it provides the total number of examples via its __len__ method.

**Listing 13.8    Tokenizing the King vignettes**

```
class ModelDataset(Dataset):
    def __init__(self, encodings, labels):
        self.encodings = encodings
        self.labels = labels

    def __getitem__(self, idx):
        item = {           #A
            key: torch.tensor(val[idx])
            for key, val in self.encodings.items()
        }    #A
        item['labels'] = torch.tensor(self.labels[idx])
        return item

    def __len__(self):
        return len(self.encodings.input_ids)

def create_king_dataset(input_phrases):
    king_phrases = input_phrases.tolist()
    king_encodings = tokenize_phrases(king_phrases)
    king_dataset = ModelDataset(
        king_encodings,
        king_encodings['input_ids'])
    return king_dataset
```

> When accessed by index, ModelDataset returns a dictionary containing token encodings for that index and the associated label.

> Create a ModelDataset instance for the king vignettes.

Next we'll tokenize the Prince and Kingdom vignettes. This code will also produce a validation dataset used in training sequence-to-sequence models.

**Listing 13.9    Tokenizing the Prince and Kingdom vignettes**

```
def create_seq2seq_datasets(input_phrases, target_phrases):
    input_phrases_list = input_phrases.tolist()
    target_phrases_list = target_phrases.tolist()
    spit = train_test_split(
        input_phrases_list,
        target_phrases_list,
        test_size=0.1
    )
    train_inputs, val_inputs, train_targets, val_targets = spit
```

> Split input and target phrases into training and validation sets.

```
    train_input_encodings = tokenize_phrases(train_inputs)
    val_input_encodings = tokenize_phrases(val_inputs)
    train_target_encodings = tokenize_phrases(train_targets)
    val_target_encodings = tokenize_phrases(val_targets)
    train_dataset = ModelDataset(
        train_input_encodings, train_target_encodings['input_ids']
    )
    val_dataset = ModelDataset(
        val_input_encodings, val_target_encodings['input_ids']
    )
    return train_dataset, val_dataset
```

**Encode the training and validation sets.**

Next, we'll write a training algorithm for the King model. This function initializes a GPT-2 model with the specified parameters, sets up the training arguments, and trains the model on the provided dataset, finally saving the trained model to the specified directory.

**Listing 13.10   Training the King model**

```
def train_king_model(output_dir, train_dataset,
                     model_name="gpt2-medium", epochs=4):
    king_model = AutoModelForCausalLM.from_pretrained(model_name)
    training_args_king = TrainingArguments(
      output_dir=output_dir,
      per_device_train_batch_size=32,
      overwrite_output_dir=True,
      num_train_epochs=epochs,
      save_total_limit=1,
      save_steps=len(train_dataset) // 16,
      max_grad_norm=1.0
    )
    data_collator = DataCollatorForLanguageModeling(
        tokenizer=tokenizer,
        mlm=False)
    trainer_king = Trainer(
        model=king_model,
        args=training_args_king,
        data_collator=data_collator,
        train_dataset=train_dataset,
    )
    trainer_king.train()
    king_model.save_pretrained(output_dir)
    return king_model
```

**Initialize and configure model with the specified parameters.**

**Configure the training settings.**

**Train the model.**

Next, we'll write a training algorithm for the sequence-to-sequence models. The function will split the provided input and target phrases into training and validation sets, tokenize them, and then create and return PyTorch `Dataset` objects for both sets using the `ModelDataset` class. The `train_seq2seq_model` function initializes a sequence-to-sequence model with the specified parameters, configures its training settings, and then trains the model using both training and validation datasets, finally returning the trained model.

---

**Listing 13.11     Function for training the sequence-to-sequence models**

```
def train_seq2seq_model(output_dir, train_dataset, val_dataset,
                        model_name="facebook/bart-base",
                        epochs=4):
    model = AutoModelForSeq2SeqLM.from_pretrained(model_name)
    training_args = Seq2SeqTrainingArguments(
        output_dir=output_dir,
        per_device_train_batch_size=16,
        predict_with_generate=True,
        logging_dir=f"{output_dir}/logs",             Initialize and configure
        save_total_limit=1,                           sequence-to-sequence
        save_steps=len(train_dataset) // 16,          model with the
        learning_rate=3e-5,                           specified parameters.
        num_train_epochs=epochs,
        warmup_steps=500,
        weight_decay=0.01,
    )
    trainer = Seq2SeqTrainer(
        model=model,
        args=training_args,                    Configure the
        train_dataset=train_dataset,           training settings.
        eval_dataset=val_dataset,
    )
    trainer.train()                   ◁       Train the model using both training
    model.save_pretrained(output_dir)         and validation datasets, finally
    return model                              returning the trained model.
```

Now we'll use this function to train the models. We'll specify some directories for saving checkpoints.

> **NOTE**   In listing 13.14, I'll provide code that downloads a pretrained model from Hugging Face, so if you don't wish train the model, you can skip ahead to that step.

---

**Listing 13.12     Training the King, Prince, and Kingdom models**

```
import os

king_model_path = os.path.join(os.getcwd(), 'king_model')
prince_model_path = os.path.join(os.getcwd(), 'prince_model')       Provide the output
kingdom_model_path = os.path.join(os.getcwd(), 'kingdom_model')     directories where
prince2king_model_path = os.path.join(                              you want to save
    os.getcwd(), 'prince2king_model')                               your model.


king_dataset = create_king_dataset(df["King"])                      Train the King model
king_model = train_king_model(king_model_path, king_dataset)        using Seq2Seq.


datasets = create_seq2seq_datasets(df["King"], df["Prince"])        Train the Prince
train_dataset_prince, val_dataset_prince = datasets                 model using Seq2Seq.
prince_model = train_seq2seq_model(                                 The King vignettes
    prince_model_path,                                              are used to predict
    train_dataset_prince,                                           the Prince vignettes.
```

```
        val_dataset_prince,
        epochs=6
)
```
**Train the Prince model using Seq2Seq. The King vignettes are used to predict the Prince vignettes.**

```
king_and_prince = [f"{k} {p}" for k, p in zip(df["King"], df["Prince"])]
df["King and Prince"] = king_and_prince
train_dataset_kingdom, val_dataset_kingdom = create_seq2seq_datasets(
    df["King and Prince"], df["Kingdom"]
)
kingdom_model = train_seq2seq_model(
    kingdom_model_path,
    train_dataset_kingdom,
    val_dataset_kingdom,
    epochs=6
)
```
**Train the Kingdom model using Seq2Seq. The combined King and Prince vignettes are used to predict the Kingdom vignettes.**

Finally, we'll train another model for inferring the King vignette given a Prince vignette. We'll use this in inference later.

**Listing 13.13  Function to train the Prince to King model**

```
p2k_data = create_seq2seq_datasets(
    df["Prince"], df["King"])
train_dataset_prince2king, val_dataset_prince2king = p2k_data
prince2king_model = train_seq2seq_model(
    prince2king_model_path,
    train_dataset_prince2king,
    val_dataset_prince2king,
    epochs=6
)
```

Running the preceding training procedure will take some time, especially if you're not using GPU. Fortunately, there are saved versions of the trained models in the Hugging Face Hub. The following code pulls the Transformer models from the Hugging Face Hub and generates from them. It also provides a function that calculates the log probability of each generated sequence.

**Listing 13.14  Pull Transformer models from the Hugging Face Hub and generate**

```
import matplotlib.pyplot as plt
import pandas as pd
import torch
from sklearn.feature_extraction.text import TfidfVectorizer
from transformers import (
    AutoModelForCausalLM, AutoModelForSeq2SeqLM,
    AutoTokenizer, GPT2LMHeadModel,
    PreTrainedModel, BartForConditionalGeneration)
DEVICE = torch.device("cuda" if torch.cuda.is_available() else "cpu")

king_model = AutoModelForCausalLM.from_pretrained(
    "osazuwa/causalLLM-king").to(DEVICE)
prince_model = AutoModelForSeq2SeqLM.from_pretrained(
```
**Load the components of our model.**

```
    "osazuwa/causalLLM-prince").to(DEVICE)
kingdom_model = AutoModelForSeq2SeqLM.from_pretrained(
    "osazuwa/causalLLM-kingdom").to(DEVICE)
prince2king_model = AutoModelForSeq2SeqLM.from_pretrained(
    "osazuwa/causalLLM-prince2king").to(DEVICE)

tokenizer = AutoTokenizer.from_pretrained("facebook/bart-base")
tokenizer.pad_token = tokenizer.eos_token
```

**Load the components of our model.**

**Load the Bart-base tokenizer and set the pad token to end-of-sequence tokens.**

Next, we'll write some functions to encode text to tokens, decode tokens to text, and generate text from the model given input text.

**Listing 13.15   Helper functions for encoding, decoding, and generation**

```
def encode(text:str, device=DEVICE) -> torch.tensor:
    input_ids = tokenizer.encode(text, return_tensors="pt")
    input_ids = input_ids.to(device)
    return input_ids

def decode(text_ids: torch.tensor) -> str:
    output = tokenizer.decode(text_ids, skip_special_tokens=True)
    return output

EMPTY_TEXT = torch.tensor(tokenizer.encode("")).unsqueeze(0).to(DEVICE)

def generate_from_model(model: PreTrainedModel,
                        input_sequence: torch.tensor = EMPTY_TEXT,
                        max_length: int = 25,
                        temperature=1.0):
    output = model.generate(
        input_sequence,
        max_length=max_length,
        do_sample=True,
        pad_token_id=tokenizer.pad_token_id,
        eos_token_id=tokenizer.pad_token_id,
        temperature=temperature,
        top_p=0.9,
    )
    return output

def convert_to_text(output):
    return decode(output[0]).strip().capitalize()
```

**Encode text into tensor.**

**Decode tensor into text.**

**Get the encoding for empty text, for convenience.**

**A function for generating from models. These parameters do slightly different things for the GPT-2 and BART models, but they more or less overlap.**

We want to use our probabilistic ML approach, so we need a way of computing the log probabilities of generated sequences so we can use these in inference. The following function computes the log probability of a generated sequence based on related values produced by the GPT-2 and BART models.

**Listing 13.16   Computing log probabilities of generated sequences**

```
def compute_log_probs(model, output_sequence):
    if isinstance(model, GPT2LMHeadModel):
        outputs = model(
            input_ids=output_sequence,
            labels=output_sequence
        )
        log_softmax = torch.nn.functional.log_softmax(
            outputs.logits, dim=-1)
        log_probs = log_softmax.gather(2, output_sequence.unsqueeze(-1))
        log_probs = log_probs.squeeze(-1).sum(dim=-1)
    elif isinstance(model, BartForConditionalGeneration):
        outputs = model(
            input_ids=output_sequence,
            labels=output_sequence)
        loss = outputs.loss
        log_probs = -loss * output_sequence.size(1)
    else:
        raise ValueError("Unsupported model type")
    return torch.tensor(log_probs.item())
```

> **Convert logits to logprobs for GPT-2.**

> **Convert logits to logprobs from BART cross-entropy.**

Finally, we'll put these pieces together to generate a full story from our three models.

**Listing 13.17   Generating a full story**

> **Generate from the GPT-based model of vignettes about the King and calculate the log probabilities of the generated sequence.**

> **Generate from the BART-based sequence-to-sequence model that generates vignettes about the Prince given vignettes about the King, and then calculate the log probability of the generated sequence.**

```
king_output = generate_from_model(king_model)
king_statement = convert_to_text(king_output)
print("Generated from king_nodel:", king_statement)
log_prob_king = compute_log_probs(king_model, king_output)
print("Log prob of generated king text:", log_prob_king)

prince_output = generate_from_model(prince_model, king_output)
prince_statement = convert_to_text(prince_output)
print("Generated from prince_model:", prince_statement)
log_prob_prince = compute_log_probs(prince_model, prince_output)
print("Log prob of generated prince text:", log_prob_prince)

king_prince_statement = king_statement + ". " + prince_statement
king_prince_output = encode(king_prince_statement)
kingdom_output = generate_from_model(kingdom_model, king_prince_output)
kingdom_statement = convert_to_text(kingdom_output)

print("Generated from kingdom model:", kingdom_statement)
log_prob_kingdom = compute_log_probs(kingdom_model, kingdom_output)
print("Log prob of generated kingdom text:", log_prob_kingdom)
```

> **Generate from the BART-based sequence-to-sequence model that generates vignettes about the Kingdom given vignettes about the King and the Prince, and then calculate the log probability of the generated sequence.**

```
king_output_infer = generate_from_model(prince2king_model, prince_output)
king_statement_infer = convert_to_text(king_output_infer)
print("Generated statement from prince2king:", king_statement_infer)
log_prob_prince2king = compute_log_probs(prince2king_model, prince_output)
print("Log prob of generated inference text:", log_prob_prince2king)
```

**Another BART-based sequence-to-sequence model that maps a vignette about the Prince to a vignette about the King. We'll use this to infer the vignette about the King from a vignette about the Prince.**

The output is nondeterministic, but one example of the output you'll get is as follows:

```
Generated statement from king_model: The king, driven by ambition, declares
    war on a neighboring nation to expand his kingdom's territories,
    declares war on.
Log probability of generated king_model: tensor(-325.8379)
Generated statement from prince_model: The prince, disillusioned by his
    father's actions, abdicates the throne in protest.
Log probability of generated prince text: tensor(-18.2486)
Generated statement from kingdom model: As the war drags on, resources are
    depleted, and the once-prosperous kingdom falls.
Log probability of generated kingdom text: tensor(-38.3716)
Generated statement from prince2king: A king, driven by greed, declares war
    on a neighboring kingdom.
Log probability of generated inference text: tensor(-297.3446)
```

Note that the generated output isn't perfect—for example, the first generated statement ideally should have stopped after "…kingdom's territories". We could try to train it more or switch to a more powerful model, but this is pretty good for a start.

Next, we'll use these Transformers library models to define distributions in Pyro, and then use Pyro to build a causal generative model. First, we'll use Pyro's `Torch-DistributionMixin` to model the causal Markov kernels with the language models. We'll use the GPT-2 model of the King vignettes to create the causal Markov kernel of the `King` variable.

Next, we'll use the BART model to create the causal Markov kernel for the `Prince` variable. The `King` variable causes this variable, so the seq2seq model uses the `King` variable's value to generate a value for this model.

Finally, we'll create the causal Markov kernel for the `Kingdom` variable. The `King` and `Prince` variables are causal parents, so we concatenate their generated outputs into one string, and use that string to generate the `Kingdom` output, again using a BART seq2seq model. We rely on a mixin called `TorchDistributionMixin`, which is useful for wrapping PyTorch distributions for use in Pyro.

**Listing 13.18   Building a Torch distribution from a Transformer model**

```
import pyro
from pyro.distributions.torch_distribution \
import TorchDistributionMixin

class TransformerModelDistribution(TorchDistributionMixin):
    def __init__(self, model: PreTrainedModel,
```

```
                    input_encoding: torch.tensor = EMPTY_TEXT,
                ):
        super().__init__()
        self.model = model
        self.input_encoding = input_encoding

    def sample(self, sample_shape=torch.Size()):
        output = generate_from_model(
            self.model, self.input_encoding
        )
        return output

    def log_prob(self, value):
        return compute_log_probs(self.model, value)
```

**Use TorchDistributionMixin to turn a Transformers model into a Pyro distribution. TorchDistributionMixin is used to make PyTorch distributions compatible with Pyro's utilities.**

**The log_prob method returns the log probabilities used in inference algorithms.**

Now we'll use that distribution in Pyro.

**Listing 13.19   Incorporating Transformer models into a causal model with Pyro**

```
def causalLLM():          ⬅—| Build the causal LLM.
    king = pyro.sample(
        "King", TransformerModelDistribution(king_model)
    )
    prince = pyro.sample(
        "Prince", TransformerModelDistribution(
            prince_model, king)
    )
    king_and_prince = torch.cat([king, prince], dim=1)
    kingdom = pyro.sample(
        "Kingdom", TransformerModelDistribution(
            kingdom_model, king_and_prince)
    )
    king_text = convert_to_text(king)
    prince_text = convert_to_text(prince)
    kingdom_text = convert_to_text(kingdom)
    return king_text, prince_text, kingdom_text

for _ in range(2):
    king, prince, kingdom = causalLLM()
    vignette = " ".join([king, prince, kingdom])
    print(vignette)
```

**Create the causal Markov kernel for the King variable.**

**Create the causal Markov kernel for the Prince variable.**

**Create the causal Markov kernel for the Kingdom variable.**

**Concatenate all the generated vignettes into one overall vignette and return the result.**

**Confirm our causal model generates the full vignette.**

The preceding code generates and prints two vignettes, such as the following:

```
And beloved king falls gravely ill, leaving the kingdom in despair in
    uncertainty over the inexperienced prince to lead the kingdom. The young
    prince, eager to prove himself, leads the army into a costly and ill-
    advised war. As a result, the kingdom's resources are depleted, plunging
    the once-prosperous land into.
King, fueled by ambition, declares war on a neighboring realm, leaving his
    subjects anxious and. The prince, disillusioned by his father's actions,
    abdicates the throne in search of a new life. Without strong leadership,
    the kingdom spirals into poverty and despair.
```

We see that the generated texts are pretty good, though they seem to cut off a bit early. This, and other issues with the generations, can be addressed by tweaking the generation parameters.

And just like that, we've built a causal LLM, an LLM build on a causal DAG scaffold. Let's prove we have a causal model by comparing the observational and interventional distributions entailed by the DAG.

### 13.3.3 Sampling from the interventional and observational distributions

By now, you know the distribution $P(Kingdom|Prince=x)$ will be different from $P(Kingdom_{Prince=x})$, but let's demonstrate the fact with this causal LLM. First, we'll model $P(Kingdom|Prince=x)$, where $x$ is

> *His courageous Prince takes command, leading the kingdom's army to victory in battle after battle*

To infer $P(Kingdom|Prince=x)$, we'll have to infer the distribution of the latent confounder, *King*. We'll do this using the prince2king_model we trained. We'll use a probabilistic inference algorithm called "importance resampling." We'll start by creating a proposal function (what Pyro calls a "guide function") that will generate samples of *King* and *Kingdom*, given *Prince*.

**Listing 13.20  Listing 13.20 Proposal distribution for *P(Kingdom|Prince=x)***

```
import pyro.poutine as poutine
from pyro.distributions import Categorical

PRINCE_STORY = (                                            We condition
    "His courageous Prince takes command, leading "         the model on
    "the kingdom's army to victory in battle after battle") this value of the
cond_model = pyro.condition(                                Prince variable.
    causalLLM, {"Prince": encode(PRINCE_STORY)})

def proposal_given_prince():      ◁──  We'll use a proposal function to generate from our target
    prince = encode(PRINCE_STORY)       distribution P(King, Kingdom | Prince=PRINCE_STORY).
    king = pyro.sample(
        "King",
        TransformerModelDistribution(prince2king_model, prince)
    )
    king_and_prince = torch.cat([king, prince], dim=1)
    kingdom = pyro.sample(
        "Kingdom",
        TransformerModelDistribution(kingdom_model, king_and_prince)
    )
    vignette = (convert_to_text(king) +                Given the value of Prince, and
        PRINCE_STORY +                                  the inferred value of King,
        convert_to_text(kingdom))                       use the king_and_prince
    return vignette                                     model to sample Kingdom.
```

Concatenate the generated king tokens and provided prince tokens to return a generated vignette so we can inspect what is sampled.

The proposal uses the prince2king_model to infer values of King given Prince=PRINCE_STORY.

Now we'll weigh each sample by the ratio of the probability of the sample under the conditioned model, over the probability of the sample under the proposal. Resampling the samples using these weights will generate samples from the target distribution. Pyro provides a utility for importance sampling, but because of the varying length of the generated sequences, it will be easier to implement importance sampling directly.

First, we'll write a function to process a sample and get its importance weight.

##### Listing 13.21 Function to draw a sample for resampling

```
def process_sample(model, proposal):
    sample_trace = poutine.trace(proposal).get_trace()
    king_text = convert_to_text(sample_trace.nodes['King']['value'])       Extract a
    kingdom_text = convert_to_text(                                        sample from
        sample_trace.nodes['Kingdom']['value'])                           the proposal.
    proposal_log_prob = sample_trace.log_prob_sum()          ◁─┐ Calculate the total
    replay = poutine.replay(model, trace=sample_trace)         │ log probability of
    model_trace = poutine.trace(replay).get_trace()            │ the sampled
    model_log_prob = model_trace.log_prob_sum()                │ values of King
    log_importance_weight = model_log_prob - proposal_log_prob │ and Kingdom.
    sample = (king_text, kingdom_text, log_importance_weight)
    return sample
```
Calculate the log         Calculate the total log probability
importance weight.        of the sample values of King and
                          Kingdom under the original model.

Now we'll run the importance resampling.

##### Listing 13.22 Listing 13.22 Importance resampling of *P(Kingdom|Prince=x)*

```
def do_importance_resampling(model, proposal, num_samples):    ◁─┐ Use importance
    original_samples = []                                          resampling as
    for _ in range(num_samples):                                   our inference
        sample = process_sample(model, proposal)                   procedure.
        original_samples.append(sample)
    unique_samples = list(set(original_samples))
    log_importance_weights = torch.tensor(                         Resample using
        [sample[2] for sample in original_samples])                the importance
    resampling_dist = Categorical(logits=log_importance_weights)   weights. Pass in
    resampled_indices = resampling_dist.sample_n(num_samples)      the log weights
    samples = pd.DataFrame(                                        to the "logits"
        [unique_samples[i] for i in resampled_indices],            argument.
        columns=["King", "Kingdom", "log_importance_weight"]
    )
    samples["Prince"] = PRINCE_STORY
    samples["Distribution"] = "observational"
    return samples[['King', 'Prince', 'Kingdom', 'Distribution']]

num_samples = 1000
posterior_samples = do_importance_resampling(
    cond_model, proposal_given_prince, num_samples)
```

Next, we'll infer $P(Kingdom_{Prince=x})$. Given our causal model in Pyro, we can use Pyro's do-operator to apply the intervention. We know that given the intervention on Prince, the edge from King to Prince is removed, so we don't need to use `prince2king_-model`. We can simply do ordinary forward generation from our intervention model.

**Listing 13.23   Inferring *P(KingdomPrince=x)* using vanilla forward Monte Carlo sampling**

```
intervention_model = pyro.do(                          Forward sample from the
    causalLLM, {"Prince": encode(PRINCE_STORY)})       interventional distribution.
intervention_samples = pd.DataFrame(
    [intervention_model() for _ in range(num_samples)],
    columns=["King", "Prince", "Kingdom"]
)
intervention_samples["Distribution"] = "interventional"    Label the samples, and
all_samples = pd.concat(                                   combine them with the
    [posterior_samples, intervention_samples],             observational samples.
    ignore_index=True
)
```

Generating the samples will take some time. Since we're working directly with the encoded sequence tensors in Pyro, we could leverage the potentially faster gradient-based inference algorithm. For convenience, you can access presaved samples in the book's directory of the GitHub repo: https://github.com/altdeep/causalml.

Next, let's visualize the difference in the distributions. We need a way to visualize sampled text from the interventional and observational distributions. We can do so using TF-IDF (term frequency-inverse document frequency), a numerical statistic that reflects how important a word is to a sample within the collection of samples, emphasizing words that are unique to specific samples.

**Listing 13.24   Get TF-IDF of generations for *P(Kingdom_Prince=x)* and *P(Kingdom|Prince=x)***

```
import pandas as pd
import numpy as np
from sklearn.feature_extraction.text import TfidfVectorizer

kingdom_samples_url = (
    "https://raw.githubusercontent.com/altdeep/causalML/"
    "master/book/chapter%2013/kingdom_samples.csv")
all_samples = pd.read_csv(kingdom_samples_url)

observational_texts = all_samples[
    all_samples["Distribution"] == "observational"]["Kingdom"]
interventional_texts = all_samples[all_samples[
    "Distribution"] == "interventional"]["Kingdom"]
```
                                              Extract generated Kingdom
                                              vignettes from observational and
                                              interventional distributions.

```
vectorizer = TfidfVectorizer(stop_words='english')
X_obs = vectorizer.fit_transform(observational_texts)
X_int = vectorizer.transform(interventional_texts)
```

**Compute the TF-IDF values for generated Kingdom vignettes in each group.**

```
k = 10
feature_names = vectorizer.get_feature_names_out()
obs_indices = X_obs.sum(axis=0).argsort()[0, -k:][::-1]
int_indices = X_int.sum(axis=0).argsort()[0, -k:][::-1]
combined_indices = np.concatenate((obs_indices, int_indices))
combined_indices = np.unique(combined_indices)
```

**Get the top k=7 words by TF-IDF for each set.**

Finally, we'll visualize the two distributions.

**Listing 13.25   Visually contrast *P(Kingdom_{Prince=x})* and *P(Kingdom|Prince=x)***

```
import matplotlib.pyplot as plt

labels = [feature_names[i] for i in combined_indices]
labels, indices = np.unique(labels, return_index=True)
obs_values = np.array(X_obs.sum(axis=0))[0, combined_indices]
int_values = np.array(X_int.sum(axis=0))[0, combined_indices]
obs_values = [obs_values[0][i] for i in indices]
int_values = [int_values[0][i] for i in indices]
combined = list(zip(labels, obs_values, int_values))
sorted_combined = sorted(combined, key=lambda x: (-x[1], x[2]))
labels, obs_values, int_values = zip(*sorted_combined)
```

**Prepare data for the bar plot.**

```
width = 0.35
x = np.arange(len(labels))
fig, ax = plt.subplots()
rects1 = ax.bar(x - width/2, obs_values, width,
                label='Observational', alpha=0.7)
rects2 = ax.bar(x + width/2, int_values, width,
                label='Interventional', alpha=0.7)
ax.set_xlabel('Words')
ax.set_ylabel('TF-IDF Values')
ax.set_title(
    'Top Words in Generated Kingdom Vignettes by TF-IDF Value')
ax.set_xticks(x)
ax.set_xticklabels(labels)
ax.legend()
fig.tight_layout()
plt.xticks(rotation=45)
plt.show()
```

**Produce the plot.**

This produces figure 13.9.

Figures 13.9 shows similar TF-IDF scores for words in the observational case. This is due to the lack of variation in the observational case, since observing the Prince constrains the likely values of King. When we intervene on Prince, King can vary more, leading to more variation in the results.

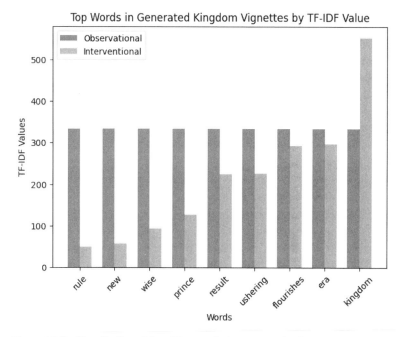

**Figure 13.9** **Visualization of the difference between samples from** $P(Kingdom_{Prince=x})$
**and** $P(Kingdom|Prince=x)$ **using TF-IDF, where** $X$ **is the Prince taking the army to battle.**
**The observational values are flat because of little variation in the inferred King vignettes.**
**The intervention enables more variation in the King vignettes and, consequently, the**
**Kingdom vignettes.**

### 13.3.4 *Closing thoughts*

This is a toy problem with a simple DAG trained on simple data with simple LLMs. But
we could extend it to more complicated DAGs and fine-tuning more advanced models. There may also be other ways to combine causal assumptions in foundation models. We're only at the beginning of exploring this exciting space.

### *Summary*

- Large language models (LLMs) are powerful AI models that generate text and
  other modalities and achieve high performance across a variety of benchmarks.
- LLMs have proven use cases for supporting causal analysis.
- LLMs can help build a causal DAG. Moreover, they can leverage common and
  expert knowledge about causal relations and mechanisms.
- The causal frame problem is the challenge of selecting the causal variables relevant to a given problem and excluding the irrelevant. Cutting-edge LLMs emulate how humans set the causal frame, which is useful for applications such as
  building DAGs and root cause analysis.
- LLMs can help us understand nuanced causal concepts and how to contextualize them within our domain of interest.

- LLMs can help us put causal queries into formal terms.
- LLMs are prone to hallucinations—convincing yet incorrect responses to our queries.
- At their core, LLMs are probabilistic machine learning models that model a joint probability distribution on sequences of tokens.
- The attention mechanism enables the LLM to learn higher-level representations that make cutting-edge LLMs so powerful.
- Just because an LLM learns a higher-level representation doesn't mean it learns a causal representation. Even if that did work in some special cases, it would be hard for the user to verify that it is working.
- We can build our own causal LLM by composing fine-tuned LLMs over a causal DAG scaffold. This allows us to work with cutting-edge LLMs while admitting causal operations, such as a do-operator.
- Use the causal hierarchy theory as your North Star in your exploration of how to combine causality with LLMs and multimodal models, as well as exploring how well these models can learn causal representations on their own.

# index